W9-BMY-033

RECIPE
encyclopedia

RECIPE
encyclopedia

CRESCENT BOOKS
New York

© Text, design, photography and illustrations Murdoch Books® 1995.
All rights reserved under International and Pan-American Copyright Conventions.

No part of this book may be reproduced or transmitted in any form or by any means electronic or mechanical including photocopying, recording, or by an information storage and retrieval system, without permission in writing from the publisher.

This 1997 edition is published by Crescent Books, a division of Random House Value Publishing, Inc., 201 East 50th Street, New York, NY 10022.

Crescent Books and colophon are trademarks of Random House Value Publishing, Inc.

Random House
New York ◆ Toronto ◆ London ◆ Sydney ◆ Auckland
http://www.randomhouse.com/

Printed and bound in the United States of America

A CIP catalog record for this book is available from the Library of Congress.

ISBN 0-517-18442-7

8 7 6 5 4 3 2 1

CONTENTS

RECIPE ENCYCLOPEDIA

Find a good cook and you find someone who *enjoys* food, someone for whom every stage of producing a meal—buying, preparing and ultimately serving—can be a source of pleasure. Such enthusiasm comes with an understanding of the ingredients, a knowledge of cooking techniques and, of course, inspiring recipes.

With this in mind we have created the *Recipe Encyclopedia*, a complete reference to food and cooking. The comprehensive dictionary of ingredients helps you make the most of everyday foods as well as giving an insight into more exotic fare. It covers cooking terms, famous dishes, national cuisines and the colorful history of food. Guidelines on choosing and using foods are given throughout the book, and 26 special sections will tempt you to try out new techniques.

The book is packed with recipes—more than 800 of them—all of which have been carefully tested. There are 1500 color photographs to whet your appetite and a star rating to help you choose recipes that suit your cooking expertise.

This beautifully crafted book is a pleasure in its own right; as your companion in the kitchen, the *Recipe Encyclopedia* will ensure that good food and cooking remain a constant delight.

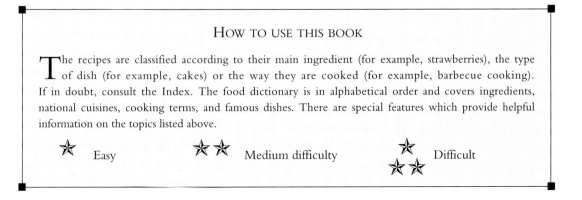

HOW TO USE THIS BOOK

The recipes are classified according to their main ingredient (for example, strawberries), the type of dish (for example, cakes) or the way they are cooked (for example, barbecue cooking). If in doubt, consult the Index. The food dictionary is in alphabetical order and covers ingredients, national cuisines, cooking terms, and famous dishes. There are special features which provide helpful information on the topics listed above.

★ Easy   ★★ Medium difficulty   ★★★ Difficult

ALMOND AND COCONUT LAMB CURRY

★★ **Preparation time:** 25 minutes
Total cooking time: 50 minutes
Serves 4

8 lamb rib chops, each about 4½ oz
¼ cup olive oil
1 medium onion, sliced
1 medium cooking apple, peeled and chopped
2 medium carrots, chopped
1 tablespoon fresh cilantro leaves
3 dried curry leaves
½ teaspoon garam masala
½ teaspoon ground cumin
½ teaspoon turmeric
5 oz can coconut milk
1 tablespoon ground almonds
1¼ cups slivered almonds, toasted

1 Trim chops of bone and excess fat and tendons. Cut meat into 1¼ inch cubes.
2 Heat 2 tablespoons of the oil in a heavy-bottom skillet. Cook meat quickly in small batches over medium-high heat until well-browned; drain on paper towels.
3 Heat remaining oil in pan. Add onion, stir over medium heat for 5 minutes or until soft. Add meat, apple, carrot, herbs, spices and coconut milk; bring to boil. Reduce heat to a simmer and cook, covered, for 35 minutes or until the meat is tender. Stir in ground almonds just before serving. Serve curry sprinkled with toasted slivered almonds.

ABOUT ALMONDS

■ To blanch almonds, place them in a small bowl, cover with boiling water and let stand for 4 minutes. Use a spoon to remove each nut, then press nut between finger and thumb: the skins should slip away easily.

■ To toast almonds, place them in a single layer on a baking sheet; bake in a moderate oven 350°F for 4 minutes (for slivered almonds) to 8 minutes (for whole almonds), checking regularly to prevent burning. Take care during the last minutes of cooking since the almonds tend to darken quickly.

■ Ground almonds are best purchased. It can be difficult to achieve the right texture by grinding in a food processor—overprocessing can result in a paste. If you wish to grind your own almonds, work in short bursts and with small batches only.

■ Store almonds in an airtight container in the refrigerator for up to two months.

RIGHT: ALMOND AND COCONUT LAMB CURRY

Abalone A large sea mollusk with a shallow, ear-shaped shell. It lives close to the shoreline, clinging to the underside of rock ledges with a broad, fleshy foot. Found throughout the world, abalone at one time became so rare in California that it was not allowed to be canned, dried or sent out of the state; the advent of farm-raised abalone eased these restrictions. In the Channel Islands, when seasonal low tides temporarily exposed the abalone's rocky haunts, the locals would race to gather as many as possible before the waters rolled back in, leading to a decline in abalone numbers. In Australia, divers harvest them in southern waters.

The flesh is tough and must be tenderized by pounding before it can be eaten. It may be thinly sliced and sautéed, fried, stewed, ground or minced, or used in a chowder.

Abbacchio The Italian term for meat from an unweaned lamb. Abbacchio is roasted with garlic and rosemary. Traditional fare at Easter,

it has been eaten since ancient times.

Aberdeen Sausage
A beef sausage that is wrapped in a cloth, boiled, and then coated in bread crumbs.

Acidulated water
Water with lemon juice or vinegar added. It is sprinkled on cut raw fruit such as apples, bananas and pears to prevent browning.

Acorn Squash A medium-sized golden squash with light orange meat and a sweet, dry flavor.

Agar-agar A white, semi-translucent, tasteless and odorless seaweed-based stabilizing agent that does not requre refrigeration.

Aïoli A garlic mayonnaise from Provence, France. In Marseilles it is said that aïoli should contain at least two garlic cloves per serving. Used over fish, meats and cold boiled potatoes, it is also added to soup.

À la French for "in the style or manner of." For example, *à la Niçoise* means typical of the cooking style of Nice. See individual entries.

Albacore A species of white meat tuna. It is usually baked or grilled.

Al dente An Italian cooking term, literally "to the tooth," which is used to describe food, particularly pasta, that is cooked until firm to the bite rather than soft.

Alfalfa Sprouts The fine, short sprouts of alfalfa seeds, with pale stalks and deep green tips; the sprouts are a good source of protein and calcium. Used in salads and sandwiches, the sprouts have a nutty taste that goes well with cheese. The alfalfa plant was first grown by Arabs as food for their horses.

Allemande, à l' A French term for food cooked in the German style: traditionally, dishes containing smoked sausages or garnished with sauerkraut and pork. It is also used to describe dishes served with allemande sauce, a white sauce made with veal or poultry stock.

All-Purpose Flour A white flour that is a combination of hard and soft wheat that works well in most home baking recipes.

Allspice A spice made from the berries of a tropical tree which grows throughout Central America and is especially abundant in Jamaica. Its

ALMOND AND PEAR TART

★ ★ **Preparation time:** 35 minutes + 20 minutes refrigeration
Total cooking time: 40 minutes
Serves 4–6

1¼ cups all-purpose flour
¼ cup confectioners' sugar
⅓ cup butter, chopped
1 egg yolk, lightly beaten
1–2 tablespoons iced water

Filling
2 large firm pears

3 tablespoons butter
¼ cup sugar
1 egg, lightly beaten
1 teaspoon vanilla
1 tablespoon all-purpose flour
⅓ cup ground almonds
2 tablespoons apricot jam, warmed and sieved

1 Place flour, sugar and butter in food processor bowl. Using the pulse action, press button for 15 seconds or until the mixture is fine and crumbly. Add egg yolk and almost all the water, process for 20 seconds or until mixture comes together, adding more water if necessary. Turn onto a lightly floured surface, press mixture together until smooth. Brush a 14 x 4½ inch oblong flan or 9 inch round tart pan with melted butter or oil. Roll out pastry to cover base and sides of pan. Ease pastry into pan; trim. Cover with plastic wrap; refrigerate for 20 minutes.
2 Preheat oven to moderate 350°F. Cut a sheet of parchment paper large enough to cover pastry-lined pan. Place over pastry and spread a layer of dried beans or rice evenly over the paper. Bake 10 minutes, remove from oven and discard paper and beans. Return to oven for 10 minutes or until pastry is lightly golden. Set aside to cool.
3 To make Filling: Peel pears, cut in half, remove cores. Place in small pan of boiling water and cook over medium heat for 5–10 minutes or until just tender. Drain, cool and slice thinly.
4 Using electric beaters, beat butter and sugar until light and creamy. Add the beaten egg gradually, beating well after each addition. Add vanilla and beat until combined. Using a metal spoon, fold in flour and almonds. Spread into pastry shell and arrange slices of pear on top. Bake for 20 minutes, or until set and golden. While still warm, brush the pears with jam.

Note: If using ripe pears, do not pre-cook them.

SPICY ALMONDS

Heat 3 tablespoons olive oil in a heavy-bottom frying pan. Add ½ teaspoon each ground cumin, ground coriander, garlic powder and chili powder, and ¼ teaspoon each ground ginger and ground cinnamon. Stir over low heat for 2 minutes. Remove pan from heat, add 2 cups whole blanched almonds and stir until almonds are coated with spice mixture. Spread almonds on baking sheet, place in a preheated 300°F oven, cook for 15 minutes. Remove from oven, sprinkle with a little salt; cool.

aroma and flavor is similar to a blend of cloves, cinnamon and nutmeg. The berries are picked while green and dried in the sun until dark red. Whole berries are used to flavor stews, pot roasts and chutney; the ground spice is added to apple dishes, milk puddings, gingerbread and tomato sauce. It is sometimes called pimento or Jamaica pepper.

Almond The oval-shaped seeds of a tree closely related to the peach and apricot. Originally from the Middle East, almonds are one of the most widely used and longest cultivated nuts. They were eaten in ancient Babylon and mentioned in the Bible. The ancient Greeks mixed the crushed nut with honey to make marzipan (see Almond Paste) and it was also popular with the Romans, who called it "the Greek nut." The prevalence of the almond in medieval cooking is thought to be connected to religious fast days when it replaced meat and milk.

There are two types of almond: the sweet almond, from a pink-flowering tree, the type most widely used; and the strongly

ALMOND MACAROONS

⭐⭐ **Preparation time:** 30 minutes
Total cooking time: 10–20 minutes
Makes 24

1 cup confectioners' sugar, sifted
1 egg, beaten
2 cups ground almonds
2 teaspoons finely grated lemon rind
1 teaspoon vanilla
1/4 teaspoon ground cinnamon
additional confectioners' sugar, for garnish

1 Place powdered sugar and egg in a small mixing bowl, beat until mixture turns white.
2 In another bowl, combine ground almonds, lemon rind, vanilla and cinnamon. Gradually mix into beaten sugar and egg mixture.
3 Knead dough in bowl for 5 minutes, or until pliable. Cover with a cloth towel, leave 15 minutes.
4 Preheat oven to 350°F. On a lightly floured surface, roll dough to a 1 1/2 inch thick sausage shape. Cut into 24 pieces, roll each into a ball.
5 Lightly oil the palms of your hands and flatten each ball into a round about 1 1/2 inches in diameter. Place on greased baking sheet, leaving plenty of room for spreading and sprinkle with confectioners' sugar. Bake for 10–20 minutes or until golden. Cool on wire rack. Store in an airtight container.

OPPOSITE PAGE: ALMOND AND PEAR TART.
ABOVE: ALMOND MACAROONS

ALMOND BREAD

⭐ **Preparation time:** 10 minutes
Total cooking time: 45 minutes
Makes about 36

4 egg whites
1/4 teaspoon cream of tartar
2/3 cup sugar
1 1/4 cups all-purpose flour, sifted
1/8 teaspoon salt
1 cup unblanched whole almonds
few drops almond extract

1 Preheat oven to 400°F; grease and flour an 8 x 4 inch small loaf pan. Beat egg whites with cream of tartar until stiff peaks form. Gradually add sugar, beating constantly until stiff. Lightly fold in flour, salt, almonds and extract.
2 Spoon mixture into prepared pan; bake for 25–30 minutes. Cool in pan for 5 minutes, then turn out onto a wire rack to cool completely.
3 Cut loaf into wafer-thin slices with a sharp, thin-bladed knife. Place on ungreased baking sheet. Reduce oven temperature to 300°F and bake slices for 10–12 minutes. Cool and store in an airtight container.

Note: Try a combination of macadamias, pecan, walnut and pistachio nuts for a delicious alternative to almonds. Partially cooked loaf can be frozen; bake as many slices as required at a time, straight from the freezer. These are excellent to serve with tea, coffee, after dinner or as an accompaniment to soft desserts.

flavored bitter almond, from a white-flowering tree. A broader and shorter nut, the bitter almond contains poisonous prussic acid, and is not sold in the United States. Slivered almonds are thinly sliced

lengthwise. The French term *amandine* is used to describe foods made with or garnished with almonds. California is the world's largest producer of almonds, followed by Italy and Spain. Almonds are eaten raw, roasted or grilled and salted, pounded or ground. They are used to accompany drinks, in stuffings, as a garnish for cooked vegetables, and in cakes and candy.

Almond Paste A mixture of finely ground almonds, sugar and glycerine or other liquid which is rolled out and used to cover rich fruit cakes with a smooth and even surface before they are iced. It also helps to preserve the cake and prevent icing discoloration.

Used for candies and pastries, almond paste is available in most supermarkets. Once it has been opened, it should be wrapped tightly and refrigerated.

AMERICAN CLASSICS

CRUNCHY FRIED CHICKEN

★★ **Preparation time:** 10 minutes
Total cooking time: 20 minutes
Serves 6

12 chicken drumsticks (about 3 lb)
1/3 cup finely crushed cornflakes
1 1/2 cups all-purpose flour
1 teaspoon celery salt
1 teaspoon onion salt
2 tablespoons chicken bouillon powder
1/2 teaspoon garlic powder
1/2 teaspoon white pepper
oil for deep frying

1 Place chicken drumsticks in a large pan of boiling water; reduce heat and simmer, uncovered, 8 minutes or until chicken is almost cooked through. Drain.
2 Combine cornflake crumbs, sifted flour, celery salt, onion salt, bouillon powder, garlic powder and white pepper in a medium bowl. Place chicken in large bowl, cover with cold water.
3 Dip wet drumsticks, one at a time, into the seasoned flour mixture; shake off excess.
4 Heat oil in deep heavy-bottom skillet. Gently add drumsticks and cook a few at a time over medium-high heat for 8 minutes, or until chicken is golden and cooked through. Drain on paper towels; keep warm. Repeat with remaining pieces. Serve warm.

CORNED BEEF HASH

★ **Preparation time:** 20 minutes
Total cooking time: 15 minutes
Serves 2

3 tablespoons butter
4 medium potatoes, cooked, peeled and cubed
12 oz cooked corned beef, cubed
1 medium onion, diced
salt and pepper to taste
tomato ketchup or chili sauce
2 poached or fried eggs (optional)

1 Melt butter in a heavy-bottom pan. Add potatoes, corned beef, onion, salt and pepper. Cook, stirring, for 1 minute.
2 Press mixture evenly over the pan, patting it down firmly with a spatula. Cook over medium heat, uncovered, for about 15 minutes, or until the hash mixture forms a brown crust on its underside.
3 Serve hash hot, accompanied by ketchup or chili sauce. It can be topped with poached or fried eggs, if desired.

Note: Use any variety of potatoes to make Corned Beef Hash. They can be prepared by whatever method you prefer: boiled, baked or cooked in a microwave oven.

ABOVE: CRUNCHY FRIED CHICKEN.
OPPOSITE PAGE: CORNBREAD

BOSTON BAKED BEANS

★ **Preparation time:** 10 minutes
Total cooking time: 30 minutes
Serves 4

1 oz salt pork or bacon, diced
28 oz can baked beans in tomato sauce
1 large onion, diced

3 tablespoons molasses
2 teaspoons dry mustard
1 tablespoon chili or Worcestershire sauce

1 Preheat oven to moderate 350°F. Lightly brush an 8-cup capacity ovenproof dish with melted butter or oil.
2 Cut the salt pork or bacon into ³/₄ inch pieces and cook in a dry pan until crisp. Drain.
3 Combine the undrained beans with the salt pork or bacon and add the onion, molasses, mustard and chili or Worcestershire sauce. Spoon the mixture into the prepared dish and bake for 30 minutes or until bubbly. Serve hot.

CORNBREAD

★ **Preparation time:** 10 minutes
Total cooking time: 45 minutes
Makes 8–9 servings

1 cup all-purpose flour
1 tablespoon baking powder
¹/₂ teaspoon salt
1 cup yellow cornmeal
2 tablespoons sugar

2 eggs, beaten
1 cup buttermilk
¹/₄ cup vegetable oil
3 tablespoons butter, melted

1 Preheat oven to moderate 350°F. Heat a 9 x 9 x 2 inch baking pan in preheated oven for about 5 minutes.
2 Sift flour, baking powder and salt into a large bowl; stir in cornmeal and sugar. Make a well in the center. Combine eggs, milk and oil in a small bowl and mix thoroughly. Stir mixture into dry ingredients and mix well.
3 Brush heated baking tin with butter and pour in the batter. Smooth top. Bake for 25 minutes. Brush extra melted butter evenly over top and bake for another 15 minutes or until firm.
4 Cut cornbread into squares and serve warm.

PECAN PIE

★ ★ **Preparation time:** 40 minutes
Total cooking time: 1 hour 15 minutes
Serves 6-8

1¹/₄ cups all-purpose flour
¹/₄ teaspoon baking powder
¹/₃ cup butter, cut into pieces
3–4 tablespoons water

Filling
¹/₄ cup soft brown sugar

¹/₄ cup all-purpose flour
1¹/₄ cups dark corn syrup
4 eggs, lightly beaten
2 tablespoons butter, melted
1¹/₂ teaspoons vanilla
1 cup pecan halves

1 Sift flour and baking powder into a bowl. Rub in butter with fingertips until mixture resembles fine bread crumbs. Add 3 tablespoons water to make a firm dough, adding remaining water if necessary. Turn dough onto a lightly floured surface, knead for 1 minute or until smooth. Store, covered in plastic wrap, in the refrigerator for 15 minutes.
2 Preheat oven to moderately hot 425°F. Roll out the pastry between 2 pieces of wax paper until it is large enough to fit a deep, 9 inch pie plate. Trim the edges. Prick the pastry evenly all over with a fork.
3 Bake for 15 minutes or until the pastry is lightly golden; remove from oven. Reduce oven temperature to moderately slow 325°F.
4 To make Filling: Stir the sugar and flour together in a bowl. Using electric beaters, gradually beat in the syrup, eggs, butter and vanilla. Stir in the pecans, mix well. Pour the mixture into the prepared pastry shell. Bake for 45 minutes or until the filling is evenly risen. Do not overbake—the filling should be firm but still custardy. Cool on a wire rack (the filling will sink slightly as it cools). Serve with cream or ice cream.

Amaranth The greens of this plant are slightly sweet. The high-protein seeds are used as cereal or ground into flour.

Amaretti A crisp almond macaroon from Italy,

where it was originally made with bitter almonds. The name comes from the Italian word *amaro*, meaning bitter.

Ambrosia A semisoft, cow's milk cheese, originally from Sweden, with a slightly tart taste and a number of small, irregular holes in the interior. Ambrosia is also a chilled dessert or salad made with layers of sliced orange, banana and pineapple and a mixture of shredded coconut.

Américaine, à l'
A French term for meat, seafood, eggs or vegetables served with a spicy, tomato-based sauce and often garnished with grilled bacon and tomatoes. The name was originally applied to a dish, created in the 1860s in Paris by a chef who had worked in North America, in which a cut lobster cooked in a tomato and wine mixture was served with a sauce made from the stock. Some say the term "*américaine*" is a mistranslation of "*armoricaine*," referring to

Armorica, the ancient name for Brittany, and that this style of cooking originated there.

American Cheese An orange, rindless, smooth flavored cheese that has a long shelf life. It is usually sold in bricks or in individual slices.

Ammonium Bicarbonate Also called *hartshorn, carbonate of ammonia* and *powdered baking ammonia*, this leavener was used in cooking before baking powder and baking soda were available. Ammonium bicarbonate is found in drugstores and must be ground to a powder before using.

Amontillado A nutty-flavored Spanish sherry made from the palomino grape. It is aged longer than a Fino sherry and has a dark color and naturally dry taste.

Anadama Bread An early American yeast bread that originated in New England. An angry farmer with a lazy wife invented this molasses and cornmeal bread while he muttered, "Anna, damn 'er!"

Anaheim Chili Pepper Also called California chili pepper, this mild pepper comes in green and red. It is used for chili rellenos, stews and sauces. Dried red

DEEP DISH APPLE PIE

★ ★   *Preparation time:* 1 hour
Total cooking time: 50 minutes
Serves 6–8

2 cups all-purpose flour
½ cup chilled butter, cut
   into pieces
2 tablespoons sugar
1 teaspoon baking
   powder
¼ teaspoon salt
1 egg
1–2 tablespoons milk
1 egg, lightly beaten

Filling
8 large Granny Smith
   apples, peeled, each cut
   into 12 wedges
2 thick strips lemon rind
6 whole cloves
1 cinnamon stick
2 cups water
½ cup sugar

1 Preheat oven to moderate 350°F. Brush a deep, 8 inch round springform pan with melted butter or oil. Line base with parchment paper; grease paper. Dust lightly with flour, shake off excess.
2 To make Filling: Combine apples, lemon rind, cloves, cinnamon stick, water and sugar in large pan. Cover and simmer for 10 minutes or until apples are only just tender. Remove from heat, drain well. Discard rind, cloves and cinnamon stick. Set aside.
3 Place flour and butter in a food processor bowl; add sugar, baking powder and salt. Using pulse action, process for 15 seconds or until mixture has a fine, crumbly texture. Add egg and almost all

the milk; process for another 15 seconds until mixture comes together, adding more liquid if necessary. Turn dough onto a lightly floured surface; knead for 2 minutes or until smooth. Store, covered in plastic wrap, in the refrigerator for 15 minutes.
4 Roll two-thirds of the pastry between 2 sheets of wax paper until large enough to cover base and side of pan. Spoon apple filling into pastry shell. Roll remaining pastry into a circle large enough to cover top of pie. Brush pastry edge with a little of the beaten egg to seal. Trim excess pastry with a sharp knife and press around edge with a fork; brush top of pie with beaten egg. Bake for 50 minutes or until pastry is golden and cooked through. Leave pie in pan for 10 minutes before removing to a serving plate. Serve warm or cold with cream, ice cream or custard.

Note: Apple pie is traditionally served, warm or cold, with a wedge of aged cheddar cheese.

VARIATIONS

■ Add ¾ cup cooked rhubarb or mincemeat to apple pie filling.
■ Use any combination of ground cinnamon, nutmeg, cloves, mace or allspice to flavor.
■ If apples are very sweet, sprinkle with a little lemon juice for extra tartness.

Anaheim chili peppers
are used to make chili
pepper wreaths called
ristras.

Ancho Chili Pepper
A dried poblano chili
pepper which is widely
used in
South-
west
and
Mexican cooking. The
ancho pepper, which
means "wide" in Spanish,
has a mild flavor with
tones of coffee, plums
and raisins and is most
commonly used in mole
sauces.

Anchovy A small,
slender, herring-like
saltwater fish with
slightly oily flesh and a
strong, sardine-like taste.
Although

anchovies are eaten fresh
in the regions in which
they occur, they are
probably best known in
their preserved form.
Traditionally the whole
fish, packed in brine in
kegs, was used for
flavoring and salting
meat dishes. In
Renaissance Italy a dish
of anchovy fillets
marinated in olive oil
and vinegar was a
popular first course, and
for centuries salted
anchovy fillets have been
an important ingredient
in the cooking of
Provence. Today they
are widely available as
salted fillets marinated in

A N C H O V I E S

PAN-ROASTED POTATOES WITH ANCHOVIES

Preparation time: 10 minutes
Total cooking time: 30 minutes
Serves 4–6

1½ lb potatoes
⅓ cup olive oil
2 tablespoons butter
4 flat anchovy fillets
salt and freshly ground
    black pepper to taste

2 cloves garlic, peeled and
    finely chopped
2 tablespoons chopped
    fresh rosemary

1 Peel potatoes and cut into ½ inch thick slices;
soak potatoes in cold water for at least
5 minutes. Drain; pat dry thoroughly with paper
towels. Heat oil and melt butter in a large frying
pan. Add chopped anchovies and cook for
1 minute, mashing slightly with a wooden spoon.
2 Add potatoes to frying pan and cook over high
heat for 2–3 minutes until potatoes are crisp on
the outside and well-coated with butter-oil
mixture. Reduce heat; cover pan with lid and
cook 7 minutes more, turning occasionally.
Remove lid from pan and cook another
15 minutes or until potatoes are tender. Season
with salt and pepper. Add garlic and rosemary.
Cook 1 minute and combine well. Serve
immediately as an accompaniment to roast meat,
or serve as a light meal with bread and salad.

Opposite page: Deep dish apple pie.
Above: Pissaladière

P I S S A L A D I E R E

Preparation time: 15 minutes
Total cooking time: 35 minutes
Serves 6–8

1 frozen puff pastry
    sheet, thawed
1 tablespoon olive oil
2 medium onions, thinly
    sliced
¼ teaspoon dried thyme
½ teaspoon dried
    oregano

2 medium tomatoes, sliced
½ cup grated mozzarella
    cheese
1½ oz can anchovy
    fillets
¼ cup black pitted olives,
    halved
1 egg, lightly beaten

1 Preheat oven to moderate 350°F. Brush baking
sheet with oil or melted butter. Place pastry on
prepared baking sheet.
2 Heat oil in a frying pan and cook onions and
herbs over medium heat for 10 minutes or until
soft. Spread on top of pastry, leaving a ¾ inch
border. Arrange tomato slices over onion
mixture; sprinkle with cheese.
3 Drain anchovies and cut each fillet in half
lengthwise. Arrange in a lattice pattern over
filling. Place an olive half in the center of each
diamond. Brush edges of pastry with beaten egg.
Bake for 25 minutes or until pastry is golden
brown. Serve warm.

A B O U T   A N C H O V I E S

■ To de-salt anchovies soak them in cold milk
for 5 minutes. Use fingers to remove the soft
backbone from each fillet.
■ Store canned anchovies, once opened, in their
oil in an airtight glass container for up to 5 days
in the refrigerator.

ANTIPASTO

Shopping at a good deli is often the only thing you need to do to put together an impressive antipasto platter. It makes a lively and appetizing start to an Italian meal, or add a bottle of wine and some crusty bread for an ideal summer lunch.

MARINATED OLIVES

Use cracked green or uncracked black olives. (To crack olives, tap lightly with a meat mallet. Alternatively you can make small slits in the olive with a sharp knife.) Place 8 oz olives into a bowl. Pour over 3 tablespoons olive oil, add 1 tablespoon each of finely chopped fresh oregano and chives, ½–1 teaspoon red chili flakes, 1 clove crushed garlic, 1 teaspoon grated lemon rind and 1 teaspoon cracked black pepper. Mix together, making sure the olives are well coated. Heat 1 tablespoon olive oil in a small pan. Add 1 finely sliced onion and cook over medium heat until soft; cool. Stir into olive mixture.

Marinated olives will keep for a month in an airtight jar. If storing in the refrigerator, remove about 10 minutes before serving to soften the olive oil. Serve marinated olives on pizzas and in salads. They are also delicious sliced and served with cheese on herb bread.

FRESH PEARS AND PARMESAN

Prepare the pears just before serving, otherwise they will turn brown. Choose ripe pears with unblemished skin. Wash and dry them, cut in half, remove cores and slice pears thinly. Using a vegetable peeler make fine shavings of Parmesan cheese and scatter over the pears.

MELON WITH PROSCIUTTO

Use cantaloupe or honeydew melon for this dish. Peel it, remove seeds and slice into long, thin wedges. Wrap paper-thin slices of prosciutto around the wedges.

FROM LEFT: MARINATED OLIVES, FRESH PEARS AND PARMESAN, MELON WITH PROSCIUTTO, TOMATO SALAD, COPPA AND SALAMI, MARINATED ARTICHOKES, CHAR-GRILLED RED PEPPER, CHILI-GARLIC OCTOPUS.

TOMATO SALAD

Cut 1–2 bocconcini (fresh baby mozzarella) into thin slices. Choose tomatoes of about the same diameter as cheese and thinly slice. Arrange bocconcini and tomato in alternate slices on serving platter. Drizzle with olive oil, sprinkle with balsamic vinegar and scatter with shredded basil leaves.

COPPA AND SALAMI

An antipasto selection should always include a variety of sausage-type meats. Paper-thin slices of salami or coppa (cured pork, served raw) are ideal. There are many types of salami—some spicy, some with crusted coatings. Arrange in cornets, fans, folds or simply in overlapping slices.

MARINATED ARTICHOKES

Fresh artichokes may be used but canned artichoke hearts are simpler to prepare. Drain and rinse well to remove brine. Cut into quarters. Place in a bowl. For 14 oz artichokes, pour over 6 tablespoons olive oil, add 1 clove crushed garlic, 1 teaspoon grated lemon rind, 2-3 tablespoons finely chopped fresh herbs, and, if desired, a finely chopped fresh chili pepper. Toss gently but well, cover and set aside. Artichokes will keep in an airtight container for a week, if covered in oil.

CHAR-GRILLED RED PEPPER

Cut red peppers in half, remove seeds and membranes. Place peppers, skin-side up, under a hot broiler, or rotate over a gas flame, until skin blisters and blackens. Wrap in damp cloth towel for a few minutes, then peel off blackened skin. Cut peppers into wide strips and drizzle with olive oil and a few drops of balsamic vinegar.

CHILI-GARLIC OCTOPUS

Mix together, in a large bowl, 3 tablespoons olive oil, 1 tablespoon soy sauce, 2 tablespoons each chopped fresh oregano and parsley, and 1 finely chopped fresh red chili pepper. Wash 1 lb baby octopus, dry well. Slit open the head and remove the gut. Grasp body firmly and push the beak out with your index finger. Place octopus in the bowl with the marinade and toss well to coat.

Drain octopus and reserve marinade. Cook on a hot grill 3–5 minutes until flesh turns white. Turn octopus frequently, brush with reserved marinade during cooking.

oil and sold in jars or cans.

Sadly, pollution has largely banished the anchovy from its home in Mediterranean waters, although it is still netted off the coasts of France and Spain in May. The anchovy is caught in the Atlantic, and off the Pacific coasts of the Americas. A similar species is found in the coastal waters of Australia.

Preserved anchovy fillets are used in hors d'oeuvres, pizza toppings, in salads and as a garnish; boned anchovies are pounded into a paste which is the basis for many sauces.

Angel Food Cake A white cake with an airy texture resulting from the high proportion of beaten egg white in the mixture. Angel food cake originated in North America in the late nineteenth century.

Angelica A tall herb with thick hollow stems and large serrated leaves. It is best known for its

candied stalks, used to flavor and decorate cakes and desserts. It was once eaten raw, like celery, and its fresh leaves can be used in salads. In parts of Iceland and Norway the dried root is ground into flour and made into a type of bread.

APPLES

BAKED APPLES

★ **Preparation time:** 20 minutes
Total cooking time: 1 hour 15 minutes
Serves 4

4 Granny Smith apples
½ cup finely chopped dates
1 tablespoon chopped walnuts
1 tablespoon grated lemon rind
½ cup water
½ cup brown sugar
2 tablespoons butter
¼ teaspoon ground cinnamon
¼ teaspoon ground nutmeg
ice cream or whipped cream

1 Preheat oven to 350°F. Cut cores neatly out of apples; peel the skin from the top quarter only of each apple.
2 Combine dates, walnuts and rind, mix well. Press mixture into centers of apples.
3 Place apples into baking pan or loaf pan. Put water, brown sugar, butter, cinnamon and nutmeg in small pan. Bring to boil; pour mixture over the apples. Bake for about 1¼ hours, basting apples occasionally with the liquid. Serve warm with vanilla ice cream or whipped cream.

APPLE CHUTNEY

★ **Preparation time:** 30 minutes
Total cooking time: 2 hours
Makes about 7 cups

10 small green apples
5 large ripe tomatoes, chopped
3 large onions, diced
1 tablespoon grated ginger
4 cloves garlic, crushed
2 small chili peppers, chopped
1 cup raisins
½ cup orange juice
⅓ cup lemon juice
3 cups soft brown sugar
2 cups cider vinegar

1 Peel, core and chop apples. Combine with tomatoes, onions, ginger, garlic, chili, raisins, juices, brown sugar and vinegar in large, deep heavy-bottom pan. Stir over low heat until the sugar is completely dissolved.
2 Increase heat, stirring occasionally until mixture boils. Simmer, uncovered, 2 hours or until fruit and vegetables are tender and chutney is thick. Stir mixture occasionally.
3 Allow to stand 5 minutes. Using a funnel, pour into warm, sterilized jars and seal immediately. Label and date jars when cool. Store in a cool, dark place for up to 12 months.

APPLESAUCE

★ **Preparation time:** 20 minutes
Total cooking time: 30 minutes
Makes 2 cups

4 large green apples, peeled, cored and chopped
2 tablespoons butter
⅓ cup sugar
2 teaspoons grated lemon rind
¼ cup water

Place apples, butter, sugar, lemon rind and water in a heavy-bottom pan. Cook over low heat, stirring frequently, until apples become soft and pulpy. Serve sauce warm with roast pork, roast duck or goose.

Note: Applesauce may be made up to 3 days in advance and stored, covered, in the refrigerator.

ABOUT APPLES

■ Buy apples with blemish-free skin and no bruises. As a guide, the lighter the ground coloring, the crisper the apple is.
■ To avoid discoloration after cutting apples, brush with lemon juice diluted with a little water, or place cut or peeled apples in a bowl of water containing 2 tablespoons lemon juice.
■ To stew apples, peel, core and thickly slice green cooking apples, place in a pan with a little water or apple juice and a few whole cloves. Bring to boil, reduce heat and simmer covered for 15 minutes, stirring occasionally.
■ To prevent baking apples from bursting, score skin around center with tip of a sharp knife.

ABOVE: BAKED APPLE. OPPOSITE PAGE, ABOVE: APPLE CRUMBLE; BELOW: APPLE CHARLOTTE

APPLE CHARLOTTES

★★ **Preparation time:** 30 minutes
Total cooking time: 25 minutes
Serves 6

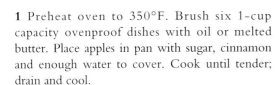

5 cooking apples, peeled, cored and sliced	**Jam Sauce**
2 tablespoons soft brown sugar	1 cup strawberry jam
¼ teaspoon ground cinnamon	1 cup water
1 loaf day-old white bread, crusts removed	1 teaspoon grated lemon rind
⅓ cup butter, melted	½ cup sugar

1 Preheat oven to 350°F. Brush six 1-cup capacity ovenproof dishes with oil or melted butter. Place apples in pan with sugar, cinnamon and enough water to cover. Cook until tender; drain and cool.
2 Using a cookie or biscuit cutter, cut 12 rounds from bread slices to fit top and base of each dish. Cut remaining slices into fingers ¾ inch wide; trim to fit height of dish. Dip 6 rounds into melted butter and place in base of dishes. Dip each finger of bread into melted butter and press around sides of dish vertically, overlapping a little.
3 Fill each bread-lined dish with cooked apple; top with last rounds of butter-dipped bread. Place on a baking sheet and bake for 20 minutes. Turn onto plates. Serve warm with Jam Sauce and whipped cream.
4 To make Jam Sauce: Place sauce ingredients in small pan; bring to boil and simmer for 15 minutes. Strain and serve warm.

APPLE CRUMBLE

★ **Preparation time**: 30 minutes
Total cooking time: 25–30 minutes
Serves 4–6

4 large green cooking apples, peeled and sliced	**Topping**
1 tablespoon soft brown sugar	½ cup all-purpose flour
2 tablespoons light corn syrup	½ cup shredded coconut
2 tablespoons lemon juice	½ cup rolled oats
	½ cup soft brown sugar
	⅓ cup butter

1 Brush a shallow 6-cup capacity casserole dish with melted butter or oil. Place apples, sugar, corn syrup and lemon juice in a large pan; cover with tight-fitting lid and cook over low heat for 10 minutes or until apples soften. Spoon apple mixture into dish. Preheat oven to moderate 350°F.
2 To make Topping: In a bowl combine flour, coconut, rolled oats and sugar; mix well. Make a well in the center. Melt butter and pour into bowl with dry ingredients. Mix to form a crumble. Scatter crumble mixture over apples.
3 Bake for 25–30 minutes or until top is crisp and golden. Serve with whipped cream or ice cream.

Note: Apple Crumble can be eaten hot or cold. Other fruits such as peaches, apricots, cherries or nectarines can be stewed and substituted for apples. Canned peaches or apricots, well-drained, can also be used.

Angelica seeds are used in the preparation of vermouth chartreuse and gin. A member of the carrot family, angelica has small pinkish white flowers in starburst clusters. Originally from northern Europe, it was brought to the warmer south by Vikings in the tenth century. It was believed to have supernatural powers and was used for protection against witches. In the seventeenth century the root was chewed or taken in a mixture called "angelica water."

Preparations made from angelica root have been used to relieve colic and toothache and to treat deafness and bronchial disorders; a North American species was used for similar medicinal purposes by early European settlers. To Native Americans, it was known as "hunting or fishing root" and was rubbed onto the hands so the smell would attract fish and game.

Angels on Horseback
An appetizer consisting of oysters wrapped in thin strips of bacon, grilled or baked until the bacon is crisp.

Anglaise, à l' A French term for boiled vegetables served with butter and chopped parsley, and for meat and poultry cooked in white stock. It is also applied to grilled fish served with melted butter.

Anise European anise is a member of the parsley family and has a licorice-like flavor and fragrance. The plant is native to Egypt, where it still grows wild, and to Greece and parts of southwest Asia. The aromatic seeds are sprinkled on some types of bread, and are used to flavor coffee cakes, salads and chicken dishes. Oil extracted from anise is used to flavor desserts and beverages.

Anisette A very sweet clear liqueur that is made with anise seeds and tastes like licorice.

Antipasti (Antipasto) The Italian term for appetizers, literally "before the pasta." It includes a vast array of meats, cheeses and pickles. There are three main categories of traditional antipasti: *affettati*, consisting of sliced cured meats such as hams and salamis; *antipasto misto*, an assortment of dishes, often without meat, including mini pizzas, cheese and raw, cooked and marinated vegetables; and *antipasto misto mare*, dishes of shellfish and small fish. See also Canapés; Hors d'oeuvre.

APRICOTS

APRICOT VEAL BIRDS

★★ **Preparation time:** 30 minutes
Total cooking time: 30 minutes
Serves 4–6

8 thin veal cutlets, about 3½ oz each
1 cup cooked rice
4 oz finely chopped dried apricots
1 tablespoon finely chopped candied ginger
¼ cup chopped fresh cilantro
2 tablespoons oil

2 tablespoons butter

Sauce
1 onion, sliced in rings
1 cup apricot nectar (juice)
½ cup good quality white wine
¼ cup French onion soup mix

1 Preheat oven to warm 325°F. Trim meat of any excess fat or tendons. Using a meat mallet or rolling pin, flatten cutlets, between plastic wrap, to an even thickness.
2 Combine rice, apricots, ginger and cilantro in a small mixing bowl; mix well. Place cutlets on a flat surface. Place spoonful of filling along one end of each piece; roll and tie up securely with string at regular intervals.
3 Heat oil and butter in a heavy-based frying pan. Cook meat rolls quickly in a single layer over medium-high heat until well browned; drain on paper towels. Arrange the rolls in casserole dish.
4 To make Sauce: Remove excess oil and butter from pan, leaving about 1 teaspoon. Add onion and cook for 2–3 minutes over medium heat until well browned. Add combined apricot

nectar, wine and soup mix. Stir over low heat until the mixture boils and thickens. Remove from heat and pour over meat rolls in casserole dish. Cover and bake for 25 minutes or until the meat is cooked through and tender. Remove string from rolls before serving. Apricot Veal Birds may be served with a green salad or steamed vegetables.

APRICOT AND LEMON JAM

★★ **Preparation time:** 15 minutes + overnight soaking
Total cooking time: 1 hour
Makes 10 cups

1 lb dried apricots
5 cups water
5 lemons
2 lb sugar, warmed

1 Soak apricots in half the water for 24 hours. Boil lemons in remaining water until soft.
2 When lemons are cold, slice thinly, removing but not discarding the seeds.
3 Boil apricots in soaking water until tender. Add the sugar and sliced lemons, together with the water in which they were boiled and the seeds, tied in a small cheesecloth bag. Boil the jam mixture until it gels (see JAMS). Discard the cheesecloth bag.
4 Ladle jam into warm, sterilized jars and seal. When cool, label and date.

ABOUT APRICOTS

■ Buy apricots that are heavy for their size, firm and plump with a bright color. Store them in a cool place. To ripen apricots, store them in a brown paper bag in a dark place. Fully ripe fruit will deteriorate very quickly at room temperature.

■ To cook fresh apricots, halve fruit and remove pits, if desired. Place in a pan, cover with water, add 2 tablespoons sugar. Bring to the boil, reduce heat and simmer until tender.

■ To quickly process dried apricots, place in a pan, cover with cold water, bring to boil. Reduce heat and simmer, covered, until tender.

■ Apricot jam can be heated, sieved and used as a glaze for fruit tarts and cakes. To make it into a sauce for baked fruits and ice cream, heat ¾ cup apricot jam with 4 tablespoons water. Sieve into a sauce boat and stir in 1 tablespoon apricot brandy. Serve warm.

ABOVE: APRICOT VEAL BIRDS. OPPOSITE PAGE, ABOVE: APRICOT PIE; BELOW: CHOCOLATE GLACE APRICOTS

APRICOT PIE

★★ **Preparation time:** 40 minutes
Total cooking time: 35 minutes
Makes 9 inch round pie

2 cups all-purpose flour	1 can (16 oz) apricot
3/4 cup cornflakes	halves in light syrup,
3/4 cup butter, chopped	drained
2 tablespoons sugar	1 can (21 oz) apricot pie
1/2 cup milk	filling
1 egg, lightly beaten	1 egg yolk
1/3 cup packed brown	1 tablespoon water
sugar	2 tablespoons sugar

1 Brush a 9 inch round pie plate with melted butter or oil. Place flour, cornflakes and butter in food processor bowl; add 2 tablespoons sugar. Cover and process for 15 seconds or until mixture is fine and crumbly. Stir together milk and egg. Add egg mixture to food processor bowl. Cover and process for 15 to 20 seconds or until mixture comes together. Wrap pastry in plastic wrap and refrigerate for 10 minutes. Roll half of the pastry between 2 sheets of waxed paper, until large enough to cover base and sides of pie plate. Place pastry in pie plate.
2 Preheat oven to moderate 350°F. Sprinkle brown sugar over the pastry and top with the apricot halves. Spoon on apricot pie filling; smooth surface. Roll the other half of the pastry to fit over the top of pie. Stir together egg yolk and 1 tablespoon water. Brush pastry edges with egg yolk mixture; gently press together to seal. Trim edges. Brush the surface of the pie with egg yolk mixture.

3 Sprinkle pie with 2 tablespoons sugar. Bake for 35 minutes or until pastry is golden. Cool completely on a wire rack.

CHOCOLATE GLACE APRICOTS

★ **Preparation time:** 45 minutes
Total cooking time: 5–10 minutes
Makes about 24

8 oz candied apricots	2 oz white chocolate,
3 oz dark (semisweet) or	chopped
milk chocolate, chopped	

1 Line a tray with waxed paper or foil. Cut each apricot into three pieces.
2 Place the dark chocolate in a small heatproof bowl. Stand bowl over a pan of simmering water and stir until the chocolate has melted and is smooth. Cool slightly. Dip the apricot pieces one at a time into chocolate, coating half of each. Drain off the excess chocolate. Place on prepared tray. Set aside.
3 Place white chocolate in a small heatproof bowl. Stand over pan of simmering water, stir until chocolate has melted and is smooth. Cool slightly. Spoon chocolate into small paper icing bag, seal open end. Snip the tip off the piping bag. Pipe white chocolate in squiggles, lines, initials or other design onto dark chocolate. Allow to set.

Note: Chocolate Glacé Apricots can be made up to 3 weeks ahead. Store in an airtight container.

Anzac Biscuit An oat and coconut cookie that originated in Australia during World War I, when eggs were scarce.

Apéritif A French term for a light, dry alcoholic drink such as dry white wine or a dry sherry. It is served before a meal to stimulate the appetite.

Appetizers Food eaten before the main meal to stimulate or excite the appetite.
See also Canapés; Hors d'oeuvre.

Apple A round, thin-skinned fruit that has a center core. Apples are the most widely cultivated of all fruits; they can be red, golden, or green in color, with sweet to tart flavors and crisp or mealy textures. The tens of thousands of apple varieties available today are believed to have descended from a tree native to the Middle East and the Balkans. The apple was introduced in North America during the eighteenth and nineteenth centuries. Folk hero Johnny Appleseed is credited with spreading the fruit to every part of the United States. Over 300 varieties are available commercially in the country and over 2500 varieties are grown. There are both eating and cooking varieties of apple. They can be cooked, dried, or made into apple juice and cider. Apples are on the market throughout the year; however, they are at their peak from October through March. For canning or freezing, preserve apples as promptly after picking as possible to retain their sweet tart flavor. Commercial apple growing is concentrated in the north where the trees flower and fruit best. Apples are a good source of dietary fiber, vitamin C and potassium. Mealiness in apples indicates a long storage period. The skins should be tight and blemish free. Apple flavor can be improved in cooking by adding lemon juice.

Applejack A potent apple-flavored brandy made from apple cider. France is famous for its apple brandy called *Calvados.*

Applesauce A thick cooked purée of apples, sugar and spices.

Apple Snow A dessert made with beaten egg whites, applesauce, lemon juice, spices and gelatin. It is set and sprinkled with cinnamon.

Apricot The apricot was first cultivated in China more than 4000 years ago. It grew in Nebuchadnezzar's

ARTICHOKES

ARTICHOKE AND ASPARAGUS SALAD

Preparation time: 20 minutes
Total cooking time: 10 minutes
Serves 4

1 bunch fresh asparagus
5 oz green beans
5 oz button mushrooms
5 canned or marinated
   artichoke hearts
2 tablespoons butter
½ teaspoon ground sweet
   paprika

2 cloves garlic, sliced thinly
2 tablespoons olive oil
2 tablespoons lemon juice
¼ teaspoon black pepper
2 tablespoons finely
   chopped mint

1 Cut the asparagus spears into 2 inch lengths. Trim the tops off the beans, leaving the tails on. Cut the mushrooms and artichoke hearts into quarters.
2 Half fill a medium saucepan with water; bring to boil. Place asparagus and beans into boiling water for 1–2 minutes or until they turn bright green. Remove from heat. Plunge into a bowl of ice water and leave until chilled; drain.
3 Heat butter in a small pan. Add paprika and garlic, cook for 1 minute. Add mushrooms, cook 2–3 minutes; remove from heat.
4 Combine oil, lemon juice, pepper and mint in a small bowl. Mix well. Place asparagus, beans, mushrooms and artichokes in a medium bowl. Pour over oil mixture and toss well. Transfer salad to serving bowl.

PENNE WITH ARTICHOKE HEARTS

Preparation time: 10 minutes
Total cooking time: 15 minutes
Serves 8

1 lb penne pasta
1 tablespoon olive oil
2 leeks, thinly sliced
2 medium red peppers,
   cut into ½ inch strips
2 garlic cloves, crushed

13 oz can artichoke
   hearts, drained and
   quartered
1 tablespoon lemon juice
2 tablespoons butter
½ cup freshly shaved
   Parmesan cheese

1 Cook pasta in a large pan of boiling water until just tender. Meanwhile, heat oil in a medium heavy-bottom pan, add leeks and cook, stirring, on medium heat for 3 minutes.
2 Add peppers and garlic and cook, stirring, for 3 minutes. Stir in artichoke hearts and lemon juice.
3 Drain pasta and return to large pan. Add butter and stir through to coat pasta, then add artichoke mixture and combine well. Serve immediately, with shavings of fresh Parmesan.

ABOUT ARTICHOKES

■ To prepare artichokes, trim stalks, remove hard outer leaves and wash well under cold water. Artichokes may be steamed or baked (see specific recipes); cook only until center leaves can be easily pulled out.

LEFT: ARTICHOKE AND ASPARAGUS SALAD; ABOVE: PENNE WITH ARTICHOKE HEARTS. OPPOSITE PAGE: ARTICHOKES WITH TARRAGON MAYONNAISE

ARTICHOKES WITH TARRAGON MAYONNAISE

★★

Preparation time: 30 minutes
Total cooking time: 30 minutes
Serves 4

4 medium artichokes
1/4 cup lemon juice

1 egg yolk
1/2 teaspoon French mustard

Tarragon Mayonnaise
1 tablespoon tarragon vinegar

2/3 cup olive oil
salt and white pepper to taste

1 Trim stalks from base of artichokes. Using scissors, trim points from outer leaves. With a sharp knife, cut top from artichoke. Brush all cut areas with lemon juice to prevent discoloration.
2 Steam the artichokes for 30 minutes, until they are tender. Add more boiling water to the pan if necessary. Remove from heat and set aside to cool.

3 To make Tarragon Mayonnaise: Place vinegar, egg yolk and mustard in a medium mixing bowl. Using a wire whisk, beat for one minute. Begin to add the oil a teaspoon at a time, whisking constantly until the mixture is thick and creamy. As mayonnaise thickens, continue to add oil by pouring in a thin, steady stream. Keep whisking until all the oil has been added; season to taste. Place a cooled artichoke on each plate and top with a little Tarragon Mayonnaise.

Note: Cooked artichokes can be eaten with the fingers; pull leaves off one at a time, dip the base of the leaf into sauce or melted butter and scrape the fleshy part off with the teeth (the leaves at the center of the artichoke are more tender, and more of each is edible). When the furry center or "choke" is reached, it should be removed and discarded. Use a fork to eat the tender base of the artichoke. Finger bowls should be provided, as well as a bowl for the discarded leaves.

1

2

3

Hanging Gardens of Babylon and was an expensive delicacy in Ancient Rome. The Persians called the soft golden fruit "eggs of the sun". The apricot was taken to Britain from Italy in the mid-1500s by the gardener of Henry VIII.

Fresh ripe apricots, usually available from late May to mid August, should be firm in texture; if wrinkled they lack flavor. Store firm apricots at room temperature and refrigerate ripe fruit. Apricots are eaten raw or cooked as a dessert, made into jams and teamed with lamb and chicken in main dishes. Dried, canned and glacé apricots are available throughout the year.

Arborio Rice A variety of rice, originally grown in Italy. It has a short, plump, oval shape and cooks to a smooth,

creamy consistency. Readily available in speciality stores and some supermarkets, it is used in risotto.

Arrowroot A fine white powder obtained from the root of the maranta, a white-flowered plant of the Caribbean. An easily digestible starch, it is used as a thickener in sauces. Because it thickens at a lower temperature than either flour or cornstarch, arrowroot is often used in delicate sauces that should not be boiled.

Arroz con Pollo
A Spanish or Mexican dish consisting of green pepper, rice, chicken, garlic, olive oil, and herbs and spices. Saffron gives it its characteristic yellow color.

Artichoke Two vegetables carry the name artichoke: the globe artichoke, which is the silvery-gray leafy bud of a large thistle-like plant; and the Jerusalem artichoke, the white-fleshed root of a relative of the sunflower.

The globe artichoke probably originated on the coasts of the western Mediterranean. It was not eaten widely until the fifteenth

century when under the patronage of the Medicis of Florence it emerged as a culinary aristocrat with a reputation as an aphrodisiac. By the sixteenth century the globe artichoke was well established in Italy and France, where it remains popular today. In North America it is not mentioned until the late 1800s when, introduced

ASPARAGUS

ASPARAGUS HOLLANDAISE ROLLS

Preparation time: 30 minutes
Total cooking time: 15 minutes
Makes about 30

1 bunch fresh asparagus
30 slices fresh white bread

Hollandaise Sauce
1 tablespoon white vinegar
5 peppercorns
1/2 teaspoon dried tarragon
2 egg yolks
1/2 cup unsalted (sweet) butter, melted
2 teaspoons lemon juice

1 Cut asparagus spears in half. Place in medium pan with a small amount of water. Cook over low heat until just tender. Plunge into cold water, drain. Pat dry with paper towels.
2 Cut out a round from each bread slice with a 3 inch cutter.
3 Place a piece of asparagus across each bread round. Spoon a teaspoonful of Hollandaise Sauce on top. Fold in half, secure edges with toothpick.
4 To make Hollandaise Sauce: Combine vinegar, peppercorns and tarragon in small pan. Bring to boil and simmer until liquid has reduced to one teaspoon. Place egg yolks in a food processor. Add strained vinegar liquid, process. Add melted butter in a thin, steady stream through chute in the food processor lid, with machine running. Process until mixture is thick; stir in lemon juice.

BEEF AND ASPARAGUS

Preparation time: 15 minutes + 30 minutes marinating
Total cooking time: 10 minutes
Serves 4

1 lb round steak
2 tablespoons soy sauce
1 tablespoon dry sherry
2 teaspoons finely grated ginger
1 teaspoon sesame oil
1 clove garlic, crushed
1 medium red chili pepper, cut into fine strips
12 spears fresh asparagus
2 tablespoons peanut oil
1 teaspoon cornstarch

1 Trim meat of any fat and tendons. Slice across the grain evenly into long, thin strips. Combine soy sauce, sherry, ginger, sesame oil, garlic and chili; add meat, stirring to coat. Leave for 30 minutes. Drain the meat, reserving marinade.
2 Cut woody ends off asparagus; cut spears into 2 inch pieces. Heat 1 tablespoon oil in wok or heavy-bottom frying pan, swirling gently to coat base and side. Add asparagus; stir-fry over medium heat for 2 minutes. Remove from wok; keep warm. Heat remaining oil in wok, cook meat quickly in small batches over high heat until browned but not cooked through. Remove and drain on paper towels.
3 Blend cornstarch with the reserved marinade until smooth. Return asparagus and meat to wok with marinade mixture. Stir-fry over high heat until meat is cooked through and sauce has thickened. Serve at once.

ASPARAGUS IN LEMON SAUCE

Preparation time: 20 minutes
Total cooking time: 10 minutes
Serves 6

3 bunches fresh
 asparagus, trimmed
2 tablespoons butter
1 tablespoon all-purpose
 flour
3/4 cup water

1 egg yolk
1/3 cup lemon juice
2 teaspoons finely grated
 lemon rind
1/3 cup whole blanched
 almonds, toasted

1 Place prepared asparagus in a large shallow pan of simmering water and cook uncovered until just tender, about 8–10 minutes. Drain on paper towels.
2 Melt butter in small pan. Add flour; cook, stirring, for one minute. Remove from heat and gradually add water. Return to heat and stir constantly until mixture boils and thickens. Remove from heat and whisk in combined egg yolk, lemon juice and rind. Return to heat and stir over gentle heat for 3–4 minutes.
3 Arrange the asparagus on one large platter or individual serving plates; pour over the lemon sauce. Garnish with the toasted almonds and serve.

ASPARAGUS WITH THAI DRESSING

Preparation time: 8 minutes
Total cooking time: 6 minutes
Serves: 6–8

2 bunches fresh asparagus
1 small onion, sliced
1/2 cup chopped mint
1/2 cup chopped cilantro
1/4 cup vegetable oil

1 tablespoon lime or
 lemon juice
1 tablespoon nuoc mam
pinch dry red chili flakes
lettuce leaves

1 Trim and diagonally slice the asparagus into 3 inch lengths. Steam over simmering water in a covered saucepan until they are just tender, about 4–6 minutes. Refresh under cold running water. Drain thoroughly on paper towels.
2 Toss the asparagus with the onion slices, mint and cilantro. Cover; chill for 2–3 hours before serving.
3 Blend together oil, citrus juice, nuoc mam and chili flakes; pour over asparagus mixture and arrange on lettuce-lined plates.

OPPOSITE PAGE: BEEF AND ASPARAGUS.
RIGHT: CREAMY ASPARAGUS SOUP

CREAMY ASPARAGUS SOUP

Preparation time: 5 minutes
Total cooking time: 5 minutes
Serves 4

2 x 11 oz cans green
 asparagus spears
1 cup chicken stock
3/4 cup heavy cream
2 egg yolks

freshly ground white
 pepper
1 tablespoon snipped
 chives

1 Place asparagus spears, liquid from cans and chicken stock in electric blender or food processor and blend until smooth. Pour mixture into a saucepan and bring to the boil. Remove from heat.
2 Beat cream lightly with egg yolks and stir slowly into soup, season with pepper. Reheat soup without boiling.
3 Serve soup sprinkled with chives.

ABOUT ASPARAGUS

■ Select crisp, straight stems of similar size for even cooking.
■ To store, keep refrigerated, wrapped in damp paper towels in a plastic bag. To prepare, scrape stalks to remove small nibs; remove hard sections from base of stalk.
■ To steam asparagus without a steamer, tie the asparagus together and stand the bundle in a large pan containing a small amount of simmering water. Cover and cook over low heat until it is just tender.

by Italian settlers in California, it was called the French artichoke. Globe artichokes can be pickled whole when small; both heart and bases are sold canned or frozen.

Despite its name, the Jerusalem artichoke has nothing at all to do with the Middle Eastern city: "jerusalem" is a corruption of *girasole*, the Italian word for sunflower, to which this plant is closely related. It comes, in fact, from North America, where it was cultivated by Native Americans, and is also known as Canadian artichoke. In the early 1600s, Samuel de Champlain, the founder of Quebec, noted in his diary that the roots had a taste somewhat like the heart of the European globe artichoke, hence the name.

By 1620 the vegetable was available in the street markets of Paris. It was first grown and eaten in England at about the same time, and not long afterwards appeared in Italy. Its reception was generally subdued, many regarding it as fit only for swine, its usual role in Europe today.

Arugula A salad green with a peppery mustard flavor that complements milder greens in a mixed green salad. Arugula is highly perishable and should be wrapped in plastic and refrigerated for no more than 2 to 3 days. It is also called *rocket*, *rugula* and *rucola*.

Asafetida A bitter, garlic-smelling condiment, prepared since the time of ancient Rome, and now used mainly in Indian and Middle Eastern cooking.

Asian Pear (Nashi) A pear with thin gold to brown skin, white meat, and a core like that of an apple. It tastes similar to an apple and a pear.

Asparagus The young shoots of a member of the lily family. There are two types: the slender-stalked green asparagus with purple buds, harvested when stalks are above ground; and the white asparagus, harvested while the stalks are still below ground. White asparagus is more expensive, and is rarely in the markets. Asparagus is available in the early spring. Choose firm stalks with tight tips.

Known since ancient times, asparagus was not widely used until the seventeenth century, when it became popular in France. By the eighteenth century it was well established in North America.

■ A V O C A D O S

HOT AVOCADO SALAD

⭐ **Preparation time**: 20 minutes
Total cooking time: 15 minutes
Serves 6 as a side dish

3 medium avocados	*2 teaspoons sugar*
1 medium tomato	*2 teaspoons sweet chili*
4 slices bacon, optional	*sauce*
1 medium red onion,	*2 tablespoons balsamic*
finely chopped	*vinegar*
1 red pepper, finely diced	*1 cup grated Cheddar*
1 stalk celery, finely diced	*cheese*

1 Preheat oven to 350°F. Brush a 10 inch pie plate with oil or melted butter. Cut avocados in half lengthwise, remove pits. Scoop out two-thirds of flesh, roughly chop. Retain shells.
2 Peel, seed and finely dice tomato. Trim bacon and place on cold broiler rack. Broil under medium-high heat until crisp; cool slightly and chop finely. Combine avocado, tomato, bacon, onion, pepper and celery in a bowl. Combine sugar, chili sauce and vinegar in a small screw-top jar; shake well. Pour over ingredients in bowl and mix well.
3 Spoon the filling into the avocado halves; sprinkle with cheese. Place in prepared dish. Bake 7–10 minutes or until heated through. Serve immediately with corn chips, crackers or thin slices of white toast.

AVOCADO WITH LIME AND CHILIES

⭐ **Preparation time**: 20 minutes
Total cooking time: none
Serves 6

1 teaspoon finely grated	*1 tablespoon olive oil*
lime rind	*2–3 jalapeño chili*
2 tablespoons lime juice	*peppers, seeded, sliced*
1 teaspoon brown sugar	*2 ripe avocados, peeled,*
1 tablespoon chopped	*sliced*
fresh parsley	

1 Thoroughly combine lime rind and juice, sugar, parsley, oil and chili peppers in a small bowl. Pour over sliced avocado.
2 Serve as a tangy side salad to fish, shellfish, chicken or meat dishes.

ABOUT AVOCADOS

■ Buy avocados 3 to 7 days before use. Choose even-colored fruit that is slightly soft at the stem end. To hasten ripening, store at room temperature in a brown paper bag with a banana. Ripe avocado flesh will yield to gentle pressure. Freezing will cause the flesh to turn black and ruin its texture.
■ Cut avocado in half lengthwise around pit; twist knife to separate halves; remove pit. Pull or peel skin off, beginning at narrow (stem) end. Brush surface of cut avocados with lemon juice to prevent discoloration.

A V O C A D O ,   T O M A T O
A N D   H A M   F L A N

★ **Preparation time** 15 minutes
Total cooking time: 40 minutes
Serves 6

8 slices bread, crusts
  removed
3 tablespoons butter, softened

Filling
3 oz sliced ham
4 large cherry tomatoes,
  sliced

½ large ripe avocado,
  sliced
1 cup grated cheddar cheese
3 eggs
⅓ cup sour cream
⅓ cup milk

1 Preheat oven to moderately hot 425°F. Flatten
bread with a rolling pin. Spread both sides of
slices with butter, cut each in half diagonally.
Press into a 9 inch round pie plate, evenly
covering base and sides. Bake for 10 minutes or
until lightly browned but crisp.
2 To make Filling: Reduce oven to moderate
350°F. Arrange ham, tomatoes, avocado and
cheese on cooked base. Combine eggs, sour
cream and milk in a bowl; mix well, pour over
pie filling. Bake for 30 minutes, or until filling is
lightly browned and set.

OPPOSITE PAGE: HOT AVOCADO SALAD.
ABOVE: AVOCADO WITH LIME AND CHILIES

A V O C A D O   A N D
S H R I M P   S A L A D   W I T H
C I T R U S   D R E S S I N G

Cut 2 large avocados in half and remove the
pits. Pile 5 oz small cooked and peeled shrimp
into the cavities in the avocados, scooping out a
little of the flesh to make room for the prawns if
necessary. Arrange the watercress on serving
plates and place filled the avocados on top. Place
3 tablespoons olive oil, 1 tablespoon lemon juice,
1 tablespoon orange juice, ½ teaspoon honey and
1 teaspoon chopped parsley in a small screw-top
jar and shake well. Drizzle the dressing over
the shrimp. Serve immediately. Serves 4 as a
first course.

A V O C A D O   V I N A I G R E T T E

Arrange 4 lettuce leaves (Romaine, leaf or
Boston lettuce) on serving plates. Peel
2 avocados and halve them lengthwise, remove
the pits and place on top of lettuce. Beat
1 tablespoon white wine or tarragon vinegar with
1 teaspoon French mustard, ¼ teaspoon sugar, salt
and freshly ground black pepper. Add
4 tablespoons of light olive oil, a drop at a time,
beating continuously so the dressing thickens.

Spoon the dressing into the avocado cavities.
Sprinkle with chopped chives or parsley and serve
immediately. Serves 4 as a first course.

Aspic A clear savory
jelly, prepared from
clarified stock made from
the gelatinous parts of
meat, chicken or fish and
usually flavored with
vegetables and herbs. It is
used to glaze cold dishes,
and to coat molds.

Avgolemono A soup
made from
chicken stock
flavored
with
lemon
juice and
thickened with egg yolk,
popular in Greece and
the Balkans. The name
also refers to a sauce
based on the same
ingredients which is
served with poached fish
or steamed vegetables.

Avocado A leathery-
skinned fruit with a large
pit and green, buttery
flesh and a slightly nutty
flavor. The avocado
comes from a tree
originating in Central
America. Avocado was
once called
"midshipmans' butter"
by the English, a name
probably dating from its
use as a crew food on
far-flung sailing ships.
Avocado is the main
ingredient of guacamole
and is used in many
Mexican dishes. Usually
served raw in salads,
sandwiches and as a first
course, it combines well
with spicy meats.

B

Baba (au Rhum) A dessert made of a yeast cake containing raisins, which is soaked in rum or kirsch one hour before serving. It has its origin in the sweetened yeast cakes, called *gugelhupf*, of central Europe and was named "Baba" by the Polish king Stanislaus for the hero of his favorite work of fiction, *The One Thousand and One Nights*. Savarin is a larger, ring-shaped version of the same cake, the center of which can be filled with fruit or ice cream before serving.

Baba Ghannouj (Imam Byildi) A dish from the Middle East, which is made from puréed eggplant flavored with tahini, garlic and lemon juice, served as a dip.

Babaco A cylindrical yellow fruit, related to the papaya, with soft yellow flesh that tastes like both banana and pineapple. Used in sweet and savory dishes, it can be used to tenderize meat and aid digestion.

Bacon Fat and lean meat, from the side and back of the pig, which

BACON

BACON, LETTUCE AND TOMATO SANDWICH

★ **Preparation time:** 10 minutes
Total cooking time: 5 minutes
Serves 2

2–4 slices bacon
1 firm ripe tomato
4 slices white or rye bread

2 large lettuce leaves
mayonnaise

1 Cut bacon slices in half. Cook in frying pan over medium heat until crisp; drain on paper towel.
2 Thinly slice tomato. Lightly toast bread slices. Spread with butter if desired.
3 Place one slice of bread on serving plate. Top with lettuce, bacon, tomato slice and a dollop of mayonnaise. Place remaining bread on top. Cut in half and serve warm.

Note: This sandwich is known throughout the world as a BLT. It is traditionally served with potato chips.

VARIATIONS:

■ Add thin slices of cooked chicken and turkey breast for a club sandwich.
■ Lay a slice of cheddar cheese on a slice of toast and broil until melted. Place remaining ingredients on top (omit mayonnaise). Serve warm.

BACON AND CHEESE BURGER

★ **Preparation time:** 30 minutes + 30 minutes standing
Total cooking time: 12 minutes
Makes 8 burgers

1 lb bacon, chopped
8 oz lean pork, trimmed and chopped
1/2 cup shredded Cheddar cheese

1/4 cup grated Parmesan cheese
1/2 cup fresh bread crumbs
pinch cayenne pepper
seasonings to taste
whole grain bread or buns

1 Place bacon, pork, cheeses, bread crumbs and seasonings in a food processor or blender. Process until finely chopped. Shape the mixture into 8 patties and chill.
2 Cook on oiled grill 6 minutes each side. Serve on whole grain bread or bun. Garnish as desired.

ABOUT BACON

■ To broil, place on a cold broiler tray, cook under a moderately high heat for 2–3 minutes each side. To pan-fry, place in a cold pan without oil or fat, cook over a low heat turning often. For really crisp bacon, drain fat from pan as bacon cooks.
■ To cook bacon in microwave, cook on 100% power until almost done. Let stand for 1–2 minutes (bacon will continue to cook slightly).

BANANAS

BANANA SPICE LOAF

⭐ **Preparation time:** 15 minutes
Total cooking time: 45 minutes
+ 5 minutes standing
Makes one 8 x 5 inch loaf

1½ cups all-purpose flour
1 teaspoon pumpkin pie
spice
1 teaspoon baking powder
¼ teaspoon baking soda
¼ teaspoon salt

½ cup unsalted (sweet)
butter, chopped
1 cup sugar
2 eggs, lightly beaten
⅓ cup plain yogurt
⅔ cup mashed ripe banana

1 Preheat oven to 350°F. Brush an 8 x 5 x 3 inch loaf pan with melted butter or oil. Line base and sides with wax paper; grease paper. Place flour, spice, baking powder, baking soda, salt, butter and sugar in food processor. Process for 10 seconds or until fine and crumbly. Add combined eggs, yogurt and banana, process 5 seconds or until mixture is combined; do not overbeat.
2 Spoon into pan; smooth surface. Bake 45 minutes or until a skewer comes out clean when inserted into center ofcake. Leave the cake in the pan for 5 minutes before turning onto wire rack to cool.

OPPOSITE PAGE: BACON, LETTUCE AND TOMATO SANDWICH. ABOVE: BANANA SPLIT

BANANA SPLIT

⭐ **Preparation time:** 5 minutes
Total cooking time: 10 minutes
Serves 4

Butterscotch Sauce
½ cup soft brown sugar
½ cup heavy cream
3 tablespoons butter

Split
4 large ripe bananas

8 small scoops vanilla
ice cream
8 oz strawberries,
hulled
12 white marshmallows
¼ cup chopped pecans

1 To make Butterscotch Sauce: Combine the brown sugar, cream and butter in a saucepan and stir over medium heat until mixture boils. Reduce heat and simmer for 3 minutes, then cool mixture to room temperature.
2 Peel bananas and cut in halves lengthwise. Arrange each banana in a long serving dish and top with two scoops of ice cream. Spoon sauce over and top with strawberries, marshmallows and pecans. Serve immediately.

ABOUT BANANAS

■ Allow bananas to ripen at room temperature. Once ripe, they can be stored in the refrigerator: the skins will turn black, but the fruit inside will not be affected. To avoid discoloration (the flesh will turn brown when exposed to the air), toss sliced bananas in lemon juice.

has been preserved by dry salting (curing) and is usually smoked as well. Bacon is sold in thin or thick slices. After cooking, bacon is about one-third of the raw weight. In separating raw bacon, tearing may be avoided if several slices are removed at one

time, then subdivided into singles. Good quality bacon has firm white fat and evenly spaced pink ribbons of meat. Canadian Bacon is lean and should be treated like ham. See also Gammon; Speck.

Bagel A ring of non-sweet, baked yeast dough with a characteristic shiny, hard crust, which is the result of being boiled in water before baking. The bagel

originated in eastern Europe and became popular in the Jewish community in Vienna, which began producing it commercially. The name is from the Yiddish word for "ring." Bagels are often served toasted with cream cheese. Raisins, nuts, minced onion or other flavorings can be added to the dough.

Bagna Cauda A garlic and anchovy-flavored sauce served hot as a dip for raw vegetables. Originally from Piedmont in Italy, it is associated with the grape harvest and the rituals and celebrations that accompany winemaking.

Baguette (French Bread) A long, thin crusty loaf of bread made of bleached white flour. The baguette, which can be up to two feet long, is the classic bread of France. It appears on the table at every meal and its price is set by law.

Bake Blind To bake a pie shell before it is filled. After placing dough in pan, prick with a fork and weigh down with dried beans or rice to prevent rising during baking.

Baked Alaska A dessert made of cake and ice cream covered with meringue. Browned rapidly in the oven, the ice cream does not melt.

Baking Powder A leavening agent made of baking soda, an acid (usually cream of tartar), and starch or flour (usually cornstarch). When mixed with liquid, the soda reacts with the acid to produce bubbles of carbon dioxide,

BANANA PEANUT BUTTER CAKE

⭐ *Preparation time:* 20 minutes
Total cooking time: 1 hour
Makes one 9 inch loaf cake

1/3 cup unsalted (sweet) butter	1 cup all-purpose flour
1 cup firmly packed light brown sugar	3/4 cup whole-wheat flour
2 eggs, lightly beaten	1 1/2 teaspoons baking powder
1/3 cup crunchy peanut butter	1/2 teaspoon baking soda
3/4 cup mashed banana	1/2 cup milk
	confectioners' sugar, sifted

1 Preheat oven to 350°F. Brush a 9 x 5 x 3 inch loaf pan with melted butter or oil. Line base and sides with parchment paper; grease paper.
2 Using electric mixer, beat butter and brown sugar until mixed. Add eggs gradually, beat well after each addition. Add peanut butter; beat until combined.
3 Add banana. Stir flours, baking powder and soda together. Stir flour mixture alternately with milk into butter mixture, stir until just combined and mixture is almost smooth.
3 Spoon the mixture into the pan; smooth the surface. Bake for 1 hour or until skewer comes out clean. Leave in pan for 15 minutes, turn out onto wire rack to cool. Dust with powdered sugar just before serving.

HOT BANANAS WITH CINNAMON COCONUT SAUCE

⭐ *Preparation time:* 5 minutes
Total cooking time: 10 minutes
Serves 4

4 large bananas	2 tablespoons sugar
	1/2 teaspoon ground
Cinnamon Coconut Sauce	cinnamon
1 tablespoon all-purpose flour	1 1/3 cups canned coconut milk

1 Rinse bananas and remove ends. Place bananas into a covered steamer over a pan of boiling water; cook for 5 minutes. Use tongs and a knife to peel off banana skins (skins will be black but the fruit inside will be golden).
2 To make Cinnamon Coconut Sauce: Place flour, sugar and cinnamon in a pan and stir until well combined. Add coconut milk and blend until smooth. Stir constantly over medium heat until mixture boils and thickens. Simmer for 2 minutes. Serve with hot bananas.

BANANA SMOOTHIE

Combine in a blender or food processor 1/2 cup cold milk, 1 banana, 1/4 cup plain or fruit yogurt, 1 teaspoon honey, 1–2 scoops vanilla ice cream and a pinch of ground nutmeg. Process or blend until smooth. Pour into a long tall glass. Sprinkle with extra nutmeg to serve.

BANANA AND PASSIONFRUIT SMOOTHIE

Place in blender 1 banana, pulp of 2 passionfruit and 1/2 cup frozen fruit yogurt. Blend until smooth.

VARIATIONS

■ Add 1–2 tablespoons chocolate chips to banana smoothie mixture before blending.
■ Add 1–2 tablespoons wheat germ to banana smoothie mixture before blending for a high-protein hunger stopper.
■ Crushed ice, added before blending, produces a much thicker drink. This applies not only to banana smoothies but to all blended drinks.

ABOVE: HOT BANANAS WITH CINNAMON COCONUT SAUCE. OPPOSITE PAGE: STEAK WITH SPEEDY BARBECUE MARINADE

BARBECUE COOKING

STEAK WITH SPEEDY BARBECUE MARINADE

★ **Preparation time:** 5 minutes +
2 hours marinating
Total cooking time: 6-12 minutes
Serves 4

2 lb boneless chuck steak	*1 tablespoon tomato paste*
1 cup red wine	*1 tablespoon Dijon mustard*
2 tablespoons olive oil	*1 clove garlic, crushed*
1 tablespoon balsamic vinegar	*2 teaspoons soft brown sugar*

1 Trim meat of excess fat and tendons. Combine wine, oil, vinegar, tomato paste, mustard, garlic and sugar in a small bowl, whisk for one minute or until well combined. Place the meat in a large dish; pour marinade over. Store in the refrigerator, covered with plastic wrap, for 2 hours or overnight, turning occasionally. Drain the meat, reserving the marinade.
2 Place the meat on a lightly oiled grill. Cook over a high heat for 2 minutes on each side, turning once. For rare, cook for a further minute on each side. For medium and well-done, move the meat to a cooler part of the barbecue, continue to cook a further 2-3 minutes on each side for medium and 4-6 minutes on each side for

well-done; brush the meat with the reserved marinade during cooking.
3 Leave the meat in a warm place, covered with foil, for 2-3 minutes. Cut it across the grain into ¾ inch thick slices for serving.

SKEWERED GINGER PORK

★ **Preparation time:** 20 minutes +
1 hour marinating
Total cooking time: 10 minutes
Serves 6

1 lb boneless pork	*1 teaspoon sesame oil*
2 tablespoons grated fresh ginger	*1 tablespoon lemon juice*
½ teaspoon ground pepper	*1 small onion, grated*
	salt and pepper to taste

1 Cut the pork into cubes. In a small bowl, combine grated ginger, pepper, sesame oil, lemon juice and onion. Pour mixture over pork cubes and marinate for 1 hour.
2 Thread pork onto skewers and grill over medium-high heat for 5 minutes each side, or until slightly pink. Serve with a salad and hot bread rolls.

Note: For boneless pork, choose from center loin, tenderloin or boneless chops.

ABOUT BARBECUING

■ Give the barbecue plenty of time to heat. A good way to find out if the heat is right is to hold the palm of your hand about 4 inches above the glowing coals. If you pull it away in two seconds, you know the barbecue is ready for the food. Likewise, when cooking over a wood fire, make certain that the flames have died down completely to leave glowing coals covered with ash before starting to cook.
■ Cooking times depend on the thickness of the meat and the efficiency of the barbecue.
■ To test meat for doneness, press with blunt tongs. If it feels springy, it is rare; if slightly resistant, it is medium-cooked; if firm to the touch, it is well-done.
■ When barbecuing kabobs, oiled metal skewers are ideal because it is easier to remove the cooked meat from them. Or use bamboo skewers that have been soaked in water for an hour—this will prevent them from burning.
■ You can give food a smoked flavor with the addition to the fire of water-soaked mesquite or hickory chips just before cooking.

causing the mixture to rise and become porous.

Baking Soda See Bicarbonate of Soda.

Baklava A cake made of alternate layers of filo (phyllo) pastry and chopped nuts, which is doused in honey syrup while still hot and then cut into diamond or triangular pieces. Of Greek or Turkish origin, baklava first appeared in the 1300s. It is popular in the Middle East.

Balsamic Vinegar A richly flavored, dark-colored vinegar. It has a bittersweet taste, is almost syrupy in consistency and is used in salads or as a meat marinade. The vinegar is made from unfermented sweet Trebbiano grapes boiled to a thick syrup, to which wine vinegar is added. The mixture is aged in a series of aromatic hardwood casks for at least five years and sometimes a century or more. It is a specialty of the Modena region of Italy. Less expensive products attempt to imitate the flavor by adding caramel to red wine vinegar.

Bamboo Shoots The young, tender and slightly crunchy cone-shaped shoots of an edible bamboo plant found throughout tropical Asia. Their use as a food dates from sixth century China and they are also an important ingredient in Japanese and Korean cooking.

Banana The yellow-skinned, crescent-shaped fruit of a tall, long-leaved plant (actually a giant herb, not a tree) cultivated throughout the tropics. It has a creamy colored flesh with tiny edible black seeds. The many varieties range from finger-sized to a short red-skinned banana.

Bananas have been grown in tropical America since their introduction by the Spanish and Portuguese in the sixteenth century. Improved transport methods in the mid-twentieth century made the fruit common in Europe and North America.

The banana, which recently became the most popular fruit in America, is now available in fresh and dried form. As a general

BARBECUED PORK SPARERIBS

⭐ **Preparation time:** 15 minutes + 3 hours marinating
Total cooking time: 30 minutes
Serves 4–6

2 lb pork spareribs
2 cups tomato ketchup
1/2 cup sherry
2 tablespoons soy sauce
2 tablespoons honey
3 cloves garlic, crushed
1 tablespoon grated fresh ginger

1 Trim spareribs of excess fat and tendons. Cut racks of ribs into pieces, so that each piece has three or four ribs. Combine ketchup, sherry, soy sauce, honey, garlic and ginger in a large pan and mix well.
2 Add the ribs to mixture. Bring to the boil. Reduce heat and simmer, covered, for 15 minutes. Move ribs occasionally to ensure even cooking. Transfer ribs and sauce to a shallow non-metal dish; allow to cool. Refrigerate, covered with plastic wrap, for several hours or overnight. Prepare and heat barbecue 1 hour before cooking.
3 Place ribs on a hot, lightly oiled barbecue grill. Cook over the hottest part of the fire for 15 minutes, turning and brushing with sauce occasionally. Serve with barbecued corn-on-the-cob and potato salad, if desired.

RIGHT: GARLIC SHRIMP;
ABOVE: BARBECUED PORK SPARERIBS.
OPPOSITE PAGE: CHICKEN SATAY WITH
PEANUT SAUCE

GARLIC SHRIMP

⭐ **Preparation time:** 10 minutes + 3 hours marinating
Total cooking time: 3–5 minutes
Serves 4

1 lb raw jumbo shrimp

Marinade
2 tablespoons lemon juice
2 tablespoons sesame oil
2 cloves garlic, crushed
2 teaspoons grated fresh ginger

1 Remove the heads from the shrimp, peel and devein, leaving the tails intact (reserve the heads and shells for fish stock, if you like). Make a cut in each shrimp body, slicing three-quarters of the way through the flesh from head to tail, as if to butterfly them.
2 To make Marinade: Combine the lemon juice, sesame oil, garlic and ginger in a cup; mix well. Place the shrimp in a bowl; pour over the marinade; mix well. Cover and refrigerate for several hours or overnight. Prepare and light the barbecue 1 hour before it is required.
3 Cook shrimp on hot, lightly greased grill for 3–5 minutes or until pink in color and cooked through. Brush frequently with marinade while cooking. Serve immediately.

CHICKEN SATAY WITH PEANUT SAUCE

★ **Preparation time:** 30 minutes +
2 hours marinating
Total cooking time: 10 minutes
Makes 12

2 lb boneless chicken
thighs
1/4 cup soy sauce
1 tablespoon honey
2 tablespoons oil

Peanut Sauce
1 tablespoon oil
2 teaspoons dried onion
flakes

3/4 cup crunchy peanut
butter
1/2 cup coconut milk
1 tablespoon soy sauce
2 tablespoons sweet chili
sauce
1/2 cup water
salt, to taste

1 Remove skin and trim chicken of excess fat and tendons. Cut chicken into 3/4 inch strips, thread onto skewers. Place in a shallow glass dish. Combine soy sauce, honey and oil, pour over chicken. Cover with plastic wrap, chill 2 hours.
2 **To make Peanut Sauce:** Heat oil in a small heavy-bottom pan. Add onion flakes, cook over low heat 30 seconds. Add peanut butter, coconut milk, soy sauce, sweet chili sauce, water and salt; combine well. Cook until heated through.
3 Drain chicken, reserve marinade. Cook satay skewers over medium-high heat for 8 minutes on a greased grill. Turn often and brush with marinade. Serve immediately with Peanut Sauce.

Note: Soak the bamboo skewers in cold water for at least 30 minutes to prevent scorching. Alternatively, cover the ends with foil.

SWEET AND SPICY CORNISH GAME HENS

★ **Preparation time:** 40 minutes +
24 hours standing
Total cooking time: 40 minutes
Serves 8

4 frozen Cornish game
hens, thawed, halved
and cleaned

Marinade
30 oz can plums, drained
and pitted
1 onion, coarsely chopped

2 cloves garlic, crushed
1/4 cup red wine
1/4 cup teriyaki sauce
2 tablespoons chili sauce
juice of 1 lemon
1 teaspoon sesame oil
freshly ground pepper

1 Make several deep slashes in the flesh of each hen half. Set aside.
2 **To make Marinade:** Place all ingredients in a food processor or blender. Process until smooth. Place hens cut-side-down in a non-metal dish. Pour over marinade. Cover. Marinate in the refrigerator, turning and basting frequently, for at least 24 hours.
3 Drain the hens. Grill over medium coals for 20 minutes each side, basting frequently with Marinade.

rule, the smaller the banana variety, the sweeter the flesh. The fruit can be eaten raw or used in a variety of cooked sweet and savory dishes. A relative, the green-skinned plantain, contains less sugar and more starch and is cooked as a vegetable accompaniment to West Indian, South American and African dishes.

Bananas Foster A popular New Orleans dessert of sliced bananas that are cooked in rum, brown sugar and banana liqueur and served warm with ice cream.

Banbury Tart A small English tart consisting of a puff or flaky pastry shell filled with mincemeat.

Bannock A flat oatmeal and wheat flour Scottish cake cooked on a griddle.

Bap A soft, white bread roll which originated in Scotland.

Barbecue Cooking Roasting, grilling, broiling or smoking food over an open fire is the oldest form of cooking. Meat, poultry, fish, shellfish, vegetables and even fruit can be barbecued. The word also refers to the equipment used in the cooking. A barbecue can hold charcoal or wood, or employ gas or electricity. Food flavors are enhanced by basting with marinades and sauces during cooking, and by the fragrant smoke from aromatic woods and herbs thrown on the coals.

Barley A grain related to wheat, barley originated in the hilly areas of the Middle East. It was the chief grain of the ancient Greeks and in Rome was used to make bread as well as being the main food of gladiators. Pearl barley, the shiny grains that have been hulled and milled until they resemble small pearls, has been used in cooking since ancient times. It is still used in soups and stews. Barley water, prepared from the grain, has been a popular health drink since the time of the Greek physician Hippocrates. Today, barley is used to make malt for beer brewing and as a livestock food.

Barley Flour Ground barley; it should be combined with wheat flour when used to make bread.

Barley Sugar A brittle candy, traditionally made with water, in which barley has been simmered for several hours (barley water), and

TERIYAKI STEAKS WITH BLUE CHEESE AND HERB BUTTER

★★☆ **Preparation time:** 20 minutes + 2 hours marinating + 4 hours refrigeration
Total cooking time: 6-16 minutes
Serves 8

8 rib eye steaks, about 6½ oz each, or 8 boneless sirloin steaks
¼ cup teriyaki sauce
2 cloves garlic, crushed

Blue Cheese and Herb Butter
4 oz blue vein cheese, chopped

½ cup butter, softened
1 tablespoon dry white wine
1 teaspoon finely chopped fresh mint
½ teaspoon dried rosemary leaves
½ teaspoon dried oregano leaves

1 Trim the meat of excess fat and tendons. Combine the steaks with teriyaki sauce and garlic. Refrigerate, covered, for 2 hours or overnight, turning occasionally. Drain the meat, reserving the marinade.
2 Place the steaks on a lightly oiled grill. Cook over high heat for 2 minutes each side to seal, turning once. For rare meat, cook another minute on each side. For medium and well-done, move the meat to cooler part of barbecue and cook each side another 2–3 minutes (medium),

or 4–6 minutes (well-done); brush with the remaining marinade in the last minutes of cooking. Serve with slices of Blue Cheese and Herb Butter on top.
3 To make Blue Cheese and Herb Butter: Using electric beaters, beat cheese and butter in a small mixing bowl until light and creamy. Add wine and herbs; beat until just combined. Spoon mixture onto a large sheet of foil. Use foil to wrap, roll and shape cheese mixture into a log measuring 2 x 6 inches. Refrigerate 4 hours or overnight.

FISH CAKES IN CORN HUSKS

★★ **Preparation time:** 30 minutes + 10 minutes standing
Total cooking time: 20 minutes
Serves 4

foil for wrapping
4 corn cobs, complete with husks
1 lb firm white fish fillets, diced
2 cloves garlic, crushed
2 teaspoons chili powder (see Note)
⅓ cup finely chopped fresh cilantro

1 tablespoon chopped canned jalapeño peppers
1 egg, beaten
½ teaspoon ground black pepper
1 tablespoon lemon juice
2 tablespoons chopped scallions
1 teaspoon ground cumin

1 Cut foil into eight 6½ inch squares. Remove only four husks from each corn cob and set these aside. Turn back the remaining husks (being careful not to detach them) and remove the thread-like cornsilk. Pull husks back into position to enclose corn. Soak cobs in cold water for 10–15 minutes.
2 Purée the fish fillets in a food processor until just smooth. Add the garlic, chili powder, cilantro, jalapeño, beaten egg, pepper, lemon juice, green onions and cumin to the food processor and blend until all ingredients are well combined. Divide mixture into eight equal portions.
3 Wrap each portion in two of the reserved corn husks, making eight parcels. Wrap each parcel in a square of foil.
4 Grill corn cobs on barbecue for 20 minutes, turning once or twice during cooking.
5 Place wrapped fish cakes on medium-hot grill for last 8 minutes of corn cob cooking time.

Note: Chili powder contains a mixture of chilies, cumin and oregano.

BASIL

MOZZARELLA, BASIL AND TOMATO SALAD

⭐ **Preparation time:** 10 minutes
Total cooking time: none
Serves 6

6 medium, ripe tomatoes	4 tablespoons virgin
3–4 fresh small	olive oil
mozzarella (bocconcini)	shredded basil leaves
cheeses	freshly ground black
1 tablespoon lemon juice	pepper

1 Slice the tomatoes thickly; slice the mozzarella thinly. Arrange on a serving plate, alternating between the slices of tomato and the slices of mozzarella.
2 Combine lemon juice and olive oil in a small bowl. Mix well using a wire whisk. Drizzle dressing over salad. Sprinkle with basil leaves and black pepper.

Note: This salad is best made just before serving. Have tomatoes at room temperature to make the most of their flavor.

OPPOSITE PAGE: TERIYAKI STEAKS WITH BLUE CHEESE AND HERB BUTTER. ABOVE: MOZZARELLA, BASIL AND TOMATO SALAD

PESTO

⭐ **Preparation time:** 10 minutes
Total cooking time: none
Makes 2 cups

4 cloves garlic, peeled	1 1/2 cups grated Parmesan
2 cups fresh basil leaves	cheese
1 cup parsley sprigs	1 1/2 cups olive oil
2/3 cup pine nuts	

1 Place garlic, basil, parsley, pine nuts and Parmesan cheese in a food processor or blender. Blend at medium speed, adding oil in a thin stream until smooth.
2 Place in a clean jar, cover with a thin layer of oil, store in the refrigerator for up to 2 weeks. Pour away oil before using.

ABOUT BASIL

■ Of the many types now grown, sweet basil is the most widely used; other varieties include an extravagantly ruffled purple version, often used as a garnish; the small-leaved, spicier Greek or perennial basil; and dark opal, which is a decorative red-leafed variety.
■ Store fresh basil in the refrigerator standing upright in a bottle or jar of water up to 3 days. Cover the leaves loosely with a plastic bag.
■ Dried basil has a stronger flavor than ground basil. Store in airtight jars in a cool, dark place.

sugar. Today it is made of boiled sugar, without barley, but with other flavorings.

Barquette A small boat-shaped tart shell made of either pie dough or puff pastry. Pressed into small molds and baked blind, they are filled with sweet or savory ingredients.

Basil A robust, pungent herb related to mint. Its color varies from green to purple, and the flavor combines well with tomatoes, zucchini and spinach; it has a concentrated lemon flavor that is a good accompaniment for fish. Basil is also used in salads, sauces and

stuffings.
Pesto, a purée of basil, nuts, olive oil and cheese, is popular on pasta.

Basmati An aromatic, long-grained rice with a nutty flavor that is aged to decrease its moisture content. Much used in India, it has been grown for thousands of years in the Himalayan foothills.

Bass A variety of fresh and saltwater fish with rough scales. Sold fresh or frozen, it can be broiled, grilled or baked.

Baste To moisten food while it is cooking with

pan juices, melted fat or a marinade.

Batter A mixture of flour and liquid which can be cooked by itself, in pancakes, waffles, doughnuts or

funnel cakes, or used to coat foods such as fish, vegetables, or edible flowers and fruits. The term fritter is used to describe foods covered in a batter and deep-fried. Batter-dipped fish probably originated in China. The word *batter* comes from the French, *battre*, to beat, and also refers to a cake mixture.

Bavarian Cream (Bavarois) A cold, molded custard made by folding gelatin and an egg and whipped cream mixture together, with fruits or flavorings, and then chilling until firm.

Bay (Bay Leaf) The stiff leaf of the evergreen bay (laurel) tree, native to the Mediterranean. It imparts a pungent woody aroma when added to stews, soups and tomato dishes.

The entire leaf, dried or fresh, is used, and then removed before eating. Fresh bay leaves are not readily

BEAN CURD

HONEY-BRAISED VEGETABLES WITH BEAN CURD

Preparation time: 30 minutes
Total cooking time: 20 minutes
Serves 6

8 dried Chinese mushrooms
3 thin slices, pared fresh ginger
20 dried lily buds (optional)
2 tablespoons peanut oil
1 medium sweet potato, halved and sliced
2 tablespoons soy sauce
1 tablespoon honey
2 teaspoons sesame oil

2 oz fried bean curd, cut into 1/2 inch strips
2 teaspoons cornstarch
4 scallions cut into 1 1/2 inch lengths
1 can (8 3/4 oz) whole baby sweet corn, drained
1 can (8 oz) whole water chestnuts, drained

1 Soak mushrooms in hot water for 30 minutes. Drain, reserving 1 cup liquid. Squeeze mushrooms to remove excess liquid. Remove stems and thinly slice caps. Slice ginger into very thin strips. Soak the lily buds separately, if using, in warm water for 30 minutes; drain well.
2 Heat the oil in a wok or large nonstick skillet over medium-high heat. Add ginger. Stir-fry for 1 minute. Add mushrooms and lily buds. Stir-fry for 30 seconds. Add sweet potato, soy, honey, sesame oil, mushroom liquid and fried bean curd.

Reduce heat. Simmer, uncovered, for 15 minutes.
3 Dissolve cornstarch in a little water. Push vegetables from the center of the wok. Add liquid to the center of the wok. Cook, stirring, until liquid thickens. Stir in scallions, corn and water chestnuts. Cook, stirring, for 1 minute or until heated through.

Note: Dried lily buds may be found in Chinese food stores. Used for their texture and subtle flavor, they have no substitute, but may be omitted without radically altering the dish.

ABOUT BEAN CURD

■ Fresh bean curd or tofu is sold in plastic containers, packaged in water, in the vegetable and refrigerator section of most supermarkets, and Asian and health-food stores; refrigerated, it will keep after opening for 4 days; change water daily. Firm (pressed) bean curd comes in square cakes and is best for slicing, cubing and stir-frying; silken (soft) bean curd is good for blending with other ingredients or for enriching dishes. Fried bean curd (aburage) is sometimes available, vacuum-packed; if not, firm bean curd can be deep-fried in oil.
■ Long-life bean curd will last for up to 6 months unrefrigerated.
■ Powdered bean curd is also available.

ABOVE: HONEY-BRAISED VEGETABLES WITH BEAN CURD. OPPOSITE PAGE: CHINESE CHICKEN AND NOODLES

BEAN SPROUTS

CHINESE CHICKEN AND NOODLES

Preparation time: 10 minutes
Total cooking time: 15 minutes
Serves 4

6 boneless chicken thighs, about 1½ lb	4 oz snow peas
⅓ cup satay sauce	4 cups chopped bok choy (Chinese cabbage)
2 tablespoons soy sauce	2 cups bean sprouts
2 tablespoons sherry	2 tablespoons cornstarch
2 tablespoons oil	1 cup chicken stock
1 onion, cut into eighths	salt, to taste
2 medium carrots, thinly sliced	4 oz fresh Chinese egg noodles

1 Trim chicken of excess fat and tendons. Cut into 1 inch cubes. Combine with satay sauce, soy sauce and sherry in a large mixing bowl.
2 Heat oil in a heavy-bottom frying pan. Add onion and carrot and cook over high heat for 2 minutes, stirring occasionally. Add snow peas and bok choy and cook, stirring, over high heat for 1 minute. Remove from pan; set aside.
3 Add chicken mixture to pan. Cook, stirring occasionally, over high heat for 4 minutes or until chicken is tender and cooked through.
4 Return the vegetables to the pan. Add the bean sprouts and blended cornstarch and stock. Add salt, stir for 2 minutes or until the sauce boils and thickens. Cook the noodles in a medium pan of rapidly boiling water until just tender, for about 2 minutes. Drain. Place the noodles in deep individual serving plates, spoon the chicken and vegetables over the noodles. Serve immediately.

ABOUT BEAN SPROUTS

■ To grow bean sprouts: Place ¼ to ½ cup mung beans in a large glass jar (the beans will take up to 10 times the volume once sprouted). Rinse well, then soak in cold water for 12 hours. Drain the water from the beans, cover mouth of the jar with a piece of loosely woven fabric held in place with string, or an elastic band. Lay the jar on its side in a warm, well-lit place (not in direct sunlight); rinse and drain the beans twice a day for 3–4 days. Do not let the sprouting beans dry out or they will die. Sprouts are ready to eat when they are about 1 inch long.
■ Place sprouts in a large bowl of water and swish to release the husks. Remove husks with a slotted spoon (the husks are edible, but bean sprouts look more appetizing without them).
■ Alfalfa and other legumes can also be sprouted.

available to consumers. Dried leaves, which have a fraction of the flavor of fresh, can be found in supermarkets and are used in a bouquet garni. The aromatic leaves were used by the ancient Greeks to crown the victors in contests. In the Middle Ages, bay leaves were used to banish odors; only later were their culinary qualities appreciated.

Bay Scallop A small shellfish whose lean meat can be baked, fried, broiled or grilled.

Bean Curd Also called tofu, bean curd is a processed extract of the soy bean. It is made by soaking, boiling and sieving to produce a liquid which, after the addition of a coagulant, is similar in appearance and texture to fresh white cheese. Bean curd takes on the flavor of other ingredients in cooking. It can be stir-fried, broiled, grilled or baked and used in dips, spreads and salad dressing. Mashed bean curd can be used instead of cottage cheese or ground beef. Low calorie and high protein, bean curd is sold fresh or waterpacked in plastic containers.

Bean Sprouts The sprout of the mung bean and, less commonly, the soy bean, used in salads or as a stir-fry vegetable. They are very low in calories.

Beans, Dried The dried seeds of various plants in the legume family. Dried beans come in a wide variety of shapes and colors. Most popular are oval black beans (turtle beans); white, spotted blackeyed peas (cow peas); large white cannellini; chickpeas (garbanzos); white, kidney-shaped great northern beans; red or white kidney beans; small, greenish lima beans; small white navy beans; oval red beans; and soy beans are all available in markets. Traditionally, dried beans have played an important role in the diet of peoples of Central and South America and the Middle East.

Beans, Fresh The edible pods or seeds of a number of bean varieties, the most common varieties being green, lima and broad (fava) beans. Fresh beans range in color from pale yellow to deep purple. They include the string bean (called haricot vert in France), Italian green bean, yellow wax bean, Chinese long bean and

BEANS
DRIED AND CANNED

HEARTY BACON AND BEAN STEWPOT

★ **Preparation time:** 25 minutes
Total cooking time: 40 minutes
Serves 4–6

½ lb piece of boneless smoked ham hock or thick-sliced bacon (see Note)	3 large carrots, cut into ½ inch cubes
2 tablespoons oil	4 medium potatoes, about 1½ lb, peeled and cut into ½ inch cubes
2 small leeks, thinly sliced	15 oz can red kidney beans, rinsed and drained
2 tablespoons all-purpose flour	½ cup finely chopped parsley
2 cups chicken stock	½ teaspoon black pepper

1 Cut ham hock into ½ inch cubes. Place in a large pan; cook over low heat until crisp. Remove from pan and drain on paper towels. Remove excess fat from pan.
2 Heat oil in pan, add leeks and cook for 5 minutes until soft. Add the flour to pan. Stir over low heat for 2 minutes or until the flour mixture is lightly golden.
3 Add chicken stock gradually to the pan, stirring until mixture is smooth. Stir constantly over medium heat for about 3 minutes or until the

mixture boils and thickens; boil for another minute. Reduce heat; simmer.
4 When mixture is at simmering point, add the potatoes, carrots and ham hock; cover and cook gently over medium heat for 20 minutes or until potatoes and carrots are tender.
5 Add the beans, parsley and pepper and stir to combine. Cook over low heat for 5 minutes. Serve with a green vegetable such as steamed broccoli or green beans.

Note: Ham hock is the lower portion of a hog's hind leg and is often cut into 2 to 3 inch pieces. It is used to flavor soups, beans and stews.

SWEET BEAN SALAD

★ **Preparation time:** 35 minutes
Total cooking time: 15 minutes
Serves 4

1 lb frozen fava beans or lima beans	½ cup olive oil
2 cloves garlic, crushed	⅓ cup cider vinegar
1 leek, sliced	¼ cup soft brown sugar
1 large carrot, sliced	¼ cup chopped parsley

1 Cook beans in boiling water until tender, then drain.
2 Return beans to saucepan, add garlic, leek, carrot and olive oil; cook gently for 5 minutes. Add vinegar and brown sugar and cook 5 minutes longer, making sure brown sugar is dissolved.
3 Chill well. Garnish with chopped parsley.

ABOUT DRIED BEANS

■ Soak dried beans overnight in cold water, or cover with boiling water and stand for 2 hours; drain and rinse well. Place in a large pan, cover with water and cook over low heat for 40–50 minutes or until tender. (Some beans, such as soy beans, take much longer to cook.) To test beans, remove one or two from the water and press between thumb and finger—beans should feel soft but not mushy. If the center is still hard, cook for a little longer. Dried beans are much more economical than canned beans, but take a long time to prepare and cook. Canned beans can be substituted in all recipes that call for dried beans. They require no special preparation, needing only to be heated through.

■ Around 1 lb or 2½ cups dried beans yields 6 cups of cooked beans.

ABOVE: HEARTY BACON AND BEAN STEWPOT.
OPPOSITE PAGE: COUNTRY BEAN SALAD

COUNTRY BEAN SALAD

⭐ **Preparation time:** 15 minutes + 1 hour
standing + 1 hour refrigeration
Total cooking time: 45 minutes
Serves 4

1 cup dried cannellini
   beans
2 tomatoes
1 onion, thinly sliced
3 scallions, chopped
1/3 cup coarsely chopped
   parsley
1/2 red pepper, cut into
   strips
Dressing

1/4 cup olive oil
1 tablespoon lemon juice
2 teaspoons finely
   chopped fresh dill
salt and freshly ground
   black pepper, to taste
5 canned anchovy fillets,
   drained

1 Put beans into a medium pan; cover with water. Bring to boil, remove from heat; leave, covered, for one hour. Drain and rinse. Return beans to pan; cover with water. Bring to boil, reduce heat. Cover and simmer 40 minutes or until tender; drain.
2 To peel tomatoes, make a small cross on the top, place in boiling water for 1–2 minutes, then plunge immediately into cold water. Remove and peel down skin from the cross. Cut tomatoes in half; gently squeeze to remove seeds and roughly chop the flesh.
3 Place beans into a large bowl. Add tomato, onions, scallions, parsley and pepper; mix well.
4 To make Dressing: Combine oil, juice, dill,

salt and pepper and pour over salad; mix well. Cover salad and refrigerate for one hour.
5 Cut anchovies into long thin strips and arrange over salad just before serving.

PORK AND BEAN SOUP

⭐ **Preparation time:** 30 minutes
Total cooking time: 1 hour 40 minutes
Serves 4–6

1 tablespoon olive oil
2 cloves garlic, crushed
1 large onion, chopped
6 slices lean bacon,
   chopped
8 oz boneless pork, fat
   removed, diced
2 large ripe tomatoes,
   peeled and chopped
1 stalk celery, chopped

1 carrot, chopped
1/2 small cabbage, shredded
1/2 fennel bulb, chopped
2 teaspoons fresh thyme
   or 1/2 teaspoon dried
   thyme
6 cups chicken stock
2 x 10 oz cans mixed
   beans, drained

1 Heat oil in a large pan, add the garlic and onion and fry for one minute.
2 Add bacon and pork and cook over medium heat until the pork is well browned. Add tomatoes, celery, carrot, cabbage, fennel, thyme and chicken stock. Cover pan, bring to the boil, reduce heat and simmer for 1 1/4 hours.
3 Add the mixed beans and cook for another 15 minutes. Serve soup hot with some fresh, crusty bread or rolls.

the runner bean which has purple pods that turn green when cooked. Fresh beans can be steamed, boiled, microwaved or stir-fried. The bean pods are usually cut lengthwise, or in 1 or 2 inch lengths. Beans are available fresh, frozen or canned. Fresh bean pods should have a vivid color and a velvety feel.

The fresh bean is native to America where it was often found planted with corn. At first only its seeds were used, but by the late eighteenth century whole pods were eaten. The Chinese long bean (snake bean) has been cultivated since ancient times and is featured in Asian cooking.

Bean Thread See Cellophane Noodles.

Béarnaise Sauce A creamy golden sauce made with butter, egg yolk, and vinegar. It may include finely chopped

BEANS & BROCCOLI

If you overcook beans they lose their bright green color. When quickly cooked (they don't have to be hard, but they should never be flabby) beans are among the sweetest-tasting vegetables. When preparing broccoli, include the stems too. Don't overcook broccoli.

MINTED TOMATO AND BEANS

Cut 20 beans in half crosswise. Heat 1 teaspoon oil in frying pan. Add 1 clove crushed garlic, 1 teaspoon grated ginger, 1/2 teaspoon each of ground coriander, cumin and garam masala, 2 chopped ripe tomatoes. Cook, stirring, for 1 minute. Add beans, cook 2–3 minutes or until just tender.

GARLIC AND BASIL BEANS

BEAN AND WALNUT SALAD

Shred 20 green beans. Combine with 1/4 cup cilantro leaves, 4 torn red leaf lettuce leaves, 1/4 shredded red pepper, 1/4 cup walnut halves, 2 tablespoons tarragon vinegar, 1–2 tablespoons peanut oil and 2 tablespoons chopped fresh mint. Mix well. Serve immediately.

BEAN BUNDLES

Trim ends of 20 beans. Divide beans into bundles of five. Tie together with the green end of a scallion or chives. Steam or microwave until just tender. Sprinkle with lemon pepper. Serve warm.

GARLIC AND BASIL BEANS

Trim ends of 20 beans. Heat 1 tablespoon olive oil in frying pan or wok. Add 1 clove crushed garlic and beans. Cook, stirring, 2–3 minutes or until beans are just tender. Stir in 1 tablespoon shredded basil leaves. Serve warm.

BEAN BUNDLES

MINTED TOMATO AND BEANS

BEAN AND WALNUT SALAD

BROCCOLI AND ONION STIR-FRY

BROCCOLI AND ONION STIR-FRY

Cut 8 oz broccoli into small florets. Slice a medium onion into 8 wedges. Heat 2 teaspoons sesame oil and 2 teaspoons vegetable oil in pan. Add broccoli and onions, cook until just tender. Stir in 2 teaspoons soy sauce and 1 tablespoon sweet chili sauce. Sprinkle with herbs.

BROCCOLI AND MUSHROOMS

Cut 8 oz broccoli into small florets. Heat 2 tablespoons butter and 1 clove crushed garlic in heavy-bottom frying pan. Add 4 sliced button mushrooms. Cook over medium heat 2 minutes or until tender. Remove from pan, set aside. Add broccoli, stir-fry 3–4 minutes until tender. Return mushrooms to pan, and stir until just heated through.

BROCCOLI WITH BACON AND PINE NUTS

Cut 8 oz broccoli into small florets. Heat 2 teaspoons oil in wok or heavy-based frying pan. Add 2 slices of bacon, cut into strips. Cook over medium heat 2 minutes. Add broccoli, stir-fry 3–4 minutes until just tender. Stir in 2 tablespoons toasted pine nuts and 1 tablespoon chopped fresh chives. Serve warm.

BROCCOLI WITH MUSTARD BUTTER

Cut 8 oz broccoli into medium florets. Steam broccoli until just tender. Combine ¼ cup softened butter, 1 tablespoon Dijon mustard and ground black pepper to taste. Mix well. Serve over hot broccoli.

BROCCOLI WITH MUSTARD BUTTER

BROCCOLI WITH BACON AND PINE NUTS

BROCCOLI AND MUSHROOMS

41

shallots or onions and tarragon. Served hot over grilled or roast meats, fish and chicken, Béarnaise sauce is named for the city of Béarn, in the Pyrenees.

Béchamel Sauce A creamy sauce made with flour, butter and milk and served hot. The original Béchamel sauce was named for the Marquis

de Béchamel, a French financier, noted art lover and gourmet, who in the late 1600s became chief steward in the household of Louis XIV. The sauce was a marked departure from the coarse mixtures in use at the time, and has since become the basis of many other sauces. Béchamel is also known as white sauce.

Beef The meat from cattle raised for food. In America, beef is the most popular meat. Beef is graded by the US government, with Prime, juicy and well marbled with fat, being the highest grade. Prime is followed by Choice,

BEEF

ROAST BEEF WITH YORKSHIRE PUDDING

★ ★   *Preparation time:* 15 minutes
Total cooking time: 1½–2 hours
Serves 6

4 lb standing rib roast
½ teaspoon dry mustard
½ teaspoon ground black pepper
salt, to taste
¼ cup pan drippings or oil

Yorkshire Pudding
1 cup all-purpose flour
salt, to taste
1 egg, lightly beaten
¼ cup water
½ cup milk
2 tablespoons pan drippings or butter,

1 Preheat oven to moderate 350°F. Trim the meat; score the fat and rub the surface with a mixture of mustard, pepper and salt. Heat the drippings in frying pan until hot; place meat in pan, fat-side down, seal quickly. Brown all sides.

2 Place meat on a roasting rack in a baking dish, fat-side up. Roast meat for 20–22 minutes per

1 lb for medium roast beef, or follow times indicated below. Allow the meat to stand for 15 minutes before carving.

3 To make Yorkshire Pudding: Sift flour and salt into a bowl. Add combined egg and water, and mix to a paste. Heat the milk and pour it into mixture; beat until smooth. Set aside. Pour drippings into a 12-cup muffin pan; heat in a 425°F oven for 5 minutes. Remove from oven. Spoon pudding batter into the cups in the muffin pan; bake for 10–15 minutes or until puddings are puffed.

ABOUT ROASTING BEEF

Roast beef according to how well done you want it to be, using the following times as a guide (times given are per 1 lb of meat):

■ **Rare:** 18–20 minutes (140°F internal temperature on a meat thermometer);

■ **Medium:** 20–22 minutes (160°F internal temperature);

■ **Well-done:** 25–30 minutes (170°F internal temperature).

■ If using a meat thermometer, insert it into the thickest part of the meat, away from fat or bone.

BRAISED OXTAIL

★ **Preparation time:** 15 minutes
Total cooking time: 2 hours 20 minutes
Serves 6

¼ cup oil
16 small pieces oxtail, about 3 lb
4 new potatoes, peeled and quartered
1 large onion, chopped
2 medium carrots, sliced
4 oz baby mushrooms, halved

2 tablespoons all-purpose flour
3 cups beef stock
1 teaspoon dried marjoram leaves
2 tablespoons Worcestershire sauce

1 Preheat oven to moderate 350°F. Heat 2 tablespoons of oil in heavy-bottom pan. Cook the oxtail quickly in small batches over medium-high heat until well browned; place in a deep casserole dish; add potatoes.
2 Heat remaining oil in pan. Add onion and carrots, stir over medium heat 5 minutes. Place in casserole dish. Add mushrooms to pan, stir over medium heat 5 minutes. Stir in flour. Reduce heat to low and stir for 2 minutes.
3 Add stock gradually, stirring till liquid boils and thickens. Add marjoram and sauce. Pour mixture over ingredients in casserole dish. Transfer to oven. Cook, covered, for 1 hour 30 minutes. Stir, then cook, uncovered, for another 30 minutes.

OPPOSITE PAGE: ROAST BEEF WITH YORKSHIRE PUDDING. ABOVE: BRAISED OXTAIL

BEEF STOCK

Place about 1 lb stewing beef, including bones, in a large heavy-bottom saucepan, add 8 cups water and bring very slowly to the boil without stirring (stirring will make the stock cloudy). Cover pan, reduce heat and simmer for 3–4 hours. Occasionally remove any scum that rises to the top with a slotted spoon. In last hour of cooking, add large pieces of carrot, leek, celery, whole onions and unpeeled whole garlic cloves (peeled garlic cooks to a purée and clouds stock). If desired, add a bouquet garni of bay leaf, thyme and parsley. When the stock has cooked, carefully strain the liquid through a fine sieve and into a large bowl. Remove any fat from surface with paper towels; cover and refrigerate (remaining fat will solidify on top and can be removed easily). Makes about 6 cups.

ABOUT BEEF STOCK

■ Good stock must be made from the finest fresh ingredients. It is a mistake to think that any meat and vegetables, or even leftover cooked meat, will give the same results.
■ Stock will keep for one week in refrigerator, and for up to 4 months if frozen. To freeze, decide how stock will be used. If you are using it as the basis of a soup, freeze in a plastic container with a snap-on lid. For small quantities to flavor sauces or casseroles, or to cook vegetables in, freeze stock in ice-cube trays, remove when frozen and store in plastic bag in the freezer. Don't forget to label and date the bag.

the most popular grade, which can be cooked with dry heat and stay tender. Select is the least expensive grade and is considered an economy meat, but has been gaining in popularity with those on a low-fat diet. The front of the animal, called the brisket, is best braised or cooked slowly. Chuck meat from the shoulder, arm, and neck is used in ground meat. The most tender cuts come from the loin and include steaks: porterhouse steaks, shell steaks and strip steaks. T-bone steaks can be called New York or Kansas City steaks because of the popularity of that cut in those cities. Good quality beef has a rich red color, firm texture, shiny appearance and is firm to the touch. Carving across the grain makes the meat easier to eat and serve. Rare beef is red in the center; well done is brown throughout. The French are the greatest per capita eaters of beef in Europe, while the Argentinians, followed by the Americans, hold the world record for production and consumption.

Beef Wellington A fillet of beef that is browned, topped with liver or mushroom pâté, wrapped in pastry dough and then baked. It is a popular dish for dinner parties.

Beer An alcoholic drink obtained from the fermentation of extracts of malted cereals, mainly barley, and flavored with hops. A form of beer was known to the Sumerians and ancient Babylonians, who brewed a cloudy version from barley or wheat, or a mixture of the two. In the Middle Ages most monasteries had breweries and the ale they made provided income for the orders. Millet and rice beers are made in Africa and Asia. In colonial New England it was common to start the day with beer. The colonists had brought barley seeds with them for the purpose of brewing beer. Most beer now brewed in the United States is pale, and light-bodied. Beer is used in cooking to flavor stews and sauces and to make a light batter.

Beer Bread Bread made using beer, instead of yeast, as a leavening agent.

Beet (Beetroot) A bulbous root vegetable with sweet, purple-red

flesh and deep green leaves. The root has a sweet, spicy flavor and the leaves can

BEEF WELLINGTON

⭐⭐ **Preparation time:** 25 minutes
Total cooking time: 50 minutes –
1 hour 35 minutes
Serves 6–8

2 lb beef tenderloin or rib eye roast
freshly ground black pepper
1 tablespoon oil
2 tablespoons brandy
4 oz peppercorn pâté
2 sheets frozen puff pastry, thawed
1 egg, lightly beaten

1 Preheat oven to hot 425°F. Trim the meat of excess fat and tendons; fold the tail-end under. Tie the meat with string at regular intervals to help it hold its shape; rub with pepper.
2 Heat the oil in a large, heavy-bottom pan. Add the meat and cook over high heat, browning well all over to seal in juices. Remove the pan from heat. Add the brandy and ignite carefully, using a long match or taper. Shake the pan until the flames subside. Remove the meat from the pan and leave to cool. Remove the string. Spread pâté over top and sides of the beef.
3 Place the pastry sheets on a lightly floured surface. Brush one edge with a little beaten egg and overlap the edge of the other sheet, pressing well to join. Place the beef on the pastry and fold the pastry over to enclose the meat completely; trim the excess pastry and use it to decorate the top, if desired. Brush the edges of the pastry with egg and seal; cut a few slits in the top to allow the steam to escape during cooking. Brush the top and sides with egg.
4 Transfer to a baking dish; cook for 45 minutes for rare, 1 hour for medium and 1 hour 30 minutes for well-done. Remove from the oven. Leave in a warm place for 10 minutes, lightly covered with foil. Cut into ¾ inch thick slices and serve with horseradish cream made by combining 1 tablespoon bottled horseradish with 1 cup sour cream.

STEAK, ONION AND TOMATO PIES

★★ **Preparation time:** 10 minutes
Total cooking time: 2 hours
Makes 4

1¹/₂ lb chuck roast
all-purpose flour
2 tablespoons oil
1 large onion, thinly
  sliced
1¹/₂ cups beef stock
1 teaspoon soy sauce
2 teaspoons cornstarch

1 tablespoon water
15 oz package
  refrigerated pie crust
  (2 sheets)
1 tomato, sliced
1 egg, lightly beaten
2 sheets frozen puff
  pastry, thawed

1 Trim meat of excess fat and tendons. Cut meat into ¹/₂ inch cubes. Toss with flour in plastic bag, shake off excess. Heat oil in a heavy-bottom pan. Cook meat quickly in small batches over medium-high heat until well browned; drain on paper towels.
2 Add onion to pan, cook over medium heat until soft. Return meat to pan. Add stock and soy sauce. Bring to boil; reduce heat. Simmer, covered, 1¹/₄ hours, stirring occasionally, or until tender. Blend cornstarch and water in small jug or bowl until smooth; add to pan. Simmer, stirring, until thickened. Remove from heat, cool slightly.
3 Preheat oven to moderately hot 425°F. Cut each pie crust sheet in half. Line four 4³/₄ inch individual pie plates with pie crust pastry, trim edges. Place one-quarter of the filling in each pastry shell. Top with tomato slices. Brush edges with a little beaten egg, top with a circle of puff

OPPOSITE PAGE: BEEF WELLINGTON.
ABOVE: STEAK, ONION AND TOMATO PIES

pastry, seal and trim edges. Cut the remaining pastry scraps into leaf shapes. Place on pies. Brush tops with egg, bake for 25 minutes or until pastry is golden. Remove the pies from pie plates, place them on a baking sheet and bake for a further 5 minutes or until the pastry base is cooked through.

ROAST BEEF TENDERLOIN WITH EASY BEARNAISE SAUCE

★ **Preparation time:** 10 minutes
Total cooking time: 45 minutes –
1 hour 10 minutes
Serves 6

3 lb whole beef tenderloin
freshly ground black
  pepper, to taste
1 tablespoon oil
2 tablespoons butter
1 clove garlic, crushed
1 cup water

Easy Béarnaise Sauce
2 bay leaves
¹/₂ cup tarragon vinegar
2 teaspoons black
  peppercorns
4 scallions, chopped
5 egg yolks, lightly
  beaten
1 cup butter, melted

1 Preheat oven to hot 425°F. Trim the beef fillet of excess fat and tendons. Tie securely with string at regular intervals to retain its shape. Rub meat all over with pepper.
2 Heat the oil, butter and garlic in a deep baking dish on top of the stove, add the meat; brown it all over on high heat. Place a rack in the dish and put the meat on top; add the water to the dish. Transfer to the oven. Roast the meat for 45 minutes for rare, 1 hour for medium, and 1 hour 10 minutes for well-done. Baste the meat occasionally with pan juices during cooking. Remove from the oven and leave in a warm place for about 10 minutes, covered with foil. Remove the string from the meat before slicing.
3 **To make Easy Béarnaise Sauce:** Combine the bay leaves, tarragon vinegar, black peppercorns and scallions in a small pan. Bring to the boil, reduce the heat to a simmer and cook, uncovered, until the liquid has reduced to 2 tablespoons. Strain, reserving the liquid. Place the liquid and the egg yolks in a food processor or blender and process for 30 seconds. With the motor constantly running, add the hot melted butter slowly in a thin stream, processing until all the butter is added. Serve Easy Béarnaise Sauce with the sliced tenderloin.

be cooked and eaten. Beets, available all year, are the most plentiful from March through July. Beets are also packed in jars or cans, and can be used in salads. The present varieties are thought to have been developed by German gardeners. Beets are the chief ingredient in the Eastern European soup *borscht.*

Beignet Small, fluffy fritter made of deep-fried pastry, usually served with a generous dusting of powdered sugar. Beignets are popular in New Orleans,

and the name comes from the French word for "fritter." The term "beignet" is also used to refer to a food that has been coated in batter and then fried, such as beignets d'aubergines, eggplant fritters, and beignets de pommes, apple fritters.

Belgian Endive See Endive.

Bel Paese A soft, creamy, mild-tasting, cow's milk cheese with a sweet, moderately robust flavor. First made in the Lombardy area of Italy in the 1920s, it is now produced in other European countries as well as in North America. The name "Bel Paese" comes from the

Italian for "beautiful country."

Berry A variety of small plump fruits. Usually available in late spring, they are highly perishable.

Besan Flour A pale yellow flour made from dried chickpeas (garbanzo beans). It is a source of protein and is used in Indian cooking.

Betty A baked dessert of fruit with a crumb topping.

Beurre Manié A paste of butter and flour used to thicken soups, stews and sauces by whisking into simmering liquid.

Bibb Lettuce A sweet mild-flavored green with soft,

buttery-textured leaves.

Bicarbonate of Soda (Baking Soda) A fine white powder, the alkaline component of baking powder. Used alone it has no leavening properties, but combined with an acid or acid salt (such as cream of tartar, the other main ingredient of baking powder) and moistened, it produces carbon dioxide.

Bigarade, Sauce A classic French sauce flavored with oranges and served with duck.

BEEF IN BLACK BEAN SAUCE

★ **Preparation time:** 10 minutes
Total cooking time: 10 minutes
Serves 4

2 tablespoons canned salted black beans
1 medium onion
1 small red pepper
1 small green pepper
2 teaspoons cornstarch
1/2 cup beef stock
2 teaspoons soy sauce

1 teaspoon sugar
2 tablespoons oil
1 teaspoon finely crushed garlic
1/4 teaspoon ground black pepper
13 oz tenderloin steak, finely sliced

1 Rinse the black beans in several changes of water, then drain and mash them. Cut the onion into wedges. Halve the peppers, discard the seeds and cut them into small pieces. Dissolve the cornstarch in the stock, add the soy sauce and sugar.
2 Heat one tablespoon of the oil in a wok or heavy-bottom frying pan, swirling gently to coat base and side. Add the garlic, onion and peppers and stir-fry over high heat for one minute; remove to a bowl.
3 Add the remaining tablespoon of oil, swirling gently to coat the base and side of the wok. Add the beef and stir-fry over high heat for 2 minutes, until it changes color. Add the black beans, cornstarch mixture and vegetables. Stir until the sauce boils and thickens. Serve with steamed rice.

BEEF POT ROAST WITH EGGPLANT AND SWEET POTATO

★ **Preparation time:** 20 minutes
Total cooking time: 1 hour 15 minutes
Serves 4

2 lb beef top round
2 tablespoons oil
1 cup beef stock
1 medium onion, sliced
1 clove garlic, crushed
4 large tomatoes, peeled, seeded and chopped
1 teaspoon ground cumin
1 teaspoon turmeric
1 teaspoon finely grated lemon rind

2 tablespoons lemon juice
1 medium eggplant, cut into 1 inch cubes
1 medium sweet potato, halved, cut into 1 1/2 inch slices
2 tablespoons all-purpose flour
3 tablespoons water
1 tablespoon chopped fresh cilantro

1 Trim the meat. Heat the oil in deep, heavy-bottom pan, add the meat and brown over medium-high heat.
2 Remove the pan from heat, add stock, onion, garlic, tomato, cumin, turmeric, lemon rind and juice. Return the pan to low heat. Cover, slowly bring to simmering point and simmer 45 minutes.
3 Add eggplant and sweet potato, cook for 30 minutes, uncovered, until meat and vegetables are tender. Remove meat from sauce. Cover with foil for 10 minutes before slicing. Add combined flour and water to sauce with cilantro, stir over medium heat until sauce boils and thickens. Cook 3 minutes. Pour over sliced meat to serve.

PIQUANT COUNTRY BEEF WITH HERB BISCUITS

★ ★ **Preparation time:** 30 minutes
Total cooking time: 2 hours
10 minutes
Serves 4

2 lb beef chuck steak
1/4 cup all-purpose flour
3 tablespoons oil
4 medium onions,
  coarsely chopped
2 cloves garlic, crushed
1/3 cup plum jam
1/3 cup brown vinegar
1 cup beef stock
2 teaspoons sweet chili
  sauce

Herb Biscuits
2 cups all-purpose flour
1 teaspoon baking powder
1/4 teaspoon salt
2 tablespoons butter
2 tablespoons chopped
  fresh chives
2 tablespoons chopped
  fresh parsley
3/4 cup (6 fl oz) milk

1 Preheat oven to 350°F. Trim meat of excess fat
and tendons. Cut into 1inch cubes. Toss in flour.
Heat 2 tablespoons oil in a heavy-bottom pan.
Cook meat quickly, in small batches, over
medium-high heat until well browned. Drain
meat on paper towels.
2 Heat remaining oil in pan, add onion and garlic
and cook, stirring, for 3 minutes or until soft.
Combine onion mixture and meat in large bowl.
3 Add jam, vinegar, stock and chili sauce, mix
well. Transfer to ovenproof dish. Cover and bake
for 1 hour 30 minutes or until meat is tender.
4 Uncover dish, turn oven up to 475°F. Place
Herb Biscuits on top of meat, bake, uncovered,
for 30 minutes or until biscuits are golden brown.
5 To make Herb Biscuits: Sift flour, baking
powder and salt into a bowl; rub in butter until
mixture resembles fine bread crumbs. Stir in
chives and parsley. Add milk, stir until just
combined. Turn onto a lightly floured surface,
knead until smooth. Press dough out to a 1 1/2 inch
thickness; using a pastry cutter, cut into
2 inch rounds.

Note: Casserole can be cooked 2 days ahead
without the biscuits and refrigerated, or frozen for
up to 2 weeks.

VARIATION

■ CHEESE BISCUITS: Reduce flour by 1/4 cup
and replace with the same quantity of grated
Parmesan. Add 2 finely chopped scallions.

OPPOSITE PAGE: BEEF POT ROAST.
ABOVE: PIQUANT COUNTRY BEEF

Bind To hold a dry crumbly mixture together by moistening it with egg, moist bread crumbs, milk or a sauce.

Bing Cherry A large cherry ranging in color from deep red to almost black. Used for cooking and eating.

Biryani (Biriani) A Mongol dish from India consisting of layers of rice pilaf and spicy lamb or chicken.

Biscotti A crunchy Italian cookie that is available in many flavors. They are ideal for dipping into dessert wine or coffee.

Biscuit Small savory quick breads leavened with baking powder or baking soda.

Bisque A rich, thick soup that is made of puréed shellfish, stock and cream. Originally made of boiled game or fowl, the most popular bisques today are crab, lobster, shrimp and, especially in the United States, clam.

Bitter Melon A cucumber-like melon with wrinkled skin that is native to Asia. In India it is usually pickled. In China it is peeled, par-boiled, and added to stir-fry dishes; it is often

cooked with beans or meat to offset its somewhat bitter taste.

Blackberry The black, juicy berry of a prickly shrub. Also see Berries.

Black Bottom Pie A rich pie with a bottom chocolate layer and a top custard-rum layer garnished with whipped cream.

Black Currant The black, sour, juicy fruit of a northern European shrub.

Blackened Fish Any fish prepared in Cajun (Louisiana) style: cooked over high heat until charred on the surface.

Black-Eyed Pea (Cow Pea) An oval cream-colored bean with a black dot in the center.

Black Forest Cake A rich chocolate cake moistened with kirsch, filled and topped

with whipped cream and decorated with cherries and shaved chocolate.

B E E T S

S P I C E D   B A K E D   B E E T S

⭐ **Preparation time:** 15 minutes
Total cooking time: 1 hour 25 minutes
Serves 6

12 small beets, about 2¹/₂ lb	¹/₂ teaspoon ground cardamom
2 tablespoons olive oil	¹/₂ teaspoon nutmeg
1 teaspoon ground cumin	1 tablespoon sugar
1 teaspoon ground coriander	1 tablespoon red wine vinegar

1 Preheat the oven to moderate 350°F. Brush a baking sheet with oil or melted butter. Trim the leafy tops from the beets and wash thoroughly. Place them on a baking sheet and bake for 1 hour 15 minutes, until very tender. Cool slightly. Peel away the skins and trim the tops and tails.
2 Heat the oil in a large pan. Add the spices and cook for one minute, stirring constantly, over medium heat. Add the sugar and red wine vinegar, and stir for 2–3 minutes, until the sugar dissolves.
3 Add the beets to the pan, reduce the heat to low and stir gently for 5 minutes, until the beets are well glazed. Serve warm or cold with hot or cold roast meats or poultry.

Note: This dish can be cooked up to 2 days ahead. Store it in a covered container in the refrigerator until it is needed.

B E E T   S A L A D

⭐ **Preparation time:** 25 minutes
Total cooking time: none
Serves 4-6

3 whole fresh beets, peeled and grated	1 tablespoon tahini paste
2 large carrots, peeled and grated	¹/₂ small red chili, finely chopped
¹/₃ cup orange juice	1 tablespoon toasted sesame seeds
2 teaspoons grated orange rind	

1 Combine the grated beets and carrot in a large bowl.
2 For dressing, combine orange juice, rind, tahini paste and chili in a small bowl. Mix ingredients well, using a wire whisk.
3 Pour dressing over beet mixture. Toss well and serve sprinkled with sesame seeds.

B O R S C H T

⭐ **Preparation time:** 5 minutes
Total cooking time: 1 hour 15 minutes
Serves 8

2 lb beef shanks	2 carrots, peeled, cut into thin strips
8 cups water	¹/₂ lb beets, cut into thin strips
1 onion, chopped	
3 bay leaves	2 teaspoons vinegar
1 teaspoon whole allspice	freshly ground pepper
2 tomatoes, peeled and chopped	¹/₄ cup chopped parsley
2 potatoes, peeled, cut into thin strips	2 tablespoons snipped fresh dill
1 small cabbage, shredded	

1 Put the beef, water, onion, bay leaves and allspice into a large saucepan; bring to boil. Skim if necessary and simmer, covered, for one hour or until tender.
2 While the meat is cooking, use a sharp knife to cut the vegetables rather than grating them (this would make the soup cloudy). When the meat is cooked, remove from the pot. Cut thick strips of meat from the bone, return them to the pot. Add the vegetables; boil, uncovered, for about 15 minutes (if lid is left on, the soup will not retain its bright attractive color).
3 Stir in the vinegar, pepper, parsley and dill. Serve warm with black bread and a spoonful of sour cream with horseradish cream if desired.

ABOVE: SPICED BAKED BEETS. OPPOSITE PAGE: BLUEBERRY MUFFINS

BERRIES

BLUEBERRY MUFFINS

⭐ **Preparation time:** 20 minutes
Total cooking time: 20 minutes
Makes 8 large or 15 regular muffins

3 cups all-purpose flour
2 teaspoons baking
powder
1/2 teaspoon baking soda
1 cup soft brown sugar
1/2 cup butter, melted

2 eggs, lightly beaten
1 cup milk
1 cup blueberries
powdered (confectioners')
sugar, for sprinkling

1 Preheat oven to 425°F. Grease 8 large muffin cups or 15 regular muffin cups. Place the flour, baking powder and baking soda in a large bowl. Stir in sugar; make a well in the center.
2 Add combined melted butter, eggs and milk all at once; stir until just blended. (Do not overbeat; the batter should look quite lumpy.)
3 Fold in the blueberries thoroughly, but very lightly. Spoon the batter into prepared muffin cups. Bake 20 minutes for large muffins or 12–13 minutes for regular muffins, or until they are golden brown. Loosen the muffins from the pans with a flat-bladed knife and transfer them to a wire rack to cool. Sprinkle the tops with powdered sugar.

Note: If fresh blueberries are unavailable, use frozen ones. Thaw and drain very well before using. Other berries can also be used. Try raspberries, blackberries or mulberries, or a combination of these.

STRAWBERRY AND PASSIONFRUIT MUFFINS

⭐ **Preparation time:** 20 minutes
Total cooking time: 25 minutes
Makes 12

2 cups all-purpose flour
1 1/2 teaspoons baking
powder
1/2 teaspoon baking soda
1/3 cup sugar
1/8 teaspoon salt

1 cup chopped fresh
strawberries
1/2 cup canned or fresh
passionfruit pulp
1 egg
1 cup milk
1/4 cup butter, melted

1 Preheat oven to 425°F. Brush 12 muffin cups with melted butter or oil. Sift flour, baking powder, soda, sugar and salt into bowl. Add the strawberries and make a well in the center.
2 Add passionfruit pulp and combined egg and milk. Pour melted butter into flour mixture all at once and stir until combined. (Do not overbeat; the batter should look quite lumpy.)
3 Spoon into muffin cups and bake 20–25 minutes or until golden brown. Turn muffins out onto a wire rack to cool. Top with whipped cream, strawberry halves and sprinkle with confectioners' sugar, if desired.

STRAWBERRY PAVLOVA SQUARES

⭐ **Preparation time:** 25 minutes
Total cooking time: 45 minutes
Serves 8–10

6 egg whites
1 1/2 cups sugar
1 teaspoon vanilla
1 teaspoon white vinegar
1 1/2 cups heavy cream,
whipped

8 oz fresh strawberries,
sliced
8 oz fresh blueberries
6 oz fresh raspberries

1 Preheat oven to 300°F. Line an 11 x 7 inch rectangular pan with parchment paper. Place egg whites in large bowl. Beat egg whites with electric beaters until soft peaks form. Gradually add the sugar, beating after each addition. Beat 5–10 minutes until thick and glossy and sugar has dissolved. Fold in vanilla and vinegar.
2 Spread mixture into pan. Bake 45 minutes or until pale and crisp. Turn off oven, cool pavlova in oven with door ajar. Lift pavlova out of pan, cut into squares. Spread with whipped cream and decorate with berries. Refrigerate until serving time.

Black Pudding (Blood Sausage) A sausage traditionally made of seasoned pig's blood and fat mixed with finely ground cereals, cooked, and then either re-boiled or sliced and broiled, grilled or fried. It is

classified as a country sausage.

Blanch (Parboiling) To lightly cook food in boiling water. Blanching preserves the color and texture of vegetables and fruits before freezing. The term also describes covering fruit and nuts with boiling water to loosen skins for peeling.

Blancmange A white molded dessert pudding made with cornstarch and milk that has been cooked, sweetened and flavored. It may be topped with fruit.

Blanquette A meat or poultry stew in which the meat is covered in a white sauce and enriched with milk or cream and egg yolk.

Blend To combine two or more ingredients into a smooth mixture.

Blender An electrical appliance for chopping, blending, puréeing and liquefying foods.

Blini Small, thick pancakes made from buckwheat flour and yeast dough. Russian in origin, blini are served topped with sour cream and caviar or smoked salmon.

Blintz A thin pancake with either a savory or sweet filling. The batter is cooked on one side, until just set, and the filling is placed in the center. The blintz is then folded into an envelope, and sautéed until golden brown. It can be topped with sauce or sour cream. Blintzes are a traditional Jewish food.

Blueberry A small, dark, purplish berry native to North America. Available fresh in the early spring, they can be frozen or dried.

Blueberries can be eaten raw or cooked in a pie filling or muffin batter. North America produces most of the world's crop. See also Berry.

Blue Vein Cheese (Blue Cheese) A soft, cow's milk cheese with veins of blue-green mold culture criss-crossing the interior. It is made by adding mold spores to

CHOCOLATE, BERRY AND MERINGUE LAYERS

Preparation time: 40 minutes
Total cooking time: 45 minutes
Serves 8–10

6 egg whites	2 cups heavy cream,
1½ cups sugar	whipped
5 oz dark baking	8 oz fresh raspberries or
chocolate	quartered strawberries
¼ cup water	extra berries for decoration
	cocoa powder for dusting

1 Preheat oven to slow 300°F. Line three baking sheets with parchment paper. Mark an 8½ inch circle on each. Place the egg whites in a large, dry mixing bowl. Beat with electric beaters until soft peaks form. Gradually add the sugar, beating constantly after each addition. Beat 5 minutes or until thick and glossy and the sugar has dissolved.
2 Divide the meringue mixture between the baking sheets and spread evenly over the marked circles. Bake for 45 minutes or until pale and crisp. Turn off the oven, cool the meringues in the oven with the door ajar.
3 Combine the chocolate and water in a small pan over low heat, stir until the chocolate has

melted and the mixture is smooth. Cool slightly until just thickened. Spread the chocolate sauce carefully over the two meringue disks and allow to set.
4 Place one chocolate-coated disk on a serving plate. Spread with one-third of the cream and top with half of the berries. Top with the remaining chocolate disk, repeat with half the remaining cream and remaining strawberries. Place the plain meringue disk on top of the berries and spread with the remaining cream. Decorate with extra berries if desired. Refrigerate. Dust with cocoa and cut into wedges to serve.

MARINATED FRUITS WITH MASCARPONE

Preparation time: 20 minutes
Total cooking time: 10 minutes
Serves 4–6

2 oranges	⅓ cup water
1 cup raspberries	3 tablespoons sugar, extra
1 cup blueberries	8 oz mascarpone cheese
¼ cup sugar	

1 Place each orange on a board and cut a ¾ inch-wide slice from each end—cut down to where pulp starts. Carefully remove the rind in wide strips, including all pith and white membrane. Using a small, sharp knife, cut the pith from the rind and discard; cut the rind into thin strips.
2 Separate the orange segments by carefully cutting between the membrane and the flesh. Combine the orange segments and berries in a medium bowl, sprinkle with ¼ cup sugar and toss lightly. Cover and refrigerate.
3 Combine the water and 3 tablespoons sugar in a small pan and stir over low heat without boiling until the sugar has completely dissolved. Bring to the boil then reduce heat and add the orange rind. Simmer gently for about 2 minutes until the rind is tender, remove from heat and cool. Reserve 1 tablespoon of rind, combine the syrup and the remaining rind with the berry mixture. Spoon into goblets and garnish with the reserved rind; serve with large dollops of mascarpone.

Note: Mascarpone cheese is a rich double- or triple-cream cheese made from cow's milk. It is available in some large supermarkets and specialty food stores.

ABOVE: CHOCOLATE, BERRY & MERINGUE LAYERS.
OPPOSITE PAGE: SUMMER BERRY TART

1

2

3

S U M M E R   B E R R Y   T A R T

⋆ ⋆ **Preparation time:** 35 minutes + 20 minutes refrigeration
Total cooking time: 35 minutes
Serves 4–6

1¼ cups all-purpose
  flour
1/3 cup butter
2 tablespoons
  confectioners' sugar
1–2 tablespoons water

Filling
3 egg yolks

¼ cup sugar
2 tablespoons cornstarch
1 cup milk
1 teaspoon vanilla
8 oz strawberries,
  halved
4 oz blueberries
4 oz raspberries
2 tablespoons apple jelly

1 Preheat oven to moderate 350°F. Process the flour, butter and confectioners' sugar in a food processor, using the pulse action, for 15 seconds or until the mixture is a fine and crumbly texture. Add almost all of the water, and process for another 20 seconds or until the mixture comes together; add a little more water if necessary. Turn onto a lightly floured surface and press the mixture together until a smooth dough is formed.
2 Roll out the pastry to fit an 8 inch round fluted flan pan. Line the pan with pastry and trim the edges. Refrigerate for 20 minutes. Cut a sheet of waxed paper to cover the pastry-lined pan. Spread a layer of dried beans or rice evenly over the paper. Bake for 15 minutes. Remove the pastry shell from oven and discard the paper and the rice. Return to the oven for a further 15 minutes, or until the pastry is lightly golden.
3 To make Filling: Place the egg yolks, sugar and cornstarch in a medium bowl and whisk until pale. Heat the milk in a small pan until it is almost boiling; remove from heat. Add the milk gradually to the egg mixture, beating constantly. Strain the mixture back into the pan. Stir constantly over low heat for 3 minutes or until the mixture boils and thickens. Remove from heat and add the vanilla. Transfer to a bowl and cover with plastic wrap. Allow to cool.
4 Spread the filling evenly into the cooled pastry shell. Top with the strawberries, blueberries and raspberries. Place the apple jelly in a small custard cup and microwave until the jelly liquefies. Brush the jelly over the fruit with a pastry brush.

Note: Cook the pastry up to a day ahead and store in an airtight container. Fill up to 4 hours before serving.

maturing curds, and then aiding their spread. Ageing is an important part of the process for this sharp and strong-flavored cheese with a crumbly texture. The many varieties of blue vein cheese include Gorgonzola, Danish Blue, Roquefort and Stilton.

Boar Meat The meat of the domestic version of the wild pig. It is usually eaten during the Christmas holidays.

Bok Choy A leafy vegetable with thick, fleshy white stalks. It has a cabbage-like flavor and a crisp texture. Native to southern China, its name comes from the Chinese words *bok,* white, and *choy,* vegetable; it is also known as Chinese cabbage.

Bologna A cooked spicy sausage that is eaten hot or cold as a sandwich meat.

Bolognese Sauce A thick meat and tomato sauce, served with pasta (usually spaghetti). It often includes minced or chopped ham, Canadian bacon, lean pork, chicken livers and white wine. Originally from the city of Bologna in northern Italy.

Bombay Duck A variety of fish found in the Arabian Sea; a shoal fish that is caught in large numbers. In India it is eaten fresh; in the West it is best known in its dried and salted form, deep-fried and served with curry.

Bombe A frozen dessert set in a mold, usually consisting of an outer layer of ice cream and a center of custard, mousse, fruit purée or cream.

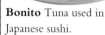

Bonito Tuna used in Japanese sushi.

Bones Marrow bones and bones with gelatin extracts are used in stocks, gravies and sauces.

Borage An herb with long green leaves. The dark blue blooms are used as a garnish. Young

RICE PUDDING WITH LEMON THYME AND MARINATED STRAWBERRIES

⭐ **Preparation time:** 20 minutes + 1 hour standing
Total cooking time: 1 hour 15 minutes
Serves 6–8

³/₄ cup long grain rice	3 egg yolks
1¹/₂ cups water	1 egg
3 cups milk	1 1b fresh strawberries
6 x 1 inch sprigs lemon thyme	2 tablespoons balsamic vinegar
¹/₂ cup sugar	additional ¹/₃ cup sugar

1 Preheat oven to 325°F. Brush a 6-cup capacity shallow baking dish with oil or melted butter. Rinse rice well. Place in a medium pan. Add water, bring to boil. Cover and cook rice over low heat 10–15 minutes; remove from heat. Leave pan with lid on for 5 minutes or until all the liquid is absorbed and the rice is soft.
2 Heat the milk with the lemon thyme and ¹/₂ cup sugar in a small pan. When bubbles form at the edge, remove from heat. Leave milk to stand

ABOVE: RICE PUDDING WITH LEMON THYME AND STRAWBERRIES. RIGHT: SALAD BASKETS WITH RASPBERRY DRESSING. OPPOSITE: INDIVIDUAL STRAWBERRY MERINGUES

10 minutes so it absorbs the flavor from the lemon thyme. Strain. Beat yolks and egg in a large bowl; add rice. Gradually stir in warm milk. Pour into prepared dish. Place dish in a deeper baking dish, pour in enough warm water to come halfway up the sides. Bake for 1 hour or until pudding is just set (timing may vary according to type of baking dish used). Remove from the oven, and allow to stand 10 minutes.
3 Hull and rinse the strawberries. Cut strawberries into halves. Place in a medium bowl. Add vinegar.
4 Sprinkle ¹/₃ cup sugar over the strawberries, stir to combine. Leave for 1 hour to absorb flavors, turning occasionally.

SALAD BASKETS WITH BERRY DRESSING

⭐⭐ **Preparation time:** 20 minutes
Total cooking time: 15 minutes
Serves 4

12 sheets frozen filo dough	1 cup blueberries
¹/₄ cup butter, melted	**Blueberry Dressing**
6–8 oz mixed greens	¹/₂ cup olive oil
8 cherry tomatoes, halved	¹/₄ cup balsamic vinegar
¹/₂ small red bell pepper, thinly sliced	1 tablespoon soft brown sugar
1 small cucumber, thinly sliced	¹/₃ cup frozen blueberries, thawed, lightly crushed

1 Preheat oven to moderate 350°F. Brush four ¹/₂ cup capacity custard cups with melted butter or oil. Line two baking sheets with parchment

paper. Place one sheet of filo dough on work surface. Brush lightly with melted butter, place another sheet on top. Repeat with a third layer. Fold dough in half. Using a plate as a guide, cut an 8¼ inch circle out of the dough with a sharp knife. Place dough over base of prepared custard cups. Carefully fold dough around the cup to form a basket shape. Place on prepared baking sheets. Repeat process for three more baskets. Bake 15 minutes or until golden. Carefully remove filo basket from custard cup while hot; place baskets on wire rack to cool.

2 To make Blueberry Dressing: Combine greens, tomatoes, pepper, cucumber and dressing in bowl. Mix well. Spoon into pastry baskets, top with extra blueberries.

Note: A salad mix (mesclun) is available from most grocery stores. It includes a wide variety of baby lettuce leaves and edible flowers.

RASPBERRY CHEESECAKE

⭐ **Preparation time:** 25 minutes +
3 hours refrigeration
Total cooking time: none
Makes one 8 inch cheesecake

5 oz vanilla wafers	2 tablespoons unflavored
2 tablespoons sugar	gelatin
2 tablespoons butter,	2 tablespoons lemon juice
melted	½ cup heavy cream,
8 oz cream cheese	whipped
½ cup sugar	14 oz fresh raspberries
½ teaspoon vanilla	

1 Brush the base and sides of an 8 inch springform pan with melted butter or oil. Place wafers in a food processor and process until finely crushed. Transfer to a medium mixing bowl and add 2 tablespoons sugar, stir to combine. Pour in melted butter and stir until all the crumbs are moistened. Spoon into the pan and smooth over the base with the back of a spoon. Refrigerate.

2 Using electric beaters, beat the cream cheese and the extra sugar until light and creamy. Add the vanilla and beat until combined.

3 Combine the gelatin with the lemon juice in a small bowl. Stand in hot water, stir until dissolved. Add to the cream cheese mixture and beat until combined. With a metal spoon, fold in whipped cream, then half of the raspberries until just combined. Pour filling onto prepared base; smooth surface. Arrange remaining raspberries on top and refrigerate for at least 3 hours.

INDIVIDUAL STRAWBERRY MERINGUES

⭐⭐ **Preparation time:** 25 minutes
Total cooking time: 40 minutes
Serves 6

4 egg whites	1¼ cups heavy cream,
1 cup sugar	whipped
1 lb fresh strawberries,	
hulled	

1 Preheat oven to slow 300°F. Brush two baking sheets with melted butter or oil. Cut parchment paper to fit baking sheets. Using a 3 inch round cutter as a guide, mark 12 circles onto paper, and place pencil-side down on trays.

2 Place egg whites in a medium, clean dry mixing bowl. Using electric beaters, beat until soft peaks form. Add the sugar gradually, beating constantly until the mixture is thick and glossy and the sugar has dissolved. Spread the meringue into rounds on prepared baking sheets. Bake 40 minutes then turn off heat and allow to cool in oven.

3 Place half the strawberries in a food processor or blender and blend until liquid. Slice the remaining strawberries and fold into the whipped cream.

To serve, sandwich two meringue rounds together with the cream mixture and place on each plate. Pour the strawberry sauce around base of the meringue. Garnish the dish with strawberry leaves to serve.

Note: For a sweeter sauce, add a little sugar.

leaves are added to drinks and used in spring salads; more mature leaves are cooked like spinach, or fried with a batter coating. Its cucumber-like flavor is often added to fish sauces. Borage is native to the Middle East and the Mediterranean region, where it still grows wild.

Bordelaise, à la A French term for a dish of roasted or broiled meat served with a brown sauce made from the reduction of red wine, bone marrow, chopped shallots, thyme, bay leaf and pepper; a sauce made with white wine is served with seafood. The cooking style originated in the Bordeaux region of France.

Börek A pastry which can contain a variety of fillings, usually a cheese mixture, and is served hot as an appetizer. Böreks are originally from Turkey and are found throughout the Middle East. They are often made in small cigar-shaped rolls and half-moon shapes.

Borlotti Bean A dried kidney-shaped bean, pale brown in color with darker speckled markings. It has a smooth texture and ham-like flavor when cooked and is used in soups, stews and casseroles, or cooled, dressed and mixed with onion rings or tuna and served as a salad.

Borscht A beet soup, originally from Eastern Europe, it became popular in France in the 1920s. Served hot or chilled, traditionally it is topped with sour cream.

Boston Brown Bread A sweet steamed bread flavored with molasses.

Boston Cream Pie A single-layered white cake, split horizontally and filled with a thick creamy vanilla custard. Usually covered with chocolate glaze.

Bouchée A small, round shell or puff pastry, filled shortly before serving. The shells are suitable for luncheons or appetizers.

Bouillabaisse A soup made from a variety of fish (traditionally white-fleshed rock fish) and shellfish and usually containing tomato, onion, garlic, herbs, wine and saffron. Originally it was served as two courses; first the broth, then the seafood.

BISQUE

LOBSTER BISQUE

★ ★ **Preparation time:** 20 minutes
Total cooking time: 1 hour 20 minutes
Serves 4–6

1 lobster tail, about 14 oz
1/3 cup butter
1 large onion, chopped
1 large carrot, chopped
1 stalk celery, chopped
1/4 cup brandy
1 cup white wine
6 sprigs fresh parsley
1 sprig fresh thyme
2 bay leaves

1 tablespoon tomato paste
2 tomatoes, peeled, seeded and chopped
4 cups fish stock or bottled clam juice
2 tablespoons cornstarch
1/2 cup heavy cream
salt and freshly ground black pepper
fresh oregano leaves and paprika, to serve

1 Remove meat from lobster tail, wash and retain shell. Chop the lobster meat, cover and refrigerate.
2 Heat butter in a pan and cook onion, carrot and celery over low heat for 20 minutes, stirring occasionally, until softened but not brown.

3 In a small pan heat brandy; ignite with a long match and carefully and quickly pour over vegetables. Shake the pan until flame dies down. Add white wine and lobster shell. Increase heat, boil mixture until it has been reduced by half.
4 Add parsley, thyme, bay leaves, tomato paste, tomato, and fish stock. Simmer without lid for 45 minutes, stirring occasionally.
5 Strain mixture through a fine sieve or cheesecloth, pressing down gently to extract all the liquid. Discard vegetables and shells.
6 Return liquid to cleaned pan. Blend cornstarch with the cream. Add to the liquid. Stir over medium heat until thickened. Add lobster meat, season to taste. Cook gently without boiling about 10 minutes or until lobster meat is just cooked. Garnish with oregano leaves and paprika and serve.

Note: Lobster Bisque can be made up to a day ahead and refrigerated. Reheat gently. Do not freeze. The long cooking time ensures optimum flavor for this delicate soup.

ABOVE: LOBSTER BISQUE

BOUILLABAISSE

BOUILLABAISSE

★ ★ **Preparation time:** 40 minutes + 2
hours soaking
Total cooking time: 1 hour 10 minutes
Serves 4–6

12 mussels, scrubbed,
  beards removed
1–2 fish heads, with bones
1 lb large shrimp, peeled,
  shells and heads
  retained
1 lobster tail, meat
  removed, shell retained
1 cup white wine
2 cups water
1/2 red onion, chopped
2 cloves garlic, chopped
1 bay leaf
1/4 cup olive oil
2 red onions, finely
  chopped, extra
1 small leek, finely sliced
4 cloves garlic, extra,
  crushed
4–6 tomatoes, skinned
  and chopped
3 tablespoons tomato
  paste
1/4 teaspoon saffron
  powder

2 bay leaves, extra
1 teaspoon dried basil
  leaves
1 teaspoon fennel seeds
2 inch piece orange rind
salt and freshly ground
  black pepper
1 lb white-fleshed fish,
  skinned, boned, cut
  into 1 1/4 inch pieces
1/2 cup fresh parsley,
  finely chopped

Rouille

4 thick slices white bread,
  crusts removed
water for soaking
4 cloves garlic, crushed
2 red chili peppers, finely
  chopped
1/4 cup egg substitute
salt and freshly ground
  black pepper
3/4 cup olive oil

1 Soak mussels for 2 hours in cold water. Discard open mussels.
2 Place fish head, bones, shrimp and lobster shells in large pan. Add wine, water, onion, garlic and bay leaf. Bring to boil, reduce heat, simmer 20 minutes. Strain and reserve liquid.
3 Heat oil in large pan. Add extra onions, leek, and garlic. Cover and cook over low heat 20 minutes, stirring occasionally, until softened but not browned. Add tomato, tomato paste, saffron, bay leaves, basil, fennel seeds, rind, salt and pepper. Stir well, remove lid; continue to cook for 10 minutes, stirring frequently.
4 Add reserved fish stock; bring to boil. Boil for 10 minutes, stirring often. Reduce heat; add fish pieces, lobster meat cut in 1 1/4 inch pieces and mussels. Cover and simmer 4–5 minutes until mussels have opened (discard any opened mussels). Add shrimp and simmer, covered, for 3–4 minutes or until just cooked.
5 Remove rind and bay leaves. Transfer to serving bowls. Sprinkle with parsley. Serve with a spoonful of Rouille.
6 To make Rouille: Place the bread and water in a bowl for 5 minutes. Squeeze the water from the bread. Place the bread, garlic, chilies, egg substitute, salt and pepper in a food processor. Process for 20 seconds. With the motor running, add the oil in a slow stream. Process until thick. Place in serving bowl; cover and refrigerate until needed.

ABOVE: BOUILLABAISSE

Bouillon A clear stock or broth that is served as is or is used as a base for soups and sauces. Compressed cubes or dehydrated bouillon powder are used for concentrated flavor.

Bouquet Garni A bundle of herbs, either tied together or enclosed in a cheesecloth bag, used to flavor soups, stews and casseroles and removed after cooking. Thyme, bay leaf, parsley and other fresh or dried herbs are used in the bouquet.

Bourguignonne, à la French term for a dish slowly cooked with red wine, onions and mushrooms.

Bourride A thick soup made with white-fleshed fish and flavored with aïoli, a strong garlic-flavored mayonnaise.

Boysenberry A large, juicy, purplish-black fruit that is a hybrid of the blackberry, loganberry and raspberry.
  Developed in California in the 1920s by Rudolph Boysen, the berries can be eaten fresh, cooked as jam or used as a filling for pies and tarts.
See also Berry.

Brains A soft, white variety meat (offal), usually lamb or calf brains, which have a high fat content.

Braise To cook slowly over a low heat in a covered pan using very little liquid.

Bran The husk or the inner casing of wheat and other cereal grains removed during the refining of white flour. Bran is a good source of dietary fiber and minerals such as zinc. It has a high vitamin B and phosphorus content.

Brandade A purée of salt cod, olive oil and milk, eaten hot; it is a specialty of the town of Nîmes, in southern France. Garlic is added to the mixture in some regions. Its name comes from a Provençal word, *brandar*, to stir.

Brandy A spirit distilled from wine and used in cooking to flavor a variety of sweet and savory dishes including sauces, casseroles, pâtés and terrines, consommés, fruit cakes and fruit desserts, and flambés. Brandies are aged in wood which adds to their color and flavor. Cognac is considered by many to be the finest of all brandies.

B R A N

B A N A N A   B R A N   M U F F I N S

⭐ **Preparation time:** 20 minutes + 1 hour standing
Total cooking time: 20–25 minutes
Makes 12

½ cup boiling water
¾ cup unprocessed wheat bran
½ cup mashed ripe banana
1 egg, beaten
2 tablespoons vegetable oil
½ cup firmly packed brown sugar
1 teaspoon vanilla
1 cup all-purpose flour
¼ cup non-fat dry milk powder
2 teaspoons baking powder
½ teaspoon baking soda

1 Pour the boiling water over the bran in a medium bowl. Set aside.
2 Preheat the oven to 400°F. Brush oil into bottoms only of 12 muffin cups. Add banana, egg, oil, brown sugar and vanilla to bran mixture and mix well.
3 Sift the flour, milk powder, baking powder and soda in a medium bowl. Add the bran and banana mixture all at once to the flour mixture. Stir gently with fork until all the ingredients are just moistened.
4 Spoon batter evenly into each muffin cup, filling them only two-thirds full. Bake 20–25 minutes, until golden. Serve warm with butter.

B R A N   A N D   F R U I T   L O A F

⭐ **Preparation time:** 15 minutes
Total cooking time: 50 minutes
Serves 8

1½ cups all-purpose flour
2 teaspoons baking powder
1 teaspoon pumpkin pie spice
1 cup unprocessed wheat bran
⅔ cup soft brown sugar
½ cup vegetable oil
2 eggs, beaten
¾ cup milk
½ cup golden raisins
½ cup chopped dried apricots
2 apples, peeled and grated

1 Preheat oven to moderate 350°F. Brush a 9 x 5 inch loaf pan with melted butter or oil. Place the flour, baking powder and spice in a large mixing bowl; stir in bran and sugar. Make a well in the center of the dry ingredients. In a small bowl combine the oil, beaten eggs and milk.
2 Pour liquids onto the dry ingredients. Using a wooden spoon, stir until well combined; do not overbeat. Stir in raisins, apricots and apple.
3 Pour the mixture into the prepared pan. Bake for 50 minutes or until a skewer comes out clean when inserted into the center of the loaf. Leave loaf in pan for 10 minutes before turning out.

Note: This loaf is best eaten within 1 or 2 days.

ABOVE: BRAN AND FRUIT LOAF.
OPPOSITE PAGE: SPICED BRAN CAKE

Bratwurst A fresh, pale, ground pork or veal link sausage.

Braunschweiger A spreadable smoked liverwurst best served at room temperature.

Brazil Nut The hard-shelled, creamy-fleshed nut of a tree native to tropical South America. Most of the world's supply comes from trees growing in the wild along the Amazon. Brazil nuts are

three-sided, with rough, hard, dark brown shells. The large oily nuts can be eaten fresh, baked in fruit cakes or coated with chocolate.

Bread A kneaded mixture of flour and water, usually with a leavening agent, which is baked. Flat cakes of grain paste cooked on hot stones are the oldest known form of prepared food, dating from over 10,000 years ago. Varieties of unleavened bread are still made in

India, the Middle East and Latin America. Today's baker uses

FIG AND OAT BRAN MUFFINS

★ **Preparation time:** 20 minutes
Total cooking time: 20 minutes
Makes 12

1 1/2 cups all-purpose flour	1 cup chopped dried
1 tablespoon baking	figs
powder	1 egg
1 teaspoon cinnamon	3/4 cup milk
1 cup oat bran	1/3 cup oil
1/2 cup soft brown sugar	1/4 maple syrup

1 Preheat oven to 425° F. Brush 12 muffin cups with melted butter or oil. Sift the flour, baking powder and cinnamon into a large bowl. Add the oat bran and sugar and stir thoroughly until all ingredients are thoroughly combined. Stir in the chopped figs. Make a well in the center of the mixture.
2 Add the combined egg, milk, oil and syrup all at once. Mix quickly with a fork until all ingredients are just moistened. (Do not overbeat)
3 Spoon the mixture into the prepared muffin cups. Bake for 20 minutes or until golden. Remove from the oven and leave in muffin cups for 5 minutes. Turn out onto a wire rack to cool.

Note: Other dried fruits such as apricots, dates, raisins and mixed dried fruits are suitable for this recipe. Add half a cup of chopped pecans or hazelnuts to the muffin batter, if desired.

SPICED BRAN CAKE

★ **Preparation time:** 20 minutes
Total cooking time: 25–30 minutes
Makes one 8 inch round cake

1/3 cup butter	1 teaspoon vanilla
1 1/2 cups all-purpose flour	1/3 cup milk
1 teaspoon ground	
cinnamon	**Icing**
1 teaspoon baking powder	4 oz cream cheese
1/8 teaspoon salt	1/4 cup sour cream
2/3 cup sugar	1/4 cup honey
1/4 cup wheat or oat bran	1/2 teaspoon ground
2 eggs, lightly beaten	cinnamon

1 Preheat oven to moderate 350°F. Brush an 8 inch round cake pan with melted butter or oil; line the base with parchment paper. Melt the butter in a small pan over low heat. Place the flour, cinnamon, baking powder and salt in a large bowl. Add sugar and bran. Make a well in center and add eggs, butter, vanilla and milk. Stir with a wooden spoon for 30–60 seconds. Do not overbeat.
2 Pour mixture into prepared pan; smooth surface. Bake for 25 minutes or until skewer comes out clean when inserted into center of cake. Turn onto a wire rack to cool before icing.
3 To make Icing: Beat cream cheese until smooth. Stir in sour cream and honey. Spread over cooled cake. Dust with cinnamon. Garnish with oranges, if desired.

many grains. Wheat, oat, rye, barley, rice, soy and peanut flours can be the base for bread dough. Fruits, nuts, vegetables and cheese can be added. Breads are made in a variety of shapes and sizes.

Breadfruit A starchy fruit of a tropical tree, it has a round shape and a bumpy green skin.

Brie A soft creamy-yellow cow's milk cheese with a thin, white, edible skin. It is aged from the outside by mold and bacteria that grow on the rind. Brie is made in a large flat wheel shape and cut into wedges for serving.

Brine A strong salt solution used for pickling and preserving meat, fish and vegetables.

Brioche A slightly sweet bread roll with a soft, spongy texture made from yeast dough enriched with butter and eggs. Brioche is a popular breakfast item in France, where it is eaten warm, spread with butter and jam. It is often bun-shaped with a small crown.

Brittle A hard, crunchy sugar candy into which nuts are folded. The hot candy batter is spread on cookie sheets to harden.

PUMPKIN BRAN BREAD

✶✶ **Preparation time:** 35 minutes + 2 hours standing
Total cooking time: 40 minutes
Makes 1 round loaf

1 envelope active dry yeast
¼ cup reserved warm pumpkin cooking liquid or water, 110–115°F
4 – 4½ cups unbleached all-purpose flour
¼ cup unprocessed bran
1 teaspoon salt
1 cup mashed pumpkin (10 oz uncooked)
¼– ½ cup reserved warm pumpkin cooking liquid or water, extra
1 egg, beaten
2 teaspoons water, extra
pumpkin seeds to sprinkle

1 Brush a deep 8 inch round cake pan with melted butter or oil; line the base with parchment paper. Dissolve yeast in ¼ cup reserved pumpkin liquid or water; cover with plastic wrap and leave in a warm place for 5 minutes or until frothy. Sift 4 cups of the flour and salt into a large bowl. Add the pumpkin, yeast mixture and ¼ cup of the extra liquid. Mix thoroughly using a wooden spoon, then your hands, until well combined. The dough will form a rough, slightly sticky ball. Add more liquid if the mixture is too dry—the amount of liquid will depend on the moistness of the pumpkin.
2 Turn onto a floured surface. Knead for 10 minutes or until the dough is smooth and elastic. Incorporate remaining ½ cup of flour as necessary to form a smooth dough. Place the dough in a lightly oiled bowl and brush the surface of the dough with oil. Cover with plastic wrap and leave in a warm place for 1 hour or until the dough is well risen.
3 Punch down dough and knead for 1 minute. Pull away a golf ball-sized piece of dough. Shape the remaining large piece of dough into a smooth round ball and place in the prepared pan. Roll the smaller ball into a rope 14 inches long. Tie into a loose knot, place across top of dough and seal with a little water to hold it in place. Cover with plastic wrap and leave to rise in a warm place for about 45 minutes or until well risen to top of the pan.
4 Preheat oven to 425°F. Brush the dough with the combined beaten egg and extra water. Sprinkle with pumpkin seeds. Bake for 20 minutes and then reduce oven to 350°F. Bake for 20 minutes more or until cooked. Cover with foil during last 10 minutes of cooking if bread is browning too much. Remove from the oven and cool on a wire rack. Pumpkin bread is delicious served plain with butter.

Note: Pumpkin bread will keep for up to 3 days in an airtight container, it also freezes well.

ABOVE: PUMPKIN BRAN BREAD.
OPPOSITE PAGE: WHITE BREAD

BREAD

BREAD (WHITE LOAF)

★ **Preparation time:** 30 minutes +
standing time
Total cooking time: 40 minutes
Makes 2 loaves

1 package active dry yeast	5½– 6 cups all-purpose
2¼ cups water	flour
1½ teaspoons salt	1 tablespoon butter, melted

1 Combine yeast and 2–3 tablespoons of warm water in a small bowl. Dissolve salt in remainder of water. Sift flour into a large bowl. Make a well in center and add yeast mixture, sprinkling flour over yeast. Add the salt and water mixture and the melted butter; combine with hands or a wooden spoon.
2 Gently knead on a lightly floured surface, adding more flour if necessary, for about 10 minutes. Shape dough into a ball, place in a large, lightly oiled mixing bowl. Stand, covered with plastic wrap, in a warm place for 1½ hours or until dough doubles in volume.
3 Brush two 8 x 4 x 2 inch loaf pans with oil or melted butter. Remove dough from the bowl, knead for 2–3 minutes until smooth. Divide in half. Press half of the dough into one loaf pan, repeat with remaining dough. Cover pans with plastic wrap and leave dough to rise for about 45 minutes or until it reaches top of pans.
4 Preheat oven to moderately hot 375°F. Bake bread for 40 minutes or until cooked. Remove from pans, cool on a wire rack.

VARIATIONS

■ OLIVE AND HERB ROLLS: Add ⅓ cup sliced black olives and 2–3 tablespoons chopped fresh herbs (oregano, lemon thyme, parsley or chives) to flour mixture in step 1. Follow recipe to kneading stage in step 3. Divide dough into 8–10 portions (depending on size of roll required). Knead each portion. Shape into rounds, flat rounds, sausage shapes or knots. Place on greased baking sheets. Brush tops with milk and sprinkle with flour if desired. Cover with plastic wrap and leave to rise for 40 minutes or until rolls are well-risen. Bake in preheated oven for 40–50 minutes or until rolls are golden and cooked through.
■ HERB AND CHEESE SCROLL: Follow bread recipe to step 3. Remove dough from bowl and knead for 2–3 minutes. Press dough into a flat rectangular shape, about 8 x 10 inches. Combine ½ cup grated cheese, 2 tablespoons fresh chopped parsley and pepper and sprinkle on top of dough. Roll up dough from the shortest side, as for a jelly roll. Place dough in prepared pans. Continue baking as for bread recipe.

Broad Bean (fava bean) A bean with a flat green pod containing large, pale green seeds. The broad bean was a staple of the poor in ancient Egypt. The ancient Greeks ate the beans green, in the pod, and also used the large dried seeds as voting tokens in the election of magistrates. Dried broad beans look like large lima beans and have a mealy texture and strong flavor. Their thick skins must be peeled before eating. The beans combine well with herbs and are popular in Italian cooking, where bean dishes are eaten as part of the funeral ceremony. See also Beans, Fresh.

Broccoli A member of the cabbage and cauliflower family. The most common variety, sprouting or heading broccoli, has deep green or purplish-green heads of tightly clustered buds and thick, juicy stalks. It was known to the ancient Romans, and was taken to France in the sixteenth century by Catherine de Medici. Both the stalk and head may be cooked or eaten raw.

Broth The liquid in which meat, fish or vegetables have been cooked. It can be eaten as a clear soup or thickened with vegetables, meat and grain.

Brownie A rich, thick chocolate bar cookie. It ranges in texture from heavy and chewy to light and cake-like. Nuts, bits of chocolate (Rocky Road Brownie) or candies can be sprinkled throughout or on top.

Brown Sauce A sauce made from meat stock thickened with flour and butter and flavored with onions, mushrooms and tomatoes. Also called Sauce Espagnole, it is the basis of other sauces, such as Bordelaise.

Brunch An informal light meal served in the late morning.

Brussels Sprout A green vegetable that resembles a tiny cabbage. Small compact sprouts have the best flavor and are available in the winter or frozen. Although its name suggests a Belgian origin, the Belgians themselves believe it was brought to their country by the Romans.

Bubble and Squeak A dish of leftover meats and vegetables, named for the sound it makes while sizzling in the pan.

WHOLE-WHEAT BREAD

★★ **Preparation time:** 30 minutes + standing
Total cooking time: 40-45 minutes
Makes 1 loaf

1/4 cup soft brown sugar
1 package active dry yeast
1 1/4 cups warm water or milk
2 cups whole-wheat flour

1 1/4 cups all-purpose flour
1 teaspoon salt
2 tablespoons butter, melted

1 Brush a 9 x 5 x 2 inch loaf pan with oil or melted butter. Combine sugar and yeast in a medium bowl. Gradually add water or milk; blend until smooth. Let stand covered with plastic wrap in a warm place for about 10 minutes or until foamy.
2 Sift flour and salt into large mixing bowl. Make a well in center. Add yeast mixture and melted butter using a wooden spoon, mix to a soft dough.
3 Turn onto lightly floured surface, knead for 5–10 minutes or until smooth. Shape dough into a ball, place in large, lightly oiled mixing bowl. Leave covered with plastic wrap in warm place for 15–20 minutes or until well risen. Punch air out of dough using your fist. Knead dough again for 3–5 minutes or until smooth. Place dough in prepared pan. Leave covered with plastic wrap in warm place until well risen and dough has doubled.
4 Preheat oven to moderately hot 375°F. Brush loaf with a little milk. Make slits or patterns in the top with a sharp knife and/or sprinkle with a little extra flour. Bake for 40–45 minutes or until well browned and cooked through. Stand bread in pan 5 minutes before transferring to wire rack to cool.

VARIATIONS

■ After punching air from dough and kneading again, divide into portions for individual rolls. Shape into rounds; roll into sausage shapes and tie in knots, or divide dough into three, roll in sausage lengths and braid together. Place rolls or decorative loaves on greased baking sheets. Leave room for spreading. Brush with milk and sprinkle with poppy seeds, sesame seeds or dried herbs and coarse salt. Bake until golden and cooked through.
■ For a lighter loaf use half all-purpose white flour and half whole-wheat flour.
■ CHEESE, BACON AND CHIVE LOAF: Combine 1/2 cup grated Cheddar cheese, 2 slices finely chopped cooked bacon, and 1/4 cup finely chopped chives with the sifted flour; proceed as recipe indicates.
■ After punching air from dough and kneading again, press into rectangle 1/2 inch thick. Sprinkle 1/2 cup chopped fresh mixed herbs, 1–2 cloves crushed garlic, salt and pepper on top. Roll dough from shortest end. Place seam-side down in prepared pan. Continue recipe as indicated.

ABOVE: WHOLE-GRAIN BREADS.
OPPOSITE PAGE: GARLIC FOCACCIA

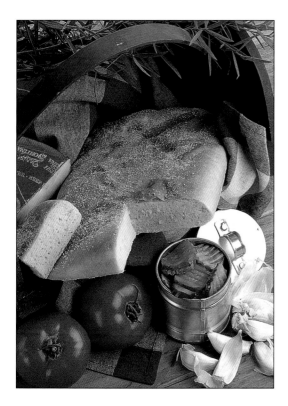

dough into pan; prick deep holes with a skewer. Sprinkle lightly with water and place in oven. Bake 10 minutes, sprinkle again with water. Bake 10 minutes more, brush with extra olive oil, sprinkle with sea salt, then bake 5 more minutes. Serve warm or at room temperature, cut into squares.

VARIATIONS

■ CHEESE AND CHIVE Add ⅓ cup finely grated Parmesan cheese and ¼ cup finely chopped chives to mixture in step 2.

■ CHEESE AND BACON Sprinkle ¾ cup grated Cheddar cheese, 2–3 slices finely chopped cooked bacon and 1 small finely sliced onion over the focaccia after pricking holes on its surface with a skewer. Bake as required. Omit sprinkling with water.

■ OLIVE, PEPPER AND ANCHOVY Sprinkle ½ cup sliced black olives, ½ small red pepper, finely chopped, and a 1½ oz can drained and finely sliced anchovy fillets over focaccia after pricking holes on surface with a skewer. Bake as required. Omit sprinkling with water.

GARLIC FOCACCIA

★ **Preparation time:** 20 minutes +
70 minutes standing
Total cooking time: 25 minutes
Serves 4–6

½ package active dry yeast	2 tablespoons olive oil
1 teaspoon sugar	1 tablespoon cornmeal or semolina
2½ cups all-purpose flour	1 tablespoon olive oil, extra
¾ cup lukewarm water	½ teaspoon finely crushed sea salt
1 teaspoon salt	
3 cloves garlic, crushed	

1 Combine the yeast, sugar, 1 teaspoon flour and water in a small mixing bowl. Stand, covered with plastic wrap, in a warm place 10 minutes or until foamy.
2 Sift the remaining flour and salt into a large mixing bowl. Add the garlic and stir with a knife to combine. Make a well in the center, stir in the yeast mixture and olive oil. Using a wooden spoon, mix to a firm dough.
3 Turn the dough onto a lightly floured surface and knead for 10 minutes. Shape the dough into a ball and place in a large, lightly oiled mixing bowl. Stand, covered with plastic wrap, in a warm place for 1 hour or until well risen.
4 Preheat the oven to moderately hot 400°F. Sprinkle the base of a 7 x 11 inch shallow pan with cornmeal or semolina. Knead the dough again for 2 minutes or until it is smooth. Press

OLIVE AND ONION FLAT BREAD

★★ **Preparation time:** 20 minutes
Total cooking time: 35 minutes +
15 minutes standing
Serves 8

1 tablespoon olive oil	3 cups whole-wheat flour
2 medium onions, finely sliced	3 cups all-purpose flour
1 teaspoon sugar	1 tablespoon caraway seeds
½ cup warm milk	1¾ cups warm water
1 package active dried yeast	⅓ cup olive oil, extra
	1 egg, beaten
	1 cup pitted black olives

1 Preheat oven to 375°F. Oil a 13 x 9 x 2 inch shallow baking dish. Heat the oil in a pan, add onions and cook for 10 minutes or until golden. Allow to cool.
2 Combine the sugar and milk, sprinkle with yeast. Mix and stand for 5 minutes. Sift the flours into a bowl, add caraway seeds.
3 Combine yeast mixture, water, extra oil and egg. Add to the flours, mix well—mixture will be tacky. Spread into baking dish; smooth with oiled hands. Let stand 15 minutes.
4 Sprinkle with cooked onions and olives, patting them firmly into top of dough. Bake for 35 minutes or until golden and firm.

Buckwheat The seeds of a plant native to Central Asia. They are roasted and available in 3 forms: buckwheat flour, used in pancakes; buckwheat grits, which are ground kernels used in cereals; and, the hulled, crushed kernels called buckwheat groats or kasha. See also Kasha.

Buffalo The lean meat of the American bison.

Bulgur Cracked wheat, which is made by steaming, drying and crushing wheat into rough fragments. Bulgur is rich in protein and is used in Middle Eastern cooking.

Bun A small, round, yeast roll, usually slightly sweetened and

sometimes containing spices and dried fruit.

Burgoo A thick, long-simmering stew of chicken or meat.

Burrito A dish consisting of a flat bread (tortilla) made of wheat flour, wrapped around a filling of shredded meat, beans and sometimes cheese. After the ends have been turned in to seal it, it is either eaten immediately or baked. The burrito is of Mexican origin. Its name comes from "burro," a small pack donkey, because the modest tortilla wrapping can accommodate a generous load of filling. A deep-fried burrito is called a *chimichanga*.

Butter A dairy product made by churning cream into a solid fat. Butter must contain at least 80 percent fat and not more than 16 percent water. Butter is used as a spread, as a cooking medium and as an ingredient in a range of sweet and savory dishes. It is salted to improve its keeping qualities; unsalted butter is also available. Clarified butter has been heated, the water content removed, and then strained to remove any nonfat solids. Whipped butter has had air beaten into it; this makes it fluffy, soft and more spreadable.

The first people to make butter from cow's milk were probably the Sumerians, although most early butter was made from the milk of goats and sheep.

FRUIT AND NUT BREAD

★★ **Preparation time:** 35 minutes + standing
Total cooking time: 40–50 minutes
Makes 1 loaf

1¼ cups all-purpose flour
1 cup whole-wheat flour
½ cup soft brown sugar
pinch of salt
¼ teaspoon ground cinnamon
¼ teaspoon ground nutmeg
¼ teaspoon ground ginger
¼ teaspoon allspice
1 package active dry yeast

⅔ cup warm milk
2 tablespoons butter, melted but not hot
⅓ cup sultanas
⅓ cup currants
⅓ cup candied peel
⅓ cup brazil nuts, chopped

Glaze
⅓ cup milk
2 tablespoons sugar

1 Combine flours, sugar, salt and spices in a large bowl. Dissolve the yeast in a little of the milk. Make a well in the center of the dry ingredients, add the milk and yeast mixture. Add the butter and remaining milk and use a wooden spoon to mix to a soft dough, adding more flour or warm water if necessary.
2 Turn dough onto a lightly floured surface and knead for about 4 minutes or until the dough is soft and elastic. Return to bowl and leave to stand, covered with plastic wrap, in a warm place for about 1½ hours or until well risen.
3 Preheat oven to 350°F. Brush a small loaf pan with melted butter or oil. Add the fruit, peel and nuts to the dough and knead again until well mixed, place in the pan. Leave the dough covered with plastic wrap in a warm place for about 1 hour, until the dough rises to top of pan. Bake for 45–50 minutes or until the loaf has shrunk slightly in pan and is brown on top. Turn onto a wire rack, tap and if the loaf is very soft return it to the oven, upside down without the pan, for a further 5 minutes.
4 When cooked and still hot, paint with Glaze. Leave on wire rack to cool.
5 To make Glaze: Combine milk and sugar in saucepan and bring to boil, stirring constantly until sugar has dissolved. Boil for 3–5 minutes until glaze thickens slightly.

VARIATIONS

■ Fruit and Nut Bread can be formed into twists or made into individual rolls.
■ For hot cross buns, place a pie crust pastry cross on top of each bun before baking. Brush with glaze as usual.
■ Bread is lighter if made with all white flour and much denser if made with all whole-wheat.
■ Use different fruit and nuts: chopped hazelnuts, and glacé cherries make a lovely tea bread.

ABOVE: FRUIT AND NUT BREAD.
OPPOSITE PAGE, ABOVE: WHOLE-WHEAT RYE SOURDOUGH BREAD; BELOW: OLIVE SODA BREAD

O L I V E   S O D A   B R E A D

★ **Preparation time:** 20 minutes
Total cooking time: 25 minutes
Serves 8

2 cups all-purpose flour
2 teaspoons baking
  powder
½ teaspoon salt
2 tablespoons butter,
  chopped
½ cup shredded
  Parmesan cheese

½ cup black pitted olives,
  sliced
1 tablespoon chopped
  fresh rosemary
½ cup milk
¼ cup water
1 tablespoon milk, extra
2 tablespoons shredded
  Parmesan cheese

1 Preheat oven to moderately hot 375°F. Brush a baking sheet with melted butter or oil and sprinkle lightly with flour. Sift flour, baking powder and salt into a mixing bowl. Add chopped butter. Using fingertips, rub butter into flour until mixture is fine and crumbly.
2 Add Parmesan, olives and rosemary; stir. Combine milk and water, add to dry ingredients. Mix to a soft dough with a flat-bladed knife.
3 On a lightly floured surface, knead dough until smooth. Shape into a ball, flatten out to a round approximately ¾ inch thick.
4 Place dough on prepared baking sheet. Using a large knife, score dough deeply to mark into eight portions. Brush with extra milk and sprinkle with extra cheese. Bake for 25 minutes or until golden brown and crusty.

W H O L E - W H E A T   R Y E   S O U R D O U G H   B R E A D

★ ★ **Preparation time:** 50 minutes
Total cooking time: 40 minutes
Makes 1 large or 2 small loaves

Sourdough Starter
1 package active dry yeast
1 cup warm water
1 cup all-purpose flour

Bread Dough
1½ cups water
1 package active dry yeast

1 tablespoon soft brown
  sugar
1 cup whole-wheat flour
2 cups all-purpose flour
1½ cups rye flour
1 teaspoon salt
2 teaspoons caraway seeds
extra rye flour for
  kneading

1 To make Sourdough Starter: Dissolve yeast in warm water. Sift in all-purpose flour, mix until smooth. Cover and leave at room temperature for at least 2 days.
2 To make Bread Dough: Combine water, yeast and brown sugar. Leave to stand in warm place until mixture starts to bubble.
3 Place whole-wheat, 1 cup plain and rye flour in a large bowl with salt. Make a well in the center of flours and add yeast mixture and ½ cup Sourdough Starter. Mix until well combined. Stir in remaining 1 cup plain flour. Knead until dough is smooth and elastic. Place in lightly oiled bowl and leave in warm position until dough has doubled in bulk.
4 Preheat oven to 400°F. Punch dough down, place on floured work surface; knead 5 minutes. Shape dough into one or two long loaves.
5 Place loaves on a greased baking sheet; stand for 10 minutes. Glaze with water, sprinkle tops with caraway seeds. Bake for 30–40 minutes until golden.

Butter Bean See Lima Bean.

Buttercup Squash A dark green squash with a turban-like cap and sweet, dry, orange-colored flesh.

Butterfly To cut a boneless piece of meat almost in half and spread the sections flat to resemble butterfly wings.

Buttermilk Originally the thin liquid left after cream had been churned into butter. Today buttermilk is made from skim milk, to which a culture has been added, giving it a thick texture and tangy flavor. It is also available dry or powdered. Buttermilk is used as a drink and in baking. It is added to hot soups and casseroles or used as a low-fat substitute for oil or cream in salad dressings.

Butternut Squash A member of the marrow family, shaped like a long pear. It has smooth buff-colored skin and bright orange flesh with a sweet flavor and is widely used as a cooked vegetable.

Butterscotch A slightly cloudy, boiled candy made with water, brown sugar and butter. Butterscotch also refers to the flavor of butter and brown sugar, popular in cookies, ice cream toppings and frostings. See Index for recipes.

C CABBAGE & CAULIFLOWER

Cabbage, so often overcooked, has not always been kindly looked upon. One of the most nutritious vegetables, it can be delicious if imaginatively prepared. Cauliflower has also suffered by being buried under thick white sauces. Here are some tasty alternatives.

QUICK COLESLAW

Finely shred ¹/₂ small green cabbage. Combine with 2 grated carrots, 1 stalk finely chopped celery, 1 finely chopped onion, 1 finely chopped small green or red pepper and ¹/₂ cup prepared coleslaw dressing in a large bowl. Toss well to combine. Add ¹/₄ cup freshly chopped mixed herbs if desired. Chill before serving.

CABBAGE AND POTATO CAKES

Combine 1 cup cooked shredded cabbage, ¹/₂ cup roughly mashed potato, 1 finely chopped scallion, 2 lightly beaten eggs and salt and freshly ground pepper to taste and mix well. Heat some oil or butter in a frying pan. Cook spoonfuls of the mixture in small batches for about 2 minutes each side or until it is golden. Drain on paper towels. Serve warm.

SWEET RED CABBAGE WITH CARAWAY SEEDS

Finely shred ¹/₂ small red cabbage. Heat 2 tablespoons butter, 1 teaspoon caraway seeds, 1 teaspoon balsamic vinegar and 1 teaspoon soft brown sugar in pan. Add cabbage, cook, stirring, for 2–3 minutes or until just tender. Serve warm.

GARLIC PEPPER CABBAGE

Finely shred ¹/₂ small green cabbage. Heat 2 tablespoons butter and 1 teaspoon oil in heavy-bottom frying pan or wok. Add 2 teaspoons garlic pepper seasoning and cabbage. Stir-fry 2–3 minutes or until tender.
Serve warm.

QUICK COLESLAW

CABBAGE AND POTATO CAKES

SWEET RED CABBAGE WITH CARAWAY SEEDS

GARLIC PEPPER CABBAGE

CAULIFLOWER WITH BACON

Cut 1 small cauliflower into florets. Steam or microwave until just tender. Heat 1 teaspoon of oil in a medium pan. Add 2 slices of julienned bacon and cook until browned. Add the cauliflower and 2 finely chopped scallions; stir to combine. Serve warm.

CAULIFLOWER WITH BACON

CAULIFLOWER WITH TOMATO SAUCE

Cut 1 small cauliflower into medium florets. Steam or microwave cauliflower until just tender. Heat 1 tablespoon oil in medium pan. Add ½ teaspoon cracked pepper, 1 teaspoon mixed Italian herbs and 1 clove crushed garlic. Cook 1 minute. Add one 14 oz can crushed tomatoes. Bring to boil, reduce heat, simmer 5 minutes or until reduced slightly. Pour sauce over vegetables and serve warm.

CAULIFLOWER WITH TOMATO SAUCE

PARMESAN CAULIFLOWER

Cut 1 small cauliflower into florets. Combine, in a bowl, ¼ cup all-purpose flour, 2 tablespoons finely grated Parmesan cheese and 1 teaspoon dried mixed herbs. Toss florets in this mixture. Heat 2 tablespoons oil and 3 tablespoons butter in a heavy-bottom frying pan. Gently cook cauliflower in batches until just tender. Drain on paper towels. Serve warm.

HOT CHILI CAULIFLOWER

Cut 1 small cauliflower into florets. Steam or microwave until just tender. Mix together 3 tablespoons melted butter, 1 tablespoon tomato paste, 2 tablespoons chopped fresh cilantro and ¼ teaspoon chili powder (or to taste) in a large bowl. Add cauliflower and toss. Serve warm.

PARMESAN CAULIFLOWER

HOT CHILI CAULIFLOWER

Cabanossi A thin, spicy, precooked sausage made from seasoned ground pork or beef, or a mixture of the two. Cabanossi originated in Poland as a snack for hunters far from home. It can be served as finger food and packed in lunches.

Cabbage A vegetable with green leaves formed into a tightly packed head. It has a mild flavor, and can be eaten raw finely chopped in salads, or thinly sliced and steamed, boiled or microwaved and served as a vegetable, or added to soups and stews; the curved outer leaves are used as wrappings for meat fillings.

Native to Europe and western Asia, cabbage is one of the oldest cultivated vegetables. It can range in color from almost white to green and red, and is available year-round; select heavy firm heads. The high vitamin C content of cabbage was recognized by eighteenth-century navigators, who carried it on board to prevent scurvy. The Ancient Greeks and Romans believed it could prevent drunkenness.

CAJUN CLASSICS

CAJUN SPICES

Mix together 1 tablespoon garlic powder, 1 tablespoon onion powder, 2 teaspoons white pepper, 2 teaspoons cracked black pepper, 1½ teaspoons cayenne pepper, 2 teaspoons dried thyme and ½ teaspoon dried oregano. Store the mixture in a spice jar.

CAJUN VEGETABLES

Peel, trim and finely dice 1 large onion, 1 green pepper and 2 short celery stalks. Makes 3–3½ cups.

ROUX

Roux is one of the most important elements in Cajun cooking. To make it, use equal parts oil and flour. Heat a heavy pan (preferably cast-iron since high heat can damage a nonstick surface) and add the oil. When oil is very hot, sprinkle on one-quarter of the flour and whisk in briskly. Add remaining flour gradually, whisking constantly until the desired color is reached. The mixture should be on a slow boil with tiny bubbles constantly breaking the surface. Light roux needs about 2 minutes cooking on high heat, red-brown roux about 5 minutes. For best results, keep the heat reasonably high, sliding the pan off the heat for 30 seconds every so often.

Whisking must be constant and fast to avoid scorching, which will make the roux bitter. Be careful not to allow hot roux to splash on your skin—it is a good idea to wear long rubber gloves when preparing it. Store roux in the refrigerator and heat gently to room temperature before use.

BLACKENED FISH

★ *Preparation time:* 5 minutes
Total cooking time: 6–8 minutes
Serves 6

½ cup unsalted (sweet) butter　　*3 tablespoons Cajun spices*
6 large white fish fillets　　*1 tablespoon sweet paprika*

1 Melt the butter in a small pan.
2 Brush each fish fillet generously with melted butter. Mix together Cajun spices and paprika and sprinkle thickly over the fish.
3 Heat a large skillet over high heat. Place fish fillets, one or two at a time, in the dry, hot pan to cook for 1–2 minutes on high heat. Turn and cook a few minutes more until done. The surface should be well charred on each side. Add a little extra butter if needed. Cook remaining fillets. Serve hot with remaining melted butter and plain white rice.

ABOVE: BLACKENED FISH
OPPOSITE PAGE: SHRIMP GUMBO

SHRIMP GUMBO

★★ **Preparation time:** 20 minutes
Total cooking time: 1 hour
Serves 6

10 oz package frozen cut okra	2 teaspoons dried red chili flakes
14¹/2 oz can diced tomatoes	1 teaspoon Worcestershire sauce
2 cups Cajun vegetables	pepper, to taste
¹/4 cup butter	2 cups seafood stock
2 cloves garlic, minced	¹/4 cup red-brown roux
2 teaspoons tomato paste	1¹/4 lb medium shrimp, peeled and deveined
2 teaspoons Cajun spices	1 teaspoon filé powder, optional
2 bay leaves	
¹/4 teaspoon ground allspice	

1 Combine the okra and crushed tomatoes in a pan. Bring to the boil, reduce the heat, cover and simmer gently for 15 minutes.
2 Cook the Cajun vegetables in butter for 2–3 minutes, add the minced garlic and cook for 20 minutes.
3 Add the okra and tomato mixture to the Cajun vegetables, with the tomato paste, Cajun spices, bay leaves, allspice, chili flakes, Worcestershire sauce and pepper. Stir for 2 minutes, then add the seafood stock and roux and cook for 15 minutes more.
4 Add the shrimp and simmer gently until just cooked. Season to taste with salt and pepper and stir in the filé powder if using.

DIRTY RICE

★★ **Preparation time:** 15 minutes
Total cooking time: 30 minutes
Serves 6

2¹/2 cups Cajun vegetables	¹/4 cup red-brown roux
¹/4 cup butter	¹/2 teaspoon Tabasco sauce
2 cloves garlic, minced	2 teaspoons Cajun spices
6 oz chicken livers, chopped	freshly ground black pepper
8 oz ground pork	2 cups long-grain white rice
1¹/2 teaspoons chicken bouillon powder	3 cups chicken stock

1 Cook the vegetables in half the butter until tender; add the garlic and cook briefly. Remove from pan.
2 Cook livers and pork for about 2–3 minutes, breaking up lumps in pork with a fork as it cooks. Add vegetables, cook for 2–3 minutes.
3 Stir in the chicken bouillon granules, roux, Tabasco sauce, Cajun spices, pepper, rice and stock and bring to the boil. Reduce heat and simmer for about 20 minutes.
4 Check seasoning, stir well and serve.

Note: Stir in chopped scallions, if desired. Wedges of hard-boiled egg, cubes of cooked chicken or ham, cooked shrimp and red kidney beans can be added to make a substantial main course dish.

Cabécou A soft-textured goat's milk cheese made in small cakes, originally produced on farms in the Quercy region of south-western France. Cabécou has a zesty, nutty flavor which becomes more intense with age. It can

be eaten fresh, or at varying stages of ripening.

Cactus Pad (Prickly Pear) The fleshy oval cactus leaves (Nopales) that are gathered in the early spring, when they are less than 3 inches in diameter. The pads, chopped and boiled, were eaten by Native Americans of the southwest; now they are often sold in markets. Slippery and crunchy, the thorns must be removed before cooking. The flavor is a cross between green beans and avocados.

Caerphilly Cheese A crumbly, semihard, cow's milk cheese with a mild, slightly salty flavor. It is almost white in color, and takes only two weeks to mature. Caerphilly takes its name from the Welsh town, and perhaps because of its easy digestibility or because it stayed fresh and moist, it was a popular ingredient in the packed lunches of coal miners.

Caesar Salad A salad of romaine lettuce, croutons, Parmesan cheese, Worcestershire sauce, and anchovies. It is dressed with olive oil, vinegar and coddled egg.

Named after its inventor, Caesar Cardini, a Mexican restaurateur, and popular in Hollywood in the 1920s, Caesar salad is now considered a classic American salad.

Café au Lait Hot black coffee mixed with scalded milk, usually in equal proportions. It is a traditional breakfast beverage in many European countries

Caffè Latte An Italian style of coffee in which very strong espresso coffee is combined in a glass with very hot milk. It is generally drunk at breakfast.

Cajun Food Cajun country takes in the bays, bayous and hinterland of southern Louisiana. In the mid-1750s it was refuge to the French Huguenots expelled by the English from Arcadia, in Nova Scotia, Canada ("Cajun" is derived from "Arcadian"). Cajun food is earthy and robust; its roots are in the peasant

CHICKEN AND SMOKED HAM JAMBALAYA

⭐ **Preparation time:** 45 minutes
Total cooking time: 1¾ hours
Serves 6

2 lb chicken pieces, deboned
1 small carrot, chopped
1 small onion, chopped
6 peppercorns
2 sprigs parsley
1 sprig fresh thyme
4 cups water
1 lb tasso (smoked ham), cubed
2 tablespoons vegetable oil
2 cups Cajun vegetables
2 cloves garlic, minced
14 oz can diced tomatoes
2½ cups long-grain white rice
2 teaspoons Cajun spices

1 Place the chicken bones and skin, carrot, onion, peppercorns, parsley and thyme in a pan, add 4 cups water. Bring to the boil, reduce heat and simmer, uncovered, for 30 minutes. Strain, reserving stock.
2 Cut the chicken meat into cubes and cook with the ham in the oil for about 6 minutes. Add chopped Cajun vegetables and garlic and cook until golden. Add tomatoes, rice, 3 cups of reserved chicken stock and the Cajun spice mix; bring to the boil.
3 Pour into a greased casserole dish and bake, uncovered, at 350°F for about 1 hour. The rice should be slightly crisp on top.

HUSH PUPPIES

⭐ **Preparation time:** 10 minutes
Total cooking time: 10 minutes
Makes 18–20

¾ cup fine cornmeal
¼ cup all-purpose flour
1 tablespoon sugar
1 teaspoon baking powder
½ teaspoon baking soda
¼ teaspoon onion salt
¼ teaspoon chili powder
1 teaspoon Cajun spices
1 clove garlic, minced
2 tablespoons grated onion
1 egg, lightly beaten
½ cup buttermilk
1 tablespoon water
oil, for deep frying

1 In mixing bowl combine cornmeal, flour, sugar, baking powder, soda, onion salt, chili powder and spices. Add garlic and onion.
2 Stir together egg, buttermilk and water. Pour over the dry mixture; stir well.
3 Heat oil in deep, heavy-bottom pan until moderately hot (375°F). Carefully spoon tablespoonfuls of mixture into oil. Cook only four or five at time; fry until puffy and lightly golden, turning once or twice.
4 Remove from oil with a slotted spoon or strainer. Drain on paper towels. Serve warm.

ABOVE: HUSH PUPPIES; LEFT: CHICKEN AND SMOKED HAM JAMBALAYA.

OPPOSITE PAGE: BASIC BUTTER CAKE

CAKES BUTTER

BASIC BUTTER CAKE

⭐ **Preparation time:** 30 minutes
Total cooking time: 35 minutes
Makes one 8 inch 1-layer cake

1/4 cup unsalted butter,
  softened
1 cup sugar
1 egg, lightly beaten
1 1/2 teaspoons vanilla
  extract
1 1/4 cups all-purpose flour
1 1/2 teaspoons baking
  powder
1/4 teaspoon salt
2/3 cup milk

thin strips of candied
  orange peel, optional,
  for decoration

Lemon Butter Icing
3 tablespoons unsalted
  butter, softened
2 1/4 cups confectioners'
  sugar, sifted
2 tablespoons lemon juice

1 Preheat oven to moderate 350°F. Grease one 8 inch round cake pan. Line bottom and side with parchment paper. Lightly grease paper. Using an electric mixer, beat butter and sugar in a small mixing bowl until well mixed. Add the egg gradually, beating thoroughly after each addition. Add vanilla; beat until combined.
2 Stir together flour, baking powder and salt. Transfer butter mixture to a large mixing bowl. Stir flour mixture and milk alternately into butter mixture. Stir until the mixture is almost smooth.
3 Spoon mixture into prepared pan; smooth surface. Bake 35 minutes or until a skewer comes out clean when inserted into center of cake. Leave in pan for 10 minutes before turning onto wire rack to cool. Remove paper.
4 To make Lemon Butter Icing: Using electric mixer, beat 3 tablespoons butter and half of the powdered sugar until well mixed. With mixer on low speed, beat in lemon juice. Gradually beat in remaining powdered sugar. Spread icing over cake using a flat-bladed knife. Decorate with thin strips of candied peel if using.

Note: Sugar assists with incorporating air into fat in cake making, so it is important to use the type of sugar called for in the recipe. Most cake recipes use granulated sugar (called for as "sugar"). Icing and frosting recipes often call for powdered sugar which is usually called confectioners' sugar.

MARBLE CAKE

Divide basic butter cake mixture equally into three separate bowls. Add 2 tablespoons sifted unsweetened cocoa powder and an extra 1 tablespoon of milk to the first bowl; mix well. Add enough red food coloring to the second bowl to tint the mixture pink. Leave the third bowl plain. Drop spoonfuls of alternating colors into the prepared pan until all the mixture has been used. Draw a skewer or knife through to swirl colors. Bake as directed.

cooking of rural France, but its distinctive style comes from a combination of Native American uses of local herbs and roots, ingredients introduced by African slaves (okra, sesame seeds, melons and hot spices) and the culinary legacy of earlier Spanish settlers. Cajun cooking features simple, one-pot meals using fresh farm produce: onions, hot and sweet peppers, okra, celery, chicken and pork, bacon and ham (pigs were easier to raise than sheep or cattle), as well as the bounty of both the brackish bayous and the waters of the Gulf of Mexico, such as crayfish (called crawfish and sometimes crawdad in Louisiana), shrimp, lobster, crab, oysters and fish. Many dishes are based on a brown roux; rice or beans are served with most meals. Filé powder, made from dried sassafras leaves, adds a distinctive flavor. Cajun specialties include spicy gumbos, peppery jambalayas (rice, pork, sausage, ham and shellfish), étouffée (shellfish cooked in a seasoned sauce and served over rice) and custard tarts.

Cake A term describing a variety of sweet, baked foods with a texture similar to bread, usually made from flour, sugar, eggs and a liquid. Cakes are grouped according to the relative proportions of these basic ingredients used in their preparation, and the method in which they are made. Many cakes have a ceremonial or symbolic significance, such as that of the rich Christmas

cake (originally part of a religious feast), the wedding cake (which dates from the time of ancient Greece), christening cakes and birthday cakes.

Cake Decorating The technique of covering cakes with icing or frosting and other sweet, edible trimmings, usually for a festive occasion such as Christmas, a wedding, birthday or christening.

Calamari The Italian name for squid, a saltwater mollusk related to the octopus and cuttlefish and prized for its delicately flavored flesh.

LEMON CUPCAKES

⭐ ⭐ **Preparation time:** 40 minutes
Total cooking time: 20–22 minutes
Makes 24

1/2 cup butter, softened	*2 1/4 teaspoons baking*
1 1/3 cups sugar	*powder*
1 egg, lightly beaten	*1/4 teaspoon salt*
1 teaspoon grated lemon	*3/4 cup milk*
rind	*1 cup heavy cream*
1 tablespoon lemon juice	*1 tablespoon sugar*
1 teaspoon vanilla	*1/4 cup raspberry jam*
2 1/4 cups all-purpose flour	*sifted confectioners' sugar*

1 Preheat oven to 350°F. Line 24 muffin cups with paper bake cups. Using electric mixer beat butter and 1 1/3 cups sugar in a mixing bowl until well mixed. Add egg gradually, beating after each addition. Add lemon rind, lemon juice and vanilla; beat until combined.
2 Combine the flour, baking powder and salt in a mixing bowl. Stir the flour mixture and milk alternately into the butter mixture until almost smooth. Spoon into prepared cups: each should be about half full. Bake 20–22 minutes until golden. Leave in pans 5 minutes, transfer to wire racks to cool.
3 When cool, cut a small circle from the top of each cupcake, cut down about 3/4 inch to allow for the filling. Set circles aside.
4 Beat cream and 1 tablespoon sugar until peaks form. Spoon 1/2 teaspoon jam into each cupcake; top with a tablespoon whipped cream and a circle of cake. Dust with powdered sugar before serving.

MADEIRA CAKE

⭐ **Preparation time:** 20 minutes
Total cooking time: 60 minutes
Makes 1 loaf cake

2/3 cup butter	*2 cups all-purpose flour*
1 cup sugar	*1 teaspoon baking*
3 eggs, lightly beaten	*powder*
2 teaspoons finely grated	*1/4 teaspoon salt*
orange or lemon rind	*confectioners' sugar, for*
1/2 cup ground almonds	*dusting*

1 Preheat oven to moderate 350°F. Lightly brush a 9 x 5 x 2 inch loaf pan with melted butter or oil. Line the base and sides with parchment paper. Using electric beaters, beat the butter and sugar in a medium mixing bowl until light and creamy. Add the eggs gradually, beating thoroughly after each addition. Add the orange or lemon rind; beat until combined.
2 Stir together flour, baking powder and salt. Using a metal spoon, fold in ground almonds and flour mixture. Stir until just combined and mixture is smooth.
3 Spoon mixture into prepared pan; smooth surface. Bake for about 60 minutes, until a skewer comes out clean when inserted in center of cake. Leave in pan 10 minutes before turning onto wire rack to cool. Dust top of cake lightly with confectioners' sugar.

ABOUT CAKES

■ For successful cake baking, read the recipe entirely beforehand and assemble all ingredients and equipment. Preheat oven to correct temperature, prepare baking pans.
■ Measure ingredients accurately—do not guess quantities. Use standard measuring cups, spoons and kitchen scales. Have eggs and butter at room temperature.
■ Butter and sugar should be thoroughly creamed. Beat in a bowl with electric beaters until mixture is light and creamy—it should almost double in volume and have no trace of sugar granules. Fold in ingredients carefully, mixing lightly yet evenly (overbeating can result in a heavy, coarse-textured cake).
■ Check oven temperature. Avoid opening oven door until two-thirds of the way through baking. Total cooking times given are approximate and may vary according to oven accuracy. Leave cake in pan for the specified time before turning onto a wire rack to cool.

ABOVE: LEMON CUPCAKES.
OPPOSITE PAGE: PANFORTE

CAKES CHOCOLATE

PANFORTE

★ **Preparation time:** 30 minutes
Total cooking time: 50–55 minutes
Makes one 8 inch round cake

²/3 cup slivered almonds	1 teaspoon ground cinnamon
²/3 cup chopped macadamia nuts	2 oz dark (semisweet) chocolate, chopped
²/3 cup chopped walnuts	¼ cup unsalted (sweet) butter
1½ cups mixed dried fruit, chopped	½ cup sugar
¾ cup all-purpose flour	⅓ cup honey
2 tablespoons unsweetened cocoa powder	confectioners' sugar

1 Preheat oven to 350°F. Brush an 8 inch round cake pan with oil or melted butter. Line base with paper; grease paper. Combine nuts and dried fruit in a large mixing bowl. Add flour, cocoa and cinnamon, stir until combined. Make a well in the center.

2 Stir the chocolate, butter, sugar and honey in a small pan over low heat until melted and well combined; remove from heat. Add the butter mixture to the dry ingredients and stir until all ingredients are well combined. Be careful not to overbeat.

3 Spoon into prepared pan; smooth surface. Bake 50–55 minutes until cake is firm to touch in the center. Allow to cool in the pan before turning out. Decorate with confectioners' sugar. Serve thin wedges with coffee or liqueur.

EASY CHOCOLATE CAKE

★ **Preparation time:** 20 minutes
Total cooking time: 25–30 minutes
Makes two 8 inch round cakes

½ cup butter	¾ teaspoon baking powder
1 cup sugar	
1 egg	½ teaspoon baking soda
1 teaspoon vanilla	⅛ teaspoon salt
1⅓ cups all-purpose flour	¾ cup milk
2 tablespoons unsweetened cocoa powder	½ cup heavy cream, whipped
	confectioners' sugar
	strawberries

1 Preheat oven to 350°F. Brush two 8 inch round cake pans with melted butter or oil, line base with waxed or parchment paper; grease paper.

2 Beat butter and sugar with electric beaters in medium mixing bowl until light and creamy. Add egg and beat thoroughly. Add vanilla; beat until combined.

3 Stir together flour, cocoa powder, baking powder, baking soda and salt. Stir in dry ingredients alternating with milk until just combined and mixture is smooth.

4 Spoon into prepared pans; smooth surface. Bake 25–30 minutes or until skewer inserted in center of cakes comes out clean.

5 Cool cakes in pans 5 minutes before turning onto wire rack to cool.

6 Sandwich together with whipped cream. Dust with confectioners' sugar and decorate with strawberries.

Camembert A cow's milk cheese, produced in small, flat disks with a tangy, creamy flavor. Like Brie, Camembert is ripened from the outside by surface molds that form a soft white skin encasing the creamy center. Though originally from Normandy, France, and known since the seventeenth century, the modern cheese is credited to Marie Harel, a farm woman. During the French Revolution she is said to have sheltered a fugitive priest from the Brie region, from whom she learned cheese-making methods. She combined these with local techniques to produce an improved version. In the 1890s it became available to a wider audience when packaging in small wooden boxes allowed it to be sent, without risk of spoilage, into new markets far afield.

Camomile (Chamomile) A plant of the daisy family, native to western Europe. Camomile has been used since the days of ancient Egypt. It can be either eaten or applied to treat sprains, muscle strain, cramps and colic. Camomile tea is made from the flower heads; it makes a soothing drink or can be used as a grooming aid for skin and hair.

MUD CAKE

⭐ ⭐ **Preparation time:** 15 minutes
Total cooking time: 65–70 minutes
Makes one 8 inch round cake

2½ cups all-purpose flour
⅓ cup unsweetened cocoa powder
1½ teaspoons baking soda
1 teaspoon baking powder
¼ teaspoon salt
2 cups sugar
1 cup butter
6 oz semisweet chocolate, chopped
1¼ cups hot water
2 eggs
1 tablespoon vegetable oil

Icing
6 oz semisweet chocolate, chopped
½ cup unsalted butter
3 tablespoons heavy cream
heavy cream, whipped
white chocolate to decorate, if desired

1 Preheat oven to 325°F. Brush an 8 inch round springform pan with melted butter or oil. Line base and sides with wax or parchment paper; grease paper.
2 Sift together the flour, cocoa powder, baking soda, baking powder and salt. Make a well in the center.
3 Combine sugar, butter, chocolate, water and oil in a medium pan. Stir over low heat until butter and chocolate have melted and sugar has dissolved; remove from heat.
4 Add butter mixture and eggs to dry ingredients. Stir with wooden spoon until ingredients are just combined; do not overbeat.
5 Pour mixture into prepared pan. Bake for

65–70 minutes or until a skewer inserted into center comes out clean.
6 Cool cake in pan at least 2 hours before turning out onto a wire rack.
7 To make Icing: Combine chocolate, butter and cream in small pan. Stir over low heat until chocolate and butter have melted; remove from heat. Cool.
8 Spread the icing over cake. Serve with whipped cream. Garnish with white chocolate if desired.

ABOUT MELTING CHOCOLATE

■ Chop chocolate into even-sized pieces and place in a glass bowl. Place bowl over a pan of simmering water and stir gently until the chocolate has melted. Do not allow any water to fall into the chocolate or it will immediately stiffen and be unworkable. Cool chocolate slightly before use.

■ Melting chocolate in the microwave is easy. Chop the chocolate for your recipe into even sized pieces and place in a microwave-safe bowl. Microwave on Medium (50% power), using short bursts of power to avoid "hot spots." Remove the bowl from the microwave and stir the chocolate gently until it is quite smooth. Chocolate will hold its shape when melted in the microwave—in order to avoid scorching it is essential to stir it before microwaving again.

ABOVE: MUD CAKE.

OPPOSITE PAGE: WHOLE-WHEAT FRUIT AND NUT CAKE

CAKES
FRUIT AND NUT

WHOLE-WHEAT FRUIT AND NUT CAKE

⭐ **Preparation time:** 45 minutes
Total cooking time: 1¼ – 1½ hours
Makes one 9 inch 1-layer cake

⅔ cup unsalted butter, softened
1¼ cups firmly packed dark brown sugar
3 eggs, lightly beaten
6 oz dried figs, chopped
1¼ cups dried apricots, chopped
1¼ cups walnut pieces
¾ cup currants
⅔ cup golden raisins
⅔ cup sunflower seeds
2 cups whole-wheat flour
⅔ cup all-purpose flour
1 teaspoon baking powder
1 teaspoon ground cinnamon

1 teaspoon ground nutmeg
1 teaspoon ground allspice
¼ teaspoon salt
1 can (5½ oz) apricot nectar (about ⅔ cup)

Spicy Nut Topping
⅓ cup finely chopped walnuts
1 tablespoon sunflower seeds
½ teaspoon ground cinnamon
½ teaspoon ground nutmeg
½ teaspoon ground allspice

1 Preheat oven to 325°F. Grease a 9 inch square cake pan. Line bottom and sides with parchment paper. Lightly grease paper. Using electric mixer, beat butter and brown sugar in small bowl until well mixed. Add eggs gradually, beat well after each addition. Transfer to large bowl. Stir in figs, apricots, walnuts, currants, golden raisins and sunflower seeds.
2 Stir together whole-wheat flour, all-purpose flour, baking powder, 1 teaspoon cinnamon, 1 teaspoon nutmeg, 1 teaspoon allspice and salt. Stir flour mixture and apricot nectar alternately into butter mixture. Stir until well mixed. Spoon mixture into prepared pan; smooth the surface.
3 To make Spicy Nut Topping: Combine all topping ingredients. Spoon mixture onto top of cake, press down firmly with the back of spoon.
4 Bake 1¼ to 1½ hours until a skewer comes out clean when inserted in center of cake. Cool in pan on wire rack. Remove from pan. Remove paper.

ABOUT FRUIT CAKES
■ Traditional fruit cakes must be left to cool in the pan. If turned out while still hot, they will break.
■ Fruit cakes will keep well. They can be stored for up to 2 months, covered with several layers of plastic wrap, in the refrigerator.

Canola Oil Also known as rapeseed or colza oil, the pale yellow, almost colorless and odorless oil extracted from the seed of the rape or colza plant. Used in salads, cooking and the manufacture of margarine, canola oil is mainly mono-unsaturated fat and is a source of vitamin E.

Cantaloupe A round melon with a light netting over a greenish rind. The inside orange

flesh is extremely juicy and sweet with small pale seeds. Widely available in the summer and early fall, it is also known as muskmelon.

Cape Gooseberry The edible berry of a tropical plant native to Peru, but widely grown in warm countries throughout the world, especially in the Cape region of South Africa. Golden in color, the fruit is the size of a cherry and is encased in a gauzy sack which must be removed before use. The cape gooseberry has a tart flavor and may be eaten as a fresh

fruit, puréed and added to sorbets and ice creams or cooked in syrups and jams.

Caper The unopened, olive-green flower bud of a prickly shrub native to the Mediterranean, the Middle East and northern Africa. Preserved in jars of seasoned vinegar or packed in salt in wooden boxes, the buds range in size from very tiny to pea-sized. Capers have been used as a condiment since the time of ancient Greece. Their sharp, sour taste adds flavor to fish, cheese and creamed dishes, as well as white sauces, salads and mayonnaise. They are also used as a garnish on appetizers, pizzas and canapés.

Capon A male chicken that has been neutered to produce tender flesh. It has a high proportion of white breast meat to dark meat. Capons usually weigh between 4 and 10 pounds.

Cappuccino Espresso coffee topped with milk which has been frothed by passing steam through it. Cappuccino coffee is often topped with a dash of cinnamon.

Carambola (Star Fruit) The small oval, golden yellow fruit of a tree originally from Indonesia

FESTIVE FRUIT CAKE

⭐ **Preparation time:** 25 minutes
Total cooking time: 1¼–1½ hours
Makes one 9 inch 1-layer cake

½ cup unsalted butter
½ cup firmly packed light brown sugar
2 eggs, lightly beaten
¼ cup dark corn syrup
8 oz pitted whole dates
½ cup candied pineapple, cut into ¾ inch pieces
½ cup dried apricot halves, halved
½ cup candied red cherries
½ cup whole Brazil nuts
½ cup whole hazelnuts
½ cup whole macadamia nuts
1⅔ cups all-purpose flour
¾ teaspoon baking powder
¼ teaspoon salt
¼ cup orange juice
2 tablespoons port or brandy
food-safe cheesecloth
extra orange juice

1 Preheat oven to 300°F. Grease a 9 x 5 x 3 inch loaf pan. Line base and sides with parchment paper. Use electric mixer to beat butter and sugar until well mixed. Add eggs gradually, beating well after each addition. Add syrup; beat until combined.
2 Add fruits and nuts. Combine flour, baking powder and salt and orange juice, port and brandy. Stir flour mixture and orange juice mixture alternately into butter mixture until combined.
3 Spoon into prepared pan. Bake 1¼–1½ hours or until skewer inserted into cake comes out clean. leave cake in pan 1 hour before turning out. Remove paper. Moisten food-safe cheesecloth with extra orange juice. Wrap cake in cheesecloth, then plastic wrap, refrigerate in airtight container at least 24 hours. Remoisten cheesecloth as needed.

DUNDEE CAKE

⭐ **Preparation time:** 30 minutes
Total cooking time: 2–2¼ hours
Makes one 9 inch 1-layer cake

⅔ cup unsalted butter, softened
1 cup firmly packed light brown sugar
3 eggs, lightly beaten
1¼ cup currants
1 cup raisins
1 cup golden raisins
⅔ cup slivered almonds
½ cup candied orange peel, chopped
¼ cup candied cherries, chopped
1 teaspoon grated orange rind
1 teaspoon grated lemon rind
2 cups plain (all-purpose) flour
¾ cup ground almonds
1 teaspoon baking powder
⅔ cup milk
½ cup rum
⅓ cup whole blanched almonds, optional, for decoration

1 Preheat oven to 300°F. Grease a 9 inch round springform pan. Line base and side with parchment paper. Using electric mixer, beat together butter and brown sugar until well mixed. Add the eggs gradually, beating well after each addition.
2 Add rind, dried fruit and nuts. Combine flour, ground almonds and baking powder. Combine milk and rum. Stir dry ingredients and milk mixture alternately into fruit mixture until almost smooth.
3 Spoon into pan. Arrange whole almonds on top of cake. Bake 2–2¼ hours, until a skewer comes out clean. Cool in pan several hours before turning out.

ABOVE: DUNDEE CAKE.

OPPOSITE PAGE: ORANGE SPONGE CAKE

CAKES
SPONGE AND ANGEL FOOD

BASIC SPONGE CAKE

Preparation time: 25 minutes
Total cooking time: 20–25 minutes
Makes one 8 inch round layer cake

1 cup all-purpose flour	2 teaspoons vanilla
1/4 teaspoon salt	1 cup heavy cream
6 eggs, separated	1 teaspoon vanilla extract
1/2 teaspoon cream of tartar	2/3 cup strawberry jam
1 1/4 cups sugar	confectioners' sugar, sifted

1 Preheat oven to 350°F. Grease and flour two 8 inch round cake pans. Sift together flour and salt. Place egg whites and cream of tartar in a clean, dry bowl. Beat until stiff peaks form. Gradually beat in sugar. Beat until thick and glossy.
2 Beat egg yolks and 1 teaspoon vanilla; add to egg-white mixture and beat 20 seconds more. Fold in sifted flour mixture.
3 Spread evenly into prepared pans. Bake for 25 minutes or until cakes spring back when touched in center. Leave in pans 5 minutes before turning onto wire racks to cool.
4 Beat cream and 1 teaspoon vanilla. When the cakes are cool, spread with the jam and cream. Sandwich the layers together and dust with confectioners' sugar.

VARIATIONS

■ **Chocolate Sponge Cake:** Replace 1 cup flour with 3/4 cup flour, sifted with 1/4 cup unsweetened cocoa powder.
■ **Coffee Sponge Cake:** Sift 2 teaspoons instant coffee with the flour.
■ **Lemon Sponge Cake:** Add 2 teaspoons grated lemon rind with the sugar; ice with lemon icing.
■ **Orange Sponge Cake:** Add 2 teaspoons grated orange rind with the sugar. Fill with orange liqueur-flavored cream, ice with orange-flavored glaze. Decorate with orange rind.
■ **Nut Sponge Cake:** Fold in 1/4 cup finely ground almonds, hazelnuts, walnuts or pecans. Sandwich together with coffee-flavored cream.

ABOUT SPONGE CAKES
■ Eggs are the most important ingredient in sponge cakes. To ensure success, use fresh eggs from the refrigerator. Separate each egg over two small bowls before transferring to a larger bowl for mixing. Bring to room temperature before use. Add sugar to egg whites or whole eggs gradually, 1 tablespoon at a time; beat well after each addition. The folding technique for dry ingredients is critical: use a large metal spoon, run it along the bottom of bowl and up in one sweeping action. Cut down through the bowl, rotating the bowl as you fold.

and Malaysia and now grown throughout Southeast Asia, China, India, the Caribbean and parts of South America. The carambola has five prominent ribs which result in star-shaped slices when cut crosswise—hence its common names, star fruit and five-corner fruit. It has a sharp, sour-sweet taste and can be eaten fresh, added to salads, served with cheese, used as a garnish or puréed for use in sorbets and ice creams, or cooked in Southeast Asian dishes. Carambolas are available fresh and dried; store ripe, yellow fruit in the refrigerator.

Caramel Sugar heated until it melts into a brown syrup. It is used in cakes, sweet sauces and desserts; to line molds for desserts and custards; as a sweet, brittle coating for fruits; and to color soups, stews and gravies. Caramel hardens and becomes brittle when cool. A soft caramel is candy made of caramelized sugar, butter and milk or cream.

Caraway A plant that is related to parsley and is native to southern Europe, the Mediterranean and parts of western Asia. Its highly aromatic, hard, brown, crescent-shaped seeds have a sharp flavor similar to anise. Caraway seeds were used by the ancient Egyptians to treat stomach complaints and flatulence, but were first used as a flavoring by the Arabs. For centuries they have been added to cakes, rye bread, cheeses, casseroles, potatoes, salads and sauerkraut. They are widely used in German, Austrian and Hungarian cooking. Oil from the the seeds is used to flavor a liqueur known as kümmel.

Carbonnade de Boeuf Thin slices of beef that are browned quickly over a high heat and then cooked with beer and onions. The dish is originally from Belgium, but its name comes from the Italian word *carbonata* which means charcoal-grilled. In France the name carbonnade is also given to broiled pork loin, and in the south of France it is used for a beef stew that is prepared with red wine.

CITRUS GENOISE SPONGE TORTE

★
★ ★   **Preparation time:** 40 minutes
Total cooking time: 20–25 minutes
Makes one 8 inch 4-layer torte

6 eggs, lightly beaten
1 cup sugar
1 1/4 cups sifted cake flour
1/3 cup unsalted butter, melted and cooled
2 teaspoons grated orange rind
1 teaspoon grated lemon rind
confectioners' sugar, sifted
sliced strawberries

Lemon Curd Filling
3/4 cup sugar
3 tablespoons cornstarch
1 tablespoon grated lemon rind
3/4 cup lemon juice
1/2 cup water
1 tablespoon unsalted butter
5 egg yolks, lightly beaten

1 Preheat oven to 350°F. Grease two 8 inch round cake pans. Line bases with parchment paper. Dust sides with all-purpose flour, tap out excess. Combine eggs and sugar in large heatproof mixing bowl. Place bowl over pan of simmering water. Beat with electric mixer until mixture is thick and pale yellow (about 5 minutes). Remove from heat, beat until mixture has cooled and increased greatly in volume (about 15 minutes).
2 Sift one-third of flour over egg mixture. Use a metal spoon to fold quickly and lightly until combined. Sift another third of flour over egg mixture; fold in quickly and lightly. Repeat with

remaining flour. Fold in melted butter, orange and lemon rind. Spread mixture into pans. Bake 20–25 minutes or until cakes spring back when touched lightly in centers. Leave in pans 5 minutes, turn onto wire racks to cool. Remove paper.
3 To make Lemon Curd Filling: Combine sugar and cornstarch in pan. Stir in lemon rind, juice, water and butter. Stir over medium heat until it bubbles and thickens. Stir half of cornstarch mixture into yolks. Stir yolk mixture into remaining cornstarch mixture in pan. Bring to boil over medium heat; stir 2 minutes. Transfer to small bowl; cover with plastic wrap and chill.
4 Cut each cake layer in half horizontally. Place a layer on serving plate. Spread with a scant 1/2 cup of filling. Continue layering with cake and filling, ending with a cake layer. Dust with sifted powdered sugar just before serving. Decorate with strawberries.

ANGEL FOOD CAKE

★ ★   **Preparation time:** 15 minutes
Total cooking time: 45 minutes
Serves 8

1 cup sifted cake flour
1 cup sugar
1 1/2 cups egg whites (use about 10 eggs)
1/4 teaspoon salt
1 1/2 teaspoons cream of tartar
1 teaspoon vanilla extract
1/4 teaspoon almond extract
1 1/2 cups confectioners' sugar
strawberries for serving

1 Preheat oven to 350°F. Sift flour with powdered sugar three times. Place egg whites in a large dry mixing bowl with salt and cream of tartar. Using electric beaters, beat egg whites until soft peaks form. Add sugar gradually, beating until mixture is thick and glossy and the sugar is dissolved.
2 Stir in the vanilla and almond extract lightly. Sift flour mixture over the egg whites one-fourth at a time, folding in gently after each addition.
3 Pour mixture into an ungreased angel cake pan or a 10 inch tube pan. Tap tin gently on bench to release any air bubbles. Bake on lowest rack in oven for 45 minutes, or until a skewer comes out clean when inserted in cake. Remove from oven and invert pan. Allow cake to cool completely before turning out.
4 Serve cake dusted with icing sugar and decorated with strawberries.

ABOVE: ANGEL FOOD CAKE.
OPPOSITE PAGE: FROSTED CHRISTMAS FRUIT CAKE

CAKES CELEBRATION

FROSTED CHRISTMAS FRUIT CAKE

Preparation time: 40 minutes
Total cooking time: 2–2¼ hours
Makes one 8 inch 1-layer cake

2/3 cup unsalted butter
1¼ cups firmly packed
    dark brown sugar
2 eggs, lightly beaten
2 tablespoons orange
    marmalade
2 tablespoons dark corn
    syrup
1 teaspoon vanilla extract
8 oz pitted prunes,
    chopped
6 oz dried apricots,
    chopped
6 oz dried mixed fruit bits
½ cup raisins
2 cups all-purpose flour
2 teaspoons ground
    cinnamon
1 teaspoon baking powder

½ teaspoon ground allspice
½ teaspoon ground nutmeg
¼ teaspoon baking soda
1/3 cup orange juice
¼ cup rum, brandy or
    port

Seven-Minute Frosting:
1½ cups sugar
1/3 cup cold water
2 egg whites
¼ teaspoon cream of tartar
½ teaspoon lemon extract

Decoration:
tiny Christmas
    ornament, optional

1 Preheat oven to 300°F. Grease an 8 inch square cake pan. Line base and sides with parchment paper. Lightly grease paper. Using electric mixer, beat butter and brown sugar in small mixing bowl until well mixed. Add eggs gradually, beat well after each addition. Add marmalade, syrup and vanilla; beat until combined.

2 Transfer to a large mixing bowl; stir in prunes, apricots, dried mixed fruit and raisins. Stir together flour, cinnamon, baking powder, allspice, nutmeg and soda. Combine orange juice and rum. Use a metal spoon to fold dry ingredients and orange juice mixture alternately into butter mixture. Stir until just combined. Spoon mixture into pan; sprinkle top with cold water, smooth surface with a wet hand.

3 Tap pan gently on counter top to settle mixture. Bake 2–2¼ hours or until skewer comes out clean when inserted in center. After baking 1 hour, cover pan loosely with foil to prevent cake from getting too brown. Cool overnight in pan on wire rack. Remove from pan. Remove paper. Place cake on large flat plate or cake board.

4 To make Seven-Minute Frosting: Combine sugar, cold water, egg whites and cream of tartar in top of double boiler. Beat with an electric mixer on low speed for 30 seconds. Place over boiling water (make sure top pan does not touch water). Cook, beating constantly with the electric mixer on high speed, for 7 minutes. Remove from the heat; add lemon extract. Beat 3 minutes more or until frosting is of spreading consistency.

5 Using a flat-bladed knife, cover cake completely with frosting. Use the knife to work frosting into fluffy peaks all over cake. Position ornament on cake, secure with frosting.

Cardamom The aromatic, round seed pod from an Asian shrub that must be picked by hand. The pods, used since ancient times, contain tiny black seeds, and must be picked and dried before they ripen. They should be stored in an airtight container and the seeds ground as required. Cardamom is used in curry powder and in pickles, rice and sweet dishes. In Arab countries the seeds are often added to coffee beans before grinding.

Cardoon Native to southern Europe and related to the artichoke, cardoon's celery-like stalk is eaten boiled, braised or baked, usually served with a sauce. Most tender and delicate in flavor are those that have been wrapped in paper as they grow to produce white stalks. It is popular in France, Italy and Spain.

Carob The fruit of the carob tree, native to the Mediterranean region. The long, leathery pod contains hard, reddish seeds in a brown pulp. The fresh pods and pulp can be eaten raw and have a sweet chocolate-like flavor. A powder from the dried, ground pod and pulp can be used in cooking as a caffeine-free substitute for cocoa powder.

Carp A freshwater fish that is used by the Chinese in poached or steamed dishes, and by Eastern European Jews in a sweet and sour poached dish called gefilte fish. The coarse flesh can also be baked or broiled.

Carpaccio A dish consisting of paper-thin slices of raw meat, usually beef, which is dressed with oil and lemon juice or a creamy vinaigrette made with olive oil, and served as a first course. It was named by its inventor, the proprietor of Harry's Bar in Venice, after Vittore Carpaccio, a fifteenth-century Venetian painter.

Carpetbag Steak A thick piece of tender steak with a pocket cut into it which is filled with raw oysters. The steak is then pan-fried, broiled or grilled.

Carrot A root vegetable, related to parsley, parsnip and celery, with crisp, orange flesh. Its ancestor was a wild plant. It was introduced to Europe by the Dutch during the Middle Ages. It is eaten raw in salads or cooked in both sweet and savory dishes. Baby carrots (sometimes known as Dutch carrots) and young carrots need only be scrubbed clean with a stiff brush before use. Tiny carrots can be

BLACK FOREST CAKE

⭐ ⭐   *Preparation time:* 1 hour 15 minutes
Total cooking time: 1–1¼ hours
Makes one 9 inch 3-layer torte

³/4 cup unsalted butter
2 cups sugar
3 eggs, lightly beaten
2 teaspoons vanilla
   extract
2¹/2 cups all-purpose
   flour
1 cup unsweetened cocoa
   powder
1 tablespoon instant
   coffee granules
1¹/2 teaspoons baking soda
¹/4 teaspoon salt
1 cup buttermilk
¹/2 cup milk

1 cup heavy cream
3 tablespoons sugar
3 cans (16 oz each)
   pitted dark sweet
   cherries, drained
white and dark chocolate
   curls, for decoration

Chocolate Cream
12 squares (1 oz each)
   semisweet chocolate,
   chopped
1¹/2 cups unsalted butter,
   softened
1 teaspoon vanilla extract

1 Preheat oven to 350°F. Grease a 9 inch round springform pan. Line base and sides with parchment paper. Grease paper. Beat butter and 2 cups sugar until well mixed. Add eggs and vanilla gradually, beating well after each addition.
2 Sift together flour, cocoa powder, instant coffee, soda and salt. Combine buttermilk and milk. Stir flour mixture and buttermilk mixture alternately into butter mixture. Stir until almost smooth.
3 Spoon into pan; smooth surface. Bake 1–1¼ hours or until a skewer comes out clean. Leave in

pan for 30 minutes, turn onto wire rack to cool. Using electric mixer, beat heavy cream and 3 tablespoons sugar until stiff peaks form.
4 To make Chocolate Cream: Place chocolate in heatproof bowl. Stir over barely simmering water until melted; remove from heat, let stand 30 minutes to cool. Beat butter and vanilla until light and creamy. Gradually add melted chocolate, beat 2 minutes, until glossy and smooth.
5 Cut cake into three layers horizontally. Place first layer on serving plate. Spread with half whipped cream; top with half the cherries. Continue layering with remaining cakes, cream and cherries, ending with cake on top.
6 Spread two-thirds of the Chocolate Cream over top and sides. Using a piping bag fitted with large star tip (about ¹/2 inch opening), pipe remaining Chocolate Cream around top edge of cake. Decorate with chocolate curls if desired.
7 To make Chocolate Curls: Spread 8 oz melted chocolate onto a marble slab or cool work surface to a depth of ¹/2 inch; smooth surface lightly. Allow to cool until almost set. Hold a sharp, flat-bladed knife horizontally against the surface of the chocolate. Applying constant pressure to the blade with both hands, pull the knife towards you. Varying the pressure will determine the thickness of the curls.

ABOVE: BLACK FOREST CAKE
OPPOSITE PAGE, ABOVE: HONEY AND COCONUT
CAKE; BELOW: CHERRY TEACAKE

CHERRY TEACAKE

⭐ **Preparation time:** 15 minutes
Total cooking time: 30 minutes
Makes one 9 inch round cake

1/4 cup unsalted butter
2/3 cup sugar
1/2 teaspoon coconut extract
2 eggs, lightly beaten
1/2 cup chopped candied
  cherries
1/4 cup flaked coconut
1 1/4 cups all-purpose
  flour
1/4 cup cornstarch

2 teaspoons baking powder
1/8 teaspoon salt

Pink Icing
2 cups confectioners' sugar
1 tablespoon unsalted
  butter
2 tablespoons boiling water
2–3 drops pink food
  coloring

1 Preheat oven to moderate 350°F. Brush deep, 9 inch round cake pan with oil or melted butter. Line base with paper; grease paper. Using electric beaters, beat butter, sugar and extract in small bowl until light and creamy.
2 Add eggs and beat for 3 minutes or until just combined. Transfer to a large mixing bowl. Add cherries, coconut, flour, cornstarch, baking powder, salt and milk. Beat for 1 minute or until mixture is almost smooth. Spoon evenly into pan; bake 30 minutes or until skewer comes out clean when inserted in center. Leave cake in pan for 10 minutes before turning onto wire rack to cool.
3 To make Pink Icing: Combine the sifted confectioners' sugar, butter and water in bowl to form a firm paste. Stand the bowl in pan of simmering water, stir until smooth and glossy; remove from heat, tint with coloring. Spread over top of cake.

HONEY AND COCONUT CAKE

⭐ **Preparation time:** 40 minutes
Total cooking time: 30 minutes
Makes one 11 inch cake

1/2 cup unsalted butter
2/3 cup sugar
2 eggs, lightly beaten
1 teaspoon vanilla
1/3 cup honey
1/2 cup flaked coconut
2 1/4 cups all-purpose flour
2 teaspoons baking
  powder
1/8 teaspoon salt
1 teaspoon ground
  nutmeg
1/4 teaspoon ground
  cinnamon

1/4 teaspoon ground allspice
2/3 cup milk
ground nutmeg, for
  decoration

**Honey and Cream
Cheese Icing**
8 oz cream cheese,
  softened
1 1/2 cups confectioners'
  sugar
2 tablespoons honey

1 Preheat oven to 350°F. Brush shallow, 11 x 7 x 1 1/4 inch rectangular cake pan with oil or melted butter, line base and sides with paper; grease paper. Using electric beaters, beat butter and sugar in mixing bowl until light and creamy. Add eggs gradually, beating well after each addition. Add vanilla and honey; beat until combined.
2 Transfer to large mixing bowl; add coconut. Using a metal spoon, fold in flour, baking powder, salt and spices alternately with milk. Stir until just combined and mixture is almost smooth. Pour mixture into pan; smooth surface.
3 Bake 30 minutes or until skewer comes out clean when inserted in center of cake. Leave cake in pan 10 minutes before turning onto wire rack.
4 To make Honey and Cream Cheese Icing: Using electric beaters, beat cream cheese in small bowl until creamy. Add sifted powdered sugar and honey, beat 3 minutes or until smooth and fluffy. Spread on cake; sprinkle with nutmeg.

cooked whole. Older carrots should be scraped or peeled and then sliced, diced or cut into julienne strips for cooking. If carrots are to be used raw, grate them for use in salads and

sandwiches or cut them into sticks for dips.

Carrot Cake A moist, crumbly, spicy, dark brown cake that can be made in layer or loaf pans; often served frosted with cream cheese.

Casaba A large, round melon that has a pale yellow, deeply wrinkled skin and a sweet, white, very moist flesh. The seeds are inedible.

Cashew Nut The creamy, kidney-shaped nut of a tall tree native to South America. The hard-shelled nut develops inside a fleshy fruit and protrudes when ripe. Cashew nuts can be eaten roasted and salted. They can be used in stuffings for chicken, made into nut butter or used in salads.

CAKE DECORATING

Sprinkle a simple sponge cake with sifted confectioners' sugar, or cover a chocolate cake with rich buttercream, pipe with rosettes of chocolate cream and decorate with chocolate curls and fanned strawberries. The way you decorate a cake depends on the type of cake, your level of skill and, most of all, your own taste.

TECHNIQUES

Always work with completely cooled cakes when decorating, unless the recipe states otherwise. If the cake is even slightly warm, the icing will be difficult to handle and there is every possibility that it will crack or break when sliced.

When baked, some cakes may have a slight dome which can be trimmed to give a better appearance when the cake is iced. Use a long, sharp, serrated knife to slice off the dome—only trim enough cake to obtain an even surface. Cut with a gentle sawing motion, using your other hand to steady the cake while you slice. Turn the cake over onto a serving plate, base side up, before icing.

Many cakes are cut in half, or in one or more layers, horizontally before they are filled. To make the job easy, mark the midpoint round the side of the cake with toothpicks. Use a long, sharp, serrated knife for slicing the cake; cut with a gentle sawing action. Repeat the marking and cutting procedure for each layer of cake.

HOW TO ICE A CAKE

Use a pastry brush to brush off any loose crumbs. For a smoothly iced surface, spread icing over the cake using a flat-bladed knife. To assemble layers, slice the cake as described above. Place a dab of icing or filling on a serving plate and center the first layer on it (the icing stops it from moving). Brush with jam if specified in recipe, then evenly spread the filling mixture. Using a flat-bladed knife or spatula, spread filling to within about 1/4 inch of the edge of the cake.

Warming the knife or spatula by dipping it into hot water as you spread the filling will make it easier to work; wipe knife with a clean cloth before continuing.

Place the second layer on top and spread with filling mixture, as described above. Place the final layer, base side up, on top. Spread a thin layer of cream or frosting around sides and top of cake to seal in any crumbs and to fill any gaps.

Spread a final layer of cream or frosting evenly around the sides and then on top of the cake, blending at the edges. Use even strokes.

ICINGS AND FILLINGS

Buttercreams make excellent fillings or coverings for cakes. Cakes that are covered in either buttercream or another type of icing will keep moist and fresh for far longer than cakes that have not been iced.

Buttercreams can range from a fairly simple mixture of confectioners' sugar, butter and flavorings, to rich combinations of butter, egg yolks and sugar syrups which result in smooth, velvety fillings. The secret of making a good buttercream is to use unsalted (sweet) butter and to beat the mixture thoroughly until it reaches a light, creamy consistency.

COOLING THE CAKE

A cake is quite fragile when just removed from the oven. It is best to leave it in the pan for the specified time before turning it onto a wire rack to cool. Leave the cake on the wire rack until it is completely cold.

If a cake seems to be stuck to its pan, run a flat-bladed knife around the sides to release it. Cakes lined with paper are easiest to release: gently lever with a thin spatula or knife before turning upside down; remove paper lining immediately. Spray wire racks with vegetable oil to prevent sticking.

MAKING PIPING BAGS

MAKING PIPING BAGS Here is a quick and easy way to make a small paper piping bag. Cut a 10 inch square of strong parchment paper and fold it in half diagonally to form a triangle.

Working with the long side at the bottom, roll a corner to the center and tape it into place. Wrap the other corner to the back and tape that in place. Use scissors to trim the tip of the bag to suit the size of your decorating. You can also insert into the bag a nozzle of the right size for icing.

Using a knife or metal spatula, half-fill the bag with chocolate or icing. Fold in the top, then roll the top down to the level of the icing to seal the bag. Grip the bag at the top with the full end resting in your palm. Use pressure from the palm of your hand to push the icing out through the hole.

VIENNA BUTTERCREAM

Beat ⅓ cup plus 1 tablespoon unsalted (sweet) butter in a bowl until soft. Gradually add 8 oz sifted confectioners' sugar, beating until mixture is light and fluffy. Add 2 tablespoons of hot water and 1 teaspoon of vanilla and stir in well. This can be used as a filling for cakes and cookies as well as an icing.

VANILLA BUTTERCREAM

In a bowl, beat together 1 cup unsalted (sweet) butter and ¼ cup confectioners' sugar until the mixture is light, fluffy and pale. Add, a little at a

time, another 1½ cups of confectioners' sugar, beating well between each addition. Then add 2 beaten egg yolks and 2 teaspoons boiling water. Whisk the mixture thoroughly until it reaches a smooth and even consistency. Add vanilla to taste.

GLAZE

This is a thin, shiny icing poured onto the center of the cake as soon as it reaches a coating consistency. Allow glaze to run down the sides, guiding it with a flat-bladed knife.

In a heatproof bowl, mix together 1¼ cups confectioners' sugar, 1 tablespoon butter, the flavoring of your choice, and sufficient liquid to make a smooth firm paste. Stand the bowl over a pan of simmering water and stir until the glaze has become smooth and glossy.

■ **LEMON GLAZE:** to the sugar and the butter, add 1 teaspoon finely grated lemon rind and 1–2 tablespoons lemon juice.

■ **ORANGE GLAZE:** to the sugar and the butter, add 1 teaspoon finely grated orange rind and 1–2 tablespoons orange juice.

■ **PASSIONFRUIT GLAZE:** to sugar and butter, add 1–2 tablespoons passionfruit pulp.

■ **COFFEE GLAZE:** to the sugar and the butter, add 1 teaspoon instant coffee powder and 1–2 tablespoons water.

■ **CHOCOLATE GLAZE:** to the sugar and the butter, add 1 tablespoon unsweetened cocoa powder and 1–2 tablespoons hot milk.

CREAM CHEESE ICING

Using electric beaters, beat ⅓ cup plus 1 tablespoon cream cheese and 1 cup sifted confectioners' sugar together in a small bowl until the mixture becomes light and creamy. Add the flavorings of your choice, and a little milk if necessary. Beat for 2 minutes or until mixture takes on a smooth and fluffy consistency. Spread the icing thickly over the cake, using a wide, flat-bladed knife.

■ **LEMON ICING:** to the cream cheese and the sugar, add 1–2 teaspoons finely grated lemon rind and 2 teaspoons milk.

■ **ORANGE ICING:** to the cream cheese and the sugar, add 1–2 teaspoons finely grated orange rind and 2 teaspoons milk.

■ **HONEY ICING:** to the cream cheese and the sugar, add 1–2 teaspoons warmed honey and 2 teaspoons milk.

■ **PASSIONFRUIT ICING:** to the cream cheese and sugar, add 1 tablespoon passionfruit pulp.

CAKE DECORATING

CHOCOLATE DECORATIONS

Chocolate provides an easy way of dressing up a simple cake or a batch of cookies. It can be used not only for making icing and fillings, but for scrolls, curls and leaves to decorate the top of the cake. Melted chocolate may be used to drizzle over cookies in decorative patterns. While good eating chocolate is superior in flavor, baking chocolate is much easier to work with. It sets at room temperature and melts easily over a bowl of hot water.

CHOCOLATE SHAPES

Line a flat, cold baking sheet with parchment paper, brush lightly with oil. Break dark (semisweet) or milk chocolate into small pieces, place in a bowl over a pan of gently simmering water. Make sure that no water or steam gets into the bowl. Stir chocolate until it has just melted. Using a flat-bladed knife to guide it, pour chocolate over oiled paper to form a thick, even coating. Leave in a cool place until chocolate is almost set.

Using a knife or a shaped cutter (star, flute, round, etc), cut chocolate into desired shapes. Chill chocolate before lifting off the cut-out shapes. The shapes should be stored in a cool, dry place. Chocolate shapes are useful not only as cake decorations, but also make very attractive garnishes for desserts such as ice cream.

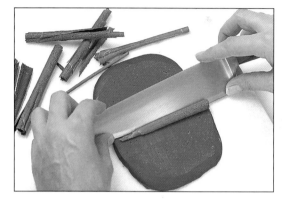

CHOCOLATE CURLS

Melt dark (semisweet) or milk chocolate in a bowl over a pan of hot water. Spread thinly over a smooth board using a palette knife. Set aside until chocolate is almost set. Using a large flat-bladed knife, pull the blade towards you along the length of the chocolate to make long curls.

CHOCOLATE SHAVINGS

Use a vegetable peeler to shave off curls from the flat side of a large block of chocolate. Work over parchment or waxed paper or a plate, using long, even strokes. Leave chocolate in a warm spot for 10–15 minutes before shaving. For best results chocolate should be warmed, but only sufficiently to enable you to work it. Spoon or shake the shavings onto the iced cake.

CHOCOLATE PETALS

Cut foil into several squares in the sizes of your choice. Melt dark (semisweet) or milk chocolate in a bowl over a pan of hot water and cool slightly. Hold a square of foil in the palm of your hand. With a palette knife or a spoon, thinly spread melted chocolate onto the foil in the shape of a flower petal. While the chocolate is still soft, lift your fingers under the foil to slightly bend the petal into a natural shape. Leave aside until set. Repeat procedure with remaining chocolate. Peel off foil before using. Petals can be formed into the shape of a flower using melted chocolate to join them together.

CHOCOLATE WEDGES

Cover the base of an 8 inch round baking pan with foil. Melt about 5 oz dark (semisweet) or milk chocolate in a bowl over a pan of hot water.

Spread melted chocolate in an even layer over foil and refrigerate until semi-set. Using a sharp, flat-bladed knife, carefully mark the chocolate into 12 wedges of equal size. Return to refrigerator until chocolate is completely set. Peel away foil. Wedges are an ideal decoration for the top of an 8 inch round cake.

SQUARES

These are an easy and impressive way to decorate the sides of a cake or a special dessert. Using a 13 x 11 inch baking sheet, cover the base with foil. Spread 7 oz of melted chocolate evenly over it and swirl a fork lightly through the chocolate to create a wavy effect; make sure you do not push the fork right down to the base of the baking sheet. Refrigerate until chocolate is semi-set.

Using a sharp, flat-bladed knife and a ruler, mark off the chocolate into squares of about 2½ inches. Return oven tray to the refrigerator until chocolate has cooled and completely set. Peel away the foil. Carefully press the chocolate squares around the edges of the iced cake to decorate. Squares can also be used as garnishes for ice cream desserts.

OTHER DECORATIONS

Cakes can look marvelous when decorated with crystallized (candied) fruit and flowers, marzipan fruit, spun sugar, silver dragées or colored sprinkles.

CRYSTALLIZED (CANDIED) FLOWERS

Lightly beat an egg white until it is broken up and foamy. Pour 1 cup sugar into a shallow bowl. Using small fresh flowers such as violets or rosebuds, or the petals of large flowers such as roses, brush petals with egg white (use a small paintbrush) then dip them into sugar, making sure petals are well coated. Place flowers on a rack to dry. Store in an airtight container.

SUGAR PATTERNS

Cut parchment or wax paper into long thin strips and place in a criss-cross or other pattern on top of a plain cake. Dust with sifted confectioners' sugar. Carefully remove paper strips to reveal a sugar pattern. A simpler way to make a sugar pattern is to lay a paper doily on top of the cake. Sift sugar over the doily and then remove it. This will leave a pretty, lacy pattern.

MELTING CHOCOLATE

Use the best chocolate you can for decorations and icing. Baking chocolate is easier to work with, although it does not have the flavor of good quality eating chocolate. Chop the chocolate into even-sized pieces and place in a glass bowl. Place bowl over a pan of simmering water; stir gently until chocolate has melted. Do not allow even a drop of the water to fall on the chocolate or it will immediately stiffen and be unworkable for decoration purposes. Cool the chocolate slightly before using.

SPUN SUGAR

Combine 1 cup of sugar and ½ cup of water in a pan. Place over medium heat and stir constantly until sugar has dissolved. Make sure you do not bring the mixture to the boil until the sugar has dissolved completely. Then bring to the boil, and boil rapidly without stirring until the mixture is a light golden-brown color. Remove the pan from the heat and, using a metal spoon, drizzle toffee in a thin stream backwards and forwards over lightly oiled baking sheets. When set, break the toffee up into small pieces and place on the cake. The toffee may also be spun over an iced cake. Place two forks back to back and dip them into the toffee mixture. Carefully pull the toffee in thin strands over the cake.

FLAKED ALMOND DECORATION

Scatter 6 oz slivered almonds over an ungreased baking sheet. Bake almonds at 350°F for about 5 minutes or until they are light golden brown. Take a generous tablespoon of the roasted almonds in the palm of your hand and press them lightly and evenly onto the icing on the side of a cake, before the icing has completely set. Toasted slivered almonds are a popular way of finishing off cake decorations as they are easy to place on the icing around the sides and they impart a wonderful flavor and texture to the cake.

Cassata An iced dessert which originated in Italy. It usually consists of layers of ice cream, at least one of which contains chopped nuts and glazed fruit, and sometimes also a layer of sweetened whipped cream. Sicilian cassata consists of strips of sponge cake soaked in a liqueur or

sweet dessert wine, encasing ricotta cheese mixed with nuts and glazed fruit cake. Both types are traditionally made in a rectangular mold—hence the name, which is derived from the Italian word for "little brick."

Cassava (Manioc) A plant native to tropical America. The starchy, tuberous roots can be prepared and cooked in the same way as the potato, the tender leaves cooked like spinach and the larger tougher ones used as wrappings for food to be baked. A powder preparation made from the dried root is used as a thickener.

Casserole A selection of meat, poultry or fish, vegetables, herbs, seasonings and liquid cooked slowly in a covered dish in the oven. It is usually served from the dish at the

CANAPES

Canapés are usually served with drinks before dinner, or at a cocktail party. They should be small enough to allow them to be held in one hand and eaten in a single bite.

QUICK BASES AND TOPPINGS

■ Spread crisp bread circles with pesto and top with halved cherry tomatoes.
■ Fill tiny cooked pastry shells with a mixture of light cream cheese, finely chopped smoked salmon and finely chopped chives.
■ Top freshly cooked mini blinis or thin pancakes with thick sour cream and caviar.
■ Top thick slices of unpeeled cucumber with blue cheese and walnuts, or slices of smoked salmon and a spoonful of sour cream.
■ Top crisp bread circles with tapenade and sliced hard-boiled egg or poached quail egg.
■ Spread crisp bread circles with thick garlic-flavored mayonnaise. Top with a green asparagus tip and garnish with a strip of roasted red pepper.
■ Top tiny wedges of spinach frittata with fine strips of ham.
■ Top fresh oysters on the shell with thick mayonnaise containing finely chopped herbs.

■ Spread crisp bread circles with chicken liver or salmon pâté and top with sliced dill cucumber.
■ Spread pumpernickel circles with herbed cream cheese and top with sliced stuffed olives.
■ Wrap slices of fresh pear or cubes of cantaloupe in wafer-thin slices of prosciutto.
■ Spread crisp bread circles or pumpernickel circles with seeded mustard, top with sliced rare roast fillet of beef and top with a piece of mango.
■ Fill fresh white button mushrooms with a mixture of chopped ham and cream cheese. Top with toasted pine nuts and finely chopped fresh parsley.
■ Fill tiny uncooked pastry shells with chopped sun-dried tomato, chopped basil and crumbled fresh goat cheese. Bake until cheese melts.
■ Make mini pizza bases, top with sautéed onion, chopped anchovy fillets and Parmesan cheese.

CRISP BREAD CIRCLES

Trim crusts from sliced white or brown bread. Using a biscuit cutter, cut 1½ x 1½ inch circles from each slice. Brush both sides of bread with melted butter, place on tray and bake at 350°F for 10 minutes until golden. Cool, store in an airtight container.

ABOVE: A SELECTION OF CANAPES.

OPPOSITE PAGE: PEANUT BRITTLE AND CARAMELS

CANDY

PEANUT BRITTLE

⭐⭐ **Preparation time:** 20 minutes
Total cooking time: 30–45 minutes
Makes about 1 lb

2 cups sugar
1 cup brown sugar, lightly packed
½ cup light corn syrup
½ cup water
¼ cup butter
2½ cups roasted unsalted peanuts

1 Line the base and sides of a shallow 15 x 10 x 1 inch baking pan with foil or wax paper. Brush the foil with oil or melted butter. Combine sugars, corn syrup and water in a large, heavy-bottom pan. Stir over medium heat without boiling until sugar has completely dissolved. Brush sugar crystals from side of pan with a wet pastry brush. Add butter, stir until melted. Bring to boil, reduce heat slightly and boil without stirring for 15–20 minutes; OR until a teaspoon of the mixture dropped into cold water reaches soft-crack stage; OR, if using a candy thermometer, until mixture reaches 275°F.
2 Fold in peanuts. Continue cooking until thermometer registers 295°F, hard-crack stage. Pour into pan. Stand pan on wire rack to cool; break into pieces when almost set.

CARAMELS

⭐⭐ **Preparation time:** 10 minutes + 30 minutes refrigeration
Total cooking time: 25 minutes
Makes 36

½ cup butter
14 oz can sweetened condensed milk
1 cup sugar
½ cup light corn syrup

1 Line base and sides of shallow 8 inch square cake pan with foil, leaving edges overhanging. Brush foil with oil or melted butter. Combine butter, condensed milk, sugar and syrup in medium, heavy-bottom pan. Stir over low heat without boiling until sugar has completely dissolved. Bring to boil; reduce heat slightly. Stir constantly (to prevent burning) 15–20 minutes, until mixture turns dark golden caramel color (do not undercook or it will not set).
2 Pour mixture into prepared pan; smooth surface. Mark into squares. Refrigerate 30 minutes or until firm. Remove from pan; cut through. Store in airtight container in the refrigerator for up to 3 weeks.

TIPSY FUDGE

⭐ **Preparation time:** 10 minutes
Total cooking time: 25 minutes
Makes 36 pieces

¾ cup golden raisins
2 tablespoons rum
3 cups sugar
1 cup milk
2 tablespoons light corn syrup
⅓ cup unsalted butter

1 Brush an 8 inch square cake pan with melted butter or oil. Line base and sides with foil; grease foil. Combine raisins and rum, set aside.
2 Combine sugar, milk and syrup in a large, heavy-bottom pan. Stir over medium heat without boiling until sugar has dissolved. Brush sugar crystals from sides of pan with a wet pastry brush. Bring to boil, reduce heat slightly and boil without stirring for about 20 minutes; OR boil until a teaspoon of mixture dropped into cold water reaches soft-ball stage; OR if using a candy thermometer, until the mixture reaches 240°F. Remove from heat immediately.
3 Add butter to pan without stirring. Let stand for 5 minutes, add raisin mixture and beat until thick and creamy. Pour into prepared pan, leave to cool. Cut into squares when cold. Store in an airtight container in a cool dark place for up to 1 week.

table. The term is for both the covered dish and the cooking method.

Cassoulet A hearty bean and meat stew originally from southern France. Recipes vary, but the essential ingredient is white beans, to which various meats are added.

Catfish A scaleless, bottom-feeding, fresh-water fish. Farmed in the south, catfish grow quickly when fed grain pellets, producing a snow-white, firm flesh.

Catsup See Ketchup.

Cauliflower A member of the cabbage family with a large head of tight flower buds that range in color from creamy white (the most popular and readily available) to green and purple. Cauliflower can be eaten raw, cut into small sprigs and dipped in various dressings, or it can be steamed, boiled or stir-fried. Available all year, select solid heads with bright green leaves.

Caviar The roe (eggs) of the sturgeon fish, salted and served as a delicacy. Caviar ranges in color from gray or yellowy-brown to shiny black; and in size from eggs as small as pinheads (Sevruga) to the highly prized seed-pearl sized eggs of the Beluga sturgeon. Pressed caviar is made from ripe eggs, salted and pressed into a block. Salmon and lumpfish roe are sometimes called "red caviar." Caviar should be well chilled and served on a bed of crushed ice for spreading on thin triangles of toast.

Cayenne Pepper A fiery spice made from the dried and powdered pods and seeds of several

varieties of small red chili peppers, used sparingly to flavor cheese and fish dishes.

Celeriac The bulbous, white-fleshed root of a variety of celery. It became popular in Italy during the Renaissance and by the eighteenth century had spread to France, Germany and Italy. Peeled like a potato, it can be served raw in salads (grated and mixed with dressing), or steamed or boiled and served hot with a sauce. Also called celery root.

Celery A vegetable valued primarily for its long, juicy stem,

CHERRY CHOCOLATES

⭐
⭐⭐ **Preparation time:** 30 minutes
Total cooking time: 10 minutes
Makes about 40

1/2 cup unsalted butter	3 1/2 oz dark (semisweet)
2 cups confectioners' sugar	chocolate, chopped
1/3 cup heavy cream	1 oz white vegetable
2 cups flaked coconut	shortening
pink food coloring	2 oz white cooking
7 oz glacé cherries	chocolate

1 Heat the butter in a small pan until lightly browned then remove from heat. Add sifted confectioners' sugar, cream, coconut and few drops of food coloring. Stir until combined.
2 Take about 2 teaspoons of mixture and press evenly around each cherry.
3 Place dark chocolate and shortening in a small heatproof bowl. Stand over a pan of simmering water, stir until the chocolate and shortening have melted and the mixture is smooth.
4 Place a wire rack over a baking sheet. Using two forks, dip the cherries into the melted chocolate; drain excess. Leave on wire rack to set.
5 Place white chocolate in a small heatproof bowl. Place over a pan of simmering water until chocolate has melted. Cool mixture slightly; spoon into a small paper icing bag. Seal the open end and snip off the tip of the bag. Drizzle over cherry chocolates to decorate; allow to set.

ABOVE: CHERRY CHOCOLATES; LEFT: SPICED FRUIT AND NUT BARS. OPPOSITE PAGE: CARROT CAKE.

SPICED FRUIT AND NUT BARS

⭐⭐ **Preparation time:** 20 minutes
Total cooking time: 40 minutes
Makes 32

2/3 cup blanched almonds	1/2 teaspoon ground
2/3 cup walnuts	cinnamon
1/2 cup mixed peel	1/4 teaspoon ground cloves
1/3 cup mixed dried fruit	1/4 teaspoon ground
2 tablespoons	nutmeg
unsweetened cocoa	1/3 cup sugar
powder	1/4 cup honey
2 tablespoons all-purpose	1/4 cup water
flour	8 oz dark (semisweet)
	chocolate, chopped

1 Preheat oven to moderate 350°F. Line an 8 inch square cake pan with aluminum foil; grease foil. Spread almonds and walnuts on a baking sheet and bake for 5 minutes or until just golden. Remove from baking sheet to cool and chop finely. Combine nuts, peel, dried fruit, cocoa, flour and spices in a large mixing bowl.
2 Combine sugar, honey and water in a heavy-based pan. Stir over medium heat without boiling until sugar has dissolved. Brush sugar crystals from sides of pan with wet brush. Bring to boil, reduce heat slightly, boil 10 minutes without stirring. Remove from heat, pour onto fruit mixture and combine well. Press into prepared pan with back of oiled spoon and bake 20 minutes. Cool in pan. Remove from pan and peel away foil. Cut crusts from edges and discard. Cut cake into four long bars, then each bar into eight short fingers.
3 Line a baking sheet with foil. Place chocolate in a heatproof bowl. Stir over a pan of simmering water until chocolate is melted and smooth. Cool slightly. Dip each bar into melted chocolate. Using a spoon, coat in chocolate, lift out on a fork, drain and place on the baking sheet to set.

CARROTS

CARROT CAKE

Preparation time: 15 minutes
Total cooking time: 35 minutes
Serves 8

1/2 cup butter
1 1/4 cups sugar
1/8 teaspoon cinnamon, nutmeg and allspice
grated rind of 1 orange
2 eggs
1 large carrot, grated (about 1 cup)

2 oz sliced almonds, chopped (about 2/3 cup)
1 1/2 cups all-purpose flour
1 1/2 teaspoons baking powder
pinch salt
1/4 cup warm water

1 Preheat oven to 350°F. Brush an 8 inch square cake pan with butter or oil. Line base and sides with parchment paper; grease paper.
2 Beat the butter in an electric mixer or with a wooden spoon until it is light and fluffy. Add the sugar and mix until combined. Add the spices and orange rind and mix well. Add the eggs, one at a time, and stir until well mixed, then add the carrot and nuts. Add the sifted flour, baking powder and salt. Add the warm water a little at a time until the consistency is smooth, without overbeating.
3 Spoon the mixture into the prepared pan; smooth the surface. Bake for 35 minutes or until a skewer comes out clean when inserted into the center of the cake. Leave in pan for 10 minutes before turning out onto wire rack to cool. Decorate with lemon icing or a thick cream cheese frosting.

CARROT SOUP

Preparation time: 12 minutes
Total cooking time: 33 minutes
Serves 4

2 tablespoons butter
6 carrots, sliced
1 clove garlic, crushed
1 onion, chopped
2 medium potatoes, peeled and diced

4 cups chicken stock
3/4 cup sour cream or yogurt
2 tablespoons chopped herbs to garnish

1 Melt butter in a large saucepan, add carrot, garlic and onion and cook for 2–3 minutes. Stir in potatoes, reduce heat to low, cover and cook vegetables for 4–5 minutes.
2 Pour in stock and bring to the boil. Season to taste. Reduce heat and allow soup to simmer, covered, for 25 minutes.
3 Purée soup in food processor or blender. Serve garnished with a spoonful of sour cream or yogurt and sprinkle with herbs.

GRATED CARROT SALAD

Preparation time: 15 minutes
Total cooking time: none
Serves 6

10 large carrots
2 small cucumbers
1/2 cup raisins
1 tablespoon lemon juice
1/2 teaspoon ground ginger
1 tablespoon honey

1 teaspoon ground cinnamon
1/3 cup olive oil
ground pepper
1/2 cup flaked almonds

1 Peel and coarsely grate carrots. Cut cucumbers in quarters lengthwise, then cut into thick slices. Place carrots and cucumber in a bowl, add raisins and stir until combined.
2 Combine the lemon juice, ginger, cinnamon, honey, olive oil and pepper in a small bowl or screw-top jar. Shake the jar well to combine ingredients.
3 Place flaked almonds in a small pan, stir over low heat until lightly golden.
4 Pour dressing over salad, garnish with almonds and serve.

ABOUT CARROTS

■ Buy carrots which are firm and smooth and have a deep orange color. To prepare, wash and lightly scrape or peel, if desired. Young carrots will not need peeling.

■ The flavors of ginger, cloves, dill, honey and marjoram team well with carrots.

although the leaves and seeds are also eaten. The ancient Egyptians gathered shoots of wild celery from seaside marshes and the Greeks used it as a seasoning. In seventeenth-century France, celery was used to flavor soups and stews; the technique of "blanching" (heaping earth against growing stems to make them paler) dates from the time of Louis XIV and was first used in the royal gardens at Versailles, outside Paris. Celery can be eaten raw or cooked in soups, stews and casseroles.

Celery Salt A blend of ground celery seed and salt used to season foods.

Celery Seed A tiny seed with a strong celery flavor; used in salad dressings or sauces.

Cellophane Noodles Thin, flavorless, transparent noodles made from ground mung beans. Used in Asian Cooking, they are also known as bean threads.

Cèpe (Cep, Boletus, Porcini) A large, wild mushroom with a stout stem and a spongy brown cap. Cèpes have a meaty, woody flavor. Sometimes available fresh, they are most often found dried.

CARVING

Skillful carving makes the most of roast dishes, and leaves them attractive enough to serve cold. Always allow roast meat and poultry to rest for 15 minutes, loosely covered with foil, before carving. Carve with a light slicing rather than sawing action to avoid tearing the flesh.

TO CARVE A TURKEY

1 Use a sharp carving knife and a carving fork to steady the bird. Cut into the turkey where the ball joint of the wing meets the breast, and loosen the meat.
2 Continue cutting around the wing, until the wing can be separated from the rest of the body.
3 Tilt the bird to see the angle of separation between the breast and thigh. Starting at the top, cut down through skin and meat to hip joint.
4 Continue cutting through the hip socket until the thigh and leg section can be loosened and removed from the body. Place section on carving board.

5 Separate thigh from leg (drumstick) by cutting through joint. Cut meat from thigh into long, thin slices. Serve legs whole or sliced, according to size and individual preference.
6 The breast is now ready to be carved. Start at the top of the breast, carving at an angle into thin, even slices.

■ Repeat all steps to carve the other side. The wishbone can be removed by snipping the tendons on either side. Serve a piece of leg with a piece of breast and a portion of the stuffing.
■ Place a dampened napkin under the board or platter before carving on a glass or marble table.

TO CARVE A STANDING RIB ROAST

Carving will be easier if you have the backbone removed by the butcher and the rib bones cut short. Usually a rib roast is carved into slices, as shown here, but hearty eaters may like a whole rib.

If the roast has been left to stand for 15 minutes before carving, the meat will settle and very little of the juices will be lost during carving.

1 Place the roast on a board with rib side down and bone ends to the left of the board. Using the tip of the knife, release the meat from the base of the rib bone.

2 Slice meat parallel to rib bones, from top to rib; cut into thick slices.

3 Using the tip of the knife, cut along each rib bone, close to the bone, to release slices.

TO CARVE A DUCK

Sharp poultry shears or kitchen scissors are useful for carving all poultry. This method is also suitable for chicken and small game birds.

1 Starting at the tail opening, cut with poultry shears through breast and up to the neck.

2 Turn the bird over; cut with the shears on one side of the backbone and separate into halves.

3 Place each half skin-side up and, following the natural line between breast and thigh, cut crosswise into quarters.

Note: Duck may also be carved Chinese fashion, by removing legs and wings, separating thigh from drumstick, and chopping the duck into small pieces with a cleaver.

TO CARVE HAM

Ham can be sliced on a board or a ham stand. The important thing is that it's kept steady as you slice. Use a clean cloth towel or napkin to firmly grasp the bone while carving. A ham knife is a good investment if you eat ham often. Otherwise, use the sharpest knife, sharpening beforehand with a knife sharpener.

1 Hold the leg firmly and slice down into the meat about 4 inches from the knuckle.

2 Make another cut at an angle to the first and remove the wedge of ham. Cut several thin slices right down to the bone. To release the slices, run knife along the bone.

3 Lift off slices on the flat of the knife and arrange attractively on a serving platter.

Cereal Plants cultivated for their grains and seeds, such as wheat, oats, rye, and barley. They provide protein, vitamins and minerals and have a high carbohydrate content.

Ceviche A dish of raw fish or raw scallops marinated in lemon or lime juice until the flesh becomes opaque. It is often served with raw onion rings and tomatoes. Ceviche is popular in South America and the South Pacific.

Champignon (Button Mushroom) The cultivated common mushroom, picked when very young before the gills are visible. Valued for their delicate flavor champignons are available throughout the year. They can be eaten raw in salads or with dips; or, sliced or whole, they can be fried, stir-fried, broiled, baked or microwaved.

Chapatti A flat unleavened bread from India. It is made with wheat flour and cooked on a hot griddle. Chapattis are served with curries and other savory dishes, and are sometimes used like edible plates to hold the food eaten with them.

CAULIFLOWER

CAULIFLOWER FRITTERS WITH TOMATO RELISH

★★ **Preparation time:** 35 minutes
Total cooking time: 30 minutes
Serves 4-6

1 small cauliflower
3/4 cup all-purpose flour
1 teaspoon ground cumin
1/2 teaspoon baking soda
2/3 cup water
1 egg
6 1/2 oz plain yogurt
vegetable oil for deep
  frying

Tomato Relish
2 tablespoons vegetable oil
1 medium onion, finely
  chopped
14 1/2 oz can diced tomatoes
1/2 cup white wine vinegar
3/4 cup sugar
1 clove garlic, crushed
1 teaspoon ground cumin
1/2 cup raisins
3/4 cup finely chopped
  cilantro

1 Cut the cauliflower into large florets. Remove as much stem as possible without breaking the florets. Wash and drain, pat dry with paper towels. Combine the flour, cumin and soda in a medium mixing bowl; make a well in the center of the ingredients. Beat the water, egg and yogurt together and pour onto the dry ingredients. Stir with a wooden spoon until the batter is smooth. Leave for 10 minutes.

2 Heat the oil in a deep heavy-bottom pan. Dip the florets in the batter, drain off excess. Using a metal spoon or tongs, gently lower the cauliflower florets into the hot oil in small batches. Cook 3–5 minutes or until they are golden brown. Lift out with a slotted spoon and drain on paper towels. Serve warm with Tomato Relish.

3 To make the Tomato Relish: Place the oil, onion, tomato, vinegar, sugar, garlic, cumin and raisins in a pan. Bring to boil, reduce heat and simmer, covered, for 20 minutes. Increase heat and cook, stirring occasionally, until the mixture thickens. Remove from heat. Stir in cilantro.

CAULIFLOWER SOUP

Melt 3 tablespoons of butter in a pan, add 1 medium onion, chopped, and cook gently until just softened. Add 1 lb trimmed cauliflower, chopped, 2 cups milk, 2 cups chicken or vegetable stock and 1 small bay leaf; bring to boil. Cover the soup and simmer for 15–20 minutes, until the cauliflower is tender. Remove the bay leaf, cool. Place the mixture in a food processor or blender and blend until smooth. Return to the rinsed saucepan. Heat gently until boiling and stir in 1/2 cup heavy cream. Serve Cauliflower Soup hot or cold, sprinkled with 1 tablespoon chopped chives. Serves 4–6.

ABOVE: CAULIFLOWER FRITTERS WITH TOMATO RELISH. OPPOSITE PAGE: BRAISED CELERY

CELERY

BRAISED CELERY

⭐ **Preparation time:** 15 minutes
Total cooking time: 40 minutes
Serves 6

1 bunch celery	2 egg yolks
2 tablespoons butter	1 tablespoon cornstarch
2 cups chicken stock	1/4 cup chopped parsley
2 teaspoons finely grated	white pepper and
lemon rind	salt to taste
1/4 cup lemon juice	1/2 teaspoon ground mace
1/4 cup heavy cream	

1 Lightly brush a 6-cup capacity shallow heatproof dish with melted butter or oil. Preheat the oven to moderate 350°F. Trim the celery and cut it into 2 inch lengths. Melt the butter in a large pan. Add the celery, toss to coat evenly in butter. Cover and cook for 2 minutes.
2 Add the chicken stock, lemon rind and juice; cover and simmer for 10 minutes. Remove the celery from the pan with a slotted spoon and place in the prepared dish. Reserve 1/4 cup of the cooking liquid.
3 Blend the cream, egg yolks and cornstarch. Whisk in the reserved cooking liquid. Return to heat and cook until the mixture boils and thickens. Add parsley, pepper, salt and mace.
4 Pour the sauce over the celery in a heatproof dish. Cook in the oven for 15–20 minutes or until the celery softens.

CURRIED CHICKEN, APPLE AND CELERY SALAD

⭐ **Preparation time:** 30 minutes
Total cooking time: 20 minutes
Serves 8

	Curry Mayonnaise
4 lb chicken thighs	1/4 cup butter
1 1/4 cups orange juice	1 small onion, finely
2 1/2 cups water	chopped
2 medium red apples	1 tablespoon curry powder
2 celery stalks	1/2 cup mayonnaise
1 1/4 cups green seedless	2/3 cup sour cream
grapes	1/3 cup heavy cream
3/4 cup walnuts, coarsely	3 tablespoons lemon juice
chopped	1 tablespoon soft brown
	sugar
	salt, to taste

1 Trim chicken of excess fat and tendons and place in a large heavy-bottom pan. Add orange juice and water. Cover and bring to the boil. Reduce heat; gently simmer, covered, until tender. Remove from heat, drain and cool. Discard bones; cut meat into 3/4 inch pieces.
2 Halve apples, remove cores and cut into 1/2 inch cubes. Slice celery. Combine chicken, apples, celery, grapes and walnuts in a large bowl.
3 To make Curry Mayonnaise: Melt butter in a small pan. Add onion, cook 2 minutes or until onion is soft. Stir in curry powder, cook 30 seconds. Transfer mixture to a small bowl. Add mayonnaise, creams, juice, sugar and salt; mix well. Gently fold through chicken mixture.

Charlotte A dessert consisting of puréed fruit (usually apple) cooked in a mold lined with thin slices of buttered bread. It is served warm with cold custard. Charlotte russe is a cold dessert

made by lining a mold with lady fingers, then filling it with a mixture of eggs, gelatin and cream, or whipped cream.

Chateaubriand A thick slice of beef fillet broiled or sautéed, and served with sauces, traditionally béarnaise. It was reputedly the favorite dish of the eighteenth-century French statesman, writer and gourmet, Vicomte François René de Chateaubriand, for whom it is named.

Chayote (Choko) The pale green, pear-shaped fruit of a climbing vine related to the gourd. It can be peeled like an apple, cooked as a squash, stuffed or used as an ingredient in chutney.

Cheddar A semihard cow's milk cheese with a creamy texture and rich, nutty flavor that can range from mild to very sharp, depending its age. Cheddar varies in color from near white for young cheeses, to deep yellow for mature, full-flavored Cheddars. Traditionally made in large cylindrical shapes or in wheels, Cheddar takes its name from the Somerset village in England where it was first made. Today it is duplicated in factories around the world. Cheddar is an all-purpose cheese, used for cooking, in sandwiches and snacks.

Cheese A nutritious food prepared from milk treated with enzymes or coagulants, so that it separates into curds (milky white solids) and whey (a cloudy liquid). Most of the world's cheese is made from cow's milk, but it can be made from the milk of sheep, goats, buffaloes, reindeer, camels or other domesticated grazing animals. The type of milk used (skimmed, partly skimmed, whole or enriched with cream) is the main factor which alters texture and flavor. Other determinants include the additive used to curdle the milk, the culture used in the fermentation process, and the methods of processing the curd. Processed cheese is made from a natural cheese that has undergone additional steps, such as pasteurization. If categorized by texture, cheese falls into four main types: fresh,

CHEESE

HERBED CHEESE CRACKERS

★★ **Preparation time:** 20 minutes
Total cooking time: 8 minutes each tray
Makes 20

Cracker Pastry
1 cup all-purpose flour
½ teaspoon baking powder
¼ cup butter, chopped
1 egg, lightly beaten
1 tablespoon iced water
½ cup grated Cheddar cheese
1 teaspoon chopped chives
1 teaspoon chopped fresh parsley

Cheese Filling
2½ oz cream cheese
2 tablespoons butter
1 tablespoon chopped fresh chives
1 tablespoon chopped fresh parsley
¼ teaspoon lemon pepper
¾ cup grated Cheddar cheese

1 Preheat oven to 425°F. Line 2 baking sheets with baking paper.
2 Place flour and baking powder in food processor; add butter. Process 30 seconds or until mixture is fine and crumbly. Add egg, water and cheese to bowl and process 40 seconds or until mixture comes together. Turn out onto floured surface, and knead in herbs until smooth.
3 Roll the pastry between sheets of baking paper so that it is about ⅛ inch thick. Cut it into rounds, using a 2 inch fluted cutter. Place on prepared sheets. Bake for 8 minutes or until lightly browned. Transfer rounds to wire rack to cool.

4 To make Cheese Filling: Using electric beaters, beat cream cheese and butter in bowl until light and creamy. Add herbs, pepper and cheese. Beat until smooth. Spread filling on half the crackers, sandwich together with other half.

CHEESE STRAWS

★ **Preparation time:** 10 minutes
Total cooking time: 10 minutes
Makes 36

1 cup all-purpose flour
½ teaspoon salt
½ teaspoon dry mustard
½ cup shredded Cheddar cheese
2 tablespoons grated
Parmesan cheese
¼ cup firm butter, diced
1 egg yolk
2 teaspoons lemon juice

1 Preheat oven to moderate 350°F. Place flour, salt, mustard, Cheddar and Parmesan cheeses in a food processor fitted with a metal blade. Process for a few seconds to combine ingredients.
2 Add butter and process until mixture resembles fine bread crumbs.
3 Beat egg yolk and lemon juice in a small bowl and add to dry ingredients while machine is running. Process only until mixture begins to form a ball around the blade. Remove dough and form ball.
4 Roll out dough to ¼ inch thickness on a lightly floured board. Cut into 2½ x ½ inch strips. Place on a greased baking sheet and bake for 10 minutes, until golden. Cool on tray, then store in an airtight container.

CHEESE TOAST

★ **Preparation time:** 10 minutes
Total cooking time: 10 minutes
Serves 6

1 cup grated Cheddar cheese
2 tablespoons chutney
1 tablespoon grated onion
1 tablespoon tomato sauce
1 teaspoon Worcestershire sauce
2 tablespoons butter
6 thick slices whole grain bread

1 Place the grated cheese in a mixing bowl. Add the chutney, onion and sauces.
2 Melt the butter and add it to mixing bowl; stir.
3 Preheat the broiler. Toast the bread under broiler on one side. Spread the cheese mixture on the untoasted side of the bread. Put it back under the broiler until the cheese is melted. Slice and serve immediately.

WARM GOAT CHEESE SALAD

⭐ **Preparation time:** 15 minutes
Total cooking time: 15 minutes
Serves 6

6 slices whole-wheat bread	**Dressing**
2 x 3 or 4 oz rounds goat cheese	1 tablespoon tarragon vinegar
3–4 oz mixed salad greens	3 tablespoons olive oil
	½ teaspoon whole-grain mustard

1 Preheat oven to 350°F. Use a biscuit cutter to cut a round out of each slice of bread that will just fit the round of goat cheese. The bread must not extend out from the cheese or it will burn. Place bread on baking sheet, and cook 10 minutes.
2 Cut cheese into six discs, place one on each bread round. Arrange salad leaves on serving plates.
3 Cook cheese under hot broiler for 5 minutes or until golden and bubbling.
4 To make Dressing: Combine vinegar, oil and mustard in a small jar. Screw lid on tightly; shake vigorously for 1 minute or until well combined. Drizzle salad leaves with dressing, place a cheese round on top and serve.

OPPOSITE PAGE: HERBED CHEESE CRACKERS.
ABOVE: WARM GOAT CHEESE SALAD;
RIGHT: CHEESE PUDDING

CHEESE PUDDING

⭐ **Preparation time:** 20 minutes + 30 minutes standing
Total cooking time: 30 minutes
Serves 4

8 slices stale bread	1 cup chicken stock
¼ cup softened butter	½ cup heavy cream
5 oz Cheddar cheese, grated	freshly ground black pepper
4 eggs	

1 Preheat oven to 300°F. Remove crusts from bread, butter each slice one side only. Sprinkle two-thirds of the grated cheese onto four slices, sandwich with remaining bread. Cut cheese sandwiches in half diagonally.
2 Grease a shallow ovenproof dish with the remaining butter. Arrange sandwiches over base.
3 Beat the eggs, stock and cream; pour mixture over the sandwiches, moistening each. Stand for 30 minutes.
4 Sprinkle remaining cheese on top and season with ground black pepper. Bake 30 minutes or until pudding is set and golden.

Note: Cheese Pudding is a traditional Irish dish, economical and comforting. It's the perfect Sunday night supper and needs only a green salad and a loaf of crusty bread to accompany it.

unripened cheeses (cottage cheese, cream cheese, mozzarella and ricotta); soft, briefly ripened cheeses, spreadable and with a high moisture and fat content (Brie, Camembert, feta and the blue-veined cheeses); semihard or firm cheeses matured with less moisture (Cheddar, Muenster and Swiss); and hard cheeses, dry, long-matured and sharp-tasting (Sapsago, Pecorino, Romano and Parmesan). When buying cheese, avoid that which is wet, sticky, shrunken or dried and cracked. Refrigerate, and use soft cheese soon after it is bought; hard cheeses can be kept longer.

Cheesecake A rich dessert in the form of an open pie. The sweet, crumbly pastry shell is filled with a custard-like mixture based on a fresh, unripened cheese, such as cottage cheese, ricotta or cream cheese. There are two types of cheesecake: in one, the cheese mixture is baked in a cool oven; in the other, the cheese mixture is chilled in the refrigerator.

CHEESECAKES

Creamy, luscious cheesecakes are always a popular dessert. Here you'll find easy recipes for both baked and unbaked versions, with suggestions for making changes in the bases, fillings and toppings to produce some spectacular versions of this favorite.

BAKED CHEESECAKE WITH SOUR CREAM TOPPING

Baked cheesecake is delicious served simply with its sour cream topping, but it also lends itself to a variety of rich fruit, nut and cream extravaganzas. The sour cream topping can be omitted if you prefer and the fruit and cream piled straight onto the plain baked cheesecake once it has cooled.

■ Place 1¼ cups crushed vanilla wafers in a food processor and add 1 teaspoon mixed spice. Melt ⅓ cup butter and add to the crushed wafers, processing until all the crumbs are moistened. Line the base of an 8 inch round springform pan with foil, brush with oil. Press cookie crumbs over base and sides of pan. Refrigerate for 20 minutes.

To make filling: Preheat oven to 350°F. Using electric beaters, beat 1 lb cream cheese until smooth. Add ¾ cup sugar, 1 teaspoon vanilla extract and 1 tablespoon lemon juice. Beat until smooth. Add 4 whole eggs, one at a time, beating well after each addition. Pour mixture into chilled cookie base, bake for 45 minutes or until cheesecake is just firm to the touch.

To make topping: Put 1 cup of sour cream in a bowl and add ½ teaspoon vanilla extract, 1 tablespoon sugar and 1 tablespoon lemon juice. Beat well. Spread over the hot cheesecake, sprinkle with nutmeg and return cheesecake to the oven for 7 minutes. Cool in the oven and then refrigerate.

VARIATIONS

■ **BLUEBERRY AND STRAWBERRY CHEESECAKE**
Beat 1 cup heavy cream until stiff peaks form. Spread over cheesecake, top with fresh blueberries and strawberry halves. Dust lightly with sifted confectioners' sugar.

■ **BRAZIL NUT CHEESECAKE**
Using a vegetable peeler, finely peel ¼ cup whole Brazil nuts in thin strips. Beat 1 cup heavy cream until stiff peaks form. Decorate cheesecake with whipped cream and Brazil nut shavings. Sprinkle with ground nutmeg if desired.

■ **MANGO CHEESECAKE**
Thinly slice 1–2 fresh mangoes. Arrange slices decoratively over cheesecake. Heat ⅓ cup apricot jam and 2–3 teaspoons brandy in small pan. Stir over heat until melted. Strain through a sieve. Brush warmed jam mixture over mango slices. Cool and serve in wedges.

■ **KIWIFRUIT AND COCONUT CHEESECAKE**
Beat 1 cup heavy cream until stiff peaks form. Spread cheesecake with whipped cream, arrange 1–2 peeled and thinly sliced kiwifruit on top and sprinkle with ¼ cup toasted flaked coconut.

NEW YORK CHEESECAKE

This is a dense cheesecake with a pastry base instead of the usual crumb crust. This version has a citrus-flavored filling and a candied rind topping.

■ In a bowl stir together ¾ cup all-purpose flour and 2 tablespoons sugar. Add 1 egg, ¼ cup softened butter and ½ teaspoon vanilla extract. Beat with an electric mixer until well combined.

With greased fingers, press dough onto the bottom and up the sides of a greased 9 inch springform pan.

Bake in a 350°F oven for 10–12 minutes or until pastry is light brown. Cool. Place three 8 oz packages cream cheese in a large bowl. Add 1 cup sugar, 2 tablespoons flour and 1 teaspoon vanilla extract. Beat with electric beaters until smooth. Add 1 teaspoon each of grated orange and lemon rind; beat until smooth. Add 2 eggs and 1 egg yolk, one at a time, beating well after each addition. Add 1/4 cup heavy cream; beat well. Pour filling into pastry crust; bake in a 375°F oven for 35–40 minutes or until firm to touch. Allow to cool; refrigerate until firm.

To make candied rind: Combine 1 cup sugar and 1/4 cup water in a medium pan. Stir over heat without boiling until the sugar has dissolved. Add the shredded rind of 3 limes and 3 oranges. Bring to the boil, reduce heat, simmer, uncovered, for 10 minutes. Remove from heat and cool. Drain rind and reserve syrup. Beat 1 cup heavy cream until stiff peaks form. Spread it over the cooled cheesecake and decorate with candied rind. Serve in wedges with reserved syrup, if desired.

TRIPLE CHOCOLATE CHEESECAKE

This is an example of an unbaked cheesecake, made with gelatin and set in the refrigerator before serving. Much simpler recipes are available, but this one shows just how spectacular a gelatin-based cheesecake can be.

■ Line the base of a 8 inch springform pan with greased foil.

Place 4 oz plain chocolate wafers in a food processor and crush. Add 1/2 teaspoon ground cinnamon and 1/4 cup melted butter. Blend well. Press chocolate crust into base of pan. Refrigerate for 20 minutes.

To make filling: Sprinkle 1 tablespoon gelatin over 1/4 cup water in a small bowl. Stand the bowl in a pan of hot water and stir until gelatin is dissolved; cool slightly. Beat 12 oz cream cheese

in a bowl with electric beaters until smooth. Beat in 1/2 cup milk and 1/2 cup sugar. Divide the mixture into three equal portions in three separate bowls. Fold 2 oz melted white chocolate into one portion, the same quantity of milk chocolate into the second, and the same quantity of dark chocolate into the third portion. Fold one-third of the gelatin mixture into each portion. Whip 1 cup heavy cream until stiff, divide into three and gently fold one-third of it into each portion. Spread the white chocolate mixture over the cookie base. Cover carefully with the milk chocolate mixture, then the dark chocolate mixture. Refrigerate for 3 hours, or until the filling has set. Decorate top of the cheesecake with whipped cream, halved chocolate discs and curls. Sprinkle with confectioners' sugar.

To make chocolate curls: Spread 8 oz melted chocolate onto a marble board to a depth of about 1/2 inch, smoothing the surface lightly. Allow to cool until almost set. Use a sharp, flat-bladed knife and hold it horizontally. Applying constant pressure to the blade with both hands, pull the knife towards you. The pressure applied to the blade will determine how thick or thin the curls will be. Chocolate curls take time, practice and patience to master, but they look splendid as a decoration on chocolate cakes, desserts and cheesecakes.

ALL CHEESECAKES ARE SHOWN FROM ABOVE AS WELL AS IN CROSS-SECTION. FROM TOP LEFT, OPPOSITE PAGE: BAKED CHEESECAKE WITH BLUEBERRY AND STRAWBERRY TOPPING, WITH BRAZIL NUT TOPPING AND WITH MANGO TOPPING; NEW YORK CHEESECAKE; TRIPLE CHOCOLATE CHEESECAKE AND BAKED CHEESECAKE WITH KIWIFRUIT AND COCONUT TOPPING.

Chelsea Bun A bun made from a rich yeast dough rolled out, spread with butter, sprinkled with currants and sugar, then rolled up and cut into slices.

Cherimoya The fruit of a Peruvian tree, now cultivated in many tropical regions. Its sweet-scented, creamy white flesh tastes like a combination of banana, pineapple and strawberry.

Cherry The small, single-pitted juicy fruit of several species of tree related to the plum. It probably originated in Asia, but spread to Europe and North America. The Romans introduced it to Britain. From medieval times the cherry fair marked the start of summer and was a time of merry-making.

Cherries have a short season in early summer. Raw, they are best eaten as fresh as possible.

Cherrystone Clam See Quahog.

Chervil A small herb, similar in appearance to parsley, with lacy, bright green

C H E R R I E S

C H E R R I E S   J U B I L E E

★ **Preparation time:** 20 minutes
Total cooking time: 15 minutes
Serves 4

½ cup water	1 tablespoon arrowroot or
1 cup sugar	cornstarch
2 strips lemon rind	vanilla ice cream for
1 lb sweet red or black	serving
cherries, pitted	¼ cup brandy

1 Heat water in a pan, add sugar and stir to dissolve. Bring syrup to the boil, add lemon rind and cherries and simmer until cherries are tender.
2 Remove cherries from syrup with a slotted spoon, discard lemon rind and boil syrup rapidly for 3 minutes. Blend arrowroot with a little extra cold water in a small bowl and stir in some of the cherry syrup. Return mixture to pan and stir until it boils and thickens. Add cherries.
3 Spoon ice cream into heatproof serving dishes. Have cherries at boiling point. Heat brandy, add to cherries and carefully ignite. Pour flaming cherries and sauce over ice cream and serve immediately.

Note: A 13½ oz can sweet cherries in syrup can be used if desired. It is then unnecessary to make a syrup. Simply add 1–2 tablespoons sugar and lemon rind to syrup from can of cherries.

B L A C K   C H E R R Y   J A M

★ ★ **Preparation time:** 35 minutes +
overnight standing
Total cooking time: 1 hour
Makes 4 cups

2 lb black cherries	1 cup water
juice of 2 lemons	2½ cups sugar

1 Rinse cherries, drain well and remove pits. Put lemon juice and water in a bowl; add some of the sugar, then a layer of cherries. Continue with remaining sugar and cherries. Cover and leave overnight.
2 Next day, strain the syrup into a large saucepan and stir over medium heat until sugar has dissolved. Bring to boil, add cherries and boil for 45 minutes or until setting point is reached (see Jams & Marmalades). Stir frequently to prevent the mixture from burning.
3 Remove from heat and stand 5 minutes. Pour jam into warm, sterilized jars and seal immediately. When cool, label and date.

C H E R R Y   C L A F O U T I S

★ **Preparation time:** 25 minutes
Total cooking time: 50 minutes
Serves 8

1 lb cherries, stems	pinch salt
removed	⅓ cup sugar
2 tablespoons unsalted	4 eggs, lightly beaten
(sweet) butter	1½ cups milk
¼ cup sugar	2 tablespoons unsalted
¼ cup all-purpose flour	butter, melted, extra
½ teaspoon baking	2 tablespoons brandy
powder	

1 Preheat oven to 350°F. Melt the butter in a large frying pan and add the cherries. Cook for 2–3 minutes. Sprinkle with ¼ cup sugar and cook over medium heat for 5 minutes or until juices form. Remove from heat and allow to cool.
2 Sift the flour, baking powder and salt into a medium bowl. Add ⅓ cup sugar. Whisk the eggs and milk. Stir into the flour mixture, then stir in the combined butter and brandy. Place the cherries in a shallow ovenproof dish and pour the batter over the top and bake for 40 minutes or until puffed and just set when tapped in the center. Serve warm, dusted with sifted confectioners' sugar.

ABOVE: CHERRIES JUBILEE.
OPPOSITE PAGE: CHOCOLATE CHESTNUT MOUSSE

CHESTNUTS

CHESTNUT STUFFING FOR TURKEY

 Preparation time: 30 minutes
Total cooking time: 30 minutes
Serves 10

20–25 large chestnuts	*1 egg, beaten*
¼ cup butter	*1 lb pork sausage meat*
1 medium onion, chopped	*1 cup fresh white bread*
½ cup finely chopped	*crumbs*
celery	*2 teaspoons dried marjoram*
1 green cooking apple,	*salt*
peeled and chopped	*freshly ground pepper*

1 With a sharp knife, make a slit down one side of each chestnut. Place in a pan of cold water, bring to the boil, cover and simmer for 20 minutes or until chestnuts are tender. Leave chestnuts in water until just cool enough to handle, then peel outer and inner skins away. Chop chestnuts coarsely.

2 Melt butter in a pan and cook onion, celery and apple slowly until tender. Transfer to a large mixing bowl and allow to cool. Add the chopped chestnuts, egg, sausage meat, bread crumbs, marjoram, salt and pepper and mix ingredients to combine well.

3 Use Chestnut Stuffing for turkey, chicken or duck. The quantity given is sufficient to stuff one turkey, or two chickens or ducks.

Note: If fresh chestnuts are unavailable, canned whole chestnuts in water, or dried chestnuts that have been soaked in cold water overnight and cooked for 15 minutes in chicken stock, may be substituted.

CHOCOLATE CHESTNUT MOUSSE

★ ★ **Preparation time:** 30 minutes
Total cooking time: 25 minutes
Serves 6

8–9 oz fresh chestnuts, or	*4 eggs, separated*
½ cup canned	*2 tablespoons brandy*
unsweetened chestnut	*2 tablespoons sugar*
purée	*whipped cream for*
5 oz dark (semisweet)	*decoration*
chocolate	*strawberries for serving*

1 To prepare chestnuts: With a sharp knife, make a slit down one side of each chestnut, place chestnuts in a pan of cold water, bring to boil, cover and simmer for 20 minutes or until tender. Leave chestnuts in water until just cool enough to handle, then peel off outer and inner skins. Grind chestnuts in a food processor until fine; measure 1 cup lightly packed ground chestnuts.

2 Break chocolate into even-sized pieces in large, clean, dry bowl; melt in microwave or over a pan of gently simmering water. Beat in egg yolks and brandy, making a smooth mixture. Add ground chestnuts.

3 Using electric beaters, beat the egg whites until stiff peaks form, then add sugar gradually while beating. Stir one tablespoon of egg white into the chocolate mixture, to lighten it, then fold in the remaining whites.

4 Spoon the mixture into six individual dishes. Refrigerate until the mousse is set. Decorate each mousse with whipped cream and strawberries before serving.

ABOUT CHESTNUTS

◼ Chestnuts do not keep well at room temperature and should be stored in a vented plastic bag in the refrigerator. Whole shelled chestnuts can be blanched in water and frozen for up to 1 month.

◼ Roast chestnuts by making a slit in the pointed end with a small sharp knife; roast in a hot 425°F oven for about 20 minutes, or over hot coals until the shells split open and the chestnuts are golden.

◼ Chestnuts contain more starch and less oil than other nuts, so are often used like vegetables.

leaves and a delicate aniseed flavor. It is an important ingredient in sauces such as béarnaise. Best used fresh; it loses its flavor if cooked.

Cheshire Cheese A hard, crumbly, slightly salty cow's milk cheese, similar to cheddar. It can be either red, white or blue in color.

Chess Pie A Southern, single-crusted custard pie, often made with lemon, nutmeg and brown sugar.

Chestnut A round, heavy, white-fleshed nut covered with a thin brown skin and encased in a glossy brown leathery shell. When cooked, the nut has a sweet, floury taste. The chestnut tree is thought to be native to southern Europe and western Asia, and since prehistoric times the easily gathered nuts have been valued as a food. Unlike most nuts, which are rich in fat and low in starch, the chestnut kernel contains less than 3 per cent fat and has a high carbohydrate content. Roasted in the shell, they are a traditional winter snack. The shelled kernels can be simmered in stock, puréed, used in soups, stuffings and cakes, or sweetened and mixed with cream as a dessert. They are also used for the French dish

◼

marrons glacés (glazed or candied chestnuts). Available dried and canned.

Chèvre The French term for cheese made from goat's milk. Fresh chèvre is soft and mild in flavor; more mature cheeses are harder and have a sharp, biting taste.

Chicken The flesh of the domestic hen, one of the most widely used meats, featured in national cuisines around the world. All breeds are descended from the red jungle fowl of India (where the bird is still found in the wild). It was domesticated some 5,000 years ago and taken by humans to every part of the world. At first, chickens were kept for eggs rather than flesh. The Romans discovered that hand-fed birds had tender, tasty meat. Broiler-fryer chickens range from 2 to 4 pounds; roasters and capons (castrated male chickens) are larger and heavier. Stewing

CHICKEN

ROAST CHICKEN WITH BREAD CRUMB STUFFING

★ ★   **Preparation time:** 25 minutes + 10 minutes standing
Total cooking time: 2 hours 15 minutes
Serves 4–6

3 slices thick-sliced bacon, finely chopped
4 cups whole-wheat bread cubes (6 slices)
3 scallions, chopped
3 tablespoons chopped pecans
1 tablespoons dried currants
1/3 cup finely chopped parsley
1/3 cup milk
1 egg, beaten

salt and freshly ground black pepper
1 whole chicken (2 1/2–3 lb)
3 tablespoons butter, melted
1 tablespoon vegetable oil
1 tablespoon soy sauce
1 1/2 cups water
1 clove garlic, finely chopped
2 tablespoons all-purpose flour, unsifted

1 Preheat oven to 350°F. In a skillet, cook bacon over high heat 5 minutes or until crisp. Drain on paper towels. In a large bowl combine bacon,

bread cubes, onion, pecans, currants and parsley. Combine egg and milk; add to mixture. Season to taste and mix well.

2 Remove the neck, giblets and any large deposits of fat from the chicken. Rinse well and pat dry with paper towels.

3 Spoon stuffing into chicken cavity; close cavity and secure with a skewer or toothpick. Tie wings and drumsticks securely in place with string. Rub chicken all over with salt and pepper.

4 Place chicken, breast-side up, on rack in a roasting pan. Combine butter, oil and soy sauce. Brush chicken with melted butter. Pour any leftover melted butter into roasting pan along with half of the water and garlic. Roast chicken for 1 1/2–2 hours or until browned and thermometer inserted into thigh registers 180°F. Brush chicken occasionally with pan juices during cooking. Transfer chicken to a serving platter. Let stand, loosely covered with foil, for 10 minutes before carving. Serve with gravy and vegetables.

5 To make gravy: Strain pan juices into a medium saucepan. Combine flour and remaining water until smooth. Add flour mixture to pan juices. Stir over medium heat for 5 minutes or until mixture boils and thickens. Season to taste. Add extra water if necessary. Serve warm.

Chicken à la King
Cooked chicken topped with cream sauce and mushrooms.

Chicken Kiev A boned and flattened chicken breast wrapped around a mixture of butter and chives, breaded and then fried until crisp and golden.

Chickpea (Garbanzo Bean) The round, pale-golden, pea-like seed of a bushy plant of southern Europe and western Asia. The chickpea has a nutty flavor and is used in

COQ AU VIN

Preparation time: 30 minutes
Total cooking time: 1 hour
Serves 4-6

2 teaspoons cooking oil	8 oz small mushrooms
1 large onion, chopped	2 cups dry red wine
10 chicken thighs, skinned	2 tablespoons cornstarch
	2 tablespoons water
2 cloves garlic, crushed	2 tablespoons chopped
4 oz ham, chopped	parsley

1 Heat the oil in a large skillet. Cook the onion in the hot oil until it is tender. Add the chicken and garlic. Lightly brown the chicken on all sides, remove from the skillet and set aside.
2 Add the ham and mushrooms to the onion mixture in the skillet. Cook and stir for 1 minute. Return the chicken to the skillet. Add the red wine and bring to boil; reduce heat. Cover and simmer for 1 hour or until the chicken is tender and no longer pink.
3 Stir together the cornstarch and 2 tablespoons of water until smooth. Add the cornstarch mixture to the wine mixture. Cook and stir until thickened and bubbly. Cook and stir for another 2 minutes.
4 Add the parsley just before serving. Serve with hot cooked rice, salad and crusty bread.

OPPOSITE PAGE: ROAST CHICKEN WITH BREAD CRUMB STUFFING. ABOVE: COQ AU VIN

CHICKEN AND CORN SOUP

Remove the skin and shred the meat from one cooked chicken (about 3 cups meat). Heat 3 1/2 cups of chicken broth in a large saucepan. Add the shredded chicken, an 8 oz can creamed corn, an 8 oz can whole kernel corn, drained, 2 scallions, thinly sliced and 1/2 teaspoon soy sauce. Bring to boil; reduce heat and simmer the soup for 2 minutes. Season to taste. Serves 4.

CHICKEN STOCK

Place 1 lb chicken bones and 1 large onion, chopped, in a baking dish. Bake in a 350°F oven for about 50 minutes or until well browned. Transfer to a large pan or stockpot. Wrap 2 bay leaves and 6 peppercorns in a piece of cheesecloth to make a bouquet garni.

Chop 1 carrot and 1 stalk of celery (leaves included) and place in a pan along with the bouquet garni and 5 cups of water. Bring the stock to boil, then reduce heat and simmer, uncovered, for 40 minutes, adding a little more water if necessary. Strain the stock. Discard the bones and vegetables. Cool stock quickly and refrigerate, then skim off any hard fat that may have risen to the surface. Refrigerate or freeze. Use the chicken stock as indicated in recipes. Makes 4 cups.

soups, stews and salads. Boiled and then ground to a paste, chickpeas are a basic ingredient in the Middle Eastern dip hummus, or formed into balls and fried as falafel. In India it is ground to make besan flour, or dry roasted and seasoned with spices as a snack food. The Phoenicians introduced it to Spain where it has been a staple food ever since.

Chicory Often known as curly endive, a loose bunch of ragged-edged leaves on a long stem. The outer leaves are deep, rich green and have a tangy

bitter taste. Chicory roots can be roasted, ground and used as a substitute for coffee. In England, Chicory is the name given to a vegetable with compact, pale, yellow-tipped leaves, called Belgian endive in the United States. Radicchio is a red-leafed Italian chicory.
See Endive, Curly.

Chili The small, smooth-skinned, long pods of a plant of the pepper family. Chilies are smaller and far hotter in taste than sweet peppers. The many species vary greatly in size, shape, color, and most importantly, in their fieriness. Most of the heat is located in the pepper's seeds and

membranes, so removing those will tone down the heat. Chili

CHICKEN CACCIATORE

⭐ **Preparation time:** 15 minutes
Total cooking time: 55 minutes
Serves 6

2 tablespoons vegetable oil
12 chicken drumsticks, about 3 lb
1 medium onion, chopped
14½ oz can tomatoes, crushed
⅔ cup chicken broth

⅔ cup dry white wine
1½ cups fresh mushrooms, quartered
1 teaspoon dried oregano, crushed
1 teaspoon dried thyme, crushed
salt and pepper

1 Preheat oven to 350°F. Heat the oil in a large skillet. Cook the drumsticks, a few at a time, over medium-high heat until well browned, 10–15 minutes; transfer to a large ovenproof casserole dish.

2 Add the onion and garlic to the skillet and cook over medium heat until golden. Add the tomatoes, broth, wine, mushrooms, oregano and thyme to the skillet. Season to taste. Bring to boil, reduce heat and simmer 10 minutes. Pour over chicken.

3 Bake, covered, 35–40 minutes or until the chicken is very tender. Serve with hot spiral or other small pasta.

ABOVE: CHICKEN CACCIATORE; RIGHT: CHICKEN WITH TARRAGON AND MUSHROOMS. OPPOSITE PAGE: GRILLED GARLIC AND ROSEMARY CHICKEN

CHICKEN WITH TARRAGON AND MUSHROOMS

⭐ **Preparation time:** 10 minutes
Total cooking time: 50 minutes
Serves 6

6 large boneless chicken breast halves, about 1½ lb, skin removed
2 tablespoons olive oil
3 slices thick-sliced bacon, cut in ¼ inch pieces, or 2 oz Canadian bacon, cut in strips
8 oz fresh mushrooms, thinly sliced

½ cup dry white wine
3 tablespoons tomato paste
1 teaspoon dried tarragon
⅔ cup heavy cream
3 scallions, finely chopped
salt and pepper

1 Preheat oven to 350°F. In a large skillet, heat oil. Add the chicken. Cook over medium-high heat 2 minutes each side, turning once, until just browned. Remove from the pan and drain. Place the chicken in a shallow baking dish; set aside.

2 Add the bacon to the pan. Cook over medium-high heat for 2 minutes; drain fat. Add the mushrooms; cook for 5 minutes. Add the wine, tomato paste and tarragon to the pan. Stir until the mixture boils. Reduce heat and add the cream; simmer for 2 minutes. Remove from heat, stir in the scallions. Season to taste.

3 Pour sauce over the chicken. Bake, covered, for 20–30 minutes or until chicken is tender.

GREEN CHICKEN CURRY

⭐ **Preparation time:** 10 minutes
Total cooking time: 45 minutes
Serves 4

8 chicken thighs, about
  2½–3 lb
2 tablespoons peanut oil
3 cloves garlic, finely
  chopped
1 tablespoon chopped
  fresh ginger
3 scallions, finely
  chopped
1 teaspoon curry powder
¼ cup chopped green
  chilies

½ teaspoon ground
  coriander
½ teaspoon ground
  cumin
1¼ cups water
⅔ cup canned coconut
  milk
⅔ cup chopped fresh
  cilantro
1 tablespoon Thai fish
  sauce (nam pla)
2 medium tomatoes,
  seeded and chopped

1 Remove the skin from the chicken, if desired. Heat the oil in a large skillet over medium-high heat. Add the garlic, ginger, green onions (scallions) and curry powder. Cook and stir for 1 minute, stir in the chilies, coriander and cumin. Add the chicken and cook over medium heat for 5 minutes, turning once. Carefully add the water; cover the pan and simmer for 15 minutes.
2 Stir in the coconut milk, cilantro, fish sauce and tomatoes. Simmer, uncovered, for 10–15 minutes more or until the chicken is tender and cooked right through. Do not cover the pan after adding the coconut milk because it may separate. Serve hot with steamed rice, if desired.

GRILLED GARLIC AND ROSEMARY CHICKEN

⭐ **Preparation time:** 10 minutes +
3 hours marinating
Total cooking time: 30 minutes
Serves 4

4 chicken legs (drumsticks
  and thighs), 2–2½ lb
1 orange
½ cup orange juice
⅔ cup olive oil
3 cloves garlic, crushed

2 tablespoons chopped
  fresh rosemary
1 tablespoon chopped
  fresh thyme
1 teaspoon Dijon mustard
salt, to taste

1 Rinse chicken; pat dry with paper towels. Use a sharp knife to make 3 or 4 deep cuts in the thickest part of the chicken pieces.
2 Using a vegetable peeler, peel long strips of orange rind from half the orange. Combine orange rind, orange juice, oil, garlic, rosemary, thyme, mustard and salt in small bowl. Place chicken in large shallow baking dish; pour garlic-herb mixture over. Cover with plastic wrap, refrigerate 3 hours or overnight, turn occasionally.
3 Preheat broiler, line pan rack with foil; brush with melted butter. Drain chicken, reserve marinade. Place chicken on prepared broiler pan. Broil 5 inches from the heat 10–15 minutes each side until tender and cooked through, brush with reserved marinade several times during cooking. Garnish with orange slices and sprigs of rosemary.

ABOUT CHICKEN

■ Chicken must be stored and handled carefully to avoid the possibility of food poisoning. Store fresh, uncooked chicken in the coldest part of the refrigerator for 1 or 2 days only; do not allow its liquid to drip onto other foodstuffs. Keep chicken away from strong-smelling items.

■ Frozen chickens or chicken portions must be fully defrosted in the refrigerator, or use the microwave oven for chicken pieces; separate pieces as they soften. Microwave defrosting is not recommended for whole frozen chickens because of uneven defrosting.

■ Never leave chicken to defrost on the kitchen counter—harmful bacteria can multiply rapidly. Poultry purchased frozen should be placed in the freezer only if still rock hard. If it has begun to defrost, defrost fully in refrigerator, then cook, cool and freeze. After chopping raw chicken, wash work surfaces and utensils in very hot water; scrub chopping boards.

■ Chicken must be thoroughly cooked: pierce the thickest part of flesh with a knife and if juices run pink, continue cooking until they run clear.

peppers contain oils that can burn the eyes and skin, so it is important to use plastic gloves when working with chili peppers; or wash hands well when finished using peppers. Chili peppers are available fresh and dried. When fresh, they should be firm and glossy. Store unwashed in the refrigerator for up to a week.

Chili con Carne A spicy dish of cubed or ground meat, red kidney beans and finely diced onions, seasoned with chili peppers, chili powder or both. Chili con Carne has its origins in the cooking of the Incas, Mayas and Aztecs, who were aware of the preservative properties of hot peppers on meat.

Chili Paste A Chinese cooking staple made of fermented fava beans, flour, red chili peppers and garlic.

Chili Powder A blend of dried chili peppers and seasonings. It has a hot, spicy, peppery taste, and is most commonly used to flavor chili con carne. It is best bought in small quantities as it rapidly loses its flavor and becomes unusable.

Chimichanga A deep-fried burrito filled with meat, beans or chicken and served with hot sauce or sour cream.

Chinese Broccoli
(Chinese Kale) A
vegetable related to
European and Middle
Eastern broccoli. It has
long, smooth stems and
larger leaves than its
Western cousins, with
clusters of small white

flowers.
Stem, leaves and
flower heads are eaten
steamed or boiled until
they are just tender and
served with oyster sauce,
or used in stir-fry dishes.

Chinese Food The
cooking and presentation
of food is a central part
of Chinese culture. It
requires a harmonious
combination of color,
aroma, flavor and
texture, and the

balancing of the five
basic flavors: sweet, sour,
salty, bitter and piquant.
A Chinese meal starts
with a soup course,
followed by dishes of
rice, meat, fish, poultry
and vegetables all placed
on the table at the same
time. Each diner has a
small bowl and a pair of
chopsticks. Dessert is
usually fruit; dairy
products are rarely eaten.
Tea is the main drink.
Regional cuisines have
been shaped by the

**CHICKEN
PRE-COOKED**

CHICKEN PROVENCALE

⭐ **Preparation time:** 15 minutes
Total cooking time: 15 minutes
Serves 4

1 whole cooked chicken
1 tablespoon olive oil
1 medium onion,
  chopped
2 cloves garlic, finely
  chopped
1 large sweet red or green
  pepper, cut in thin
  strips
14½ oz can tomatoes,
  crushed

1 tablespoon tomato
  paste
⅓ cup dry sherry
½ teaspoon sugar
⅓ cup shredded fresh
  basil leaves
⅔ cup pitted black olives,
  halved
salt and freshly ground
  black pepper

1 Cut the cooked chicken into eight or ten
portions.
2 Heat the oil in a large skillet. Add the onion,
garlic and pepper strips. Cook over medium heat
until the onion is tender. Add the undrained
tomatoes, tomato paste, sherry and sugar to the
skillet. Bring to boil, reduce heat and simmer,
uncovered for 10 minutes or until the sauce has
thickened.
3 Add the chicken pieces, basil and olives to
sauce. Stir until heated through. Season to taste
and serve immediately with a green salad and
crusty bread. Makes 4 servings.

SMOKED CHICKEN SALAD WITH SWEET AND SOUR DRESSING

⭐ **Preparation time:** 25 minutes
Total cooking time: none
Serves 4–6

5 oz alfalfa or bean sprouts
1 carrot, peeled and cut
  into thin strips
5 oz oyster mushrooms
5 oz snow peas
¼ cup cashews
2 lb smoked chicken, flesh
  removed and cut into
  chunks

Dressing
¼ cup olive oil
2 tablespoons white wine
  vinegar
2 tablespoons prepared
  sweet and sour sauce
few drops Tabasco sauce

1 Spread a layer of sprouts on a serving plate. Top
with carrot, mushrooms, snow peas, cashews and
smoked chicken.
2 To make Dressing: Place all ingredients in a
screw-top jar. Shake well.
3 Pour over salad just before serving. Serve salad
with boiled new potatoes.

WARM CHICKEN SALAD

⭐ **Preparation time:** 35 minutes
Total cooking time: 10 minutes
Serves 4

1 small onion, thinly
  sliced
2 tablespoons olive oil
2 large peppers seeded,
  cut into thin strips
2 lb cooked chicken,
  skinned and cut into
  pieces
1 tablespoon soy sauce

¼ teaspoon Chinese five-
  spice powder
pinch sugar
freshly ground black
  pepper

Dressing
1 tablespoon vinegar
¼ cup blanched slivered
  almonds, toasted

1 In a pan, cook the sliced onion in half of
the oil until the onion is golden. Add the pepper
strips and cook until they are crisp-tender, about
5 minutes.
2 Stir in the chicken pieces, soy sauce, five-spice
powder, sugar and seasonings (to taste).
Heat through. Transfer to a serving bowl or
individual plates.
3 To make Dressing: Combine the vinegar and
the remaining oil; drizzle over the salad. Serve
garnished with almonds.

ABOVE: CHICKEN PROVENCALE.
OPPOSITE: PORT AND PEPPER PATE

CHICKEN LIVERS

PORT AND PEPPER PATE WITH MOON TOASTS

⭐ **Preparation time:** 40 minutes + overnight refrigeration
Total cooking time: 20 minutes
Serves 8

2 oz can green
  peppercorns
1/3 cup butter
15 oz chicken livers,
  chopped
1 medium onion,
  chopped
2 cloves garlic, crushed

1/3 cup port
1/3 cup heavy cream
1 tablespoon chopped
  chives

Moon Toasts
10 slices bread
lemon pepper seasoning

1 Preheat oven to moderate 350°F. Line a baking sheet with foil. Drain peppercorns. Heat butter in a large, heavy-bottom pan. Add livers, onion, garlic and port. Stir over medium heat until liver is almost cooked and onion is soft. Bring to boil; simmer 5 minutes. Remove from heat. Cool slightly.
2 Place mixture in food processor. Using the pulse action, process 30 seconds or until mixture is smooth. Add cream, process 15 seconds more.
3 Transfer mixture to medium mixing bowl. Stir in chives and peppercorns. Spoon mixture into individual or one large ramekin dish. Refrigerate overnight or until firm.
4 To make Moon Toasts: Using a moon-shaped cutter, cut shapes out of bread. Place on prepared baking sheet. Sprinkle with pepper. Bake 5 minutes or until crisp. Cool on wire rack.

Note: Make pâté one day ahead. Moon Toasts can be made one week ahead and stored in an airtight container.

PASTA WITH CHICKEN LIVERS

⭐ **Preparation time:** 15 minutes
Total cooking time: 20 minutes
Serves 4–6

8 oz pasta (penne, fusilli
  or rigatoni)
1/4 cup olive oil
1 large onion, chopped
1–2 cloves garlic, crushed
1/2 cup finely chopped
  lean bacon
1 lb chicken livers,
  trimmed

1 tablespoon chopped
  marjoram or oregano
1 tablespoon chopped
  parsley
2 tablespoons red wine
  vinegar
2 cups torn spinach leaves
freshly ground pepper

1 Cook pasta in large pan of rapidly boiling water until just tender; drain.
2 Heat oil in a large pan and cook onion until soft but not brown. Add garlic, bacon and chicken livers and while stirring cook quickly until livers are almost cooked; they should still be faintly pink inside.
3 Add herbs and vinegar, spinach, pepper and warm pasta and toss ingredients over medium heat until spinach has wilted. Serve immediately.

diversity of terrain and climate over the vast lands, dictating not only local ingredients but also, because of a general lack of fuel, cooking techniques: most food is chopped into small pieces and quickly cooked, either stir-fried in a wok or steamed.

Cantonese cooking, the style best known outside China, uses stir-fried pork, fish or shellfish, crisp vegetables, steamed dumplings with fragrant dipping sauces and rice as an accompaniment to every meal.

Chinese Gooseberry See Kiwifruit.

Chinese Parsley See Coriander.

Chipolata A small sausage, about finger length, made from pork or pork and beef. Often served as a garnish for roast meat or poultry, or as a cocktail snack.

Chipotle Chili Pepper A hot chili pepper available dried, canned and pickled. It is a dried, smoked jalepeño pepper with a smoky, chocolate flavor.

Chitterlings (Chitlins) Hogs' intestines prepared by boiling.

Chive An herb related to the onion and leek with hollow, grass-like stems. Chives are used fresh and finely chopped to add a delicate onion flavor to salads and dips. They are also an ingredient in *fines herbes*.

Chocolate A food made from the seeds of the cacao tree which is native to Central America. The white seeds grow in a pod. Fermented to develop the flavor, the seeds are then roasted and ground to a dark paste and formed into blocks of pure chocolate, also called bitter or unsweetened chocolate. More than half the weight of pure chocolate is fat known as cocoa butter: cocoa powder is ground from the solids left after this fat is extracted.

The Mayan people of Central America were the first to cultivate the cacao tree and to process its seeds. The Spanish explorer Cortez brought the beans back as well as the knowledge of how to prepare them. The beans were ground to a paste and mixed with cane sugar to produce a food.

The main types of chocolate are: un-sweetened or bitter chocolate, which is unadulterated;

CHINESE CLASSICS

MINI SPRING ROLLS

★★ **Preparation time:** 45 minutes
Total cooking time: 30 minutes
Makes 20

4 dried Chinese mushrooms	1/4 teaspoon ground black pepper
3 cups finely shredded Chinese cabbage	1 tablespoon soy sauce
2 teaspoons salt	1 tablespoon oyster sauce
6 teaspoons oil	2 large carrots, grated
1/2 teaspoon crushed garlic	3 teaspoons cornstarch
1 teaspoon grated ginger	2 tablespoons water
5 oz ground pork	10 large spring roll wrappers
	oil for deep-frying

1 Soak mushrooms in hot water to cover for 30 minutes. Drain, squeeze to remove excess liquid. Remove stems and chop caps finely. Place cabbage in colander, sprinkle with salt, leave 10 minutes to draw out excess liquid. Rinse under cold, running water, squeezing to remove liquid.
2 Heat oil in wok or heavy-bottom frying pan, swirling gently to coat base and side. Add garlic and ginger, cook until pale golden. Increase heat to high, add pork and stir-fry, breaking up lumps, until meat changes color. Stir in pepper and sauces. Add mushrooms, cabbage and carrot; continue stir-frying 3 minutes. Mix cornstarch with water, add to meat mixture. Cook, stirring, until liquid is clear and thick. Leave to cool.

3 Cut spring roll wrappers diagonally in half. Work with one triangle at a time, keeping remainder covered with clean, damp towel. Place 2 teaspoonfuls of filling on a triangle. Fold in two side points, then roll up towards last point, forming a log. Seal point with a little flour and water paste. Repeat with remaining wrappers.
4 Heat the oil in wok and deep-fry rolls four at a time until they are golden—about 3 minutes. Drain on paper towels. Serve with sweet and sour sauce.

Note: Prepare rolls 1 day ahead; refrigerate. Store uncooked in freezer for up to 1 month. Deep-fry frozen rolls in moderately hot oil for 5 minutes.

PEKING DUCK WITH MANDARIN PANCAKES

★
★★ **Preparation time:** 30 minutes +
1 hour for pancakes
Total cooking time: 1 hour
45 minutes–2 hours
Serves 5

1 domestic duckling (about 4–4 1/2 lb)	**Mandarin Pancakes**
1 tablespoon honey	3 cups all-purpose flour
1/4 cup hot water	2 teaspoons sugar
1 medium cucumber	1/4 teaspoon salt
10 scallions	1 1/4 cups boiling water
hoisin sauce	sesame oil, for brushing

bittersweet, semisweet or sweet chocolate, which contains sugar, lecithin and vanilla; and milk chocolate which is sweetened chocolate with dry milk added. White chocolate is not really chocolate because it lacks chocolate liquor; it contains sugar, cocoa butter, milk solids, lecithin and vanilla. Chocolate can be purchased in squares, chips, chunks and bars.

Chop Suey A dish developed by immigrant Chinese cooks in the United States and often served in Chinese restaurants in Western countries. It consists of a mixture of bean sprouts and finely sliced vegetables and meat (usually chicken or pork), stir-fried then simmered in sauce. The name is from the Chinese and means "mixed bits."

Chorizo A highly seasoned coarse-textured, dried sausage of Spanish origin, heavily flavored with garlic and chili. It is added to many Spanish dishes, such as cocido (Spanish stew) and paella. Any spicy salami may be used in its place.

Choux Pastry (Chou paste) A light pastry used for making éclairs, cream puffs, profiteroles and croquembouche. It is

1 Prepare duck by removing neck, giblets and any large pieces of fat. Rinse the bird inside and out under cold running water. Skewer neck skin to back; tie legs to tail. Twist wing tips under back. Prick skin all over with fork. Put the duckling on a cake rack placed over a baking pan. Mix the honey and hot water together and brush two coats of this glaze over the duck, ensuring that it is entirely covered.

2 Preheat oven to moderately hot 375°F. Place duckling breast-side up, on a rack in a shallow roasting pan. Roast for 1¾–2 hours. Remove from the oven and let stand a minute or two. Slice duck; place in a warm serving dish.

3 Meanwhile, remove seeds from cucumber and slice into very thin strips. Chill in refrigerator. Take a 3 inch section from each scallion and make very thin parallel cuts from the end towards the center. Place scallions in ice water. (They will open into "brushes.") Arrange the cucumber sticks and scallion brushes on a serving plate. Place the hoisin sauce in a small dish. Serve the Mandarin Pancakes and duck on separate plates.

4 To make Mandarin Pancakes: Stir together flour, sugar and salt in a medium bowl. Pour boiling water slowly into flour mixture, stirring constantly using a table knife or a chopstick. Stir until well blended. When cool enough to handle,

knead mixture on a well-floured surface until smooth and elastic (8–10 minutes). Place dough back in bowl; cover with damp cloth. Let stand for 20–30 minutes.

5 Turn dough out onto a lightly floured surface. Shape dough into twenty 1½ inch balls. Work with 2 balls of dough, rolling each into a 3 inch circle. (Keep the remaining dough covered with a damp cloth to prevent it from drying out.) Brush sesame oil on the entire surface of one side of one of the circles; place another 3 inch circle on top. Re-roll the dough to make an 8 inch pancake. Repeat with remaining dough to make 10 "double" pancakes.

6 Heat a heavy ungreased skillet or griddle; cook the pancake stacks, a few at a time, over medium heat 25–35 seconds or until small bubbles appear on the surface of pancake. Turn over and cook the second side (a few golden spots will appear), pressing the surface with a wide spatula. The pancake should puff up when done.

7 Quickly remove from skillet and gently separate the two pancakes. Stack them on a plate and cover at once to prevent them from drying out.

8 To serve, each guest spreads a little hoisin sauce on a pancake, adds a couple of pieces of cucumber, a scallion and finally a piece of crisp duck skin. Fold into a neat envelope shape and eat immediately. Follow the same procedure with the duck meat when all the skin has been finished.

OPPOSITE PAGE: MINI SPRING ROLLS.

ABOVE: PEKING DUCK WITH MANDARIN PANCAKES

cooked twice: first in the saucepan, where water, flour, butter and sugar—for sweet choux—are mixed before the eggs are whisked in to produce a smooth, shiny paste; the mixture is then piped onto oiled sheets and cooked for a second time in the oven. The egg causes the mixture to swell, resulting in almost hollow logs or balls. When cool, they are split open and filled with custard or cream.

Chowchow A hot, spicy relish made by pickling cabbage, peppers, cucumbers and onions in a sugary vinegar.

Chowder A thick soup, usually milk-based, made with seafood, fish, vegetables or chicken.

Chow Mein A Chinese dish consisting of strips of meat (usually chicken, pork or seafood) and vegetables, stir-fried and served with fried noodles.

Churro A fritter made of deep-fried choux pastry, sprinkled with sugar and served as a dessert. The churro originated in Spain where it is often served at breakfast with a large cup of hot chocolate or coffee.

Chutney A sweet, sour or spicy condiment of fruits and vegetables cooked with sugar, spices and vinegar

WONTON SOUP

★★ **Preparation time:** 1 hour
Total cooking time: 6 minutes
Serves 10

4 dried Chinese mushrooms
8 oz ground pork
6oz medium shrimp, peeled, deveined and finely chopped
1/2 teaspoon salt
1 tablespoon soy sauce
1 teaspoon sesame oil
2 scallions, finely chopped
1 teaspoon fresh ginger, finely chopped

2 tablespoons finely sliced water chestnuts
40 wonton skins or 10 egg roll skins, quartered
8 cups water
6 cups chicken broth, preferably homemade
4 scallions, in thin strips, to garnish

1 Soak mushrooms in hot water 30 minutes. Drain; squeeze to remove excess liquid. Remove stems, chop caps finely. Stir mushrooms, pork, shrimp, salt, soy sauce, sesame oil, scallions, ginger and water chestnuts together. Work with one skin at a time, cover remainder with clean, damp towel to prevent drying out. Spoon a rounded teaspoon of filling just off center of skin.
2 Moisten edges of pastry with water, fold in half diagonally, bring two points together. Place on a plate dusted with flour to prevent sticking.
3 Bring the water to boil in a Dutch oven. Drop 20 wontons, one at a time, into boiling water. Simmer, uncovered 3 minutes. Remove with slotted spoon. Cook remaining wontons. Place in soup bowls. Bring broth to boil. Pour over wontons. Garnish with scallions. Serve immediately.

FRIED RICE

★ **Preparation time:** 20 minutes
Total cooking time: 9–10 minutes
Serves 4

2 eggs, lightly beaten
1 medium onion
4 scallions
6 oz cooked ham
2 tablespoons peanut oil

5 cups cold, cooked rice
1/3 cup frozen peas
2 tablespoons soy sauce
6 oz cooked shrimp, shelled

1 Season eggs with salt and pepper. Peel onion; cut into 1/2 inch wedges. Diagonally slice scallions into 1 inch pieces. Cut the ham into very thin strips. Heat 1 tablespoon of the oil in a wok or a large non-stick skillet over medium heat. Add the eggs; lift and tilt the wok to form a thin omelet. Cook, without stirring, for 1 minute.
2 When almost set, break into pieces, to resemble scrambled eggs. Transfer to plate, set aside.
3 Heat the remaining 1 tablespoon of oil in the wok over medium-high heat. Add the onion. Stir-fry for 4–5 minutes or until onion is soft and lightly browned. Add the ham. Stir-fry for 1 minute. Add rice and peas. Stir-fry for 3 minutes or until the rice is heated through. Add eggs, soy, scallions and shrimp. Cook and stir until heated. Serve immediately.

ABOVE: FRIED RICE; BELOW: WONTON SOUP.
OPPOSITE PAGE, ABOVE: EASY CHOCOLATE FUDGE;
BELOW: CLASSIC CHOCOLATE MOUSSE

CHOCOLATE

CLASSIC CHOCOLATE MOUSSE

Preparation time: 25 minutes +
2 hours refrigeration
Total cooking time: 5 minutes
Serves 6

6½ oz dark (semisweet)
  chocolate, chopped
3 tablespoons unsalted
  (sweet) butter
1 tablespoon
  confectioners' sugar
1 teaspoon vanilla extract

4 eggs, separated
⅔ cup cream, whipped
1 tablespoon brandy,
  cognac or orange
  liqueur
whipped cream, for
  serving

1 Place chocolate in heatproof bowl. Stand over pan of simmering water and stir until chocolate has melted and is smooth. Remove from heat. Cool slightly.
2 Using electric beaters, beat butter, sugar and vanilla until light and creamy. Add yolks, one at a time, beating well after each addition. Add chocolate, beat until smooth. Fold in a third of the cream.
3 Place the egg whites in a small, dry mixing bowl. Beat with electric beaters until stiff peaks form. Using a metal spoon, fold the egg whites, remaining cream and liqueur into the chocolate mixture. Pour the mixture into individual glasses. Refrigerate for 2 hours or until set. Serve with whipped cream.

EASY CHOCOLATE FUDGE

Preparation time: 10 minutes
Total cooking time: 5 minutes
Makes 64

4 oz dark (semisweet)
  chocolate, chopped
½ cup unsalted butter
1½ cups confectioners'
  sugar, sifted

¼ cup milk
½ cup coarsely chopped
  pecans, almonds,
  walnuts or hazelnuts

1 Line the base and sides of a shallow 8 inch square cake pan with aluminum foil. Brush the foil with oil or melted butter. Combine the chocolate, butter, sugar and milk in a medium heavy-bottom pan. Stir over low heat until the chocolate and butter have melted and the mixture is smooth. Bring to boil; boil for 1 minute only. Remove from the heat and beat the mixure with a wooden spoon until it is smooth. Fold the chopped nuts into the mixture.
2 Pour mixture into the prepared pan; smooth surface with the back of a metal spoon. Stand pan on wire rack to cool. When fudge is firm, remove from pan. Carefully peel off the foil and cut into squares. Store Easy Chocolate Fudge in an airtight container in a cool, dark place for up to 7 days.

CHOCOLATE SAUCE

Break 5 oz dark (semisweet) chocolate into small pieces and place in a pan with ½ cup heavy cream. Heat gently until the chocolate melted, stirring until smooth. Serve warm or at room temperature. Makes about 1 cup.

until thick. Chutney is served as an accompaniment to hot and cold meat, with cheese platters, with fish dishes and with Indian curries.

Cider An alcoholic drink that is made from the fermented juice of apples or other fruits. It can be bubbly, clear or cloudy. Served hot or cold, cider is also used in cooking to flavor meat, poultry and fish, and in desserts.

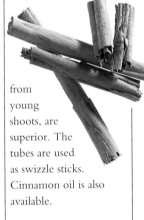

Cilantro See Coriander.

Cinnamon The light brown, aromatic, flaky bark of a small tree native to Sri Lanka. The inner bark is taken from thin branches and dried in the sun to form curled tubes. The palest,

from young shoots, are superior. The tubes are used as swizzle sticks. Cinnamon oil is also available.

Cinnamon Sugar A combination of equal amounts of sugar and ground cinnamon sprinkled on cakes and buttered toast.

Citron A pear-shaped citrus fruit resembling a lemon, but larger and with a thicker, fragrant rind. A native of China, it is grown mainly for its peel, which is candied or preserved and used in the making of fruit cakes. It is the traditional topping to Madeira cake.

Citrus Fruit A family of tropical fruits that includes the orange,

lemon, grapefruit, lime, tangerine, mandarin, clementine and kumquat.

Clam A saltwater shellfish with edible flesh protected by two large hinged shells marked by fine circular ridges. Clams are opened like oysters, and, like oysters, the flesh can be eaten fresh on the half-shell, dressed with a squeeze of lemon juice. The east coast of North America is famous for its summer

clambakes and its New England clam chowder. Popular clams include littlenecks, quahogs and cherrystones. In Italy,

SOUR CREAM AND CHOCOLATE TRIANGLES

⭐ **Preparation time:** 25 minutes
Total cooking time: 25–30 minutes
Makes 16 triangles

3 oz dark (semi-sweet) chocolate, chopped	⅔ cup butter, melted
1 cup sugar	**Icing**
1 cup all-purpose flour	3 oz milk chocolate, chopped
¼ cup unsweetened cocoa	¼ cup sour cream
3 eggs	
⅔ cup sour cream	

1 Preheat oven to 350°F. Brush an 11 x 7 inch baking pan with melted butter or oil. Line base with waxed or parchment paper; grease paper.
2 Place chocolate in glass bowl. Stir over barely simmering water until melted; remove from heat.
3 Place all ingredients in food processor bowl. Using the pulse action, process for 10 seconds or until mixture is smooth.
4 Pour into pan; smooth surface. Bake 25–30 minutes or until a skewer inserted into center comes out clean.
5 Cool in pan 10 minutes before turning onto a wire rack to cool.
6 To make Icing: Combine chocolate and sour cream in pan. Stir over low heat until smooth; remove from heat, cool slightly. Spread over bars. Cut into triangles. Store, covered, in refrigerator.

DATE AND CHOCOLATE FUDGE BARS

⭐ **Preparation time:** 35 minutes
Total cooking time: 30 minutes
Makes 18 bars

1¼ cups all-purpose flour	1 cup brown sugar, firmly packed
½ cup dates, chopped	2 tablespoons unsweetened cocoa powder
½ cup walnuts, chopped	
1 teaspoon grated lemon rind	2 tablespoons maple syrup
1 teaspoon baking powder	1 egg, lightly beaten
¼ teaspoon baking soda	2 oz dark (semisweet) chocolate, chopped
¼ teaspoon salt	
½ cup butter	

1 Preheat oven to 350°F. Brush an 11 x 7 inch baking pan with melted butter or oil. Line base with waxed or parchment paper; grease paper.
2 Combine flour, dates, walnuts, lemon rind, baking powder, baking soda and salt in large mixing bowl. Make a well in the center.
3 Combine butter, brown sugar, cocoa powder and syrup in small pan. Stir over low heat until butter has melted and sugar has dissolved; remove from heat. Cool slightly and whisk in the egg.
4 Add butter mixture to dry ingredients. Stir with a metal spoon until well combined.
5 Spoon into prepared pan; smooth surface. Bake 30 minutes or until a skewer inserted into the center comes out clean. Cool.
6 Place chocolate in a glass bowl. Stir over barely simmering water until melted; remove from heat.
7 Drizzle chocolate over bars. Cut into rectangles.

CHOCOLATE-DIPPED FRUIT OR PETALS

Chocolate-dipped petals make very attractive decorations for cakes and desserts, and chocolate-dipped fruit is a delicious way to end a meal.

Melt 4 oz dark (semisweet) chocolate in a bowl over a pan of simmering water; cool slightly. Separate the petals of small roses or other edible flowers. Work with one petal at a time, dip into the chocolate to half-coat only—this gives a lovely effect. Drain excess chocolate. Place coated petals on a foil-lined tray, set aside to harden.

Dip strawberries or glacé fruit pieces in the same way; dip them fully, or half-dip for a different effect. Serve with coffee and liqueur.

ABOVE: SOUR CREAM AND CHOCOLATE TRIANGLES, WITH DATE AND CHOCOLATE FUDGE BARS. OPPOSITE, ABOVE: PISTACHIO PRALINE TRUFFLES; below: CHOCOLATE AND CREAMY BERRY ROULADE

CHOCOLATE AND CREAMY BERRY ROULADE

Preparation time: 30 minutes
Total cooking time: 12–15 minutes
Makes 1 roulade

2 oz dark (semisweet)
chocolate, chopped
4 eggs
1 cup sugar
1 teaspoon vanilla
2/3 cup all-purpose flour
1/2 teaspoon baking
powder

1/4 teaspoon baking soda
confectioners' sugar, sifted

Filling
1 cup heavy cream,
whipped
1 cup fresh raspberries,
halved

1 Preheat oven to 375°F. Brush a 15 x 10 x 1 inch jelly roll pan with melted butter or oil. Line base with waxed or parchment paper; grease paper.
2 Place the chocolate in a glass bowl. Stir over barely simmering water until melted; remove from heat.
3 Beat eggs with electric beaters until thick and pale, add sugar gradually, beating until pale yellow and glossy and all the sugar is dissolved. Beat in vanilla and chocolate. Sift together flour, baking powder and baking soda. Fold flour mixture into egg mixture quickly and lightly.
4 Spread mixture evenly into pan; smooth surface. Bake 12–15 minutes until cake springs back when lightly touched in center. Turn onto cloth towel sprinkled with powdered sugar; let stand 1 minute. Using the towel as a guide and starting with one of the long sides, carefully roll cake up with paper; cool. Unroll cake.
5 Spread cake with whipped cream, cover with fruit; re-roll. Trim ends of roll with serrated knife; dust with confectioners' sugar to serve.

PISTACHIO PRALINE TRUFFLES

Preparation time: 50 minutes +
15 minutes refrigeration
Total cooking time: 20 minutes
Makes 55

1/3 cup shelled pistachio
nuts
1/2 cup sugar
1/4 cup water
3 tablespoons unsalted
(sweet) butter, chopped

8 oz dark (semisweet)
chocolate, chopped
1/3 cup heavy cream
2 teaspoons brandy or
cognac
1/3 cup unsweetened cocoa
powder, sifted

1 Preheat oven to moderate 350°F. Place shelled pistachios in shallow cake pan. Bake 5–10 minutes or until nuts are lightly roasted; cool. Combine sugar and water in medium pan. Stir over low heat without boiling until sugar has dissolved. Brush sugar crystals from side of the pan with a wet pastry brush. Bring to boil, reduce heat and simmer 8–10 minutes or until syrup turns golden. Remove from heat, stir in nuts. Pour mixture onto an oiled, foil-lined tray.
2 Place butter and chocolate in medium heatproof bowl. Stand over pan of simmering water until mixture has melted and is smooth. Remove from heat; cool slightly. Add the cream and brandy, mix well; cool completely.
3 Using a meat mallet or rolling pin, finely crush hardened toffee. Add to chocolate mixture, mix well. Cover and refrigerate for 45 minutes or until firm enough to handle.
4 Roll teaspoonsful of mixture into small balls. Place on paper-lined tray and refrigerate for 15 minutes. Roll in sifted cocoa and serve.

tiny clams (*vongole*) are often part of pasta sauces; in Japan, clam broth is served at wedding banquets.

Clarify To clear a liquid of impurities or sediments. Stocks and broths are clarified for use as clear soups by whisking egg white into the cold liquid: as the mixture is heated the egg white coagulates, trapping any opaque particles in a scum on the top which can then be strained off.

Clove The fragrant, sun-dried flower-bud of an aromatic evergreen tree native to the Moluccas, or Spice Islands, of Indonesia. Cloves have a sweet, peppery aroma and a warm, fruity, slightly bitter flavor. Its use, both medicinal (it was believed to ward off the plague) and culinary (as a preservative of meat and a flavoring), was widespread in the Middle Ages. Cloves are used in stewed fruit, spiced cakes and breads, in pork and ham dishes, and sauces, pickles, chutneys, marinades, wines and liqueurs. They are available whole or ground as a powder.

Cobbler A baked fruit dessert with a crusty topping.

Cock-a-Leekie A thick Scottish soup of chicken pieces simmered in stock with chopped leek and thickened with barley.

Cocktail An alcoholic drink usually made from a mixture of spirits and liqueurs, often with fruit or vegetable juice, sometimes sweetened, and blended either by shaking the ingredients in a closed container or by stirring. A cocktail is usually served chilled as a pre-dinner drink. Non-alcoholic versions combine juices and carbonated drinks. The cocktail is probably an American invention.

Cocoa A dark brown powder made from seeds of the cacao, a tree native to tropical America. The seeds are roasted and ground into a paste of pure chocolate. Cocoa powder is ground from the dry solids left when the vegetable fat known as cocoa butter is removed.

Coconut A large round nut, the fruit of the coconut palm. Grown throughout the tropics, it is an important food,

CHUTNEYS

BANANA DATE CHUTNEY

★ **Preparation time:** 45 minutes
Total cooking time: 45 minutes
Makes 8 cups

2 lb bananas	1 cup orange juice
1 lb onions	1/2 cup lemon juice
12 oz pitted dates	1 tablespoon yellow
2 cloves garlic, crushed	mustard seeds
1 1/2 cups malt vinegar	5 whole cloves
1 1/2 cups golden raisins	1 teaspoon salt
2/3 cup drained preserved	1/4 teaspoon crushed red
ginger chopped	pepper flakes

1 Peel and mash bananas; chop the onions and dates coarsely.
2 In a large, heavy saucepan combine the mashed bananas, onions, dates, garlic and vinegar. Mix until thoroughly combined, heat until boiling. Reduce heat, cover and simmer for 20 minutes. Add the golden raisins, ginger, orange and lemon juice, mustard seeds, cloves, salt and red pepper flakes. Heat until boiling. Reduce heat and simmer, stirring frequently until the chutney has thickened, about 15–20 minutes.
3 Ladle into warm, sterilized jars and seal. When cool, label and date.

APPLE, TOMATO AND MINT CHUTNEY

★ ★ **Preparation time:** 1 hour
Total cooking time: 2 1/2 hours
Makes 6 cups

2 lb green apples	1 cup raisins
2 lb tomatoes	1/3 cup lemon juice
3 onions	3 cups brown sugar
2/3 cup mint leaves	2 teaspoons salt
1/2 cup parsley	2 cups cider vinegar
1/2 cup orange juice	

1 Wash, peel and finely chop the apples, tomatoes and onions. Finely chop fresh herbs.
2 Place all the ingredients together in a large saucepan. Bring slowly to boil and simmer for about 2 1/2 hours or until the mixture is thick, stirring occasionally.
3 Remove the cooked chutney from the heat and stand for 5 minutes. Spoon into warm, sterilized jars and seal immediately. When cool, label and date.

Note: Chutneys are delicious served with cold sliced meats, especially in sandwiches.

ABOVE: BANANA DATE CHUTNEY; APPLE, TOMATO AND MINT CHUTNEY. OPPOSITE PAGE: SPICY TORTILLA TRIANGLES

CILANTRO

SPICY CILANTRO LAMB

⭐ **Preparation time:** 10 minutes
Total cooking time: 1 hour 10 minutes
Serves 6

2 lb lamb shoulder chops	2 teaspoons ground cumin
1 tablespoon olive oil	1 teaspoon turmeric
2 small onions, chopped	1/3 cup finely chopped cilantro
2 cloves garlic, crushed	
1 tablespoon ground ginger	freshly ground black pepper to taste
1 tablespoon ground coriander	2 cups chicken stock

1 Trim the meat of any excess fat and tendons. Heat the oil in a large heavy-bottom pan. Cook the meat quickly, in small batches, over medium-high heat for two minutes or until it is well browned; drain the meat thoroughly on paper towels.
2 Add the onions and garlic to the pan and cook for two minutes or until they are browned. Stir in all the remaining ingredients except chicken stock.
3 Return the meat to the pan along with the chicken stock and bring to boil. Reduce the heat slightly and simmer, tightly covered, for about 1 hour or until the meat is tender. Serve with steamed rice.

POTATO AND CILANTRO SALAD

Cut 6 large potatoes, about 4 lb, into thick slices and cook in a large pan of boiling water until just tender; drain and place in a bowl. In a small bowl, whisk together 1/2 cup white wine vinegar, 1/3 cup olive oil, 1 clove garlic, crushed, 1 tablespoon finely shredded fresh ginger and 1 teaspoon finely sliced fresh red chili pepper for 2 minutes or until well combined. Pour mixture over potato, top with 1/2 cup chopped cilantro and serve immediately. Serves 4–6.

SPICY TORTILLA TRIANGLES

⭐ ⭐ **Preparation time:** 20 minutes
Cooking time: 10 minutes
Makes 24

2 x 9 inch flour tortillas	15 oz can pinto beans, drained, mashed coarsely
1/4 cup oil, approximately	
Topping	1 cup bottled thick and chunky salsa
1 tablespoon oil	
1 onion, finely chopped	2 tablespoons chopped cilantro
2 small red chili peppers, finely chopped	1/2 cup grated Cheddar cheese
2 cloves garlic, crushed	

1 Cut tortillas into quarters. Cut each quarter into 3 triangles. Heat 2 tablespoons of the oil in a frying pan. Add a few triangles to the pan, cook for 30 seconds each side or until crisp and golden. Remove from the pan, drain on paper towels. Repeat with remaining triangles, adding more oil if necessary.
2 To make Topping: Heat oil in a shallow pan, add onion, garlic and chili, stir over medium heat 3 minutes or until onion is tender. Stir in beans, salsa and cilantro. Remove from heat and cool.
3 Spread topping on triangles, sprinkle with cheese. Cook under preheated broiler for 1 minute or until the cheese has melted.

Note: Triangles can also be cooked in oven. Place on baking sheet in preheated moderate 350°F oven 5 minutes or until crisp. Add topping, cook 3–5 minutes or until cheese melts.

ABOUT CILANTRO

■ The chopped leaves of this pungent herb add a delightful freshness and fragrance to chicken, lamb and vegetable dishes. Also known as fresh coriander.

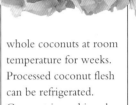

providing oil-rich white flesh and a refreshing liquid. The soft pulp of a young coconut can be eaten with a spoon and in some areas is the first solid food given to an infant. Processed coconut is canned and packaged shredded, flaked or grated. Store whole coconuts at room temperature for weeks. Processed coconut flesh can be refrigerated. Coconut is used in cakes, cookies and candy; it is often used in macaroons and custard pies.

Coconut Milk The liquid pressed from coconut flesh. It is used in many Asian dishes, especially curries. Coconut cream is made by chilling coconut milk then scooping off the surface "cream."

Cod A fish with moist, white, firm flesh that when cooked separates into large flakes. A cold water fish, it is abundant in the north Atlantic. Cod has been eaten since prehistoric times; in its dried form it provisioned the Vikings on their sea voyages. It was the first fish to be caught and salted commercially.

Coddle To cook an egg in the shell just below boiling point, until the white turns opaque and the yolk is heated.

COFFEE

Coffee, with its incomparable aroma, is one of the world's favorite beverages. It can be roasted, blended and brewed in a variety of ways, and served either hot or cold, black or enriched with milk or cream, sweetened with sugar or flavored with spices or alcohol.

COFFEE FROM LEFT:
CAFFÈ LATTE;
CAPPUCCINO; ICED
COFFEE; BLACK
COFFEE; CAFFÈ
MACCHIATO

BLENDS AND ROASTS

The type of bean, and the region, climate and soil in which it was grown, all affect coffee's flavor. Specialist coffee merchants select and blend beans from many parts of the world to produce subtle differences in flavor. The temperature at which the beans are roasted affects both the aroma and the taste of the coffee.

■ Light or pale roast enhances delicate, subtle flavors; this coffee is good with milk.

■ Medium roast gives a more distinctive flavor and aroma—good for daytime drinking, with or without milk.

■ Dark or full roast produces a strong aroma and flavor, suitable for after-dinner drinking and usually served black.

■ Double or continental roast has a powerful, smoky aroma. The beans are glossy and very dark in color and the coffee has an almost bitter taste. It is served black.

GRINDING COFFEE

Coffee can be bought as whole beans or ground, with a choice of coarse, medium, fine or superfine grinds; the latter is sometimes labelled "Espresso" or "Turkish" coffee. The type of grind depends on the brewing method to be used. Ground beans lose flavor faster than whole ones and should be ground just before use.

BREWING COFFEE

Despite the wide variety of equipment available, there are two basic methods of brewing coffee—infusion and boiling.

■ **PERCOLATOR**: Steam pressure forces boiling water up a central tube and over the grounds. This takes about 15 minutes. Use a coarse grind.

■ **PLUNGER POT** (*Cafetière*): Water is boiled, allowed to go just off the boil, then poured over grounds in a pot. A lid with attached plunger is put on and coffee allowed to infuse for several minutes before the plunger is slowly pushed down; grounds are held in the bottom of the pot while the coffee is poured. Use a medium grind.

■ **FILTER POTS**: A filter paper or gold filter fits into a holder on top of the pot (or cup); coffee is placed in the filter and just-past-boiling water is poured slowly over the grounds. The coffee filters down into the pot. Some have their own heating device. Use a fine grind.

INTERNATIONAL FAVORITES

■ **ESPRESSO** This very strong coffee (its name is Italian for "pressed out") is made in a machine which forces a combination of steam and water through very finely ground coffee. A high proportion of coffee is used—about 2 tablespoons of coffee to 6 tablespoons water. Traditionally served in a small cup with sugar to taste.

■ **CAPPUCCINO** This, too, is made in an espresso machine. The coffee is not quite as strong and is served in a larger cup, and is topped with hot milk which has been frothed by having steam passed through it. Grated chocolate, powder cocoa or cinnamon is often sprinkled on top.

■ **CAFFÈ MACCHIATO** Another Italian favorite. Fill a 3 oz glass with espresso to within ¼ inch of the rim. Add a small dash of cold milk by pouring down the side of the glass, forming a lighter, coffee-colored layer above the espresso. Place the filled glass on a saucer, accompanied by a small paper napkin.

■ **CAFFÈ LATTE** Italian breakfast coffee, made of equal parts espresso and hot milk. An 8 fl oz glass is half-filled with espresso and topped up with hot milk, which forms a slight froth on top. Serve on a saucer with a white paper napkin tied around the glass so it can be held without burning the hands.

■ **CAFÉ AU LAIT** An essential part of breakfast in France, this is strong black coffee and hot milk in equal proportions (sometimes 2 or 3 parts milk to 1 of coffee). The two are poured simultaneously into a large cup or bowl.

■ **TURKISH COFFEE** In Turkey, the Middle East and in Greece, rich, dark, sweet coffee is made in an *ibrik*, a small brass or copper pot with a long handle. For each small cup, place 1 heaped teaspoon of dark-roast coffee (pulverized to a fine powder), 2 fl oz cold water and 1 teaspoon sugar into the pot. Bring to boil over medium heat; remove from heat as soon as it froths up. Pour a little coffee into each cup, bring coffee back to the boil and again pour some into each cup; repeat a third time, making sure each cup has foam on top. Turkish coffee is traditionally drunk from tiny, stemmed cups; often a glass of iced water is offered with it.

■ **IRISH COFFEE** For each person, place 2 lumps (1 teaspoon) sugar and 1 measure 1½ fl oz Irish whiskey in a warm, tall stemmed glass, and fill two-thirds of the glass with hot, strong black coffee. Stir briefly and carefully add cream, pouring it over the back of a spoon so that it floats on the surface. Do not mix—drink the coffee and whiskey through the layer of cream.

■ **SPICED VIENNA COFFEE** Place 3 cups hot strong coffee, 2 cinnamon sticks, 4 cloves and 4 allspice berries in a pan; simmer over low heat for 10–15 minutes. Strain and pour into warmed wine glasses or mugs. Top with whipped cream, sprinkle with nutmeg. Sugar can be added. Or serve cold: omit cream and garnish with lemon.

■ **ICED COFFEE** Prepare strong black coffee and sweeten to taste while still hot. Cool and refrigerate. Pour some coffee into an ice-cube tray. To serve, pour chilled coffee into tall glasses, add a coffee ice cube, top with whipped cream.

■ **GRANITA DI CAFFÈ** This soft water ice, also known as *café frappé*, is a summer favorite in European bars. Prepare strong black coffee, sweeten to taste, cool and strain through a filter paper. Pour into a shallow tray, freeze until solid, then process briefly in a blender. Transfer the frozen granita to tall glasses, top with whipped cream and sprinkle with cocoa powder.

■ **HOT MOCHA JAVA** Mocha is a strongly flavored coffee, often combined with chocolate. Here, anise gives it a new twist. Combine zest of 1 orange and 1 lemon, 4 cinnamon sticks, ¼ cup chocolate syrup, 4 drops oil of anise and 8 cups strong, hot coffee. Steep over low heat for 15 minutes; strain and pour into demitasse cups. Add a lemon twist to each cup, top with whipped cream. Serves 12.

POINTS FOR SUCCESS
■ *Black coffee should be strong, clear and very hot. Use 1 to 1½ tablespoons of coffee per 6 oz of water. If weaker coffee is required, brew at normal strength, then dilute with hot water to taste.*
■ *Coffee kept for too long after brewing loses its flavor due to the formation of astringent and bitter residues.*
■ *Clean coffee pots thoroughly after use; oily residues can collect inside and turn rancid, tainting subsequent brews.*
■ *Buy coffee in quantities to last you not more than 2 weeks. Store it in a sealed container in the refrigerator.*

Coeur à la Crème A dessert of unripened fresh cheese, such as cream cheese, mixed with heavy cream and sometimes sugar, and drained in a perforated mold, traditionally heart-shaped—hence its name. It is served chilled with fresh fruit.

Coffee The roasted and ground beans of a tropical tree, made into a beverage and also used as a flavoring. The "beans" are the seeds of a red berry (two to each fruit); when roasted they develop the characteristic coffee aroma and flavor. The coffee tree, native to Ethiopia and Sudan, is now cultivated in New Guinea, the Americas and

Africa.
Drinking coffee did not become fashionable in Europe until the seventeenth century. Coffee is marketed in many forms: roasted beans, ground beans, granules or powder, with added flavors and decaffeinated. Coffee is made using infusion or boiling methods: vacuum, drip percolation and steeping.

Colby A soft-textured yellow cow's milk cheese similar to Cheddar. It has a mild, sweet flavor and tiny holes.

COCONUTS

COCONUT FISH CURRY

Preparation time: 20 minutes
Total cooking time: 20 minutes
Serves 4–6

1 lb 5 oz thick white fish fillets
2 teaspoons lemon juice
1 teaspoon cumin seeds
½ teaspoon fennel seeds
½ cup shredded coconut
2 dried red chili peppers, soaked for 15 minutes in hot water
2 cloves garlic
¾ inch piece ginger, chopped
1 medium onion
¾ teaspoon turmeric
2 teaspoons tamarind concentrate (see Note)
2 tablespoons butter
1½ cups water
2 tablespoons chopped cilantro

1 Cut across the fillets to make thick slices. Sprinkle with lemon juice and set aside.
2 Toast cumin, fennel seeds and coconut in a dry pan until lightly golden and aromatic. Grind to a powder in a spice grinder or mortar.
3 Grind chili peppers, garlic, ginger and onion to a paste; add ground spices, turmeric and tamarind.
4 Fry mixture in butter for 1½–2 minutes, stirring. Add water, bring to boil. Simmer for 6 minutes.
5 Add fish with half the cilantro. Simmer gently until fish is tender, about 6 minutes. Serve with rice, garnishing with the remaining cilantro.

Note: If tamarind concentrate is not available, use a tablespoon of lemon juice for tartness.

COCONUT MACAROONS

Preparation time: 15 minutes
Total cooking time: 15–20 minutes
Makes 60

3 egg whites
1⅓ cups sugar
1 teaspoon grated lemon rind
3 tablespoons cornstarch
3 cups sweetened grated coconut
¾ cup dark (semisweet) chocolate pieces, melted

1 Preheat oven to moderately slow 325°F. Line two baking sheets with parchment paper or foil.
2 Place egg whites in a small dry mixing bowl. Using electric beaters, beat egg whites on high speed until soft peaks form. Add sugar gradually, beating on medium speed until stiff peaks form and sugar is dissolved. Add lemon rind; beat until just combined. Combine cornstarch and coconut; fold into egg white mixture.
3 Drop rounded teaspoonfuls onto prepared baking sheets, about 2 inches apart. Bake 15–20 minutes or until golden.
4 Cool macaroons on baking sheet. When cool, dip half of each macaroon into melted chocolate; place on wire rack to harden.

Note: For grated coconut, place flakes of shredded coconut in food processor bowl and process until grated. If desired, drizzle with melted chocolate instead of dipping.

ABOUT COCONUT

■ Traditionally coconut milk was made by grating fresh coconut into a bowl, adding hot water and straining it. It is much easier to use shredded coconut (make sure it's unsweetened) and easiest of all is to open a can of coconut milk.
■ Coconut cream is the thick layer that forms on top of the milk after it has been left to stand in the refrigerator.

COOKIES

MONTE CREAMS

★ **Preparation time:** 35 minutes
Total cooking time: 10–12 minutes
Makes 20

½ cup butter
⅔ cup sugar
1 egg
1 teaspoon vanilla extract
2 cups all-purpose flour
1 teaspoon baking powder

Filling
¼ cup butter
½ teaspoon vanilla
1 cup confectioners' sugar
1 tablespoon milk
3 tablespoons raspberry
    jam

1 Preheat oven to 350°F. Beat the butter with an electric mixer until softened. Add the sugar and beat until fluffy. Add the egg and vanilla and beat until well combined. Stir in the flour and baking powder and mix until well combined.
2 Shape the dough into 1 inch balls. Place 2 inches apart on greased baking sheet. Flatten with the tines of a fork. Bake 10–12 minutes or until golden brown. Cool on wire racks.
3 To make Filling: In a small bowl beat the butter and vanilla until softened. Gradually add the confectioners sugar, beating until well combined. Beat in as much milk as necessary to make the filling a spreading consistency.

ABOVE: MONTE CREAMS; RIGHT: CHOCOLATE CHIP COOKIES. OPPOSITE, ABOVE: COCONUT MACAROONS; BELOW: COCONUT FISH CURRY

4 Spread filling over the flat side of one cookie, and jam over the flat side of another, press the two together to form a sandwich. Repeat with remaining cookies, filling and jam. Store in an airtight container.

CHOCOLATE CHIP COOKIES

★ **Preparation time:** 30 minutes
Total cooking time: 12 minutes
Makes 24

½ cup unsalted butter
½ cup sugar
⅓ cup light brown sugar,
    firmly packed
1 egg yolk
1 teaspoon vanilla extract
1½ cups all-purpose flour
¾ teaspoon baking powder
¼ teaspoon baking soda
1 cup (6 oz package)
    semisweet chocolate
    pieces

1 Preheat oven to moderate 350°F.
2 Beat together the butter, sugars and egg yolk in a large bowl until light and creamy. Add the vanilla and beat until combined. Mix together the flour, baking powder, soda and salt. Stir into the butter mixture. Stir in ¾ cup of the chocolate pieces. Stir or shape with hands until the dough forms a ball.
3 Shape into 1¼ inch balls. Arrange on an ungreased baking sheet about 3 inches apart. Press the remaining chocolate pieces firmly into the top of the balls. Bake for 12–15 minutes or until the cookies are lightly browned. Remove to a wire rack to cool.

Colcannon An Irish dish of cooked cabbage, onion and mashed potato, beaten with butter and hot milk.

Coleslaw A salad of shredded cabbage, carrot, celery and peppers dressed in mayonnaise.

Compote A preparation of fresh, canned or dried fruits, poached in syrup to preserve their shape and served·hot or cold in the syrup as a dessert.

Condensed Milk A thick, creamy, sweetened canned milk.

Confectioners' Sugar (Powdered Sugar) Fine sugar used for icings.

Confit A piece of duck, goose or pork which has been preserved by simmering in its own fat.

Conserve Whole berries or sliced fruit preserved by boiling with sugar. It is richer and sweeter than jam and, unlike jam, the pieces of fruit retain their shape. It is used as a spread or filling.

Consommé A rich, clear soup made of reduced and clarified stock. It can be served hot or cold.

Cookie A small, sweet, cake-like bread, which can be crisp or soft, made with baking powder or soda. In England and Australia cookies are called *biscuits* and in Italy they are called *biscotti*. The name comes from the French *bis* (twice) and *cuit* (cooked), because they were originally returned to the oven to make them crisper, thus improving their storage properties. There are six basic types of cookie: drop, bar, molded, pressed, refrigerator and rolled.

Coq au Vin Chicken cooked in red wine. Since the dish was traditionally made with a rooster which was at least twelve months old, the wine was needed to tenderize the meat.

Coquilles St. Jacques A dish in which poached scallops are returned to their shells and served topped with a rich sauce.

Coriander (Cilantro) An annual herb, a member of the carrot family, which has green, lacy leaves and a pungent flavor. Also known as Chinese parsley.

MELTING MOMENTS

⭐ **Preparation time:** 30 minutes
Total cooking time: 12 minutes
Makes 30

3/4 cup unsalted butter	*1 1/4 cups all-purpose*
1/2 cup confectioners'	*flour*
sugar, sifted	*1/2 cup cornstarch*
1 teaspoon vanilla extract	*8 oz candied cherries,*
	halved

1 Preheat oven to moderate 350°F. Lightly grease a baking sheet with melted butter or oil, or line with parchment paper or foil.
2 Beat the butter, sugar and vanilla until creamy. Sift together the flour and cornstarch; stir into butter mixture.
3 Spoon the mixture into a cookie press or piping bag fitted with a 1/4–1/2 inch fluted piping tip. Pipe the mixture into 1/2 inch diameter rosettes on the prepared baking sheet, about 2 inches apart.
4 Top each rosette with a half a candied cherry. Bake for 10–12 minutes or until the cookies are lightly golden and crisp. Transfer to a wire rack to cool.

Note: Try adding small pieces of crystallized ginger or nuts in place of the cherries. Another option is to sandwich together two Melting Moments, without cherries, with raspberry jam. Decorate with sifted confectioners' sugar. Drizzle melted chocolate over the cookies, or dip them in chocolate.

SLICED ALMOND TUILES

⭐⭐⭐ **Preparation time:** 8 minutes + 2 hours standing
Total cooking time: 5 minutes each tray
Makes 22

3/4 cup plain flour	*1/4 teaspoon almond*
2/3 cup sugar	*extract*
1/4 cup unsalted butter,	*2/3 cup toasted sliced*
melted	*almonds*
2 egg whites, lightly	
beaten	

1 In a medium bowl stir together the flour and sugar. Make a well in the center. Add melted butter, egg whites and almond extract; stir until well combined. Cover the mixture with plastic wrap; allow to rest for 30 minutes.

ABOVE: MELTING MOMENTS.
OPPOSITE PAGE: FLORENTINES

2 Preheat the oven to 350°F. Line two baking sheets with parchment paper or foil. Lightly grease the paper or foil. Drop rounded teaspoons of the mixture onto the prepared baking sheets and spread each to a 4–4½ inch circle. Sprinkle with sliced almonds.

3 Bake for 5 minutes or until lightly golden. Remove from the oven. Let the cookies remain on the baking sheet for 30 seconds, then carefully loosen then and lift them from baking sheet. Shape the cookies over a bottle or rolling pin, almond-side up.

FLORENTINES

★★ **Preparation time:** 25 minutes
Total cooking time: 7 minutes
each batch
Makes 24

⅓ cup all-purpose flour
3 tablespoons finely
chopped walnuts
3 tablespoons finely
chopped sliced almonds
3 tablespoons finely
chopped candied
cherries

3 tablespoons finely
chopped candied mixed
peel
¼ cup unsalted butter
⅓ cup light brown sugar,
firmly packed
1 cup semisweet chocolate
pieces
1 tablespoon shortening

1 Preheat oven to moderate 350°F. Line a baking sheet with parchment paper. Lightly grease paper.
2 In a medium bowl combine the flour, walnuts, almonds, cherries and mixed peel. Stir to combine and make a well in the center.
3 In a small saucepan combine butter and sugar. Stir over a low heat until butter has melted and sugar has dissolved; remove from heat. Add the butter mixture to the dry ingredients. Using a wooden spoon, stir until just combined; do not overbeat. Drop rounded teaspoonfuls of the mixture onto the prepared baking sheets, leaving about 3 inches between each one. Flatten each to a 2 inch round. Bake for 7 minutes. While still soft, use a flat-bladed knife or the back of a spoon to push the cookies into 3 inch wide rounds. Cool on the baking sheet for 5 minutes; transfer to a wire rack to cool thoroughly.
4 Melt the chocolate and shortening in a double boiler or in a small bowl over hot water. Stir until the chocolate is completely melted and smooth. Carefully spread the chocolate on the underside of the Florentines. Place chocolate-side up on a wire rack until the has chocolate hardened.

Note: Florentines are best made on the day of serving. For a variation, try white chocolate instead of semisweet.

Corn (Maize, Sweet Corn) The round, yellow or white kernels borne on long, cone-shaped "ears," encased in a fine silk and green husk. The plant is native to the Americas. First domesticated more than 7,000 years ago in Mexico. Corn is available from late spring to late summer. Frozen ears (cobs) are sold, and the kernels are canned and frozen, alone or with mixed vegetables. Use fresh corn as soon as possible, or store it in its husk for up to two days.

Corn Bread Bread made from cornmeal and flour, leavened with baking powder. Corn pone is a similar bread that is fried.

Corned Beef A cut of beef brisket which has been preserved (cured) by soaking and injecting

with brine. This causes the flesh to turn pink. Cooked corned beef is served hot, with vegetables and an onion sauce; or is eaten cold, sliced as a salad meat.

Cornish Hen (Cornish Game Hen, Cornish Rock Hen) A specially bred small tender chicken.

Cornish Pasty A mixture of finely chopped meat and vegetables in a turnover of short-crust pastry. It originated in Cornwall as a meal for tin miners. Often a savory filling was placed in one end of the pastry and an apple mixture was placed in the other.

Cornmeal A yellow-white flour made from finely ground dried corn kernels. Cornmeal is an important food in Italy (polenta), the United States and Latin America. It is used to make cornbread, muffins and as a coating for fried food. It is available in three textures: fine, medium and coarse.

Cornstarch A fine white powder obtained from corn kernels, used to thicken sauces, gravies and puddings.

Corn Syrup See Syrup.

Cottage Cheese A soft, fresh, lowfat, mild-flavored

cheese. It is made from cow's milk curds. Creamed cottage cheese is made from washed curds.

GINGERBREAD FAMILIES

★★ **Preparation time:** 30 minutes + 15 minutes refrigeration
Total cooking time: 10 minutes
Makes 16

1/2 cup unsalted butter
1/2 cup dark brown sugar, firmly packed
1/3 cup dark corn syrup
1 egg, lightly beaten
2 1/2 cups all-purpose flour
1 tablespoon ground ginger
1 teaspoon baking powder

1/2 teaspoon baking soda
1 tablespoon currants

Icing
1 1/3 cups confectioners' sugar, sifted
1/2 teaspoon lemon juice
1–2 tablespoons milk
assorted food colorings

1 Preheat oven to moderate 350°F. Lightly grease two baking sheets; set aside.

2 Beat the butter, sugar and syrup in a mixing bowl until light and creamy. Add the egg; beat well. Sift together the flour, ginger, baking powder and baking soda; add to the butter mixture. Stir until well blended. Turn the dough onto a well-floured surface and knead for 1–2 minutes or until smooth. Wrap dough and chill 15 minutes.

3 On a floured surface, roll the dough to 1/8–1/4 inch thickness (dust the folling pin with flour if necessary to prevent sticking).

4 Cut the dough into shapes with a 4–5 inch gingerbread man cutter. Press the remaining dough together and roll it out again. Cut out shapes. Place the gingerbread shapes on the prepared baking sheets. Position the currants as eyes and noses on the gingerbread family. Bake for about 10 minutes or until set and lightly browned. Allow to cool for 1 minute on the baking sheets. Remove to a wire rack to cool completely.

5 To make Icing: In a mixing bowl combine the confectioners' sugar, the lemon juice and 1 tablespoon milk. Stir in enough of the remaining milk to make the desired consistency. Divide the icing and add food coloring as desired. Using a pastry bag with small tip (or small plastic bag with a corner snipped off) pipe faces and clothing onto the gingerbread family, decorating as desired.

Note: When the icing is completely dry, gingerbread families may be stored in an airtight container for up to 3 days.

RIGHT: GINGERBREAD FAMILIES

Coulibiac A pie of Russian origin filled with salmon, rice, eggs, mushrooms and seasonings.

Coulis A liquid purée of cooked vegetables or of cooked or fresh fruit.

Court Bouillon An aromatic mixture of water, stock and a dash of vinegar, wine or lemon juice, spices, herbs and chopped vegetables, in which fish or shellfish is poached. Food cooked in the broth absorbs the flavors.

Couscous A cereal made from semolina and wheat flour pressed into tiny bead-like grains. It is cooked in water or stock until soft, then butter is added and it is served hot as a side dish, or as part of a dish of stewed meat. Couscous is a staple in the cooking of North Africa.

Crab Species vary in color when alive but when

cooked all turn red-orange; the flesh is white, moist and sweet. Found in sheltered coastal water, crabs can purchased fresh, frozen or in cans.

Crab Apple A small, sour-tasting apple, with a rosy red skin and very hard white flesh. Crab apples are used to make jellies and preserves. They make a delicious accompaniment to pork and poultry.

Cracked Wheat Whole-wheat grains that are soaked, cooked, dried and then crushed.

Cracker A bite-size, thin, dry, baked product.

Cracklings The crisp, brown skin of roast pork, eaten as a snack.

Cranberry A small, tart, red berry used in cranberry sauce, the classic accompaniment to roast turkey. Cranberries can be added to muffins and breads.

Crayfish (Crawfish) A freshwater crustacean that looks like a tiny lobster and tastes like shrimp. Most of the meat is in the tail and when cooked is white, sweet and moist.

Cream The fatty part of milk which rises to the top when milk is allowed to stand. It is made into butter and many varieties of cheese, and used on its own as an accompaniment to fruits and desserts, as a filling for cakes and pastries, or to add richness to sauces, soups and custards.

Whipping, double or heavy cream is the

CORN

HOT CHILI CORN

★ **Preparation time:** 30 minutes
Total cooking time: 10 minutes
Serves 6

3 whole ears of corn, sliced in 1¼ inch rounds
2 tablespoons butter, melted
1 tablespoon tomato paste

2 tablespoons chopped cilantro
¼ teaspoon chili powder, or to taste
sour cream, to serve

1 Half fill a large pan with water. Bring to the boil and add corn. Reduce heat, simmer until corn is tender, about 10 minutes. Drain.
2 Combine butter, tomato paste, cilantro and chili powder in a large bowl. Add hot corn. Mix well. Serve immediately with a dollop of sour cream.

CORN AND BACON HOTPOT

★ **Preparation time:** 20 minutes
Total cooking time: 25 minutes
Serves 4

8 oz thickly sliced bacon
2 onions, sliced
1 clove garlic, crushed
14½ oz can tomatoes

4 small potatoes, sliced
freshly ground pepper
4 fresh or frozen ears of corn

1 In a heavy saucepan cook bacon until crisp. Drain on paper towels, reserve drippings. Add onions and garlic to drippings and cook until tender. Stir in undrained tomatoes, potatoes, pepper, and bacon. Cover and simmer for 15 minutes.
2 Cut corn into 1 inch pieces. Add vegetable mixture, adding vegetable broth or water, if necessary. Cover; cook 10 minutes or until the corn is tender.

CORN AND CRABMEAT SOUP

★ **Preparation time:** 20 minutes
Total cooking time: 10 minutes
Serves 4–6

2 cups frozen or canned corn kernels
3½ oz crabmeat
1 scallion, finely chopped
2 teaspoons chicken bouillon powder

3½ cups water
3 tablespoons cornstarch
1½ tablespoons soy sauce
2 tablespoons chopped scallion greens to garnish

1 Thaw or drain the corn. Chop the corn in a food processor until partially ground.
2 Mix the corn, crabmeat and white parts of the scallion in a saucepan, add the bouillon powder, water, and cornstarch. Bring to boil and simmer, stirring, until thickened.
3 Season with soy sauce. Pour into soup bowls and garnish with the scallion greens.

CORNED BEEF WITH ONION SAUCE AND HORSERADISH CREAM

★ **Preparation time:** 5 minutes
Total cooking time: 1 hour 45 minutes
Serves 6–8

3 lb piece corned beef
    brisket
1 tablespoon oil
1 tablespoon white vinegar
1 tablespoon soft brown
    sugar
4 whole cloves
4 whole black peppercorns
2 bay leaves
1 clove garlic, crushed
1 large sprig parsley
4 medium carrots
4 medium potatoes,
    about 1½ lb
6 small onions

Onion Sauce
2 tablespoons butter
2 medium white onions,
    chopped
3 tablespoons all-purpose
    flour
1⅓ cups milk

Horseradish Cream
3 tablespoons prepared
    horseradish
1 tablespoon white vinegar
black pepper, to taste
½ cup heavy cream,
    whipped

1 Trim meat of excess fat and tendons. Heat oil in a deep, heavy-bottom pan. Add meat, cook over medium-high heat, turning until browned. Remove pan from heat; add vinegar, sugar, cloves, peppercorns, bay leaves, garlic and parsley.

OPPOSITE, ABOVE: HOT CHILI CORN; BELOW: CORN AND BACON HOTPOT. ABOVE: CORNED BEEF WITH ONION SAUCE AND HORSERADISH CREAM

2 Pour over enough water to cover. Return to heat. Reduce heat, cover pan and bring slowly to simmering point. Simmer for 30 minutes. Cut carrots and potatoes into large pieces; add to pan with onions and simmer, covered, for 1 hour or until tender. Remove vegetables with a slotted spoon and keep warm. Reserve ½ cup liquid to make Onion Sauce.

3 Remove meat from pan and discard remaining liquid and spices. Carve the meat into slices and serve with vegetables, Onion Sauce and Horseradish Cream.

4 To make Onion Sauce: Heat butter in a small pan. Add the onion and cook gently for 10 minutes or until soft but not browned. Transfer onion to a bowl. Add flour to the butter left in pan; stir over low heat for 2 minutes or until the flour is lightly golden. Gradually add milk and the ½ cup of reserved liquid to the pan; stir until sauce boils and thickens. Boil for 1 minute; remove from heat and stir in the cooked onion. Season to taste.

5 To make Horseradish Cream: Combine all ingredients until smooth.

ABOUT CORNED BEEF

■ Corned beef is a cured meat with a strong, rosy pink color. It is sold, ready to cook, by butchers or the meat department of most supermarkets. The meat is usually simmered in a clove-and-onion-flavored stock.

■ Cooked corned beef can also be purchased from the deli counter as a cold cut of meat and is ideal for sandwiches and salads.

richest form, with a high fat content. Whipping cream incorporates air into the fat, and gives the cream a lighter texture. Half-and-half and light cream have a lower fat content and are often served with coffee.

Cream Cheese A soft, white, fresh cheese that is made from cream or a mixture of milk and cream. It is smoother in texture and has a higher fat content than cottage cheese.

Cream of Tartar A white powder made by fermenting grape juice and used as a leavening agent.

Cream Pie A single crust pudding or custard-filled pie.

Crème Brûlée A rich baked custard topped with a shell of hard, caramelized sugar.

Crème Caramel A vanilla-flavored baked custard coated with thick caramel sauce.

Crème Chantilly Sweetened whipped cream which has been flavored with vanilla extract.

Crème Fraîche A mature cream with a nutty, slightly sour flavor. It is available in cartons or can be made by mixing pure fresh heavy cream with sour cream, yogurt or buttermilk. Crème fraîche is used in sauces for game, poultry, fish and vegetables; in salad dressings; as a garnish for soups; and in candy.

Crème Pâtissière
A stirred custard lightened with whipped egg whites. Flavored with coffee or chocolate,

it is the traditional filling for éclairs, or, flavored with vanilla or orange, it is used to fill cream puffs.

Crenshaw Melon A smooth, oval melon with orange and green skin and moist pinkish flesh.

Crêpe A light, thin pancake made with a batter of milk, eggs and flour, cooked on each side until golden. They can be filled with sweet or savory ingredients.

Cress Any of several plants of the mustard family. Eaten while still seedlings, their tiny leaves and slender stems give a peppery flavor to salads and sandwich fillings, and can be used as a garnish for meat.

Croissant A soft, flaky, buttery, crescent-shaped roll of yeast dough, baked until crisp and

CRAB

CRAB IN BLACK BEAN SAUCE

★ *Preparation time:* 40 minutes
Total cooking time: 10 minutes
Serves 4

4 fresh crabs
1 medium onion
½ red pepper
½ green pepper
2 scallions
½ cup oil
1 tablespoon finely chopped salted black beans

1 teaspoon finely chopped garlic
1 teaspoon finely chopped ginger
1 teaspoon sugar
⅓ cup water
1 tablespoon soy sauce
2 teaspoons cornstarch

1 Cut crabs in half, then in half again. Crack large claws with a mallet. Devein; remove fibrous tissue. Rinse crabs; pat dry.

2 Cut onion, peppers, and scallions into 3 inch strips. Heat wok over high heat. Add oil.
3 Shallow-fry crab in hot oil for 3 minutes. Drain. Strain oil and return 2 tablespoons to wok. Stir-fry black beans, garlic and ginger for 30 seconds. Add the sugar and vegetables. Stir-fry for 2 minutes.
4 Add the crab. Combine soy sauce, water and cornstarch and add to wok. Cook until sauce boils and thickens. Remove from heat. Serve immediately.

ABOUT CRAB

■ Both fresh and saltwater crabs are available whole (cooked or live), as cooked lumpmeat, or flaked meat. Dungeness, King, Snow, and Blue Crab are the major varieties. Live crabs should be eaten the day they are purchased. Cook raw crabmeat within 24 hours after crab dies. Crabmeat is available frozen, canned or vacuum packed.

CHILI CRAB AND SOFT NOODLES

★ **Preparation time:** 20 minutes
Total cooking time: 7–10 minutes
Serves 4–6

10–12 large Chinese
   cabbage leaves
2 tablespoons oil
6½ oz egg noodles, cooked
   and cooled
2 teaspoons grated ginger
1 clove garlic, chopped
6½ oz crabmeat pieces

1 bunch asparagus, cut
   into 1½ inch lengths,
   cooked
1 cup bamboo shoots
1 red pepper, thinly sliced
   into strips
1 tablespoon oil
2 tablespoons soy sauce
1 teaspoon chili sauce

1 Plunge cabbage leaves one at a time into boiling water for 30 seconds, remove and place into iced water. Remove and pat dry on a clean towel.
2 Heat oil in large pan, add noodles and cook for 3–4 minutes, remove and set aside. Remove oil from pan, add ginger, garlic and crabmeat, stir 2–3 minutes. Remove, add to noodles.
3 Add asparagus, bamboo shoots and red pepper to mixture. Combine oil, soy sauce and chili sauce, add to noodle mixture and toss well.
4 Place cabbage leaves on a large serving dish, with crab and noodle mixture in serving bowl. Guests can fill and roll their own cabbage leaves. Serve with Asian Sweet Chilli Sauce if desired.

OPPOSITE PAGE: CRAB IN BLACK BEAN SAUCE.
ABOVE: CHILI CRAB AND SOFT NOODLES;
RIGHT: CRAB CAKES WITH HOT SALSA

CRAB CAKES WITH HOT SALSA

★ **Preparation time:** 30 minutes +
30 minutes refrigeration +
1 hour standing
Total cooking time: 5–6 minutes
each batch
Serves 6

3½ oz vermicelli, broken
   into 3 inch lengths
1¼ lb crabmeat
2 tablespoons finely
   chopped fresh parsley
1 small red pepper,
   chopped
¼ cup finely grated
   Parmesan cheese
¼ cup all-purpose flour
2 scallions, finely chopped
freshly ground black
   pepper, to taste
2 eggs, lightly beaten

2–3 tablespoons oil, for
   frying

Hot Salsa
2 large ripe tomatoes
1 medium onion, finely
   chopped
2 cloves garlic, crushed
1 teaspoon dried oregano
   leaves
2 tablespoons sweet chili
   sauce
1 serrano chili pepper,
   finely chopped

1 Cook vermicelli in boiling water until just cooked; drain. In a large bowl, combine noodles, crabmeat, parsley, red pepper, Parmesan cheese, flour, scallions and pepper. Add egg; mix well.
2 Shape mixture into 12 flat patties; refrigerate 30 minutes. Heat oil in large heavy-bottom pan; cook crab cakes a few at a time over medium-high heat until golden brown. Serve with Hot Salsa.
3 **To make Hot Salsa:** Combine all ingredients in small bowl. Stand at room temperature 1 hour.

golden and served warm as part of a traditional French breakfast. Croissants can be eaten on their own or split open and spread with butter and jam. They can also be filled with ham, cheese, mushrooms or chicken.

Croque Monsieur A hot sandwich of a firm-textured mild cheese and ham between slices of toasted bread.

Croquembouche A pastry made up of a number of choux puffs, filled with cream piled into a cone shape, glazed with toffee and topped with sugar.

Croquette A small patty or ball of ground meat, poultry, fish or shellfish bound with a thick white sauce, coated with bread crumbs and deep-fried.

Crostini Slices of bread that are toasted, fried, or dipped in broth, then spread with a savory topping such as pâté.

Croustade A case made out of fried, hollowed bread, puff pastry or potato shell, used to hold preparations of cooked meat or vegetables.

Croûte A small, thick slice of bread, fried in butter or oil or dried in the oven, which is served with soup, casseroles or mornays.

Croûte, en The French term for food cooked, wrapped or encased in pastry or dough.

Croûtons Small cubes of bread that have been fried or toasted. They can be served as an accompaniment to soup or salads.

Crown Roast Two racks of lamb or pork ribs curved around and secured in the shape of a crown. The center is usually filled with stuffing.

Crudités Raw vegetables cut into bite-size pieces and served as finger food accompanied by dips and cold sauces.

Cucumber The crisp, juicy, pale-fleshed fruit of a vine. The thin skin does not require peeling. Cucumbers can be eaten raw, as a salad vegetable, as well as cooked or

CUCUMBERS

BREAD AND BUTTER CUCUMBERS

★ ***Preparation time:*** 30 minutes + overnight standing
Total cooking time: 10 minutes
Makes 8 cups

3 long, thin-skinned	1/2 cup hot water
cucumbers	2 teaspoons salt
salt	2 teaspoons mustard
2 cups white vinegar	seeds
3 tablespoons sugar	1 red pepper, thinly sliced

1 Cut washed, unpeeled cucumbers into very thin slices. Layer cucumbers in large bowl and sprinkle lightly with salt between layers. Cover and stand overnight.
2 Rinse cucumbers under cold water; drain well. Place vinegar, sugar, hot water, salt and mustard seeds in large saucepan or boiler. Bring to the boil, stirring until sugar is dissolved. Simmer, uncovered, for 5 minutes.
3 Add cucumber slices to pan and bring back to the boil. Remove from heat.
4 Using tongs, pack the cucumber slices into warm, sterilized jars. Add a few strips of pepper to each jar. Pour the hot vinegar mixture into the jars to cover the cucumbers. Seal the jars; cool. Label and date.

Note: Serve Bread and Butter Cucumbers with salads, or add to sandwich fillings or dips. They are also good served on crackers with cheese and can be used with chicken or steak as a relish.

CUCUMBER AND FENNEL WITH DILL

★ ***Preparation time:*** 20 minutes
Total cooking time: 10 minutes
Serves 4-6

1 tablespoon olive oil	1/3 cup chopped fresh dill
1 fennel bulb, washed,	freshly ground pepper
trimmed and sliced	2 oz roasted hazelnuts,
1 large cucumber, peeled,	coarsely chopped
halved, seeds removed	
and sliced	

1 Heat oil in a large shallow pan. Add the sliced fennel, then cover and cook over a gentle heat until fennel is just tender.
2 Add the cucumber and cook over gentle heat for 3–4 minutes. Scatter dill over top, and some freshly ground pepper. Shake the pan to combine ingredients.
3 Place on a serving plate and garnish with roasted hazelnuts. Serve.

CUCUMBER RELISH

★ ***Preparation time:*** 15 minutes + overnight standing
Total cooking time: 1 hour
Makes 4 cups

2 1/2 lb cucumbers	10 oz can corn kernels,
2 tablespoons salt	drained
1 red pepper	2 teaspoons brown
1 green pepper	mustard seeds
1 medium onion	1 cup white vinegar
2 teaspoons celery seeds	1 1/2 cups sugar

1 Slice the cucumbers thinly. Place in a large bowl, sprinkle with salt, cover with dry cloth and stand overnight. Dice the red and green peppers and chop the onion finely. Drain the cucumbers, rinse thoroughly in cold water then drain again.
2 Place the marinated cucumbers, peppers, onion, celery seeds, corn kernels, mustard seeds, vinegar and sugar in a large saucepan. Bring to boil, reduce the heat and simmer for 1 hour or until the mixture is thick, stirring occasionally.
3 Remove from heat. Spoon the relish into warm, sterilized jars and seal. When cool, label and date.

Note: Store relish in a dry place for up to 1 month. Refrigerate after opening.

ABOVE: BREAD AND BUTTER CUCUMBERS.
OPPOSITE PAGE: QUICK CHICKEN CURRY

CURRIES

BEEF CURRY WITH POTATOES

⭐ **Preparation time:** 15 minutes
Total cooking time: 1 hour 30 minutes
Serves 4

2 lb boneless chuck steak
2 tablespoons oil
³/₄ cup coconut milk
¹/₂ cup water
1 tablespoon tamarind sauce
1 lb baby potatoes, halved

Spice Paste
2 scallions, chopped
2 cloves garlic, chopped

2 teaspoons grated lemon rind
2 small red chili peppers, chopped
2 teaspoons ground coriander
2 teaspoons ground cumin
1 teaspoon turmeric
¹/₂ teaspoon ground cardamom
1 teaspoon garam masala

1 Trim meat of excess fat and tendons. Cut the meat evenly into 1 inch cubes. Heat the oil in a heavy-based pan. Cook the meat quickly in small batches over medium-high heat until well browned; drain on paper towels.

2 To make Spice Paste: Combine all the ingredients in a food processor or blender, process one minute or until very finely chopped.

3 Add the Paste to the pan, stir over medium heat for 2 minutes. Return the meat to the pan with the coconut cream, water and tamarind sauce; bring to boil. Reduce the heat slightly and simmer, covered, for about 30 minutes, stirring occasionally.

4 Add potato, cook for another 30 minutes or until the meat is tender and the liquid has almost evaporated.

QUICK CHICKEN CURRY

⭐ **Preparation time:** 10 minutes
Total cooking time: 50 minutes
Serves 4

1¹/₂ lb boned chicken thighs
3 tablespoons ghee or oil
1 large onion, halved and thinly sliced
1 teaspoon mashed garlic
1¹/₂ teaspoons grated ginger
1 cinnamon stick
2 bay leaves

2 cloves
2 cardamom pods
2 dried chili peppers
1 tablespoon ground coriander
2 teaspoons garam masala
¹/₂ teaspoon turmeric pepper
lemon juice
lemon slices, for garnish

1 Brown the chicken pieces in ghee or oil, then set aside.

2 Fry the onion until golden, add the garlic, ginger, cinnamon, bay leaves, cloves, cardamom and chili peppers. Fry for 2 minutes, stirring. Add the ground spices and pepper.

3 Return the chicken to the pan and add water to barely cover. Cover the pan and simmer for about 40 minutes until the chicken is very tender.

4 Add lemon juice to taste. Garnish with lemon slices and serve with rice and chutney.

Note: This curry is delicious when first made, but improves in flavor if made a day ahead. Store, covered, in the refrigerator.

ACCOMPANIMENTS

■ Curries, particularly Indian curries, are complemented with chutneys, relishes or pickles: sweet to go with a hot dish, fiery to pep up a mild dish, and crunchy with a smooth dish. Try the ideas below, or any of the great Indian relishes, such as mango chutney or lime pickle, available bottled.

■ Peel a large cucumber, halve it vertically, scoop out seeds and coarsely grate it into a bowl. Sprinkle on about 1 teaspoon salt and let stand for 5 minutes. Drain off the accumulated liquid. Stir in ¹/₂ cup plain yogurt and 1 tablespoon finely chopped mint. Add a sprinkling of cumin seeds.

■ Combine 1 cup plain yogurt with ¹/₂ cup cream, stir in ¹/₂ teaspoon finely chopped red chili peppers and a pinch of salt. Peel and chop two bananas into small pieces, stir into the yogurt mixture.

■ Finely chop 1 red onion. Chop 2 ripe tomatoes, combine with onion. Add salt, chili powder and fresh chopped cilantro.

Cumberland Sauce A sauce, made with redcurrant jelly and port wine, which is served cold with ham, lamb, beef or game.

Cumin A spice made from the aromatic, yellow-brown seeds of a plant, similar in appearance to parsley. Cumin has a pungent flavor (similar to caraway) and is used whole or ground in a range of Middle Eastern and Indian dishes.

Cupcake A small cake baked in a muffin tin or small mold lined with a crimped paper or foil cup.

Currant A small, round, smooth-skinned, red, black or white (rare) berry that is a member of the gooseberry family. Red currants can be eaten fresh, with sugar and cream or in salads; redcurrants and black currants are used to make jellies and sauces; black currants are used to make cordials, syrups and liqueurs (such as cassis).

Currant, Dried The dried fruit of a small, purple, seedless grape with a sweet, tangy flavor. It is used in cakes cookies, breads and pastries; in stuffings for game or fish; and in sauces and rice dishes.

Curry A meat, poultry, fish or vegetable dish flavored with spices and served with rice, pappadams and a variety of accompaniments. Curries, most strongly identified with India, are also part of the cooking of Thailand, Malaysia, Indonesia and the West Indies.

Curry Leaves The small, shiny, aromatic leaves from a tree native to South-East Asia, used whole in cooking in much the same way as bay leaves. Available fresh, dried or fried in oil, they add a curry-like flavor.

Curry Paste and Curry Powder Blends of ground spices used to flavor savory dishes. A basic Indian curry powder includes ground dried red chilies, coriander, mustard, black peppercorns, fenugreek, cumin and turmeric; other spices that can be included are cardamom, cloves, cinnamon, allspice, ginger and garlic. The addition of oil, vinegar or water

CUSTARDS

BAKED VANILLA CUSTARD

★ **Preparation time:** 10 minutes
Total cooking time: 40 minutes
Serves 4

2 cups milk
3 eggs
1/3 cup sugar

1 teaspoon vanilla extract
ground nutmeg for sprinkling

1 Preheat oven to moderate 350°F. Brush an ovenproof dish with oil. Whisk the milk, eggs, sugar and vanilla together in a mixing bowl for 2 minutes.
2 Pour the mixture into the prepared dish and sprinkle the top with nutmeg.
3 Put the custard dish into a larger baking dish. Pour enough hot water into the baking dish to come halfway up the sides. Bake for 20 minutes, then turn oven down to warm 325°F. Bake for 20 minutes more or until custard is set and a knife comes out clean when pushed into the center. Remove the dish from the water bath immediately. Serve warm or cold, with fruit if desired.

RICH CUSTARD

★ ★ **Preparation time:** 10 minutes
Total cooking time: 12 minutes
Makes 2½ cups

2 cups milk
4 egg yolks
1/3 cup sugar
1 teaspoon vanilla extract

1 Scald milk in the top of a double boiler. Beat the egg yolks and sugar together and slowly beat into hot milk.
2 Place custard over a pan of simmering water, and beat with a rotary beater until it thickens sufficiently to coat the beater. Remove from heat and beat again from time to time until custard cools. Stir in vanilla and chill.

Note: If you do not have a double boiler, make custard by scalding the milk in a saucepan, then transferring it to a heatproof bowl that will fit comfortably on top of another saucepan. Take care not to let the bowl of milk touch the simmering water.

ABOVE: BAKED VANILLA CUSTARD.
OPPOSITE PAGE: CREME BRULEE WITH PLUMS IN LIME

ABOUT CUSTARD

■ There are two types of custard: stirred and baked. Each uses the same cooking principles and similar ingredients.

■ Both types of custard are cooked over, or with, a controlled application of gentle heat (over simmering water or in a water bath). This is important if the characteristic velvety smoothness is to be achieved. The exception is when cornstarch is added. This custard can be cooked over direct heat with no danger of curdling it.

■ Also important to success is the correct beating of the eggs, sugar and milk for the custard; depending on the recipe, they should be whisked until the mixture has an even color and consistency.

■ A stirred custard has reached the correct consistency when it coats the back of a metal spoon. If the custard curdles, remove from heat immediately and pour it into a cold dish sitting in a bowl of ice cubes; beat vigorously—you may have some success in restoring smoothness.

■ If a stirred custard is removed from heat immediately it will thin on standing. Applying intense heat to a baked custard will cause it to separate and weep while standing; this cannot be corrected.

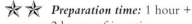

CREME BRULEE WITH PLUMS IN LIME

★★ **Preparation time:** 1 hour +
2 hours refrigeration
Total cooking time: 1 hour
10 minutes
Makes 6

3 cups heavy cream	**Plums in Lime**
2 vanilla beans	*30 oz can plums, drained*
8 egg yolks	*1 tablespoon grated lime*
½ cup sugar	*rind*
1 teaspoon vanilla extract	*½ cup lime juice*
1 tablespoon sugar	*½ cup sugar*

1 Place the heavy cream and vanilla beans in a large, heavy saucepan. Bring to boiling; remove from the heat and let stand for 15 minutes. Remove the vanilla beans. Using a whisk or spoon, beat the egg yolks and ½ cup sugar in a large heatproof bowl until well mixed. Place bowl over a saucepan of simmering water; stir constantly until just warmed through, about 2 minutes. Add the cream mixture gradually to egg mixture, stir constantly for 10 minutes. Continue to cook and stir until the mixture thickens slightly and coats the back of a metal spoon, about 4 minutes more. Remove from heat, stir in the vanilla. Spoon the mixture into six 6-oz individual soufflé dishes or custard cups. Refrigerate until set, about 2 hours.

2 To make Plums in Lime: Combine plums, lime rind, lime juice and ½ cup sugar in a heavy saucepan. Cook and stir over low heat until sugar has dissolved. Bring to the boil; reduce heat. Simmer, stirring occasionally, keeping plums whole, for 40 minutes or until liquid has reduced and thickened. Remove from heat. Cool to room temperature.

3 To serve, sprinkle ½ teaspoon of the remaining sugar over each custard. Place custards in a large baking pan. Pack ice around the dishes to prevent the custards from being heated. Place under preheated broiler about 5 inches from heat; broil until sugar caramelizes on top, about 2 minutes. Serve immediately with Plums in Lime.

CREME PATISSIERE

Beat 3 egg yolks with ⅓ cup sugar, 1 tablespoon all-purpose flour, 1 tablespoon cornstarch in mixing bowl until pale. Heat ½ cup milk in pan until almost boiling; remove from heat. Add milk gradually to egg mixture, beating constantly. Strain into pan. Stir over medium heat until mixture boils and thickens. Remove from heat; add 1 teaspoon vanilla. Place plastic wrap over surface to prevent skin forming; cool. Makes 1½ cups. Use to fill choux puffs or cakes. For a richer mixture, fold in whipped cream.

gives a curry paste, or wet masala (spices and seasonings ground together). The green and red curry pastes of Thai cooking are both based on a blend of fresh cilantro leaves, chili peppers, garlic and other spices and fresh herbs.

Custard A mixture of egg and milk, sweetened, cooked and served hot

or cold as a dessert. Custards require slow cooking and gentle heat to prevent curdling. Baked custard is cooked in the oven, usually in a water bath; stirred custard is cooked over simmering water or in a double boiler. Stirred custards are softer than baked custards and are often used as a sweet sauce or as the basis of many other desserts.

Cuttlefish A saltwater mollusk closely related to squid. It is sometimes referred to as "chameleon of the sea" because it can quickly change its skin color and pattern. It has a broad oval body; two tentacles and eight arms attached to the head. The lean flesh can be poached, steamed, baked, fried, stuffed or cut into rings. It has been eaten for centuries around the shores of the Mediterranean, either stuffed or cut into rings and fried in batter.

D

Daikon A variety of radish grown in Japan with a long, almost cylindrical, fleshy white root and a mild, peppery taste. It is eaten raw

(either grated or sliced in salads), cooked (steamed or stir-fried) as a vegetable and, in its pickled form (takuan) is served with almost every meal. Spicy tasting daikon sprouts (kaiware) are used in salads and as a garnish. Daikon is also known as Japanese white radish and mooli.

Daiquiri A cocktail made from white rum, lemon or lime juice and sugar, served in a chilled glass. The drink is named after a small village near Santiago, on the Cuban coast. Fruits such as peaches, strawberries or kiwifruit are sometimes added.

DATES

WARM DATE AND MASCARPONE TART

⭐ **Preparation time:** 25 minutes
Total cooking time: 25–30 minutes
Serves 6–8

4 sheets frozen filo (phyllo) dough, thawed
3 tablespoons unsalted (sweet) butter, melted
1/4 cup ground almonds
7 1/4 oz dried dates, pitted and sliced
2 eggs
2 teaspoons cornstarch
4 oz mascarpone or cream cheese, softened
1/3 cup sugar
1/2 cup heavy cream
2 tablespoons sliced almonds

1 Preheat oven to 350°F. Brush a shallow 4 x 14 inch fluted rectangular flan pan or 10 inch fluted pan or quiche dish with melted butter. Brush a sheet of filo dough sparingly with melted butter, sprinkle with ground almonds and fold in half lengthwise. Line flan pan lengthwise with pastry. Repeat with remaining pastry, butter and nuts. Bake for 15 minutes.
2 Spread dates evenly over the pastry base. Combine eggs, cornstarch, cheese, sugar and cream in a medium bowl; whisk until smooth. Pour mixture over dates. Sprinkle with sliced almonds. Bake 10–15 minutes or until custard is set and golden. Leave for 10 minutes before slicing. Serve warm with whipped cream.

STEAMED DATE AND PECAN PUDDING CAKE

⭐ **Preparation time:** 30 minutes
Total cooking time: 2 hours
Serves 6–8

1/2 cup butter
1 1/4 cups sugar
4 eggs
2 cups dried dates, chopped
3/4 cup chopped pecans
1/4 cup milk
1 teaspoon ground cardamom
2 cups all-purpose flour
1/2 teaspoon baking powder
1/8 teaspoon salt

Cardamom Sauce
2 tablespoons unsalted (sweet) butter
2 tablespoons soft brown sugar
1 teaspoon ground cardamom
3/4 cup orange juice
1 teaspoon cornstarch

1 Grease a 6-cup capacity mold with melted butter. Line base with wax paper, grease paper. Beat butter and sugar in a small bowl until light and creamy. Add eggs gradually, beating thoroughly after each addition.
2 Transfer to large bowl, fold in dates, pecans and milk. Stir in cardamom and flour, baking powder and salt. Spoon into prepared mold, cover with greased round of foil, secure with lid and string.
3 Place mold on a trivet in a large pan with simmering water to come halfway up side of mold. Cover and cook for 2 hours. Do not allow pan to boil dry: replenish water as necessary.
4 To make Cardamom Sauce: Combine butter, sugar and cardamom in a pan; cook over low heat, stirring until butter melts and mixture is smooth. Combine orange juice and cornstarch. Stir in orange juice mixture, blend well. Bring to boil; cook and stir 1 minute. Serve warm.

DATE AND WALNUT LOAF

Preheat oven to 350°F. Cream 1/2 cup butter and 1 cup soft brown sugar in a bowl. Add 2 eggs, one at a time, beat well after each addition. Blend in 1 cup milk, 1 1/2 cups chopped dates and 1 cup chopped walnuts. Fold in 3 cups all-purpose flour, 1 teaspoon baking powder, 1/2 teaspoon baking soda and 1/8 teaspoon salt. Pour into two greased 5 1/2 x 8 1/2 inch loaf pans. Bake 35–40 minutes. Remove from pans; cool on cake rack. Serve sliced, warm or cold, with butter. Store in an airtight container. Makes 2 loaves.

ABOVE: STEAMED DATE AND PECAN PUDDING CAKE.
OPPOSITE PAGE: PINEAPPLE UPSIDE-DOWN PUDDING CAKE AND BUTTERSCOTCH PUDDING CAKES

Damper Unleavened
bread made from a
simple dough of flour
and water. It was a staple
food for early European
settlers in outback
Australia. Traditionally
the dough was cooked
directly in the hot ashes
of an open fire (with this
method the encrusting
ashes must be knocked
off before the bread can
be eaten), or wound

around a green stick
which was placed over
the fire, the result was
known as a Johnny
Cake. In later years camp
ovens were used and,
after they became
available, baking powder
and powdered milk were
added to the mixture.
Today the term damper
refers to leavened bread,
round in shape, with a
crunchy crust and a taste
and texture similar to
white bread. The name
comes from a British
dialect word meaning
"something that takes the
edge off the appetite".

Damson A small, dark
purple variety of
European plum with a
thick skin. It is also
known as a prune plum.
The fruit is too tart to
eat raw but is delicious
cooked in compotes,
jams, jellies and as a pie
filling. The name is a
contraction of
Damascene, "from
Damascus."

DESSERTS
BAKED PUDDINGS

PINEAPPLE UPSIDE-DOWN PUDDING CAKE

⭐ ⭐ **Preparation time:** 15 minutes
Total cooking time: 40–45 minutes
Makes one 8 inch round cake

1 tablespoon butter, melted
2 tablespoons shredded
 coconut
1/3 cup soft brown sugar
8 oz can sliced pineapple,
 drained
1/3 cup butter
2/3 cup sugar
2 eggs, lightly beaten
1 teaspoon vanilla
1 cup all-purpose flour
1/2 teaspoon baking
 powder
1/8 teaspoon salt
1/3 cup coconut milk

1 Preheat oven to moderate 350°F. Brush an
8 inch tube pan or ring mold with melted butter
or oil, sprinkle with coconut and sugar. Cut
pineapple slices in half, arrange over coconut.
2 Beat butter and sugar in small bowl until light
and creamy. Add eggs, one at a time, beating well
after each addition. Add vanilla.
3 Fold in flour, baking powder and salt alternately
with coconut milk. Stir until just combined and
mixture is almost smooth. Spoon into pan;
smooth surface. Bake 40–45 minutes or until a
skewer inserted into center comes out clean.
Leave in pan 5 minutes, turn onto serving plate.
Serve with custard or cream.

BUTTERSCOTCH PUDDING CAKES

⭐ **Preparation time:** 15 minutes
Total cooking time: 45 minutes
Serves 8

1/3 cup butter, chopped
1 cup soft brown sugar
11/2 cups all-purpose flour
1/2 teaspoon baking powder
1/8 teaspoon salt
1 teaspoon pumpkin pie
 spice
3/4 cup milk
1/4 cup butter, extra
1/2 cup sugar
1/4 cup water
1 cup water, extra

1 Preheat oven to 350°F. Brush eight 6 oz
ovenproof dishes with oil or melted butter. Beat
butter and sugar in a small mixing bowl until light
and creamy. Fold flour, pumpkin pie spice,
baking powder and salt into butter mixture
alternately with milk. Spoon into dishes. Place on
a baking sheet.
2 Place extra butter, sugar and 1/4 cup water in a
pan. Stir over low heat until butter has melted
and sugar dissolved. Bring to boil, reduce heat,
simmer gently, uncovered, until golden brown.
Remove from heat. Stir in extra water. Stir over
low heat until smooth; cool slightly.
3 Pour an equal amount of mixture over each
pudding. Bake 35 minutes, or until skewer comes
out clean when inserted in center. Loosen edges
of puddings by running a knife around the edge.
Invert onto serving plates.

Dandelion A flowering plant well known as a weed. Its young leaves can be added to mixed green salad for a peppery bite. The leaves should be picked before the plant flowers, otherwise they can become tough and bitter; cut them off at the root crown. Dandelions can be blanched by covering the growing plant with an inverted flowerpot; the result is a crisp pale leaf with a milder flavor. Its roots can be dried, roasted and used as a coffee substitute.

Danish Blue A soft, creamy white, cow's milk cheese with fine blue veining and a sharp, sometimes salty, taste. It has a buttery

texture and can be either spread or sliced. Modelled on the blue-veined Roquefort cheese of France, it was developed in Denmark in the early 1900s to compete in the United States with Roquefort sales. The cheese is also known as Danablu.

Danish Open Sandwich A thin slice of bread, buttered right to each edge to seal the

INDIVIDUAL BUTTER PUDDING CAKES

★ *Preparation time:* 20 minutes
Total cooking time: 20 minutes
Serves 8

½ cup butter	⅛ teaspoon salt
1 cup sugar	½ cup milk
2 eggs	
1 teaspoon vanilla	**Maple Syrup Cream**
1½ cups all-purpose flour	¼ cup butter
½ teaspoon baking powder	½ cup maple syrup
	1¼ cups heavy cream

1 Preheat oven to 350°F. Brush eight 1-cup capacity ovenproof ramekins or molds with melted butter. Using electric beaters, beat butter and sugar in a small mixing bowl until light and creamy. Add eggs, one at a time, beating well after each addition. Add vanilla; beat until combined. Transfer to a large mixing bowl. Fold in flour, baking powder and salt alternately with milk. Stir until combined and almost smooth.
2 Spoon into molds; place on large baking sheet, bake 20 minutes or until a skewer comes out clean when inserted in center. Leave in molds 5 minutes then turn onto a wire rack to cool.

3 To make Maple Syrup Cream: Melt the butter in a small heavy-bottom pan. Add maple syrup and stir over medium heat until well combined. Add cream and bring to the boil, stirring constantly. Transfer to a jug. To serve, place a pudding on each plate and drizzle with Maple Syrup Cream. Serve with whipped cream or vanilla ice cream.

Note: Puddings can be made up to 2 hours in advance. Store at room temperature, covered with a clean towel. Make Maple Syrup Cream just before serving.

CREME CHANTILLY

Serve baked puddings, marinated fruit and sweet tarts with Crème Chantilly. Pour 2 cups heavy cream into a large bowl, add 1 tablespoon vanilla sugar and beat until soft peaks form—take care not to overbeat.

Vanilla sugar is made by placing 2 or 3 vanilla pods in a jar of sugar. Refill the jar as you use the sugar. The vanilla will continue to flavor the sugar for a year.

ABOVE: INDIVIDUAL BUTTER PUDDING CAKE.
OPPOSITE PAGE: FRUIT BREAD AND APPLE PUDDING

bread from the topping, which can include generous mounds of fresh salad vegetables, cold meats, smoked fish, cheese, mayonnaise, pickles, gherkins and relishes, garnished with fresh herbs such as parsley, dill, chervil and watercress. A Danish open sandwich is best eaten with a knife and fork. The Danish word for open sandwich is *smørrebrød*, meaning buttered bread.

Danish Pastry A sweet, light pastry consisting of a buttery yeast dough encasing a filling such as jelly, stewed fruits,

custard, preserves, nuts and cheese. The dough is shaped into rolls and twists, then glazed with spices and sprinkled with sugar before being baked. Danish pastries are usually served with coffee.

Dariole The name given to both a small, steep-sided mold and the preparation cooked in it. Dariole molds are used to make pastries, individual fruit cakes and puddings. They can also be lined with aspic, filled with a savory mixture and topped with more jelly. When the mixture has set, it is turned out onto a platter for serving.

DESSERTS
BREAD PUDDINGS

FRUIT BREAD AND APPLE PUDDING

★ **Preparation time:** 25 minutes
Total cooking time: 35–40 minutes
Serves 6

12 slices day-old raisin bread, crusts removed
½ cup apple juice
½ cup red wine
4 large green apples, peeled, cored and sliced into thin wedges
1 teaspoon cinnamon

¾ cup coarsely chopped walnuts
¼ cup soft brown sugar
1 tablespoon unsalted (sweet) butter
1 cup sour cream
3 tablespoons soft brown sugar, extra

1 Put bread into bowl, pour over half combined juice and wine, stand for 5 minutes. Remove bread, place 4 slices in base of greased ovenproof dish. Preheat oven to 350°F.
2 Combine apples, cinnamon, walnuts and sugar. Place half mixture over bread. Top with 4 bread slices, and rest of apple mixture. Cover with remaining bread, pour over rest of juice and wine. Dot with butter, bake for 35–40 minutes.

3 Combine sour cream and extra brown sugar. Leave pudding for 10 minutes then serve warm, topped with a spoonful of sour cream mixture.

BREAD AND BUTTER PUDDING

★ **Preparation time:** 10 minutes
Total cooking time: 50 minutes
Serves 4–6

2 tablespoons butter, softened
6 thin slices day-old white or brown bread, crusts removed
¾ cup mixed dried fruit

¼ cup sugar
1 teaspoon pumpkin pie spice
2 eggs, lightly beaten
1 teaspoon vanilla extract
2½ cups milk

1 Preheat oven to moderate 350°F. Grease a medium, shallow, ovenproof dish. Butter bread and cut slices in half diagonally. Layer bread into the dish, sprinkling each layer with dried fruit, sugar and pumpkin pie spice.
2 Beat the eggs, vanilla and milk together. Pour mixture over the bread and set aside for 5 minutes to soak.
3 Bake pudding for 50 minutes, or until it is set and top is browned.

Dasheen (Taro, Eddo) A tropical tuber with brown skin and white flesh, similar to a potato and tasting like chestnut.

Dashi A fish and kelp stock which gives Japanese cooking its distinctive "sea" flavor. It is made by heating a kelp leaf in water to boiling point then removing the kelp and adding flakes of dried bonito. The mixture is stirred until the flakes sink and then strained. Dashi is also eaten as a clear soup and is used as sauce and marinade. It is available from Asian or specialty food stores.

Date The oblong, amber to dark brown, sweet-fleshed fruit of the date palm. A French author described it as being "to the people of the Sahara what wheat is to the French and rice to the

Chinese." In the hot deserts of western Asia and northern Africa, the date palm is the tree of life, fringing every oasis and thriving in conditions where virtually nothing else can grow. Date palms have been known to bear fruit for up to a century.

Dates travel well and were exported (mostly from Egypt) to ancient

BERRY CHERRY CRUMBLE

Preparation time: 10 minutes
Total cooking time: 15 minutes
Serves 6

8 oz strawberries, hulled
6½ oz blueberries
13½ oz can pitted
   black cherries, strained,
   ½ cup juice
   reserved
½ teaspoon cornstarch

1 tablespoon
   confectioners' sugar

Topping
⅓ cup butter
¼ cup light corn syrup
2 cups rolled oats

1 Preheat oven to moderate 350°F. Cut the strawberries in half. Place in an ovenproof dish with the blueberries and cherries. Mix well. Blend the cornstarch with the reserved cherry juice until smooth. Pour over the fruit. Sprinkle on sifted confectioners' sugar. Set aside.
2 To prepare Topping: Combine the butter and syrup in a small pan, place over low heat until the butter has melted. Remove from the heat and stir in the rolled oats until thoroughly combined. Spoon the oat mixture evenly over the berries. Bake crumble for 15 minutes, or until the topping is golden and crunchy. Serve warm.

APRICOT BETTY

Preparation time: 10 minutes
Total cooking time: 30 minutes
Serves 6

2 x 13½ oz cans apricot
   halves, drained, ⅓ cup
   juice reserved
⅓ cup sugar

2 cups fine, fresh white
   bread crumbs
¼ cup butter, melted

1 Preheat the oven to moderate 350°F. Lightly brush an 8 inch pie dish with oil or melted butter. Place half of the apricots in the prepared dish.
2 Sprinkle half the sugar and half the bread crumbs over the apricots in the dish. Pour half the melted butter and half the juice over the bread crumbs.
3 Repeat this procedure with the remaining apricots, sugar, bread crumbs, melted butter and juice. Bake for 30 minutes. Serve warm.

LEFT: BERRY CHERRY CRUMBLE (TOP) AND
BREAD AND BUTTER PUDDING (BOTTOM)

Greece and Rome where they were sold on the streets and in the theatres as a sweet snack food, as they were again fifteen hundred years later in medieval Europe.

The fruit is available fresh or dried. Iraq is the

main exporter of dried dates; Israel, Lebanon and the United States export "fresh" frozen dates. The name comes from the Greek *dáktylos*, meaning finger.

Daube, en A French term for a method of cooking meat by braising it in red wine seasoned with herbs.

Deep-Fry To cook pieces of food by immersing them in very hot fat or oil. Deep-frying creates a crust around the food which seals in the flavor and juices. Food should be cooked in small batches to avoid lowering the temperature of the oil or fat. Fish, chicken, croquettes or soft vegetables should be protected with a coating of batter or bread crumbs before they are fried. Peanut and corn (maize) oils have a high smoking point and are therefore most suitable for deep-frying.

Deglaze To add water, stock or wine to the cooking juices and cooked-on sediments left in the pan after roasting or frying meat. The mixture is heated, stirred and reduced to make a or gravy or brown sauce. The name comes from the French *déglacer*, to dissolve into liquid.

Dégorger A French term (meaning "disgorge") for the process of soaking meat, poultry, offal or fish in cold water to free it of impurities and blood, or to eliminate any "muddy" flavor from freshwater fish. The term is also used for the process of removing excess water and strong flavors from certain vegetables.

Demerara Sugar A white cane sugar treated with molasses to produce large, slightly sticky, pale brown crystals. It is often served with coffee and is used for making cookies, cakes and candy. Brown sugar or raw sugar can be substituted. It was first produced in the Demerara region of Guyana, West Indies.

Demi-Glace A basic brown or espagnole sauce which is reduced to a rich, thick, glossy syrup. It is used to coat meat and game dishes as well as to enrich other sauces.

DESSERTS
CHRISTMAS PUDDINGS

ICE CREAM CHRISTMAS DESSERT

★ **Preparation time:** 20 minutes + 20 minutes standing + overnight freezing
Total cooking time: 4 minutes
Serves 8–10

2 cups mixed dried fruit
3 oz candied cherries, cut into quarters
1½ oz candied apricots, chopped
1½ oz candied pineapple, chopped
2 teaspoons finely chopped candied ginger
2 teaspoons grated orange rind
2 tablespoons Grand Marnier
1 tablespoon brandy

1 gallon vanilla ice cream, softened
¼ cup chocolate chips
½ cup chopped pecans

Chocolate Sauce
½ cup water
¼ cup unsweetened cocoa powder, sifted
¼ cup butter
2 tablespoons soft brown sugar
3½ oz dark (semisweet) chocolate, chopped
1 tablespoon brandy

1 Mix fruits, rind, liqueur and brandy in a large mixing bowl. Set aside for 20 minutes, uncovered; stir occasionally.
2 Using a metal spoon, break up the ice cream in a large mixing bowl. Add the fruit mixture, chocolate chips and nuts to ice cream; stir until well mixed.

3 Line a 9-cup capacity bowl with plastic wrap. Spoon in ice cream mixture; smooth surface. Cover with plastic wrap; freeze overnight. To serve, unmold and cut into wedges. Serve with Chocolate Sauce.
4 To make Chocolate Sauce: Place water, cocoa, butter and sugar in small pan. Stir over low heat 4 minutes or until mixture boils and sugar is dissolved. Remove from heat; add chocolate. Stir until chocolate has melted and mixture is smooth; stir in brandy.

STEAMED CHRISTMAS PUDDING

★ **Preparation time:** 30 minutes
Total cooking time: 6–7 hours
Serves 8–10

2 cups golden raisins
1½ cups dark raisins
¾ cup currants
1 tablespoon finely chopped mixed peel
¼ cup brandy
¼ cup rum
1 cup butter

1 cup soft brown sugar
5 eggs
1 cup all-purpose flour
½ teaspoon baking soda
1½ teaspoons pumpkin pie spice
4 oz fresh bread crumbs
¼ cup chopped almonds

1 Combine the fruits, peel, brandy and rum in a bowl. Beat the butter and sugar together until pale. Add the eggs, one at a time, beating well after each addition. Gradually add the sifted flour, baking soda and spice. Fold in the undrained fruit, bread crumbs and chopped almonds.
2 Spoon the mixture into a well-greased 8-cup bowl. Allow room for rising. Cover with greased waxed paper, then foil. Tie with string, leaving a loop handle for lifting. Place on a trivet or an upturned saucer in a large saucepan. Pour in enough hot water to come two-thirds of the way up the side of bowl. Bring to boil, boil rapidly for 5–6 hours. Check water occasionally, refill as needed. Do not let the pan boil dry. Cool pudding completely; refrigerate.
3 To serve: Reheat pudding by cooking in the same way for 1 hour before needed. Serve with hot Brandy Butter.

BRANDY BUTTER

Beat together 1 cup butter, ⅓ cup firmly packed soft brown sugar and 1 cup sifted confectioners' sugar until the mixture is smooth. Add ¼ cup brandy gradually, beating continuously. Store in the refrigerator for up to a week. Makes about 1 cup.

DESSERTS FRUIT

SUMMER PUDDING

⭐ ⭐ **Preparation time:** 20 minutes + 1 hour
standing + overnight refrigeration
Total cooking time: 13 minutes
Makes one 8 inch cake

13¹/₂ oz can
  boysenberries
13¹/₂ oz can blackberries
1 cup sugar
1 medium apple, peeled
  and coarsely grated

10 oz raspberries
15 slices thick bread,
  crusts removed
fresh blueberries, raspberries,
  strawberries and
  blackberries, to decorate

1 Drain the berries and set aside. Pour the syrup into pan, add sugar. Stir over low heat for 3 minutes until the sugar dissolves. Bring to boil, reduce heat. Simmer uncovered for 10 minutes; remove from heat.
2 Combine the canned berries with the apple and raspberries in a large bowl and mix well.
3 Cut the bread diagonally in half. Arrange half of the bread over base and sides of deep 8 inch cake pan. Brush with a little syrup. Spoon half the fruit onto bread; pour ¹/₃ of syrup over fruit. Arrange a layer of bread over fruit. Top with remaining fruit and ¹/₃ of syrup. Arrange remaining bread over fruit and cover with remaining syrup.
4 Stand pan on a plate with a lip. Cover with plastic wrap, top with a plate and a weight. Stand 1 hour. Remove plate and weight. Refrigerate overnight. Turn onto serving plate; decorate with berries.

MOROCCAN-STYLE FRESH FRUIT SALAD

⭐ **Preparation time:** 20 minutes
Total cooking time: 5 minutes
Serves 6

2 apples
2 pears
³/₄ cup orange juice
1 tablespoon lemon juice
2 bananas
2 tablespoons orange
  flower water

confectioners' sugar
8 oz strawberries, hulled
  and halved lengthwise
fresh mint leaves
rind of 1 orange

1 Core the apples and pears and cut them into thin slices. Place in serving bowl and add orange and lemon juices to prevent apples and pears discoloring.
2 Peel and cut bananas thinly. Add to fruit in bowl and toss gently. Add orange flower water and sprinkle with powdered sugar to taste. Add strawberry halves to fruit salad. Sprinkle with fresh mint leaves.
3 Remove bitter white pith from orange rind. Slice orange rind into thin matchsticks and cook in water or light sugar syrup for 5 minutes, drain. Arrange over fruit salad and serve.

Note: This fruit salad is best served plain without cream or ice cream.

OPPOSITE PAGE: ICE CREAM CHRISTMAS DESSERT.
ABOVE: MOROCCAN-STYLE FRESH FRUIT SALAD;
LEFT: SUMMER PUDDING

Dessert A sweet course eaten at the end of a meal. It can range from a simple compote of fresh fruit to ice creams, jellies, custards, sweet pies, steamed puddings and elaborate cakes. In ancient times a meal was likely to have been rounded off with fruit, honey or cheese. In medieval Europe it was customary at banquets to serve jellies and sweet tarts between meat courses. In the seventeenth century, sweet ices and sherbets (which originated in Spain and Sicily) made an appearance, as did chocolate, brought back from the Americas. Ideally, a light, fruit–based dessert should follow a heavy meal, while a sweet pie or rich pudding is appropriate after a light meal. Nowadays, dessert can also mean cheese and crackers. The word comes from the French *desservir*, to remove all that has been served: at a formal dinner, everything, including the tablecloth, was removed and the table re-laid for dessert.

Dessert Wine A sweet, full-bodied wine served at the end of a meal with the dessert. Dessert wines include muscat, madeira, sauternes and tokay. Champagne can also be served with the dessert course.

Deviled The term applied to food, such as meat, poultry, fish and shellfish, that has been spiced with a sharp flavor from seasonings and marinades before broiling, grilling or frying. Flavorings (which are often brushed on during cooking) can include mustard, Tabasco sauce, Worcestershire sauce, pepper and lemon juice.

Deviled Butter Softened butter mashed with Tabasco sauce, Worcestershire sauce, dry mustard, chopped onion and parsley, formed into a roll and then chilled. Served on broiled or grilled foods.

Devils on Horseback An hors d'oeuvre of almond-stuffed prunes wrapped in bacon and broiled or grilled until the bacon is crisp.

TRIFLE

Preparation time: 20 minutes + 50 minutes refrigeration
Total cooking time: 10 minutes
Serves 6–8

1 sponge cake, 6½ inches diameter x 1¼ inches deep
¾ cup cream sherry or port
1 x 4-serving package sweetened strawberry jello
⅓ cup sugar
2 tablespoons cornstarch

2½ cups milk
1 teaspoon vanilla
1 egg
2 x 13½ oz cans peach slices, drained
1 cup heavy cream
¼ cup confectioners' sugar
8 oz strawberries, hulled and halved

1 Cut the cake into ¾ inch cubes and place in an 8-cup capacity serving dish. Drizzle sherry over the cake.
2 Prepare the jello according to package directions. Pour into a 11 x 7 inch pan and refrigerate for about 30 minutes or until the jello is set.
3 Place the sugar and cornstarch in a medium pan, gradually blend in the milk. Stir over medium heat with a wooden spoon until the custard boils and begins to thicken. Remove from heat. Add the vanilla and egg, mix well.

Cover the surface with plastic wrap, cool to room temperature.
4 Using a plastic spatula, cut the jello into cubes. Place cubes in a layer on top of sponge. Add fruit for the next layer, then pour custard over top. Refrigerate for 20 minutes or until custard has set. Whip the cream with the cpnfectioners' sugar until thick, pipe or spoon onto the trifle and garnish with strawberries.

FRUIT SALAD WITH PORT

Preparation time: 20 minutes
Total cooking time: none
Serves 6

⅔ cup sugar
¼ cup lemon juice
¼ cup port
1 papaya, peeled and sliced

8 oz raspberries
1 kiwifruit, peeled and sliced
other seasonal fruit

1 Combine the sugar, lemon juice and port in a screw-top jar. Shake well, so that the ingredients are thoroughly combined.
2 Combine the papaya, raspberries, kiwifruit and other fruit in a serving bowl. Pour the dressing over the fruit. Cover. Refrigerate until required. Serve with whipped cream.

DESSERTS
ICE CREAMS

ICE CREAM FRUIT BOMBE

★ **Preparation time:** 20 minutes + overnight soaking + overnight freezing
Total cooking time: none
Serves 8

10 oz jar fruit mincemeat	1 cup egg substitute
1/2 cup dried figs, finely chopped	1 cup sugar
1/4 cup rum	1 1/2 cups heavy cream
1 cup sliced almonds	3/4 cup buttermilk

1 Combine the mincemeat, figs and rum in small mixing bowl. Cover and soak overnight. Toast the almonds.
2 Using electric beaters, beat egg substitute in large mixing bowl 5 minutes or until thick and pale. Add sugar gradually, beat until sugar dissolves and mixture is pale and glossy. Gradually add combined cream and buttermilk; beat for another 5 minutes.
3 Using a metal spoon, fold in fruit mixture and almonds. Pour into deep 8-cup capacity bowl, cover with foil. Freeze overnight.
4 Push a flat-bladed knife down between the bowl and frozen mixture and ease it gently onto a serving plate.

OPPOSITE PAGE: TRIFLE.
ABOVE: MANGO ICE CREAM

MANGO ICE CREAM

★ ★ **Preparation time:** 25 minutes + freezing time
Total cooking time: 10 minutes
Makes 4 cups

4 egg yolks	1/2 cup heavy cream
3/4 cup confectioners' sugar	cookie baskets, fresh mango and shredded coconut for serving
2 cups mango purée	
1 tablespoon lemon juice	
1/2 cup coconut cream	

1 Place the egg yolks and confectioners' sugar in a medium heatproof bowl. Stand the bowl over a pan of simmering water, beating until mixture is thick and creamy. Remove from heat, continue beating for 1 minute longer or until cool.
2 Place the mango purée, lemon juice, coconut cream and cream into a large bowl, mix well. Using a metal spoon, gently fold in egg mixture.
3 Spoon into a 7 x 11 inch or 4-cup capacity rectangular pan. Store, covered with foil in freezer for 3 hours, or until the mixture is almost frozen.
4 Transfer the mixture to a large mixing bowl. Using electric beaters, beat on high speed until smooth. Return the mixture to pan or container and store, covered with foil, in freezer for 5 hours or overnight. Scoop into cookie baskets and top with slices of fresh mango and shredded coconut.

Note: Buy cookie baskets from gourmet food stores and major department stores.

Devonshire Tea Scones, jam and clotted cream served with a pot of tea as a light mid-morning or mid-afternoon meal. Clotted cream, also known as Devonshire cream, was originally made by slowly warming fresh cream in an earthenware bowl which was then left on a cold stone floor to cool, allowing the cream to thicken. The process originated in the county of Devon, in southwestern England.

Dhal An Indian dish of lentils cooked with garlic, ginger and seasonings and then puréed. It has a consistency similar to porridge and can be eaten on its own, served with boiled rice or Indian breads, or as an accompaniment to a meat dish.

Diable A cooking vessel consisting of two unglazed clay pots, one of which fits the other as a lid. It is used for cooking foods such as potatoes, onions, beets and chestnuts without water; halfway through cooking the diable is turned upside down. The vessel can be used in the oven or, with a heat diffuser, on an electric range or gas stove. A diable should never be washed.

Dibs A chocolate-flavored syrup made from the carob pod. In Syria and Lebanon it is mixed with tahini and used as a spread.

Dibs Roman Also known as grenadine molasses, a thick, dark, purple-red syrup with a strong, sour-sweet flavor. Made from concentrated pomegranate juice, it is used in the cooking of the Middle East to sharpen the flavor of lamb fillings for pies, as a marinade for lamb and to add a tart sweetness to soups and stews. It is also the basis of a drink. The name is derived from the Arabic word for "pomegranate sugar."

Dijon Mustard A pale yellow mustard, originally from Dijon, France. It has a clean sharp flavor which can range from mild to hot.

Dijonnaise French term for a dish prepared with Dijon mustard, one of the traditional French mustards. *Dijonnaise* is also the name given to a mustard-flavored mayonnaise served with cold meats. Both are named after Dijon, capital of the Burgundy region of France, an ancient city famous for its castles and museums, an annual International Food Fair, and black currant syrup (cassis).

DESSERTS
JELLIES AND MOUSSES

EASY ORANGE MOUSSE

⭐ **Preparation time:** 12 minutes + 10 minutes standing
Total cooking time: none
Serves 8

1 cup orange juice
2 tablespoons lemon juice
3/4 cup sugar
1 tablespoon unsweetened gelatin
1/4 cup water
1 tablespoon orange liqueur
3 egg whites
3/4 cup cream, whipped until stiff

1 Combine orange and lemon juice in a bowl; add the sugar. Leave for 10 minutes until sugar has softened.
2 Sprinkle gelatin over water in a small bowl. Stand in boiling water, stirring until the gelatin has dissolved. Add to juices, with orange liqueur. Mix well. Refrigerate until mixture is the consistency of unbeaten egg white.
3 Beat orange and lemon mixture until fluffy and light. Using electric beaters, beat egg whites until stiff peaks form. Using a metal spoon, fold the cream and egg whites together. Fold gelatin mixture into egg white mixture. Spoon into eight individual dessert dishes or wine glasses. Decorate with an orange segment, orange rind and a little whipped cream, if desired.

ABOVE: ORANGE MOUSSE; RIGHT: PASSIONFRUIT AND CITRUS FLUMMERY. OPPOSITE PAGE: BLUEBERRY CHEESE TART (LEFT) AND BUTTERMILK NUTMEG PIE

PASSIONFRUIT AND CITRUS FLUMMERY

⭐ **Preparation time:** 35–40 minutes + 4 hours chilling
Total cooking time: 10 minutes
Serves 8

1 tablespoon all-purpose flour
1 cup warm water
1 tablespoon unsweetened gelatin
1/4 cup cold water
1/4 cup lemon juice
2/3 cup orange juice
1 cup sugar
pulp of 5 passionfruit

1 In a medium pan, blend the flour and a little warm water to a paste, adding the remaining water a little at a time. Bring the mixture to boil, stirring or whisking constantly. Boil for 1 minute, remove from heat.
2 Sprinkle the gelatin over the combined cold water and lemon juice in a small bowl. Stand the bowl in a pan of warm water, and whisk until the gelatin has completely dissolved and there are no lumps.
3 Add juices, gelatin mixture, sugar and passionfruit pulp to the pan. Return to heat; bring to the boil. Transfer mixture to a large heatproof bowl.
4 Place the bowl over ice cubes and beat the mixture with electric beaters until it is thick and light. Transfer the mixture to a clean bowl and set aside until it is beginning to set. Whisk again lightly so that the passionfruit seeds are evenly distributed. Spoon the mixture into individual parfait glasses. Chill for about 4 hours or until lightly set. Serve with whipped cream and extra passionfruit pulp if desired.

DESSERTS
TARTS

BLUEBERRY CHEESE TART

⭐ **Preparation time:** 30 minutes
Total cooking time: 45 minutes
Serves 6

2 sheets ready-made piecrust pastry	1 lb fresh or frozen blueberries
4 oz cream cheese	2 tablespoons seedless blackberry jam
1/4 cup sugar	
1 egg, lightly beaten	2 teaspoons lemon juice
1 teaspoon vanilla extract	1 egg, extra, lightly beaten

1 Preheat oven to moderate 350°F. Line a 9 inch fluted flan pan with one sheet of pastry; trim edges. Cut remaining pastry sheet into long thin strips. Brush with extra beaten egg.
2 Using electric beaters, beat cream cheese and sugar in a small mixing bowl until light and creamy. Add the egg gradually, beating thoroughly. Beat in vanilla.
3 Spread cheese mixture over pastry, top with blueberries. Heat jam and juice together in a small pan until jam has melted. Gently spoon over top of blueberries. Cut remaining pastry into strips. Lay pastry strips in a lattice pattern over tart; gently press edges to base. Trim excess pastry. Bake for 45 minutes, or until cheese mixture has set. Leave to cool in pan for 10 minutes. Serve warm or cold with ice cream.

BUTTERMILK NUTMEG PIE

⭐⭐ **Preparation time:** 30 minutes
Total cooking time: 50 minutes
Serves 6

1 sheet ready-made piecrust pastry	1/2 cup sugar
	1 teaspoon vanilla extract
	1/2 cup heavy cream
Filling	1 cup buttermilk
1 tablespoon cornstarch	1 teaspoon ground nutmeg
3 eggs, lightly beaten	

1 Preheat oven to moderate 350°F. Brush a shallow 9 inch round ovenproof pie plate with oil or melted butter.
2 Ease pastry sheet into prepared pie plate; trim around edge. Using fingertips, pinch a fluted pattern around the edge of the pastry.
3 To make Filling: Whisk the cornstarch, eggs and sugar together in a medium bowl. Add vanilla, cream and buttermilk and mix until well combined. Pour mixture into the pie shell and sprinkle with nutmeg.
4 Place the tart on a baking sheet. Bake for 50 minutes or until custard is set and a sharp knife comes out clean when inserted into center. Leave 10 minutes before serving. Serve warm or cold with cream.

Note: Custard tarts need to cool before serving to allow the filling to set to a perfect consistency.

Dill An aromatic herb, similar in appearance and related to fennel, that is a native of southern Europe and western Asia. Both its feathery green leaves and small brown seeds are used as a flavoring (the leaves in soups, egg dishes, salads, soft cheeses and sauces to accompany fish; the seeds in breads, pickles and for flavoring vinegar and cooked cabbage). Dill is widely used in the cooking of northern Europe, where it flavors sauerkraut and potato salad, fish and vegetable dishes and pickled gherkins. Dill water was for many years given to babies to soothe them to sleep. The leaves are also known as dillweed.

Dim Sim A tiny parcel of finely chopped meat and cabbage wrapped in a wonton wrapper (a thin sheet of dry dough) and then either deep-fried until crisp and golden, or steamed. The name comes from the Cantonese word *tim-sam*, "little snack," and is sometimes applied to a range of similar bite-sized morsels such as gow gee and spring rolls.

Dip A dish of puréed or finely chopped food blended with a moist or oily base to form a creamy mixture; it is served as a snack or appetizer. Bread, crackers, corn chips or crisp raw vegetables cut into pieces are eaten with dips. Popular for entertaining, dips are often thought of as a recent invention; however, the practice of using a firm food to scoop up a softer food is far from new and is found in all parts of the world. The ancient Romans snacked on pieces of coarse bread dipped in goat's milk; the chickpea mixture hummus has been made for thousands of years in the Middle East; taramasalata, a paste of mullet roe, has a long history around the Aegean; the Mayans of Central America enjoyed guacamole for many centuries before the arrival of the Spanish in the sixteenth century; and in India, dhal, made from puréed lentils, is often eaten with chapattis, roti or one of the many other types of flat bread.

Nowadays a variety of commercially prepared dips can be found on the shelves of most large supermarkets.

DESSERTS
STEAMED PUDDINGS

DARK CHOCOLATE PUDDING WITH MOCHA SAUCE

★ **Preparation time:** 30 minutes
Total cooking time: 1 hour 30 minutes
Serves 6

2½ cups all-purpose flour
¼ cup unsweetened cocoa powder
1½ teaspoons baking powder
¼ teaspoon salt
¼ teaspoon baking soda
⅔ cup butter
⅔ cup sugar
⅓ cup soft dark brown sugar
3½ oz dark (semisweet) chocolate, chopped
1 teaspoon vanilla extract

2 eggs, lightly beaten
¾ cup buttermilk

Mocha Sauc
¼ cup butter
5 oz dark (semisweet) chocolate, chopped
1½ cups heavy cream
1 tablespoon instant coffee powder
1–2 tablespoons chocolate liqueur

1 Brush an 8-cup bowl or covered mold with oil or melted butter. Line base with parchment paper, grease paper. Grease a large sheet of aluminum foil and a large sheet of wax paper. Lay paper over foil, greased side up. Pleat paper and foil down the center. Set aside.

2 Sift flour, cocoa, baking powder, salt and soda into large mixing bowl. Make a well in center. Combine butter, sugars, chocolate and vanilla in pan. Stir over low heat until butter and chocolate have melted and sugars have dissolved; remove from heat. Add butter mixture, beaten eggs and buttermilk to dry ingredients. Using a wooden spoon, stir until well combined; do not overbeat.

3 Spoon mixture into prepared bowl. Cover with the greased foil and paper, greased side down. Place lid over foil and secure clips. If you have no lid, lay a pleated towel over foil and tie securely with string under lip of bowl. Knot ends of towel together—this will act as a handle to help lower the bowl into the pan.

4 Place bowl on a trivet in a large, deep pan. Carefully pour boiling water into pan to come halfway up side of bowl. Bring to boil; cover and cook for about 1 hour and 20 minutes. Do not allow to boil dry—replenish pan with boiling water if necessary. When cooked, uncover, invert onto plate. Serve hot with Mocha Sauce.

5 To make Mocha Sauce: Combine butter, chocolate, cream and coffee powder. Stir over low heat until butter and chocolate have melted and mixture is smooth. Add chocolate liqueur, combine well; remove from heat. Cool slightly.

ABOVE: DARK CHOCOLATE PUDDING WITH MOCHA SAUCE. OPPOSITE PAGE: MINCEMEAT PUDDING WITH CITRUS SAUCE

MINCEMEAT PUDDING WITH CITRUS SAUCE

★★ *Preparation time:* 15 minutes
Total cooking time: 1 hour 40 minutes
Serves 6

1/2 cup butter	**Citrus Sauce**
1 cup sugar	*2 tablespoons sugar*
2 eggs, lightly beaten	*3/4 cup water*
2 teaspoons finely grated	*3/4 cup orange juice*
orange rind	*2 tablespoons lemon juice*
1/2 cup mincemeat	*2 teaspoons finely grated*
1 1/2 cups all-purpose flour	*orange rind*
1 teaspoon baking powder	*2 teaspoons finely grated*
1/4 teaspoon baking soda	*lemon rind*
1/4 cup milk	*1 tablespoon cornstarch*
1/4 cup orange juice	*1 teaspoon butter*
	1 egg yolk, beaten

1 Brush a 7 inch, 6-cup capacity bowl or mold with melted butter or oil. Line base with parchment paper, grease paper. Grease a large sheet of aluminum foil and a large sheet of wax paper. Lay paper over foil, greased side up, and pleat in the center. Set aside.

2 Using electric beaters, beat butter and sugar in mixing bowl until creamy. Add eggs gradually, beating well after each addition. Stir in rind.

3 Transfer mixture to large mixing bowl; add mincemeat. Combine flour, baking powder and soda. Using a metal spoon, fold in flour mixture alternately with liquids. Stir until mixture is just combined and almost smooth.

4 Spoon mixture into prepared bowl. Cover with the greased foil and paper, greased-side down. Place lid over foil and secure clips. If you have no lid, lay a pleated towel over foil, tie securely with string under the lip of the bowl. Knot the ends of the towel together—this will act as a handle to help lower the bowl into the pan.

5 Place the bowl on a trivet in a large, deep pan. Carefully pour boiling water down the side of pan to come halfway up side of bowl. Bring to the boil, cover and cook for 1 hour 30 minutes. Do not let pudding boil dry: replenish pan with boiling water if necessary as the pudding cooks. Once it is cooked, leave pudding in bowl for 5 minutes before uncovering and inverting onto a plate. Serve warm with Citrus Sauce.

6 To make Citrus Sauce: Combine sugar and all but 1 tablespoon of water in small pan. Heat gently, stirring, until sugar dissolves. Add orange and lemon juice and rinds. Combine cornstarch with reserved water to make a smooth paste. Bring sugar and juice mixture to boil and add cornstarch paste; stir until sauce thickens and clears. Stir a small amount of hot mixture into egg yolk; return all to saucepan. Boil 1 minute. Stir in butter. Remove from heat, cool slightly. Strain through a fine sieve into serving jug.

STEAMED JAM PUDDING

★ *Preparation time:* 10 minutes
Total cooking time: 1 hour
Serves 6

1/2 cup strawberry jam	*1 1/2 cups all-purpose flour*
1/4 cup butter	*1 teaspoon baking powder*
2/3 cup sugar	*1/2 cup milk*
1 egg	

1 Grease a 4-cup pudding bowl. Spread jam in the base. Beat butter, sugar and egg until smooth and creamy.

2 Sift in flour and baking powder. Add milk and mix well. Spread mixture carefully on top of the jam in the bowl.

3 Make a foil lid for the bowl; press the edges to seal tight. Make a string handle for the bowl and lower it onto a trivet in a large pan filled with boiling water to a depth of about 2 inches. Cover the pan with a lid. Simmer over low heat for 1 hour, taking care not to let pan boil dry—refill with boiling water if necessary. Run a knife around edge of pudding, turn onto serving plate.

Dirty Rice A Creole-Cajun dish in which long grain rice is mixed with ground beef, pork or chicken livers, vegetables, onions and herbs and cooked together.

Dolmades (Dolma) Small cylindrical packages consisting of rice, ground or minced lamb, finely chopped onion, nuts and seasonings wrapped in partially cooked grapevine or cabbage leaves, braised in a little stock or wine, and sprinkled with olive oil and lemon juice. Dolmades are usually eaten cold as a first course. Of Middle Eastern origin, the dish is served throughout Greece, Turkey and Lebanon. The name comes from the Persian *dolmeh,* meaning "stuffed."

Doner Kabob Lamb slices and salad sprinkled with a tahini-based sauce and wrapped in a piece of unleavened bread. Even-sized rounds of boneless lamb, marinated for up to 24 hours in a mixture of olive oil, salt, pepper, onion, rigani (a variety of oregano), thyme, parsley and sometimes mint, are threaded onto a heavy spit. Traditionally the spit was turned over a charcoal fire; today it is usually a vertical motor-driven rotisserie. When the surface of the lamb cooks it is removed in thin slices. The salad usually consists of tabouli, raw onion rings, lettuce and tomato; the sauce can be hummus, tahini, chili or barbecue. The doner kabob originated in Turkey and is popular throughout the Middle East.

Double-Cream Cheese A fresh cheese, such as cottage cheese enriched with more cream or butterfat.

Double Gloucester A firm-textured, yellow cow's milk cheese, with a mellow Cheddar-like flavor. It is also available layered with Stilton. Originally made in England from the milk of the now virtually extinct Gloucester cattle, it has more recently been made with full-cream milk from the herds of adjoining counties such as Somerset, Dorset and Wiltshire. The cheese almost became a casualty of the disruptions caused in Britain by World War II. When peace returned it seemed that traditional methods for making Double Gloucester had been lost, and the situation was saved only by the appearance of an ancient farm woman who before her death

DIPS

SALMON DIP

⭐ **Preparation time:** 10 minutes
Total cooking time: none
Makes about 3½ cups

13 oz can pink salmon, drained
8 oz packet cream cheese, softened
½ cup mayonnaise
juice of 1 lemon
¼ cup sour cream
3–4 gherkins, chopped
1 tablespoon chopped chives
freshly ground black pepper

1 Place all the ingredients for the dip in a food processor or blender. Process until the mixture is smooth.
2 Transfer the dip to a serving dish. Refrigerate until required. Serve with crackers.

LIVERWURST COTTAGE DIP

1 Place 8 oz cottage cheese, 4 oz liverwurst, ½ cup mayonnaise, 2 chopped dill pickles, 1 chopped onion, 1 tablespoon capers (optional) and 1 tablespoon prepared mustard in a food processor or blender. Process until the mixture is smooth.
2 Transfer the mixture to a serving dish. Cover and refrigerate. Serve dip with corn chips and a selection of crackers. Serves about 10.

Note: The flavor of this dip is best appreciated if it is served at room temperature.

SUN-DRIED TOMATO DIP WITH GRISSINI AND CRUDITES

⭐ **Preparation time:** 10 minutes
Total cooking time: none
Serves 6

5 oz sun-dried tomatoes in oil
2 cloves garlic
1 tablespoon mango chutney
2 scallions, chopped
6 anchovy fillets
2 tablespoons chopped fresh basil leaves
2 tablespoons grated Parmesan cheese
1 cup sour cream
6 slices prosciutto
12 bread sticks
vegetables for crudités—
baby carrots, celery, broccoli, cucumber, red pepper

1 Drain the sun-dried tomatoes and combine them with garlic, chutney, onions, anchovies, basil, Parmesan and sour cream in a food processor. Process for 40 seconds or until mixture is smooth.
2 Cut each slice of prosciutto in half lengthwise. Wrap a half-slice of prosciutto around each bread stick.
3 Cut carrots, celery, cucumber, pepper or other vegetables for crudités into sticks or slices; separate the broccoli into small florets. Transfer the dip mixture to a serving bowl and surround with bread sticks and vegetables arranged attractively on a serving platter.

ABOVE: SUN-DRIED TOMATO DIP.
OPPOSITE: ARUGULA AND PINE NUT DIP

AVOCADO DIP

Blend 1 large ripe peeled and pitted avocado in a food processor until it is smooth. Add 1/2 teaspoon finely grated lemon rind, 1 crushed small clove garlic, crushed, 1 cup plain yogurt; salt and freshly ground black pepper. Blend until the mixture is smooth, stir in 1/4 cup of finely chopped Spanish (large red) onion and 2 teaspoons finely chopped parsley. Serve with crackers, corn chips, cooked peeled shrimp, cooked new potatoes, raw button mushrooms, crisp celery, carrot or pepper sticks or baby tomatoes.

ARUGULA AND PINE NUT DIP

Place 3/4 cup light sour cream and 1/4 cup mayonnaise in a food processor. Add 1 cup arugula leaves and process until the arugula is chopped, but not too finely. Season the mixture with salt and freshly ground black pepper, then stir in 2 tablespoons pine nuts. Serve with cooked peeled shrimp, mini lamb or beef satay sticks, baked chicken wings, dolmades, raw button mushrooms, red pepper sticks or fried eggplant fingers.

SMOKED SALMON DIP

Beat 8 oz light cream cheese until smooth. Stir in 1/4 cup heavy cream, 1/4 cup finely chopped smoked salmon, 1 tablespoon finely chopped chives and some freshly ground white pepper. Serve with crackers, bread sticks, crisp cucumber or celery sticks, baby tomatoes, cooked warm new potatoes, raw button mushrooms, cooked asparagus spears or canned artichoke hearts.

FRAGRANT COCONUT DIP

Mix 1 cup plain yogurt with 1/4 cup coconut milk. Stir in 1 tablespoon sweet chili sauce, 1 tablespoon lime juice and 1 tablespoon chopped cilantro. Chill for 30 minutes and serve with fresh oysters, grilled sea scallops, cooked peeled shrimp, grilled fish pieces, chicken or lamb satay sticks, snow peas, blanched baby beans, celery sticks, melon or mango wedges.

MEDITERRANEAN DIP

Mix 8 oz light cream cheese with 1/2 cup plain yogurt and stir until smooth. Add 1 crushed small clove of garlic, 1 tablespoon thinly sliced black olives, 1 tablespoon sliced stuffed olives, 2 tablespoons grated Parmesan cheese, 1 tablespoon finely chopped fresh basil or oregano, and some freshly ground black pepper. Mix all the ingredients until combined. Serve the dip with bread sticks, crisp crackers, mini meatballs, canned artichoke hearts, cooked asparagus spears, or raw celery, carrot, pepper or zucchini sticks.

was able to instruct cheese factory workers in the craft and so keep the cheese alive.

Dough A mixture of flour and liquid, usually water, to which other ingredients (butter, margarine, seasonings or sweeteners) are often added before it is baked into bread or pastry. Although the ingredients are basically the same as for batter, the proportions are different (dough has far less liquid and is thick enough to be kneaded). There are two main types of dough: soft dough, with a slightly higher liquid content, is used for cookies and doughnuts; stiff dough, with less liquid, is used for pastry, pie crusts and crackers. Fermented dough, called sourdough, was originally used instead of yeast as a leavening agent when baking bread. The word "dough" probably comes from the Anglo-Saxon *deawain*, meaning "to moisten."

Doughnut A small, usually ring-shaped cake, made of deep-fried yeast dough, which is dusted with spiced sugar or frosted. It has a moist, bread-like texture.

Doughnuts can be twisted or round in shape, and are sometimes filled with jam or custard. The ring doughnut is of modern North American origin, attributed to John Blondel, who in the 1870s patented a cutter with a central hole.

Drambuie A Scottish liqueur, made from whiskey and honey.

Dredge To coat food by dusting, sprinkling or rolling with a dry ingredient, such as flour or sugar.

Dresden Sauce A cold sauce made from sour cream, mustard and horseradish, usually served with smoked or boiled fish.

Dressing A liquid used to moisten and flavor a variety of foods, from salads or cooked vegetables to raw meat or fish dishes. Dressings can be based on olive oil, lemon juice, wine or vinegars, with various flavorings, or ingredients such as eggs, cream or yogurt.

Dried Beef See Jerky

Dried Fruit See Fruit, Dried

Drippings The fat that drips from meat during roasting. Drippings

DRINKS
COCKTAILS

MARTINI

Stir ice, 2½ oz gin and ½ oz dry vermouth in a mixing glass. Strain into a martini glass and garnish with an olive. Serves one.

MARGARITA

Shake ice, 1½ oz tequila, 1 oz lemon juice and ½ oz Cointreau in a shaker. Strain into salt-frosted glass and garnish with lemon peel. Serves one.

JAPANESE SLIPPER

Combine ice, 1 oz each Midori, Cointreau and lemon juice in a shaker; shake well. Strain, serve in a chilled glass. Garnish with a lemon slice and a sprig of flowers. Serves one.

PINA COLADA

Place ice, 1½ oz light rum, 1 oz coconut cream, ½ oz heavy cream, ½ oz sugar syrup and 3 oz pineapple juice in a shaker and shake well. Strain into a serving glass and garnish with a slice of fresh pineapple and a maraschino cherry. Serves one.

BRANDY ALEXANDER

Place ice, 1 oz brandy, 1 oz crème de cacao and 2 oz cream in a shaker; shake well. Strain into a serving glass and garnish with a sprinkling of ground nutmeg and a strawberry. Serves one.

LONG ISLAND ICED TEA

Place some crushed ice, ½ oz light rum, ½ oz vodka, ½ oz gin, ½ oz Cointreau and ½ oz tequila in a long glass. Top with cola and a dash of lemon juice. Garnish with a lemon slice. Serves one.

FROZEN STRAWBERRY DAIQUIRI

Blend 1½ oz light rum, ½ oz strawberry liqueur, ½ oz lime juice, 6 strawberries and some crushed ice together in a blender. Pour into a glass and garnish with a strawberry. Serves one.

ABOVE, LEFT TO RIGHT: MARGARITA, PINA COLADA, FROZEN STRAWBERRY DAIQUIRI, JAPANESE SLIPPER. OPPOSITE PAGE, LEFT TO RIGHT: RED SANGRIA, PIMM'S PUNCH, PINEAPPLE AND PASSIONFRUIT PUNCH

CHAMPAGNE PUNCH

Place 8 oz strawberries in a bowl, sprinkle with ⅓ cup sugar, and add ½ bottle Sauternes and ½ cup brandy. Place in refrigerator and chill for at least 1 hour. Just before serving, pour in 3 bottles of champagne slowly and mix all ingredients gently. Serves 18–20.

RED SANGRIA

Mix 3 bottles dry red wine, ¾ cup Grand Marnier (or other orange-flavored liqueur) and 3 tablespoons sugar in a large container such as a punch bowl, or in two or three jugs. Cut 3 oranges and 3 lemons into 24 wedges each. Add wedges to sangria and chill for up to 24 hours. Just before serving, add 3 cups soda water and ice cubes. Serves 18–20.

PINEAPPLE AND PASSIONFRUIT PUNCH

Combine 2 cups strong hot black tea with ¼ cup demerara sugar in a medium bowl. Stir until the sugar has dissolved. Cool. Place ¾ cup lemon juice, 4 cups pineapple juice, 1–2 tablespoons lime cordial, a 40 oz bottle soda water, two 40 oz bottles lemonade, 13½ oz can crushed pineapple, the cooled tea and the pulp of 5 passionfruit in a large punch bowl. Mix well. Add crushed ice, shredded fresh mint and orange slices before serving. As a variation, a few drops of Angostura bitters may be added to the recipe. Serves 18–20.

BRANDY ALEXANDER PUNCH

Combine 3 cups brandy, 1½ cups crème de cacao and 2⅓ cups heavy cream in a large bowl or jug. Whisk until well combined. Add some crushed ice to a large punch bowl, pour over the cream mixture. Sprinkle with a little nutmeg and decorate with some strawberry slices to serve. Serves 10–15.

PIMM'S PUNCH

Place ice into a large punch bowl or jug. Add 1½ cups each Pimm's No 1 and Southern Comfort, ¾ cup each sweet vermouth and dark rum (not overproof), 1½ cups orange juice, 3 cups champagne, 8 oz hulled and sliced strawberries, and orange, lime and lemon slices. Add some freshly sliced mango for a tropical touch. Mix together well. Serve immediately. Serves 10–15.

should be strained from the roasting pan and left to set so that the jellied meat juices can be removed from the bottom.

Dry Ice Crystallized carbon dioxide used for long-term refrigeration because it doesn't produce water when it melts.

Duchess Potatoes A purée of potatoes blended with butter, egg yolk

and seasonings and piped into various individual shapes. Used as a garnish for roasts or as a decorative border for fish, savory dishes and casseroles. The mixture is glazed with beaten egg yolk, then browned in a hot oven or under the broiler.

Duck A large, long-bodied waterbird with dark, moist, richly flavored flesh. Duck has been part of the human diet since the time of the earliest hunters. Always in plentiful supply on rivers, lakes, ponds and

marshlands around the world, the bird and its eggs were there for the taking. It was the first fowl to be domesticated, probably by the Chinese some 4000 years ago, although some claim the first duck farmers were the Incas of South America.

Domesticated breeds are now kept in all parts of the world; even so, some of the duck eaten today is, by preference, still taken from the wild. Ducks bred for the table include the large and lean Barbary duck of Europe; the English Aylesbury and Gadwell; the French Nantais, which is often reared semi-wild, and the Rouenais; and the Peking duck of China. In Australia the most common breed is a cross between the Peking and the Aylesbury. In the United States most ducks are raised commercially and fed a special diet to make the meat tender and sweet. Available fresh or frozen, ducks weigh between three and six pounds; ducklings younger than nine weeks weigh less. Most domestic ducks come from Long Island. Wild ducks include mallards, wigeons and teals. Wild ducks usually

DUCK

ROAST DUCK WITH MANDARIN SAUCE

⭐ **Preparation time:** 30 minutes
Total cooking time: 1 hour 50 minutes
Serves 8

3 x 3¼ lb ducks
¼ cup butter, melted

Stuffing
⅓ cup butter
12 scallions, chopped
3 garlic cloves, crushed
3 teaspoons grated ginger
8 cups fresh white bread crumbs
¼ cup chopped cilantro
2 eggs, lightly beaten

Mandarin Sauce
10 oz can mandarin orange segments
2 tablespoons cornstarch
4 cups light chicken stock
½ cup orange juice
2 tablespoons lemon juice
1 tablespoon honey
1 tablespoon soy sauce
2 teaspoons grated ginger
1 tablespoon sugar

1 Preheat oven to moderate 350°F. Rinse ducks, pat dry with paper towel.
2 To make Stuffing: Heat the butter in medium pan, add onions, garlic and ginger. Stir-fry for 3 minutes or until the vegetables are soft, add the bread crumbs, cilantro and eggs and stir until combined. Remove from heat. Spoon the stuffing into the ducks, ensuring that each has the same amount.

3 Tie wings and drumsticks securely in place. Place ducks on roasting rack over a shallow baking dish and brush with butter. Roast for one hour, basting ducks occasionally with pan juices. While the ducks are roasting, prepare the Mandarin Sauce.
4 To make Mandarin Sauce: Process the undrained mandarin segments to a smooth texture in a blender or food processor. Place the cornstarch in a small pan, add a little stock and stir until smooth. Add the remaining stock, orange and lemon juice, honey, soy sauce, ginger, sugar and mandarin purée. Stir over medium heat until the sauce boils and becomes thick.
5 Remove the ducks from the oven, drain pan juices, place the ducks in a baking dish, and pour over the Mandarin Sauce. Roast for another 40 minutes. To test if the duck is cooked, insert a skewer into the thigh. If the juice runs clear, the duck is ready. Strain sauce and serve with the ducks.

ABOUT DUCK

■ To prepare ducks for cooking, remove the fat sac at the base of the tail, rinse thoroughly in cold water and dry with paper towels. Prick the duck all over with a fine metal skewer. For roasting, skewer the neck skin to the back, tie the legs to the tail and turn the wing tips underneath.

SHERRIED DUCK WITH OLIVES AND WALNUTS

★ ★ **Preparation time:** 20 minutes
Total cooking time: 1 hour 45 minutes
Serves 4–6

2 tablespoons olive oil
4 lb duck, cleaned and
   trussed
2 onions, halved
2 carrots, cut into large
   pieces
¼ cup medium dry sherry
¼ cup chicken stock or
   water
3 tablespoons butter

2 tablespoons all-purpose
   flour
¼ cup medium dry
   sherry, extra
½ cup fresh orange juice
½ cup chicken stock or
   water, extra
½ cup stuffed green
   olives, warmed in brine
½ cup walnut halves,
   warmed in oven

1 Preheat oven to 350°F. Heat olive oil in large baking pan or dish on top of stove. Add duck, onions and carrots. Gently turn duck to brown all over, being careful not to split the skin. Pour over combined dry sherry and stock or water. Cover with aluminum foil. Bake in oven for 1 hour, basting occasionally with juices (for crisp skin, uncover during last 15 minutes).
2 Remove the duck and vegetables from the baking pan. Reserve any remaining liquid. Discard vegetables.
3 Place baking pan on top of stove over medium heat, add butter, allow to melt and brown, scraping pan; do not allow to burn. Remove from heat, stir in flour. Gradually add combined extra sherry, orange juice, extra stock and reserved liquid. Return to heat and cook, stirring constantly, until mixture boils and thickens.
4 Put duck back in pan and spoon over sauce. Cover and bake at 350°F for 15–20 minutes or until duck is tender. Place on heated serving dish, pour over sauce. Garnish with warm stuffed olives and walnut halves.

WARM DUCK SALAD

★ **Preparation time:** 15 minutes
Total cooking time: none
Serves 4

Oriental Dressing
¼ cup peanut oil
1 tablespoon cider or
   white wine vinegar
1 tablespoon honey,
   warmed
2 teaspoons grated fresh
   ginger
1 teaspoon soy sauce
¼ teaspoon five-spice
   powder

1 large Chinese
   barbecued duck,
   chopped
10 oz can mandarin
   orange segments, drained
3½ oz snow peas,
   trimmed
1 cup bean sprouts
½ cup canned water
   chestnuts, sliced
½ cup sliced scallions

1 Half an hour before serving, place all the dressing ingredients in a small jar, shake well for 1 minute.
2 Place the duck, drained oranges, snow peas, bean sprouts, water chestnuts and onions in a large bowl. Add the dressing and toss gently before serving.

OPPOSITE PAGE: ROAST DUCK WITH MANDARIN SAUCE. ABOVE: WARM DUCK SALAD

weigh a little over one pound when dressed.

The ancient Egyptians ate the ducks of the Nile. The Romans feasted on the breast and brains of wild duck. Throughout Europe until medieval times the bird, although eaten regularly, seems always to have been caught in the wild and not reared in the fowl yard.

Duck is a favorite in the cooking of France and China. The art of drying duck meat has been used in China for more than 2000 years.

Because of its fattiness duck should be roasted or braised. It is often served with fruit to offset its greasiness, as in the famous French dish, duck à l'orange. Very little of the bird need go to waste. The carcass can be used to make stock and the liver to make pâté. Duckling is best broiled, grilled or roasted—it does not need stuffing. The older the bird, the more strongly it is flavored.

Dumpling A small ball of dough, either savory or sweet, poached and served as an

accompaniment to meat dishes and desserts. Savory dumplings simmered in meat stock or stew are traditionally served with roast or boiled beef. In Asian cooking, mixtures of finely chopped pork or beef and vegetables wrapped in dough and steamed are called dumplings. Sweet dumplings are simmered in either a dessert sauce or fruit juice. The name is also given to a piece of fruit encased in a sweet pastry dough and baked.

Dundee Cake A butter cake flavored with dried fruit and nuts.

Before baking the top is closely covered with blanched and halved almonds. The cake is named after Dundee, a seaport on the east coast of Scotland.

Dungness Crab Caught off the Pacific coast of America, a popular eating crab with large legs and pinkish meat.

Durian A large, oval fruit covered with an armour of close-set, short, hard spikes. The durian is native to Southeast Asia. In Thailand it is so highly regarded that some farmers employ security guards to deter fruit thieves. The sticky, cream-colored pulp of the durian is noted

DUMPLINGS

SOUP WITH CHICKEN DUMPLINGS

★★ **Preparation time:** 25 minutes
Total cooking time: 15 minutes
Serves 6

1 boneless chicken breast, skin removed
2 eggs
½ cup finely chopped leek
½ cup finely chopped onion
½ cup finely chopped carrot
1 teaspoon pepper

1 teaspoon dried thyme
2 cups fresh white bread crumbs
1 tablespoon chopped parsley
3 cups rich chicken stock
chopped parsley, for garnish

1 Cut chicken into small pieces. Process eggs in food processor until thick and creamy. Add leek, process until smooth, add onion and carrot, process until smooth. Add chicken, blend until mixture is thick and smooth; transfer to bowl.
2 Add pepper, thyme, bread crumbs and parsley. Shape dumplings between two spoons dipped in water. Place on lightly greased tray and cover.
3 Bring stock to boil, lower heat. Spoon dumplings into simmering stock, cook until they float. Cover and simmer 10 minutes. Divide between six soup bowls, pour ½ cup of chicken stock over each. Sprinkle with chopped parsley.

DUMPLINGS (BASIC RECIPE)

★ **Preparation time:** 5 minutes
Total cooking time: 15–20 minutes
Serves 4

1 cup all-purpose flour
½ teaspoon baking powder
¼ teaspoon salt
ground white pepper

2 tablespoons butter or shortening
1 egg, beaten
¼ cup milk

1 Sift flour, baking powder, salt and pepper into a bowl. Rub in butter until mixture resembles fine bread crumbs. Combine egg and milk and add to flour, mixing to a soft dough.
2 Using lightly floured hands, shape dumplings into balls about 1¼ inches in diameter. About 20 minutes before stew or casserole is cooked, arrange dumplings in a layer on top, leaving space between them.
3 Cover and cook until dumplings are light and fluffy, about 15–20 minutes.

Note: If desired, dumplings can be steamed in a perforated steamer for 30–40 minutes.

HERB DUMPLINGS

Add 1 tablespoon chopped parsley and 1 teaspoon chopped thyme to basic dumpling recipe. Good with veal, chicken, beef or vegetable stews.

ZUCCHINI CHEESE DUMPLINGS

Add ¼ cup grated zucchini and 1 tablespoon grated Parmesan cheese to basic dumpling recipe. Serve with chicken, lamb or beef stews.

ORANGE DUMPLINGS

Add 1 teaspoon finely grated orange rind and 2 teaspoons chopped parsley to the basic dumpling recipe. Good with pork, veal or lamb stews.

HIGH FIBER DUMPLINGS

Use half whole-wheat flour and half plain flour in basic dumpling recipe and add 1 tablespoon finely chopped chives to dry ingredients. Good with beef, lamb or vegetable stews.

ABOVE: SOUP WITH CHICKEN DUMPLINGS.
OPPOSITE: BEEF GOULASH WITH CARAWAY DUMPLINGS

especially for the contrast between its putrid odor and delicious taste. The flesh of the durian is eaten raw, as a dessert, either on its own or with sugar and whipped cream or ice cream. In Java the durian is made into fruit jelly. The seeds can be roasted and eaten like nuts. Canned durian pulp is also available.

Durum Wheat A variety of wheat milled to produce semolina flour, a more durable flour than that used to make bread. It is ideal for pasta making. The wheat is noted for its extreme hardness and yellow color.

Duxelles The French name for a mixture of mushrooms finely chopped with some minced shallots, then sautéed in butter until soft and dry. Duxelles add a strong mushroom flavor to stuffings, gravies and sauces and they can also be used as a garnish.

BEEF GOULASH WITH CARAWAY DUMPLINGS

★ ★ **Preparation time:** 1 hour
Total cooking time: 1 hour 15 minutes
Serves 6

3 lb top round steak
1/2 cup all-purpose flour
1/4 teaspoon ground black pepper
1/3 cup olive oil
1 clove garlic, crushed
2 medium onions, sliced
1 teaspoon ground sweet paprika
1/2 teaspoon ground cinnamon
1/2 cup beef stock
1/3 cup red wine

1/2 teaspoon dried mixed herbs
2/3 cup bottled chunky tomato sauce
1 large red pepper

Caraway Dumplings
1 1/2 cups all-purpose flour
1 teaspoon baking powder
1/8 teaspoon salt
5 tablespoons butter
1/2 cup milk
1 teaspoon caraway seeds
1 tablespoon milk, extra

1 Preheat oven to moderate 350°F. Trim the meat and cut into 1 1/4 inch cubes. Combine flour and pepper on wax paper. Toss meat in seasoned flour, shake off excess.
2 Heat 2 tablespoons of the oil in a heavy-based pan. Cook the meat quickly in small batches over medium-high heat until well browned; drain on paper towel.
3 Heat remaining oil. Add garlic and onion, stir over medium heat for 2 minutes or until soft.

4 Return meat to pan with spices, stock, wine, mixed herbs and tomato sauce; bring to boil. Remove from heat, transfer to a deep casserole dish. Cook, covered, for 45 minutes. Remove from the oven and remove lid. Increase oven temperature to hot 475°F.
5 Cut the pepper into halves lengthwise; remove the seeds. Place on cold, greased broiler rack, skin-side-up. Place under a hot broiler for 3–7 minutes or until skin burns and blisters. Remove and cool. Carefully peel off skins, discard. Cut pepper into 3/4 inch wide strips. Arrange over meat.
6 To make Caraway Dumplings: Place flour, baking powder, salt and butter in food processor. Process 10 seconds or until mixture is fine and crumbly. Add milk, process 10 seconds or until mixture forms a soft dough. Turn onto lightly floured surface. Add caraway seeds, knead 1 minute or until smooth. Press out to 1/2 inch thickness. Cut into 1 1/2 inch rounds with a fluted cutter. Top the meat with dumplings; brush with extra milk. Return to oven, cook, uncovered, 15 minutes or until dumplings are puffed and golden.

Note: Thickly sliced potatoes can be added to the goulash at Step 4 instead of dumplings, OR slice potatoes thinly and place, overlapping, over surface. Dab with small pieces of butter. Cook until golden and crisp.

E

Eccles Cake A traditional small English cake of currants, chopped peel, brown sugar and spices encased in puff pastry. The cakes were originally made to sell during the Eccles Wakes, festival days once held in the Lancashire town of Eccles.

Eclair A finger-shaped bun made by piping lengths of

choux pastry onto greased baking sheets and baking them until crisp. The cooked pastry is split open and filled with cream or custard and topped with chocolate or coffee icing or frosting.

Edam A semihard cow's milk cheese of mellow flavor, made from a combination of full cream and skim milk. Edam is made in the shape of a sphere and coated in red wax. In Holland ripening cheeses are assessed by

E G G S

EGG, SALMON AND RICE PIE

✦✦ **Preparation time:** 50 minutes
Total cooking time: 1 hour
Serves 8

3/4 cup fish stock or clam juice
1/4 cup short-grain rice
3 tablespoons butter
2 tablespoons all purpose flour
2/3 cup milk
1 egg, lightly beaten
1/4 cup finely chopped fresh parsley
1/2 cup fresh or frozen peas
2 sheets frozen puff pastry, thawed
2 x 6 1/2 oz cans pink salmon, drained
4 hard-boiled eggs, quartered
1 egg, extra, lightly beaten

1 Preheat oven to 425°F. Line two baking sheets with parchment paper. Place stock in medium heavy-bottom pan. Bring to boil. Add rice, reduce heat. Simmer, covered, 10 minutes or until rice absorbs all liquid. Remove from heat.
2 Heat butter in medium pan; add flour. Stir over low heat for 2 minutes or until flour is lightly golden. Add milk gradually to pan, stirring until mixture is smooth. Stir constantly over medium heat for 5 minutes or until mixture boils and thickens; boil for 1 minute, remove from heat. Cool slightly, stir in egg, parsley and peas.
3 Carefully lay pastry sheets on a work surface. Place salmon in small bowl, flake with a fork. Spread evenly in an oblong shape down center of each pastry sheet, leaving a 1¼ inch border on all sides. Place the quartered eggs on top.
4 Combine rice and pea mixture in a bowl. Mix well. Spoon evenly over salmon. Brush pastry edges with extra egg. Fold in edges like a parcel. Turn over and place on baking sheet, seam-side-down. Make three diagonal slits in top of pie. Brush with egg. Bake 30 minutes until pastry is puffed and golden. Cut each pie into four to serve. Serve with a green salad.

ABOUT EGGS

■ Use eggs as quickly as possible after purchase (although eggs will last for up to five weeks); store in the carton in refrigerator with pointed ends downward. Discard eggs that are broken or cracked because they may be infected with harmful bacteria. In some countries, infants, pregnant women and the elderly are advised to avoid eating raw or lightly cooked eggs. This is because of the danger of salmonella. Dishes made with raw eggs (or almost raw eggs) such as mayonnaise, mousses or Caesar salad dressing should be eaten within two days.
■ White or brown eggs have the same nutritional value. The type of poultry feed causes variations in yolk color; some say it also affects the taste.
■ For cooking, eggs should be at room temperature. Eggs separate more easily if fresh and cold; bring to room temperature after separating. Whites can be stored for up to a week and frozen for up to nine months. Unbroken yolks can be refrigerated for up to three days, covered with water in a small bowl.

ABOVE: EGG, SALMON AND RICE PIE.
OPPOSITE PAGE: CREAMY EGGS WITH RED PEPPER

CREAMY EGGS WITH RED PEPPER

Preparation time: 10 minutes
Total cooking time: 10 minutes
Serves 4–6

1 tablespoon butter or
  olive oil
2 onions, sliced
2 small red peppers
6 eggs

½ cup heavy cream
freshly ground black pepper
chopped parsley or dill,
  optional

1 Heat butter or oil in a heavy-bottom frying pan. Add onion and cook slowly until golden brown. Cut peppers into thin strips; add to pan and cook until soft.
2 Combine eggs, cream and pepper; beat well.
3 Pour mixture over onion and peppers. Stir gently until eggs are creamy and soft.
4 Serve immediately. Sprinkle with chopped parsley or dill if desired.

Note: Do not allow the mixture to overcook or the eggs will become tough and "weep."

QUICK EGGS FLORENTINE

Tear 2 bunches spinach into pieces. Steam or microwave until tender. Combine spinach with 2 tablespoons butter, nutmeg and salt to taste. Divide into two ramekin dishes. Top each with a poached egg, sprinkle with grated Cheddar cheese. Bake in a moderate oven 350°F for 5–10 minutes until cheese melts and browns.

HUEVOS RANCHEROS

Preparation time: 1 hour
Total cooking time: 35 minutes
Serves 6

2 small red peppers,
  halved and seeded
2 teaspoons olive oil
2 teaspoons olive oil,
  extra
1 small onion, finely
  chopped
2 tablespoons tomato
  paste

1 teaspoon ground oregano
1 medium green pepper,
  finely chopped
2 jalapeño chili peppers,
  finely sliced
6 x 6 inch tortillas
6 eggs, fried or poached
½ cup grated Cheddar
  cheese

1 Brush small red peppers with oil. Broil for 5 minutes or until skin is black. Cover with damp towel until cool; peel off the skin. Cut pepper flesh into small pieces and place in a food processor. Process for 30 seconds or until smooth. Set aside.
2 Heat extra oil in a medium pan. Add onion, tomato paste, oregano and green pepper. Cook until soft. Stir in red pepper purée and chilies. Heat gently, stirring for 1 minute.
3 To serve, place a fried or poached egg onto a tortilla. Top with a tablespoon of pepper sauce and sprinkle with grated Cheddar cheese.

TO POACH EGGS

■ For best results, use eggs less than a week old. Half fill a shallow pan with cold water, bring to the boil over medium high heat then reduce heat slightly so water is just simmering. Break 1 egg into a cup, slip the cup into simmering water and slide the egg into the water by tilting the cup. Repeat with remaining eggs, allowing each an equal amount of space. Cover pan and cook for 3 minutes for soft eggs and up to 5 minutes for firmer ones. Remove pan from heat. Lift poached egg from water with slotted spoon; rest spoon on paper towel to remove any water. Transfer egg to a slice of hot toast.

TO SCRAMBLE EGGS

■ Whisk the required number of eggs in a bowl together with a small amount (1 tablespoon per egg) of milk or cream. Melt 1–2 tablespoons of butter in a pan. Pour the eggs into the pan and stir over very low heat until the eggs begin to thicken and bubble. (Add herbs or flavorings at this stage, but do not salt.) Remove from heat and continue stirring another minute. Serve immediately.

rapping knuckles against the sphere (a dull thump is the sign of a well-cured cheese ready for eating).

Eel A long, snake-like fish with a smooth, slippery, olive green or silvery skin, found throughout the world. Most commonly eaten are freshwater varieties; saltwater eels are larger and include the moray and the conger. The eel has firm, white, fatty flesh which deteriorates rapidly and so must be cooked as quickly as possible after killing. For this reason, in many parts of the world, eels are kept in large tanks and sold live. Smoked eel is also available, and in Britain and northern Europe is a popular appetizer, served either in thin slices or as fillets lifted off the bone, dressed with lemon juice on a round of rye bread. The matchstick-thin, finger-length, transparent young are called elvers or glass eels and are a delicacy in Spain, Italy, France and Belgium.

Egg An oval reproductive body enclosed in a protective shell. Most commonly eaten is the egg of the domestic hen, but duck, goose, quail, pheasant, guinea fowl, partridge, plover, ostrich and emu eggs are also used. In some parts of the world the fish-flavored, soft-skinned egg of the sea turtle is an important food. The egg is a highly nutritious and well-balanced package: two eggs provide half of the body's total daily protein and vitamin needs. The yolk, about 30 per cent of the total weight of the egg, contains more than 80 per cent of its protein.

Most eggs are from hens caged in large, temperature-controlled and artificially lit sheds. White eggs often come from the White Leghorn hen. Brown eggs, laid by the Rhode Island Red or Plymouth Rock hen are preferred in the Northeast United States, although there is no difference between the nutritive value of white and brown. Eggs are graded by quality, AA, A and B from the United States Department of Agriculture (USDA) and Peewee through Extra Large or Jumbo by size. Most cooking and baking requires large eggs.

Eggs are best used as fresh as possible. Two simple, age-old methods of testing freshness are based on the fact that the little weight and moisture lost each day by evaporation through the porous shell is replaced by air in the

EGGS VINDALOO

Preparation time: 25 minutes
Total cooking time: 30 minutes
Serves 4–6

8 eggs	1 green chili pepper, seeded and chopped
1 teaspoon vinegar	
3 tablespoons ghee or butter	2 tablespoons vindaloo or other hot curry paste
1 large onion, coarsely grated	3 tablespoons coconut milk
1 teaspoon mashed garlic	1/3 cup water
	vegetable oil for deep frying
1/2 teaspoon grated ginger	1 tablespoon chopped cilantro or mint leaves
	lemon juice

1 Boil the eggs in water to cover, with 1 teaspoon vinegar added, for 8–9 minutes. Remove to a large dish of cold water; when cooled, peel eggs and prick evenly all over with a fork. Dry well.
2 Melt the ghee or butter, cook onion, garlic, gingerroot and chili until onions are soft and golden. Add vindaloo or curry paste, cook over medium heat for 2 minutes. Add coconut milk and water. Cook, stirring, until sauce thickens.
3 Heat the oil and deep-fry the eggs until they turn golden on the surface. Transfer eggs to pan containing vindaloo mixture. Add cilantro and lemon juice to taste and simmer in the sauce for 8–9 minutes. Serve with rice.

CARROT PARSNIP FRITTATA

Preparation time: 10 minutes
Total cooking time: 20 minutes
Serves 2–4

1/4 cup butter	4 eggs
1 clove garlic, crushed	3 tablespoons chopped flat-leaf parsley
2 parsnips, peeled and grated	freshly ground black pepper
2 carrots, peeled and grated	2 teaspoons olive oil

1 Melt butter, add the garlic and fry for one minute without browning. Add the parsnip and carrot and cook gently with the lid on the pan for 10 minutes. Allow to cool.
2 Beat the eggs just enough to combine them. Add parsley and freshly ground black pepper and stir in the cooled parsnip and carrot.
3 Heat olive oil in an omelet pan or other small pan. Pour in the egg mixture to cover the base of the pan. Lift the edges of the frittata with a spatula to allow uncooked egg to run underneath. When the frittata is set on top, turn it over, or brown it under a broiler. Serve frittata warm sprinkled with parsley if desired. Serve with a crisp green salad and slices of crusty French bread.

Note: For extra flavor, freshly grated Cheddar or Parmesan cheese can be added to the frittata. Stir in with the parsnip and carrot or sprinkle on top before broiling. This recipe makes a delicious, light main meal.

LEFT: *EGGS VINDALOO;* ABOVE: *CARROT PARSNIP FRITTATA.* OPPOSITE PAGE: *SCOTCH EGGS*

SCOTCH EGGS

Preparation time: 15 minutes
Total cooking time: 8 minutes
Makes 4

4 hard-boiled eggs
8 oz ground sausage
1 small onion, grated
2 tablespoons dried
 bread crumbs
1 egg, separated

1 tablespoon chopped
 fresh parsley
salt and pepper
pinch nutmeg
1/2 cup dried
 bread crumbs, extra
oil for deep-frying

1 Remove shells from eggs. Place sausage, onion, bread crumbs, egg yolk, parsley, salt, pepper and nutmeg in a medium bowl. Stir to combine. Divide mixture into four. Using wet hands, press one portion of sausage mixture, large enough to cover egg, into palm of hand. Press around egg to enclose. Repeat with remaining sausage and eggs.
2 Coat Scotch Eggs in lightly beaten egg white, then coat with bread crumbs.
3 Heat oil in a heavy-based pan. Lower eggs into oil, cook over medium heat for 8 minutes until golden and crisp. Remove from oil. Drain.

EGGS BENEDICT

Preparation time: 10 minutes
Total cooking time: 10 minutes
Serves 2

**Quick Hollandaise
 Sauce**
1/2 cup butter
4 egg yolks
3 teaspoons lemon juice
cayenne pepper to taste

Bacon and Eggs
2 tablespoons butter
4 thick slices Canadian
 bacon
2 English muffins
4 eggs

1 **To make Sauce:** Heat butter slowly in pan until it begins to bubble. Place egg yolks, lemon juice and cayenne in electric blender, blend for 5 seconds. Slowly pour hot butter onto yolk mixture in a steady stream until it is all added. Transfer sauce to a bowl, cover and keep warm.
2 Melt butter in a pan and heat ham slices through. Split muffins, toast, then place a slice of ham on each muffin half. Keep muffins warm.
3 Poach eggs, drain, place one on each ham slice.
4 Spoon warm Hollandaise Sauce over the eggs. Garnish with parsley or caviar and serve.

sac at the round end of the egg. To assess the freshness of an egg either put it in a bowl of water; if fresh it will sink to the bottom; or hold it up to a strong light, the larger the air sac the older the egg. A fresh egg broken onto a plate will have a well-rounded yolk centered in a thick,

sticky white; in an older egg the white is runny and the yolk flattened. Never use dirty or cracked eggs.

Popular methods of cooking eggs include simmering, frying and poaching. Cook egg yolks until firm to kill any unwanted organisms. Refrigerate cooked eggs within two hours. Make sure all custards or pie fillings are cooked or baked thoroughly. Wash utensils and containers which have come into contact with raw egg carefully. The famous hundred-year-old eggs of China are usually raw duck eggs, buried in a mixture of salt, lime, ash

and tea leaves. From the time of ancient Rome, eggshells were crushed to prevent evil spirits hiding in them. The egg has long been a symbol of

renewal. The colored Easter egg originated in medieval European spring festivals.

Egg Foo Yung An American version of a Chinese omelet of meat flavored with soy sauce.

Egg Noodle A type of pasta made from wheat flour, egg and water and cut into long strips.

Eggplant (Aubergine) A fruit used as a vegetable with smooth, shiny, purple skin and creamy white, pithy flesh studded with numerous tiny, soft, pale brown edible seeds. It may be egg-shaped, from which it takes its common name, round, or long and thin; some varieties are white-skinned.

The eggplant originated in South-East Asia, where varieties still grow wild, and in antiquity was cultivated in India, China and Turkey. The eggplant is widely used in Mediterranean cookery. It can be steamed, boiled, broiled, sautéed and stuffed, or it can be added to salads or made into dips. The eggplant is a basic ingredient of classic dishes such as ratatouille and moussaka.

CLASSIC PUFFY OMELET

★ **Preparation time:** 5 minutes
Total cooking time: 10 minutes
Serves 2

4 eggs, separated
1 tablespoon milk or heavy cream
salt and freshly ground pepper
2 tablespoons butter

1 Beat egg yolks in medium bowl until thick. Add milk or cream, salt and pepper. Whisk whites in medium bowl with electric beaters until soft peaks form. Fold whites into yolk mixture.
2 Heat butter in pan until it covers base of pan and foams. Pour in omelet mixture and cook over medium heat until base of omelet sets and it turns lightly golden underneath.
3 Cook top of omelet under a hot broiler until puffed and lightly golden, or bake in a moderate oven 350°F for 5 minutes. Puffy omelet is usually served flat, not folded.

Note: For a sweet puffy omelet, omit salt and pepper; add 1 tablespoon of sugar to egg yolks before beating.

CLASSIC FRENCH OMELET

★ **Preparation time:** 2 minutes (unfilled)
Total cooking time: 1 minute
Serves 1

3 eggs
1 tablespoon water
salt
freshly ground pepper
2 tablespoons butter

1 Beat eggs in small bowl until yolks and whites are just combined. Stir in water, salt and pepper.
2 Heat butter in a pan until it covers base of pan and foams. Pour eggs into pan. Over moderate heat, draw outside edges of mixture into center with a spatula until eggs are lightly set.
3 Add a hot prepared filling if desired. Tilt the pan away from you so that the omelet can be folded or rolled easily. Carefully tip omelet onto a warmed plate. Serve.

Note: Use 2 eggs for each filled omelet and 3 eggs for each plain omelet. Suitable fillings would include grated cheese, chopped ham, cooked asparagus, mushrooms or seafood.

CLASSIC PUFFY OMELET (RIGHT);
CLASSIC FRENCH OMELET (LEFT)

Egg Roll (Spring Roll) Small, thin rice dough or egg noodle wrappers rolled around fillings of chopped vegetables, meat, poultry, or seafood, and deep-fried.

Eggs Benedict A dish consisting of a poached egg, a slice of Canadian bacon and a dollop of Hollandaise sauce, all perched on an English muffin.

Eggs Florentine A light dish consisting of two soft poached eggs in a nest of cooked spinach topped with mornay sauce and grated cheese.

Emmenthal (Swiss) A hard, pale yellow cow's milk cheese, with a mild, nutty flavor. Made in huge, flat wheels and with characteristic, large, regularly spaced, spherical holes, it is the cheese most identified with Switzerland.

Empanada A pie or pastry shell filled with meat or fish and folded over, and fried or baked. The dish originated in Spain, where it is now usually made with flaky pastry and is often eaten cold. The dish is also popular in parts of Latin America, where it often features a spicy meat filling and is served hot as an appetizer.

Enchilada A dish of Mexican origin consisting of a corn flour tortilla, wrapped around a meat, vegetable or cheese filling and then topped with a spicy chili and tomato sauce. In Mexico, enchiladas are often served with refried beans. The name comes from *enchilar*, to cover, wrap or coat with chili.

Endive, Belgian Known as chicory in England and some other parts of Europe, and as witloof in Belgium

and Australia, Belgian endive (*Cichorium intybus*) has a compact, cone-shaped head of long, pale leaves. It can be eaten raw as a salad vegetable or steamed or boiled. See also Chicory.

Endive, Curly A salad vegetable (*Cichorium endivia*) with frilly, dark green leaves and a mildly bitter taste. It is a native of the Mediterranean. It can be used in salads in the same way as

lettuce, or cooked like spinach. In the United States and France curly endive is called

EGGPLANT (AUBERGINE)

EGGPLANT AND CILANTRO SALAD

★★ **Preparation time:** 25 minutes
Total cooking time: 6 minutes
Serves 6

2 small eggplant, halved lengthwise	½ cup chopped fresh cilantro
salt	1 tablespoon lemon juice
3 small zucchini	1 tablespoon orange juice
2 tablespoons olive oil	½ teaspoon ground pepper

1 Cut the eggplant into thin slices. Place in a colander and sprinkle with salt. Allow to stand for 15–20 minutes.
2 Using a vegetable peeler, cut the zucchini lengthwise into thin slices; set aside. Wash the eggplant and pat dry with paper towels. Brush both sides of eggplant lightly with olive oil and place on a baking sheet. Cook under preheated broiler or until lightly browned on both sides. Remove the eggplant from the broiler and allow to cool.
3 Place the eggplant, zucchini, oil, cilantro, lemon juice, orange juice and pepper in a bowl and toss to combine. Serve the salad as a first course or as a side salad to accompany a main meal.

STUFFED WHOLE EGGPLANT

★ **Preparation time:** 15 minutes +
30 minutes standing
Total cooking time: 1 hour
Serves 6

3 small to medium eggplant	freshly ground black pepper
1 tablespoon salt	2 tablespoons chopped fresh parsley
½ cup olive oil	2–3 tablespoons lemon juice
2 cloves garlic, crushed	
3 medium onions, thinly sliced	½ teaspoon sugar
4 ripe tomatoes, chopped	⅓ cup water

1 Cut stems from eggplant and cut in half lengthwise. Cut a long deep slit into each half, leaving ⅝ inch at each end. Sprinkle eggplant with salt and stand in a bowl of iced water for 30 minutes. Drain and squeeze dry with paper towels.
2 Heat half the oil in a frying pan and cook the garlic and onions over medium heat for 5 minutes or until onions are soft. In a small bowl, combine onion and garlic mixture with tomato, pepper and parsley. Mix well.
3 Preheat oven to moderately slow 325°F. Heat the remaining oil in pan. Cook the eggplant over medium heat until lightly browned.
4 Remove from pan and place in an ovenproof dish. Spoon onion mixture into slits. Add combined lemon juice, sugar and water to dish. Cover; bake 45–50 minutes, basting occasionally with pan juices. To serve, sprinkle with parsley; spoon cooking juices over top of eggplant.

ABOUT EGGPLANT

■ Choose firm eggplant that are heavy for their size, and have a uniform, deep purple color. Wilted or shrivelled fruit will be bitter and poorly flavored.
■ The bitter juices of the eggplant are generally "degorged" or extracted before the flesh is used in cooking. Cut off the stem end of the eggplant, slice or cube the flesh, place in a colander, sprinkle with salt and stand for 15–30 minutes. Rinse eggplant well and dry with paper towels before use.
■ Sliced degorged eggplant make a crunchy side vegetable if coated in flour and fried in olive oil.
■ There are small varieties of eggplant which are less bitter and do not need degorging.

ABOVE: EGGPLANT AND CILANTRO SALAD.
OPPOSITE PAGE: CHELSEA BUNS

3 Spread the dough with the butter, sprinkle with sugar, mixed fruit and pumpkin pie spice. Roll up to make a long roll; cut into 12 evenly-sized pieces. Place pieces in prepared pan with sides touching. Reduce oven temperature to 350°F. Bake 25–30 minutes until brown and cooked through. Remove; place on wire cooling rack.

4 To make Glaze: Place sugar and water in a small pan. Stir over medium heat without boiling until sugar dissolves. Bring to the boil and boil without stirring for 2–3 minutes. Remove pan from heat and brush glaze over the buns while still warm. When ready to serve, split bun and serve with butter if desired.

CORNISH PASTIES

★ **Preparation time:** 30 minutes +
30 minutes refrigeration
Total cooking time: 50 minutes
Makes 6 pasties

Pastry
2½ cups all-purpose
   flour
½ teaspoon dry mustard
½ cup butter, chopped
⅓ cup water

Filling
8 oz round steak, finely
   chopped
2 small potatoes, peeled,
   finely chopped

1 medium onion, peeled
   and finely chopped
¼ cup chopped fresh
   parsley
¼ cup beef or chicken
   stock
white pepper
salt to taste
½ teaspoon English
   mustard
1 teaspoon grated
   horseradish
beaten egg to glaze

1 Brush baking sheet with oil or melted butter. Place flour, mustard and butter in food processor, process until mixture is fine and crumbly. Add almost all the water, process 20 seconds or until mixture comes together; add more water if needed. Remove pastry, form into a ball, cover with plastic wrap; refrigerate 30 minutes.

2 To make Filling: Combine steak, potatoes, onion and parsley. Add stock and season with pepper, salt, mustard and horseradish. Mix well.

3 Preheat oven to hot 425°F. Roll pastry out to ⅛ inch thickness. Cut out six circles, 6½ inch in diameter, use a saucer as a guide. Divide filling between circles, placing in center of each.

4 Glaze edge of circle with egg and bring two sides together to form a half circle. Pinch edge to form a frill. Brush with egg and place on a baking sheet in preheated oven for 10 minutes. Reduce heat to moderate 350°F and cook for another 40 minutes. Serve warm.

ENGLISH CLASSICS

CHELSEA BUNS

★★ **Preparation time:** 35 minutes
Total cooking time: 30–35 minutes
Makes 12

2 cups all-purpose
   flour
⅓ cup sugar
1 teaspoon baking
   powder
¼ teaspoon salt
2 tablespoons butter,
   chopped
⅓ cup milk
1 egg

Filling
2 tablespoons butter,
   softened
1 tablespoon soft brown
   sugar
1 cup dried mixed fruit
1 teaspoon pumpkin pie
   spice

Glaze
¼ cup sugar
¼ cup water

1 Preheat oven to moderately hot 425°F. Brush an 8 inch square cake pan with oil or melted butter. Line base of pan with parchment paper. Sift flour, sugar, baking powder and salt into a bowl; add chopped butter. Using your fingertips, rub the butter into the flour until the mixture is fine and crumbly.

2 Whisk milk and egg together, pour onto sifted ingredients and mix to form a soft dough. Turn onto a sheet of parchment paper and roll into a rectangle 14 x 8¾ inch.

chicory (the term used in England and some other parts of Europe for the cone-shaped, pale-leaved winter vegetable also known as Belgian endive and witloof).

English Food The food of England has a reputation for being stodgy and uninteresting, but the best English food is peerless. Poached salmon with cucumber salad and mayonnaise, steak and kidney pie, baked ham, summer pudding and chelsea buns are a few examples. An "English breakfast" has always meant bacon and eggs with grilled tomato, and perhaps sausage or kippers, with toast and marmalade and a cup of tea. The ploughman's lunch, another famous English meal, consists of good country bread, a piece of Cheddar or local cheese, and some pickled onions. Tea is an English institution and usually takes place at 4 pm. A "proper" tea starts with bread and butter and homemade jam, or little sandwiches. A fruitcake or rich sponge cake, an iced teacake, or little cakes may also be served, with plenty of hot tea.

Nowadays, eating a "proper" tea would probably eliminate the need for dinner. The English dinner often starts with soup, which is followed by a main course of meat or fish served with vegetables. A dessert and then cheese finishes the meal. The English, in contrast to the French, eat cheese at the end of the meal, rather than before the dessert. A "savory" such as anchovy toast or devils on horseback is sometimes served to finish off the meal, although nowadays they are generally only offered at old-fashioned clubs.

English Muffin A round, flat, unsweetened yeast bun served split and toasted, buttered and spread with jam or honey or a savory topping. Splitting a muffin is done by piercing the muffin along the midline with the tines of a fork.

Enoki Mushrooms Japanese mushrooms with long stems and small caps.

Entrecôte A tender cut of beef taken from the between the ribs; usually broiled.

Entrée The main course of a meal, traditionally served after soup, before dessert.

BANGERS AND MASH

⭐ *Preparation time:* 25 minutes
Total cooking time: 25 minutes
Serves 4

8 thick sausages
1 tablespoon oil
2 medium onions, sliced
¼ cup packaged gravy
 mix
1½ cups water

Mash
4 medium potatoes
2 tablespoons milk
2 tablespoons butter
salt and pepper
finely chopped parsley, for
 garnish

1 Prick the sausages with a fork. Heat oil in a large heavy-based frying pan; add sausages. Cook over medium heat for 10 minutes until sausages are brown and cooked through. Transfer to a plate covered with paper towel.
2 Pour off most of the fat from pan, leaving about a tablespoonful. Add onions and cook over a medium heat for 5 minutes until soft and golden.
3 Combine gravy mix with water in a jug, stir until smooth. Add to pan, stir to combine with onions. Stir gravy constantly over a medium low heat for 2 minutes or until mixture boils and thickens. Return sausages to pan. Combine with gravy and serve immediately with mash.
4 To make Mash: Cook potatoes in large pan of boiling water until tender; drain well. Mash with a potato masher until free from lumps. Add milk and butter, blend with a fork until smooth and creamy. Add salt and pepper to taste. Sprinkle parsley over potatoes to serve, and accompany with a green vegetable, such as beans or peas.

SHEPHERD'S PIE

⭐ *Preparation time:* 15 minutes
Total cooking time: 1 hour
Serves 6

1½ lb lean cooked roast
 lamb
2 tablespoons drippings
 or butter
2 medium onions, thinly
 sliced
¼ cup all-purpose
 flour
½ teaspoon dry mustard
1½ cups chicken stock
¼ cup chopped fresh
 mint
¼ cup chopped fresh
 parsley

½ teaspoon ground
 pepper
salt to taste
2 tablespoons
 Worcestershire sauce

Potato Topping
4 large old potatoes,
 cooked and mashed
¼– ⅓ cup hot milk
2 tablespoons butter
salt and pepper to taste

1 Brush an 8-cup capacity casserole with melted butter or oil. Preheat oven to hot 425°F. Trim meat and cut into small cubes. Melt drippings or butter in a large pan. Add onions and cook until golden.
2 Sprinkle in the flour and mustard. Gradually add stock and blend, stirring until smooth. Bring to boil, reduce heat, simmer for 3 minutes. Stir into meat, mint, parsley, pepper, salt and sauce. Remove from heat and spoon into dish.
3 To make Potato Topping: Combine the potato, milk, butter, salt and pepper. Mix until smooth and creamy. Spread potato mixture evenly over the meat; rough up the surface with fork. Bake for 40–45 minutes until pie is heated through and potato topping is golden.

SPOTTED DICK

⭐⭐ **Preparation time:** 15 minutes
Total cooking time: 2½ hours
Serves 4

1⅓ cups all-purpose flour	½ cup golden raisins
1½ teaspoons baking powder	¾ cup currants
½ cup sugar	4 oz shredded suet
1½ teaspoons ground ginger	2 teaspoons finely grated lemon rind
2 cups soft bread crumbs	2 eggs, lightly beaten
	1 cup milk
	custard or cream to serve

1 Brush a 5 cup capacity bowl with oil or melted butter. Line base with parchment paper; grease paper. Grease a large sheet of aluminum foil and a large sheet of waxed paper. Lay paper over foil, greased side up, and pleat in center. Sift flour, baking powder, sugar and ginger into a bowl. Add bread crumbs, fruit, suet and rind. Mix well with a wooden spoon.
2 Combine egg and milk, add to dry ingredients, mix well. Spoon into bowl. Cover with foil and paper, greased-side-down. Place lid over foil, bring clips up, secure firmly with string.
3 If you have no lid, lay a pleated towel over the foil, tie firmly with string under bowl lip. Knot towel ends together to form a handle to lower bowl into pan.
4 Place bowl on a trivet in a large, deep pan.

OPPOSITE PAGE, ABOVE: BANGERS AND MASH; BELOW: SHEPHERD'S PIE. ABOVE: ECCLES CAKES

Carefully pour boiling water down side of pan to come halfway up side of bowl. Bring to boil, cover and cook for 2½ hours. Do not allow the pan to boil dry—replenish with boiling water as pudding cooks. Unmold the pudding onto a serving plate, slice and serve with warm custard or cream.

ECCLES CAKES

⭐ **Preparation time:** 20 minutes
Total cooking time: 15–20 minutes
Makes 27

1 cup currants	3 sheets frozen puff pastry, thawed
½ cup mixed peel	1 egg white
1 tablespoon brandy	2 teaspoons sugar, extra
½ teaspoon ground cinnamon	
1 tablespoon sugar	

1 Preheat oven to hot 425°F. Brush 2 baking sheets with melted butter. Combine the currants, mixed peel, brandy, ground cinnamon and sugar in a bowl.
2 Cut nine 3 inch circles from each sheet of puff pastry. Place 2 level teaspoons of filling on each circle. Bring the edges together and pinch; turn the seam-side-down and roll out to ½ inch thick rounds.
3 Place the cakes on baking sheets. Brush them with the egg white and sprinkle with sugar. Make 3 slashes across top of each cake. Bake 15–20 minutes, until golden.

Escabèche A spicy marinade used to preserve fish, the name is also used to describe fish preserved in this way.

Escalope A thin piece of boneless white meat, usually veal or pork. Slices are beaten until thin, then coated with bread crumbs before frying. Known in Italy as scallopine and in Germany as schnitzel.

Escargot The French name for snail.

Escarole A vegetable with long, flat, irregularly shaped, green leaves. It has a slightly bitter taste and is used either in salads, mixed with milder-flavored lettuces; warmed and served in wilted salads; or as a cooked vegetable. Also known as broadleaf endive and Batavian endive.

Espagnole, Sauce Another name for brown sauce. See SAUCES for recipe.

Espresso Coffee Made by forcing steam under pressure

through finely-ground coffee beans; served in small cups.

Estouffade A dish which is slowly stewed, most usually applied to beef in wine sauce. The name is also used for beef stock.

F

Fajita Grilled marinated beef, chicken or shrimp served with tortillas, sautéed onions and sweet peppers, refried beans, guacamole, and salsa.

Falafel Deep-fried balls of ground and spiced chickpea; a snack of Middle Eastern origin.

Feijoa An oval, green-skinned, egg-sized tropical fruit. The pale yellow flesh, which can be eaten raw is similar in flavor to a mixture of pineapple and strawberry.

Feijoada The national dish of Brazil, it is a stew of black beans and pig snouts, ears and feet. It is served with rice, kale and orange slices.

Fennel A tall, feathery, aromatic plant; its finely divided, blue-green

leaves have a slightly bitter anise taste and are similar in appearance to dill. Fresh leaves can be used as a stuffing for baked fish, as a wrapping

FENNEL

CRUNCHY FENNEL SALAD

⭐ **Preparation time:** 15 minutes
Total cooking time: 3 minutes
Serves 4

4 thin slices prosciutto
1 medium fennel bulb
1 bunch spinach
2 oranges, peeled and segmented
1 tablespoon finely chopped chives

¼ cup chopped walnuts

Dressing
½ cup olive oil
2 tablespoons orange juice
2 teaspoons seeded mustard
freshly ground pepper

1 Cook prosciutto in a heated dry pan or broil until crisp. Cool and crumble coarsely. Set aside.
2 Remove green tops and outer stems from fennel. Trim top and base; cut bulb in quarters and slice thinly across ribs. Wash spinach well, dry thoroughly and tear into bite-size pieces.
3 Place fennel, spinach, orange segments, chives and walnuts in a large bowl. Add dressing and toss ingredients lightly to combine. Transfer to a salad bowl and sprinkle with crumbled prosciutto. Serve salad immediately.
4 To make Dressing: Whisk all ingredients in a small bowl until combined.

ABOVE: CRUNCHY FENNEL SALAD;
RIGHT: CREAMED FENNEL SOUP.
OPPOSITE PAGE: BAKED FENNEL PARMESAN

CREAMED FENNEL SOUP

⭐ **Preparation time:** 10 minutes
Total cooking time: 20–25 minutes
Serves 4

1 medium fennel bulb
¼ cup butter
2 medium potatoes, peeled and chopped
2 cups chicken stock
salt

freshly ground black pepper, to taste
4 oz cream cheese, chopped
1 tablespoon chopped fresh chives
1 tablespoon lemon juice

1 Trim and slice fennel. Heat butter in a medium pan; add fennel. Cook, covered, over low heat for 10 minutes, stirring occasionally. Do not allow fennel to brown. Add potatoes and stock to pan, stir. Bring to boil, reduce heat to low. Cover and cook 10 minutes or until vegetables are tender. Season to taste. Remove from heat; cool slightly.
2 Transfer mixture to a food processor; add cheese. Process until mixture is smooth and creamy. Return soup to pan. Add chives and juice, stir over low heat until just heated through. Soup can be made one day ahead. Store in refrigerator.

ABOUT FENNEL

■ The principal edible part of the fennel is the white bulb at the base of the green stem. The bulb should be crisp and white; trim the base and separate the sections and slice each section before use. Use the bulb as you would celery. It has a slight aniseed flavor and is delicious in salads, stir-fries and soups, or you can simply braise or steam and serve it with butter and freshly ground black pepper. The leafy foliage can be finely chopped and used to garnish and flavor dishes; trim away any tough stalks.

FISH BARBECUED WITH FENNEL

⭐ **Preparation time:** 10 minutes +
1 hour marinade
Total cooking time: 8–10 minutes
Serves 4

4 white-fleshed whole fish
large bunch fresh fennel
stalks

Marinade
½ cup olive oil

juice of 1 lemon
4 tablespoons cognac or
brandy
salt and freshly ground
black pepper to taste
2 cloves garlic, crushed

1 Scale, gut and clean the fish. Place one fennel stalk inside each fish. Score the fish on each side.
2 Combine marinade ingredients. Place the fish in a shallow dish, pour over the marinade, cover and refrigerate for 1 hour. Dry the remaining fennel stalks in a slow oven at 200°F. Place the fennel on a hot grill. Place the fish and marinade in foil, with the ends folded up to form a boat, on top of the fennel on the grill. Cook for 5 minutes each side or until the the fish flakes easily when tested. The fennel will burn, giving an aromatic taste to the fish.

BAKED FENNEL PARMESAN

⭐ **Preparation time:** 15 minutes
Total cooking time: 20–25 minutes
Serves 4

2 medium fennel bulbs
2 tomatoes, peeled,
seeded and chopped
2 tablespoons black pitted
olives, sliced
2 teaspoons chopped fresh
oregano

freshly ground black
pepper
3 tablespoons butter
1 clove garlic, crushed
½ cup freshly grated
Parmesan cheese

1 Preheat oven to moderate 350°F. Remove green tops and outer stems from fennel. Trim bulbs at the top and base. Cut each bulb in half and slice across ribs.
2 Cook fennel in boiling water for about 7 minutes and drain. Combine with tomatoes, olives, oregano and pepper. Place in a shallow heatproof dish.
3 Melt butter in a small pan and cook garlic gently for 30 seconds. Spoon garlic butter over fennel and top with cheese. Bake for 15–20 minutes until top is golden.

for broiled seafood, or it can be added to court bouillon. Chopped leaves are used in sauces, stuffings, dressings and seafood salads. The small brown seeds, also tasting of anise, are also used.

Fenugreek A small plant of the pea family. Its tiny, squarish, brown, aromatic seeds have a spicy, slightly bitter flavor and are so hard that they can only be ground with a mortar and pestle or a special grinder. Lightly roasted and powdered, they are an essential ingredient in curry powders and pastes.

Feta A soft, white, crumbly cheese originally made from ewe's or goat's milk, but now often made from cow's milk. Feta has been made in Greece since ancient times. It is an important ingredient in Greek salads and savory pastries.

Fettuccine (Fettuccini) Pasta cut into long flat ribbons. It can be made at home or bought fresh, frozen or dried. Sometimes colored and flavored with tomato or spinach, fettuccine is especially identified with Rome and its region.

Fig A small, soft, pear-shaped fruit with sweet, pulpy flesh studded with small, edible seeds. Varieties of fig trees grow in warm climates throughout the world. The fig is the sweetest of all fruits. The color of the skin can be purple, red, green or yellow. Calimyrna figs are large

with greenish skin and a nutty flavor; they are usually dried. Kadota figs are usually canned. Available fresh in the summer season, figs are very fragile. Store fresh figs in the refrigerator, and store dried figs for up to six months in an airtight container. The high sugar content is concentrated by the preservation process. Figs can be stewed or used in desserts. The fig probably originated in the Middle East, where it has been eaten for 5,000 years or more. Figs were grown in the Hanging Gardens of Babylon; ripe figs were covered with the hot desert sand to preserve them.

FIGS

STICKY FIG PUDDING WITH QUICK BRANDY CUSTARD

★★ **Preparation time:** 15 minutes
Total cooking time: 1 hour 35 minutes
Serves 8

2½ cups all-purpose
 flour
2 teaspoons pumpkin pie
 spice
1 teaspoon baking soda
¼ cup powdered milk
⅔ cup butter
¾ cup soft brown sugar
1 cup dried figs, chopped

¾ cup water
2 eggs, lightly beaten

Quick Brandy Custard
2½ cups prepared
 custard
1¼ cups heavy cream
¼ cup brandy

1 Brush an 8½inch, 8-cup capacity bowl with oil or melted butter. Line base with paper, grease paper. Grease a large sheet of aluminum foil and a large sheet of waxed paper. Lay the paper over the foil, greased side up, and pleat in the center. Set aside.

2 Sift the flour with the remaining dry ingredients into a large mixing bowl. Make a well in the center. Combine butter, sugar, figs and water in a small pan. Stir over low heat until butter has melted and sugar has dissolved.

3 Add butter mixture and eggs to dry ingredients. Stir until just combined—do not overbeat mixture.

4 Spoon mixture into the prepared bowl. Cover with the greased foil and paper, greased side down. Place lid over foil and secure clips. If the bowl has no lid, lay a pleated towel over the foil and tie it securely with string under the lip of the bowl. Knot the four ends of the towel together to make a handle for lowering the bowl into the pan.

5 Place the bowl on a trivet in a large, deep pan. Carefully pour boiling water down the side of the pan to come halfway up the side of the bowl. Bring to the boil, cover, cook for 1½ hours. Do not let the pudding boil dry. Remove covering, invert onto a plate. Serve warm with Quick Brandy Custard.

6 To make Quick Brandy Custard: Place all the ingredients in a small pan. Stir over a low heat until warmed through. Do not allow the mixture to boil.

ABOUT FIGS

■ Choose fresh figs that are fully colored and firm with no skin breaks. They should be sweet-smelling with no sign of sweating or sour odor (this suggests overripeness). Figs range in color from greenish yellow to purple/black. They are extremely perishable and should be stored in the refrigerator. Guard against any bruising from other produce, and enjoy them as soon as possible. Eat figs fresh, lightly poach them, or cut in half, sprinkle with sugar and briefly place under a hot broiler.

FIGS IN SYRUP

⭐ **Preparation time:** 30 minutes +
3 hours soaking
Total cooking time: 25 minutes
Serves 6

1 lb dried figs	*thin strip orange rind*
3 cups cold tea	*1 whole cinnamon stick*
3/4 cup sugar	*1 teaspoon orange flower*
1 1/2 cups water	*water*
1/2 cup orange juice	*1/3 cup slivered almonds*
1/4 cup honey	*6 1/2 fl oz plain yogurt*

1 Wash figs, cover with cold tea and leave to soak for 3 hours. Remove figs and discard tea.
2 Heat the sugar, water and orange juice in a heavy-bottom saucepan, stirring occasionally until the sugar has completely dissolved. Add the honey, orange rind and cinnamon stick. Bring to the boil.
3 Add figs, boil gently for 5 minutes. Reduce heat and simmer uncovered 20 minutes until figs are tender and syrup is reduced. For a thicker syrup, remove figs and allow syrup to cook longer. Remove orange rind and cinnamon stick. Stir in orange flower water.

OPPOSITE PAGE: STICKY FIG PUDDING WITH QUICK BRANDY CUSTARD. ABOVE: FIGS IN SYRUP

4 Pour syrup over figs in serving bowl, sprinkle with almonds and serve with yogurt.

FIG AND PROSCIUTTO SALAD

Cut 4 fresh figs in halves, wrap each half in a thin slice of prosciutto. Arrange 2 halves per person on serving plates on a bed of arugula leaves. Sprinkle with ground black pepper and drizzle with virgin olive oil and balsamic vinegar. Serves 4.

SPICED FIGS AND ORANGES

Combine 1 cup orange juice, 1/4 cup sugar and 1/2 teaspoon pumpkin pie spice in pan, bring to boil. Simmer 3 minutes; cool. Slice 6 fresh, unpeeled figs and 4 peeled oranges. Place in serving dish, pour syrup over. Chill 1 hour. Sprinkle with 1 tablespoon pine nuts. Serves 4.

FIGS WITH RICOTTA

Combine 1 cup ricotta cheese with 1 tablespoon finely chopped mixed peel, 1 tablespoon finely chopped ginger and 1/4 cup chopped toasted almonds. Place in serving bowl. Cut 4–5 fresh figs into halves and arrange around ricotta. Serves 4.

Filberts See Hazelnuts.

Filé Powder The ground dried leaves of the sassafras shrub used in Cajun cooking as a thickener and to add a thyme-like flavor to gumbos. Filé should not be cooked in the pot (as it will turn stringy), but added at the table or just before serving.

Filet Mignon A small, tender steak cut from the narrow end of a beef tenderloin. It is often cut thick and then quickly cooked by broiling, grilling or sautéing. The name comes from the French for "little fillet."

Fillet A piece of boneless meat, poultry or fish, with little or no fat. Beef fillet, also known as tenderloin, is prized for its tenderness and delicate flavor. A chicken fillet is the small strip of flesh near the breast bone. A fish fillet is the side of the fish cut along the length of the body; it contains few if any bones.

Filo (Phyllo) Pastry made with a dough of high-gluten flour, water and oil that is stretched until tissue-thin, then cut into sheets for use. Filo is widely used in the cooking of the Middle East, Turkey, Greece, Austria and Hungary. Each sheet is lightly brushed with oil or melted butter before being topped with another. The layered sheets can be twisted or wrapped around a sweet or savory filling; baking results in light, crisp, flaky layers. Filo can be made at home, but since it requires skill and time, commercially made filo, available chilled or frozen, is most often used.

Fines Herbes A mixture of finely chopped, subtly flavored fresh herbs, usually parsley, tarragon, chives and chervil, used to flavor omelets, sauces and fish. Fines herbes mixtures are commercially available in dried form.

Finger Food Small portions of hot or cold savory food that can easily be held in one hand and eaten. Finger food is served with drinks and at cocktail parties. See also Hors d'oeuvre.

Finnan Haddie Haddock that has been gutted, split, flattened and immersed in brine before being smoked (traditionally over peat smoke) until the flesh is pale golden. Finnan haddie can be broiled, poached or baked before being baked with an egg

FILO (PHYLLO) DOUGH

SWEET CUSTARD ROLLS

★★ **Preparation time:** 15 minutes + 10 minutes standing
Total cooking time: 50 minutes
Serves 6–8

1 lemon
3 cups milk
½ cup coarse semolina
¼ cup rice flour
¾ cup sugar
2 eggs, lightly beaten
1 teaspoon vanilla extract
14 sheets frozen filo (phyllo) dough, thawed

2 tablespoons unsalted (sweet) butter, melted
1 tablespoon oil
2 tablespoons confectioners' sugar
½ teaspoon ground cinnamon

1 Preheat oven to moderate 350°F. Grease a 13 x 11 inch baking sheet. Peel lemon rind into three strips ½ x 2 inches long. Combine rind with milk in small heavy-bottom pan. Stir over low heat until almost boiling. Reduce heat and simmer, covered, for 10 minutes. Remove pan from heat, leave to cool for 10 minutes. Remove peel.
2 Using electric beaters, beat semolina, rice flour, sugar and eggs on low speed 2 minutes or until smooth. Add milk gradually, beating thoroughly after each addition. Return mixture to pan. Stir over medium heat 10 minutes or until mixture boils and thickens. Remove and stir in vanilla.
3 Cover surface of custard with plastic wrap to prevent skin forming; cool. Place filo (phyllo) sheets onto work surface. Cut crosswise into three even pieces. Brush one with combined butter and oil, top with a second piece. Brush one narrow end.
4 Place 2 tablespoons of custard ¾ inch in from opposite end. Roll pastry over filling, fold ends in, roll to end. Repeat with the remaining pastry and custard.
5 Arrange the rolls on the baking sheet about ¾ inch apart. Brush with the remaining butter mixture. Bake for 30 minutes or until the pastry is puffed and lightly golden. Serve warm, dusted with combined powdered sugar and cinnamon.

ABOUT FILO (PHYLLO) DOUGH

■ Filo (phyllo) pastry can be purchased frozen. Once thawed, unused sheets can be refrigerated for up to one month (do not re-freeze). Cold filo (phyllo) is very brittle; leave it in its packaging until thawed (about 2 hours). Remove only the number of sheets needed, re-roll and store the remainder in their wrapping. Work quickly, one sheet at a time; cover reserved unrolled sheets with a clean, damp towel to prevent drying out.
■ Brush each sheet of dough with melted unsalted (sweet) butter or olive oil, or spray with olive or canola oil.

ABOVE: SWEET CUSTARD ROLLS.
OPPOSITE PAGE: SEAFOOD PARCELS

SEAFOOD PARCELS

✦ ✦ ***Preparation time:*** 25 minutes
Total cooking time: 25 minutes
Serves 4

8 oz boneless white fish fillets	1 tablespoon chopped fresh chives
3½ oz scallops	1 tablespoon chopped fresh dill
2 tablespoons butter	6½ oz peeled, cooked shrimp
1 tablespoon lemon juice	
1 tablespoon all-purpose flour	10 sheets frozen filo (phyllo) dough, thawed
1 cup milk	¼ cup butter, melted
½ cup grated Cheddar cheese	2 teaspoons poppy seeds

1 Preheat oven to moderate 350°F. Line a baking sheet with parchment paper. Cut fish into ½ inch wide strips. Wash scallops, remove brown vein, leaving corals intact.
2 Heat butter in heavy-bottom pan. Add fish, scallops and juice. Cook over medium heat for 1 minute or until tender. Remove fish and scallops from pan with slotted spoon and keep warm.
3 Stir the flour into a pan. Add the milk gradually to flour and butter mixture, stirring constantly over medium heat for 3 minutes or until the mixture boils and thickens. Simmer for another minute, stirring constantly. Remove pan from heat. Stir in the cheese, chives, dill, cooked fish, prepared scallops and shrimp. Cover surface

with plastic wrap and set aside while preparing the pastry.
4 Place two sheets of pastry on a work surface. Brush each sheet with melted butter. Place one sheet of pastry on top of the other. Cut pastry in four equal strips using a sharp knife or scissors. Place two tablespoons of mixture on one short end of each pastry strip. Fold in edges and roll up. Repeat with remaining pastry and mixture. Place seam-side down on prepared baking sheet. Brush with butter, sprinkle with poppy seeds. Bake for 20 minutes or until golden.

ASPARAGUS STRUDEL

✦ ✦ ***Preparation time:*** 20 minutes
Total cooking time: 35 minutes
Serves 4

2 bunches fresh asparagus	⅔ cup grated Cheddar cheese
2 small onions	
1 tablespoon oil	1 egg
4 oz can corn kernels, drained	6 sheets frozen filo (phyllo) dough, thawed
¼ cup chopped fresh parsley	3 tablespoons butter, melted
2 tablespoons chopped fresh basil	2 tablespoons grated fresh Parmesan cheese, extra
2 tablespoons freshly grated Parmesan cheese	

1 Preheat oven to moderately hot 425°F. Cut asparagus into 1¼ inch lengths. Trim any woody stems with a vegetable peeler. Place in a pan of boiling water. Stand for 1 minute, then drain and plunge into ice water. Drain well.
2 Chop onions finely. Heat oil in large heavy-bottom pan. Add onions. Cook, stirring, over medium heat for 3 minutes or until soft. Add asparagus, corn, parsley, basil, Parmesan and Cheddar cheese. Mix well; remove from heat. Cool to room temperature, then add egg; stir well to combine.
3 Brush pastry sheets with melted butter. Layer sheets on top of each other. Place asparagus mixture along one long end of pastry, leaving a 1¼ inch border.
4 Form into log shape with hands. Roll pastry tightly, enclosing filling, folding in short ends to form a parcel. Brush with any remaining melted butter.
5 Place parcel on greased baking sheet. Sprinkle with extra Parmesan cheese. Bake for 25 minutes or until pastry is lightly browned and filling is cooked through. Serve sliced as a first course or main meal.

sauce or in an omelet; it is an ingredient of the fish and rice dish, kedgeree.

Fire Pot An Asian main course soup served like fondue. Each diner dips pre-cut pieces of food into the stockpot.

Fish Valued for its low calorie and cholesterol counts, and its high protein content; fish is easily digestible. Fresh fish deteriorates quickly and should be cooked immediately. Fish can be broiled, baked or poached in water or stock; battered and deep-fried; steamed; wrapped in foil or buttered paper; or microwaved. Fish is cooked when the flesh becomes opaque and flakes easily and the juices are milky white. Some dishes, such as ceviche (from Peru,

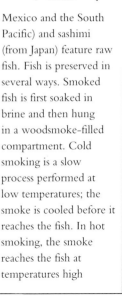

Mexico and the South Pacific) and sashimi (from Japan) feature raw fish. Fish is preserved in several ways. Smoked fish is first soaked in brine and then hung in a woodsmoke-filled compartment. Cold smoking is a slow process performed at low temperatures; the smoke is cooled before it reaches the fish. In hot smoking, the smoke reaches the fish at temperatures high

FINGER FOOD

Finger food is the perfect party food and makes entertaining easy. Going beyond canapés or appetizers, it needs to be substantial, but the name says it all. Finger food should be manageable—no runny fillings, precarious toppings or unwieldy sizes.

WONTON FRILLS

Mix together in a small bowl 5 oz ground pork and veal, 1 tablespoon finely chopped fresh cilantro, 1 clove crushed garlic, 2–3 teaspoons soy sauce, salt, pepper and 1 tablespoon plum sauce. Place 1 teaspoon of mixture towards corner of a square wonton wrapper. Brush around corner edge with water. Fold corner over, press to seal, leaving a large frilled edge. Continue with remaining mixture and wrappers. Deep-fry wontons in oil until crisp. Drain on paper towel. Serve with sweet chili sauce for dipping.

SHRIMP AND MELON SKEWERS

Scoop 12 balls from a honeydew or cantaloupe. Peel 12 cooked medium king prawns (shrimp), leaving tails intact. Thread prawns (shrimp), melon balls and slices of avocado onto bamboo skewers. Squeeze over a little lemon or orange juice. Serve.

CLOCKWISE, FROM LEFT: WONTON FRILLS, SHRIMP AND MELON SKEWER, GOAT CHEESE AND ARTICHOKE TART, FINGER SANDWICH, RICOTTA AND ONION BOAT, YAKITORI, PIZZA WEDGE, TARAMASALATA PASTRY, CAVIAR OYSTER, CORN FRITTERS AND A SALMON AND CHEESE SQUARE

GOAT CHEESE AND ARTICHOKE TARTS

Spread some goat cheese or ricotta cheese into base of baked miniature pastry shells. Top with plain or marinated artichoke hearts, drained and quartered, and a sprinkling of black or red caviar.

FINGER SANDWICHES

Cut avocado in half and remove the pit. Cut the flesh into thin slices, squeeze a little lemon juice over slices to prevent discoloration. Lay avocado slices side-by-side on a slice of brown bread and sprinkle with salt and pepper. Place a slice of white bread on top. Spread white bread with some canned pink or red salmon, mashed and drained. Top with shredded spinach or basil leaves. Place another slice of brown bread on top. Press down firmly but do not squash filling. Cut crusts from bread and cut sandwich into small fingers. Repeat process to make several more sandwiches. Substitute your own favorite fillings, varying colors and textures. Avoid ingredients that will make the bread soggy.

RICOTTA AND ONION BOATS

Place 2–3 teaspoons fresh ricotta cheese into each of 12 baked pastry boats or shells. Top with finely sliced sun-dried tomatoes and red onion rings, black olive halves and fresh baby basil leaves.

YAKITORI

Cut 1 lb chicken thigh fillets into bite-size pieces. Combine in medium bowl with ¼ cup each sake or white wine and soy sauce, 1 tablespoon each sherry and sesame oil, 1 teaspoon grated fresh ginger, and pepper to taste; mix well. Cover chicken, refrigerate several hours or overnight. Thread chicken pieces onto bamboo skewers alternately with scallions cut into ¾ inch lengths. Place on cold broiler tray. Cook under preheated broiler for 5–10 minutes or until cooked through. Serve hot.

PIZZA WEDGES

Spread 4 small ready-made pizza crusts with tomato paste. Top with thin slices of spicy salami and tomato, halved pitted black olives, 1 finely sliced onion, anchovy fillets and small sprigs of thyme or oregano. Bake in preheated oven 350°F for 15–20 minutes or until cooked through. Serve hot or cold, cut into wedges.

TARAMASALATA PASTRIES

Heat 12 small vol-au-vent or puff pastry shells on baking sheet in preheated oven 350°F for 5–10 minutes or until crisp. Cool. Beat 1½ oz cream cheese with electric beaters until smooth and creamy. Add 1 cup store-bought or homemade taramasalata and continue beating until well combined. Pipe mixture into pastry shells. Top with red caviar and serve.

CAVIAR OYSTERS

Spoon a dollop of seafood sauce on top of each fresh oyster on the shell and add a little orange or black caviar. Garnish with a small sprig of fresh dill or lemon thyme.

CORN FRITTERS

Combine ¼ cup butter and ½ cup water in a small pan and stir until the butter has melted. Bring to the boil, then remove from heat. Stir in ½ cup all-purpose flour. Return pan to heat and stir until the mixture leaves the sides of the pan. Transfer to a mixing bowl. Cool slightly. Gradually add 2 lightly beaten eggs. Beat with electric beaters until mixture is smooth, thick and shiny. Beat in ¼ cup creamed corn, salt, pepper and 1 tablespoon grated Parmesan cheese. Drop level tablespoons of the mixture into deep, moderately hot oil. Cook until golden and doubled in size. Remove and drain on paper towel. Cook only two or three fritters at a time.

SALMON AND CHEESE SQUARES

Spread some softened cream cheese onto small squares or rounds of pumperknickel. Top with pieces of smoked salmon or smoked trout and decorate with small sprigs of fresh dill. Sprinkle the squares with a little freshly ground black pepper, if desired.

enough to cook it. Salt-cured fish are split and gutted and packed in coarse salt. Unsalted dried fish are gutted and hung in an air current for about six weeks. Thaw frozen fish slowly in the refrigerator.

Fish Sauce
See Nuoc Mam.

Five Spice Powder A fragrant spice mixture used in Chinese and Vietnamese cooking, it consists of ground star anise, Szechwan pepper, cinnamon, cloves and fennel seeds.

Flambé To ignite a spirit, such as brandy, to burn off its alcohol content and at the same time create delicate flavors. The spirit must be warmed to release sufficient fumes to set alight; it is then ignited with a taper and poured over the food. Alternatively, cooking juices containing a spirit can be flambéed in a shallow pan. Sometimes fresh fruit is sautéed in butter and sugar, then flambéed with brandy or rum.

Flan A shallow, open, round pastry filled with fruit or custard and served hot or cold. Flan is also a classic caramel-flavored Spanish dessert of molded egg custard which is served cold with caramel sauce.

FISH FRESH

FISH AND CHIPS

⭐ **Preparation time:** 15 minutes + 10 minutes standing
Total cooking time: 30 minutes
Serves 6

Batter
2 cups all-purpose
  flour
1 teaspoon baking
  powder
salt to taste
⅔ cup water
¾ cup milk

1 egg, lightly beaten
2 tablespoons white
  vinegar

2 lb white fish fillets
5 large potatoes
oil for deep frying
lemon wedges, for serving

1 To make Batter: Sift flour, baking powder and salt into large bowl; make a well in the center. In jug, whisk together water, milk, egg and vinegar. Gradually pour liquid into flour well. Stir with a wooden spoon until mixture forms a smooth batter; stand for 10 minutes before using.
2 Trim fish, removing any skin and/or bones; cut into serving-sized pieces. Peel potatoes and cut into ½ inch slices, then into lengths ½ inch wide. Place cut potatoes into water until ready to use.

3 Heat oil in deep pan. Drain and dry chips with paper towels. Lower a few at a time into moderately hot oil, cook over medium heat 4 minutes or until pale golden. Drain on paper towels. Reheat oil; cook chips again in batches until crisp. Drain; keep warm to serve with fish.
4 Reduce oil temperature. Dip fish into batter, coating evenly. Deep-fry for 4–5 minutes until batter is crisp and golden. Drain on paper towels.

ABOUT FISH
■ Whole fresh fish should have bright, bulging eyes, red gills, shiny skin, close-fitting scales and firm, resilient flesh. Look for a pleasant sea smell and be wary of ammonia or musty odors. Fillets and cutlets should have moist, resilient flesh with no discoloration or dryness. Fillets should not be waterlogged, cutlets should be firmly attached to the bones. Smoked fish should have a fresh smoky smell—do not buy any with a sweaty appearance or a rancid smell.
■ Store fresh and smoked fish in the refrigerator and use within 2–3 days. Freeze fish, in a single layer, only when very fresh. Defrost overnight in refrigerator.

ABOVE: FISH AND CHIPS. OPPOSITE PAGE:
MOROCCAN FISH WITH FRESH TOMATO SAUCE

MOROCCAN FISH WITH FRESH TOMATO SAUCE

★★ **Preparation time:** 30 minutes +
3 hours standing
Total cooking time: 5–10 minutes
Serves 6

1½ lb white-fleshed fish
fillets, skinned
1 medium red onion, peeled
and finely chopped
1 clove garlic, crushed
2 tablespoons chopped
fresh cilantro
⅓ cup chopped flat-leafed
parsley
½ teaspoon ground sweet
paprika
¼ teaspoon chili powder
⅓ cup olive oil
2 tablespoons lemon juice

Tomato Sauce
4 large, red, ripe
tomatoes, peeled,
seeded and chopped
2 small red chili peppers
cut in half, seeded and
finely sliced
4 scallions, including
some green, finely
sliced
½ bunch fresh cilantro,
finely chopped
½ cup olive oil, extra
virgin
ground pepper
lemon or lime juice
(optional)
1 red onion, finely
chopped (optional)

1 Cut fish fillets across grain into ³/₄ x ³/₄ inch squares. Combine onion, garlic, cilantro, parsley, paprika, chili powder, olive oil and lemon juice and spoon over fish. Mix to coat fish

squares well. Marinate for 2 hours or overnight.
2 Place fish on metal skewers and broil, turning frequently until browned on all sides.
3 To make Tomato Sauce: Combine tomatoes, chilies, scallions and cilantro in a bowl; add olive oil and pepper to taste. Add lemon or lime juice and chopped onion, if using.
4 Allow Tomato Sauce to stand for at least an hour in the refrigerator before serving with fish.

Note: The fish could be grilled instead of broiled. This type of tomato sauce or "salsa" makes a very good quick sauce for fish. Allow the tomatoes to drain in a strainer for at least 30 minutes to get rid of excess water.

PAN FRIED FISH WITH SPICY VINEGAR SAUCE

★ **Preparation time:** 20 minutes
Total cooking time: 20 minutes
Serves 4-6

Spicy Vinegar Sauce
1 cup white wine
vinegar
¼ cup fresh thyme
leaves
1 scallion, chopped
1 teaspoon sugar
1 teaspoon sweet
paprika
½ cup all-purpose flour

½ teaspoon ground pepper
6 x 3 oz small white
fish fillets
3 eggs
1 clove garlic, crushed
1 teaspoon sweet paprika,
extra
½ cup olive oil

1 To make Spicy Vinegar Sauce: Combine the vinegar, thyme, onion, sugar and paprika in a small pan. Simmer, uncovered, for about 10 minutes.
2 Combine flour and pepper in a medium bowl. Toss fish lightly in seasoned flour; shake off any excess. In a medium bowl, lightly beat the eggs with garlic and paprika until frothy. Dip each fillet into egg mixture and hold up to drain off any excess.
3 Heat oil in a medium pan; add fish. Cook on medium-high heat 3–4 minutes each side until golden brown and cooked through. Remove from pan; drain on paper towels.
4 Serve fish immediately, accompanied by Spicy Vinegar Sauce.

Note: The egg coating on the fish results in a fine, slightly crisp coating. Fish should be served as soon after cooking as possible, otherwise the coating will become soggy.

Flapjack A thick pancake. Buttered, stacked in a pile and topped with maple syrup, flapjacks are a popular breakfast food in North America. They

are also known as griddle cakes, flannel cakes, hot cakes and wheat cakes. In Britain flapjack is the name given to a mixture of rolled oats, brown sugar and melted butter that is baked and cut into squares.
See also Pancake

Fleuron Small pieces of puff pastry, cut, glazed, and baked or fried; they are made in many shapes such as ovals or diamonds cut from thinly rolled puff pastry. Fleuron are used as decoration on pie crusts or as a garnish.

Floating Island A dessert of chilled custard topped with meringue and a dollop of caramel syrup.

Florentine Very thin cookies containing dried fruit and nuts and coated on one side with melted chocolate that has been decorated with the tines of a fork to create wavy lines on its surface.

Florentine, à la A dish featuring fish, poultry or eggs, served on a bed of spinach, sometimes with a mornay sauce.

Flounder A generic tern for different ocean flatfishes. The thin body provides fillets.

Flour Finely ground cereals, seeds or roots; those most often used include wheat, corn, barley, oats, rye and rice. In Western countries the term usually refers to wheat flour. Dried chickpeas are ground into besan flour and arrowroot is ground from the tuber of a plant.

Flower, Edible Fresh whole flowers or petals bring a bright touch to salads, sorbets and drinks;

when candied (crystallized) they are used to decorate cakes and desserts.

Not all flowers are edible; if in doubt, check with the local health center. Make sure that flowers have not been treated with pesticides or other harmful chemicals. Flowers commonly added to salads include the petals of yellow and white chrysanthemums, whole nasturtiums,

FISH PIE

⭐ ⭐ **Preparation time:** 45 minutes
Total cooking time: 50 minutes
Serves 4–6

1¹⁄₂ lb firm white fish
  fillets
1 large leek, chopped
2 strips lemon rind
¹⁄₄ teaspoon ground nutmeg
8 peppercorns
2 bay leaves
6 parsley stalks
2¹⁄₂ cups milk
2 tablespoons butter
1 clove garlic, crushed
1 chopped leek, extra

¹⁄₂ cup chopped scallions
2 lb potatoes, cooked and
  mashed
ground pepper
1 teaspoon sweet paprika,
  optional

Sauce
2 tablespoons all-purpose
  flour
extra milk or cream

1 Preheat oven to 400°F. Place fish in pan, add leek, lemon rind, nutmeg, peppercorns, bay leaves and parsley stalks. Add milk. Simmer, uncovered, over low heat for 15 minutes or until fish is cooked (cooking time depends on thickness of fillets). Remove fish, strain liquid and reserve for sauce.
2 Melt butter in pan, add garlic, leeks and scallions. Cook over low heat 7 minutes, or until leeks soften. Remove half mixture and reserve.
3 To make Sauce: Sprinkle flour over remaining mixture in pan, blend until smooth. Measure reserved liquid and make up to 1¹⁄₂ cups with extra milk or cream. Add to flour, stir until mixture boils and thickens. Cook 1 minute more.

4 Cut fish into chunks, fold gently through sauce. Add reserved leek and scallion mixture to mashed potatoes. Season both mixtures with pepper. Pour sauce into a greased shallow casserole dish. Top with potatoes, sprinkle with paprika. Bake 20 minutes or until topping browns.

ROLLMOPS

⭐ ⭐ **Preparation time:** 20 minutes +
5 days marinating
Total cooking time: 10 minutes
Serves 6

12 herrings or fresh sardines,
  gutted and rinsed
2–3 small pickles,
  chopped
¹⁄₄ cup chopped scallions
2 tablespoons chopped
  capers
2 medium onions, sliced

2 cups white wine or cider
  vinegar
2 cups water
12 black peppercorns
6 allspice berries, crushed
6 whole cloves
1 tablespoon mustard
  seeds
2 bay leaves

1 Fillet fish, leaving tails on. Lay flat on a board, skin side down. Sprinkle with pickles, scallions and capers, roll up firmly from tail end. Secure each fillet with wooden cocktail sticks; arrange in glass jar alternating with sliced onions.
2 Place remaining ingredients in pan, bring to boil. Simmer, uncovered, 10 minutes; cool. Pour over fish. Cover, refrigerate for at least five days. Serve, drained, with salad and bread.

STEAMED FISH WITH GINGER

Preparation time: 45 minutes+
refrigeration
Total cooking time: 12 minutes
Serves 4

1½ lb sea bass, cleaned
  and scaled
2 tablespoons finely
  grated ginger
2 teaspoons dry sherry
2 tablespoons soy sauce
2 tablespoons peanut oil

2 teaspoons sesame oil
2 scallions, finely sliced
  diagonally
½ cup pine nuts, toasted
1 slice bacon, diced and
  cooked until crisp,
  optional

1 Wash the fish, removing any remaining loose
scales and pat dry with paper towels. Place on
a large heatproof dish; sprinkle with ginger,
sherry and soy. Leave for 30 minutes in the
refrigerator.
2 Place a round cake-cooling rack in a wok;
balance the fish dish on top. Carefully pour 6–8
cups of boiling water into wok. Cover, steam fish
over a rolling boil for 10 minutes.
3 Test if cooked by flaking a little flesh from the
thickest part of the fish with a fork—fish is ready
when it flakes easily and is milky white. Turn off
heat and keep the dish covered.

OPPOSITE PAGE: FISH PIE.
ABOVE: STEAMED FISH WITH GINGER

4 Heat the oils in a small pan until very hot.
Carefully remove fish on its dish from wok.
Sprinkle the scallions over the fish and very
carefully pour on the hot oil. Garnish with nuts
and bacon, if desired. Serve at once with stir-fried
vegetables and steamed rice.

BAKED FISH WITH SPICES

Preparation time: 15 minutes
Total cooking time: 30 minutes
Serves 2

2 x 10 oz whole white
  fish
1 onion, chopped
1 clove garlic, crushed
1 teaspoon chopped fresh
  ginger

1 teaspoon chopped
  lemon rind
2 tablespoons tamarind
  sauce
1 tablespoon soy sauce
1 tablespoon peanut oil

1 Place fish onto 2 large sheets of foil. Make 3
deep incisions on each side of the fish.
2 In a food processor, combine onion, garlic,
ginger, lemon rind, tamarind sauce, soy sauce and
peanut oil; blend until mixture is smooth.
3 Spread the mixture on both sides, and on the
inside, of the fish.
4 Wrap the foil around the fish and secure firmly.
Place the fish in a baking dish and bake at
350°F for 30 minutes, or until the fish is just
cooked through.

marigold and calendula
petals, whole blooms
of violet, pansy,
honeysuckle and
cornflower, and herb
flowers such as borage
and chive. A salad
dressing light in vinegar
should be used, and the
flowers strewn across the
top after the greens have
been tossed, as the
dressing will
affect
their
color.
Pumpkin,
zucchini and
squash flowers can be
stuffed or dipped in
batter and fried. Candied
or crystallized petals (rose
and violet are most often
used) can be made by
dipping clean dry petals
into beaten egg white
and then into sugar; dry
on a cake rack and store
in an airtight container.

Fluke A flatfish that
belongs to the flounder
family.

Flummery A dessert
of fruit, fruit juice
and cream or milk,
thickened with gelatin
and whipped until fluffy,
it is then poured into a
wet mold and chilled
until set. It is of Welsh
origin and was originally
thickened with oatmeal.

Focaccia A flat bread
made from yeast dough,
sprinkled with coarse salt
and baked

in a shallow, well-oiled pan. It is originally from Italy. Flavorings and baked toppings such as herbs, tomatoes, onions, garlic and olives, vary according to the region. Warmed and filled with salads and cheese or meat, focaccia is popular as a snack or light meal.

Foie Gras Literally, "fat liver," the enlarged liver of a specially fattened goose or duck, seasoned, poached and often studded with truffles. Foie gras is served cold at the beginning of a meal or is made into a smooth paste, pâté de foie gras.

Fondant A sweet, smooth candy or icing made from sugar, water and cream of tartar. Fondant, with flavorings and food coloring added, is used as a center for chocolates and and to make molded fruits, flowers and icings.

Fondue Food that is cooked at the table by being immersed in simmering sauce or oil kept hot in a specially designed fondue pot. Diners using individual long-handled forks dip or retrieve the food from the communal pot. There are several types of fondue:

FISH SMOKED

SMOKED FISH FLAN

⭐ **Preparation time:** 20 minutes
Total cooking time: 45 minutes
Serves 4

8 oz smoked fish fillets	2 tablespoons all-purpose
1 small onion, sliced	flour
4 tablespoons water	1 cup milk
4 tablespoons sherry	lemon juice to taste
4 sheets frozen filo	1 egg, beaten
(phyllo) dough, thawed	1 tablespoon chopped
5 tablespoons butter	fresh parsley
	salt and pepper to taste

1 Preheat oven to 350°F. Place fish, onion, water and sherry in a pan. Bring to the boil, reduce heat and simmer for 10 minutes or until fish flakes when tested. Remove fish and flake, discarding any bones and skin.
2 Brush all pastry sheets with 3 tablespoons melted butter. Fold each sheet in half. Layer pastry, one folded piece on top of the other, to give eight layers. Using an 8 inch flan ring as a guide, cut out a circle from the pastry sheets, ½ inch larger than the flan. Lift all the layers into flan tin carefully, leaving pastry standing up around edge of flan tin.
3 Melt the remaining 2 tablespoons butter in a pan. Add flour and cook, stirring continuously, for 2 minutes. Gradually add milk and bring to the boil, stirring. Reduce heat and simmer for 5

minutes. Stir in lemon juice, beaten egg and parsley. Season to taste.
4 Spread fish and onion over base and pour over sauce. Bake for 20 minutes. Serve hot or cold.

SMOKED HADDOCK IN WHITE SAUCE

⭐ **Preparation time:** 12 minutes
Total cooking time: 20 minutes
Serves 4

1 large onion, thinly sliced	2 tablespoons butter,
1 lb smoked haddock	softened
1⅔ cups milk	2 teaspoons all-purpose
½ teaspoon cracked	flour
black pepper	1 scallion, finely chopped
1½ teaspoons dry	
mustard	

1 Spread onion over base of large saucepan. Cut haddock into ¾ inch wide pieces. Arrange over onion.
2 Blend milk, pepper and mustard; pour over fish. Bring slowly to the boil. Reduce heat to low, simmer covered for 5 minutes. Uncover and simmer for another 5 minutes.
3 Remove the fish to serving dish; keep warm. Simmer mixture in the saucepan for 5 minutes more, stirring.
4 Combine butter and flour, add to pan with scallion. Stir over low heat until mixture boils and thickens. Pour over fish.

SMOKED SALMON AND DILL CREPES

★ ★ **Preparation time:** 50 minutes
Total cooking time: 25 minutes
Makes 9 crêpes

Crêpes
1 cup all-purpose flour
1 egg, lightly beaten
1½ cups milk

1 tablespoon chopped dill
2 teaspoons chopped mint
1 tablespoon lemon juice
1 small avocado, mashed
6½ oz smoked salmon,
   thinly sliced
sprigs of dill, for garnish

Filling
5 oz cream cheese,
  softened
1 tablespoon sour cream

1 Sift flour into a medium mixing bowl; make a well in the center. Using a wooden spoon, gradually stir in combined egg and milk. Beat until all liquid is incorporated and batter is free of lumps. Transfer mixture to jug; cover with plastic wrap and leave for 30 minutes.
2 To make Filling: Using electric beaters, beat cream cheese in a small mixing bowl until creamy. Add sour cream, dill, mint, juice and avocado, beat 30 seconds or until mixture is smooth and creamy. Cover with plastic wrap, refrigerate until needed.

OPPOSITE PAGE: SMOKED HADDOCK IN WHITE SAUCE. ABOVE: SMOKED SALMON AND DILL CREPES

3 Pour 2–3 tablespoons batter onto lightly greased 8 inch crêpe pan, swirl evenly over base. Cook over medium heat one minute or until underside is golden. Turn over; cook other side. Transfer to a plate; cover with towel. Repeat with remaining batter; grease pan when necessary.
4 Spread each crêpe evenly with filling, top with salmon slices. Stack crêpes, cut into eight wedges. Garnish with dill sprigs. Serve with green salad.

SMOKED TROUT MOUSSE

★ **Preparation time:** 20 minutes +
  overnight setting
Total cooking time: none
Serves 4

1½ lb smoked trout
¾ cup mayonnaise
½ cup very finely
  chopped celery
1 tablespoon white wine
  vinegar

2 teaspoons Dijon mustard
1½ tablespoons
  unsweetened gelatin
½ cup cold water
pinch cayenne pepper

1 Skin and fillet the trout. Place in a bowl and mash finely.
2 To the trout add mayonnaise, celery, vinegar, and mustard. Mix well. Add gelatin combined with water. Season with cayenne pepper.
3 Put mixture into individual wetted molds. Set in refrigerator. Unmold onto serving plates.

cheese fondue (originally from Switzerland), a mixture of melted cheeses and white wine into which pieces of crusty bread are dipped; meat fondue, in which cubes of meat, poultry or fish, as well as vegetables, are cooked in oil or stock; and dessert fondue, where pieces of cake or fruit are dipped into a sweet sauce, often made from chocolate.

Fool A dessert of fresh or cooked fruit, which has been puréed, sweetened and then chilled. Just before it is served, the purée is mixed with whipped cream or custard.

Forcemeat A mixture of finely chopped or ground meat, herbs and seasonings. It can be used as a stuffing.

Four Spices (*Quatre Épices*) A spice mixture of ground white pepper, nutmeg, cloves and ginger, used to flavor pâtés, terrines and some slowly cooked meat and poultry dishes.

Frankfurter (Hot Dog) A lightly smoked sausage made from spiced meat, either pork, a beef and pork mixture, or poultry meat. Frankfurters are sold contained in a casing, or skinless; they are precooked and need only to be reheated in simmering water (boiling may split them), or by making several slashes in the skin and broiling until brown. Frankfurters range from finger-sized cocktail to foot-long and are served in buns.

Frappé The French term for "iced." It is used to describe both a drink that is poured over crushed ice and a refreshing dessert made of partially frozen sweetened fruit juice.

Freezing A method of preserving food by storing it at or below the freezing point. Freezing halts the growth of bacteria, yeasts and molds.

French Dressing
Also called vinaigrette, a salad dressing made up of one part vinegar to three parts olive oil, seasoned with black pepper and salt. It is also a creamy, orange-colored commercially produced salad dressing.

French Food
French cooking is still

FISH CANNED

SALMON PATTIES

⭐ **Preparation time:** 20 minutes
Total cooking time: 6 minutes
Serves 4

1 lb potatoes	all-purpose flour
6½ oz can pink salmon, drained	1 egg
	¾ cup dry bread crumbs
2 tablespoons mayonnaise	¼ cup oil
4 scallions, chopped	lemon wedges for serving

1 Peel and chop potatoes. Cook in boiling water until tender, drain. Mash until smooth.
2 Put salmon, mayonnaise and scallions in bowl with potatoes. Stir with wooden spoon until well mixed. Divide mixture into eight portions. Roll each portion into a smooth patty.
3 Dust patties lightly in flour. Beat the egg in a small bowl, and use to brush patties. Coat in bread crumbs.
4 Heat oil in frying pan. Place patties in frying pan in a single layer; cook over medium heat for 3 minutes or until underside is golden. Turn patties over and cook for 3 minutes or until golden. Drain on paper towels. Serve with lemon wedges.

Note: If preferred, drained, canned tuna can be used to replace the pink salmon in this recipe.

FETTUCCINE AND TUNA WITH CAPERS

⭐ **Preparation time:** 10 minutes
Total cooking time: 15 minutes
Serves 4–6

1 lb fettuccine	⅓ cup lemon juice
¼ cup olive oil	2 tablespoons chopped capers
2 cloves garlic, crushed	
7 oz can tuna, drained	½ teaspoon chopped chili pepper
¼ cup butter	

1 Place fettuccine in a pan of boiling water and cook until just tender.
2 Heat the oil in a pan, add the garlic and cook for 1 minute. Add the tuna and cook for 2 minutes longer. Add butter, lemon juice, capers and chili, stir into tuna and cook on low until heated through. Drain fettuccine, add to sauce and mix to combine.

TUNA MORNAY

⭐ **Preparation time:** 15 minutes
Total cooking time: 30 minutes
Serves 4–6

3 tablespoons butter	2 x 13½ oz cans tuna, drained
2 scallions, finely chopped	
2 tablespoons all-purpose flour	¼ cup fresh bread crumbs
1½ cups milk	¼ cup grated Cheddar cheese, extra
¾ cup grated Cheddar cheese	2 tablespoons finely chopped fresh parsley

1 Preheat oven to moderately hot 425°F. Heat butter in a medium pan; add scallions and cook over a low heat for 2 minutes until soft. Add flour, stir over low heat 2 minutes, until mixture is lightly golden.
2 Add milk gradually to pan, stirring until mixture is smooth. Stir constantly over medium heat for 4 minutes or until the mixture boils and thickens; boil for another minute, remove from heat. Cool slightly, stir in grated Cheddar cheese.
3 Add tuna to pan and fold through gently, taking care not to break up pieces too much. Transfer mixture to 5-cup capacity casserole dish. Sprinkle with combined bread crumbs, extra cheese and parsley. Bake for 20 minutes, or until golden brown.

ABOVE: SALMON PATTIES.

OPPOSITE PAGE: BAGNA CAUDA (TOP) AND CHEESE FONDUE (BELOW)

FONDUES

CARAMEL TOFFEE FONDUE

★ **Preparation time:** 30 minutes
Total cooking time: 20 minutes
Serves 6

½ cup sugar
½ cup demerara sugar
½ cup sweetened
  condensed milk

2 teaspoons cornstarch
1 cup heavy cream
seasonal fruits

1 Combine the sugars in a large pan. Heat gently over a low heat until the sugars have completely dissolved. Remove from heat. Combine a small amount of the condensed milk with the cornstarch and blend until smooth.

2 Add the cornstarch mixture, cream and the remaining condensed milk to the sugars. Return the pan to heat until a toffee lump forms. Continue stirring over a low heat until the lump dissolves. The fondue should be a dark, rich caramel color.

3 Transfer the mixture to a fondue pot. Stir often to prevent the toffee from burning. Serve the caramel toffee immediately with a selection of skewered fresh fruit. Fondue may also be served in a bowl and passed around on a platter with skewered fruit.

BAGNA CAUDA

★ **Preparation time:** 20 minutes
Total cooking time: 10 minutes
Serves 6

1½ oz can anchovies,
  drained and chopped
⅓ cup unsalted (sweet)
  butter
5 cloves garlic, crushed

2 egg yolks
selected raw vegetables,
  cut into 2 inch long
  sticks

1 Cook anchovies, unsalted butter and garlic in a medium pan until butter has melted. Transfer mixture to a food processor. Add egg yolks. Process until thick.

2 Pour into fondue pot, slowly bring to simmering point. Serve at once with selected vegetables and skewered crusty bread. Bagna Cauda may also be served in a bowl and passed around on a platter with the bread and vegetables.

CHEESE FONDUE

★ **Preparation time:** 20 minutes
Total cooking time: 10 minutes
Serves 10–15

2 cups grated mild
  Cheddar cheese
2 cups grated sharp
  Cheddar cheese
1 cup grated Parmesan
  cheese

¼ cup all-purpose
  flour
2 teaspoons dry mustard
2 cups white wine
2 teaspoons Dijon
  mustard
cubes French bread

1 Combine the cheeses, flour and dry mustard. Pour the wine into the fondue pot, slowly bring to simmering point. Add heaped tablespoonfuls of the cheese mixture to the simmering wine, one at a time, stirring after each addition until the cheese has melted.

2 Continue process until all the cheese has melted and mixture is thick. Stir in Dijon mustard, season with pepper to taste.

3 Stir until the fondue is bubbling and smooth. Keep hot over burner. Supply fondue forks or skewers for dipping cubes of French bread. Fondue can be made in a pan a day ahead. Keep covered in refrigerator. Reheat gently in fondue pot just before serving.

ABOUT FONDUES

■ To eat fondue spear chunks of bread or fruit with long-handled fondue forks, twirl into cheese or sweet fondue mixture and carefully tip bread or fruit directly into the mouth.

considered by many to be the finest in the world. It has become so universally accepted that many dishes we take for granted are French in origin: the humble omelet, pâté, mayonnaise, quiche, fruit

tart, beef stews, fish soups, and soufflés. Over the past decade, classic French food has given way to a more casual style of eating. Conscious of weight and health, people are eschewing rich egg- and cream-based sauces in favor of simpler French food, brasserie style. The essence of French food has not changed, but a cheese soufflé is now more likely to be served as a main course with a salad and a chunk of bread than as the first course to a big dinner. There will always be a place for French

desserts such as profiteroles, tarts, crêpes and gateaux. Croissants, served with café au lait, are fast becoming an international breakfast

FOCACCIA

Focaccia is a light yeast flatbread from Italy, traditionally brushed with oil and sprinkled with flavoring such as herbs, onions, olives, coarse salt or even nuts. Nowadays, it is popular split and served as a sandwich with hot or cold fillings. It can be toasted, grilled or even pan-fried in variations limited only by your imagination.

Focaccia has become a popular alternative to ordinary sliced bread. It is flatter and drier in texture than the familiar fresh white loaf from the bakery, and is made in large squares or rounds as well as in small rounds like flattened bread rolls. The close texture and hard crust of traditional focaccia make it perfect for carrying moist foods such as marinated vegetables and cheeses.

APHRODITE

Combine some thinly sliced marinated feta or goat cheese, 4–5 sun-dried tomatoes in oil, drained, and 4–5 green or purple basil leaves. Sprinkle with freshly cracked black pepper and Parmesan cheese shavings, if desired.

To marinate cheese: In a bowl, combine 1/4 cup olive oil, 1/2 teaspoon grated lemon rind, 1 crushed clove garlic, 1 teaspoon each chopped parsley, chives and thyme, 1/4 teaspoon dried red chili flakes, and freshly ground black pepper. Mix well. Place cheese slices in the bowl and toss gently to coat with marinade. Cover the bowl and refrigerate for up to 2 hours.

COPENHAGEN

Plunge slender baby asparagus spears into boiling water for 1 minute or until they turn bright green, then plunge them into a bowl of iced water; drain well. Split focaccia and fill with some finely sliced red or brown onion rings, slices of fresh smoked salmon, baby asparagus spears and tiny capers. Top with a dollop of horseradish cream or crème fraîche, if desired. Sprinkle with freshly cracked black pepper and serve.

MEDITERRANEAN MEDLEY

Halve 1 red pepper and remove seeds and membrane. Brush skin with olive oil. Cook under hot preheated broiler, cut-side down, until skin blisters and blackens. Cover with a damp cloth towel until cool. Peel and discard skin. Cut flesh into strips. Slice 1–2 small slender eggplant lengthways. Fry the slices in 2–3 tablespoons olive oil, with 1 clove crushed garlic, 2–3 minutes each side; drain. Layer peppers, eggplant and thin slices of provolone cheese on focaccia. Lightly toast, if desired.

ARUGULA EXPRESS

Wash some arugula or lettuce leaves. Layer onto focaccia with 2–3 slices chili-, pepper- or herb-crusted salami and thinly sliced baby bocconcini (fresh mozzarella). Drizzle with virgin olive oil and good balsamic vinegar. Thin slices of aged mozzarella can be used instead of bocconcini.

POMPEII

Halve 1 red pepper; remove all the seeds and membrane. Brush skin with olive oil. Cook under hot preheated broiler, cut-side down, until skin blisters and blackens. Cover with damp cloth towel until cool. Peel off skin; discard. Cut flesh into strips. Split focaccia, spread with olive paste. Top with strips of pepper, halved pitted green and black olives, halved marinated artichokes and thin slices of mortadella.

NAPOLI

Thinly slice 1–2 plum tomatoes, or use ripe vine tomatoes. Arrange on split focaccia. Top with fresh green or purple basil leaves and thin slices of coppa or prosciutto. Sprinkle with crushed sea salt, cracked black pepper and drizzle with olive oil. Add some fresh grated Parmesan or pecorino cheese, if desired.

OPPOSITE, FROM TOP TO BOTTOM: APHRODITE, COPENHAGEN, MEDITERRANEAN MEDLEY, ARUGULA EXPRESS, POMPEII AND NAPOLI

food; in some countries they are also served for lunch with ham and cheese.

French Fries Thin strips of potato which are deep-fried until they are a pale golden color. They are a very popular vegetable accompaniment in France, where they are known as *pommes frites*.

French Toast Slices or strips of bread, dipped in an egg and milk mixture and fried in butter until crisp and golden-brown on both sides. French toast is served hot, topped with sugar and syrup, jam or cinnamon for breakfast or dessert.

Fricassée A dish of meat or poultry (most commonly veal or chicken) first fried in butter without browning, then cooked slowly in white stock thickened with flour; cream is added just before serving. A fricassée is usually garnished with small glazed onions and lightly cooked mushrooms.

Frikadell A small fried meatball which is usually served hot. It is garnished with sour cream or a tomato-based sauce.

FRENCH CLASSICS

CASSOULET

⋆⋆ **Preparation time:** 25 minutes
Total cooking time: 2 hours
Serves 6

10 oz boneless chicken thighs, skin removed
10 oz lean lamb
10 oz lean pork loin
2 oz lard
2 medium onions, chopped
2 cloves garlic, crushed
2 stalks celery, chopped
1 tablespoon all-purpose flour
14 oz can tomatoes,

drained, juice reserved
1 cup white wine
1 teaspoon fresh thyme leaves
2 bay leaves
3 cloves
ground pepper, to taste
13 oz can white cannellini beans, drained
6½ oz chopped ham
3 oz salami, chopped

1 Trim the meat of excess fat and cut into ¾ inch cubes. Heat lard in a large pan. Cook the chicken until brown and remove from pan. Add lamb to pan and cook until brown; remove. Cook the pork until brown, and remove. Add onions to remaining fat in pan and cook until they are well browned. Add garlic and celery, stir for one minute and remove from pan.

2 Sprinkle flour over the base of the pan. Add the chopped tomatoes, tomato juice and wine; stir until the sauce boils and thickens. Add thyme

leaves, bay leaves, cloves and pepper. Bring to boil, reduce heat and simmer uncovered for 10 minutes.

3 Add meat, onion mixture and cannellini beans, cover and simmer for one hour. Remove the lid, add chopped ham and salami; cover and cook for 30 minutes.

FRENCH ONION SOUP

⋆⋆ **Preparation time:** 15 minutes
Total cooking time: 55 minutes
Serves 4–6

3 tablespoons butter
1 tablespoon olive oil
4 large onions, thinly sliced
1 clove garlic, crushed
1 tablespoon sugar
2 tablespoons red wine vinegar
⅓ cup all-purpose flour
½ cup dry sherry
1 cup dry white wine

13½ oz can beef consommé
1¼ cups water
2 tablespoons olive oil, extra
1 clove garlic, crushed, extra
1 small French baguette, cut into ¾ inch slices
½ cup grated Parmesan cheese
thyme, to garnish

1 Heat the butter and olive oil together in a large frying pan. Add the onions and cook for about

20 minutes until brown.

2 Add the garlic and sugar and stir through until the sugar has browned. Add the red wine vinegar and cook for 2 minutes. Sprinkle the flour over the onions and cook, stirring constantly, for 1 minute. Stir in the sherry, white wine, consommé and water. Continue stirring until the mixture boils and thickens. Reduce heat and simmer the soup uncovered for a further 25 minutes.

3 Preheat the oven to 425°F. Combine the extra olive oil and garlic in a small bowl. Brush the mixture over both sides of the bread, then sprinkle one side with Parmesan cheese. Bake for 5 minutes or until bread slices are crisp and golden.

4 To serve, place a slice of bread at the bottom of each soup bowl and pour over the soup. Garnish with thyme. Alternatively, lay a slice of thinly sliced Swiss cheese, such as gruyére, on the slice of bread. Float on top of the soup and place under a hot broiler for 1–2 minutes or until the cheese melts.

Note: It is important that the onions used for making French Onion Soup are well browned this gives the soup an authentic flavor. The sugar assists by caramelizing the onions. Start by cooking the onions over full heat for a few minutes, then reduce to medium heat to brown the onions slowly.

OPPOSITE PAGE: CASSOULET.

ABOVE: FRENCH ONION SOUP;

RIGHT: BEEF BOURGUIGNON

BEEF BOURGUIGNON

⭐ **Preparation time:** 25 minutes
Total cooking time: 1 hour 30 minutes
Serves 6

2 lb blade steak
2 slices bacon
2 tablespoons olive oil
12 small pearl onions, peeled
2 cloves garlic, crushed
1/3 cup all-purpose flour
2 cups dry red wine

1 teaspoon fresh thyme leaves
1 tablespoon grated or bottled horseradish
2 tablespoons butter
12 oz button mushrooms
fresh thyme, to garnish

1 Trim the meat of excess fat, cut into 5/8 inch cubes. Cut the bacon into 1/2 inch strips.
2 Heat the oil in large pan; add the bacon, cook until brown, remove. Add the onions to the pan, cook in bacon fat until browned; remove. Add the garlic, cook one minute. Brown the steak in remaining fat; stir in flour. Add the wine, thyme and horseradish, stir until the mixture boils and thickens. Return the onions and bacon to pan; reduce heat, cover, simmer one hour.
3 Heat the butter in a small pan; add mushrooms, cook until soft. Stir mushrooms and juices into casserole, cook uncovered a further 30 minutes.
4 Serve casserole garnished with fresh thyme, accompanied with fresh vegetables.

Frittata A dish using beaten eggs, frittata is similar to an omelet but the filling (diced vegetables, cheese, meat, chicken or seafood) is stirred into the egg mixture before it is cooked.

Fritter Food dipped in or mixed with a batter of flour, egg and liquid and then deep-fried until crisp and golden.

Fritto Misto Literally "mixed fry," an Italian dish of various vegetables, seafood or meat, dipped in a light batter, deep-fried and served piping hot. Perhaps best known is the mixed seafood fritto misto, a Neapolitan specialty, which usually includes baby squid and calamari rings; a version of the dish from Florence consists of chicken, rabbit and vegetables; in the Piedmont region of northern Italy, fritters of brain, sweetbreads and veal are popular.

Fromage Blanc A soft, white, unripened fresh cheese. It has a slightly sour, tangy taste and in France is widely used in sauces, as a topping for steamed or boiled vegetables, as a dressing for salad vegetables, as a dip for crudités and as a topping for fresh fruit.

Frosting A sweet cooked or uncooked topping for cakes, cookies or cupcakes, or filling between layers or cake. Often made with water, sugar, cream of tartar and egg white, frosting is spreadable, but holds its shape.

Fruit Botanically, a fruit is the pulp that covers the seeds of various flowering plants. This includes nuts and some fruits principally eaten as vegetables, such as eggplant, tomato and avocado. In general usage, the term is restricted to fruits that are fleshy, sweet and sometimes juicy. Low in fat and high in fiber, fruit is an essential part of a healthy diet. It can be eaten fresh or cooked.

Fruit Butter A preserve made with fruit pulp and sometimes thickened with sugar.

Fruit, Dried Fruit that is preserved by having its natural water content reduced by exposure to the sun in the open air or by heating. Such dehydration slows the growth of bacteria, allowing most dried fruits to be stored for up to a year. Fruits most commonly

CREPES SUZETTE

✦✦ *Preparation time:* 30 minutes
Total cooking time: 35 minutes
Serves 4–6

Crêpe Batter
1 cup all-purpose flour
2 teaspoons sugar
2 eggs, lightly beaten
1 cup milk
1 tablespoon butter, melted
1 tablespoon brandy

Suzette Sauce
¼ cup butter
¼ cup sugar
1 tablespoon grated orange rind
1 tablespoon grated lemon rind
1 cup orange juice
¼ cup lemon juice
½ cup Grand Marnier
whipped cream or ice cream, to serve

1 To make Batter: Place all ingredients into the bowl of a food processor. Using the pulse action, press button for 40 seconds or until ingredients are combined and the mixture is free of lumps. Transfer mixture to bowl or jug and stand covered with plastic wrap for one hour. The crêpe batter should be the consistency of pouring cream—if it thickens on standing, thin with extra milk or water.

2 To cook Crêpes: Pour 2–3 tablespoons of batter onto a lightly greased 4 inch crêpe pan; swirl evenly over base. Cook over medium heat for 1 minute or until the underside is golden. Turn the crêpe over and cook the other side. Transfer to plate; cover with towel and keep warm. Repeat process with the remaining batter, greasing pan when necessary.

3 To make Sauce: Heat the butter in a pan, add the sugar and stir over a medium heat until caramelized. Add the orange and lemon rind, juice and Grand Marnier; simmer uncovered for 10 minutes.

4 To assemble: Preheat oven to 400°F. Fold the crêpes into quarters and arrange them across the base of an ovenproof dish, overlapping to form a pattern. Pour the Sauce over the crêpes. Bake for 10–15 minutes and serve warm with whipped cream or ice cream. This crêpe batter can be used for all sweet crêpe recipes.

Note: Crêpes can be flambéed at the table. Heat 2 tablespoons Grand Marnier, brandy or orange liqueur in small pan. Carefully light at the table and pour over crêpes.

ABOVE: CREPES SUZETTE.
OPPOSITE PAGE, ABOVE: SPINACH FRITTATA; BELOW: CHICKEN AND ASPARAGUS FRITTATA

FRITTATA

CHICKEN AND ASPARAGUS FRITTATA

⭐ **Preparation time:** 10 minutes
Total cooking time: 20 minutes
Serves 4

2 tablespoons butter
4 scallions, finely chopped
6 eggs, lightly beaten
1 cup milk
2 teaspoons whole grain
   mustard

1½ cups chopped, cooked
   chicken
freshly ground black
   pepper to taste
8 canned asparagus
   spears, drained
¾ cup grated Swiss cheese

1 Heat the butter in a large pan. Add scallions and cook, stirring, for one minute or until the onions are soft. Whisk together the eggs, milk and mustard.

2 Stir in the chicken and pepper to taste. Pour egg mixture over onions and cook over low heat for 15 minutes or until frittata is set.

3 Preheat broiler. Arrange asparagus spears on top of frittata and sprinkle with cheese. Place under hot broiler for 2 minutes, or until the cheese is melted and golden. Serve with a crisp garden salad.

Note: Frittata can be served hot or cold. Cut into wedges for lunchbox or picnics.

SPINACH FRITTATA

⭐ **Preparation time:** 2 minutes
Total cooking time: 30 minutes
Serves 4

6 eggs, lightly beaten
1 cup milk
8 oz package frozen
   spinach, thawed
1 onion, chopped
½ cup grated Cheddar
   cheese

½ cup grated Parmesan
   cheese
1 clove garlic, crushed
1 tablespoon finely
   chopped fresh parsley
freshly ground black
   pepper to taste

1 Preheat oven to moderate 350°F. Whisk together eggs and milk. Squeeze all water from thawed spinach.

2 Stir spinach, onion, cheeses, garlic, parsley and pepper to taste into the egg mixture.

3 Pour into a greased 9 inch pie plate. Bake for 30 minutes or until set and golden. Serve hot or cold, cut into wedges. Serve with crusty whole-wheat bread.

ABOUT FRITTATAS

■ Frittatas are similar to omelets, except that the filling and the beaten eggs are combined. They can be fried and the uncooked side browned under the broiler, or baked. When frying, use a heavy-bottom, non-stick frying pan with a long, heat-resistant handle. Pour mixture into pan and cook over moderate heat until the underside is golden. Place the frittata under a hot broiler until the top is puffed and golden or you can turn it like an omelet if you prefer.

■ Experiment with fillings—any combination of meat, fish or vegetables which are suitable for an omelet or quiche can be incorporated into a frittata. Herbs can also be added.

dried include apples, apricots, bananas, dates, figs, grapes (as currants, raisins and sultanas), and peaches, pears and plums (as prunes). Dried fruit mixtures, for use in rich fruit cakes, fruit minces and boiled fruit puddings, are also available.

Fruit Cake A rich, moist cake containing dried and candied fruit, candied fruit peel, nuts and spices. Well wrapped in cheesecloth, soaked in brandy, rum or fruit juice and stored in an airtight container, a fruit cake will keep for several months, its flavor

deepening and maturing with time. Fruit cakes are traditional holiday and celebration fare (weddings, christenings and Christmas). Forms of fruit cake have been made since ancient times, when the Greeks and Romans baked cakes containing honey, pine nuts walnuts, and dried figs.

Fruit Cocktail A mixture of fruit chunks, doused with lemon juice and sprinkled with a little sugar, chilled and served as a first course or dessert. Use fruits that contrast in color and texture, such as grapes and cantaloupe or strawberries and oranges.

FREEZING

Freezing is an excellent way of preserving food; it allows economical shopping in bulk, meals or school lunches can be prepared in advance, leftovers can be stored, and favorite produce enjoyed out of season. As long as the food is carefully prepared and packaged, it will retain its color, texture, taste and nutritional value.

EQUIPMENT

■ Plastic freezer bags. Flatten contents to a thin layer, expel air and seal.

■ Sturdy plastic containers with tight-fitting lids. Useful for liquids. Allow about ½ inch space for expansion.

■ Foil containers. Cooked food can be reheated in the same container.

■ Microwave cookware, which allows food to go from freezer to microwave, and even to the table.

■ Aluminum foil, for wrapping and padding.

■ Freezer wrap for interleaving. The double layers allow easy separation of frozen foods.

■ Labels or tags and a waterproof pen or wax pencil. Label frozen items with name, number of servings, date frozen, any reminders, and "use by" date.

■ A double-edged freezer knife for cutting food frozen into solid blocks.

UNCOOKED MEAT

■ Meat purchased on styrofoam trays should be repackaged and the trays discarded. As a general rule, uncooked meat can be frozen for up to 6 months. Do not refreeze meat which has partially thawed—cook it first.

■ Steaks and chops: Wrap individually in plastic wrap, expelling air; pad bones with foil to prevent the wrap tearing. Pack number of steaks or chops required in a strong plastic freezer bag; extract air and seal. Label and freeze for up to six months.

■ Cubes or strips for stewing or braising: Store meal-sized portions in strong plastic bags, filling to the corners with meat. Flatten packages for quick thawing, expel air, seal and label. Freeze for up to 2 months.

■ Roasting joints and corned joints can be kept frozen in a strong freezer bag for 6 months.

■ Chicken: Uncooked, home-frozen chicken (without giblets) will keep for up to 9 months. The giblets can be frozen separately for 8 weeks. Stuffed poultry should never be frozen as harmful bacteria can develop.

■ Sliced processed meats: Bacon, ham, salami and other delicatessen meats can be frozen, well wrapped, for up to one month without the flavor deteriorating.

■ Liver, kidneys and brains do not freeze well and are best purchased as needed.

COOKED MEAT

■ Quickly reduce the temperature of cooked items by placing in refrigerator in a shallow container, or by plunging base of dish into cold water, then cooling completely in refrigerator.

■ Stews, casseroles, curries, soups: line suitable containers with heavy-gauge plastic bags and ladle an individual serving or meal-sized portion into each; place containers in freezer. When contents are frozen, remove bags, expel air, seal and label. Freeze for 2 months.

■ Meat sauce, meatballs in sauce and savory ground meat dishes can be three-quarters cooked, then frozen for up to a month.

■ Slices of roast meat should be covered with gravy before freezing to prevent moisture loss. Reheat gently to avoid tough, stringy meat. Whole cooked roasts do not freeze well. They tend to become waterlogged and when they are defrosted, they lose much of their goodness.

BAKED GOODS

■ Sliced sandwich bread overwrapped in a freezer bag will freeze for one month.

■ Home-baked bread or rolls, sealed in plastic bags, can be frozen for 3 months.

■ Cakes without filling or icing can be frozen for 3 months. Iced cakes lose quality after about 2 months—freeze them, unwrapped, until icing sets, then wrap in foil and pack in containers.

■ Cookies are best frozen unbaked and will keep for up to 6 months. Freeze baked cookies (cooled and without icing) in layers, interleaved with parchment or wax paper, in an airtight container.

■ Croissants and Danish pastries (baked) will keep for 1–2 months in freezer bags.

■ Sandwiches freeze well for up to 1 month. Avoid fillings with cooked egg whites, raw vegetables, mayonnaise or jam.

HERBS

■ Freeze whole sprigs of thyme or rosemary in freezer bags.

■ Mint, basil, marjoram and oregano can be chopped, mixed with a little water and set in ice-cube trays. Seal frozen cubes in plastic bags. Label (one frozen herb purée looks just like another).

■ Basil, dill, chervil, parsley or tarragon can be chopped, mixed with butter and stored as a frozen cylinder for up to 2 months. Slice and serve with grilled meat or fish.

FREEZER SAFETY HINTS

■ Make sure that meat or chicken bought frozen is completely enclosed in its package.

■ Defrost frozen chicken in refrigerator—allow 2–3 hours per 1lb—to prevent bacterial growth. Microwave defrosting of whole chickens is not recommended because of uneven thawing.

■ Thaw frozen meat in refrigerator or on defrost setting in microwave, never at room temperature. If frozen meat is accidentally defrosted (e.g. in a power failure), do not refreeze.

■ Remove frozen meat from wrapping before defrosting. Separate items as they defrost.

FRUIT AND VEGETABLES

■ Vegetables must be blanched before they are frozen and most fruit are frozen in a sugar syrup or dry sugar pack. Contact your local extension office for information on the most up-to-date method of freezing fruit and vegetables.

The exception is berries, which can be frozen without any preliminaries. Line baking sheets with freezer wrap and spread out the washed and dried fruit so that pieces do not touch. Set freezer at coldest setting and freeze fruit until hard, about 2 hours. Remove, pack in freezer bags, expel air, seal and label. Keep for up to 3 months.

Fruit Cup A refreshing drink made of a mixture of fresh fruit pieces and fruit juices, sometimes mixed with iced water, soda, lemonade or alcohol and sweetened to taste. Serve in a stemmed glass garnished with a slice of lemon and a sprig of mint.

Fruit Juice The liquid squeezed from fruit. The juice of oranges or other citrus fruits is a popular breakfast drink.

Fruit Leather A chewy candy or sweet snack made by boiling down pureed fruit (such as apricot, peach, apple, plum, strawberry or raspberry) and sugar until it forms a thick paste. This is spread on a lightly greased surface to dry and then cut into strips. Fruit leather has a sweet, tangy taste; it can be served after a meal with coffee or included in a packed lunch.

Fruit Salad
A combination of chopped, sliced or small whole fruits served as a dessert accompanied by whipped cream, ice cream or custard.

Fresh fruit (raw or poached and cooled), dried fruit (soaked, poached and cooled) or canned fruit can be used. The fruit is usually first sprinkled with sugar (for canned fruit use the syrup instead of sugar) and steeped in fruit juice,

FRITTERS

ONION FRITTERS

★ **Preparation time:** 20 minutes
Total cooking time: 15 minutes
Makes 18–24

4 large onions	1½ teaspoons baking
4 cloves garlic	soda
¾ cup besan flour	1 teaspoon chili powder
(see Note)	(or sweet paprika for a
½ cup all-purpose	milder taste)
flour	vegetable oil for shallow
1 egg	frying

1 Peel and halve the onions and then slice very thinly. Finely chop garlic.
2 Mix the flours with egg, soda, chili powder or paprika and enough water to make a smooth creamy batter. Add the onion and garlic.
3 Heat oil, about ¾ inch deep, in a wide flat pan. Add tablespoons of batter, press into patties. Fry both sides until golden brown and cooked through. Drain on a rack covered with paper towels.
4 Serve fritters hot accompanied by chili sauce or hot mango chutney.

Note: Besan flour is a soft, golden flour milled from dried chick peas (garbanzo beans). Look for it in health food stores

ABOVE: ONION FRITTERS;
RIGHT: FRITTERS WITH STRAWBERRY SAUCE.
OPPOSITE PAGE: DRIED FRUIT SALAD

FRITTERS WITH STRAWBERRY SAUCE

★ **Preparation time:** 30 minutes
Total cooking time: 35 minutes
Serves 6–8

Fritters	Strawberry Sauce
1 cup water	¼ cup sugar
¼ cup butter	¼ cup water
¼ cup sugar	8 oz strawberries
½ cup currants	2 tablespoons brandy or
1 teaspoon grated orange	strawberry liqueur
rind	oil, to deep-fry
1 cup all-purpose flour	confectioners' sugar,
3 eggs, lightly beaten	to dust
	whipped cream, to serve

1 To make Fritters: Place water, butter, sugar, currants and rind in a small pan; bring to the boil. Stir in flour and beat until smooth using a wooden spoon; cool slightly. Gradually add the eggs, beating well after each addition. Set aside.
2 To make Strawberry Sauce: Heat sugar and water until sugar dissolves. Add strawberries, simmer, uncovered, 5 minutes. Process in food processor for 30 seconds or until smooth. Flavor with brandy or strawberry liqueur, to taste.
3 Heat oil in deep pan. Lower tablespoons of the batter into the hot oil, cook over medium heat until the fritters puff and turn a golden brown color. Drain on paper towels, dust with powdered sugar.
4 Serve with Strawberry Sauce and whipped cream. As a simple variation, kiwifruit, mangoes, passionfruit or other berries can be used instead of strawberries.

FRUIT DRIED

DRIED FRUIT SALAD

★ **Preparation Time:** 20 minutes +
2 hours chilling time
Total cooking time: 15 minutes
Serves 6

12 cardamom pods
3 oz dried figs
3 oz dried pears
3 oz dried apples
6½ oz dried apricots
3 oz muscatel raisins
3 oz pitted dessert prunes
1 teaspoon orange flower
  water
1 cup toasted slivered
  almonds

**Yogurt Cardamom
Cream**
¾ cup plain yogurt
¾ cup sour cream
2 tablespoons soft brown
  sugar
¼ teaspoon ground
  cardamom

1 Tie cardamom pods in piece of cheesecloth; lightly roll with a rolling pin to bruise.
2 Cut the figs and pears into halves. Combine the fruits in large saucepan and cover with water to ¾ inch over the fruit. Bring to boil, add cardamom pods. Simmer 10 minutes, then allow to cool.
3 Remove the cardamom pods, spoon the fruit into a serving dish and stir in the orange flower water. Chill well; serve with Yogurt Cardamom Cream and sprinkle with toasted almonds.
4 To make Yogurt Cardamom Cream: Combine yogurt, sour cream, brown sugar and ground cardamom; chill before serving.

DRIED FRUIT COBBLER

★ **Preparation time:** 20 minutes
Total cooking time: 30 minutes
Serves 6

1 lb mixed dried fruit,
  chopped
2 cups hot water
⅓ cup soft brown sugar
½ teaspoon cinnamon
¼ teaspoon ground
  ginger
¼ teaspoon ground
  cloves

Topping
2 cups all-purpose flour
1½ teaspoons baking
  powder
5 tablespoons butter,
  chopped
1 tablespoon sugar
¾ cup milk
milk, extra
soft brown sugar

1 Preheat oven to moderate 350°F. Grease a 9 inch, 6-cup capacity ovenproof dish. Soak dried fruit in hot water for 10 minutes. Drain; mix sugar and spices through, spoon into dish. Cover with aluminum foil and bake in oven for 10 minutes.
2 To make Topping: Sift flour and baking powder into bowl. Using fingertips, rub butter into flour until the mixture is a crumbly texture; stir in sugar. Add almost all the liquid, mix to a soft dough, adding more liquid if necessary. Turn onto a floured surface; knead 2 minutes or until smooth. Roll dough out to ½ inch thickness. Using a 2 inch round cutter, cut out about 17 rounds. Remove dish from oven and uncover. Arrange rounds of dough on top of fruit, brush with milk and sprinkle lightly with brown sugar. Return to oven; bake for 20 minutes.

liqueur or sweet wine, and is served chilled with the flavored juices poured over. Fruit salad as a dessert was developed in France, in the early nineteenth century, prompted by the appearance in the Paris markets of numbers of new, exotic fruits.

Fry To cook a food in very hot vegetable oil or fat over a direct heat. This usually results in a crisp, golden-brown crust. Deep-frying requires sufficient fat to immerse the food. Shallow-frying involves enough fat or oil to cover the bottom of a shallow pan, it is often used in foods coated with batter. Pan-frying uses less fat again, and is suitable for foods that have a light coating of flour or bread crumbs.

Fudge A soft, sweet candy made with sugar and milk or heavy cream to which dried fruits, nuts and other flavorings, such as chocolate, coffee, and vanilla are added. The mixture is poured into a shallow pan and when cold, it is cut into squares. Fudge originated in the nineteenth century.

G

Gado Gado
A salad from Indonesia consisting of a mixture of cooked and raw vegetables garnished with sliced,

hard-boiled eggs and dressed with a thick, spicy peanut sauce.

Galangal The spicy root of two plants that are closely related to ginger and used in the cooking of Southeast Asia. Greater galangal, the more delicately flavored, is a knobby root with white flesh. The lesser galangal has orange-red flesh, a stronger flavor and is cooked as a vegetable.

Game Animals traditionally hunted for their meat, though many are now bred for the table. Often classified as: game birds (wild duck, grouse, partridge, pheasant and quail); small game (rabbit and hare); and large game (buffalo, deer, wild boar, moose and caribou). In

GAME

VENISON PIE

★★ **Preparation time:** 35 minutes
Total cooking time: 45–55 minutes
Serves 6–8

2 lb boneless venison	1 cup chicken or beef
¼ cup butter	stock
3 slices bacon, diced	1 oz dried mushrooms,
2 large onions, chopped	soaked in water for 10
3 tablespoons all-purpose	minutes
flour	½ tablespoon fresh
½ teaspoon mustard	thyme leaves
¼ cup port	pepper
½ cup red wine	¼ cup chopped parsley
6 juniper berries	12 oz puff pastry sheet
	1 egg, lightly beaten

1 Cut venison into ¾ inch pieces, heat butter and brown meat quickly; remove from pan, drain on paper towels. Add bacon to pan, cook until crisp, remove, drain. Add onion and fry until golden. Sprinkle flour over onion and stir until brown.

2 Add mustard, port, red wine, berries, stock, mushrooms and thyme leaves to pan and stir until mixture comes to the boil. Add venison and simmer gently until tender, about 30–40 minutes. Preheat oven to 425°F.
3 Using a slotted spoon, transfer the meat to a large, greased casserole dish. Continue simmering the sauce until it thickens. Season with pepper. Pour sauce over the meat and sprinkle with chopped parsley.
4 Roll the pastry out large enough to cover the top of the casserole dish. Brush edge of dish with a little egg and cover casserole with pastry. Brush top of pastry with egg and make a couple of slits to allow steam to escape. Bake in preheated oven 10–15 minutes or until pastry is golden.

Note: It is important not to overcook venison as it will become tough.

ABOVE: VENISON PIE AND RABBIT WITH DIJON MUSTARD. OPPOSITE PAGE: QUAILS WITH TARRAGON AND PANCETTA

general game meat has a darker color, stronger flavor and less fat than the meat of domesticated animals. Cuts of large game are often marinated before cooking. Older game is braised or stewed and made into pies and pâtés. Young game birds can be roasted. Small game is braised, stewed or cooked in casseroles.

Gammon The lower end of a cured side of bacon. It is eaten hot, boiled and served with parsley sauce, or sliced into thick steaks and broiled or gently fried.

Ganache An icing of sweetened chocolate and heavy cream heated until the chocolate melts. It is cooled and poured over a cake or torte.

Garam Masala A spice mixture of northern Indian origin used to flavor curries and other dishes. Basic ingredients are cumin, coriander, cardamom, cinnamon, pepper and cloves.

Garbanzo Bean See Chickpea.

Garlic A member of the onion family. Its strongly scented bulb

provides a distinctive flavoring integral to the cooking of Asia, the Middle East and the Mediterranean.

RABBIT WITH DIJON MUSTARD

★★ **Preparation time:** 35 minutes
Total cooking time: 1 hour 40 minutes
Serves 6

2 rabbits, about 2 lb each	1 parsnip, diced
1/4 cup all-purpose flour	1 cup white wine
freshly ground pepper	1/2 cup chicken stock
1/2 teaspoon dry mustard	6 whole allspice
1/4 cup butter	4 teaspoons Dijon
2 cloves garlic, crushed	mustard
8 oz small mushrooms	2 tablespoons chopped
1 tablespoon olive oil	fresh parsley
3 slices bacon, chopped	2 tablespoons heavy
2 onions, chopped	cream
2 carrots, diced	

1 Preheat oven to moderate 350°F. Clean rabbits, cut each into 6 portions. Place flour, pepper and mustard in a plastic bag, add rabbit pieces a few at a time. Toss to coat with flour.

2 Heat the butter in a pan, add the garlic and rabbit pieces, cook until meat is browned on both sides. Transfer rabbit to an ovenproof dish. Add the mushrooms to the pan and cook 1 minute, remove. Heat oil in pan. Add bacon, onion, carrot and parsnip. Stir for 3 minutes.

3 Add the vegetables, wine, stock, allspice and mustard to the rabbit in dish. Cover, cook 1½ hours or until rabbit is tender. Stir in parsley and cream. Serve.

QUAILS WITH TARRAGON AND PANCETTA

★ **Preparation time:** 20 minutes
Total cooking time: 40 minutes
Serves 4

8 small quails	1½ cups red wine
1/2 cup all-purpose	1/2 cup chicken stock
flour	1 tablespoon red currant
1/4 cup olive oil	jelly
2 onions, chopped	pepper, to taste
10 oz button	1 teaspoon chopped fresh
mushrooms	tarragon
3½ oz pancetta	

1 Tie the quails into neat shapes. Place the flour in plastic bag. Toss the quails in flour, remove excess. Heat the oil in a heavy-bottom pan and cook the quails, turning until they are brown on all sides. Remove from pan. Drain well on paper towels.

2 Add the onion to pan and cook 1 minute. Add mushrooms and pancetta; cook until mushrooms soften. Add wine and chicken stock and stir until mixture comes to the boil. Add red currant jelly, pepper and tarragon.

3 Add the quails to the sauce and simmer gently, turning the quails occasionally until they are tender and the sauce has thickened, about 20–30 minutes.

4 Serve the quails on a warm serving plate with fried polenta wedges and vegetables in season.

Each bulb is made up of a number of segments called cloves. The pungent flavor is released when a clove is cut; if it is crushed or pounded the flavor is even more powerful.

Garnish An edible trimming added to a dish before serving to enhance its visual appeal and complement its flavor. Garnishes used on savory dishes include sprigs of parsley (chopped, fresh or fried) and cilantro; dill and fennel (in sprigs or finely chopped); small bunches of watercress; leaves of basil; celery curls and young leaves; raw carrot in long, fine strips; onion rings, curls of scallion and finely chopped chives; slices of hard-boiled egg; small wedges of tomato; edible flowers, such as nasturtiums; slices of lemon, orange or cucumber. Croûtons and small pastries often garnish soups and stews, as do bits of bacon. Candied (crystallized) flower petals, fruit and fruit rind are used on sweet dishes.

Gâteau A rich, elaborately decorated cake, often a liqueur-flavored sponge layered with whipped cream. A

GARLIC

HERB AND GARLIC CORNBREAD SLICES

⭐ **Preparation time:** 20 minutes
Total cooking time: 50 minutes
Makes about 16 slices

3/4 cup all-purpose flour
2 teaspoons baking powder
1/8 teaspoon salt
1/2 teaspoon chili powder
1 1/2 cups fine cornmeal
1/3 cup butter, melted
3 eggs, lightly beaten
3/4 cup milk

Herb and Garlic Butter
1/2 cup butter, softened
1 tablespoon chopped fresh parsley
1 tablespoon chopped fresh chives
2 cloves garlic, crushed

1 Preheat the oven to moderate 350°F. Brush an 8 1/2 x 5 1/2 x 2 3/4 inch loaf pan with melted butter or oil; line the base and sides with parchment paper. Sift flour, baking powder, salt and chili powder into a bowl. Add the cornmeal and stir until combined. Make a well in the center. Add butter, eggs and milk to the dry ingredients. Using a wooden spoon, stir until just combined; do not overbeat the mixture.
2 Pour mixture into pan. Bake for 45 minutes or until bread is firm in the center and beginning to brown around the edges. Turn bread out onto a wire rack, leave at least 10 minutes or until cool. Using a sharp knife, cut loaf into thin slices.

3 To make Herb and Garlic Butter: Combine butter, parsley, chives and garlic. Spread on cornbread slices. Place slices on a baking sheet; bake for another 5 minutes or until slightly crispy.

ABOUT GARLIC

■ Look for firm compact heads of garlic. Avoid any with grayish loose papery bulbs or those which have begun to sprout. Store fresh garlic bulbs and heads in a cool, dry, dark place for about 2–3 weeks.

■ Garlic loses flavor the longer it is cooked. A whole head of garlic roasted in the oven will yield soft flesh which is surprisingly sweet, whereas a freshly crushed single clove raw will give a distinct bite to a salad. If you like garlic, add it at the end of the cooking process, rather than—as stated in most recipes—at the beginning.

■ One of the most prevalent herbs in cooking, garlic is also available powdered, dried or minced, but it is much more delicious fresh.

■ The easiest way to prepare garlic is to crush the peeled clove in a garlic press. In the absence of a press, crush the clove with the flat part of a knife, press down firmly, and work to a paste.

■ Keep aside one chopping board for processing garlic. The smell of garlic can be removed from hands by rubbing with salt or a cut lemon.

ABOVE: HERB AND GARLIC CORNBREAD SLICES.
OPPOSITE PAGE: GARLIC SOUP

GARLIC SOUP

⭐ **Preparation time:** 15 minutes
Total cooking time: 35–40 minutes
Serves 4–6

1/4 cup olive oil	*1/2 teaspoon chili powder*
6 cloves garlic, crushed	*1 teaspoon sweet paprika*
1 1/2 cups fresh white	*4 cups water*
bread crumbs	*2 eggs, lightly beaten*
3 medium ripe tomatoes,	*1/4 cup chopped fresh*
peeled and chopped	*parsley*

1 Heat the oil in large pan; add garlic. Cook over gentle heat for 1–2 minutes until soft but not brown. Add breadcrumbs and cook over medium heat 3 minutes or until they turn a light golden brown.
2 Add chopped tomatoes, chili powder, paprika and water. Bring to the boil; simmer, covered, for 30 minutes.
3 Add eggs in a thin stream to simmering soup. Cook over low heat for another 2 minutes.
4 Pour into serving bowl, sprinkle parsley over and serve. Serve hot and heavily seasoned.

GARLIC BREAD

■ Traditionally made with a long French bread stick, garlic bread can also be made with any type of crusty bread. Slice the bread almost all the way through, spread with garlic-flavored butter and bake until hot.

WALNUT AND GARLIC SAUCE

⭐ **Preparation time:** 10 minutes
Total cooking time: 5 minutes
Makes 1 cup

3 1/2 oz walnut halves	*1/3 cup white wine*
4 cloves garlic, peeled	*vinegar*
2 cups olive oil	*salt*

1 Place the walnuts on a baking sheet, bake at 350°F for 5 minutes. Cool.
2 Place the walnuts and garlic in a food processor, process until finely ground. Add the oil in a slow stream until thick and creamy. Add vinegar and salt to taste.
3 Place the sauce in a small clean jar, cover with a thin layer of oil, store in the refrigerator for up to one week. Pour away the oil before using. Use as a dip for fresh bread and raw celery, or as a sauce for cold veal and pork.

ROASTED GARLIC PASTE

⭐ **Preparation time:** 5 minutes
Total cooking time: 1 hour
Makes 1 cup

10 bulbs garlic	*1/3 cup water*
2 tablespoons olive oil	

1 Preheat oven to moderate 350°F. Remove the loose papery skin from the garlic bulbs. Place garlic in a greased baking dish, pour over the olive oil and water.
2 Cook the garlic in the oven for about 1 hour or until the garlic is very soft. Spoon the oil and water from baking dish over garlic cloves as they cook, add a little more water to the baking dish if it dries out. Remove the garlic from oven and cool.
3 Separate the garlic cloves, press the cooked garlic out of their skins into a small bowl. Mash garlic with a fork until smooth.
4 Spread on toasted slices of French bread.

ROAST GARLIC

The next time you are cooking a roast, try roasting a head of garlic at the same time. Using a sharp knife, cut off the top of the head. Place in a 350°F oven for 30–45 minutes. Serve 1 or 2 cloves to each individual. The soft, sweet flesh can be squeezed over the rest of the food, or spread on toasted slices of French bread.

gâteau can be served as dessert, for a special celebration or with coffee. Gâteau is the French word for cake.

Gazpacho A spicy, chilled soup of Spanish origin.

Gazpacho varies from region to region, but usually contains ripe red tomatoes, red peppers, cucumber, olive oil and bread crumbs or garlic croûtons.

Gefilte Fish Poached fish balls, a traditional Jewish dish made from chopped fish fillets, finely diced onion, bread crumbs or matzo meal, egg and seasonings. The mixture is formed into balls and cooked in simmering fish stock. Gefilte fish can be eaten warm or chilled.

Gelatin A setting agent prepared from a natural animal protein, collagen, extracted from the bones and cartilage of animals. Available as powdered granules or thin leaves, gelatin is odorless, virtually tasteless and creamy white in color. When mixed with hot water it forms a viscous liquid which sets as a jelly as it cools. Gelatin is used in sweet and savory dishes, and can be used with almost all foods apart from some raw fruits which contain an enzyme that prevents setting. These include pineapple, kiwi fruit (Chinese gooseberry) and papaya.

Gelato Italian ice cream, made with sweetened milk or cream, egg yolks and flavorings. It is firmer and less sweet than British and American ice creams.

Genoise A light sponge cake. Eggs and sugar are whisked over a low heat until warm and thick; flour and melted butter are added after the mixture has cooled. It is used for layered cakes, sponge fingers and bombe Alaska.

German Potato Salad A cold or hot potato salad that contains bacon bits and is dressed with vinegar.

Ghee Clarified butter, used in the cooking of northern India. It can be heated to a much higher temperature than butter without burning. To make ghee: melt butter until frothy; scoop or strain off the foam; pour the liquid butter into a heatproof glass container. When set, discard any solids from the base, reheat and repeat the process, straining through cheesecloth.

GELATIN

AVOCADO ASPIC MOUSSE

★★ **Preparation time:** 30 minutes
Total cooking time: 10–15 minutes
Serves 6

Aspic
light olive oil
1 cup chicken stock (see Note)
1 tablespoon unsweetened gelatin
garnish (pink peppercorns, finely sliced lemon and sliced avocado)

Avocado Mousse
1/2 cup chicken stock
1 tablespoon unsweetened gelatin
2 ripe medium avocados
2 tablespoons lemon juice
1 1/2 cups mayonnaise
1 teaspoon finely grated white onion
salt and white pepper
1/2 cup cream, whipped

1 To make Aspic: Lightly brush a 4-cup capacity mold with a small amount of light olive oil. Place the chicken stock in a small pan and sprinkle with gelatin. Stir over low heat until gelatin is completely dissolved; cool and pour half of the mixture into base of the mold. Chill in the refrigerator until almost set, add the garnish and carefully spoon over remaining mixture. Chill until set.

2 To make Avocado Mousse: Place stock in a small pan and sprinkle with gelatin. Heat gently and stir until gelatin is dissolved; allow mixture to cool to lukewarm.

3 Peel the avocados, cut in half and remove the pits. Chop the avocados and place in a food processor. Add the lemon juice, mayonnaise, onion, salt and pepper and process until smooth. Transfer the mixture to a medium bowl. Stir dissolved gelatin into avocado mixture and leave until partially set.

4 Fold whipped cream into mixture and pour mousse over aspic in mold. Refrigerate until set. To unmold, gently loosen sides of mousse to create an air space and invert mousse onto a serving plate.

Note: For the aspic, chicken stock must be well flavored, clear and free from fat.

FRUITS IN GELLED CHARDONNAY

★ **Preparation time:** 30 minutes
Total cooking time: 5 minutes
Serves 4

2 tablespoons unsweetened gelatin
1/2 cup water
2 cups chardonnay
1/2 cup sugar
1/4 cup blanched slivered almonds

2 cups prepared fruit (strawberries, melon balls, seedless grapes, chopped apricots)
ice cream or whipped cream, for serving

1 Sprinkle gelatin over water in a small bowl. Place chardonnay in a medium pan with sugar and heat gently while stirring to dissolve sugar. Remove from heat, add gelatin mixture and stir until dissolved.

2 Cool gelatin mixture until it begins to thicken slightly. Place a few tablespoons in a 5- or 6-cup capacity mold which has been rinsed with cold water. Arrange a layer of fruit and almonds on top, allow to set and repeat until all fruits and almonds have been used.

3 Chill the gelatin in refrigerator for several hours or until it is firmly set. Unmold and serve plain or with ice cream or whipped cream. Extra chopped fresh fruit may be served with the dessert.

Note: Clear apple juice with a tablespoon lemon juice can be used instead of chardonnay.

ABOVE: FRUITS IN GELLED CHARDONNAY.
OPPOSITE PAGE: COLD LEMON SOUFFLE

Giblets The edible inner parts of poultry (heart, liver and gizzard, and sometimes the neck). They are used for stock, gravy, soup or stuffings.

Gin A clear liquor made by distilling grains with juniper berries.

Ginger A spicy tasting root much used in Asian cooking in both savory and sweet

dishes. The longer, older roots tend to be hotter and more fibrous. Fresh ginger is peeled, then grated, finely sliced or crushed. Ground dried ginger is used in desserts. Ginger is also available pickled, preserved and candied.

Ginger Ale A ginger-flavored carbonated soda.

Ginger Beer A sweet, carbonated drink that tastes like ginger ale with a stronger flavor. It can be non-alcoholic or alcoholic.

Gingerbread A dark, aromatic, sticky cake or cookie flavored with ginger, molasses and cinnamon.

COLD LEMON SOUFFLE

★★
★ **Preparation time:** 35 minutes
Total cooking time: none
Serves 4–6

5 eggs, separated
1 cup sugar
2 teaspoons finely grated lemon rind
3/4 cup strained lemon juice
1 tablespoon unsweetened gelatin

1/4 cup water
1 cup heavy cream, lightly whipped
chopped pistachio nuts or toasted ground almonds
whipped cream, extra, for decoration

1 Cut a piece of aluminum foil 2 inches longer than the circumference of a deep 6½ inch 5-cup capacity soufflé dish. Fold foil in half lengthwise. Wrap foil around the outside of soufflé dish extending 2 inches above the rim. Secure foil with string.

2 Using electric beaters, beat egg yolks, sugar and lemon rind in a bowl 3 minutes until sugar has dissolved and mixture is thick and pale. Heat lemon juice and gradually add to yolk mixture, while beating, until well mixed.

3 Combine gelatin with water in a small bowl. Stand bowl in hot water and stir until gelatin has dissolved. Add gradually to lemon mixture, with beaters on low, until combined. Transfer mixture to a large bowl, cover with plastic wrap and refrigerate 15 minutes, until thickened but not set.

4 Using a metal spoon, fold whipped cream into lemon mixture. Using electric beaters, beat egg whites in a clean, dry mixing bowl until soft peaks form. Fold whites quickly and lightly into lemon mixture until just combined and all lumps of egg white have dissolved. Pour gently into prepared dish and chill until set. Remove foil collar, sprinkle nuts around edge of soufflé and decorate top with extra whipped cream.

ABOUT GELATIN

■ Extracted from animal bones and cartilage, gelatin is sold in powdered form. Gelatin has no taste so it can be used as a setting agent in foods from pâtés to desserts.

■ Follow any recipe calling for gelatin exactly. Measure water and gelatin carefully, as incorrect amounts will cause the gelatin to set at the wrong consistency. Use a metal teaspoon to remove any undissolved crystals or threads.

■ Take care that when adding dissolved gelatin to the mixture to be set, both are at the same temperature (slightly warm), otherwise gelatin may form into clumps called roping which can't be dissolved. Add dissolved gelatin slowly, stirring constantly until mixture begins to thicken.

Gingersnap A thin, crisp ginger cookie flavored with molasses.

Glacé A term applied to food that has been coated with a sugar syrup that hardens into a glossy surface. Glacé cakes have a smooth, thin layer of shiny icing.

Glacé Fruit Fruit that has been preserved in syrup; it is moist and sticky on the inside and has a glazed surface achieved by a final dipping in a very strong syrup. Glacé fruit has four times the calories of its fresh equivalent.

Glaze A thin glossy surface on a food which enhances its visual appeal and stops it from drying out. Glazes are used on both sweet and savory dishes; some are applied before cooking, others are brushed onto cold food. Pastry can be glazed with egg white before baking, breads can be glazed with a sprinkling of sugar and milk mixture before baking. Hot vegetables are glazed with sugar and melted butter. Cold savory food can be brushed with aspic jelly, and fruit sauce can serve as a glaze for ham. Fruit tarts and flans are coated with a glaze made of jam or jelly.

Globe Artichoke See Artichoke.

GINGER

GINGER-CHILI DRUMSTICKS WITH CUCUMBER YOGURT

★ **Preparation time:** 10 minutes + 3 hours marinating
Total cooking time: 16 minutes
Serves 6

12 chicken drumsticks (about 2 lb 10 oz)
1 tablespoon grated fresh ginger
1/4 teaspoon dried red chili flakes
1/4 teaspoon ground turmeric
1 teaspoon lemon juice
1 teaspoon grated lemon rind
1 cup plain yogurt

1 1/2 teaspoons soft brown sugar

Cucumber Yogurt
1 cup plain yogurt
1/4 teaspoon dried red chili flakes
1 small cucumber, finely chopped
salt, to taste
1/2 teaspoon sugar

1 Wipe the chicken and pat dry. Line a broiler rack with foil. Lightly brush the rack with melted butter or oil. Combine the ginger, chili flakes, turmeric, lemon juice, lemon rind, yogurt and sugar in a large bowl; mix well. Add the chicken, stir well to coat with marinade. Store, covered with plastic wrap, in refrigerator 3 hours or overnight, stirring occasionally. Drain the chicken; reserve marinade.
2 Place the drumsticks on the prepared rack and broil, brushing frequently with marinade, about 6 inches from heat for 8 minutes on each side or until cooked through. Serve hot or cold with Cucumber Yogurt.
3 To make Cucumber Yogurt: Combine all ingredients in small bowl and mix well.

GINGER CHOCOLATES

★ **Preparation time:** 10 minutes
Total cooking time: 5 minutes
Makes about 24

3 1/3 oz dark (semisweet) chocolate

4 oz crystallized ginger pieces

1 Line a 13 x 11 inch baking sheet with aluminum foil. Place the chocolate in a medium heatproof bowl. Stand over a pan of simmering water and stir until the chocolate has melted and is smooth. Cool slightly.
2 Add the ginger to the melted chocolate, stir to combine, making sure that the ginger pieces are completely coated in chocolate.
3 Place heaped teaspoonsful of mixture onto prepared baking sheet. Leave on baking sheet until set. Serve with coffee or liqueur.

Note: Ginger Chocolates can be made 4 weeks ahead. Store in an airtight container in a cool, dark place, or refrigerate in hot weather.

LEFT: GINGER CHOCOLATES; ABOVE: GINGER-CHILI DRUMSTICKS WITH CUCUMBER YOGURT. OPPOSITE PAGE: GINGERBREAD

GINGERBREAD

Preparation time: 15 minutes
Total cooking time: 30–40 minutes
Makes 8 inch square cake

½ cup butter	1½ cups all-purpose
¼ cup brown sugar,	flour
firmly packed	1 teaspoon ground
½ cup light molasses	ginger
½ cup water	¾ teaspoon ground
½ cup golden raisins	allspice
1 egg, lightly beaten	½ teaspoon baking soda
	⅛ teaspoon salt

1 Preheat oven to moderate 350°F. Brush a deep 8 inch square cake pan with melted butter, line the base with paper; grease the paper. Place the butter, brown sugar, molasses and water in a large pan. Cook over a low heat until the butter has melted and the sugar has completely dissolved. Add the golden raisins and cool slightly.
2 Add the lightly beaten egg to butter mixture.
3 Sift the flour, ground ginger, allspice, baking soda and salt into a large bowl. Make a well in the center of the ingredients and add the butter and egg mixture; stir until the ingredients are just combined and moistened. Spoon into the prepared cake pan; bake for 30 minutes, or until the gingerbread is cooked through.
4 Gingerbread may be served warm with whipped cream, or cold, dusted with confectioners' sugar; or serve spread with butter.

GINGERED GREEN BEANS

Preparation time: 5 minutes
Total cooking time: 7–8 minutes
Serves 6

½ inch piece fresh ginger,	2 tablespoons finely
finely grated	chopped fresh mint
1 teaspoon ground	1 lb green beans, trimmed
fenugreek	and sliced
	2 tablespoons olive oil

1 Pour enough water into a pan to cover the bottom and heat. Add ginger and fenugreek and cook for 2 minutes.
2 Add mint and beans and toss lightly. Cook over low heat until beans are just tender.
3 Remove from pan and refrigerate until chilled. Toss in olive oil before serving.

GINGER APPLE MARMALADE

Preparation time: 30 minutes
Total cooking time: 45 minutes
Makes 5 cups

2 lb cooking apples	2 tablespoons grated fresh
4 cups sugar, warmed	ginger
1 cup water	grated rind and juice of
	2 large lemons

1 Peel, core and chop the apples finely.
2 Place sugar and water in large pan and bring to the boil, stirring until sugar has dissolved. Add the grated fresh ginger, lemon rind, lemon juice and chopped apples. Reduce heat, simmer, stirring occasionally, until setting point is reached.
3 Spoon into warm, sterilized jars, seal, label and date the jars.

ABOUT GINGER

■ Fresh ginger is used extensively in Asian cooking, with fish, chicken, duck, shrimp or vegetables. To prepare fresh ginger, scrape the tough skin from the root and either grate or thinly slice the flesh. Bruise dried ginger to open its fibers and release its flavors.
■ Leftover peeled fresh ginger can be stored for several months if packed tightly into a clean glass screw-top jar. Pour in enough sherry to completely cover the ginger, seal the jar and store in the refrigerator.
■ Ground ginger is traditionally used in ginger cookies, brandy snaps or gingerbread. It can also be sprinkled over melons—offering a surprising, but pleasant contrast between hot and cool.

Gnocchi Small savory dumplings made with potato, semolina flour or puff pastry. Gnocchi are poached and served with a sauce or melted butter and grated cheese as a first course, accompanied by a salad as a main course or served as a side dish to roast meat or chicken. The word is Italian for "lumps"; similar dumplings,

knödel, *noques* and *knepfe*, are found in the cooking of Austria, Hungary and northeastern France.

Goat Cheese See Chèvre.

Goat Milk The milk of goats is whiter and sweeter than cow's milk. Used mainly to make cheese, it is more easily digestible than cow's milk and can be used by those allergic to cow's milk. Goat milk is available from health food shops.

Golden Syrup (Light Treacle) A smooth, clear, golden syrup that is derived from the processing of sugar cane. It is used in cooking and as a sweetener for porridge and desserts.

GNOCCHI

POTATO GNOCCHI WITH RICH TOMATO SAUCE

★★ **Preparation time:** 40 minutes
Total cooking time: 45 minutes
Serves 4–6

*3 medium potatoes
  1 lb 5 oz, peeled and
  chopped
2 cups all-purpose flour,
  sifted
2 tablespoons butter,
  melted
¼ cup freshly grated
  Parmesan cheese
freshly ground pepper*

Sauce
1 tablespoon olive oil

*1 large onion, finely
  chopped
1 clove garlic, crushed
14½ oz can tomatoes,
  undrained
2 teaspoons capers, finely
  chopped
4 anchovy fillets, chopped
1 tablespoon finely
  chopped fresh basil
shavings Parmesan
cheese, extra, for
serving*

1 Cook potatoes in large pan of boiling water until just tender; drain and mash. Transfer to large bowl. Add flour, butter, Parmesan and pepper. Mix until combined. Turn onto a lightly floured surface. Knead 4 minutes or until smooth.
2 Form dough into a long roll; divide into 1 inch pieces. Form into small rounds. Indent with fingertips or fork prongs to shape.
3 Heat a large pan of water until boiling. Gently lower batches of gnocchi into the boiling water and cook for 5 minutes or until gnocchi float to the top. Drain and keep warm.
4 To make Sauce: Heat oil in a pan, cook onion over low heat 5–8 minutes until soft. Add

garlic, cook for another minute, add crushed tomatoes and juice. Cook for 15 minutes, uncovered, add capers, anchovy fillets and fresh basil. Cook 1 minute. Pour sauce over gnocchi and serve with Parmesan.

SPINACH GNOCCHI

★★ **Preparation time:** 40 minutes
Total cooking time: 45 minutes
Serves 4

*1½ lb fresh spinach,
  cleaned, trimmed and
  finely chopped
15 oz ricotta cheese
2 eggs
1 cup grated Parmesan*

*freshly ground pepper
pinch ground nutmeg
all-purpose flour for
  rolling
¼ cup butter, melted*

1 In a bowl combine spinach, ricotta, eggs, half the Parmesan, pepper, and nutmeg. Mix well.
2 On a floured surface and with floured hands, shape mixture into 2-inch balls. Lightly coat balls with flour to prevent sticking. Set aside on waxed paper.
3 Bring a large saucepan of water to boil; reduce heat. Drop 3 or 4 gnocchi into water. Simmer until they float to the surface. Remove with a slotted spoon, drain, transfer to a greased shallow baking dish. Repeat with remaining gnocchi.
4 Top gnocchi in baking dish with remaining Parmesan. Drizzle with butter. Bake, uncovered, in a 400°F oven 15 minutes.

ABOVE: POTATO GNOCCHI WITH RICH TOMATO SAUCE. OPPOSITE PAGE: PUMPKIN GNOCCHI WITH SAGE BUTTER

PUMPKIN GNOCCHI WITH SAGE BUTTER

 Preparation time: 30 minutes +
5 minutes standing
Total cooking time: 1 hour 45 minutes
Serves 4

1 lb pumpkin
1½ cups all-purpose
flour
¼ cup freshly grated
Parmesan cheese
freshly ground black
pepper

Sage Butter
⅓ cup butter
2 tablespoons chopped
fresh sage
¼ cup freshly grated
Parmesan cheese, extra

1 Preheat oven to moderate 350°F. Brush a baking sheet with oil or melted butter. Cut pumpkin into large pieces and place on baking sheet. Bake for 1½ hours or until very tender. Allow to cool slightly. Scrape flesh from skin, avoiding any tough or crispy parts. Place pumpkin flesh in a large mixing bowl. Sift flour into bowl, add Parmesan cheese and pepper. Mix until well combined. Turn onto a lightly floured surface and knead for 2 minutes or until smooth.

2 Divide dough in half. Using floured hands, roll each half into a sausage about 16 inches long. Cut into 16 equal pieces. Form each piece into an oval shape and indent with fork prongs.

3 Heat a large pan of water until boiling. Gently lower small batches of gnocchi into water. Cook until gnocchi rise to the surface, and then cook for another 3 minutes. Drain in a colander and keep warm.

To make Sage Butter: Melt the butter in a small pan, remove pan from heat and stir in the chopped sage. Set pan aside for 5 minutes; keep warm.

To serve, place equal portions of gnocchi in individual serving bowls, drizzle with Sage Butter and sprinkle with extra Parmesan cheese.

its veining is more green than blue. Named after an Italian village, Gorgonzola is often served with fresh fruit, especially apples or pears.

Gouda A semi-hard Dutch cow's milk cheese with a mild, buttery flavor that deepens as the cheese matures. Gouda is made in wheel shapes which are coated with red or yellow wax; the interior of the cheese is dotted with small unevenly shaped holes.

Gougère Choux pastry flavored with cheese, baked in a ring shape and served either sliced as a finger food with drinks (in Burgundy it is traditional in wine-tasting cellars) or, with a chicken or meat mixture, as a first course.

Goulash A rich meat stew of Hungarian origin that contains beef or veal and onions and is seasoned with paprika. It is served topped with chopped parsley and accompanied by sour cream.

Graham Cracker A thin cookie-like wafer made with whole-wheat flour.

Granadilla See Passionfruit.

Granita A sorbet made with fruit juices, soft fruit, coffee, wine or liqueur and frozen until grainy crystals form.

Granola A cereal consisting of grains, dried fruits and nuts.

Grape A small, sweet-fleshed, smooth-skinned fruit that grows in tight clusters on vines.

Varieties range in color from pale green to dark purple-black, some with seeds, others seedless. Grapes are eaten fresh, often with cheese, or dried as raisins, sultanas and currants. They are also used to make jelly and wine.

Grapefruit A large round citrus fruit with juicy segmented flesh and yellow to golden-pink skin.

Grapefruit is a popular breakfast fruit, cut in half crossways and served in the skin (the segments can be loosened from the membrane with a special knife). The fruit is made into marmalade and the juice is used in cooking and as a drink.

Gratin The crisp, golden crust formed when crumbs or grated cheese, spread over food, is dotted with butter, and then browned. See also Au Gratin.

GOOSE

ROAST GOOSE

⭐ ⭐   *Preparation time:* 40 minutes
Total cooking time: 2 hours 45 minutes
Serves 6

6 lb goose	*2 teaspoons grated lemon*
2 tablespoons butter	*rind*
1 onion, finely chopped	*½ cup chopped fresh*
2 green apples, peeled,	*parsley*
cored and chopped	*2 tablespoons all-purpose*
1½ cups chopped, pitted	*flour*
prunes	*2 tablespoons brandy*
3 cups small cubes of bread	*1½ cups chicken stock*

1 Remove all the loose fat from goose. Using a fine skewer, prick the skin across the breast. Set aside.

2 Melt butter in pan, add onion and cook, stirring, until golden. Combine butter and onion with apples, prunes, bread, rind and parsley; mix thoroughly. Spoon stuffing loosely into cavity of goose, then join edges of cavity with skewer. Tie legs together.

3 Preheat oven to 400°F. Sprinkle 1 tablespoon of flour over the goose. Place goose on a rack in a baking dish and bake for 15 minutes. Remove and discard any fat from the baking dish. Prick skin of goose to remove excess fat. Cover with foil. Reduce oven temperature to 350°F and return goose to oven and bake for 2 hours, basting occasionally. Discard the fat as it

accumulates in the baking dish. Remove the foil, bake for a further 15 minutes or until goose is golden. Remove the goose from the baking dish. Allow to stand for 15 minutes before carving; keep warm.

4 Drain all but 2 teaspoons of fat from baking dish and place dish over a low heat. Add remaining flour and stir well to incorporate all the sediment. Cook, stirring constantly, over medium heat until well browned, taking care not to burn. Gradually stir in brandy and stock. Heat, stirring constantly, until gravy boils and thickens. Serve the goose with gravy, roast potatoes and creamed onions.

Note: During roasting, baste goose with its own, plentiful fat. This helps crisp the skin.

ABOUT GOOSE

■ Geese usually weigh from 6 to 10 lb making goose a meal for at least six people; one serve is approximately 1 lb. Choose a young bird in the mid-weight range and, if possible, a hen.

■ Always baste the goose as it cooks. Scattering flour over the top of the bird will coat the skin in dark, crusty speckles. Alternatively, increase the heat of the oven for a few minutes, then splash the bird with a few drops of cold water; this will leave the skin crisp.

ABOVE: ROAST GOOSE.

OPPOSITE PAGE, ABOVE: GRAPEFRUIT WATERCRESS SALAD; BELOW: GRAPEFRUIT MARMALADE

GRAPEFRUIT

GRAPEFRUIT WATERCRESS SALAD

★ **Preparation time:** 20 minutes
Total cooking time: none
Serves 6

7 oz watercress
1 large orange
1 medium grapefruit

3 tablespoons olive oil
1 tablespoon raspberry
vinegar

1 Wash and dry watercress thoroughly. Tear into large sprigs, discarding thick stems. Place in a serving bowl.
2 Cut a slice off each end of orange to where the flesh starts. Using a small knife cut the skin away from the orange in a circular motion, cutting only deep enough to remove all white membrane. (Reserve a 1½ inch long piece of orange peel.) Separate segments by cutting between the membrane and flesh. Repeat process with the grapefruit and scatter segments over watercress.
3 With a sharp knife, cut away white pith from reserved peel. Cut peel into long strips.
4 Drizzle oil over salad, then vinegar. Toss lightly to combine. Garnish with strips of orange peel.

Note: Raspberry vinegar can be made by mixing ⅔ cup crushed raspberries with 2 cups white wine vinegar. Place in a glass bottle with a cork or plastic (not metal) lid. Leave 3 days in cool dark place, shaking occasionally. Strain before use.

GRAPEFRUIT MARMALADE

★ **Preparation time:** 35 minutes
Total cooking time: 1 hour 40 minutes
Makes 4 cups

1½ lb grapefruit
2 medium lemons

8 cups water
6 cups sugar, warmed

1 Peel grapefruit and lemons thinly. Cut the peel into very fine strips and place in a large saucepan. Remove pith from fruit and cut flesh into small pieces, reserving seeds.
2 Tie seeds and some pith in a piece of cheesecloth and add to the peel with the water. Bring water to boiling point then simmer until peel is tender and liquid reduced by half.
3 Add sugar, stir until dissolved then boil rapidly until setting point is reached. Leave 10 minutes. Skim gently, turn into warm, sterilized jars and seal. When cool, label and date.

ABOUT GRAPEFRUIT

■ Grapefruit come as large yellow or smaller pink fruit. In either case, choose ones which are evenly colored and unblemished. They will keep well, for several weeks, in a cool place because of their thick skin.

■ Grapefruit are popular as a breakfast dish; simply cut in half and sprinkle lightly with sugar. Special double-sided serrated grapefruit knives help loosen segments from the membrane.

Gravlax Salmon fillets cured in a marinade of sugar, salt and dill. Traditionally served with caraway-flavored Scandinavian spirit aquavit. (Gin, vodka or brandy can be substituted).

Gravy A sauce made in the pan from the juices released by roasting meat or poultry, thickened with flour, diluted with stock, wine or water and served over meat, poultry or vegetables.

Grecque, à la A French term for food cooked in a marinade flavored with olive oil and lemon juice and served cold.

Greek Food In the early evening, sitting in outdoor cafes, the Greeks enjoy a glass of ouzo and a selection of little morsels, collectively called *mezze*. The selection may include taramasalata, tsatziki (a mixture of yogurt, cucumber and garlic), dolmades, marinated vegetables, cold meats, octopus and fish. It is served with pita bread. Greek yogurt, thick and creamy, is often eaten for breakfast with honey. And feta, the famous goat's milk cheese, is crumbled over many dishes, not just the familiar Greek salad. Lamb, or more often mutton, plays an important role in Greek cooking, especially in the north of the country. It is slowly roasted until very tender and served with baked potatoes. The Greeks like to serve their food tepid rather than hot. Greek vegetables are often marinated: the most commonly used are eggplant, zucchini and artichokes. Vegetables à la grecque are some of the most delicious of vegetable dishes. Greek desserts are rich and sticky. Pastries filled with nuts and honey (baklava) are traditionally served with a glass of cold water and a cup of very strong sweet coffee.

Greengage Plum A variety of plum with pale yellow-green skin and sweet, fragrant yellow flesh. It is eaten fresh, cooked as jam or stewed as a filling for tarts.

Green Goddess An anchovy-flavored mayonnaise used on fish and shellfish. It gets its green color from the addition of finely chopped parsley.

Green Pepper See Peppers.

Green Tea Tea leaves processed by steaming to retain their green color.

Gremolata A mixture of finely chopped parsley, finely grated

GRAPES

GRAPE AND CURLY ENDIVE (CHICORY) SALAD

Preparation time: 15 minutes
Total cooking time: none
Serves 4–6

1/2 head curly endive (chicory)
7 oz seedless green grapes
7 oz black grapes
1 Spanish (large red) onion, chopped

Dressing
3 tablespoons red wine vinegar
3 tablespoons olive oil
1 teaspoon Dijon mustard
freshly ground black pepper

1 Wash and dry curly endive. Shred leaves. Place endive, grapes and onion in a large salad bowl.
2 To make Dressing: Mix vinegar, olive oil, mustard and black pepper in a small jar. Shake well until combined. Pour dressing over salad and toss gently to combine. Serve.

FROSTED GRAPES

Lightly whisk 1 egg white in a medium bowl. Gently wash and pat the grapes dry (either individually or in small bunches) with a paper towel. Carefully dip or brush the grapes with egg white, then sprinkle or lightly roll in sugar, covering all sides. Shake off excess. Place on a paper-lined tray to dry. Repeat process. Use to decorate cakes, desserts or drinks.

SPICY GRAPE SAUCE

Preparation time: 15 minutes
Total cooking time: 40–50 minutes
Makes 4 cups

4 lb grapes, washed
2 cups vinegar
2 cups soft brown sugar
1 teaspoon ground ginger
1/2 teaspoon ground cloves
6 peppercorns
1/4 teaspoon chili powder
2 cloves garlic

1 Place grapes and vinegar in a large saucepan or Dutch oven and squash grapes with a wooden spoon. Simmer gently 20 minutes or until grape skins are tender. Strain and push grapes through a coarse sieve. Discard skins and seeds.
2 Return to saucepan and add remaining ingredients. Stir until boiling and simmer another 20–30 minutes. Remove from heat and strain again. Pour into warm, sterilized jars and seal. When cool, label and date.

Note: Either white or black grapes may be used for this recipe. Serve Spicy Grape Sauce with pork, duck or goose.

GRAPES WITH CHEESE

Make a very simple but elegant cheese board with black grapes and a soft cheese. Choose goat cheese, Brie or Camembert, or cream cheese mixed with sour cream or whipped cream. Serve with slices of fruit bread and walnuts or pecans.

TZATZIKI

★ **Preparation time:** 15 minutes + 2 hours refrigeration
Total cooking time: 20 minutes
Serves 6

3 small cucumbers, coarsely grated
16 oz thick natural yogurt
3 cloves garlic, crushed
1 teaspoon finely chopped fresh dill

1 tablespoon olive oil
salt and freshly ground black pepper, to taste
2 pita breads
2 tablespoons olive oil, extra

1 Line a fine strainer with cheesecloth. Spoon cucumber into strainer, cover with cloth to enclose. Press and squeeze firmly to remove the moisture from the cucumber. Place cucumber in mixing bowl.
2 Add yogurt, garlic, dill and oil; mix well to combine. Season to taste. Cover with plastic wrap; refrigerate for at least 2 hours or overnight.
3 Preheat oven to moderate 350°F. Cut through the center of pita breads with a sharp knife. Brush rough side with oil. Cut each round into eight wedges. Bake bread on ungreased baking sheet 20 minutes or until crisp. Serve cool with chilled yogurt dip.

Note: If preferred, you can serve tzatziki with savory crackers or crisps instead of pita bread. It is a very refreshing dip.

GREEK CLASSICS

TARAMASALATA

★ **Preparation time:** 20 minutes + 2 hours refrigeration
Total cooking time: 20 minutes
Makes 1½ cups

2 large potatoes, peeled
4 oz cod roe or tarama
2/3 cup olive oil

1/3 cup lemon juice
2 tablespoons fresh parsley

1 Cut the potatoes into ¾ inch cubes. Place into small pan; cover with water. Bring to boil, reduce heat and simmer, covered, for 15 minutes or until tender. Drain well. Mash potato with a fork until almost smooth; cool.
2 Using electric beaters, beat the roe in a small mixing bowl on high speed 2 minutes. Add the potato gradually, beating thoroughly after each addition.
3 Add oil and juice gradually, beating thoroughly after each addition. When all the oil and juice has been added, beat mixture on high speed for 5 minutes or until light and fluffy.
4 Refrigerate for 2 hours. Finely chop parsley. Transfer purée to serving dish; sprinkle with parsley. Serve at room temperature with bread and olives.

OPPOSITE PAGE: GRAPE AND ENDIVE SALAD.
ABOVE: TARAMASALATA;
RIGHT: TZATZIKI

lemon zest, crushed garlic and sometimes chopped anchovy. It is often sprinkled over veal.

Gribiche Sauce
A cold sauce similar to mayonnaise, but using the yolk of a

hard-boiled egg instead of a raw yolk; capers, gherkin, chopped egg white and fines herbes can be added.

Griddle Cake Small flat sweet or savory cake made from batter. Cakes are cooked on a griddle, a heavy flat rimless pan or in a frying pan. See also Flapjacks.

Grill To cook food quickly by direct or indirect heat with little or no fat. Grilling is done over hot coals or other heat source over a grill. One side of the food at a time is exposed to the heat source.

Grissini Long, thin, crisp, bread sticks. In Italy

they are served along with bread and bunched in tumblers in restaurants.

Grits Finely ground corn kernels, a form of hominy.

Groats See Buckwheat.

Ground Beef See Hamburger.

Grouse (Prairie Chicken) A game bird. Birds are roasted or grilled, older ones stewed or braised.

Gruel A thin porridge made by boiling meal, usually oatmeal, in water, broth or in milk. It is one of the oldest forms of cooked food. The Egyptians made millet, barley and wheat gruel.

Gruyère A Swiss hard cow's milk cheese, pale in color and with a sharp but creamy nutty flavor. The curd is "cooked" in heated whey and then pressed into wheel-shaped molds to mature; the interior is dotted with small holes. Gruyère is often served on a cheeseboard, or in fondues and quiches.

Guacamole A Mexican dish consisting of mashed ripe avocado, finely chopped onion, lime or lemon juice, cilantro and sometimes tomato, and seasoned with chili peppers. It is served with tortilla chips or as a dip.

SOUVLAKIA

⭐ **Preparation time:** 20 minutes + overnight refrigeration
Total cooking time: 10 minutes
Serves 4

2 lb leg of lamb, boned
1 green pepper cut into ¾ inch squares
1 red pepper, cut into ¾ inch squares
⅓ cup lemon juice
⅔ cup olive oil

1 tablespoon white wine vinegar
2 cloves garlic, crushed
3 teaspoons dried oregano leaves
2 bay leaves, crumbled
salt and freshly ground black pepper, to taste

1 Trim the lamb of excess fat and tendons. Cut lamb evenly into 1¼ inch cubes.
2 Thread the meat and the red pepper pieces alternately onto oiled skewers; place in a shallow non-metal dish.
3 Combine the lemon juice, olive oil, white wine vinegar, garlic, oregano, bay leaves, salt and pepper. Pour the marinade over the meat on skewers. Cover with plastic wrap and refrigerate overnight, turning occasionally. Drain the skewers and reserve the marinade.
4 Place the skewers on a lightly greased grill. Cook over medium heat for 10 minutes or until the lamb is tender, brushing with reserved marinade several times during cooking. Serve Souvlakia with warm pita bread and Greek salad or Tzatziki (cucumber yogurt dip).

CHEESE TRIANGLES

⭐⭐ **Preparation time:** 35 minutes
Total cooking time: 20 minutes
Serves 4–6

6½ oz feta cheese
3½ oz ricotta cheese
¼ cup grated mozzarella cheese
1 egg, lightly beaten
white pepper to taste

15 sheets frozen filo (phyllo) dough, thawed
2 tablespoons olive oil
2 tablespoons butter, melted

1 Preheat oven to moderate 350°F. Place feta in medium mixing bowl; mash with a fork. Add ricotta, mozzarella, egg and pepper; mix well.
2 Place one sheet of pastry lengthwise on work surface. Brush all over with combined oil and butter. Fold into thirds lengthwise.
3 Place 1 tablespoon cheese mixture on corner of pastry strip. Fold this corner over the filling to edge of pastry to form a triangle. Continue to fold until filling is enclosed and end of pastry is reached. Repeat process with remaining pastry and filling.
4 Place triangles on lightly greased baking sheet. Brush with oil and butter mixture. Bake for 20 minutes or until crisp and golden.

Note: While working with filo (phyllo), keep it covered with a clean, damp towel to prevent drying out. Cooked triangles can be frozen for up to 3 months. Reheat before serving.

MOUSSAKA

⭐⭐ **Preparation time:** 20 minutes
+ 1 hour standing
Total cooking time: 1 hour 45 minutes
Serves 6

3 medium eggplants
1 tablespoon salt
½ cup olive oil

Meat Sauce
2 tablespoons olive oil
1 large onion, finely
  chopped
1 lb ground beef
2 tablespoons dry white
  wine
13½ oz can tomato
  puree
1 tablespoon finely
  chopped fresh flat-leaf
  parsley

2 teaspoons finely
  chopped fresh mint
  leaves
½ teaspoon ground
  cinnamon
¼ teaspoon ground white
  pepper

Cheese Sauce
⅓ cup butter
⅓ cup all-purpose flour
2 cups milk
2 eggs, lightly beaten
⅔ cup grated Romano
  cheese

1 Cut unpeeled eggplant into ½ inch slices. Sprinkle both sides with salt; stand in a colander for 1 hour. Rinse in cold water; drain well. Squeeze out excess moisture with paper towels.
2 To make Meat Sauce: Heat the oil in a pan. Add the onion and ground beef. Stir over high heat 10 minutes or until well browned and all the liquid has evaporated. Add the wine, tomato puree, herbs, cinnamon and pepper; bring to boil. Reduce heat, simmer, covered, 20 minutes, stirring occasionally. Remove lid and simmer 10 minutes.
3 To make Cheese Sauce: Heat butter in small pan; add flour. Stir over low heat for 2 minutes. Add milk gradually to pan, stirring until smooth. Stir over medium heat for 5 minutes or until mixture boils and thickens. Cook for 1 minute; remove pan from heat. Add eggs and cheese, beat until smooth.
4 Preheat oven to moderate 350°F. Heat the oil in a heavy-bottom pan. Cook the eggplant a few slices at a time until golden; remove from pan, drain on paper towels. Divide the eggplant into three. Arrange one portion over the base of a shallow ovenproof dish. Spread with half the meat sauce, add a second layer of eggplant, then the remaining meat sauce and eggplant. Spread Cheese Sauce over the top layer of eggplant. Bake for 45 minutes or until golden. Leave in dish for 5 minutes before serving.

OPPOSITE PAGE, ABOVE: SOUVLAKIA; BELOW: CHEESE TRIANGLES. ABOVE: BAKLAVA

BAKLAVA

⭐⭐ **Preparation time:** 15 minutes
Total cooking time: 40 minutes
Serves 4–6

12 oz walnuts, finely
  chopped, not ground
5 oz almonds, finely
  chopped
½ teaspoon ground
  cinnamon
½ teaspoon pumpkin pie
  spice
1 tablespoon sugar
2 tablespoons butter, melted

1 tablespoon olive oil
16 sheets frozen filo
(phyllo) dough, thawed

Syrup
1 cup sugar
⅔ cup water
3 whole cloves
3 teaspoons lemon juice

1 Preheat oven to moderate 350°F. Brush sides and base of shallow 7 x 11 inch ovenproof dish with oil. Combine walnuts, almonds, spices and sugar in a bowl; divide into three. Place one sheet of pastry on work surface. Brush half the sheet with combined butter and oil; fold in half crosswise. Trim edges to fit dish. Place in dish. Repeat process with another three sheets of pastry.
2 Sprinkle one portion of the walnut mixture over the pastry. Repeat this process using four sheets of pastry at a time and walnut mixture in between. When the last four sheets of pastry are on top, trim the edges.
3 Brush the top of pastry the with remaining butter and oil mixture. Cut the slice in four lengthwise. (Do not cut through the base). Bake 30 minutes.
4 Pour cooled syrup over hot slice. When cold, cut slice into squares or diamonds.
5 To make Syrup: Stir ingredients in pan over low heat until mixture boils and sugar dissolves. Reduce heat, simmer without stirring 10 minutes.

Guava The fruit of a tree native to Central America and the Caribbean. It is about the size and shape of a small apple with a thin green to yellow skin and a pulpy flesh that ranges in color from off-white to red, is studded with tiny edible seeds and has a flavor reminiscent of pineapple and lemon. Available most of the year, guavas can be eaten fresh, added to fruit salad, puréed for use in ice creams and sorbets or cooked as jam and jelly. Guava juice is a popular drink in Hawaii.

Gugelhopf (Kugelhupf) A yeast cake containing almonds with sultanas, currants or raisins, and the cherry liqueur kirsch, and baked in a high, fluted ring mold.

Guinea Hen A domesticated bird with dark meat, related to chicken and turkey.

Gumbo A thick, spicy soup-stew made from vegetables and seafood, meat, poultry or sausage and often served with rice. The dish is named for the gumbo, or okra, which thickens it but is not used in all gumbos; filé powder can also be added. Gumbo is a specialty of Louisiana.

Gyro Seasoned chopped meat roasted on a spit.

HERBS

Herbs, especially fresh ones, can lift dishes from out of the ordinary into the realms of the exceptional. You can be generous with them, although it is wise to be discreet when using dried herbs—their flavor is concentrated and too much can ruin a dish.

BASIL: Bright-green herb with distinctive taste and aroma. Staple ingredient in Italian cuisine. Essential to pesto sauce. **BUY:** fresh, store in water 5 days; or dried. **USE:** whole or chopped leaves as ingredient or garnish. Cooking diminishes flavor. **FOODS:** tomato, eggplant or zucchini, green salads, pasta dishes.

BAY: Glossy, dark-green leaves essential to bouquet garni and many marinades. **BUY:** dried (whole leaves); fresh not usually available. **USE:** whole leaves for flavor. Cooking makes the flavor more pronounced; discard before serving. **FOODS:** meat and chicken dishes, baked fish, pickling mixtures.

CHIVES: Thin, grassy herb with delicate flavor suggestive of onions. **BUY:** fresh, keep in water 5 days; or dried, use a third less than fresh. **USE:** chopped or whole stalks for garnishing, or chopped as an ingredient. Cooking diminishes flavor, add just before serving. **FOODS:** egg dishes, green salads, potato salad, tomato dishes, soups, yogurt dips.

CORIANDER: Light-green herb with delicate leaves (cilantro) and distinctive flavor. **BUY:** fresh (in bunches, with roots attached), store in water 2 days; or ground seeds. **USE:** whole leaves as garnish, or the chopped leaves or roots as a cooking ingredient; use ground coriander in baked goods. **FOODS:** stir-fries, salads, seafood, salsa, chutneys. **OTHER NAME:** Chinese parsley.

DILL: Fern-like herb with slightly aniseed flavor and aroma. **BUY:** fresh, store in water 2–3 days; or dried. **USE:** fresh as garnish, whole sprigs or chopped just before serving; dried, use one-third quantity of fresh. **FOODS:** potatoes, egg dishes, creamy sauces, pickled cucumbers, rice dishes, salads and seafood.

GARLIC: Strongly flavored aromatic bulb used in many savory dishes. **BUY:** fresh (in bulbs), store for 2–3 weeks; dried, as powder, flakes or minced. **USE:** peeled cloves, chopped or crushed. **FOODS:** chicken and meat dishes, pasta sauces, pizza, garlic bread, curries, shellfish, salad dressings.

GARLIC CHIVES: Flat, dark, grass-like herb with taste of garlic. Much used in Asian dishes. **BUY:** fresh, store 5 days in refrigerator, wrapped in plastic. **USE:** chopped green parts as garnish or ingredient, add 2–3 minutes before serving; cooking diminishes flavor. **FOODS:** soups, scrambled eggs, dips.

LEMON GRASS: Long, thick grass-like plant with a strong citrus flavor. Used in Asian cooking. **BUY:** fresh, store in water for 2–3 days; dried powder form (1 teaspoon equals one stalk). **USE:** first 4 inches only of chopped and bruised stem, as ingredient. Cooking enhances flavor; do not use uncooked. **FOODS:** fish, chicken, curries.

MARJORAM: Small, dark-green herb related to oregano but less strongly flavored. **BUY:** fresh, store in water 5 days; or dried. **USE:** chopped leaves as ingredient or as a garnish. Cooking will diminish the flavor. **FOODS:** savory scones or dumplings, savory pies, meatloaf, fish.

MINT: Dark-green herb with strong, fresh flavor. Many varieties, of which spearmint is the most common. **BUY:** fresh, store in water 5 days; or dried. **USE:** whole leaves as garnish, chopped leaves as ingredient. Cooking diminishes flavor. **FOODS:** peas, potatoes, lamb dishes, roast duck, Asian-style salads, fruit drinks. **VARIETIES:** Peppermint, Apple, Vietnamese, Pineapple.

OREGANO: Small-leafed aromatic plant with strong flavor used widely in Greek and southern Italian dishes. **BUY:** fresh, store in water for 5 days; or dried. **USE:** chopped leaves as ingredient or garnish. Cooking diminishes flavor. **FOODS:** pizza, Greek salad, moussaka, salad dressings, tomato-based sauces, risotto, casseroles, pasta dishes.

PARSLEY: Curly-leafed herb with mild, crisp flavor. **BUY:** fresh, refrigerate 2 weeks; or dried. **USE:** chopped leaves as ingredient or garnish. Cooking will diminish flavor. Part of bouquet garni with thyme and bay leaf. **FOODS:** all savory dishes, especially egg dishes, casseroles, mornays, soups, salads, fish and shellfish, chicken, tomatoes, eggplant.

PARSLEY (FLAT-LEAF): Dark-green herb with a stronger flavor than curly variety. **BUY:** fresh, store in water for 7 days. **USE:** chopped or whole leaves as garnish, chopped as ingredient. Cooking diminishes flavor, although it withstands heat better than the curly-leafed variety. **FOODS:** salads, soups, omelettes, tabouli, chicken, fish, shellfish, pasta dishes, vegetables and soft cheeses.

ROSEMARY: Dark-green herb with spiny leaves and a strong taste and aroma. Traditional affinity with lamb. **BUY:** fresh, store 5 days in refrigerator; or dried, use third quantity of fresh. **USE:** whole sprigs or leaves or finely chopped leaves as ingredient. Cooking enhances flavor. Discard whole sprigs or leaves before serving. **FOODS:** lamb dishes, roast chicken, veal, pork, beef, fish.

SAGE: Greenish-grey, long-leafed plant with a savory, dry aroma and strong taste. Traditionally used to counteract oily, rich meats. **BUY:** fresh, store in water 5 days; or dried, use half quantity of fresh. **USE:** whole or chopped leaves as an ingredient. Cooking will enhance its flavor; discard whole leaves before serving. **FOODS:** in stuffing mixtures for chicken, goose, duck; with veal, liver, sausages, oily fish. **VARIETIES:** Purple, Golden, Pineapple.

SORREL: Large-leafed herb, closely resembling young spinach, with a slightly bitter taste and lemony aroma. **BUY:** fresh, store in water 5 days. **USE:** whole leaves as ingredient or (used sparingly) as garnish. Cooking diminishes flavor. **FOODS:** soup, omelettes, salads. **VARIETIES:** Garden, Wild.

TARRAGON: Thin-leafed, dark green herb with distinctive flavor and aroma. Used widely in French cuisine. **BUY:** fresh, store in water for 2–3 days; or dried, use a third of the quantity of fresh. **USE:** chopped as ingredient or garnish. Cooking diminishes flavor. **FOODS:** chicken dishes, omelettes, fish, salad dressings, Béarnaise sauce. **VARIETIES:** French, Russian.

THYME: Fragrant herb with tiny leaves and strong flavor. **BUY:** fresh, store in water for 7 days, or dried. **USE:** whole sprigs as a garnish or whole or chopped leaves as ingredient. Cooking will enhance flavor. Discard whole sprigs before you serve. **FOODS:** roast meats, pâtés, terrines, herb breads, marinades, stuffings. **VARIETIES:** Lemon, Orange.

Haddock A fish of northern Atlantic waters, related to the cod. Fresh haddock has firm, white, delicately flavored flesh. It can be cooked in a variety of ways. Smoked haddock, usually poached in milk, is a traditional breakfast dish in Britain. It can also be baked, grilled or gently fried. Haddock is the main ingredient in the classic Anglo-Indian kedgeree.

Haggis A traditional Scottish dish, is widely regarded as the national dish of Scotland. The ground innards of a sheep are mixed with ground beef or mutton, suet and oats, seasoned with cayenne pepper and chopped onion, and boiled in the stomach of the sheep. It is served hot, scooped out of its casing, and accompanied by pureed turnips and potatoes. Haggis is considered by some to be a great delicacy.

Half-and-Half A mixture of milk and cream substituted for cream.

Halibut A large, flat saltwater fish with delicate white flesh.

Haloumi A sheep's milk cheese with a firm texture and sharp, creamy taste similar to feta. Made in Cyprus, Syria and Lebanon for at least 2000 years, it is

HAM

HAM STEAKS IN WHISKEY SAUCE

★ **Preparation time:** 20 minutes
Total cooking time: 35 minutes
Serves 4

4 x ⁵⁄₈ inch thick ham
  steaks
1 tablespoon butter
1 large onion, thinly sliced
1 tablespoon butter, extra
2 green apples, peeled,
  cored and cut into
  ¼ inch slices

1 tablespoon brown sugar
2 tablespoons Irish
  whiskey
1 tablespoon all-purpose
  flour
¾ cup chicken stock
ground pepper
2 tablespoons heavy cream

1 Trim the ham steaks and snip the edges to prevent curling during cooking. Heat the butter until foaming, then quickly cook the steaks on both sides until they are brown, remove and keep warm. Add onion to pan, cook until golden, remove and keep warm.
2 Heat extra butter in pan, add apple, cook until tender, remove and keep warm. Sprinkle sugar over juices in pan and cook until sugar dissolves. Add whiskey and swirl it with pan juices.
3 Blend in flour, cook 1 minute, add chicken stock and stir until mixture is smooth. Cook until sauce boils and thickens, season with pepper. Add cream just prior to serving.

4 Arrange ham steaks on a serving plate, pour sauce over meat. Arrange cooked onion and apple slices on top. Serve with mashed potatoes and steamed cabbage.

ABOUT HAM

■ Ham is an ideal food for large-scale entertaining, particularly over the Christmas and New Year period. Your butcher will be able to help you choose the appropriate cut and size for the number of guests—generally, half a leg serves 5–10 people, and a whole ham up to 20 people.
■ Ham can be roasted in the oven or cooked on a kettle-style barbecue. Remove the rind and most of the fat, score the skin in a criss-cross pattern. Traditionally, ham is coated with fruit glaze, such as orange or cherry, and studded with whole cloves. Carve thickly and serve warm or cold with a variety of sauces.
■ Store ham in the refrigerator, covered loosely with a clean cloth—a small tablecloth or pillowcase, for example, changing the cloth every 2–3 days. Stored carefully, ham will last for up to 3 weeks. Serve cold slices with fried eggs, chop and toss into fried rice or pasta sauces, or simply make up into sandwiches. The bone can be frozen for up to a month and makes an excellent base for soups.

ABOVE: HAM STEAKS IN WHISKEY SAUCE;
OPPOSITE PAGE: ORANGE-GLAZED HAM

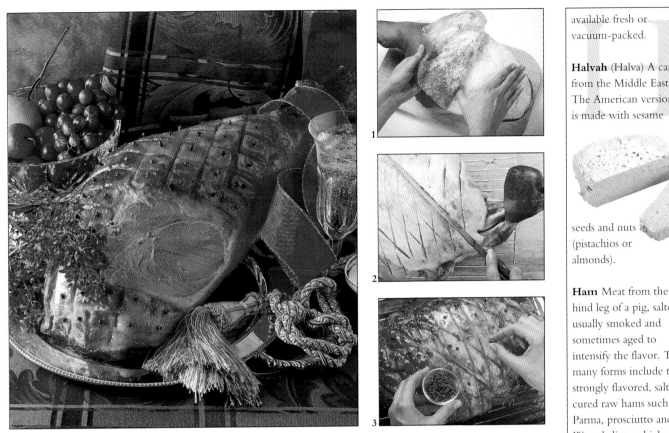

available fresh or vacuum-packed.

Halvah (Halva) A candy from the Middle East. The American version is made with sesame seeds and nuts (pistachios or almonds).

Ham Meat from the hind leg of a pig, salted, usually smoked and sometimes aged to intensify the flavor. The many forms include the strongly flavored, salt-cured raw hams such as Parma, prosciutto and Westphalian, which are often served thinly sliced as a first course; and the cooked hams which can be baked and served hot, but are also served cold in salads, sandwiches or cooked in a variety of other dishes. York ham, lightly smoked, is a British specialty; also known as country hams, Virginia (sugar-cured and smoked) and

Kentucky (smoked over hickory and apple wood), are firmer than other hams and very salty and need to be soaked and simmered before they are baked.

ORANGE-GLAZED HAM

★★ **Preparation time:** 10 minutes + 1 hour standing
Total cooking time: 3 hours 45 minutes
Serves 20

1 x 14 lb leg ham
1 large orange
2 cups water
6 whole cloves
1¼ cups soft brown sugar
1 tablespoon dry mustard
1 cup light corn syrup

1 teaspoon yellow mustard seeds
whole cloves

Mustard Cream
2 tablespoons Dijon mustard
½ cup sour cream
½ cup cream

1 Preheat oven to moderate 350°F. Remove the rind from the ham by running a thumb around the edge, under the rind. Begin pulling from the widest edge. When rind has been removed to within 4 inches of the shank end, cut through the rind around the shank. Using a sharp knife, remove the excess fat from the ham and discard. Squeeze the juice from the orange and reserve juice. Peel the orange rind into long, thin strips. Place the ham on a roasting rack in deep baking dish; add water, rind and cloves to dish. Cover the ham and dish securely with foil and cook for 2 hours.

2 Remove baking dish from oven. Drain meat and reserve 1 cup of the pan juices. Using a sharp knife, score across the fat with deep cuts crosswise and then diagonally to form a diamond pattern. Combine the sugar, dry mustard and corn syrup in a medium bowl; mix to a thick paste. Spread half the paste thickly over the ham. Return the ham to a moderately hot oven 400°F, and cook, uncovered, for 30 minutes.

3 Combine the reserved orange juice and mustard seeds with the remaining brown sugar paste to make a glaze; stir until smooth. Remove the ham from the oven; brush with a little of the glaze. Press a clove into each diamond and return to the oven. Roast, uncovered, for another hour; brushing with the glaze every 10 minutes. Place the reserved pan juices and any remaining orange and brown sugar glaze in a small pan. Stir mixture over low heat until it boils. Allow to boil, without stirring, for 3 minutes. Serve ham sliced, warm or cold with glaze and Mustard Cream.

To make Mustard Cream: Place the Dijon mustard, sour cream and cream in a bowl. Stir to combine. Leave, covered, 1 hour.

Note: Ham will keep in the refrigerator for about 3 weeks. Cover ham with a damp cloth; change cloth regularly.

Hamburger A flat, round patty of ground meat, usually beef, seasoned, cooked and served with lettuce, tomatoes, dill pickles, ketchup and mustard on a soft bun. It evolved in the United States in the early years of the twentieth century.

Hard Sauce A topping made with butter, sugar and flavoring. It is beaten until smooth and then refrigerated until hard.

Hare An animal similar to the rabbit, but larger, with darker flesh and a rich and gamey flavor. Young hare is roasted. Older meat is marinated and cooked slowly.

Haricot Vert A long, thin, fresh green bean. In French *haricot* means "bean" and *vert* means "green." More expensive than regular fresh green beans, they require less cooking time.

Harissa A fiery condiment for meats, couscous and soups; used as a marinade for chicken, lamb or fish.

HAM AND MUSHROOM CROQUETTES

⭐ **Preparation time:** 15 minutes + refrigeration
Total cooking time: 10 minutes
Serves 4

1/4 cup butter	salt and freshly ground
1/3 cup all-purpose flour	pepper, to taste
1 cup hot milk	1 tablespoon heavy
4 oz ham, finely chopped	cream
1 tablespoon butter, extra	1 tablespoon chopped
3 1/2 oz button	parsley
mushrooms, chopped	dry bread crumbs
1 teaspoon lemon juice	1 egg, beaten lightly
	light olive oil for frying

1 Melt butter in a small pan, remove from heat. Stir in flour and add hot milk. Return pan to heat and stir continuously until mixture boils and thickens, add ham and simmer 1 minute.
2 In a separate pan melt extra butter and toss mushrooms over high heat for 2 minutes; add lemon juice. Add mushrooms to hot ham sauce, beat in salt, pepper, cream and parsley. Spread mixture into a shallow dish and refrigerate until firm, preferably overnight.
3 Form mixture into 8 cylinder shapes. Roll in breadcrumbs, dip in beaten egg, roll in bread crumbs again. Refrigerate croquettes for at least 1 hour. Heat oil in a pan and fry croquettes until golden. Serve.

HAM SALAD

⭐ **Preparation time:** 20 minutes
Total cooking time: 1–2 minutes
Serves 4–6

6 1/2 oz mixed green	3 eggs, hard-boiled
lettuce leaves or salad	8 slices smoked ham
mix (mesclun)	vinaigrette dressing,
1 red onion, finely	mayonnaise or
sliced	chutney, optional
1 bunch thin fresh	
asparagus spears	

1 Wash lettuce leaves or salad mix (mesclun) thoroughly and pat dry gently with paper towels. Combine lettuce in large bowl with onion. Set aside.
2 Trim any woody ends from the asparagus. Plunge into medium pan of boiling water 1–2 minutes or until bright green in color and just tender. Drain and plunge into bowl of iced water. Drain well.
3 Peel eggs and cut into quarters. Arrange salad leaves, onion, asparagus, eggs and ham slices on individual serving plates. Drizzle with vinaigrette or a thin mayonnaise dressing, or serve with a fruity chutney if desired.

ABOVE: HAM SALAD. OPPOSITE PAGE, ABOVE: BEEF BURGERS WITH CARAMELIZED ONIONS; BELOW: CHICKEN BURGERS

HAMBURGERS

BEEF BURGERS WITH CARAMELIZED ONIONS

⭐ **Preparation time:** 25 minutes
Total cooking time: 46 minutes
Serves 6

2 lb ground beef	**Caramelized Onions**
¼ cup sour cream	1 tablespoon olive oil
1 teaspoon dried thyme	3 medium red onions,
1 teaspoon dried basil	sliced into rings
1 teaspoon dried rosemary	1 tablespoon balsamic
	vinegar
	2 teaspoons honey

1 Place ground beef, sour cream and herbs in a large mixing bowl and combine thoroughly. Divide mixture into six equal portions and shape into ⅝ inch thick patties. Refrigerate, covered, until required.
2 To make Caramelized Onions: Heat oil in a large pan, add onion and cook over medium-low heat for 20 minutes. Onions should be very soft and golden brown. Add vinegar and honey and cook, stirring, for another 10 minutes.
3 While onions are cooking, heat grill or frying pan and brush lightly with oil. Cook burgers over medium-high heat for 8 minutes each side, turning once only. When burgers are cooked through, remove from pan and serve with salad and warm Caramelized Onions.

CHICKEN BURGERS WITH GRAINY MUSTARD CREAM

⭐ **Preparation time:** 12 minutes + 20 minutes standing
Total cooking time: 10 minutes
Makes 6

1 lb ground chicken	salt and freshly ground
⅔ cup dry bread crumbs	black pepper, to taste
1 tablespoon mild curry powder	
2 tablespoons mango chutney	**Grainy Mustard Cream**
2 tablespoons finely chopped flat-leaf parsley	¼ cup sour cream
	1 tablespoon seeded mustard
1 egg, lightly beaten	1 tablespoon mango chutney
	¼ cup olive oil

1 Place ground chicken, bread crumbs, curry powder, chutney, parsley, egg, salt and pepper into mixing bowl.
2 Using hands, press the mixture together until ingredients are well combined. Cover mixture with plastic wrap and refrigerate for 20 minutes.
3 Divide mixture into six equal portions. Shape each portion into a patty with lightly oiled hands and flatten slightly. Place the patties on a lightly oiled grill. Cook over medium-high heat for 5 minutes each side or until the burgers are well browned and cooked through, turning once. Serve hot with Grainy Mustard Cream.
4 To make Grainy Mustard Cream: Place cream, mustard and chutney in a bowl. Using a wire whisk, stir to combine. Add oil a few drops at a time, beating until all the oil has been added.

The main ingredients are chilies and olive oil.

Hash A fried mixture of diced potatoes and meat, developed to use leftovers.

Hash Brown Potatoes Grated cooked potatoes pan-fried in bacon fat to form a crusty pancake.

Havarti A loaf-shaped, semi-hard cow's milk cheese. The interior has small, irregular holes.

Hazelnut A small round hard-shelled nut with mild sweet flavor; it can be eaten fresh, or roasted and salted.

The filbert is a large cultivated hazelnut.

Head Cheese Stewed, boned meat from the head of a calf or pig. It is seasoned with spices and set in aspic from the cooking liquid. Head cheese is sliced and served cold.

Heart Dark red lean muscle surrounded by fatty tissue. Heart requires long slow cooking such as stewing.

Hearts of Palm The tender, pale-colored interior of cabbage palm trees.

Herb The leaves and stems of various aromatic plants used in cooking to enhance the flavor and color of food. Among the most often used herbs are parsley, mint, thyme, rosemary, sage, basil, dill, marjoram,

tarragon, oregano and bay leaf. Some herbs have a particular affinity with certain foods.

Hero (Subway, Grinder, Hoagie, Poor Boy) A large sandwich of meats, cheeses, peppers, onions and lettuce on a small oval crusty bread loaf.

Herring A saltwater fish of the north Atlantic with dark, richly flavored, soft-textured, oily flesh. Fresh herring, sold whole or in fillets, is best broiled or fried, but can also be baked and poached. Because of its high fat content the herring is well suited to smoking and pickling.

Hoisin Sauce A sweet and spicy, red-brown sauce that is made from fermented soy beans and red rice, a natural coloring agent. Hoisin sauce gives a red glaze to meat dishes. It is used on pork and chicken, as a seasoning for braised dishes and, sparingly, in stir-fried dishes.

VEGEBURGER WITH CHICKPEA SAUCE

⭐ **Preparation time:** 20 minutes + 2 hours refrigeration
Total cooking time: 20 minutes
Serves 4

½ cup olive oil
1 medium onion, finely chopped
1 tablespoon curry powder
½ cup fresh or frozen peas
½ cup finely chopped carrot
½ cup finely chopped pumpkin
1 ripe tomato, peeled and chopped
¾ cup fresh white bread crumbs
1 egg
salt and pepper
10 oz canned chickpeas (garbanzo beans), drained
4 whole-wheat rolls

lettuce
1 small cucumber, thinly sliced lengthwise
1 tomato, thinly sliced
1 red onion, cut in thin rings

Hummus
10 oz canned chickpeas (garbanzo beans), extra, drained
2 cloves garlic, crushed
2 tablespoons lemon juice
2 tablespoons sour cream
1 tablespoon peanut butter
1 teaspoon ground cumin
2 tablespoons toasted sesame seeds

1 Heat 2 tablespoons oil in medium pan, add onion and curry powder. Cook over medium heat 3–4 minutes or until softened. Stir in peas, carrot and pumpkin; cook for another 2 minutes. Add chopped tomato, reduce heat, cover and cook 3–5 minutes or until vegetables are soft. Remove from heat, cool slightly. Stir in bread crumbs, egg, salt and pepper. Transfer mixture to bowl.
2 Place chickpeas in food processor. Process until smooth. Add to vegetable mixture and mix well.

Cover; refrigerate 2 hours. Divide mixture into four portions, shape each into a flat round patty.
3 Heat remaining oil in frying pan. Cook patties over medium heat 3–4 minutes each side or until golden and cooked through. Cut rolls in half horizontally. Lightly toast if liked. Place bases of rolls on serving plates. Top with lettuce, cucumber, tomato, onion rings and cooked patties. Spoon over Hummus mixture. Place remaining roll halves on top. Serve.
4 To make Hummus: Place chickpeas, garlic, lemon juice, sour cream, peanut butter, cumin and sesame seeds in food processor. Process for 20–30 seconds or until smooth.

CARPETBAG BURGERS WITH HORSERADISH CREAM

⭐ **Preparation time:** 20 minutes
Total cooking time: 16 minutes
Serves 6

1½ lb ground beef
1 cup fresh white bread crumbs
½ teaspoon finely grated lemon rind
5 drops Tabasco sauce
1 egg, lightly beaten
6 oysters

6 hamburger buns
shredded lettuce

Horseradish Cream
½ cup sour cream
2 teaspoons horseradish relish

1 Place the ground beef, bread crumbs, lemon rind, Tabasco and egg in a large mixing bowl and combine thoroughly. Divide the mixture into six equal portions and shape into patties about ⅝ inch thick. With your thumb, make a cavity in the top of each burger. Place an oyster in each cavity and smooth the ground beef over the oyster to enclose it completely. Refrigerate until required.
2 To make Horseradish Cream: Place sour cream and horseradish relish in a small bowl, stir to combine. Refrigerate until required.
3 Heat grill or a frying pan and brush lightly with oil. Cook the prepared patties on medium-high heat for about 8 minutes on each side, turning once only. Halve the hamburger buns and lightly toast and butter if desired. Place the bases of the buns on individual serving plates. Spread shredded lettuce over buns and add a cooked mince patty to each. Add Horseradish Cream and finish with bun top.

ABOVE: CARPETBAG BURGERS WITH HORSERADISH CREAM. OPPOSITE: COFFEE HAZELNUT COOKIES

HAZELNUTS

COFFEE HAZELNUT COOKIES

★★ **Preparation time:** 15 minutes +
30 minutes freezing
Total cooking time: 15 minutes
Makes 25

1¹⁄₃ cups all-purpose
  flour
¹⁄₃ cup unsalted butter,
  chopped
¹⁄₂ cup sugar
1 tablespoon instant coffee
  granules
2 teaspoons boiling water
1 large egg yolk
¹⁄₂ cup ground hazelnuts
³⁄₄ cup finely chopped
  hazelnuts

13 whole hazelnuts,
  halved

Coffee Icing
²⁄₃ cup confectioners'
  sugar, sifted
¹⁄₂ teaspoon instant coffee
  powder
2 teaspoons butter,
  softened
2 teaspoons milk

1 Sift flour into large mixing bowl; add butter and sugar. Using fingertips, rub butter into the flour until fine and crumbly (or cut butter into mixture with a pastry cutter). Make a well in the center. Dissolve coffee in water. Add beaten egg, cooled coffee and ground hazelnuts to flour mixture. Mix until almost smooth.

2 Turn dough onto lightly floured surface. Knead for 1 minute or until smooth; shape into a log about 1¹⁄₂ x 12 inches. Roll log in chopped hazelnuts. Wrap in plastic wrap and chill for 30 minutes in the freezer or for 1 to 2 hours in the refrigerator.

3 Preheat oven to 350°F. Lightly grease a baking sheet. Using a sharp knife, cut log into 25 slices. Place on baking sheet about 1¹⁄₂ inches apart. Bake 15 minutes or until set. Cool on baking sheet 1 minute. Remove to rack to cool completely.

4 To make Icing: In a small bowl combine confectioners' sugar, coffee and softened butter. Stir in milk. Place the bowl in a larger bowl of hot water. Stir the icing until smooth. Spread a small amount of icing in center of each cookie; top with a half hazelnut.

ABOUT HAZELNUTS

■ Hazelnut meal is frequently used as a substitute for flour in cookies and cakes, although their mild sweet flavor also suits savory food. Chop coarsely and combine with melted butter, then scatter over trout or lobster, toss through a green salad or sprinkle over mushroom or vegetable soup.

■ Hazelnuts are difficult to shell (the nut needs to be toasted and the skin rubbed off with a towel) so are probably best bought shelled. They are available whole, chopped or ground. Ground hazelnuts can be substituted for ground almonds in many recipes.

■ Hazelnut oil is rare and expensive, but makes a delicious salad dressing.

Hollandaise Sauce A rich, golden yellow sauce made with butter, egg yolk, lemon juice or vinegar, and seasonings.

Hominy Dried corn kernels that have been hulled and the germ removed by soaking in slaked lime or lye. Ground hominy, called grits or hominy grits, is a popular breakfast cereal in the south. Coarsely ground hominy is also called pearl hominy or samp. Hominy can be served as a vegetable, added to casseroles, soups and stews, or mixed with egg and flour and fried as cakes.

Honey A sweet viscous fluid made by bees from flower nectar and stored sealed in wax

honeycombs. Color and flavor depend upon the species of flower the nectar came from. In general, the darker the color, the stronger the flavor.

Thyme honey is clear and dark golden and ranked by some as the finest in the world; orange blossom yields an amber-colored citrus-flavored honey. Clover honey, the most common in North

America, is pale, clear and mild.

Liquid honey is the honey as extracted from the honeycomb. Candied, creamed or whipped honey has some of the moisture removed and is finely crystallized (all honeys will crystallize and harden with age).

Honey is used as a spread, in baking, as a sweetener for beverages and cereals and in making candy.

Honeycomb A waxy structure made by bees consisting of rows of adjacent hexagonal cells in which they store honey, lay eggs and allow larvae to develop. Resembling this in its structure is a brittle candy with an aerated interior made by

adding baking soda to a boiling syrup of honey and sugar.

Honeydew Melon A round, pale-skinned melon with honey-scented, juicy, pale green flesh and slender, pale seeds. The flesh can be eaten raw on its own, added to fruit salads or served

HAZELNUT CHOCOLATE ROLL

⭐ **Preparation time:** 30 minutes
Total cooking time: 12 to 15 minutes
Serves 10

1/2 cup all-purpose flour
2 tablespoons unsweetened cocoa powder
1/4 teaspoon baking soda
1/8 teaspoon salt
4 eggs, separated
1/2 teaspoon cream of tartar
1/3 cup sugar
1 1/2 teaspoons vanilla extract
1/2 cup sugar

1/4 cup ground hazelnuts or almonds
1 square (1 oz) semisweet chocolate, finely chopped
1/4 cup sifted confectioners' sugar

Cream Filling
1 cup heavy cream
3 tablespoons confectioners' sugar
1 tablespoon creme de cacao

1 Preheat oven to 375°F. Grease a 15 x 10 x 1 inch jelly roll pan. Line with parchment paper; grease. Sift flour, cocoa, soda and salt. Place egg whites and cream of tartar in mixing bowl. Beat with electric mixer until soft peaks form. Add 1/3 cup sugar gradually, beat 3 minutes until glossy and thick and sugar is almost dissolved.
2 Beat egg yolks and vanilla 3 minutes until thick and pale yellow. Add 1/2 cup sugar gradually, beat 3 minutes until sugar is almost dissolved. Add yolks and beat 20 seconds. Fold in hazelnuts, chocolate and confectioners' sugar. Spread into pan. Bake 12 to 15 minutes until golden. Turn onto a towel covered with waxed paper sprinkled with powdered sugar. Roll up and leave to cool.
3 To make Cream Filling: Beat the cream, confectioners' sugar and creme de cacao into stiff peaks.
4 Unroll cake; Spread with Cream Filling; re-roll. Trim ends with knife.

SPICED HAZELNUTS

⭐ **Preparation time:** 6 minutes
Total cooking time: 30 minutes
Makes 4–5 cups

1 egg white
1/3 cup sugar
3 teaspoons ground cinnamon
1/4 teaspoon ground nutmeg
1/4 teaspoon ground cloves
8 oz roasted hazelnuts

Preheat oven to 325°F. Beat egg white until stiff; fold in sugar, cinnamon, nutmeg and cloves. Toss nuts in mixture to coat. Spread on greased baking sheet. Bake for 30 minutes. Cool completely. Cut into bite-size bits.

HAZELNUT SHORTBREAD

⭐ **Preparation time:** 30 minutes
Total cooking time: 12 to 15 minutes
Makes about 40

1 cup butter
1/2 cup sugar
1 egg
1 teaspoon vanilla extract
1 1/2 cups all-purpose flour
1/2 teaspoon baking powder
1/4 teaspoon baking soda
1/2 cup finely ground hazelnuts
30 whole hazelnuts

1 In a bowl beat butter with an electric mixer until softened. Add sugar and beat until fluffy. Add egg and vanilla and beat until well combined. Stir in flour, baking powder and baking soda until well combined. Stir in ground hazelnuts.
2 Shape tablespoonfuls of dough into balls. Place 2 inches apart on a baking sheet. Press a whole hazelnut into the center of each cookie.
3 Bake in a 350°F oven for 12 to15 minutes or until light brown. Cool on wire racks.

HONEY

HONEY MINT ROASTED CHICKEN

⭐ **Preparation time:** 15 minutes
Total cooking time: 1 hour 10 minutes
Serves 4–6

3¼ lb chicken
2 cloves garlic, crushed
2 tablespoons finely chopped fresh mint
¼ cup butter

juice of 1 lemon
¼ cup honey
1½ cups water
preserved ginger, to serve
chopped almonds, to serve

1 Preheat oven to 350°F. Remove excess fat from chicken. Wash the chicken and pat dry with paper towels.
2 Combine crushed garlic and mint. Using your fingers or a spoon, spread mixture under the chicken skin. Heat butter, lemon juice and honey in a medium pan, stirring well to combine.
3 Brush chicken all over with honey mixture; tie wings and drumsticks securely in place. Place chicken on a roasting rack in a baking dish. Pour water into dish.
4 Bake 1 hour or until golden, brushing with honey mixture. Serve with preserved ginger and chopped almonds.

OPPOSITE, PAGE, ABOVE: HAZELNUT CHOCOLATE ROLL; BELOW: HAZELNUT SHORTBREAD.
ABOVE: HONEY MINT ROASTED CHICKEN;
RIGHT: BARBECUED HONEY SEAFOOD

BARBECUED HONEY SEAFOOD

⭐ **Preparation time:** 15 minutes + 3 hours marinating
Total cooking time: 5 minutes
Makes 8 skewers

1 lb medium uncooked shrimp
8 oz fresh scallops, with corals intact
¼ cup honey

2 tablespoons soy sauce
¼ cup bottled barbecue sauce
2 tablespoons sweet sherry

1 Soak 8 wooden skewers in water. Remove heads from shrimp. Peel and devein shrimp keeping tails intact. Clean scallops, removing brown thread.
2 Thread the shrimp and scallops alternately onto skewers (about 3 shrimp and scallops per skewer). Place in a shallow non-metal dish. Combine the honey, soy sauce, barbecue sauce and sherry and pour over the skewered shrimp and scallops. Cover and refrigerate for several hours or overnight.
3 Remove the skewers from dish and cook on a hot lighly greased grill for 5 minutes or until cooked through. Brush frequently with marinade while cooking.

ABOUT HONEY

■ Honeys range in color from light and clear to thick and opaque. Each offers a distinct flavor and taste, depending on the flower the honey is harvested from. Usually, the paler the honey, the milder its taste.
■ Cooking honey will caramelize its sugars and diminish its flavor, so choose darker, more strongly flavored honeys for cooking.

with prosciutto as a light first course.

Hopping John Rice and black-eyed peas; a southern dish, traditional for New Years Day.

Hors d'Oeuvre A French term used to describe small portions of hot or cold savory foods served with drinks prior to a meal. Cold hors d'oeuvres can range from olives and nuts to dips, spreads, crudités, and marinated and smoked foods. Hot ones can include croquettes, fritters, tiny pizzas and bacon-wrapped tidbits.

Horseradish A plant of the mustard family native to Eastern Europe and now cultivated around the world for its pungent hot-flavored root, which is grated to flavor sauces (such as those served with roast beef and seafood dishes) and soups. Grate

horseradish just before use, as it quickly loses its bite. Fresh horseradish is available in many large supermarkets. Bottled horseradish is sold white (in vinegar) and red (in beet juice). Horseradish cream is a preparation of grated horseradish root, oil, white vinegar and sugar. The young leaves of the horseradish plant can be added to salads.

Hot Cross Bun A small bun made with a yeast dough flavored with spices and dried fruits. It is slashed on top with a cross and glazed with a sugar syrup. Nowadays it is traditionally eaten on Good Friday, but the hot cross bun was originally baked to honor the pagan goddess of spring. The round shape represents the moon, and the cross the four seasons.

Hot Dog A hot frankfurter served on a split soft bread roll of the same length and garnished with mustard,

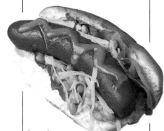

ketchup, pickles, relish, sauerkraut, chopped onion, or cheese (or a mixture of any of these). The frankfurter is said to have been brought to St. Louis, Missouri, in the 1880s and it was served on a bread bun for the first time at the 1904 St. Louis World's Fair. See also Frankfurter.

Hotwater Pastry A pastry made with hot water, lard, flour and salt that even before baking sets into a shell firm enough to stand by itself. It must be used while still warm, as it becomes brittle when cold. It is used for traditional English raised pies.

HONEY DATE CAKE

Preparation time: 10 minutes + 10 minutes standing
Total cooking time: 30 minutes
Makes one 8 inch round cake

1 one-layer package
yellow cake mix
1/2 cup finely chopped
fresh or vacuum packed
dates
1 teaspoon pumpkin pie
spice
1 egg
1/2 cup buttermilk
1/4 cup honey
1 tablespoon unsalted
(sweet) butter
1 tablespoon water

1 Preheat oven to moderate 350°F. Brush a shallow 8 inch round cake pan with melted butter or oil, line base and side with paper; grease paper.
2 Place cake mix, dates, pumpkin pie spice, egg and buttermilk in a small bowl. Using electric beaters, beat ingredients together on low speed for 1 minute or until just combined. Beat on medium speed 2 minutes or until mixture is smooth.
3 Spread mixture in prepared pan. Bake for 30 minutes or until a skewer comes out clean when inserted in center of cake. Leave cake in pan for 10 minutes before carefully turning out onto a wire rack.
4 Combine honey, unsalted butter and water in a small pan. Stir over low heat 1 minute or until butter has just melted. Brush warm honey mixture over warm cake. Serve warm with custard or ice cream. Decorate cake with sifted confectioners' sugar, if desired.

HONEY PEANUT BUTTER COOKIES

Preparation time: 15 minutes
Total cooking time: 10 minutes
Makes about 30

1 1/2 cups all-purpose flour
1 cup rolled oats
1 teaspoon baking powder
1/8 teaspoon salt
1/2 cup unsalted (sweet)
butter
2/3 cup sugar
2 tablespoons peanut
butter
1/3 cup honey

1 cup roasted unsalted
peanuts, finely chopped

Topping
3/4 cup confectioners'
sugar
2 tablespoons butter,
softened
1 tablespoon warm water

1 Preheat oven to 350°F. Brush 2 baking sheets with melted butter or oil. Sift flour into a large mixing bowl; stir in oats, baking powder and salt.
2 Combine butter, sugar, peanut butter and honey in pan, stir over medium heat until melted. Add to flour mixture. Stir to combine. Roll teaspoonfuls of mixture into balls. Arrange on baking sheets, with room for spreading, press lightly. Bake 10 minutes or until golden. Cool on baking sheets.
3 To make Topping: Combine powdered sugar, butter and water. Stir until smooth. Dip tops of cookies into topping, then into nuts.

ABOVE: HONEY DATE CAKE.

OPPOSITE PAGE: BARBECUED TROUT WITH HORSERADISH CREAM AND LEMON SAUCE

HORSERADISH

BARBECUED TROUT WITH HORSERADISH CREAM AND LEMON SAUCE

★ **Preparation time:** 20 minutes
Total cooking time: 15 minutes
Serves 4

¼ cup chopped fresh dill
2 tablespoons chopped fresh rosemary
⅓ cup coarsely chopped fresh flat-leaf parsley
2 teaspoons chopped fresh thyme
6 teaspoons crushed green peppercorns
⅓ cup lemon juice
salt and pepper, to taste
2 lemons
4 whole fresh trout
⅓ cup dry white wine

Horseradish Cream
1 tablespoon prepared horseradish
½ cup sour cream
2 tablespoons heavy cream
salt and pepper, to taste

Lemon Sauce
2 egg yolks or ¼ cup of egg substitute
⅔ cup butter, melted
3–4 tablespoons lemon juice
salt and pepper, to taste

1 Prepare and heat the grill. Lightly grease four large sheets of foil, each double-thickness. Place herbs, peppercorns, juice, salt and pepper in a bowl; mix well. Cut each lemon into eight slices, cut each slice in half. Place 2 lemon pieces in each fish cavity. Spoon equal portions of herb mixture into each fish cavity.

2 Place each fish on foil layers, sprinkle each with 1 tablespoon of wine. Seal the fish in foil to form neat parcels. Cook on a grill over medium–high heat for 10–15 minutes or until the fish is just cooked. (Test for doneness by gently flaking flesh with a fork.) Allow the fish to stand, wrapped in foil, for 5 minutes, serve with Horseradish Cream and Lemon Sauce.

3 To make Horseradish Cream: Combine horseradish, sour cream, cream, salt and pepper in bowl; mix well.

4 To make Lemon Sauce: Place yolks or egg substitute in food processor. Process 20 seconds or until blended. With motor constantly running, add butter slowly in a thin, steady stream. Continue processing until all butter has been added and mixture is thick and creamy. Add juice, season with salt and pepper.

FRESH HORSERADISH

★ **Preparation time:** 5 minutes
Total cooking time: none
Makes 6 fl oz

6 tablespoons grated fresh horseradish
2 teaspoons salt
2 tablespoons raw sugar
3 tablespoons vinegar

Place horseradish in a small bowl and stir in salt, sugar and vinegar to taste. Pack in sterilized jars and refrigerate until required.

Note: Horseradish is a delicious accompaniment to roast beef, oily fish and grilled meats. Add to cream cheese or cottage cheese and use as a spread or dip.

ABOUT HORSERADISH

■ Grated horseradish in salt and vinegar is available from most supermarkets and delicatessens.

■ When buying fresh horseradish, look for firm roots without sprouting or traces of green—these will be bitter. Peel the roots thoroughly and grate or process the flesh finely. Prepare only the quantity you need as grated horseradish loses its pungency quickly.

■ Plants should be stored in a cool, dark place to prevent the roots turning green. (Alternatively, use a commercially prepared grated horseradish or powdered dried horseradish, which is reconstituted with liquid.)

■ Grated horseradish can be combined with softly whipped cream, a good mayonnaise, sour cream or a good white vinegar for use as a relish or a sauce.

Hubbard Squash A large winter squash. The bumpy skin can be blue to orange; the orange flesh is mildly flavored.

Huckleberry See Blueberry.

Huevos Rancheros Eggs served on tortillas topped with a tomato salsa, a popular breakfast throughout the southwest. Traditionally, the eggs are poached in the salsa; they can also be fried or scrambled. The name is Spanish for country-style eggs.

Hummus bi Tahini A dip of Middle Eastern origin made from cooked and ground chick-peas (garbanzo beans), tahini (a paste of ground roasted sesame seeds), garlic and lemon juice. It can be served with pita bread or vegetables as a dip, topped with olive oil mixed with paprika or cayenne pepper.

Hushpuppy A deep-fried dumpling or fritter made from a cornmeal batter, often served with fried fish. It is said to have originated in the south of the United States, from the practice of tossing fried batter to the dogs to keep them from barking.

I

Ice (Sorbet) A frozen dessert made from sugar, water and frozen fruit juice or puréed fruit; no dairy product is used.

Ice Cream A frozen dessert made of sweetened cream or rich milk, sometimes thickened with egg or gelatin, alternately flavored and churned while partially frozen until it reaches a smooth consistency. Ice cream is available commercially in many forms and flavors (including low-fat versions) or it can be made at home. It can be flavored with vanilla, chocolate, caramel, honey, coffee, spirits or liqueurs; chopped nuts, pieces of honeycomb or puréed fruit can be added. A home-made ice cream will freeze harder than a commercial variety; if it is too hard, move it from the freezer to the refrigerator half an hour before serving. Home-made ice cream is best eaten within 48 hours.

Ice cream is descended from the flavored ices eaten in China some

BEEF SAMOSAS WITH MINT CHUTNEY DIP

★ **Preparation time:** 1 hour 30 minutes
Total cooking time: 12–15 minutes
Makes 40

1 tablespoon vegetable oil
1 medium onion, finely chopped
2 teaspoons finely chopped ginger
12 oz lean ground beef
1 tablespoon curry powder
1/2 teaspoon salt
1 medium tomato, peeled and chopped
1 medium potato, chopped
1/3 cup water
1 tablespoon finely chopped fresh mint

2 packages (171/4 oz each) frozen puff pastry, thawed
1 egg yolk, lightly beaten
1 tablespoon milk

Mint Chutney Dip

21/2 cups fresh mint sprigs
8 green scallions
2 red chili peppers, seeded
1/4 cup water
2 tablespoons lemon juice
4 teaspoons sugar
1/2 teaspoon garam masala
1/4 teaspoon salt

1 Heat oil in a large skillet over medium heat. Add onion and ginger. Cook, stirring frequently, for 5 minutes or until onion is soft and lightly browned. Crumble ground beef into skillet; stir in curry powder and salt. Cook over medium-high heat until beef is browned. Stir in tomato, potato and water. Simmer, covered, 5–7 minutes or until potato is tender. Remove from the heat,

cool. Stir in mint.

2 Preheat oven to 400°F. Cut pastry into 5-inch circles; cut circles in half. Form cones by folding each semi-circle in half and pinching the sides together.

3 Spoon 2 teaspoons of the meat mixture into each cone. Pinch edges together to seal. Place on a lightly greased baking sheet. Beat egg yolk with milk, brush over puffs. Bake 12–15 minutes until golden brown.

4 To make Mint Chutney Dip: Cut up mint sprigs, scallions and red chilies; place in a food processor or blender. Add water, lemon juice, sugar, garam masala and salt. Process or blend until well combined. Serve with the hot samosas.

VEGETABLE PAKORAS

★ ★ **Preparation time:** 30 minutes
Total cooking time: 20 minutes
Makes about 40

1 large potato
1 small cauliflower
1 small red pepper
1 medium onion
2 cabbage or 5 spinach leaves
1/2 cup sweet corn kernels, parboiled
3/4–1 cup cold water
2 teaspoons garam masala

2 teaspoons ground coriander
11/2 cups besan (chickpea/ garbanzo bean) flour
3 tablespoons all-purpose flour
1 teaspoon baking soda
1 teaspoon chili powder
1 tablespoon lemon juice
vegetable oil for deep frying

1 Boil potato until just tender, peel and chop finely.
2 Finely chop cauliflower, pepper and onion. Shred the cabbage or spinach.
3 Make a creamy batter with the water and remaining ingredients. Stir until smooth. Add the vegetables and mix in evenly.
4 Heat the oil. Drop tablespoonsful of mixture into oil, about eight at a time; fry until golden. Remove to a rack covered with paper towels.
5 Serve hot with sweet mango chutney or sweet chili sauce if desired.

BEEF VINDALOO

 Preparation time: 15 minutes
Total cooking time: 1 hour 15 minutes
Serves 4–6

2 lb round steak
3–5 tablespoons vindaloo
   paste (to taste)
1/2 cup ghee

1 large onion
2 tablespoons toasted
   sliced almonds

1 Trim meat of excess fat and sinew. Cut meat into 3/4 inch cubes. Place the beef cubes and vindaloo paste in a bowl. Stir until beef is coated on all sides.
2 Heat ghee in heavy-bottom pan. Finely chop the onion, add to pan and cook until quite dark

OPPOSITE PAGE: BEEF SAMOSAS WITH MINT CHUTNEY DIP. ABOVE: VEGETABLE PAKORAS

in color. Add the meat and cook until brown.
3 Add water to cover, partially cover the pan and cook for 40 minutes. Remove lid from pan and cook until the meat is tender and the sauce is well reduced.
4 Serve vindaloo garnished with the sliced almonds and accompanied by boiled rice.

YOGURT AND CUCUMBER RAITA

Preparation time: 10 minutes
Total cooking time: none
Serves 4–6

1 large cucumber
1 1/4 teaspoons salt
1/2 cup plain yogurt

1 tablespoon chopped
   fresh mint

1 Peel cucumber, cut in halves, and scoop out seeds with a teaspoon. Coarsely grate the cucumber into a bowl, sprinkle with the salt, and leave for 5–6 minutes. Drain off the accumulated liquid.
2 Stir yogurt and mint into the cucumber. Serve in small containers with curry meals.

CHAPATTIS

Preparation time: 10 minutes +
30 minutes standing
Total cooking time: 25 minutes
Makes 12

1 1/4 cup all-purpose flour
1 1/4 cup whole-wheat
   flour
1/2 teaspoon salt

1 tablespoon ghee or
   shortening
3/4 cup warm water
   (105°–115°F)

1 Stir flours and salt together in a mixing bowl. Using fingertips, rub in ghee until mixture resembles fine crumbs. Pour water slowly into flour mixture, stirring constantly with a knife. Stir until blended, form into a ball. Turn onto lightly floured surface. Knead 5 minutes until smooth Place back in bowl, cover with damp cloth. Stand 30 minutes.
2 Divide dough into 4, divide each piece into 3, making 12 small balls. Roll out each ball to a 7–8 inch circle. Keep the other balls covered with a clean, damp towel to prevent drying out.
3 Heat a heavy, ungreased skillet or griddle over medium heat. Cook chapattis, one at a time, 1 minute each side, pressing edges lightly with a broad spatula during cooking to encourage them to puff up slightly. As they are cooked, stack them on a plate and cover with a clean cloth towel to keep warm. Serve warm.

3,000 years ago, from the semisolid iced fruit drinks of ancient Persia (the word "sherbet" comes from *sharbia*, the Arab word for "drink") and from the ice sorbets of the Mongol emperors of sixteenth century India. Thirteenth-century Venetian traveller Marco Polo returned from China with tales of a frozen sweet cream dish; kulfi is an ancient Indian dish made with milk boiled until thick and then frozen. In the sixteenth century the Florentine cooks of Catherine de' Medici, bride of France's Henri II, introduced the French to the frozen cream confection gelati; it was quickly taken up by fashionable Parisian cafés who served it in small silver bowls.

The ice cream churn, invented by American Nancy Johnson in 1846, enabled good quality ice cream to be made at home; it also made it possible to mass produce ice cream and sell it commercially. The best ice cream churns are electric or hand operated with rock salt and ice placed around the outside of the bucket containing the ice cream. When the paddles stop, the ice cream is ready.

Iced Coffee Strong black coffee, sweetened, chilled and served in a tall glass with milk or it can be topped with whipped cream. If required, it is sweetened before being chilled. Iced coffee is said to have been first made in Vienna in the seventeenth century, after coffee beans were left behind by the vanquished Turkish army which had unsuccessfully besieged the city.

Iced Tea Tea brewed extra strong, sweetened or not to taste, strained and chilled. Serve in a tall glass over ice cubes and garnish with a slice of lemon and a sprig of mint. For a stronger mint taste, add bruised mint leaves to the brewing tea. Iced tea originated in St. Louis, Missouri, where it was served as a cool and refreshing drink for patrons of the 1904 World's Fair.

Icing A sweet coating, usually made with confectioners' sugar

LAMB KORMA

⭐ **Preparation time:** 15 minutes
Total cooking time: 1 hour
Serves 6

1½ lb boneless lamb
2 large onions, chopped
2 teaspoons finely chopped ginger
3 cloves garlic, finely chopped
3 large dried chili peppers, or to taste
2 tablespoons ghee or vegetable oil
¾ teaspoon ground turmeric
2 teaspoons ground cumin
1 tablespoon ground coriander
⅔ cup tomatoes, peeled and chopped
¼ teaspoon ground cloves

½ teaspoon ground cinnamon
¼ teaspoon ground cardamom
¼ teaspoon black pepper
½ cup water
⅔ cup heavy cream
fresh cilantro sprigs, for garnish

Onion and Mint in Yogurt

1 medium onion, very thinly sliced
¼ cup white vinegar
¼ teaspoon salt
1 tablespoon chopped fresh mint
2 tablespoons plain yogurt

1 Trim fat from lamb. Cut into 1-inch cubes; set aside. Place the chopped onion, ginger, garlic and chilies in a food processor bowl or blender container. Cover and process or blend until well combined. Add a little water, if necessary.
2 Heat the ghee or oil in a large saucepan over medium–high heat. Add the onion mixture. Cook until soft and lightly browned. Stir in the turmeric, cumin and coriander. Cook, stirring frequently, until the moisture has evaporated and the mixture has a rich appearance. Add the lamb. Cook lamb, stirring frequently, until browned.
3 Stir in the remaining ingredients. Reduce heat; simmer, covered, 30–40 minutes, stirring occasionally to prevent mixture sticking to bottom of pan. Garnish with sprigs of cilantro, serve with steamed long-grain rice and the Onion and Mint in Yogurt.
4 To make Onion and Mint in Yogurt: Place onion slices in a small glass bowl. Pour on the vinegar, leave for 30 minutes. Drain off the vinegar; discard. Rinse onion slices twice in cold water. Drain well. Add salt, mint and yogurt; stir to combine. Cover and refrigerate until well chilled.

Note: Lamb Korma can be cooked three days ahead and refrigerated. It can also be frozen for up to one month.

TANDOORI CHICKEN KABOBS

⭐ **Preparation time:** 10 minutes +
5 hours marinating
Total cooking time: 10 minutes
Serves 4–6

1 lb boneless chicken breasts, skin removed
½ cup plain yogurt
½ teaspoon mashed garlic
1 tablespoon tandoori or vindaloo paste

2 tablespoons ghee, melted
2 small limes
1½ teaspoons garam masala

1 Cut chicken into 1¼ inch cubes. Thread cubes onto oiled skewers, use about three or four pieces on each skewer. Arrange side by side in a flat dish.
2 Place yogurt, garlic and tandoori or vindaloo paste in a bowl. Mix to form a paste, spread evenly over chicken. Refrigerate, covered with plastic wrap, 4–5 hours, turning several times.
3 Line broiler rack with aluminum foil, brush with ghee. Broil kabobs 5 inches from heat 4 minutes each side until surface is flecked brown and chicken is tender. Brush with melted ghee when kabobs are half cooked to keep meat moist.
4 Arrange on serving plates. Serve with steamed rice, several small wedges of lime, and sprinkle with garam masala.

ABOVE: TANDOORI CHICKEN KEBABS.
OPPOSITE PAGE, BELOW: SEAFOOD LAKSA;
ABOVE: PANDANG CHICKEN

INDONESIAN CLASSICS

SEAFOOD LAKSA

Preparation time: 25 minutes
Total cooking time: 10 minutes
Serves 4

1 lb medium-sized raw shrimp	1 teaspoon sambal oelek
1 lb white fish fillets	1 teaspoon shrimp paste
5 oz vermicelli	1 teaspoon ground turmeric
6 cups fish stock or clam juice	1 cup coconut milk
4 scallions, chopped	1½ cups finely shredded lettuce
stem of lemon grass, 4 inches long	2 tablespoons chopped mint
1 tablespoon curry paste	

1 Peel and devein the shrimp; cut fish fillets into ¾ inch cubes.

2 Place the vermicelli in a large bowl. Pour over enough hot water to cover. Stand for 10 minutes; drain.

3 Combine fish stock in a pan with scallions, lemon grass, curry paste, sambal oelek, shrimp paste and turmeric, bring to the boil. Reduce the heat to low and simmer for 3 minutes.

4 Add the shrimp, fish and coconut milk to the pan and simmer for a further 3 minutes. Remove lemon grass.

5 To serve, place lettuce and vermicelli in bowls, add soup, sprinkle with mint.

PANDANG CHICKEN

Preparation time: 15 minutes +
1 hour standing
Total cooking time: 40–50 minutes
Serves 4

2 lb boneless chicken thighs, skin removed, cut into 1¼ inch cubes	2 teaspoons grated fresh ginger
½ cup lime juice	2 cloves garlic, crushed
8 oz ripe tomatoes	1 teaspoon ground turmeric
1 cup water	stem of lemon grass, 4 inches long
3 small red chili peppers, seeded and sliced in short, thin strips	1 cup coconut milk

1 Place chicken cubes in a bowl. Add lime juice, stir to combine and stand for about 1 hour.

2 Peel and chop the tomatoes and combine in a bowl with water, mix until smooth; strain into a pan.

3 Add the sliced chilies, grated ginger, crushed garlic, turmeric, lemon grass and undrained chicken. Bring to the boil, reduce heat, cover and simmer for 30 minutes.

4 Stir in the coconut milk and simmer, uncovered, for approximately 10 minutes. Using tongs or a fork, remove lemon grass before serving. May be served with boiled rice.

and butter. It is used to decorate cakes and cookies.

Icing Sugar (Powdered or Confectioners' Sugar) Finely powdered granulated sugar used to make icings and frostings. Icing sugar has a small amount of cornstarch added to it to prevent it from drying out and turning lumpy while it is being stored.

Idaho Potato America's most popular baking potato. Also called russet potato.

Île Flottante (Floating Island) A dessert of rich custard topped with an island of baked meringue coated in toffee or caramel. It can be topped with crushed praline (a confection of nuts and caramelized sugar) or toasted slivered almonds.

Indian Food Although most people think of hot curries when they think of Indian food, many Indian dishes are not hot at all (although those from the south generally are). Some curries and rice dishes, especially those from the northern regions, have a rich deep flavor and are spicy but not at all pungent.

Indian food differs according to the region that it originates from and according to the religious practices of its people. Hindus will not eat beef, Muslims will not eat pork. Southern Indians are for the most part vegetarian: this is partly because they are poorer, and partly because vegetables grow very well in the hot climate. Rice is eaten in the south, chapattis (made from wheat flour) in the north. Delhi is famous for its tandoori dishes, Kashmir for its lamb, Madras for its vegetarian dishes and Bombay for its fish.

Curry powder is never used in traditional Indian cooking: fresh spices are ground into a powder, mixed together and fried. Nearly every family has its own recipes for spice mixtures. In India, meals are eaten with the fingers of the right hand only. Chapattis are always torn with the fingers and used to scoop up small quantities of food. When serving an Indian meal, be generous with the rice; an Indian meal uses a lot more rice and less meat or vegetables than a Western meal would. Snacks are popular, especially fried dishes, and are served at teatime.

Indian Pudding
(Hasty Pudding) A baked pudding made from corn-meal, milk, maple syrup, molasses and spices.

NASI GORENG

★ *Preparation time:* 15 minutes
Total cooking time: 8 minutes
Serves 4 as a main course

1 lb medium-sized raw shrimp
2 boneless chicken thighs, skin removed
2 eggs
3 tablespoons peanut oil
1 large carrot, cut into fine julienne strips
1 clove garlic, crushed
1 teaspoon sambal oelek
1 tablespoon soy sauce
4 cups cooked rice (see note)
4 scallions, sliced diagonally
scallions and red pepper, for garnish

1 Peel and devein shrimp. Slice chicken into thin strips.
2 Lightly beat the eggs. Heat 1 tablespoon of oil in a frying pan, pour in the eggs, cook over low heat until the eggs have set, lift out. When the omelet is cold, roll it up, slice thinly.
3 Heat remaining oil in a frying pan, add shrimp, chicken, carrot and garlic, stir until browned.
4 Add the sambal oelek, soy sauce, rice and scallions, stir-fry until heated through. Serve garnished with omelet strips and scallion and red pepper curls.
5 To make green onion and pepper curls: Cut into fine strips and place in iced water, refrigerate.

Note: You will need to cook 1½ cups of raw rice for this recipe. Cooked rice should be cooled before using for fried rice to prevent stickiness.

BEEF RENDANG

★ *Preparation time:* 15 minutes
Total cooking time: 2 hours
Serves 4

2 lb round steak
2 onions, chopped
4 cloves garlic, chopped
1 tablespoon chopped fresh ginger
4 small red chili peppers, chopped
½ cup water
2 teaspoons ground coriander
2 tablespoons tamarind sauce
1 teaspoon ground turmeric
10 curry leaves
stem of lemon grass, 4 inches long
4 cups coconut milk

1 Remove excess fat and tendons from steak, cut meat into 1¼ inch cubes, place in a bowl.
2 In food processor, combine onions, garlic, ginger, chilies and water; blend until smooth. Add the mixture to steak.
3 Add the coriander, tamarind sauce, turmeric, curry leaves and lemon grass, stir until well combined. Transfer to a pan. Stir in the coconut milk. Slowly bring to the boil, reduce heat to medium, simmer, uncovered, for 1 hour, stirring occasionally. Reduce the heat to very low, simmer for 30 minutes, stirring frequently, until the meat is very tender and the liquid has been absorbed. Remove the lemon grass before serving.

Note: Stir Beef Rendang often during last 30 minutes of cooking to prevent coconut milk from separating, and to avoid sticking.

INDONESIAN CHICKEN IN COCONUT MILK

⭐ **Preparation time:** 15 minutes + 1 hour marinating
Total cooking time: 45–50 minutes
Serves 4

8 chicken drumsticks (about 2 lbs)
2 cloves garlic, finely chopped
1/2 teaspoon salt
1/2 teaspoon black pepper
2 teaspoons ground cumin
2 teaspoons ground coriander
1/2 teaspoon ground fennel
1/2 teaspoon ground cinnamon

3 tablespoons vegetable oil
2 medium onions, finely sliced
1 cup coconut milk
1¼ cups water
1 tablespoon lemon juice, malt vinegar or tamarind liquid
sliced scallions, for garnish

1 Rinse chicken, pat dry with paper towels. Combine garlic, salt, pepper, cumin, coriander, fennel, cinnamon and 2 tablespoons oil. Rub the mixture over chicken, cover and refrigerate 1 hour.
2 Heat remaining oil in large skillet. Add onion, cook, until soft and golden. Add chicken, cook quickly over medium-high heat until well browned.
3 Combine coconut milk, water and lemon juice. Pour over chicken, cover, simmer 35–40 minutes until chicken is tender and sauce is reduced. Garnish with scallions. Serve with plain steamed rice.

OPPOSITE PAGE, ABOVE: NASI GORENG; BELOW: BEEF RENDANG. ABOVE: GADO GADO WITH PEANUT SAUCE

GADO GADO

⭐ **Preparation time:** 35 minutes
Total cooking time: 36–40 minutes
Serves 6

3 eggs
2 medium sweet potatoes
2 medium potatoes
2 medium pattypan squash
1/2 small head cabbage
2 medium carrots, cut into thin strips

1 medium cucumber
1/2 cup fresh bean sprouts, trimmed watercress sprigs, for garnish
3/4 cup Peanut Sauce (see recipe below)
3/4 cup coconut milk

1 Place eggs in saucepan, add enough cold water to cover. Bring to boiling over high heat. Reduce heat so water is just below simmering; cover, cook 15 minutes. Pour off water; fill saucepan with cold water. Stand 2 minutes until eggs are cool enough to handle; drain. Cut sweet potato into 1/2-inch thick slices. Cut potatoes in half, then into 3/4-inch thick slices. Halve squash. Cut cabbage into 6 wedges. Bring a large saucepan of water to boiling.
2 Blanch each type of vegetable separately in boiling water; they must be firm and not overcooked. Sweet potato and potato will each need 8–10 minutes; squash, 1 minute; carrots, 2 minutes; cabbage, 2 minutes. Remove from water and plunge into a bowl of ice water to stop the cooking process and set the color.
3 Shell eggs and cut in halves or quarters. Slice cucumbers into thin strips. Arrange vegetables in decorative groups on a large platter. Garnish with sliced eggs, bean sprouts and watercress sprigs. Mix Peanut Sauce and coconut milk in a small saucepan; heat through. Serve in a small bowl.

PEANUT SAUCE

⭐ **Preparation time:** 5 minutes
Total cooking time: 5–10 minutes
Makes 2 cups

8 oz roasted unsalted peanuts
1 small onion, chopped
1 clove garlic, chopped
1 teaspoon chopped fresh ginger

1 teaspoon shrimp paste
1 teaspoon sambal oelek
1 tablespoon soy sauce
1 tablespoon lemon juice
1/2 cup mango chutney
1 cup water

1 Chop peanuts and onions coarsely. Combine all ingredients in a food processor, blend until smooth.
2 Pour mixture into a pan, bring to the boil. Reduce heat to low and simmer, stirring occasionally, for about 5 minutes, or until sauce has reduced and thickened.

Indonesian Food
In an Indonesian meal, all the food is laid out at once. The soup, if there is one, is sipped between mouthfuls of other food. Rice is important in the diet; it is eaten with every meal. Indonesian cooking makes use of fresh,

aromatic seasonings such as chili peppers, galangal, lemon grass, turmeric (both root and leaves), basil, mint and curry leaves. The food is a ready mixture of spicy and salty, pungent and sweet. The sweetness of the dishes comes from fresh coconuts and sweet soy sauce, sourness from limes and tamarinds, and texture from nuts. Indonesian cuisine is also characterized by its Dutch-Indonesian dishes: the most famous are rijstafel and nasi goreng. Tempeh is an

Indonesian ingredient which has been gaining popularity in the West. Made from soy beans, it is cut into thin matchsticks and fried with peanuts, onions, chilies and tamarind. Tempeh is used in the

ICE CREAMS & SORBETS

Home-made ice cream, sorbet or gelato are among the most elegant desserts. Ice cream and gelato can be made in an ice cream machine, as well as by hand. Sorbets are made in freezer trays.

FROM LEFT TO RIGHT: BASIC VANILLA ICE CREAM, LEMON SORBET, BLACKBERRY AND RASPBERRY SORBET, AND RICH CHOCOLATE GELATO

ICE-CREAM

Old-fashioned vanilla ice cream will complement most desserts, and fruit, nut, chocolate or other flavored ice creams are delicious by themselves. Home-made ice cream freezes much harder than commercial ice cream. Remove it from the freezer half an hour before serving time.

BASIC VANILLA ICE CREAM

Place in a medium bowl ³/₄ cup sugar and 2 vanilla beans, split lengthwise. Stir in 1 cup milk, place bowl over a pan of simmering water and stir until sugar has dissolved and mixture starts to simmer.

Warm 6 egg yolks in a large bowl and gradually whisk in hot milk. Place bowl over simmering water, stir constantly (never allow it to boil) until mixture coats the back of the spoon. Set bowl aside to cool with a piece of plastic wrap over the surface of the custard to prevent a skin forming.

Stir 2 cups of heavy cream into the custard and chill for 2 hours. Remove the vanilla beans and scrape the seeds into the custard, discarding the pods. Pour the custard into an ice cream machine and churn for about 30 minutes or until the ice cream has become firm and thick.

To make by hand: Pour the custard into metal freezer trays and freeze for 2–3 hours or until just solid around the edges. Transfer to a medium bowl and beat with electric beaters until smooth.

VARIATIONS

Other ingredients may be added to the custard mixture before chilling. These include :

■ **COFFEE**: Add 2 tablespoons instant coffee dissolved in 1 tablespoon hot water.

■ **COCONUT:** Add 2 cups coconut cream or 1 cup flaked coconut.

■ **CHOCOLATE CHIP:** Add 8 oz finely chopped semisweet chocolate with 2 tablespoons orange juice or liqueur.

■ **BANANA:** Add 3 small ripe bananas, mashed or puréed with 1 tablespoon lemon juice.

■ **BERRY:** Add 8 oz puréed fresh strawberries, blackberries or raspberries.

■ **PASSIONFRUIT:** Place the pulp of 8 passionfruit in a sieve placed over a bowl to extract as much juice as possible. Discard seeds. Add 1 teaspoon lemon juice to the passionfruit juice, and fold into the ice cream mixture before churning.

■ **MACADAMIA OR PISTACHIO NUTS:** Before starting to churn ice cream, add 2 cups coarsely chopped nuts to the mixture.

SORBET AND GELATO

A sorbet is a water ice served to refresh the palate between courses or as a light dessert. Fruit sorbets are the simplest and freshest-tasting, but tea, coffee, champagne, wine, spirits, liqueur or spices are also used as flavorings. Gelato is slightly richer and is always served as a dessert.

LEMON SORBET

Pour 1/2 cup cold water into a medium pan, sprinkle with 1 tablespoon gelatin. Stand for 10 minutes. Pour 1/2 cup boiling water over gelatin mixture, stirring over low heat until gelatin is dissolved. Add 1 cup sugar and stir over low heat without boiling until sugar is dissolved. Remove from heat. Add 1 cup cold water and 1 cup strained lemon juice. Cool, then pour into freezer trays. Freeze 2-3 hours or until just firm. Scrape into chilled dessert dishes.

BLACKBERRY AND RASPBERRY SORBET

Place 6 cups fresh or frozen blackberries and 2 cups raspberries in a large pan with 1 cup water. Bring to the boil, reduce heat and simmer for 2 minutes. Strain through a fine muslin sieve. Return mixture to pan; add 1 cup water. Add 1½ cups sugar and 1 tablespoon lemon juice, stir over low heat until sugar dissolves. Set aside to cool. Pour mixture into freezer trays and freeze until sorbet is mushy. Transfer to a bowl. Beat 2 egg whites until stiff. Using a metal spoon, fold the egg whites into berry mixture.

Return to freezer trays and freeze, stirring occasionally to ensure egg whites are evenly distributed. Scrape mixture into serving dishes.

RICH CHOCOLATE GELATO

Place 4 cups milk, 1¼ cups sugar and ½ teaspoon vanilla into a large pan. Stir over low heat until sugar has dissolved but don't allow to boil. Remove pan from heat and stir in ¼ teaspoon instant coffee powder and 5 oz of chopped dark (semisweet) chocolate. Continue to stir until chocolate has melted and mixture is smooth. Pour the mixture into an ice cream machine and churn for about 30 minutes or until gelato is firm.

To make by hand: Pour the chocolate mixture into metal freezer trays and freeze until mixture is set around the edges. Transfer mixture to a large bowl. Beat with electric beaters until thick. Return to freezer trays and freeze 3-4 hours or until firm.

POINTS FOR SUCCESS

■ Most ice cream and sorbet mixtures taste oversweet before freezing. This compensates for the numbing effect coldness has on our tastebuds. Ices with too little sweetening are flat-tasting and bland. As fruits differ in the amount of sugar and water they contain, the proportions of sugar to water in the syrup vary. It is important to dissolve the sugar completely by stirring over direct heat—undissolved crystals give a grainy texture to frozen mixtures.

■ Working utensils such as bowls, freezer trays or containers should be icy cold. The mixture should always be chilled before freezing. If using an ice cream machine, refrigerate prepared mixture for at least 4 hours, preferably over-night, before churning, for a smoother result. Freeze handmade ice creams at the coldest setting of your freezer, especially when freezing in trays—slow freezing can produce coarse crystals. To avoid crystallization in sorbets and handmade ice creams and gelatos, beat the mixture at least twice, at hourly intervals, during the freezing process.

same way as tofu and added to many dishes. Satay is made by threading small pieces of meat onto a skewer, grilling and serving with a peanut sauce. Sambal, a fiery mixture of ground fresh chili peppers, salt and sometimes lime juice, tomatoes or brown sugar, is served with almost every meal.

Iodized Salt Table salt that has been nutritionally enhanced with potassium iodide.

Irish Coffee A mixture of Irish whiskey and freshly brewed coffee, sweetened with sugar, topped with a layer of chilled cream and served at the end of an evening meal. It should be served in a tall coffee cup or a heatproof glass. Do not stir once the cream has been added: the hot beverage should be sipped through the layer of cream. The drink is said to have been invented in the 1950s by a barman at Dublin's Shannon Airport.

Irish Food The traditional cooking of Ireland is functional rather than fancy and is intended to sustain rather than excite. The style is straightforward and has been little influenced by the cuisines of France or other European countries. The sheer quality of many of its ingredients

BROWN SODA BREAD

⭐ **Preparation time:** 10 minutes
Total cooking time: 20–30 minutes
Serves 4–6

2 cups whole-wheat flour
2 cups all-purpose flour
2 teaspoons baking soda
¼ teaspoon salt
2–2½ cups buttermilk

1 Preheat oven to 375°F. Grease a baking sheet with melted butter or margarine. Sift the flours, soda and salt into a large mixing bowl. Use sufficient buttermilk to moisten the ingredients and form a soft dough—the amount of buttermilk required will depend on the strength of the flour.

2 Turn the dough out onto a lightly floured surface and knead lightly until smooth. Press the dough into an 8 inch round. Place the round on a greased baking sheet. With a floured knife score a deep cross, one-third of the depth of dough. Brush with water and sprinkle with a little flour. Bake for 20–30 minutes, or until the bread sounds hollow when tapped with the fingers.

Note: No yeast is used in this bread. The baking soda and buttermilk give rise, texture and flavor. If buttermilk is unavailable, use sour milk. This is made by adding a teaspoon of lemon juice or vinegar to a cup of milk. Allow to stand for about 15 minutes before using.

COLCANNON

⭐ **Preparation time:** 15 minutes
Total cooking time: 20 minutes
Serves 4

4 medium potatoes
10 oz shredded cabbage
¼ cup butter
½ cup chopped scallions
⅔ cup warm milk
freshly ground black pepper
1 tablespoon chopped parsley, for garnish

1 Peel potatoes, cut into quarters and cook in boiling water for 15 minutes, or until tender. Drain, mash with a fork.

2 Cook the cabbage in boiling water for 10 minutes, remove from the pan with tongs, drain well. Melt the butter in a large pan, add cabbage and stir in the scallions, cook for 1 minute.

3 Combine the cabbage mixture with mashed potatoes. Add enough warm milk to give a creamy consistency. Season with black pepper and serve, garnished with chopped parsley. Drizzle over extra melted butter for a richer dish.

Note: This is similar to England's Bubble and Squeak. Leftover vegetables can be added or substituted.

LEFT: BROWN SODA BREAD; ABOVE: COLCANNON.
OPPOSITE PAGE, BELOW: GUINNESS BEEF STEW;
ABOVE: DUBLIN CODDLE

GUINNESS BEEF STEW

Preparation time: 20 minutes
Total cooking time: 2 hours
Serves 4–6

2 lb round steak	2 large carrots, sliced
2 tablespoons dripping	2 bay leaves
2 large onions, chopped	1 sprig fresh thyme
2 cloves garlic, crushed	ground pepper
1/4 cup all-purpose flour	1/2 cup prunes, halved
1 cup beef stock	and pitted (optional)
1 cup Guinness stout	chopped parsley, for garnish

1 Remove excess fat from the meat, cut meat into 1/2 inch cubes. Heat half the drippings in a pan, cook the onion until golden. Add garlic, cook for another minute. Remove from the pan, drain on paper towels.

2 Heat remaining dripping in a large pan, add meat and cook quickly to brown on all sides. Reduce heat, stir in flour until all meat is coated.

3 Add stock, stir until mixture forms a thick, smooth sauce. Add Guinness and stir until mixture comes to simmering point. Add onion and garlic, carrots, herbs and pepper, stir until combined.

4 Cover and simmer gently for 1 1/2 hours, stirring occasionally to prevent sticking. Remove lid and cook uncovered until sauce is reduced and thickened. If using prunes, add to pan in the final 30 minutes of cooking. Serve garnished with chopped parsley.

Note: Prunes add sweetness to this dish and balance the characteristic bitterness of Guinness.

DUBLIN CODDLE

Preparation time: 40 minutes
Total cooking time: 1 hour 15 minutes
Serves 4

8 thick pork sausages	4 medium-sized potatoes
4 slices bacon, 1/4 inch thick	1/4 teaspoon dried sage
	ground pepper
2 tablespoons dripping	3/4 cup chicken stock
2 large onions, chopped	2 tablespoons chopped
2 cloves garlic, crushed	fresh parsley

1 Preheat oven to 350°F. Place sausages in a pan, cover with cold water and bring to boil. Reduce heat, simmer uncovered for 7 minutes, drain and cool. Cut the bacon into 3/4 inch strips.

2 Heat dripping in a pan, cook the bacon for 1 minute. Add the onion and cook until golden. Add the garlic and cook for 1 minute. Remove bacon, onion and garlic, drain on paper towels. Add the sausages to the pan and cook on all sides until well browned, remove and drain on paper towels.

3 Peel the potatoes and cut into 1/8 inch slices. Arrange the potato slices in the base of a large heatproof dish, top with the bacon, onion and garlic. Sprinkle sage and pepper over dish and add the chicken stock. Place the drained sausages on top, cover and cook in a preheated oven for 1 hour. Serve garnished with the chopped parsley.

(salmon fresh from the streams, high quality dairy products, succulent lamb and excellent bacon) are a delicious compensation for any lack of culinary sophistication. In Ireland the day begins with a substantial cooked breakfast of porridge, bacon

and eggs or fish, followed by toast and marmalade and tea or coffee. The midday meal, known as dinner, is the main meal of the day. A light supper is eaten in the evening.

The history of Ireland has been greatly influenced by the potato, the humble "pratie," said to have been introduced to the island by Sir Walter Raleigh in the late sixteenth century. It was a godsend to a country constantly on the edge of famine, for when planted with potato, Ireland's poor soils yielded up to six times as much nourishment as when sown with grain. Ireland became a one-crop country, with both people and livestock dependent upon the potato for sustenance.

The failure of the blight-infested 1845 potato harvest triggered a national disaster, and families across the land faced starvation. It was a time when many of Ireland's people, its greatest export, were forced to flee to more fruitful soils. Potatoes remain a staple food throughout rural Ireland. There are many traditional potato dishes: pratie cakes are scones made from mashed potato cooked on a griddle and served, buttered, for supper; champ is fluffy mashed potatoes enriched with milk and butter and sprinkled with chopped scallions. The potato is also a basic ingredient in soups,

stews, breads and pastry, and is predominant in Irish stew, traditionally made from a neck of mutton or lamb, onions and potatoes. Soda bread, made with buttermilk and leavened with baking soda, is found throughout Ireland.

A fine array of seafood can be had in the fishing villages and the fish markets of the coastal towns; delicious smoked mackerel is available throughout the year. Regional specialties include crubeen, pig's feet, from Cork and coddle, pork sausage and

IRISH STEW

⭐ **Preparation time:** 20 minutes
Total cooking time: 1 hour 15 minutes
Serves 4

8 lamb neck chops
4 slices bacon
1 tablespoon dripping
2 lb potatoes, cut into
   thick slices
3 carrots, sliced
   diagonally
3 medium onions, thickly
   sliced

freshy ground black
   pepper
2 cups beef stock
1 teaspoon chopped fresh
   thyme
chopped fresh parsley, for
   garnish

1 Trim chops, removing excess fat. Cut bacon into ³⁄₄ inch strips. Heat the dripping in a pan, add bacon and cook until crisp and brown, remove from pan, drain on paper towels. Cook chops until brown on both sides, remove from pan, drain.
2 Arrange half the potato, carrot and onion in the base of a deep, heavy-bottom pan. Season with pepper, and add half the bacon. Place chops over this layer. Cover the chops with remaining potato, carrot, onion and bacon.
3 Add stock and thyme. Cover, bring to boil, reduce heat, simmer for 1 hour or until lamb is very tender. Serve garnished with chopped parsley.

ABOVE: IRISH STEW; BELOW: IRISH MIST CREAM.
OPPOSITE PAGE: CARPACCIO

IRISH MIST CREAM

⭐ ⭐ **Preparation time:** 30 minutes +
1 hour 30 minutes setting
Total cooking time: 10 minutes
Serves 8

2¼ cups milk
4 eggs, separated
4 tablespoons sugar
2 tablespoons
   unsweetened gelatin
¼ cup boiling water

⅓ cup Irish Mist
   liqueur
½ cup cream, whipped
extra whipped cream
chocolate, for decoration

1 Bring the milk to boil in a pan. Remove from heat. In a bowl, whisk egg yolks and 2 tablespoons sugar. Add milk and whisk to combine. Pour mixture back into pan, cook over low heat for 7 minutes; do not boil.
2 Dissolve the gelatin in boiling water, add to the hot milk mixture, stir well. Pour in Irish Mist, refrigerate for 40 minutes, or until mixture begins to set.
3 Beat egg whites until soft peaks form, sprinkle with remaining sugar and beat until it dissolves. When milk and egg mixture begins to set, fold through whipped cream and beaten egg whites. Pour even portions into eight glass serving dishes and refrigerate until set.
4 Decorate each portion with whipped cream and chocolate curls. Sprinkle with grated chocolate.

Note: Prepare Irish Mist Cream one day ahead.

ITALIAN CLASSICS

MINESTRONE

⭐ **Preparation time:** 20 minutes
Total cooking time: 1 hour 30 minutes
Serves 6–8

1/3 cup olive oil
2 cloves garlic, finely chopped
2 onions, chopped
1/2 cup chopped bacon or salt pork
2 carrots, chopped
3 stalks celery, sliced
2 potatoes, peeled and diced
2 zucchini, chopped
4 oz green beans, chopped

8 oz savoy cabbage, shredded
14 1/2 oz can diced tomatoes
1 teaspoon dried oregano
8 cups chicken or beef stock
1 cup elbow macaroni
10 oz canned cannellini beans, drained
1 tablespoon chopped fresh basil
freshly grated Parmesan cheese for serving

1 Heat oil in a large pan and cook garlic, onions and bacon until onions are soft but not brown. Add carrot and celery and cook for 3 minutes, stirring occasionally. Add remaining vegetables, tomato and tomato juice from the can.
2 Stir in oregano and stock, bring to the boil and simmer soup for 1 hour. Add macaroni, cook for 10 minutes; add cannellini beans and basil and simmer for 5 minutes.
3 Serve minestrone sprinkled liberally with Parmesan cheese. May be served with thick, crusty bread or warm bread rolls.

CARPACCIO

⭐ **Preparation time:** 20 minutes + 2 hours refrigeration
Total cooking time: none
Serves 4

12 oz beef tenderloin
olive oil
fresh Parmesan cheese

freshly ground black pepper
salt (optional)
lemon wedges

1 Wrap the beef in plastic wrap; place in the freezer for about 2 hours or until firm but not frozen solid. Using a sharp knife, trim away any fat. Slice the beef into wafer thin slices. Arrange beef on serving plates.
2 Drizzle the oil lightly over beef slices. Using a vegetable peeler, shave thin pieces of Parmesan cheese, sprinkle over beef.
3 Season beef with pepper and, if desired, salt. Serve with lemon wedges.

Note: Choose high quality beef with low fat and sinew content for this recipe.

VEAL SCALOPPINE WITH EGGPLANT

⭐ **Preparation time:** 25 minutes
Total cooking time: 20 minutes
Serves 4

4 large pieces veal scaloppine (about 1 lb)
all-purpose flour
1/4 cup butter
1 small eggplant, thinly sliced

1 large tomato, sliced
4 slices fontina cheese
2 teaspoons dried oregano, crushed
freshly ground black pepper

1 Dust the veal with flour. In a large skillet melt the butter over medium heat until it begins to brown. Add the veal in a single layer. Brown the veal quickly in the hot butter for about 1 minute on each side. Remove the veal from the skillet.
2 Add the eggplant to skillet. Brown on both sides. Remove.
3 Lay one piece of veal on each of the four sheets of aluminum foil. Top with the eggplant, tomato and cheese. Sprinke with oregano and black pepper.
4 Bring the foil loosely up around the veal. Seal the foil at the top, leaving a space between the foil and cheese. Place the foil packages on a baking sheet. Bake in a 350°F oven for 20 minutes. Remove from foil and serve.

potato from Dublin. Ireland is also known for its rich black stout, introduced to the world in 1759 by Arthur Guinness. A favorite in the pub, it also features in the kitchen as a slightly bitter flavoring for beef stew and rich fruit cake. Irish whiskey, made from barley malt and wheat or oats and matured for seven years, is the secret to a successful Irish coffee. The Irish were the first to make whiskey, which they called *uisge breatha*, "blessed water". Legend has it they were taught the art of distilling, in which alcohol is produced from cereal grain instead of grapes, by St. Patrick, patron saint of Ireland, in the fifth century; it seems certain that Irish monks were busy at their stills long before they began selling the warming spirit outside the monasteries in the eleventh century.

Irish Soda Bread Bread made with buttermilk or sour milk and leavened with baking soda. Currants, raisins and caraway seeds are often added to this bread. Soda bread is a specialty of Ireland and is baked in homes and bakeries throughout the country.

Irish Stew A hearty stew in which mutton or lamb is arranged in alternate layers with sliced potatoes and onions, moistened with water and simmered. It is called a "white stew" because the meat is not browned before being cooked with the vegetables. There should be more potato than meat; during the long, slow cooking the potatoes break up and thicken the gravy. To serve, first lift out the potatoes, place the meat on top, cover with the gravy and garnish with chopped parsley.

Italian Food Italy produces some of the best-loved food in the world. The culinary differences that existed between northern and southern Italy have become hazy, with pizza napolitana eaten not only

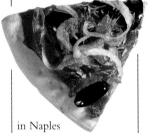

in Naples but also in the north and all over the world, and risotto alla milanese being enjoyed in Sicily as well as Milan. But it is the fact that Italian food is regional, and that it uses fresh local produce, that has made it so popular.

From the south come olive oil, olives, tomatoes and wheat. The cooking of southern

SPAGHETTI PUTTANESCA

★ **Preparation time:** 15 minutes
Total cooking time: 15 minutes
Serves 4

4 large ripe tomatoes (about 1½ lb)
1 tablespoon olive oil
2 small red chili peppers, chopped
2 cloves garlic, crushed
⅔ cup water
12 pitted ripe olives, sliced
8 canned anchovy fillets, drained and chopped

¼ cup chopped parsley
1 tablespoon chopped fresh basil or 1 teaspoon dried
2 teaspoons chopped capers
8 oz dried spaghetti
freshly grated Parmesan (optional)
Italian parsley (optional)

1 Peel, seed and chop tomatoes.
2 Heat the oil in a saucepan over a medium heat. Cook the chili peppers and garlic in hot oil for 1 minute. Add the tomatoes and water. Bring to a boil; reduce heat. Cover; simmer for 10 minutes or until the tomatoes are soft. Add additional water if the sauce sticks to the pan during cooking.
3 Add olives, anchovies, parsley, basil and capers to saucepan. Simmer, uncovered, for 3 minutes.
4 Meanwhile, cook the spaghetti until al dente. Drain. Add to the tomato mixture; toss until combined. If desired, sprinkle each serving with freshly shredded Parmesan; garnish with parsley.

TRADITIONAL THIN-CRUST PIZZA

★ **Preparation time:** 30 minutes
Total cooking time: 30 minutes
Serves 4

Crust
1 package active dry yeast
2 teaspoons sugar
1 cup warm water (105°–115°F)
3¼ cups all-purpose flour
pinch salt

Topping
¾ cup tomato sauce
4 oz Italian salami, sliced and cut into strips

¼ cup chopped fresh basil
4 oz small mushrooms, sliced
1 onion, sliced into thin wedges
½ green pepper, sliced
12 pitted ripe olives, halved
6 canned anchovy fillets, drained
1¼ cups shredded mozzarella cheese

1 To make Crust: Combine yeast and sugar in a bowl; stir in warm water. Leave until yeast dissolves.
2 In another bowl stir together flour and salt. Add yeast mixture, stir until well combined. Turn dough onto a floured surface, knead for 10 minutes or until smooth and elastic.
3 Roll dough to a circle large enough to fit a 12-inch round pizza pan. Transfer dough to pizza pan.
4 Spread dough with tomato sauce and top with salami, basil, mushrooms, onion, pepper, olives and anchovies. Sprinkle with cheeses.
5 Bake uncovered in a 375°F oven 30 minutes or until crust is crispy and topping is heated through.

Italy reflects this: pizza with tomato sauce, mozzarella, olives, anchovies; pasta with rich tomato sauce, olives and fresh oregano. Eggplant dishes are popular as are red peppers and artichokes. Seafood is prepared simply, and is usually grilled or fried.

The food of the north is more sophisticated. More meat is eaten, especially beef, and the charcoal-grilled bistecca of Florence is thought to be the best beef dish in Italy. Pasta is popular all over Italy, but rice in the form of risotto is a northern speciality. In northern Italy, butter is used in preference to olive oil, and many cheeses are made there, notably gorgonzola, mascarpone, and bel paese. The most famous cheese of the south, mozzarella, is made from sheep's milk.

Polenta is a batter made from cornmeal and is one of the favorite accompaniments of meals in northern Italy. It is cooked, cooled, cut into squares, and then fried. Polenta is served with quail as well as other meat and poultry dishes.

VEAL CHOPS WITH SAGE AND LEMON

⭐ **Preparation time:** 10 minutes
Total cooking time: 10 minutes
Serves 4

4 veal loin chops	1 tablespoon chopped
all-purpose flour	fresh sage or
1 egg, beaten	1 teaspoon dried sage
¼ cup milk	2 tablespoons butter
1 cup fine dry bread	1 tablespoon olive oil
crumbs	1 clove garlic, crushed
	lemon wedges

1 Trim the fat from the chops. Curl up the tail of each chop and secure with toothpicks.
2 Place the flour in a plastic bag. Place chops, one at a time, in the bag and coat thoroughly with flour, shake off excess. In a shallow bowl combine the egg and milk. Combine the bread crumbs and sage on a plate. Dip the floured chops into the egg mixture, then press lightly into the bread crumb mixture, making sure each one is coated thoroughly.
3 In a skillet heat the butter, oil and garlic over medium heat. Add the chops in a single layer and cook for 2–3 minutes on each side. Serve with lemon wedges.

LEMON ZABAGLIONE

⭐ **Preparation time:** 5 minutes
Total cooking time: 10 minutes
Serves 4

3 egg yolks	1 tablespoon Marsala
¼ cup sugar	8 almond cookies
½ cup dry white wine	fresh strawberries
¼ cup lemon juice	(optional)

1 In a heatproof bowl beat the egg yolks and sugar together with a wire whisk until light and creamy. Add the white wine, lemon juice and Marsala. Whisk until thoroughly combined.
2 Place the heatproof bowl over a saucepan of simmering water, making sure that the bottom of the bowl does not touch the water. Cook and stir for 10 minutes or until the mixture thickens.
3 Spoon into decorative serving glasses and serve with the almond cookies and strawberries.

Opposite page, below: Spaghetti puttanesca; above: Traditional thin-crust pizza.
Above: Lemon zabaglione

Note: Zabaglione can be served on its own or as a topping for fruit or ice cream. It is quite rich so only small amounts are served.

J JAMS & MARMALADES

Jam (jelly) and marmalade are made by boiling together sugar and fruit in a concentration high enough to preserve the mixture and prevent spoilage. While jam does not store indefinitely, it usually has a shelf life of about two years.

JAM (JELLY)

Jam should set to a firm consistency and have a good, clear color characteristic of the fruit used to make it. The flavor should be that of the fruit without being excessively sweet or acidic. What makes jam set is the combination of pectin and acid (naturally occurring in fruit) and added sugars. Because pectin and acid are present to varying degrees in different fruits, two or more fruits are often combined in one jam. Alternatively, lemon juice or commercial pectin may be added. Pectin is highest in slightly underripe fruit; it is concentrated in the core and skin, and in the white pith and pips of citrus fruit.

FROM LEFT: ORANGE MARMALADE, LIME MARMALADE, APRICOT JAM; RIGHT: STRAWBERRY JAM

PECTIN CONTENT

The pectin content of fruits varies considerably. Some fruits are rich in pectin and acid and make jam which sets easily, while others contain less pectin. Pectin levels of some common fruits are:

High	Medium	Low
citrus fruits	apricots	bananas
cooking apples	blackberries, early	blackberries, late
crab apples	eating apples	boysenberries
cranberries	greengages	cherries
currants (red & black)	loganberries	figs
damson plums	mulberries	guavas
gooseberries	raspberries	melons
grapes	peaches	nectarines
plums (some varieties)	pears	
quinces	pineapples	
	rhubarb	
	strawberries	
	tomatoes	

STEPS IN MAKING JAM

1 PREPARING THE FRUIT

Choose slightly underripe fruit. Wash fruit thoroughly, drain, remove leaves and stalks, and cut off any bruised or damaged sections. Peel, cut or slice fruit according to recipe.

2 RELEASING THE PECTIN

Cook fruit with or without water (see individual recipes) to soften it and to release the pectin. Place in a large pan, add water as specified, bring to boil, reduce heat and simmer, covered. If not following a recipe, test the pectin content when fruit has softened.

To test for pectin: Place 1 teaspoon of liquid from pan in a glass. Cool, add 3 teaspoons methylated spirits (grain alcohol), leave for 3 minutes. If pectin is high, liquid will form a firm, jelly-like clump. If jelly is only partially set, pectin level is not enough to set jam. Boil mixture a little longer, adding 1 tablespoon lemon juice per 2 lb fruit; test again. If it still does not gel, use commercial pectin.

3 COOKING WITH SUGAR

Use amount of sugar specified in recipe. For best results, warm sugar in oven before adding to fruit—this minimizes the amount of scum on the surface during cooking. Bring fruit to boil, add sugar; stir until sugar has fully dissolved. Bring to boil; boil without stirring for time specified. (Check with a wooden spoon that mixture is not burning.) Setting point of jam is reached when correct concentration of sugar is achieved. If testing with a candy thermometer, it should reach 221°F.

Alternatively, spoon a little jam onto a cold plate; cool. When setting point has been reached, the jam holds its shape and wrinkles when it is pushed gently with the finger. If this does not happen the first time, continue to cook jam and test again at frequent intervals.

4 BOTTLING

Before bottling, remove any scum from surface of jam with a metal spoon. Allow jam to stand for 10 minutes to prevent fruit sinking to the bottom of the jar. Ladle hot jam into warm sterilized jars, filling to within ½ inch of top, and seal immediately. Plastic or plastic-coated metal lids are suitable, or seal jars with wax or special cellophane-like jam covers (follow directions on packet).

MARMALADE

Marmalade is essentially jam made from citrus fruit, and methods are the same. However, because citrus rind is tough, prepared fruit is often soaked overnight, and the initial cooking period is longer, with more water used. It is important to boil the peel until it is soft enough before adding sugar, as no further softening will be achieved once sugar has been added.

The cutting of citrus fruit takes time, but this can be minimized by using a food processor or a vegetable slicer.

Citrus fruits are high in pectin and acid, so it is not necessary to test for pectin.

1 Slice citrus fruit thinly. Place fruit and water in a large bowl. Cover and set aside for fruit to soak overnight.

2 Place fruit and water in a large pan and bring to the boil. Simmer until the citrus rind has softened.

3 Add warmed sugar to the pan, stirring until sugar has completely dissolved.

4 Boil without stirring until mixture reaches setting point 221°F. Use a candy thermometer to check temperature.

5 Carefully pour the marmalade into warm jars that have been sterilized.

6 To seal, carefully pour melted wax over marmalade. When cool, label and date.

TO STERILIZE JARS

Wash jars thoroughly, then rinse in very hot water and invert them on a rack to drain. Place jars upright in a 300°F oven for 30 minutes. Use the jars straight from the oven to minimize the risk of them cracking when filled with hot mixture. Lids should be boiled or rinsed in very hot water. To prevent burns, use oven mitts when handling hot jars.

SLICE CITRUS FRUITS THINLY. PLACE IN A BOWL, COVER WITH WATER AND SOAK OVERNIGHT.

WARM SUGAR IN A LOW OVEN AND ADD IT TO THE SOFTENED FRUIT IN THE PAN.

SPOON MARMALADE INTO WARMED STERILIZED JARS. USE COTTON GLOVES TO HOLD JARS.

Jack Cheese Monterey Jack, unaged jack cheese, has a semisoft texture, ivory color and mild flavor. Aged jack cheese is yellow to orange, salty and sharp-flavored. It resembles Cheddar cheese.

Jackfruit A large, barrel-shaped fruit with yellow-green knobby skin and sweet, pungent-smelling, creamy white flesh and many large

white seeds. A relative of the breadfruit, it is now grown throughout the tropics. The crunchy flesh has a potato-like taste and can be eaten fresh on its own, added to fruit salad or puréed for use in ice cream. It can be boiled or deep-fried or added to curries. The seeds are cooked in the same way as chestnuts; in Africa they are ground into flour. Jackfruit weigh up to 100 pounds and are in season in summer.

Jalapeño Chili Pepper A small, tapered, thick-fleshed, fiery-tasting chili, the most common variety in North America. Fresh jalapeño chilies are

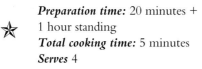

JAPANESE CLASSICS

SUNOMONO (CUCUMBER AND SHRIMP SALAD)

★ **Preparation time:** 20 minutes + 1 hour standing
Total cooking time: 5 minutes
Serves 4

1 long cucumber
salt
12 oz medium raw shrimp
¼ cup rice vinegar
1 tablespoon sugar
¼ teaspoon soy sauce
¼ teaspoon finely grated fresh ginger
1 tablespoon toasted sesame seeds

1 Halve the cucumber lengthwise; remove the seeds with a teaspoon. Cut cucumber into thin slices, sprinkle with salt and allow to stand for 5 minutes. Gently squeeze the moisture from cucumber.
2 Place the shrimp in a pan of lightly salted boiling water and simmer 2 minutes or until just cooked. Drain and plunge into cold water. Allow to cool, then peel and devein.
3 Place the vinegar, sugar, soy sauce and ginger in a large bowl and stir until the sugar dissolves. Add the prepared shrimp and cucumber and leave to stand for 1 hour.
4 Drain the shrimp mixture in a colander. Place on serving plates and sprinkle with the toasted sesame seeds.

Note: To toast sesame seeds quickly, place in a small dry pan and toss over low heat until seeds are golden brown. Remove to a plate to cool.

MISOSHIRU (MISO SOUP)

★ **Preparation time:** 10 minutes
Total cooking time: 10 minutes
Serves 4

4 cups dashi (bonito stock)
3½ oz red miso
1 tablespoon mirin
4 oz tofu, diced
4 button mushrooms
2 scallions

1 Place dashi in a medium pan and bring to the boil. Blend miso with mirin and add to hot stock.
2 Simmer soup gently, uncovered, for 2 minutes. Add diced tofu to soup and simmer for another 5 minutes.
3 Trim mushroom stems level with caps and finely slice mushrooms. Finely slice the scallions. Pour soup into warmed bowls and sprinkle mushrooms and scallions on top.

Note: Instant dashi is available in powdered form or as a concentrated liquid in Japanese food stores. Add boiling water as directed on the package.

ABOVE: SUNOMONO. OPPOSITE PAGE: SUSHI ROLLS

SUSHI ROLLS

★★ **Preparation time:** 45 minutes
Total cooking time: 10–15 minutes
Makes about 30

1 cup short-grain white
   rice
2 cups water
2 tablespoons rice vinegar
1 tablespoon sugar
1 teaspoon salt
3–4 sheets nori
1–2 teaspoons wasabi

4 oz smoked salmon,
   trout or fresh sashimi
   tuna
½ long thin cucumber,
   peeled
½ small avocado
¼ cup pickled ginger
soy sauce for dipping

1 Wash rice in cold water, drain well. Place rice and water in medium pan. Bring to boil, reduce heat, simmer uncovered 4–5 minutes or until water is absorbed. Cover, reduce heat to very low and cook for another 4–5 minutes. Remove pan from heat, cool. Stir combined vinegar, sugar and salt into rice. Place 1 sheet of nori onto a piece of wax paper on a flat work surface. Place a quarter of the rice along one end of the nori, leaving a ¾ inch border around the three sides. Spread a very small amount of wasabi evenly down center of the rice.

2 Cut the fish into thin strips, and the cucumber and the avocado into small pieces. Place the pieces of fish, cucumber, avocado and ginger over the wasabi.

3 Using the paper as a guide, roll up firmly from the bottom, enclosing in the rice the ingredients placed in the center. Press nori to seal edges. Using a sharp flat-bladed or electric knife, cut roll into 1 inch rounds. Repeat the process with remaining ingredients. Serve sushi rolls with small shallow bowls of soy sauce or extra wasabi mixed with soy sauce, for dipping.

usually sold green, but bright red, fully ripe and slightly sweeter-tasting forms can also be found; both green and red are also pickled in brine.

Jalousie A pastry dessert of French origin consisting of a layer of thinly rolled puff pastry spread with a sweet filling such as marzipan (almond paste), stewed fruit or jam, then topped with a second layer of pastry which is glazed with beaten egg yolk and milk and cut into fine slats before baking.

Jam A sweet spread made by cooking fruit in sugar and water until set. The setting power depends on the pectin content of the fruit (pectin occurs naturally in many ripe fruits, but commercial pectin can be added if there is an

insufficient amount in the mixture). Fruits abundant in pectin include blackberries, apples, lemons, oranges, quinces and red currants. One of these can be combined with a strong-flavored fruit which is low in pectin to produce a good-setting jam. Jam is made from whole fruit that is either crushed or chopped and so differs from conserve, in which the fruit or fruit pieces remain intact, and from fruit jelly, which is made from fruit juice strained to remove all other matter and then boiled with sugar. Marmalade is similar in preparation to other jams, but only citrus fruit (either a single fruit or a mixture) is used. See also Jelly.

Jambalaya A peppery Cajun dish featuring rice, chicken, shrimp and ham and derived from the Spanish paella. It is a specialty of Louisiana; the name is thought to come from *jamón*, the Spanish word for "ham."

Japanese Food Rice is the staple of Japanese food and a meal without rice is not considered a meal, it is a snack. The three major ingredients used in Japanese cooking are fish stock, rice and soy bean products. Sashimi (raw fish) is a delicacy considered the high point of any meal. The fish must be very fresh. It is sliced and served with a dipping sauce into which is mixed a little wasabi (green horseradish paste). Sushi are little rolls of vinegared rice wrapped in seaweed with a filling of fish and vegetables. Tempura is probably the best-loved Japanese food in the West. It is made by dipping shrimp and vegetables in a very light batter,

VEGETABLE TEMPURA

⭐ *Preparation time:* 30 minutes +
1 hour refrigeration
Total cooking time: 5 minutes per batch
Serves 6

1¼ cups all-purpose flour	1 medium carrot
1 egg	2 oz green beans
1¼ cups iced water	light vegetable oil for deep frying
4 oz broccoli	
1 small onion	**Dipping Sauce**
1 small red pepper	3 tablespoons soy sauce
1 small green pepper	2 tablespoons mirin

1 Sift the flour into a large mixing bowl. Make a well in the center, add the egg and water and whisk until combined. Cover, refrigerate for 1 hour.
2 Cut broccoli into small florets. Finely slice onion, and cut peppers and carrot into thin strips about 2½ inches long. Cut the beans to about 2½ inches long, and halve lengthwise. Add vegetables to batter and mix.
3 Heat the oil in a medium pan. Using tongs, gather a small bunch of batter-coated vegetables (roughly two pieces of each vegetable) and lower into oil. Hold submerged in the oil for a few seconds until the batter begins to set and the vegetables hold together. Release from the tongs and cook until the batter is crisp and golden. Drain on paper towels. Repeat until all the vegetables are cooked. Serve immediately with dipping sauce.
4 To make Dipping Sauce: Place soy sauce and mirin in a small bowl and combine.

CHICKEN TERIYAKI

⭐ *Preparation time:* 20 minutes +
2 hours marinating
Total cooking time: 6 minutes
Makes 12

1½ lb boneless chicken breasts, skin removed	2 teaspoons grated fresh ginger
¼ cup soy sauce	1 medium red pepper, cut into ¾ inch squares
2 tablespoons mirin	
2 tablespoons sherry	4 scallions, cut into 1¼ inch lengths
2 tablespoons soft brown sugar	2 tablespoons oil

1 Trim the chicken of excess fat and tendons. Soak the bamboo skewers in water to prevent them from burning. Place the chicken in a shallow glass or ceramic dish. Combine the soy sauce, mirin, sherry, brown sugar and ginger in a small bowl. Stir to dissolve the sugar; pour over the chicken. Cover and refrigerate for up to 2 hours, turning occasionally. Drain and cut the chicken breast halves in half lengthwise.
2 Thread the chicken onto the bamboo skewers alternating with pepper and green onion pieces.
3 Brush the kabobs with oil and place on a lightly oiled grill. Cook over medium-high heat for 6 minutes or until tender, turning and brushing with oil occasionally. Serve immediately, with steamed rice or egg noodles and stir-fried or grilled vegetables.

JELLIES

GUAVA JELLY

⭐ **Preparation time:** 30 minutes + overnight standing
Total cooking time: 45 minutes
Makes 3½ cups

2 lb slightly underripe guavas
1 green apple, peeled and cored
½ cup lemon juice
4 cups water
sugar

1 Cut guavas and apple into thick slices.
2 Combine guava, apple, lemon juice and water in large pan. Bring to the boil and boil slowly, uncovered, for 10 minutes. Break up guava and apple with a wooden spoon and boil slowly for another 10 minutes.
3 Strain the mixture through some cheesecloth suspended over a bowl, and leave to stand overnight. Measure the strained juice and return to the pan. Add 1 cup of warmed sugar for each cup of juice; stir over heat until the sugar is dissolved. Bring to boil; boil rapidly until setting point is reached.
4 Remove from heat and pour into warm, sterilized jars. When cool, seal jars, label and date. Serve on toast or muffins.

OPPOSITE PAGE, ABOVE: VEGETABLE TEMPURA; BELOW: CHICKEN TERIYAKI. THIS PAGE, ABOVE: GUAVA JELLY; RIGHT: ROSEMARY, TOMATO AND APPLE JELLY

ROSEMARY, TOMATO AND APPLE JELLY

⭐⭐ **Preparation time:** 25 minutes
Total cooking time: 1 hour 45 minutes
Makes 7 cups

7 medium green apples
2 medium pears
1 ripe tomato
1 cup fresh rosemary leaves
⅔ cup lemon juice
sugar

1 Wash the apples, pears and tomato; drain. Finely chop apples, pears and tomato; coarsely chop rosemary.
2 Combine apple, pear (including cores and seeds), tomato and rosemary in a large pan and cover with water. Bring to the boil and simmer, covered, for about 1 hour or until fruit is soft and pulpy.
3 Strain fruit mixture through a cheesecloth bag suspended over a bowl. Measure juice and return to pan with lemon juice. Heat until boiling. Add ¾ cup warmed sugar per cup of juice. Return to boil, stirring until sugar dissolves. Boil rapidly, uncovered, for 45–60 minutes or until setting point is reached.
4 Remove the cooked jelly from heat; allow to stand for 5 minutes. Skim any scum off surface of jelly with a metal spoon. Pour into warm, sterilized jars and cool before sealing. When almost set, a sprig of fresh rosemary may be suspended in the jelly using a clean bamboo skewer. When cool, label and date. Serve with roast lamb.

deep-frying and serving immediately. Miso soup can be sipped through the meal or eaten at the beginning or the end. One-pot dishes such as sukiyaki are favorite restaurant dishes, where everyone cooks their own meat and vegetables in a central pot of stock. Cooking on a teppan is popular in the West. In teppan restaurants you sit and watch the chef cook the food for you on a hot griddle. The chef often shows wonderful skill with his knife as he slices through vegetables and omelet rolls: the meal is a show as well as a feast. Japanese food is among the most visually beautiful in the world. Appearance is rated as highly as taste.

Jarlsberg A deep yellow, semihard, cow's milk cheese with a sweet nutty flavor similar to Swiss cheese. The interior is dotted with large irregularly shaped holes  sometimes called "eyes"; the rind is covered with yellow wax. Best at room temperature, it is a good eating cheese and can be used in sandwiches, salads, fondues and sauces. The cheese was developed in the late 1950s at the Jarlsberg estate in Norway.

Jasmine Tea Any tea that is blended with dried jasmine flowers.

Jelly A clear or semiclear food preparation with a soft elastic consistency due to the presence of gelatin or pectin. There are several types of jelly: a spread made from fruit juice boiled with sugar to which commercial pectin is often added; a cold dessert made with sugar and fruit juice, sometimes flavored with a liqueur, then set with gelatin, often in a mold;

aspic, made from meat, fish or vegetable stock, set with gelatin and used as a garnish and glaze; and jellied candies such as marshmallow and Turkish delight, made from thick syrup set with gelatin. See also Jam.

Jelly Roll A flat, thin sponge cake rolled around a filling of jam or jelly and sprinkled with confectioners' sugar.

Jerky Meat, usually beef, which is cut into thin strips, salted and then cured by being either smoked or dried. An early method of making

SAGE JELLY

⭐ ⭐ **Preparation time:** 35 minutes + 3 hours standing
Total cooking time: 1 hour 50 minutes
Makes 8 cups

8 medium green apples
2 medium red apples
40 fresh sage leaves

2 teaspoons grated lemon rind
²/₃ cup lemon juice
sugar

1 Wash and dry fruit. Finely chop fruit and coarsely chop sage leaves.
2 Combine fruit including cores and seeds, leaves and rind in a large saucepan. Cover with water, bring to boil and simmer, covered, for 1 hour or until fruit is soft and pulpy.
3 Strain fruit through a cheesecloth bag suspended over a bowl and stand for 3 hours. Measure the juice and return to saucepan. Add lemon juice and heat until boiling. Add ¾ cup warmed sugar per cup of juice. Return to the boil, stirring until the sugar dissolves. Boil rapidly for 45 minutes or until the jelly reaches setting point.
4 Remove jelly from the heat and allow to stand for 5 minutes. Pour into warm, sterilized jars. Allow to cool completely. When almost set, sage leaves may be suspended in the jelly using a clean bamboo skewer. Seal jars. When cool, label and date the jars. Serve with roast pork.

MINT JELLY

⭐ **Preparation time:** 30 minutes + overnight standing
Total cooking time: 45 minutes
Makes 3½ cups

2 lb green apples
4 cups water
½ cup lemon juice

2 cups fresh mint leaves
sugar
green coloring, optional

1 Cut the apples into thick slices but do not peel or core.
2 Combine apples, water, lemon juice and mint leaves in a large pan. Bring to the boil and boil slowly, uncovered, for about 10 minutes. Break up apples with a wooden spoon and boil slowly for another 15 minutes or until apples are soft and pulpy.
3 Strain mixture through a cheesecloth bag suspended over a bowl and stand overnight. Measure strained juice and return to pan. Add 1 cup of warmed sugar for each cup of juice and stir over heat until sugar is dissolved. Bring to the boil and boil rapidly until setting point is reached. Add a few drops of coloring to mixture until the desired color is achieved.
4 Remove pan from heat; leave to stand for 2 minutes. Pour into warm, sterilized jars. Seal when cold. Label and date jars. Serve with roast lamb.

2 Add Matzo Balls and simmer, uncovered, for 15 minutes. Return shredded chicken meat to pan and simmer for another 5–10 minutes.
3 To make Matzo Balls: Heat fat or oil in a medium pan, cook onion until golden. Transfer contents of pan to a bowl. Add matzo meal, eggs and parsley. Season mixture with salt and pepper; mix. If necessary, add sufficient almond meal to bind mixture. Cover, refrigerate 1 hour. With hands dipped in cold water, roll mixture into ¾ inch balls.

CHOPPED LIVER

Preparation time: 15 minutes
Total cooking time: 10 minutes
Serves 4

1 tablespoon chicken fat	1 tablespoon fresh white
1 medium onion,	bread crumbs
chopped	chicken fat, extra
1 clove garlic, crushed	salt
8 oz chicken livers,	freshly ground black
trimmed	pepper
2 hard-boiled eggs	nutmeg

1 Melt chicken fat in a pan and cook onion and garlic until onion is soft. Add livers and cook quickly until tender. Do not overcook.
2 Allow mixture to cool for a few minutes; place in a food processor with hard-boiled eggs and bread crumbs. Process until the mixture is fine, adding a little more chicken fat if necessary to make a smooth paste.
3 Season mixture with salt, pepper and nutmeg.

meat non-perishable and easily transportable.

Jerusalem Artichoke
Not really an artichoke, this lumpy brown tuber is a variety of sunflower. It resembles ginger. The white flesh is nutty, sweet and crunchy. Also called sunchoke.

Jewish Food Although Jewish food comes from many different countries, and has been

influenced by the local produce of these diverse regions, a surprising number of dishes are quite similar. Jewish cooking is closely linked to religious feast days. Plaited bread (challah), honey and eggs are all parts of feast-day food, and they all have biblical connotations.

All fruit and vegetables are kosher (permitted) but there are strict rules regarding meat, fish and dairy products. Pork is forbidden, as is game, shellfish and fish without scales. Dairy products may not be eaten in the same meal as meat dishes, nor prepared using the same

JEWISH CLASSICS

CHICKEN SOUP WITH MATZO BALLS

★★ **Preparation time:** 30 minutes + 1 hour refrigeration
Total cooking time: 2 hours 30 minutes
Serves 6

Soup	Matzo Balls
3½ lb chicken	2 tablespoons chicken fat
4 quarts water	or vegetable oil
3 onions, sliced	1 medium onion, finely
4 carrots, chopped	chopped
4 stalks celery, chopped	1 cup matzo meal (coarse)
1 leek, chopped	2 eggs, beaten
2 large parsley sprigs	1 tablespoon chopped
1 bay leaf	fresh parsley
8 peppercorns	salt and pepper
1 tablespoon salt	almond meal

1 Remove excess fat from chicken and reserve. Cut chicken into 8 or 9 pieces, place in large pan with water and remaining soup ingredients. Bring to boil slowly; skim the surface. Reduce heat, simmer 2 hours or until chicken meat leaves the bone. Strain and return soup to the rinsed pan and bring to the boil. Reserve chicken meat for soup.

OPPOSITE PAGE, ABOVE: MINT JELLY; BELOW: SAGE JELLY. THIS PAGE, ABOVE: CHICKEN SOUP WITH MATZO BALLS; RIGHT: CHOPPED LIVER

equipment. Many Jewish traditions have been taken up by non-Jews, for example the cooking of fish in olive oil. The oil must be fresh and hot, the fish is dusted with flour and cooked until brown on both sides. Even non-orthodox Jews eat traditional dishes on feast days: soup with matzo balls and charoseth (fruit and nuts with red wine) at Passover and teiglach (honey cake) at Rosh Hashanah (Jewish New Year).

Jicama A root with brown skin and crisp, white flesh. It is similar in taste to a water chestnut and used raw in salads or in stir-fries.

Johnnycake A flat, round, unleavened bread made from a dough of cornmeal, water or milk and salt and cooked on a griddle; eggs and butter are sometimes added.

Julienne Food, especially vegetables such as carrot, turnip, celery and leek, cut into thin, matchstick-sized pieces; it is used raw

in salads or lightly cooked as a garnish.

Juniper Berry The aromatic, slightly resinous-flavored dark berry of a small

LATKES

⭐ **Preparation time:** 35 minutes
Total cooking time: 30 minutes
Serves 4

3 lb medium potatoes
1 tablespoon oil
1 egg, beaten
1 small onion, grated

salt and freshly ground
    black pepper
2 tablespoons all-purpose
    flour
vegetable oil for frying

1 Scrub potatoes well. Peel and coarsely grate potatoes; rinse and drain. Squeeze out excess moisture using paper towels. Place in a bowl.
2 Add oil, egg and onion to potatoes, mixing well. Season with salt and pepper and stir in flour.
3 Shape into round flat cakes with floured hands. Heat oil and shallow fry potato cakes until golden brown on both sides.

ROAST BRISKET OF BEEF

In a baking dish, brown a 5 lb lean beef brisket in oil on both sides. Remove from the pan. Fry 3 sliced onions in the same oil and baking dish until the onion is transparent. Add the brisket and 1 cup of water. Sprinkle the meat with 1 tablespoon of flour, salt and garlic, to taste, and bake in a preheated moderately slow oven 325°F for 3 1/2 hours.

GEFILTE FISH

⭐⭐ **Preparation time:** 5 minutes
Total cooking time: 1 hour 45 minutes
Serves 4

2 lb cod, bream or
    haddock, with skin and
    bones for stock
2 stalks celery, chopped
2 onions, chopped
2 medium carrots, sliced
3 cups water

1 tablespoon chopped
    parsley
2 tablespoons ground
    almonds
2 eggs, beaten
salt and ground white
    pepper
matzo meal

1 Remove skin and bones from fish and place in a large pan with celery, half of the onion and half of the carrot. Add water, bring to the boil and simmer for 30 minutes. Strain stock.
2 Chop fish roughly and place in a food processor with remaining onion and parsley. Process until fine, add ground almonds, eggs, salt and pepper and sufficient matzo meal to bind. Roll mixture into 8 balls with floured hands.
3 Simmer remaining sliced carrot in fish stock for 10 minutes and remove. Add fish balls to stock, cover and simmer gently for 1 hour. Remove fish balls with a slotted spoon to a serving plate and top each with a slice of carrot.
4 Strain fish stock and spoon a little over each fish ball. Chill remaining stock which will set to a jelly. Chop jelly and use to garnish fish balls.

COTTAGE CHEESE BLINTZES

⭐⭐ **Preparation time:** 15 minutes +
1 hour standing
Total cooking time: 30 minutes
Serves 4–6

1 cup all-purpose flour	2 tablespoons sour cream
1/2 teaspoon salt	2 egg yolks
3 eggs	2 tablespoons sugar
1/4 cup milk	finely grated rind of
3 tablespoons butter, melted	1 lemon
	1/2 teaspoon vanilla extract
Filling	1/4 cup golden raisins
12 oz cottage cheese	

1 Sift flour and salt into a medium bowl. Make a well in the center. Add eggs one at a time, beating well after each addition. Stir in milk and melted butter. Cover batter and allow to stand for 1 hour.

2 Heat a 7–8 inch crêpe pan and brush with oil. Pour 2–3 tablespoons batter into pan; swirl evenly over base. Cook on medium heat until underside is golden. Turn pancake over and cook the other side. Place pancakes on a plate and cover with a

towel. Repeat process with remaining batter, brushing pan with oil when necessary.

3 Place a heaped tablespoon of filling on one side of each pancake and roll up firmly, tucking sides in to form a parcel.

4 Place the pancakes in a shallow, greased heatproof dish and bake in a hot oven 425°F for 10 minutes. Dust the blintzes with sifted powdered (confectioners') sugar and serve hot.

5 To make Filling: Place the cottage cheese in a medium bowl and stir in the sour cream and egg yolks. Add sugar, lemon rind, vanilla and golden raisins to bowl and mix thoroughly to combine.

CHAROSETH

⭐ **Preparation time:** 15 minutes +
1 hour refrigeration
Total cooking time: none
Serves 6

2 medium red apples	1 teaspoon cinnamon
1/4 cup finely chopped blanched almonds or walnuts	2 tablespoons red wine
	1 tablespoon honey

1 Halve and core the apples, leaving the skin on. Chop the apples very finely and place in a small bowl.

2 Add the almonds or walnuts, cinnamon, wine and honey to bowl and mix well. Chill for 1 hour before serving.

Note: Charoseth should be eaten on the day it is made, because it does not keep well. If the wine that you use is sweet, you may wish to reduce the amount of honey.

BAGELS AND LOX

Slice the bagels in half horizontally (allow 1 per person). Spread both sides of bagels with softened cream cheese. Top with 2–3 slices of fresh smoked salmon (lox) and sandwich the two sides of the bagel together. Capers and onion slices can also be added.

Note: This is the classic bagel combination, although there are many ways to serve them. Any sandwich filling can be used on a bagel. Traditionally, they are served unfilled and lightly toasted with scrambled eggs. Bagels can be purchased in many flavors such as onion, garlic, poppy seed, whole-wheat or cinnamon.

evergreen tree. Juniper berries are used to flavor gin (the word "gin" comes from the Dutch *jenever*, "juniper") and other spirits. Dried berries are added to marinades; used in stuffings for poultry and game birds and in the curing of hams; and often add flavor to slowly cooked meat dishes and sauerkraut. Crush berries before cooking to release the spicy pine aroma. Juniper berries are sold in jars.

Junket A sweet milk pudding, often flavored with chocolate or vanilla, that is set by the curdling action of the enzyme rennet and served topped with grated nutmeg or cinnamon or garnished with crystallized (candied) lemon rind.

Junket is easily digested and is often served to the sick.

Jus, au A French term applied to meat served in its own juice or gravy. Water or stock is added to pan juices and it is boiled until reduced and concentrated. *Au jus* means "with the juice."

OPPOSITE PAGE, ABOVE: LATKES;
BELOW: GEFILTE FISH.
THIS PAGE, ABOVE: COTTAGE CHEESE BLINTZES

K

Kabob Small pieces of meat, poultry or seafood (often marinated), threaded on a skewer and broiled or barbecued.

Kale A strong-flavored leaf vegetable native to the Mediterranean. It is prepared and cooked in the same way as collard greens or beet greens.

Kangaroo A lean, dark, high-protein meat with a taste similar to venison. It can be pan fried, roasted, barbecued or cooked in a casserole.

Kasha An Eastern European dish made from buckwheat, butter and milk.

Kedgeree An Indian mixture of rice and fish.

Ketchup (Catsup) A thick, spicy tomato-based condiment served with french fries, hot dogs and hamburgers.

Kibbi A Middle Eastern dish of lean lamb, bulgur (cracked wheat) and minced onion.

Kidney Classed as a variety meat, lamb, calf,

KABOBS

GRILLED TERIYAKI BEEF KABOBS

⭐ **Preparation time:** 15 minutes + 2 hours marinating
Total cooking time: 6–14 minutes
Serves 6

6 top round steaks, about 11 oz each
1 cup beef stock
¼ cup teriyaki sauce
2 tablespoons hoisin sauce
2 tablespoons lime juice
1 tablespoon honey
2 scallions, finely chopped
2 cloves garlic, crushed
1 teaspoon finely grated fresh ginger

1 Trim meat of excess fat and tendons. Slice meat across the grain into long, thin strips. Thread meat onto skewers, "weaving" them in place.
2 Combine the stock, teriyaki and hoisin sauces, lime juice, honey, scallions, garlic and ginger in a small bowl, whisk for 1 minute or until well combined. Place the skewered meat in a shallow dish, pour marinade over. Store in refrigerator, covered with plastic wrap, for 2 hours or overnight, turning occasionally. Drain, reserving marinade.
3 Place the skewered meat on a cold, lightly oiled broiler rack. Cook under high heat for 2 minutes each side to seal, turning once. For rare, cook for another minute each side. For medium and well done, lower the broiler rack, and cook for another 2–3 minutes each side for medium

and 4–6 minutes each side for well done. Brush occasionally with the reserved marinade during cooking.

FISH AND CUMIN KABOBS

⭐ **Preparation time:** 10 minutes + 3 hours marinating
Total cooking time: 5–6 minutes
Serves 4

1½ lb firm white fish fillets

Marinade
2 tablespoons olive oil
1 clove garlic, crushed
1 tablespoon chopped fresh cilantro
2 teaspoons ground cumin
1 teaspoon ground pepper

1 Cut fish fillets into 1¼ inch cubes. Thread onto oiled skewers and set aside.
2 To make Marinade: Combine oil, garlic, cilantro, cumin and pepper in a small bowl. Brush fish with marinade. Cover with plastic wrap and refrigerate several hours or overnight, turning occasionally. Drain and reserve marinade.
3 Place skewers on cold, lightly oiled broiler rack. Cook under medium-high heat 5–6 minutes or until tender, turning once and brushing with reserved marinade several times during cooking. Serve with pita bread and lime wedges.

ABOVE: FISH AND CUMIN KABOBS.
OPPOSITE PAGE, BELOW: GREEK LAMB KABOBS;
ABOVE: GARLIC CHICKEN KABOBS

GARLIC CHICKEN KABOBS

⭐ **Preparation time:** 20 minutes
Total cooking time: 12 minutes
Makes 12

6 boneless chicken thighs,
skin removed (1½ lb)
1 medium red pepper, cut
into 1¼ inch pieces
1 medium green pepper,
cut into 1¼ inch pieces
1 large red onion, cut
into 12 wedges
½ cup oil

2 cloves garlic, crushed
1 tablespoon chopped
fresh chives
1 tablespoon chopped
fresh mint
1 tablespoon chopped
fresh thyme
½ teaspoon seasoned
pepper

1 Soak bamboo skewers in water for several hours. Trim the chicken of excess fat and tendons. Cut chicken into 1¼ inch cubes.
2 Thread the chicken, peppers and onion alternately onto bamboo skewers. Combine the oil, garlic, herbs and pepper in a small bowl.
3 Place the kabobs on a lightly oiled grill. Cook the skewers over a medium-high heat for 6 minutes each side or until they are cooked through, brushing with herb mixture several times during cooking.

ORIENTAL VEAL STICKS

⭐ **Preparation time:** 6 minutes
Total cooking time: 6–8 minutes
Serves 4

1½ lb veal strips
½ cup plum sauce
2 teaspoons soy sauce
1 clove garlic, crushed

½ teaspoon grated fresh
ginger
¼ teaspoon minced chili
pepper

1 Thread meat onto 8 bamboo skewers.
2 Combine plum and soy sauces, garlic, ginger and chili. Brush the kabobs with the chili-plum mixture. Barbecue kabobs over hot coals 3–4 minutes each side, brushing constantly with the sauce.
3 Serve veal sticks with brown rice and salad. Any leftover baste may be used as a dipping sauce.

GREEK LAMB KABOBS

⭐ **Preparation time:** 20 minutes +
2 hours marinating
Total cooking time: 12 minutes
Makes 20 kebabs

3 lb boned leg of lamb
⅓ cup olive oil
¼ cup lemon juice
2 tablespoons dry white
wine
2 cloves garlic, crushed
2 tablespoons soy sauce

1 teaspoon dried oregano
leaves
½ teaspoon ground black
pepper
1 large onion, finely
chopped
¼ cup finely chopped
fresh parsley

1 Trim meat of excess fat and tendons. Cut meat evenly into 1¼ inch cubes. Thread cubes onto oiled skewers. Place oil, juice, wine, garlic, sauce, oregano and pepper in a bowl. Whisk for 2 minutes or until well combined. Pour over meat.
2 Refrigerate, covered with plastic wrap, 2 hours or overnight. Drain meat, reserving the marinade.
3 Place meat on a cold, lightly oiled broiler rack. Cook 5–6 inches from heat 12 minutes or until tender, turning once. Brush with reserved marinade several times during cooking. Combine onion and parsley; serve sprinkled over kabobs.

beef and pig kidneys are eaten. Lamb kidney can be broiled; calf kidney, braised; pork kidney is best cooked slowly in a casserole.

Kidney Bean Dried, red-brown, kidney-

shaped seed used in Mexican foods.

King Crab A large crab from the Alaskan coast.

Kipper Pickled herring, a favorite British breakfast.

Kiwifruit Also known as Chinese gooseberry, an egg-shaped, hairy fruit with

sweet, juicy flesh and tiny black seeds. Eat fresh, cut in half, or add to desserts.

Kofta A Middle East dish of ground meat or chicken balls cooked in a spicy sauce.

Korma An Indian dish of lean meat or chicken braised in a spicy yogurt or cream sauce.

Kumquat A berry-sized, orange-color citrus fruit with bitter flesh.

L

Ladyfingers A term used for several different foods, all slender and

finger-shaped. Okra, a vegetable much used in North African and Caribbean dishes is known in some places as ladies' fingers, as is a small sweet variety of banana. A small, finger-shaped, crisp sponge cookie also carries the name. In Middle Eastern cooking the name can refer to thin rolls of filo pastry filled with either a spicy meat mixture or crushed nuts and honey.

Lamb Meat from a sheep under one-year-old; milk-fed or baby lamb is under 3 months old; spring lamb, 3 to 9 months. Lamb should be firm with fine-grained, reddish-pink meat with an even edge of white fat; it is succulent and is suitable for roasting, broiling and barbecuing. It is suitable for cooking with or without liquid. It is featured in the cuisines of many countries. In Greece it is slow-roasted in *kleftico*; in the Middle East kabobs of lamb are

LAMB

CROWN ROAST OF LAMB WITH ROSEMARY STUFFING

★★ **Preparation time:** 20 minutes
Total cooking time: 45 minutes
Serves 6

1 lamb crown roast (minimum 12 chops)
2 medium onions, peeled and chopped
1 green or cooking apple, peeled and chopped
1 tablespoon butter
2 cups (about 4 oz) fresh bread crumbs

2 tablespoons chopped fresh rosemary
1 tablespoon chopped fresh parsley
1/4 cup unsweetened apple juice
2 eggs, separated

1 Preheat the oven to moderately hot 400°F. Trim meat of excess fat and tendons. Cook onion and apple in butter until soft. Remove from heat and stir in bread crumbs and herbs. Whisk apple juice and egg yolks together. Stir into bread crumb mixture.
2 Place egg whites in a small, dry mixing bowl. Using electric beaters, beat egg whites until soft peaks form. Fold lightly into stuffing mixture.
3 Place crown roast in a baking dish. Place a sheet

of lightly greased foil underneath the roast to hold stuffing. Spoon stuffing into cavity. Roast meat for 45 minutes, or until cooked to your liking. Use a sharp knife to cut between cutlets to separate.

Note: Order the crown roast in advance and ask your butcher to shape and tie it with string. Wrap foil around the ends of the chop bones to prevent them burning; discard before serving.

ABOUT LAMB

■ In recent years, the variety of boneless cuts of lamb has increased its popularity at the table. A flavorsome and nutritious alternative to beef, lamb steaks and fillets are usually cooked quickly and served rare, or medium. (To test for doneness, press the meat gently with tongs—rare lamb will be very soft, and medium slightly firm.) Ground lamb is an alternative to recipes that usually use beef, such as hamburgers.
■ More traditional (and just as delicious) is the practice of cooking lamb until it is almost ready to fall apart or away from the bone. Lamb curries, stews and casseroles should be cooked very slowly until the meat almost melts in the mouth.

ABOVE: CROWN ROAST OF LAMB WITH ROSEMARY STUFFING. OPPOSITE PAGE, BELOW: ROAST LEG OF LAMB; ABOVE: LAMB NAVARIN WITH VEGETABLES

ROAST LEG OF LAMB WITH SAGE AND TARRAGON

Preparation time: 15 minutes
Total cooking time: 1 hour 30 minutes
Serves 6

4 lb leg of lamb
1/4 cup roughly chopped
 fresh sage leaves
2 tablespoons roughly
 chopped fresh tarragon
 leaves
1 clove garlic
1 medium onion, chopped
1 tablespoon oil
2 tablespoons plum sauce
1 cup white wine
1/4 cup chicken stock

1 Preheat oven to moderate 350°F. Using a small, sharp knife, trim meat of excess fat and tendons. Combine sage, tarragon, garlic, onion, oil and plum sauce in food processor. Process for 30 seconds or until mixture is smooth.
2 Place meat in a deep baking dish. Rub meat all over with sage mixture. Add a little water to the base of the dish to prevent burning. Bake, uncovered, for 1 hour 15 minutes. Remove from oven, place on carving platter. Cover loosely with foil and leave in a warm place for 10 minutes before slicing.
3 Place baking dish on top of stove. Add wine and stock to pan juices, stirring well to incorporate browned bits off the bottom of the pan. Bring to boil, reduce heat, simmer for 5 minutes. Pour over sliced lamb when serving.

LAMB NAVARIN WITH VEGETABLES

Preparation time: 20 minutes
Total cooking time: 1 hour 45 minutes
Serves 6

2 lb lamb shoulder chops
2 tablespoons butter
1/4 cup olive oil
2 medium onions, chopped
1 clove garlic, crushed
2 parsnips, sliced
2 carrots, sliced
2 stalks celery, sliced
1/4 cup all-purpose flour
14 oz can tomatoes,
 drained, juice reserved
1/2 cup water
1 cup chicken stock
2 tablespoons chopped fresh
 mint
1/2 cup frozen green beans
1/2 cup chopped fresh
 parsley
1 teaspoon fresh thyme
 leaves
ground pepper, to taste
1 tablespoon Dijon
 mustard
1/2 cup chopped fresh
 parsley, extra

1 Preheat oven to 300°F. Trim meat of bones and excess fat, cut into 3/4 inch cubes. Heat butter and oil in a large pan. Cook the meat in batches over medium heat until well browned; drain on paper towels.
2 Cook onion until golden, add garlic, parsnip, carrot and celery; cook until all vegetables are lightly browned. Stir through flour, add roughly chopped tomatoes and reserved juice, water, stock, mint, beans, parsley, thyme, pepper and mustard, to taste. Stir until sauce thickens.
3 Add meat, place in a casserole dish and cover. Cook for 1 1/2 hours. Garnish with the extra chopped parsley.

marinated and grilled and the feast dish *mansaaf* is lamb simmered in a spicy yogurt sauce; *mechoui*, eaten in North Africa and the Middle East, is whole lamb roasted on the spit; in France roasting joints of lamb are basted with buttery stock; in Iran lamb is stewed; spicy-sauced Mongolian lamb is a Chinese favorite; and in the British Isles lamb is the essential ingredient in Irish stew and Lancashire hot pot. In Muslim India lamb is the main meat.

Lamington A small cube of sponge or butter cake dipped in thin chocolate icing and then coated in shredded coconut. The lamington originated in Australia. It is said to be named after Lord Lamington, governor of Queensland, Australia, from 1895 to 1901.

Lancashire Hot Pot A warming stew of lamb, onions and potatoes, topped with a crust of overlapping potato slices. It originally also contained mushrooms and oysters and was cooked in a special earthenware pot.

Langue de Chat (Cats' Tongues) A crisp, flat, oblong cookie served with iced desserts, fruit salad, dessert wines and champagne. Its name is French for "cat's tongue," a reference to its shape.

Lard Rendered pork fat, pure white in color and virtually odorless, used to make pie crusts and biscuits or as a frying and roasting medium. It is found in the refrigerator section of supermarkets.

Larding The process of inserting strips of pork or bacon fat into cuts of lean meat and game to give it additional juiciness and flavor during cooking. The strips, called lardoons, are inserted with a larding needle, a hollow stainless steel skewer.

Lasagne A variety of Italian pasta. It is flat and wide with either straight or wavy edges. Lasagna sheets are boiled in water, drained, then combined with various sauces, topped with cheese and baked. There is a pre-cooked

LAMB CHOPS WITH TOMATO-MINT SAUCE

★ **Preparation time:** 20 minutes + 1 hour standing
Total cooking time: 15 minutes
Serves 6

12 lamb chops, about
2½ oz each
1 tablespoon olive oil

Tomato-Mint Sauce
3 medium tomatoes

1 teaspoon cider vinegar
2 teaspoons soft brown
sugar
1 scallion, finely chopped
2 teaspoons finely
chopped fresh mint

1 Trim excess fat and tendons from each chop. Scrape bone clean, and trim meat to a neat disk. Heat oil in pan: Cook chops over high heat 2 minutes each side to seal, then another minute each side. Serve with Tomato-Mint Sauce.
2 To make Tomato-Mint Sauce: Mark a small cross on the top of each tomato. Place in boiling water for 1–2 minutes, then plunge immediately into cold water. Remove and peel skin down from the cross. Cut tomatoes in half and gently squeeze seeds out. Remove any remaining seeds with a teaspoon. Chop tomatoes finely.
3 Combine tomato, vinegar, sugar, and onion in a pan over medium heat. Bring to boil, reduce heat, simmer 5 minutes. Remove from heat, transfer to a bowl, leave at room temperature for at least 1 hour. Stir in mint just before serving.

MONGOLIAN LAMB

★ **Preparation time:** 15 minutes + 1 hour marinating
Total cooking time: 10 minutes
Serves 4

1½ lb lamb fillets
2 cloves garlic, crushed
1 teaspoon grated fresh
ginger
1 tablespoon sesame oil
2 tablespoons peanut oil

4 medium onions, cut in
wedges
1 tablespoon cornstarch
1 tablespoon soy sauce
¼ cup dry sherry
1 tablespoon toasted
sesame seeds (see note)

1 Trim meat of any fat and tendons. Slice meat across the grain evenly into thin slices. Combine garlic, ginger and sesame oil; add meat, stir to coat. Store in refrigerator, covered with plastic wrap, 1 hour or overnight, turning occasionally.
2 Heat peanut oil in wok or heavy-bottom frying pan, swirling gently to coat base and side. Add onion, stir-fry over medium heat for 4 minutes or until soft, remove from wok; keep warm. Reheat wok, cook the meat quickly in small batches over high heat until browned but not cooked through. Remove from wok; drain on paper towels.
3 Combine cornstarch, soy sauce and sherry to make a smooth paste. Return meat to wok with cornstarch mixture, stir-fry over high heat until meat is cooked and sauce has thickened. Remove from heat, top with onion and sprinkle with toasted sesame seeds.

Note: To toast sesame seeds, place in a dry pan and stir over low heat until golden.

LANCASHIRE HOT POT

★ ★ **Preparation time:** 20 minutes
Total cooking time: 2 hours
Serves 8

8 lamb shoulder chops, 1 inch thick

1/4 cup all-purpose flour

3 tablespoons dripping or butter

2 large onions, sliced

2 stalks celery, chopped

1 large parsnip, peeled and sliced

1 3/4 cups chicken or beef stock

6 1/2 oz mushrooms, sliced

1/2 teaspoon white pepper

salt to taste

2 teaspoons dried mixed herbs

1 tablespoon Worcestershire sauce

4 medium potatoes, peeled and very thinly sliced

1 Preheat oven to moderately slow 325°F. Brush a large 6-cup capacity heatproof casserole dish with melted butter or oil. Trim meat of excess fat and tendons. Place flour in a plastic bag and toss chops in flour to coat thoroughly. Shake off excess and reserve for later use. Heat dripping or butter in frying pan. Add chops and cook until both sides are brown. Remove chops and place in a casserole dish.

2 Add onion, celery and parsnip to pan, cook until slightly softened. Place mixture on top of chops in casserole dish.

3 Sprinkle reserved flour over base of pan and cook, stirring, until dark brown. Gradually pour in stock and stir until mixture comes to the boil. Add mushrooms, pepper, salt, herbs and Worcestershire sauce, simmer for 10 minutes. Remove from heat and pour over chops.

4 Place overlapping slices of potato on top to completely cover the meat and vegetables. Cover casserole dish with lid and place in preheated oven. Cook for 1 1/4 hours. Remove lid and continue cooking for another 30 minutes or until potatoes are brown and crisp.

JHAL FARAZI

Heat a little oil in a pan and cook 1 sliced onion for 8 minutes. Add 1/2 teaspoon grated ginger and cook for another minute. In a bowl mix 1/2 teaspoon ground turmeric, 1/2 teaspoon garam masala, 1/4 teaspoon chili powder and 1/2 teaspoon salt. Add a little cold water and mix to a paste. Add this to the pan and cook, stirring for another minute, being careful not to allow mixture to burn. Add 6 1/2 oz sliced leftover roast lamb and toss well. Add a sliced cooked potato and toss gently, moistening with 2–3 tablespoons water. Cover pan and cook over low heat until heated through. Sprinkle with lemon juice and chopped mint just before serving.

OPPOSITE PAGE, ABOVE: LAMB CHOPS WITH TOMATO-MINT SAUCE; BELOW: MONGOLIAN LAMB. ABOVE: LANCASHIRE HOT POT

lasagna noodle which does not need boiling.

Lassi A refreshing yogurt drink popular in India and the Middle East. It is made by blending plain yogurt with iced water and traditionally is seasoned to taste with salt and pepper, although for a sweetened version sugar can be added. Serve in a tall glass with ice cubes.

Lebanese Food The ingredients that predominate in Lebanese cooking are sesame seeds, pistachios, cracked wheat (bulgur), filo (phyllo) pastry, chickpeas and yogurt. Outside of the country, the most famous Lebanese dishes are tabbouleh, a salad made from bulgur, parsley, mint and tomatoes; falafel, little balls of crushed chickpeas; and hummus,

a dip made from puréed chickpeas, sometimes with sesame seed paste (tahini) added. These three are often rolled into a round of pita bread, the result of which is known as a falafel sandwich. That's about as much as many Westerners know about Lebanese food. In fact, like the food of many

Middle Eastern countries, it is a subtle and elegant cuisine. Kibbe, one of Lebanon's most famous meat dishes, is made from lamb and there are many varieties of lamb pastries too. The most common vegetables in Lebanese cooking are the vegetables popular throughout the

Mediterranean: eggplant, zucchini and tomatoes. Okra, fava beans and cucumbers are also used in Lebanese cuisine. The Lebanese are fond of sweet, fragrant desserts and use orange flower water and rose water, honey, nuts and spices.

Leek A member of the onion family valued for its fleshy, mild-flavored stem. When preparing leeks, remove the outer layers, cut off roots and base and tough dark green tops. Thoroughly wash to remove all dirt and grit. Leeks can be steamed, boiled or braised as a hot vegetable; cooked in soups, pies, tarts and stir-fries; or served cold, as a salad with a mayonnaise or vinaigrette dressing. They are in season during winter.

The leek was grown

ROGHAN JOSH

★★ **Preparation time:** 25 minutes
Total cooking time: 1 hour 10 minutes
Serves 6

1 tablespoon coriander seeds	4 whole cloves
1/2–1 1/2 teaspoons red chili flakes	3/4 cup plain yogurt
2 lb boneless lamb, cut into 1 inch cubes	1/2 teaspoon nutmeg
	1/2 teaspoon ground cardamom
1/2 teaspoon grated fresh ginger	1 cup water
4 tablespoons ghee or unsalted (sweet) butter	3 teaspoons garam masala
	1/4 teaspoon powdered saffron
	1/2 cup heavy cream

1 In a dry pan, toast the coriander seeds until they are very aromatic. Add the chili flakes and cook very briefly. Remove from pan and grind both to a fine powder.
2 Season the meat with ginger, and brown in the ghee or butter with the cloves. Sprinkle with the coriander and chili. Add yogurt, nutmeg and cardamom to the pan and cook for 8 minutes, stirring occasionally.
3 Add the water, cover the pan and simmer for about 50 minutes until the meat is very tender. Uncover halfway through cooking to reduce the sauce if a drier curry is preferred. Add the garam masala.
4 Stir saffron into the cream and add to the pan. Cook gently, stirring, for 3–4 minutes. Serve with steamed white rice.

LAMB SHANKS WITH ROASTED GARLIC

★ **Preparation time:** 20 minutes
Total cooking time: 1 hour 40 minutes
Serves 6

6 large lamb shanks	2 medium leeks, sliced
freshly ground black pepper, to taste	1 medium sprig rosemary
	1 cup dry white wine
1 tablespoon oil	1 head garlic

1 Preheat oven to moderate 350°F. Season the shanks with pepper. Heat the oil in a heavy-based pan. Cook the shanks quickly in batches over medium-high heat until well browned; drain on paper towels. Place in the meat in a heatproof casserole dish.
2 Add the leek and cook in pan until tender. Add to the casserole with rosemary and wine.
3 Cut the whole garlic through the center horizontally. Brush cut surfaces with a little oil. Place cut side up in casserole, but not covered by liquid. Cover pan and bake for 1 hour. Remove lid and cook for another 15 minutes. Discard rosemary before serving. Serve with steamed vegetables and crusty bread on which to spread the roasted garlic.

LEFT: ROGHAN JOSH; ABOVE: LAMB SHANKS WITH ROASTED GARLIC. OPPOSITE PAGE, BELOW: LADIES' FINGERS; ABOVE: HUMMUS

LADIES' FINGERS

⭐⭐ **Preparation time:** 25 minutes
Total cooking time: 30–35 minutes
Makes 24

2 tablespoons olive oil
1 onion, finely chopped
⅓ cup pine nuts
1 lb ground lamb
¼ cup raisins, chopped
1 cup grated Cheddar
   cheese
2 tablespoons chopped
   fresh cilantro
1 teaspoon ground pepper

2 tablespoons chopped
   fresh mint
10 sheets frozen filo
   (phyllo) dough, thawed
⅓ cup butter, melted

Yogurt Sauce
¼ small cucumber
¾ cup plain yogurt
1 tablespoon chopped
   fresh cilantro

1 Preheat oven to 375°F. Line a 13 x 11 inch baking sheet with parchment paper. Heat oil in heavy-bottom pan. Cook onion and pine nuts over medium heat 5 minutes until golden brown. Add lamb and cook over medium heat 5–10 minutes until well browned and almost all liquid has evaporated. Use a fork to break up any large lumps of lamb as it cooks.
2 Remove from heat, cool slightly. Add raisins, cheese, cilantro, pepper and mint; mix.
3 Place 10 sheets of pastry on work surface. Using a sharp knife or scissors, cut pastry lengthwise into 4 strips. Cover pastry strips with a dry towel. Brush two strips with melted butter, place one on top of the other. Place a tablespoon of lamb mixture at one end of top sheet. Fold in ends and roll into a finger shape. Repeat process with remaining pastry and filling.

4 Place pastries on prepared baking sheet and brush with remaining butter. Bake for 15–20 minutes or until golden brown. Serve warm or cold with Yogurt Sauce if desired.
5 To make Yogurt Sauce: Peel skin from cucumber. Scoop out the seeds. Chop the flesh and place in a bowl. Add yogurt and cilantro and mix to combine.

HUMMUS

⭐ **Preparation time:** 10 minutes +
4 hours soaking
Total cooking time: 1 hour
Serves 8–10

1 cup chickpeas
   (garbanzo beans)
3 cups water
¼ cup lemon juice
¼ cup olive oil

2 cloves garlic, coarsely
   chopped
2 tablespoons water, extra
½ teaspoon salt
sweet paprika, to garnish

1 Soak chickpeas in water for 4 hours or overnight. Drain chickpeas, place in a pan, add water and bring to the boil. Simmer, uncovered, for 1 hour, drain.
2 Place chickpeas, lemon juice, olive oil, chopped garlic, water and salt into a food processor, process for 30 seconds or until the mixture is smooth. Sprinkle with paprika and serve as a dip with pita bread.

in ancient Egypt, and 3500 years ago was mentioned in a Chinese food guide. The emperor Nero is said to have supped daily on leek soup, believing it would strengthen his voice for delivering orations. In Celtic Britain the vegetable patch was called a *leactun,* "leek enclosure." The leek has a particular association with Wales and is that country's national emblem. On St. David's Day, pieces of leek are worn in the buttonhole to commemorate the famous seventh century victory over the Saxons by the Welsh warriors of King Cadwallader.

Legumes A group of plants which bear their seeds in pods, especially beans, peas and lentils. Legumes are a good source of

protein in meatless diets. They have been used since the earliest times, from the soy bean of Asia to the lentils of ancient Egypt and the beans of the Americas.

Leicester Cheese A semihard cow's milk cheese with a moist, crumbly texture and mellow flavor; its deep orange color comes from annatto dye. A good snack and sandwich cheese, it goes well with fruits and salad vegetables and is an excellent cooking cheese. It originated near the village of Melton Mowbray, in Leicestershire, England.

Lemon An oval, yellow-skinned citrus fruit with pale yellow, tart-tasting flesh. It is not usually eaten on its own but is the most versatile and widely used of all fruits as its acid juice and fragrant rind are used to flavor a wide range of sweet and savory dishes. It is also used in drinks, marinades, sauces and icings. Slices and wedges of lemon are a common garnish. Its juice stops cut fruit from turning brown when exposed to the air. Lemon is a good source of vitamin C. Fresh lemons are available throughout the year; lemon juice can be bought frozen or as a concentrate.
The lemon probably originated in northern India, from where it spread to China and to the Middle East.

Lemon Balm A member of the mint family with leaves that

FALAFEL WITH TOMATO RELISH

★★ **Preparation time:** 25 minutes + 30 minutes standing + 4 hours soaking
Total cooking time: 20–25 minutes
Serves 6

Falafel
2 cups chickpeas (garbanzo beans)
3 cups water
1 small onion, finely chopped
2 cloves garlic, crushed
2 tablespoons chopped fresh parsley
1 tablespoon chopped fresh cilantro
2 teaspoons ground cumin
1 tablespoon water, extra
1/2 teaspoon baking powder
oil for deep-frying

Tomato Relish
2 medium tomatoes, peeled and finely chopped
1/4 small cucumber, finely chopped
1/2 green pepper, finely chopped
2 tablespoons chopped fresh parsley
1 teaspoon sugar
2 teaspoons chili sauce
1/2 teaspoon ground black pepper
grated rind and juice of 1 lemon

1 To make Falafel: Soak chickpeas in water 4 hours or overnight. Drain, place chickpeas in food processor. Process until finely ground.
2 Add onion, garlic, parsley, cilantro, cumin, extra water and baking powder, process for 10 seconds or until mixture resembles a rough paste. Leave to stand for 30 minutes.
3 To make Tomato Relish: Place all ingredients in a bowl, mix to combine; set aside.
4 Shape heaped tablespoons of falafel mixture into balls. Squeeze out excess liquid using your hands.

Heat oil in a deep heavy-bottom pan. Lower falafel balls on a large spoon into moderately hot oil. Cook in batches of five at a time, for about 3–4 minutes each batch. When well browned, carefully remove from the oil with a large slotted spoon. Drain falafel on paper towels. Serve hot or cold on a bed of Tomato Relish or in pita bread with relish and hummus.

BABA GHANNOUJ

★ **Preparation time:** 20 minutes
Total cooking time: 20 minutes
Serves 6–8

2 small eggplants, halved lengthwise
salt
2 cloves garlic, crushed
2 tablespoons lemon juice
1/4 cup tahini (sesame seed paste)
1 tablespoon olive oil
salt, extra, to taste
1 tablespoon finely chopped fresh mint

1 Preheat oven to 375°F. Sprinkle eggplant flesh with salt. Stand for 10–15 minutes then rinse off salt and pat dry with paper towels.
2 Place eggplant, flesh-side up, on a baking sheet. Bake for 20 minutes or until flesh is soft. Peel off the skin and discard.
3 Place eggplant flesh, garlic, lemon juice, tahini and olive oil in a food processor. Process for 30 seconds or until smooth. Season to taste with salt. Garnish with fresh mint and serve with pita bread wedges.

TABBOULEH

⋆ **Preparation time:** 20 minutes
Total cooking time: none
Serves 6–8

1 cup medium bulgur
  (cracked wheat)
2 cups water
3/4 cup chopped flat-leaf
  parsley
3/4 cup chopped fresh
  mint

4 scallions, finely chopped
2 medium tomatoes,
  finely chopped
2 tablespoons lemon juice
1 tablespoon olive oil
1 teaspoon ground pepper

1 Soak the bulgur wheat in water for
10 minutes, drain and squeeze remaining water
from wheat in a sieve, pressing down hard with
the back of a spoon.
2 Place wheat, parsley, mint, scallions, tomato,
lemon juice, oil and pepper in a bowl and mix to
combine. Serve as a first course with small crisp
lettuce leaves to scoop up the tabbouleh or as a
side salad to a main meal.

Note: Tabbouleh can be stored for up to
2 days, covered in plastic wrap, in the refrigerator
but is best eaten soon after making.

Opposite page, above: Falafel with tomato
relish; below: Baba ghannouj. This page,
above: Tabbouleh; below: Spicy lamb in pita

SPICY LAMB IN PITA BREAD

⋆ **Preparation time:** 10 minutes +
  2 hours marinating
Total cooking time: 10 minutes
Serves 6

2 lamb loins
2 teaspoons olive oil
4 large pita breads
2 medium tomatoes,
  sliced
hummus, to serve
tabbouleh, to serve

Marinade
2 cloves garlic, crushed
2 teaspoons onion powder
1 teaspoon grated fresh
  ginger
1 teaspoon ground pepper
1 tablespoon finely
  chopped fresh cilantro
1/2 cup red wine

1 **To make Marinade:** Combine all of the
ingredients for the marinade in a medium bowl.
2 Trim lamb of excess fat or tendons. Add lamb
to marinade, toss to coat well; refrigerate, covered
with plastic wrap, several hours or overnight,
turning occasionally. Drain; reserve marinade.
3 Heat oil in medium pan; add lamb. Cook over
medium-high heat for 5 minutes each side. Add
the reserved marinade during the last 3 minutes
and reduce to 2 tablespoons over high heat. Slice
the lamb thinly.
4 Place lamb on warmed, opened-out pita bread.
Place tomato slices over top followed by hummus
and tabbouleh. Roll bread to encase filling; serve.

are crinkle-edged, heart-
shaped and lemon-
scented. The leaves can
be added to almost any
dish using lemon juice.
They are also used to
make a soothing tea. The
sweet-scented flowers
are the basis of the
cordial Eau des Carmes.
Lemon balm is easy to
grow and is best used
when fresh.

Lemon Curd A sweet
spread made from lemon
juice, lemon rind, egg
yolks, butter and sugar.
It can be used as filling
for tarts, cakes and
cookies.

Lemon Grass A tall,
tufted, sharp-edged grass
with a strong citrus
flavor, common in
tropical Southeast Asia.
The whitish, slightly
bulbous base of the stem
is used
especially
in the
cooking of Thailand
and Vietnam; it flavors
curries, soups, stews and
casseroles, particularly
those made with chicken
and seafood. To prepare
lemon grass for adding to
a dish either pound the
stem to bruise the flesh
and release the fragrant
juices, or make cuts
down the stem, leaving
the bottom intact;
remove the stalk before
serving. Lemon grass is
available fresh in some
supermarkets and Asian
food stores; dried ground
and shredded stalks are
also available (ground

stalks can be added directly to the dish; shredded stalks must first be soaked). Lemon grass is very easy to grow in tropical and warm climates. Grated lemon rind and a pinch of finely shredded ginger can be substituted for fresh lemon grass.

Lentil The tiny, flat disk-shaped seed of an annual plant of the legume (pod-bearing) family. Lentils are a good source of vegetable protein and have been used as a food since prehistoric times. The brown lentil (sometimes called the continental lentil) has a bland, nutty flavor when cooked; it is often added to stews and casseroles, and can be used in salads. Red lentils (which can be yellow or orange and are also known as split lentils) are often used in Asian cooking; they have a subtle spicy flavor and are used for the Indian dish dhal. Both brown and red lentils are used to make vegetarian loaves and patties. Lentils are sold in dried form or pre-cooked in cans; they are also processed into flour. In ancient Egypt, lentils were grown, eaten and exported in large quantities, mainly to Greece and Rome, where they provided protein in the diets of the poor.

LEEKS

LEEK TART

★★ **Preparation time:** 30 minutes + 30 minutes refrigeration
Total cooking time: 30–40 minutes
Makes one 9 inch flan

Pastry
2 cups all-purpose flour
1/2 cup butter, cut into small pieces
2 tablespoons shortening, chilled
2 tablespoons lemon juice
2–3 tablespoons ice water

Filling
2 slices bacon, finely chopped
5 leeks, cleaned and thinly sliced
1/3 cup all-purpose flour
1 cup milk
2 eggs, lightly beaten
1 cup shredded Cheddar cheese
1/2 teaspoon pepper
1 beaten egg

1 Preheat oven to 400°F.
2 To make Pastry: Place the flour, butter and shortening in a food processor. Cover and process until the mixture has a fine crumbly texture. Add the lemon juice and water. Process for a further 30 seconds or until the mixture is smooth. Refrigerate the dough, covered with plastic wrap, for about 30 minutes.
3 To make Filling: In a medium skillet cook the bacon until it is crisp. Add the sliced leeks and cook for 5 minutes or until tender. Stir in the flour. Add the milk and cook, stirring until it is thickened and bubbly. Cook, stirring for 1 minute more. Allow to cool slightly, then stir in 2 eggs, the shredded cheese, and pepper.
4 Roll two-thirds of the pastry out to fit the bottom and up the sides of a 9-inch flan pan or quiche dish. Place the pastry in the pan and spoon the filling over. Roll out the remaining pastry to cover the top of the pie. Trim, seal and flute the edges. Brush with 1 beaten egg. Cut three deep slits in the pastry lid to allow steam to escape. Bake, uncovered for 30–40 minutes or until crust is golden brown and crisp. Cut into wedges to serve.

LEEKS IN HERB SAUCE

Cut off and discard the green tops of 12 baby leeks. Wash the leeks thoroughly and simmer them in salted water for about 10 minutes or until they are tender. Drain and place on a serving dish. Make a sauce by mixing together 5 tablespoons olive oil, 1 tablespoon white wine vinegar, 1 finely chopped large scallion, 2 teaspoons finely chopped capers, 1 teaspoon chopped parsley, 1/2 teaspoon chopped fresh tarragon, 1/2 teaspoon chopped fresh chervil and 1/2 cup of heavy cream. Pour the sauce over the leeks and put them aside until they are cool. Serve at room temperature.

ABOVE: LEEK TART.

OPPOSITE PAGE: FROZEN LEMON TART

L E M O N S

F R O Z E N   L E M O N   T A R T

★★ ***Preparation time:*** 40 minutes +
30 minutes refrigeration +
overnight refrigeration
Total cooking time: 25 minutes
Serves 6

1¼ cups all-purpose flour	1 tablespoon finely grated lemon rind
1 tablespoon sugar	½ cup lemon juice
⅛ teaspoon salt	4 egg yolks, lightly beaten
6 tablespoons butter	2 tablespoons butter, extra
3 tablespoons iced water	2 medium lemons
1½ cups sugar	½ cup sugar, extra
⅓ cup cornstarch	½ cup water, extra
1¼ cups water	

1 Place flour, sugar and salt in a large mixing bowl; add chopped butter. Using fingertips or pastry blender, rub butter into flour for 2 minutes until mixture is fine and crumbly. Add almost all the water and mix to a firm dough, adding more liquid if necessary. Turn onto a lightly floured surface, knead 1 minute or until smooth. Roll pastry until it is large enough to cover base and sides of a 9 inch flan pan. Line pan with pastry, trim edge. Cover with plastic wrap and refrigerate for 30 minutes. Preheat oven to moderate 350°F. Cut a sheet of waxed paper large enough to cover pastry-lined pan. Spread a layer of dried beans or rice evenly over paper. Bake 10 minutes, remove from oven. Discard paper and beans. Return pastry to oven for another 5–8 minutes or until lightly golden. Set aside to cool.

2 Combine sugar, cornstarch and water in a medium pan and stir until smooth. Add lemon rind and juice and cook, stirring, over medium heat until mixture boils. Reduce heat slightly, add egg yolks, whisking to combine, and cook for 1 minute. Remove from heat and stir in butter. Set aside to cool.

3 Slice lemons very finely, being careful to retain round shape. Combine sugar and water in a small heavy-bottom pan. Stir over medium heat without boiling until sugar has completely dissolved. Bring to the boil, reduce heat slightly, add lemon slices and boil for 1 minute without stirring. Remove lemon slices from syrup and drain thoroughly. Spread cool lemon mixture into cool pastry shell and cover top with overlapping lemon slices. Freeze overnight. Stand for 5 minutes at room temperature before serving. Cut into wedges and serve with whipped cream.

A B O U T   L E M O N S

■ Lemons do not ripen after picking, so choose fruit with deep yellow skins.

■ There is no need to cut a whole lemon if all you require is a tablespoon of juice. Simply pierce the skin with a sharp metal skewer and squeeze out the required amount. (Microwave on 50% power for 20 seconds first, if possible.) An average lemon will yield about 3 tablespoons of juice.

Lettuce A plant valued for its large, succulent leaves which are mainly used in salads, although they are sometimes braised or steamed and served as a hot vegetable. Today's lettuces descend from loose-leafed plants native to the Middle East and they have been cultivated there since ancient times. Lettuce was eaten by the Greeks, Persians and Egyptians; by 500 BC it was one of the most popular vegetables in Italy and remained a favorite with the Romans over the following centuries. In its wild form it spread into northern and western Europe, where it was gathered but, until the ninth century, not cultivated. In China lettuce has been cultivated since the fifth century; Christopher Columbus introduced it into the Americas.

There are three main types of lettuce: butterhead (including Boston and bibb) with soft-textured, loosely packed leaves; crisphead (including iceberg) with crisp,

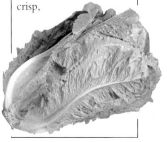

tightly packed leaves; and leaf lettuce (oak leaf and romaine), with long dark green leaves. Lettuce, either a single variety or a mixture, can be made into a green salad or can be used as the basis of a number of other salad dishes.

Leyden A semihard cow's milk cheese with a tangy taste and a dark yellow, dry texture. It is usually spiced with caraway seeds; varieties flavored with cumin and cloves or a mixture of the three spices are also available. Leyden is made in cylinder shapes, is colored with annatto dye, and has a dark yellow rind covered in red wax stamped with two crossed keys, the symbol of the Dutch city of Leyden.

Lima Bean A bean with pale green or white slightly kidney-shaped seeds. They are mainly used in

their dried form (added to soups and casseroles or served in salads), although they can also be cooked fresh as a vegetable. The lima bean does not come from Lima, in Peru, but from Guatemala. It is available fresh, dried, canned and frozen.

Limburger Cheese A semisoft cow's milk

CHINESE LEMON CHICKEN

Preparation time: 15 minutes
Total cooking time: 1 hour 10 minutes
Serves 4

3¼ lb chicken
1 tablespoon soy sauce
1 tablespoon dry sherry
1 tablespoon lemon juice
2 teaspoons soft brown
 sugar

Lemon Sauce
2 scallions

½ cup lemon juice
½ cup sugar
2 teaspoons dry sherry
1 teaspoon soy sauce
1 tablespoon cornstarch
½ cup water
salt and white pepper, to
 taste

1 Preheat oven to moderate 350°F. Remove the giblets and any large deposits of fat from the chicken. Wipe chicken, pat dry with paper towels. Tie the wings and drumsticks securely in place. Place the chicken on a rack in a baking dish. Brush with combined soy sauce, sherry, juice and sugar.
2 Bake the chicken for 1 hour or until the juices run clear when the flesh is pierced with a skewer. Baste occasionally with remaining soy mixture. Remove from oven, leave covered with foil 10 minutes. Remove string before serving hot with Lemon Sauce.
3 To make Lemon Sauce: Cut the scallions into long thin strips; place in iced water until curly. Combine lemon juice, sugar, sherry and sauce in pan. Blend the cornstarch with water in a bowl until smooth. Add to pan. Stir over medium heat 4 minutes or until sauce boils and thickens slightly. Season to taste; stir in scallions.

LEMONADE

Preparation time: 15 minutes
Total cooking time: 15 minutes
Serves 6

6 lemons
1½ cups sugar
6 cups water

ice cubes, for serving
lemon slices, for serving

1 Wash and dry lemons. Using a potato peeler remove the peel very thinly from three of the lemons. Place peel in a medium pan, add sugar and half of the water. Cover and simmer gently for 15 minutes. Allow to cool.
2 Squeeze juice from all of the lemons and strain into a large jug. Strain syrup over lemon juice and add remaining water, stirring to combine. Cover and chill.
3 Serve lemonade in glasses, over ice cubes. Float lemon slices on top.

LEMON BUTTER

Preparation time: 10 minutes
Total cooking time: 15 minutes
Makes about 2 cups

3 eggs, beaten
1 cup sugar
1 tablespoon grated lemon
 rind

½ cup lemon juice
¼ cup butter, chopped

1 Combine all ingredients in a heatproof bowl. Whisk constantly over simmering water until mixture thickens and coats the back of a metal spoon.
2 Remove from heat and pour into warm, sterilized jars. When cool, label and date. Store in the refrigerator until required.

SEMOLINA CAKE WITH LEMON SYRUP

★ **Preparation time:** 30 minutes
Total cooking time: 1 hour
Serves 6–8

1 cup unsalted butter
1 cup sugar
3 eggs, lightly beaten
1 teaspoon vanilla extract
1 cup fine ground semolina
3/4 cup flaked coconut
1 1/2 cups all-purpose flour

1 teaspoon baking powder
1/4 teaspoon salt

Lemon Syrup
1 cup sugar
1 cup water
1 lemon, thinly sliced

1 Preheat oven to 350°F. Brush a deep 9 inch springform pan with melted butter or oil. Line base and sides with parchment paper; grease paper. Beat butter and sugar in small mixing bowl 10 minutes. Add eggs gradually, beating thoroughly after each addition. Add vanilla and semolina; beat 5 minutes.
2 Transfer to large mixing bowl; add coconut. Fold in flour, baking powder and salt. Stir until combined and mixture is smooth.
3 Spoon mixture into pan; smooth surface. Bake 55–60 minutes or until a skewer comes out clean. Pour syrup over hot cake in pan. When cold, remove paper. Serve with lemon slices and whipped cream.
4 To make Lemon Syrup: In a pan, stir sugar and water over low heat until sugar dissolves; add lemon. Bring to boil, reduce heat, simmer uncovered, without stirring 15 minutes. Remove lemon slices for garnish; cool syrup before serving.

CHOCOLATE LEMON SWIRLS

★ **Preparation time:** 10 minutes
Total cooking time: 12 minutes
Makes 60

1/2 cup unsalted (sweet) butter
2/3 cup confectioners' sugar
1 egg, lightly beaten
2 teaspoons grated lemon rind

1 1/2 cups all-purpose flour
1/3 cup unsweetened cocoa powder
2 tablespoons finely chopped mixed citrus peel

1 Preheat oven to moderate 350°F. Line a 13 x 11 inch baking sheet with parchment paper. Using electric beaters, beat butter and sugar until light and creamy. Add egg and rind, beat until well combined.
2 Add sifted flour and cocoa. Using a metal spoon, stir until ingredients are just combined and mixture is almost smooth.
3 Spoon mixture into a piping bag fitted with a fluted 1/2 inch wide piping nozzle; pipe swirls about 1 inch in diameter onto prepared baking sheet. Top each swirl with mixed peel. Bake for 12 minutes; cool on tray.

Note: Chocolate Lemon Swirls may be stored in an airtight container for up to two days.

OPPOSITE PAGE, BELOW: LEMON BUTTER; ABOVE: CHINESE LEMON CHICKEN. LEFT: SEMOLINA CAKE; ABOVE: CHOCOLATE LEMON SWIRLS

cheese with a powerful aroma, distinctive, tangy taste, and a yellow, creamy textured interior covered by a thin, red-brown rind. Limburger cheese should be served at room temperature accompanied by dark bread and strong-flavored vegetables such as onion and radish.

Lime A green-skinned citrus fruit about the size of a

small lemon with tart greenish-yellow pulp. Its juice and grated zest adds a piquant flavor to both sweet dishes (ice creams, sorbets, mousses, soufflés and pie fillings) and savory dishes (curries and stews, especially chicken and fish). It is cooked as marmalade and its juice is used in cordial and other drinks. The lime is native to the tropics and is often used in the cooking of those regions; the Spanish introduced it to the Caribbean in the sixteenth century. In South America and the Pacific Islands lime juice is used to "cook" raw fish in the dish ceviche. Its sharpness in key lime pie (named for the lime variety that grows semi-wild on the Florida Keys) gives a truly agreeable bite to the sweet creamy filling. Pickled lime is served with meat and fish dishes; the peel can be candied (crystallized) for a garnish. Fresh limes are available all year long.

Linzer Torte A rich jam tart consisting of a cinnamon and nut–flavored shortbread base filled

with raspberry jam and covered with a lattice of pastry strips. It is served in thin wedges. The linzer torte takes its name from the Austrian town of Linz.

Liqueur An alcoholic syrup distilled from wine or brandy and flavored with fruit, herbs or spices. Liqueurs are available in a wide variety of flavors and alcoholic content. Crème de cacao is made from the cocoa bean, kümmel is flavored with caraway seed and ouzo with

aniseed. Cointreau gets its strong orange tang from orange peel, while many other fruit liqueurs are made by macerating the fruit with spirit and adding sugar. Some liqueurs are flavored with herbs or spices. Liqueurs are used to flavor a range of sweet

L E M O N   M E R I N G U E   P I E

★ ★   **Preparation time:** 40 minutes +
1 hour chilling time
Total cooking time: 22–25 minutes
Serves 8

Pastry
1¹/2 cups all-purpose
  flour
1 tablespoon sugar
¹/2 cup butter, chopped
1 egg yolk
1–2 tablespoon cold
water

Filling
¹/2 cup sugar
¹/2 cup cornstarch

1¹/2 cups water
3 eggs yolks
1 tablespoon butter
2 teaspoons finely
  shredded lemon rind
¹/2 cup lemon juice

Meringue
3 egg whites
¹/2 teaspoon vanilla
  extract
¹/4 teaspoon cream of

1 To make Pastry: Combine flour and sugar. Cut in the butter until mixture resembles coarse crumbs. Stir together egg yolk and cold water. Add to flour mixture, stir to form a firm dough. Wrap and chill for 1 hour. On a floured surface, flatten dough with hands, roll into a circle about 12 inches in diameter. Place in a 9 inch pie plate, trim, fold under pastry. Flute edge. Prick with a fork. Bake in a 450°F oven 10 minutes. Cool.

2 To make Filling: Combine sugar and cornstarch in a saucepan. Stir in water. Cook and stir until thick and bubbly. Cook and stir 2 minutes more. Remove from heat. Beat egg yolks slightly. Gradually add 1 cup of hot mixture to egg yolks; return all to saucepan. Bring to a gentle boil. Cook and stir for 2 minutes. Remove from heat; stir in butter and lemon rind. Gradually stir in lemon juice, gently mixing.

3 To make Meringue: In a bowl, beat egg whites, vanilla and cream of tartar until soft peaks form. Gradually add the sugar, 1 tablespoon at a time, until stiff peaks form and sugar dissolves.

4 Pour hot filling into baked pastry shell. Spread meringue over hot filling; seal to edge. Bake in a 350°F oven for 12–15 minutes or until golden. Cool on a wire rack. Cover; chill to store.

Note: To bake a flan "blind," line pierced pastry with parchment paper, waxed paper or foil. Fill with dry beans, rice or ceramic baking beads to weigh down pastry. Bake pastry until firm, then remove weights and paper. Return flan to oven and continue baking until pastry is evenly browned.

ABOVE: LEMON MERINGUE PIE. OPPOSITE PAGE, BELOW: WARM LENTIL AND RICE SALAD; ABOVE: SPICY CREAMED LENTILS

LENTILS

WARM LENTIL AND RICE SALAD

★★ **Preparation time:** 15 minutes
Total cooking time: 50 minutes
Serves 6

1 cup brown lentils	2 teaspoons ground
1 cup Basmati rice	cinnamon
4 large red onions, finely	2 teaspoons sweet paprika
sliced	2 teaspoons ground cumin
4 cloves garlic, crushed	2 teaspoons ground
1 cup olive oil	coriander
3 tablespoons butter	3 scallions, chopped
	ground pepper

1 Cook the lentils and rice in separate pans of water until grains are just tender; drain.
2 Cook the onion and garlic in oil and butter for 30 minutes, on low heat until very soft.
3 Stir in the cinnamon, paprika, cumin and coriander and cook for another few minutes.
4 Combine the onion and spice mixture with the well-drained rice and lentils. Stir in chopped scallions until combined and add ground pepper, to taste. Serve warm.

Note: Do not use red lentils, which become mushy very quickly and do not retain their shape. Rinse brown lentils thoroughly before using them for cooking.

SPICY CREAMED LENTILS

★ **Preparation time:** 5 minutes
Total cooking time: 45 minutes
Serves 4

1 cup red lentils	1/2 teaspoon turmeric
2 tablespoons ghee or oil	2 1/2 cups water
1 large onion, finely	1/2 teaspoon salt
sliced	1 teaspoon garam masala
2 teaspoons finely	fresh cilantro sprigs, for
chopped garlic	garnish
1 teaspoon finely chopped	
ginger	

1 Wash lentils and drain thoroughly. Heat ghee in a pan. Add the onion, garlic and ginger and cook until soft and golden. Add turmeric and drained lentils, cook 1–2 minutes.
2 Add water and bring to the boil, reduce heat to a simmer. Add the salt and cook lentil mixture, uncovered, for 15 minutes.
3 Add the garam masala and cook for another 15 minutes until lentils are soft and most of the liquid has evaporated. Garnish with sprigs of fresh cilantro and serve with rice or bread.

ABOUT LENTILS

■ Red lentils are sold split and require no soaking. They will soften and become mushy after 20 minutes or so, and are used in soups, purées and casseroles.
■ Green and brown lentils (sometimes known as continental lentils) take longer to cook than red lentils—up to 1 1/2 hours depending on their age—and can be soaked in cold water for 2 hours before using to shorten the cooking time.

dishes and savory dishes; they are also served in special small glasses to be sipped with coffee.

Littleneck Clam A small hardshell clam that is used in soups or eaten raw on the half shell.

Liver Classed as a variety meat, the liver of lamb, sheep, calf, steer, pig, poultry and game are eaten. Liver is the organ that purifies the blood of an animal. It is a red-brown meat with a distinctive flavor. To prepare liver for cooking, first wash and pat dry; remove the thin outer skin and cut away any fat, gristle and veining. Slice thinly and cook until the pink color disappears (do not overcook as the meat toughens easily). Liver can be fried, broiled, braised or cooked in a casserole. Calve's liver or lamb's liver sautéed with onions and bacon is a popular dish. Goose and chicken liver are used to make pâté.

Liverwurst A soft sausage containing a smooth mixture of liver, ground pork, garlic, onion and seasonings. Liverwurst is used as a spread on bread or crackers and can also be added to stuffings. It has a long history in many regions of

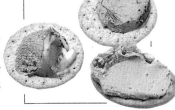

Europe and was often used to garnish roast meats on festive occasions.

Lobster A large saltwater crustacean related to the crayfish and crab. The shell of the living lobster is bluish green to pinkish brown, depending on the species; the shell of the cooked lobster is bright red. The lobster has a pair of huge claws that are actually modified legs, and uses its tail to move through the water in quick, backward movements. Lobster can be boiled or broiled. The cooked meat is firm textured, white, sweet and moist; it is usually served in the shell with various sauces. The coral-colored roe, sometimes called coral butter,

present in female lobsters, is considered a delicacy and should either be served with the meat or added to the sauce. Most of the meat is in the claws and the tail; use a nutcracker to break open the claws. Live lobsters are available throughout the year. Keep live lobsters moist by covering them with damp towels or keeping them in ice in an

LIMES

LEMON-LIME PIE

★ ★   ***Preparation time:*** 1 hour + overnight standing
Total cooking time: 1 hour
Makes 9 inch round flan

¼ cup rice flour
⅔ cup all-purpose flour
2 tablespoons confectioners' sugar
1 tablespoon sugar
¼ cup flaked coconut
¼ cup ground almonds
½ cup chilled unsalted (sweet) butter, chopped

Filling
2 tablespoons cornstarch
½ cup sugar

¼ cup lemon juice
¼ cup lime juice
½ cup sour cream
1 cup cream, whipped

Candied Rind
1 cup sugar
¼ cup water
rind of 3 lemons
rind of 3 limes

1 Preheat the oven to moderate 350°F. Brush the inside of a shallow, 9 inch round fluted flan pan with melted butter. Coat the base and sides with flour; shake off the excess. Place the flours, sugars, coconut, almonds and butter in food processor. Process for 20 seconds or until the mixture has a fine, crumbly texture. Process for another 10–15 seconds. Turn the pastry onto a lightly floured surface, knead for 5 minutes or until smooth.

Refrigerate, covered, for 15 minutes.
2 Press the pastry evenly to cover the base and sides of the prepared pan. Cover the pastry with a sheet of wax paper. Spread a layer of dried beans or rice evenly over the paper. Bake for 15 minutes. Remove from the oven; discard the paper and beans or rice. Return to the oven for another 8–10 minutes or until the pastry is very lightly golden. Stand pastry in the pan on a wire rack to cool.
3 To make Filling: Combine the cornstarch, sugar and lemon and lime juice in a medium, heavy-bottom pan. Cook over a low heat, stirring constantly, until the mixture boils and thickens; remove from heat. Cool slightly. Transfer the mixture to a bowl. Using a metal spoon, stir in the sour cream until smooth. Fold in the whipped cream. Stir until the mixture is smooth. Pour the mixture into the pastry shell; smooth surface. Refrigerate overnight.
4 To make Candied Rind: Combine the sugar and water in a heavy-based pan. Stir over low heat without boiling until the sugar has dissolved. Add the lemon and lime rind, bring to boil, reduce heat, simmer for 10 minutes. Remove from heat, cool. Drain rind and reserve syrup. Decorate outer edge with whipped cream, place candied rind over cream. Serve with syrup.

ABOVE: LEMON-LIME PIE.

OPPOSITE PAGE: CEVICHE

LIME PIE

★★ **Preparation time:** 40 minutes +
20 minutes standing
Total cooking time: 30–35 minutes
Serves 6–8

1⅓ cups all-purpose
 flour
1 teaspoon confectioners'
 sugar
6 tablespoons butter,
 chopped
1 egg yolk
1–2 tablespoons iced

water

Filling
2 eggs, separated
½ cup sweetened
 condensed milk
finely grated rind of
 2 limes

1 Place flour, sugar and butter in food processor. Process 30 seconds or until mixture is fine and crumbly. Add egg yolk and almost all the water and process 20 seconds or until mixture just comes together when squeezed. Add more water if necessary. Turn onto lightly floured surface and knead gently to form a smooth dough. Cover with plastic wrap and refrigerate for 20 minutes.
2 Preheat oven to 325°F. Brush a 9 inch fluted round flan pan or dish with melted butter or oil. Roll pastry between two sheets of baking paper large enough to cover the base and sides of prepared tin. Ease pastry into pan; trim edges with rolling pin or sharp knife. Cut a sheet of wax paper to cover pastry-lined pan. Line pan with paper and spread a layer of dried beans or

rice evenly over paper. Bake for 10 minutes, remove from oven and discard paper and beans or rice. Bake for another 7 minutes or until lightly golden; cool.
3 To make Filling: Using electric beaters, beat egg yolks in a medium bowl until thick and creamy. Gradually add condensed milk in a thin stream. Continue beating until mixture is thick and pale. Add rind; mix well. Gradually beat in juice until combined. Beat egg whites in separate bowl until soft peaks form. Using a metal spoon, fold egg whites into yolk mixture. Stir until smooth. Spoon mixture into prepared pastry base. Bake 15–20 minutes or until filling is set and top is lightly golden. Serve cool or chilled, with whipped cream. Dust pie with sifted powdered (confectioners') sugar to serve, if preferred.

CEVICHE

★ **Preparation time:** 20 minutes +
2 hours marinating
Total cooking time: none
Serves 4

1½ lb white fish fillets
3 onions, thinly sliced
3 cloves garlic, crushed
1 small red chili pepper,
 finely chopped
¾ cup lime juice
1 teaspoon salt
1 teaspoon ground pepper

Garnish
3 tomatoes, sliced
1 large green pepper,
 chopped
4 hard-boiled eggs,
 quartered

1 Wash and skin the fish fillets. Cut into thin strips. Place in a bowl. Add onion, garlic and chili pepper.
2 Place juice, salt and pepper in a small bowl; whisk to combine. Pour over fish. Marinate for 2 hours, covered, in refrigerator. The fish is ready when the flesh turns white.
3 Serve the fish accompanied by sliced tomato, chopped pepper and quartered hard-boiled eggs.

ABOUT LIMES
■ Buy limes with dark green skins—yellowish limes are over-mature and without tang. Limes will perish quickly; store at room temperature for a week, then keep in the refrigerator.

■ Use limes in sweet or savory dishes as a sweeter, milder substitute for lemons. Lime juice may be used as a marinade for meat and fish. Grated lime peel is delicious in sherbets, sorbets and ice cream.

■ Make curls, knots or spirals from the rind of limes to use as a decoration for summer drinks.

insulated bag until ready to use. They are also available frozen and uncooked, either whole or as tails. Pre-cooked lobsters should have bright eyes, a curled tail and all limbs intact; pre-cooked tails are also available. Cooked meat is sold frozen or in cans.

Loganberry A large, soft, pink to red berry fruit. The loganberry is a hybrid between the blackberry, from which it takes its shape, and the raspberry, from which it takes its flavor. It was developed in the 1880s by Scottish-born Californian judge and amateur horticulturist James H. Logan. The loganberry can be eaten fresh, served topped with whipped cream, ice cream or liqueur, puréed or cooked as a filling for pies or as jam.

London Broil A beef flank steak that has been marinated, broiled or grilled, and thinly sliced.

Longan An oval-shaped fruit of Asian origin. It is similar to the lychee, but smaller, and has dull, red-brown skin and sweet, firm, translucent flesh surrounding a dark brown pit. Longans can be eaten fresh, added to fruit salad or poached in sweet and savory dishes. They are in season in summer and are also available canned (preserved in

syrup) and dried. Dried longan can be added to braised meats and sweet and sour Chinese dishes. The fruit's Chinese name *lung-yen* means "dragon's eye."

Long Grain Rice Rice with a long grain such as Carolina or basmati rice.

Loquat The pear-shaped fruit of a small evergreen tree native to Asia and now widely grown in Mediterranean lands. It is the size of a small plum with glossy yellow-orange skin and crisp, juicy, tart-sweet yellow flesh. It can be eaten fresh on its own, added to fruit salads or other desserts (in Asia it is often set in a jelly of agar-agar) or cooked as jellies and jam.

Lord Baltimore Cake A yellow three-layer sponge cake filled with nuts and cherries, and covered with a fluffy white frosting.

Lotus A type of water lily native to China and India. All parts of the plant are edible, but it is the crunchy, reddish root that is most widely used. It can be stir-fried, braised, coated in batter and deep-fried or simmered in stock. Lotus seeds can be used as a filling for Japanese and

L O B S T E R S

L O B S T E R   M O R N A Y

Preparation time: 15 minutes
Total cooking time: 20 minutes
Serves 2

1 medium cooked lobster, halved	¼ cup heavy cream
1¼ cups milk	½ cup grated Cheddar cheese
1 bay leaf	salt and ground white pepper
1 onion, chopped	1 tablespoon butter, melted, extra
6 peppercorns	
2 tablespoons butter	½ cup fresh white bread crumbs
2 tablespoons all-purpose flour	

1 Remove tail meat from lobster and reserve shells. Cut lobster into cubes and set aside.
2 Place milk in a pan with bay leaf, onion and peppercorns. Heat slowly to boiling point. Remove from heat; leave, covered, 10 minutes.
3 In a separate pan, melt butter and remove from heat. Stir in flour and blend in strained, hot milk. Return pan to heat and stir continuously until sauce boils and thickens. Simmer sauce for 1 minute. Remove from heat, add cream, cheese, salt and pepper. Stir sauce until cheese melts and add lobster to sauce.
4 Divide lobster mixture between shells and place shells in a shallow heatproof dish. Melt extra butter in a small pan and add bread crumbs,

stirring lightly to combine. Scatter crumbs over filling and cook under a broiler until crumbs are golden brown and filling is hot.

C H I L L E D   L O B S T E R   W I T H   H O M E M A D E   S E A F O O D   S A U C E

Preparation time: 20 minutes + chilling time
Total cooking time: none
Serves 4

2 x 2 lb cooked lobsters	2 tablespoons tomato paste
1½ cups homemade mayonnaise	½ cup sour cream
1 tablespoon Worcestershire sauce	1 teaspoon horseradish cream
	¼ teaspoon dry mustard

1 Cut lobsters in half lengthwise. Wash inside lightly and remove tail meat.
2 Cut tail meat into medallions and return to each tail shell. Cover and place in refrigerator to chill well before serving.
3 Combine remaining ingredients for sauce. Serve half a lobster with sauce to each person.

ABOVE: LOBSTER MORNAY. OPPOSITE PAGE, BELOW: LOBSTER MEDALLIONS IN HOISIN MARINADE; ABOVE: BARBECUED LOBSTER TAILS WITH AVOCADO SAUCE

BARBECUED LOBSTER TAILS WITH AVOCADO SAUCE

★ ★ **Preparation time:** 15 minutes + 3 hours marinating
Total cooking time: 10 minutes
Serves 4

1/4 cup dry white wine
1 tablespoon honey
1 teaspoon sambal oelek (bottled chopped chilies)
1 clove garlic, crushed
1 tablespoon olive oil
4 fresh green lobster tails, about 13 oz

Avocado Sauce
1 medium ripe avocado, mashed
3 teaspoons lemon juice
2 tablespoons sour cream
1 small tomato, chopped finely
salt and pepper, to taste

1 Combine the wine, honey, sambal oelek, garlic and olive oil in a jug and mix well. Using a sharp knife or kitchen scissors, cut along the soft shell on the underside of the lobster. Gently pull the shell apart and ease the raw flesh out with fingers.
2 Place the lobster flesh in a shallow non-metal dish. Pour the marinade over the lobster and stir well. Cover and refrigerate for several hours or overnight. Prepare and light the barbecue. Cook the lobster tails on a hot lightly greased barbecue grill for 5–10 minutes, turning frequently. Brush lobster tails with the marinade until they are cooked through. Slice into medallions and serve with Avocado Sauce and a green salad if desired.

3 To make Avocado Sauce: Combine the avocado, juice and sour cream in a bowl; mix well. Add chopped tomato and mix to combine with avocado mixture; add salt and pepper, to taste.

LOBSTER MEDALLIONS IN HOISIN MARINADE

★ **Preparation time:** 20 minutes + 1 hour marinating
Total cooking time: 15 minutes
Serves 4

3 lb cooked lobster tails
1 bunch asparagus, cut into 1 1/2 inch lengths

Marinade
1/2 cup hoisin sauce
3 tablespoons tomato paste
2 tablespoons lemon juice
2 tablespoons honey
2 tablespoons soy sauce

1 Preheat oven to 350°F. Remove the flesh from lobster tails. Discard the shells. Cut the tails into medallions approximately 1/2 inch thick.
2 Place the lobster medallions in a shallow ovenproof dish. Combine the marinade ingredients and pour over the lobster. Cover and refrigerate for 1 hour.
3 Steam the asparagus until just tender. Add to lobster.
4 Place the dish in oven and cook for 10 minutes or until heated through. Serve immediately.

Chinese pastries and cakes. Dried leaves are used as food wrappers. Lotus root is available fresh and canned; seeds are dried and canned.

Lox Cured and smoked salmon, thinly sliced.

Luau A traditional Hawaiian feast with roast pig. It includes dancing.

Lychee (Litchi) A small oval fruit about the size of a

large cherry with sweet, pale pink flesh similar in flavor to a grape, and thin, bumpy, reddish skin. It has a shiny brown pit. Lychees can be eaten fresh, added to fruit salads and served as a dessert with whipped cream or ice cream; poached, they can be added to both sweet and savory dishes. Lychees are in season in summer; the fruit is also available canned and

dried. The lychee is native to southern China and has been cultivated there for 4,000 years.

Lyonnaise, à la
A French term for food cooked with chopped and sautéed onions, a style characteristic of the Lyonnaise region of eastern France.

M

Macadamia Nut The round, hard-shelled, creamy-meat nut of a tree grown in Australia and Hawaii. Fresh or roasted nuts are eaten as a snack; crushed nuts can be added to ice cream or used in cookies, cakes or breads; whole nuts are coated with chocolate as a candy.

Macaroni Pasta in the form of short, dried, hollow tubes.

Macaroon A small, round drop cookie, crunchy on the outside and soft and moist on the inside, made from ground almonds mixed with sugar and egg white; coconut is often added. Macaroons originated in France and are a specialty of the Nancy region.

Mace The fibrous, lacy skin that envelops the nutmeg, but which has its own distinctive flavor and is used as a spice. It is made up of numerous tendrils called blades; the spice is also sold in ground

CHICKEN CURRY WITH MANGO AND CREAM

★ **Preparation time:** 10 minutes
Total cooking time: 20 minutes
Serves 4

1½ lb boneless chicken breasts, skin removed
2 tablespoons ghee or oil
2 large onions, finely sliced
2 red chili peppers, seeded and sliced
1 teaspoon grated fresh ginger
¼ teaspoon saffron threads
1 tablespoon hot water
½ teaspoon salt
¼ teaspoon ground white pepper

½ teaspoon ground cardamom
½ cup heavy cream
2 ripe mangoes

Mint and Yogurt Raita
1 cup plain yogurt
¼ cup finely chopped fresh mint leaves
1 green chili pepper, seeded and chopped
1 teaspoon finely chopped ginger
½ teaspoon salt

1 Wash chicken under cold water. Pat dry with paper towels. Cut chicken into 1¼ inch wide strips. Heat ghee in a pan, add onion, chili and ginger and cook until onion is soft.
2 Heat saffron in a dry pan over low heat until it is crisp, stirring constantly. Cool. Place saffron in a bowl, crush with the back of a spoon. Add hot water to dissolve. Add chicken strips, salt, pepper and cardamom to the onion mixture in the pan and stir to coat chicken with spices. Add saffron and cream to pan. Simmer, uncovered, for 10 minutes.

3 Peel mangoes and slice flesh from the pit. Add to the pan and cook for another 4 minutes until mango is heated through and slightly softened.
4 To make Mint and Yogurt Raita: Mix ingredients together. Serve chilled.

HOT CARAMEL MANGO

★ **Preparation time:** 20 minutes
Total cooking time: 5 minutes
Serves 6

3 large mangoes
¾ cup heavy cream

2 tablespoons soft brown sugar
1 tablespoon sugar

1 Peel the mangoes. Cut the mango flesh into thin slices. Arrange the slices in six individual ramekin dishes. Pour the cream evenly over each dish and sprinkle with the combined brown and white sugars.
2 Preheat the broiler. Broil dishes 5–6 inches from the heat for 5 minutes or until the sugar has caramelized and the mango is warm. Serve immediately, with a wafer cookie or tuille.

ABOUT MANGOES

■ Mangoes continue to ripen after picking so unless using immediately, choose mangoes that are slightly green and firm.

LEFT: HOT CARAMEL MANGO; ABOVE: CHICKEN CURRY WITH MANGO AND CREAM. OPPOSITE PAGE, BELOW: SPLIT PEA SOUP WITH MEATBALLS; ABOVE: HERB MEATBALLS WITH RICH TOMATO SAUCE

MEATBALLS

HERB MEATBALLS WITH RICH TOMATO SAUCE

Preparation time: 40 minutes
Total cooking time: 10–15 minutes
Makes about 45

1 medium onion, finely
    chopped
1 1/2 lb ground beef
1 egg, lightly beaten
2 cloves garlic, crushed
2 teaspoons cracked black
    pepper
1/4 teaspoon salt
2 tablespoons plum sauce
1 tablespoon
    Worcestershire sauce
2 tablespoons finely
    chopped fresh rosemary

1–2 tablespoons finely
    chopped fresh mint or
    sweet basil
oil for frying

Rich Tomato Sauce
1 1/2 cups red wine
1 clove garlic, crushed
3/4 cup tomato purée
1/3 cup chunky bottled
    spaghetti sauce
2–3 teaspoons Dijon
    mustard
2 tablespoons butter,
    chopped

1 Combine onion, beef, egg, garlic, pepper, salt, sauces and herbs in a bowl. Use hands to combine well. Shape level tablespoons of mixture into balls.
2 Heat oil in a large frying pan. Cook meatballs in batches over medium heat for 5 minutes or until browned. Shake pan during cooking to prevent sticking. Drain on paper towels. Keep warm.
3 To make Rich Tomato Sauce: Drain oil

from pan, add wine and garlic to pan juices. Bring to boil, reduce heat, simmer to reduce liquid by half. Strain into medium pan. Add tomato purée, sauce and mustard. Bring to boil, reduce heat and reduce liquid by half. Gradually whisk in butter.

SPLIT PEA SOUP WITH MEATBALLS

Preparation time: 1 hour 30 minutes
Total cooking time: 1 hour 30 minutes
Serves 6

2 cups green split peas
6 cups chicken stock or
    water
1/2 cup chopped celery
1 large onion, chopped
1/2 teaspoon dried
    marjoram
1/4 teaspoon pepper
1 lb ground pork and veal

2 slices bacon, chopped
2 tablespoons chopped
    fresh parsley
2 teaspoons grated lemon
    rind
1/2 teaspoon dried sage
3 potatoes, peeled and
    diced
juice of 1 lemon

1 Wash peas in cold water. Drain, place in large pot, add stock or water, celery, onion, marjoram and pepper. Bring to boil. Reduce heat, cover, simmer 1 hour or until peas are tender. Do not drain.
2 Combine ground pork and veal, bacon, parsley, lemon rind and sage. Mix well with hand. Using wet hands, shape into walnut-sized balls.
3 Gently drop meatballs and potatoes into the soup mixture. Return soup to boiling. Reduce heat, cover and simmer for 20–30 minutes or until meatballs and potatoes are cooked. Add lemon juice to taste before serving.

form. Blade mace is used to flavor clear soups, jellies and pale sauces; ground mace is used to season English potted meats, pork dishes and béchamel sauce.

Mackerel A saltwater fish with oily, dark, firm-textured flesh. It can be baked, broiled, pan-fried and poached.

Madeira Cake A rich cake flavored with lemon or orange juice and baked with a slice of citron peel on top. In Victorian England the cake was traditionally served with a glass of Madeira wine.

Madeleine Small cake baked in shell-shaped mold and often served dusted with finely powdered sugar. They are a specialty of the town of Commercy, in northeastern France.

Madrilène A clear soup (chicken or vegetable) thickened and flavored with tomato pulp and usually served chilled.

Maître d'Hôtel Butter Softened butter mixed with chopped parsley, lemon juice and freshly ground white pepper, then chilled until firm. It

is served on top of broiled steak and fish.

Maize See Corn.

Malt The term given to a grain, usually barley, which has been soaked, sprouted, roasted and crushed. During this process the starch content of the grain is converted by partial fermentation into sugar. Further processing of malt produces beer; distillation results in whiskey. Malt extract, which comes in syrup or dried form, can be added to drinks, cakes, bread dough and puddings.

Mandarin Orange A small, loose-skinned category of citrus fruit with sweet, juicy, easily separated segments. They can be eaten as a

fruit, used in fruit salad or made into marmalade. The most common mandarin found in the United States is the tangerine.

Mango A tropical fruit with juicy, sweet, golden flesh clinging to a large pit. Mangoes are delicious eaten fresh; perhaps the least messy way is to slice a cheek from each side of the pit and score the flesh into small squares, then push the skin upwards

SPAGHETTI AND MEATBALLS

✯✯ **Preparation time:** 25 minutes
Total cooking time: 50 minutes
Serves 6

Sauce
1 tablespoon oil
1 small onion, chopped
14½ oz can diced
    tomatoes
4 tablespoons tomato
    paste
½ cup water
½ cup dry red wine
1 small clove garlic,
    crushed
1 bay leaf
pinch black pepper

Meatballs
½ cup milk
1 cup soft bread crumbs

1 lb ground beef
1 small onion, very finely
    chopped
1 tablespoon grated
    Parmesan cheese
1 egg, beaten
1 tablespoon chopped
    fresh parsley
pinch black pepper
¼ teaspoon dried oregano
    leaves

4 tablespoons oil
1 lb spaghetti
grated Parmesan cheese,
    to serve

1 To make Sauce: Heat oil in a pan. Add onion and fry until soft. Add remaining sauce ingredients and simmer for 20 minutes until thick, stirring occasionally.

2 To make Meatballs: Add the milk to bread crumbs, leave for 5 minutes. Combine the soaked bread crumbs with remaining meatball ingredients. Form into balls, brown on all sides in 3 tablespoons hot oil. Add to the sauce and simmer gently for about 15 minutes. Remove bay leaf.

3 Bring a pan of water to the boil, add remaining oil. Add spaghetti, cook 10–12 minutes. Drain. Spoon meatballs and sauce over spaghetti and serve with grated Parmesan cheese.

MEATBALLS IN SHERRY SAUCE

✯ **Preparation time:** 35 minutes
Total cooking time: 30 minutes
Serves 4–6

1 lb ground pork and
    veal
½ cup fresh white bread
    crumbs
¼ cup chopped fresh
    parsley
2 cloves garlic, crushed
2 teaspoons sweet paprika
2 tablespoons olive oil
2 tablespoons butter
1 medium onion, finely
    chopped

1 teaspoon sweet paprika,
    extra
1 tablespoon all-purpose
    flour
½ cup dry or sweet
    sherry
1 cup chicken stock
10 small new potatoes
¼ cup chopped fresh
    parsley, extra

1 Combine meat, bread crumbs, parsley, garlic and paprika in a medium bowl. Mix well. Using wet hands, roll the mixture into meatballs the size of walnuts.

2 Heat the oil and butter in a medium pan; add meatballs. Cook over medium-high heat for 3–4 minutes until well browned. Remove from pan; drain.

3 Add onion, paprika and flour to pan and cook, stirring, for 2 minutes. Add sherry and stock gradually to pan, stirring until mixture is smooth. Stir constantly over medium heat 2 minutes or until sauce boils and thickens.

4 Return meatballs to pan, add potatoes. Cover, cook over low heat 20 minutes. Serve with parsley.

M E A T L O A V E S

G O U R M E T   M E A T L O A F

⭐ **Preparation time:** 20 minutes
Total cooking time: 1 hour 20 minutes
Serves 6

1 lb ground pork and veal	1 tablespoon green peppercorns, drained, chopped
1/2 lb ground sausage	
1 1/2 cups fresh white bread crumbs	2 tablespoons chopped fresh mint
1 small green pepper, chopped	2 teaspoons sweet paprika
1 medium onion, finely chopped	1 tablespoon toasted sesame seeds
2 cloves garlic, crushed	**Tomato Cream Sauce**
1/2 cup bottled spaghetti sauce	1 1/2 cups bottled spaghetti sauce
1/2 cup fruit chutney	1/2 cup heavy cream
1 egg, lightly beaten	1 tablespoon seeded mustard
1/2 cup chopped dried apricots	

1 Grease a 9 x 5 inch loaf pan. Preheat oven to moderate 350°F. Combine ground pork and veal and ground sausage in a bowl. Add bread crumbs, pepper, onion, garlic, tomato sauce, chutney, egg, apricots, peppercorns, mint and paprika, mix.
2 Press prepared mixture into loaf pan, bake, uncovered, 1 hour 15 minutes. Carefully pour off the juices. Turn out the meatloaf and sprinkle with sesame seeds. Slice meatloaf and serve

OPPOSITE PAGE, ABOVE: SPAGHETTI AND MEATBALLS; BELOW: MEATBALLS IN SHERRY SAUCE. ABOVE: GOURMET MEATLOAF

with Tomato Cream Sauce.
3 To make Tomato Cream Sauce: Combine all the ingredients in a pan. Bring to boil. Reduce the heat and simmer 3 minutes stirring occasionally.

B E E F   A N D   P I M I E N T O   L O A F   W I T H   C H E E S E

⭐⭐ **Preparation time:** 20 minutes
Total cooking time: 1 hour
Serves 6

2 lb ground beef	2 garlic cloves, crushed
2 cups fresh white bread crumbs	1 egg, lightly beaten
	1 cup chopped pimiento
1/4 cup tomato paste	1/3 cup chopped fresh basil
1 tablespoon dry mustard powder	2 tablespoons chopped black olives
2 teaspoons dried mixed herbs	8 oz ricotta cheese
	4 oz feta cheese

1 Preheat oven to moderate 350°F. Line a 4-3/4 x 5-1/2 x 2-3/4 inch loaf pan with aluminum foil. Combine beef in a large bowl with bread crumbs, tomato paste, mustard, mixed herbs, garlic and egg. Divide into 3 portions.
2 Combine pimiento, basil and olives.
3 Press 1 portion of the meat mixture evenly over the base of the pan. Top with half the pimiento mixture. Top with another portion of meat, then the remaining pimiento mixture, then the remaining meat mixture. Bake for 1 hour or until cooked through. Drain off liquid, stand loaf for 5 minutes, turn out, serve sliced.
4 Combine ricotta cheese and crumbled feta cheese; serve as an accompaniment to sliced loaf.

so that the cubes bristle like a porcupine. Mango is cooked in curries and other savory dishes (it goes well with chicken) and is made into chutney and pickles which are often served with curries. Mango pulp can be used in ice cream, mousse and sorbet. Mangoes are in season in summer; they are also available canned.

Mangosteen A tropical fruit, about the size and shape of an apple, with a shiny, thick, purple skin containing segments of soft, white, lychee-like flesh. It is eaten fresh.

Manicotti Pasta tubes that are cooked, stuffed with cheese or meat filling and baked.

Manioc See Cassava.

Maple Syrup The sap of various species of maple tree, boiled into a syrup that varies from pale amber (the finest) to dark amber (used mainly in cooking). Maple syrup is poured over pancakes, waffles, ice cream and other desserts. Maple-

flavored syrup is a blend of pure maple syrup and corn syrup.

Maraschino A colorless liqueur made from a bitter black cherry called *marasca.* Maraschino cherries are cherries that have been bleached, stoned, then steeped in a sugar syrup flavored with maraschino liqueur; they are used in baking and as a garnish for cocktails.

Marble Cake A cake which, when sliced, has a marbled appearance, achieved by coloring the portions of the batter (pink, chocolate and plain) and mixing them in the pan before baking.

Marengo A dish of chicken, tomato, mushroom, garlic and wine. It was created in 1800 for Napoleon following his victory at the battle of Marengo.

Margarine A butter-like spread usually made from vegetable oil but also from a combination of vegetable and animal oils. In most recipes regular margarine (not diet margarines or spreads) can be substituted for butter. Several types are available: stick form, either salted or unsalted, is the most common; whipped and soft margarines have a smooth spreadable consistency; liquid margarine is formulated to remain liquid at room temperature; and diet margarine has a high percentage of water.

MELONS

MELON WITH GINGER SYRUP

⭐ **Preparation time:** 40 minutes
Total cooking time: 5 minutes
Makes about 25 skewers

1 cantaloupe, halved
1 honeydew melon, halved
half a small watermelon

Ginger Syrup
1 cup sugar
1 cup water
2 tablespoons brandy
2 tablespoons preserved ginger syrup or green ginger wine

1 Remove seeds from each of the melons. Using a melon baller, scoop the flesh of each melon into balls. Place balls in a large bowl. Cover with plastic wrap. Chill well.
2 To make Ginger Syrup: Place sugar and water in a small saucepan. Heat gently until sugar has dissolved. Simmer until slightly thickened.
3 Stir in brandy and ginger syrup or green ginger wine. Allow the mixture to cool before pouring over the melons. Cover with plastic wrap and return to refrigerator until well chilled.
4 For serving, skewer one of each type of melon ball onto a bamboo skewer. Repeat until all the fruit is used. May be served with dollops of freshly whipped cream or ice cream.

SUMMER MELON SALAD

⭐ **Preparation time:** 15 minutes
Total cooking time: none
Serves 6

11 oz honeydew melon
11 oz cantaloupe
11 oz watermelon (optional)
2 small red onions

1 tablespoon chopped fresh parsley
2 tablespoons lemon juice

1 Cut the melon flesh into pieces roughly 1½ inches square and ½ inch thick. Slice the onions into very thin rings.
2 Place the onion, parsley and lemon juice in a small bowl; toss to combine.
3 Layer the melons and onion in a glass bowl, pour over the lemon juice mixture. Serve immediately.

ABOUT MELONS

■ The tough skin of a melon (which belies its soft, sweet interior) can make judging its ripeness difficult. Choose melons which have a sweet smell and are slightly soft at the stalk end.
■ Once cut, melons should be used quickly. Even well wrapped in the refrigerator, melons can quickly taint the flavor of other foods.

ABOVE: MELON WITH GINGER SYRUP.
OPPOSITE PAGE: APRICOT AND ALMOND VACHERIN

MERINGUES

APRICOT AND ALMOND VACHERIN

★ ★ **Preparation time:** 40 minutes
Total cooking time: 50 minutes
Serves 8–10

4 egg whites
1 cup sugar
1½ teaspoons vanilla
    extract
1½ teaspoons white
    vinegar
1 cup ground almonds

1 cup water
½ cup sugar
2 tablespoons butter

Topping
1½ cups cream, whipped
½ cup chopped dried
    apricots, extra
½ cup toasted sliced
    almonds

Filling
6½ oz chopped dried
    apricots

1 Preheat oven to slow 300°F. Line 2 baking sheets with parchment paper, mark a 9 inch circle on each. Place egg whites in small dry mixing bowl. Using electric beaters, beat egg whites until soft peaks form. Gradually add sugar, beating constantly after each addition. Beat for 5–10 minutes or until thick and glossy and sugar has dissolved. Gently fold in vanilla, vinegar and almonds.

2 Divide the mixture between baking sheets, spread evenly over the marked circles. Bake for 45 minutes or until the meringues are pale and

crisp. Turn the oven off and cool meringues in the oven with the door ajar.

3 To make Filling: Place the apricots and water in a pan, stir over medium heat until the apricots are just tender. Add the sugar and simmer, uncovered, over low heat for 3–5 minutes or until nearly all the liquid has been absorbed. Transfer the apricot mixture into a food processor, process until smooth. Add butter, process until butter has melted and the mixture is smooth. Cool.

4 To assemble: Place one meringue disk on serving plate, spread with apricot mixture, top with half the whipped cream, then other meringue disk. Spread top with rest of cream, decorate with extra apricots and almonds. Refrigerate until required for serving.

MERINGUE NESTS WITH KAHLUA CREAM AND STRAWBERRIES

★ ★ **Preparation time:** 40 minutes
Total cooking time: 30 minutes
Serves 4

3 egg whites
¾ cup sugar

Filling
¾ cup heavy cream
1 tablespoon sugar
2 teaspoons instant coffee
    powder

1 teaspoon water
1 tablespoon Kahlua or
    coffee liqueur
8 oz strawberries
2 oz dark (semisweet)
    cooking chocolate,
    melted

1 Preheat oven to very slow 250°F. Line 2 baking sheets with parchment paper. Mark two 4 inch circles on each baking sheet. Place egg whites in small dry mixing bowl. Using electric beaters, beat egg whites until soft peaks form. Gradually add the sugar, beating constantly after each addition. Beat 5–10 minutes until thick and glossy and sugar has dissolved.

2 Place the meringue mixture into a piping bag fitted with a ⅝ inch star-shaped nozzle. Pipe some of the meringue over the marked rounds to form a base. Pipe the remaining mixture around the edge of the base to form a wall (or nest). Bake for 30 minutes or until the meringue nests are pale and crisp. Turn the oven off and cool nests in the oven with door ajar.

3 To make Filling: Using electric beaters, beat cream with the sugar until soft peaks form. Fold in blended coffee powder, water and Kahlua and beat until firm peaks form. Divide cream between nests, top with whole strawberries, drizzle with melted chocolate.

Margarita A drink of tequila, orange-flavored liqueur and lime juice.

Marinade A seasoned mixture in which raw meat, poultry, fish or seafood is marinated before cooking, to add flavor and tenderize by softening the fibers.

Marinara Sauce An Italian sauce of tomatoes, onions, garlic and oregano.

Marjoram Also known as sweet

marjoram, an aromatic herb with spicy flavored, small gray-green leaves which are used in meat, poultry, egg, cheese, cabbage, green bean and tomato dishes. Oregano, a similar herb, is also known as wild marjoram.

Marmalade A thick, jam-like spread made from citrus fruit and peel (either a single fruit or a combination). It is usually eaten at breakfast, on hot buttered toast.

Marrow, Bone A fatty tissue found in the center of animal bones. It is pale-colored and when cooked and cooled has a smooth, jelly-like texture. Raw marrow extracted from larger beef bones may be chopped and added to stuffings; cooked marrow is spread on toast as an hors d'oeuvre or cooked in dishes such as risotto Milanese.

Marrow, Vegetable A sausage-shaped summer squash belonging to the same family as the zucchini. Young marrows have the best flavor and most delicate flesh and can be cooked in the same way as zucchini. Large older marrows have a high water content and bland flavor and are best stuffed with a savory filling and baked, or cooked gently in butter and their own juice.

Marshmallow A whipped candy with a springy, puffy texture made from gelatin, sugar, flavoring and coloring. It is commercially available in bite-sized, sugar-

dusted portions or can be made at home.

Marzipan A candy made from a sugar and water syrup, almond paste and sometimes egg white cooked together, cooled, and then kneaded into a smooth

PAVLOVA WITH FRUIT SALAD TOPPING

Preparation time: 15 minutes
Total cooking time: 40 minutes
Serves 6–8

4 egg whites	1 banana, sliced
1 cup sugar	8 oz strawberries, sliced
3 teaspoons cornstarch	2 kiwifruit, sliced
1 teaspoon white vinegar	2 passionfruit
1 cup cream, whipped	

1 Preheat the oven to a slow 300°F. Line a baking sheet with parchment paper. Mark an 8 inch circle on the paper. Place the egg whites in a large, dry mixing bowl. Using electric beaters, beat the egg whites until soft peaks form. Gradually add the sugar, beating constantly after each addition. Beat for 5–10 minutes until the sugar has dissolved. Fold in the cornstarch and vinegar.

2 Spread the meringue mixture onto the marked circle. Shape evenly, running a flat-bladed knife around edge and over top of meringue. Run the knife up the edge of the meringue mixture, all the way around, making furrows. This will strengthen the pavlova and gives a nice decorative finish.

3 Bake for 40 minutes or until the meringue is pale and crisp. Turn the oven off, cool pavlova in the oven with the door ajar. Top with cream and arrange the fruit decoratively. Drizzle with passionfruit pulp.

ABOUT MERINGUE

■ For successful meringues, separate eggs very carefully—even the smallest amount of yolk will cause the egg foam to break down. Use only fresh, dry sugar, or fine powdered (confectioners') sugar, if the recipe calls for it. Make sure you clean and thoroughly dry the bowl and all the utensils you are going to use.

■ Meringues are cooked at a very low temperature—they are, in fact, dried rather than baked. Cooked meringues should lift off the baking sheet easily and feel light and dry to the touch. (The centers can be slightly soft and chewy, or completely dry, depending on the type of dessert you are making.)

■ When spooning or piping meringue onto a pie, spread the mixture to the very edges. Cover the entire filling well and evenly, as the meringue will shrink slightly during baking.

MERINGUE NESTS WITH KAHLUA CREAM (LEFT) AND
PAVLOVA WITH FRUIT SALAD TOPPING

firm paste. It is cut or molded into small shapes which are used to decorate cakes or it is boxed as gift candy. It is also used as a coating under the top icing of rich fruit cakes.

Mascarpone A fresh, unripened, soft, creamy cheese, made from cow's milk cream, with a high fat content and a rich, buttery taste. It is usually served as a dessert with sweetened fruit or mixed with brandy or liqueurs.

Matzo A thin sheet of unleavened bread, usually made with wheat flour and water only. It is traditionally eaten during the Jewish Passover when only unleavened products are eaten. Matzo meal, made from ground matzo crackers, is used in place of bread crumbs at Passover.

Mayonnaise A cold uncooked sauce that is made by whisking oil and egg yolks into an emulsion. It is flavored with lemon juice,

vinegar or mustard and seasonings. Mayonnaise is served as a salad dressing and accompaniment to cold meat, fish and egg dishes; it is the basis of many other cold sauces.

Meat The flesh of animals used for food. The term is often used to refer only to lamb, beef, pork and some game, and

not to poultry, fish and seafood.

Meatballs Small balls made of ground beef, lamb, veal or pork, seasoned and bound together with beaten egg or bread crumbs. Meatballs can be cooked in a variety of ways and served as finger food or as a first or main course.

Meat Loaf A mixture of ground beef, pork or veal, or a combination of these, seasoned, bound with beaten egg, bread crumbs or rice, formed into a loaf shape and baked. It can be eaten hot or cold.

Meat Tenderizer A product containing an enzyme that breaks down the meat's connective tissue.

Medlar A plum-sized fruit with yellowish-brown skin and firm grayish flesh from a tree

MEXICAN CLASSICS

LAMB EMPANADAS

⭐ **Preparation time:** 1 hour
Total cooking time: 20 minutes
Serves 6

8 oz ground lamb
½ small onion, finely chopped
½ medium green pepper, finely chopped
1 small carrot, finely chopped
2 tablespoons tomato paste
1 teaspoon ground cinnamon
2 teaspoons brown sugar

Pastry
2 cups all-purpose flour
¼ teaspoon salt
½ cup cold butter; chopped
½ cup cold milk
2 tablespoons butter; softened
1 beaten egg

1 In a medium skillet cook lamb and onion over medium heat until meat is brown. Drain. Add pepper, carrot, tomato paste, cinnamon and sugar. Mix well. Remove from heat; cool.
2 Preheat oven to 400°F. Lightly grease a baking sheet. Set aside.
3 To make Pastry: Place flour and salt in a food processor. Process until combined. Add butter and process mixture until it resembles fine bread crumbs. Add cold milk and process to make a soft dough. Turn dough out onto a lightly floured surface. Knead gently. Divide dough into three equal portions.
4 On a lightly floured surface, roll each portion into an 8 inch square. Spread two of the squares with softened butter. Stack all three dough squares on top of each other, with the unbuttered square on top. Roll out the layers together.
5 To assemble: Cut out six 6 inch circles from pastry. Divide meat mixture evenly between the circles. Brush edges with egg. Fold in half, pressing edges together with the tines of a fork. Place on prepared baking sheet, brush pastry with remaining egg. Bake for 15–20 minutes or until puffed and golden. Serve with a green salad.

Note: Freeze unbaked empanadas in an airtight plastic bag for 4 weeks. To bake, place frozen pastries on baking sheet in a 400°F oven 25–30 minutes or until golden and heated through.

GUACAMOLE

⭐ **Preparation time:** 20 minutes
Total cooking time: none
Serves 6

2 ripe avocados
1 small onion
1 medium tomato
1 tablespoon chopped fresh cilantro

¼ cup sour cream
1 tablespoon lemon juice
Tabasco sauce, to taste

1 Cut avocados in half, remove pit with the blade of a sharp knife. Peel avocados, place flesh in medium bowl. Mash with a fork until smooth.
2 Peel and finely chop onion and tomato; mix with chopped fresh cilantro. Add to avocado in bowl with remaining ingredients, mix well. Serve as a dip with corn chips or add to taco filling.

native to central Asia. Edible only when over-ripe, it has a wine-like flavor. It can be made into preserves.

Melba Toast Thin, crisp slices of crustless bread served with dips, pâtés and creamy soups. It was originally created for the Australian

opera singer Dame Nellie Melba.

Melon Large fruit with a thick rind and juicy flesh. Melons are a good source of potassium and vitamin C. The many varieties fall into three main groups: round with netted, bark-like skin, fragrant orange flesh and a cluster of pale seeds in the center, such as the cantaloupe, muskmelon and Persian melon; oval and smooth skinned with creamy-white to dark green sweet flesh and a central cluster of seeds such as the honeydew, Juan Canary, casaba, crenshaw and Santa Claus melon; and watermelons, larger with moist reddish flesh studded with dark seeds. Melon is eaten fresh as a fruit and added to fruit salads; some

BURRITOS

Preparation time: 15 minutes
Total cooking time: 40 minutes
Serves 4

1 lb boneless top round roast or boneless shoulder pot roast
1 tablespoon olive oil
1 cinnamon stick

1 medium onion, finely sliced
4 cloves
1 bay leaf
2½ cups beef stock
8 x 8 inch flour tortillas

1 Trim meat of excess fat; cut into 1 inch cubes. Heat oil in a large saucepan, add onion. Cook until golden brown.
2 Add meat, cinnamon stick, cloves, bay leaf and beef stock. Bring to boil; reduce heat. Simmer, uncovered, for 40 minutes or until meat is tender and liquid is almost absorbed. Remove and discard the cinnamon stick, cloves and bay leaf.
3 Shred meat with two forks. Roll meat up in tortillas. Serve with Tomato Salsa and salad.

OPPOSITE PAGE, ABOVE: LAMB EMPANADAS; BELOW: GUACAMOLE. THIS PAGE, ABOVE: BURRITOS AND TOMATO SALSA

TOMATO SALSA

Preparation time: 10 minutes
Total cooking time: none
Serves 4–6

1 medium tomato, finely chopped
1 medium red onion, finely sliced
3 tablespoons lemon juice

2 tablespoons chopped fresh cilantro
2 teaspoons grated lemon rind

1 Thoroughly combine all ingredients in a medium bowl.
2 Serve as an accompaniment to Empanadas, a filling for Tacos, wrapped in a tortilla for Burritos or as a refreshing sauce with meat, chicken or seafood dishes. It tastes best when served at room temperature.

Note: Use scallions if a milder flavor is preferred. Or add a little finely chopped green or red chili pepper for spiciness. The size of the tomato and onion will determine the quantity that this recipe makes. It is at its best when eaten fresh, but it can be stored, covered, for up to two days in the refrigerator.

varieties are served with ham as an hors d'oeuvre.

Melt To liquify using gentle heat.

Merguez A spicy sausage of Algerian origin made from ground goat meat.

Meringue A mixture of stiffly beaten egg white and granulated sugar, used in various

desserts such as pies, shells and baked Alaska.

Mesclun A mixture of the slightly bitter leaves and young shoots of wild plants such as chicory (curly endive), arugula, dandelion and chervil. It originated in the Nice region of the south of France and the name is derived from the local word *mesclumo*, a mixture. A similar salad from the area around Rome is called *mescladissei* and is served with walnuts.

Meunière A fillet or small whole fish, dusted with flour, then pan-fried in butter. It is served with a sauce of butter, lemon juice and chopped parsley.

TEX-MEX CHILI CON CARNE

★ **Preparation time:** 30 minutes
Total cooking time: 50 minutes
Serves 4

1 tablespoon olive oil
2 cloves garlic, crushed
1½ lb top round steak, cut into ¾ inch cubes
1 large onion, chopped
2 bay leaves
1 cup tomato juice
16 oz can whole tomatoes, crushed

16 oz can red kidney beans, drained
1–2 tablespoons chili powder
1 teaspoon ground cumin
½ teaspoon ground oregano
¼ teaspoon cayenne pepper

1 Heat the olive oil and crushed garlic in a large pan. Add the meat and cook in batches over medium heat until well browned.
2 Stir in the onion, bay leaves, tomato juice and tomatoes. Bring to a boil; reduce heat.
3 Cover and simmer for 40 minutes or until the meat is very tender and the liquid has reduced by half. Stir in the kidney beans and spices. Cook for 10 minutes more. Serve with Guacamole and corn chips.

ABOVE: TEX MEX CHILI CON CARNE;
RIGHT: SPICY BEEF AND BEAN TACOS.
OPPOSITE PAGE: MINCEMEAT TARTS

SPICY BEEF AND BEAN TACOS

★ **Preparation time:** 25 minutes
Total cooking time: 15 minutes
Serves 4

8 oz ground beef
1 small onion, finely chopped
⅓ cup tomato paste
1 teaspoon chili powder
1 teaspoon ground cumin
1 teaspoon ground coriander
16 oz can refried beans

12 taco shells
½ cup shredded Cheddar cheese
2 small carrots, grated
2 medium tomatoes, sliced
½ small lettuce, shredded

1 In a medium skillet cook ground beef and onion until meat is brown and onion is tender. Drain off fat.
2 Add tomato paste, chili powder, cumin, coriander and beans. Mix well. Cook, stirring occasionally, 2–3 minutes or until mixture is hot.
3 To serve, preheat oven to 350°F. Place taco shells over the rungs of the oven rack. (This will prevent them from closing up while they heat.) Heat for about 8 minutes until they are crisp. Alternatively, taco shells can be heated in a microwave oven. Follow the instructions on the package. Fill the shells with beef mixture, cheese, carrots, tomatoes and lettuce. Sour cream or Guacamole can also be added if desired.

Note: The beef mixture can be cooked and frozen for 4 weeks in an airtight container. Thaw and reheat in a saucepan over low heat.

MINCEMEAT

BASIC MINCEMEAT

★ **Preparation time:** 20 minutes
Total cooking time: none
Makes 3½ cups

8¾ oz finely chopped raisins

5 oz golden raisins, chopped

¼ cup finely chopped dried apricots

2 tablespoons finely chopped candied cherries

2 tablespoons chopped almonds

½ cup mixed peel

⅓ cup currants

1 cup soft brown sugar

1 apple, peeled, coarsely grated

1 teaspoon grated lemon rind

1 teaspoon grated orange rind

1 tablespoon lemon juice

1 teaspoon pumpkin pie spice

¼ teaspoon ground nutmeg

¼ cup brandy

¼ cup butter, melted

1 Place all ingredients together in a large mixing bowl. Mix well with a wooden spoon.

2 Spoon mincemeat mixture into airtight containers or sterilized jars and seal well.

3 Keep the containers in a cool, dark place for up to three months. Stir the mixture occasionally, sealing the jars or containers well after each opening. Mixture may be frozen if desired.

Note: Traditionally mincemeat is made with suet; we used butter in this recipe. Suet is sold in clumps and must be grated or melted if it is to be used in fruit mince, cakes or puddings. Mincemeat made with suet will keep for several years, if stored in a dry, dark place.

TO MAKE MINCEMEAT TARTS

Place 2½ cups of plain flour, ⅔ cup of chopped butter and 2 tablespoons sugar in a food processor. Process the mixture for 20 seconds or until it is fine and crumbly. Add 2 egg yolks and 1 tablespoon of water and process for 20 seconds or until mixture comes together. Add a little more water if necessary. Turn onto a lightly floured surface. Knead gently until dough is smooth. Cover with plastic wrap and refrigerate for about 15 minutes. Roll the pastry between two sheets of wax paper until it is ⅛ inch thick. Cut pastry into circles, using a 3 inch round cutter. Ease circles into greased shallow muffin or tart pans. Spoon 1–2 teaspoonfuls of filling into each. (You will need about 1 cup mincemeat altogether.) Re-roll the pastry trimmings. Cut into shapes; use to decorate tops of the pies. Bake in a preheated moderate 350°F oven for 10–15 minutes or until golden. Dust with confectioners' sugar.

Mexican Food This cuisine evolved from a mixture of the food of Aztec, Maya and other native groups, and the food of the Spanish colonists. It uses local foods such as corn, tomatoes, beans, chili peppers, avocados and squash. Chili pepper is the one ingredient common to all

Mexican food. There are over a hundred varieties, ranging from mild to fiery. Large chili peppers are stuffed with meat and nuts; smaller varieties are ground or crushed. Tortillas (cornmeal or flour flatbreads) are central to Mexican food. They are crisply fried and folded to make taco shells; torn into pieces and fried to use as scoops (tostadifas); stuffed with beans, cheese and sour cream and baked (enchiladas); or fried and stacked with filling between (quesadillas). Chocolate, from the cacao bean, is cooked with water and flavored with cinnamon, to make a popular drink. Tex-Mex food is often accepted as Mexican. It is milder in flavor and uses more meat, cheese and sour cream, and fewer exotic ingredients.

Microwave Cooking
 A method of cooking or warming food using

MICROWAVE

Use your microwave oven to cook vegetables, heat milk for sauces or coffee, melt butter and chocolate, heat prepared meals and defrost raw and cooked food. Most foods normally steamed or poached can be successfully cooked in the microwave.

Microwave ovens vary a great deal and cooking times are therefore approximate. They depend on how well done you like your food and on the power rating of your microwave.

MICROWAVE COOKWARE

■ Glass: Use ordinary glass dishes for short-term or low-power heating and defrosting. Ovenproof glass can be used for all microwave cooking.
■ Pottery or earthenware: This should be non-porous and well-glazed with no metallic content. Use only for defrosting or low-power cooking.
■ China: For reheating only. Do not use any china with a metallic trim or pattern.
■ Paper: Use parchment (not wax) paper, microwave-safe paper towels or plastic-coated paper containers for quick heating and reheating.

■ Aluminum foil: Use only to shield food parts (e.g. bones) from overcooking. Never completely cover the food. Keep foil 1 inch from interior oven walls.
■ Plastic: Plastic cookware and wraps that are designated microwave-safe can be used for most cooking and reheating purposes. Never use metal twist ties to secure bags and always poke holes in, or vent, plastic wrap to allow steam to escape. Do not let plastic wrap touch the food. Ordinary plastic containers and wraps should be used only for reheating or quick cooking.

DEFROSTING IN THE MICROWAVE

■ Remove the food from its original wrapping or container. Many rigid plastic containers are not designed for use in a microwave. Discard any metal twists or clips. For convenience foods, follow the instructions given on the package.
■ Place food, preferably on a rack, in a shallow microwave-safe dish with sides high enough to catch and hold liquids as the food thaws.
■ Defrost all foods, loosely covered unless specifically stated otherwise, according to oven manufacturer's instructions.
■ Where practical, large dense foods such as roast meats, may be turned over once or twice during defrosting to assist equal heat distribution.
■ When defrost time is complete, allow to stand as required. Continue specific food preparation and microwave cooking or reheating as required.

MICROWAVING VEGETABLES

A microwave oven comes into its own when used to cook vegetables. The vegetables should be placed in a microwave-safe dish, with a little water and seasonings, covered and cooked on HIGH (100%) for the stated time. The vegetables will retain their color, crispness and nutrients.

DEFROSTING MEAT AND POULTRY
USE MEDIUM-LOW (30%) POWER LEVEL

CUT	MICROWAVE TIME PER 1 lb	STANDING TIME
Roast beef	8-10 minutes	10-15 minutes
Steaks	4-6 minutes	5-10 minutes
Ground beef	5-8 minutes	5-10 minutes
Roast pork	8-12 minutes	5-10 minutes
Pork chops	5-8 minutes	5-10 minutes
Pork ribs	6-8 minutes	5-10 minutes
Ground pork	6-8 minutes	5-10 minutes
Roast lamb	8-10 minutes	10-15 minutes
Lamb shoulder	7-10 minutes	10-15 minutes
Lamb chops	5-8 minutes	5-10 minutes
Whole turkey	6-10 minutes	20-30 minutes
Turkey breast	5-10 minutes	15-20 minutes
Turkey pieces	7-10 minutes	10-15 minutes
Whole chicken	5-8 minutes	10-15 minutes
Chicken pieces	5-7 minutes	10-15 minutes
Duck	8-10 minutes	10-15 minutes

VEGETABLES	QUANTITY USE HIGH (100%) POWER LEVEL	PREPARATION	COOKING TIME (MINUTES)
Artichokes	8 oz	1/4 cup water	8–9
Asparagus, fresh	8 oz	2 tablespoons water	2–4
Asparagus, frozen	8 oz	2 tablespoons water	2–3
Beans, fresh	8 oz	1–2 tablespoons water	3–4
Beans, frozen	8 oz	1 tablespoon water	5–7
Broccoli, fresh	8 oz	2 tablespoons water	3–4
Broccoli, frozen	8 oz	2 tablespoons water	5–7
Brussels Sprouts, fresh	8 oz	2 tablespoons water	3–4
Brussels Sprouts, frozen	8 oz	2 tablespoons water	5–7
Cabbage, shredded	½ small	only water remaining after washing, butter	6–8
Carrots, fresh	8 oz	2 tablespoons water	3–4
Carrots, frozen	8 oz	2 tablespoons water	6–8
Cauliflower, fresh	½ head	slit stalks, 2 tablespoons water	7–8
Cauliflower, frozen	8 oz	2 tablespoons water	5–7
Corn on cob, fresh	2	remove husks, dot with butter, wrap in plastic wrap	6–8
Corn on cob, frozen	8 oz	dot with butter	8–10
Eggplant, sliced	8 oz	brush with oil	3–4
Leeks, whole	8 oz	2 tablespoons water	5–7
Mushrooms, fresh	8 oz	whole or sliced, dot with butter	3–5
Onions, sliced	8 oz	1 tablespoon butter	3–4
Parsnips, sliced	8 oz	2 tablespoons water	5–6
Peas, fresh	8 oz	2 tablespoons water	3–5
Peas, frozen	8 oz	1 tablespoon water	2–4
Potatoes, boiled	8 oz	cut into quarters, 2 tablespoons water (place flat in plastic bag)	6–8
Potatoes, baked	8 oz	pierce skin, rub with oil, turn over after 3 minutes	4–6
Pumpkin or winter squash	8 oz	cut into serving pieces, 2 tablespoons water	4–6
Spinach, fresh	8 oz	only water remaining after washing, 1 tablespoon butter, dash nutmeg and pepper	4–5
Spinach, frozen	8 oz		5–7
Tomatoes, halved	8 oz	dot with butter and pepper	3–4
Zucchini, sliced	8 oz	1 tablespoon butter and pepper	3–4

electromagnetic waves that are absorbed by food molecules. The waves cause the molecules to vibrate, creating friction which produces heat. It is much faster than conventional cooking. The microwave is also used to defrost or reheat food.

Milk Commonly cow's milk but goat and sheep's milk are also used. Types available are whole milk, low-fat milk, skim milk, buttermilk, powdered milk, sweet acidophilus milk, chocolate milk and canned milk.

Mille-Feuille A pastry consisting of layers

of crisp puff pastry and whipped cream or crème pâtissière and jam. The top pastry layer is dusted with confectioners' sugar or glazed with icing (frosting). Savory mille-feuille, filled with creamed fish or chicken, is served as a first course or as a buffet dish.

Mincemeat Finely chopped dried fruit and fresh apple, mixed with suet, sweet spices and nuts, and soaked with

MINT

MINTED LAMB SALAD

Preparation time: 25 minutes
Total cooking time: 10 minutes
Serves 4

1 lb lamb fillets	1/2 teaspoon Dijon
1 tablespoon olive oil	mustard
1 bunch red leaf lettuce	1 tablespoon chopped
2 oz yellow pear	fresh mint
tomatoes	3 1/2 oz haloumi cheese
2 oz cherry tomatoes	(see note)
1/4 cup olive oil, extra	1 tablespoon olive oil,
1/2 teaspoon sugar	extra
1 tablespoon white wine	
vinegar	

1 Trim the meat of excess fat and tendons. Heat olive oil in a heavy-based pan; add meat. Cook meat over medium-high heat, turning frequently, 7–8 minutes for medium-rare. Do not overcook, meat should be pink in the center. Remove to a plate, cover loosely with foil. Let thinly slice diagonally.
2 Wash and dry lettuce thoroughly, and tear leaves into bite-size pieces. Arrange lettuce on individual serving plates and arrange the teardrop and cherry tomatoes and lamb slices on top. Place the oil, sugar, vinegar, mustard, and mint in a small screw-top jar and shake well.
3 Drain cheese and cut into fingers about 1/2 inch thick and 1 1/2 inches long. Pat dry. Add extra oil to pan, heat on moderate heat. Add cheese, cook for

2 minutes or until golden, turning occasionally. Drain on paper towels. Arrange warm cheese on top of salad, shake dressing again, drizzle over salad and serve immediately.

Note: Haloumi is a firm, salty white cheese from Cyprus. It is delicious grilled or fried, and does not melt and stick to the pan. Haloumi cheese is available from Greek or Cypriot delicatessens. You can substitute fingers of uncooked feta cheese.

HOT MINTED POTATO SALAD

Preparation time: 30 minutes
Total cooking time: 20 minutes
Serves 8

2 lb tiny new potatoes	1/4 cup chopped fresh
5 large sprigs fresh mint	parsley
1 cup sour cream	2 tablespoons chopped
1 medium white onion,	fresh dill
grated	2 tablespoons chopped
2 tablespoons mayonnaise	chives
	salt and ground pepper

1 Place potatoes and mint in large saucepan; add enough water to cover. Heat until boiling; reduce heat and cover. Gently simmer until potatoes are just tender, about 10–12 minutes. Drain well; discard the mint.
2 In a bowl, stir together sour cream, onion, mayonnaise, fresh herbs and seasonings to taste. Add to hot potatoes and mix well. Serve warm.

MINT SAMBAL

Preparation time: 5 minutes
Total cooking time: none
Makes 3/4 cup

1 cup fresh mint leaves	1 green chili pepper,
1 medium onion, peeled	chopped (optional)
1/2 cup plain yogurt	

Chop mint and onion in a blender. Add enough yogurt to form a smooth, creamy mixture. Add chopped chili to taste. Serve with curries or barbecued chicken. This sambal can also be used to marinate chicken pieces, by adding chopped fresh ginger and 1/4 teaspoon turmeric. Marinate overnight, then grill or broil the chicken.

ABOVE: MINTED LAMB SALAD.
OPPOSITE PAGE: VEGETABLE COUSCOUS

MOROCCAN CLASSICS

VEGETABLE COUSCOUS

⭐⭐ **Preparation time:** 40 minutes + overnight soaking
Total cooking time: 2 hours
Serves 6

2 cups dried chickpeas
(garbanzo beans)
1/3 cup vegetable oil
1 onion, finely chopped
1 small stick cinnamon
6 1/2 oz eggplant, cut into
3/4 inch cubes
3 medium carrots, cut in
1/4 inch rounds
3 medium new potatoes,
cut into 1/2 inch cubes
5 oz pumpkin, cut into
1/2 inch cubes
1/4 teaspoon pumpkin pie
spice
3 teaspoons harissa, or to
taste
2 cups boiling water

3 1/2 oz small stringless
beans, cut in 2 inch
diagonal slices
2 zucchini, unpeeled,
cut in 1/2 inch rounds
1 medium, ripe tomato,
cut into eight pieces
1 tablespoon chopped
flat-leaf parsley
1 tablespoon chopped
fresh cilantro
ground pepper

Couscous
1 cup couscous (semolina)
3/4 cup boiling water
2 teaspoons butter

1 Cover the chickpeas with cold water, soak overnight. Drain, wash well and cook in a large pan, on low simmer, for 1 1/2 hours. Drain.
2 Heat oil in a large heavy-based pan; cook onion and cinnamon stick over a low heat until the onion softens. Add eggplant, carrot and potatoes. Cover and cook on low heat for 10 minutes, stirring occasionally with a wooden spoon.
3 Add the pumpkin, spice and harissa. Pour boiling water over the mixture and add the chickpeas, beans and zucchini. Simmer, covered, for another 15 minutes. Stir in the tomato just before serving. Garnish with the fresh parsley and cilantro. Sprinkle with pepper.
4 **To prepare Couscous:** Pour boiling water over the couscous in a bowl. Stir in the butter, cover tightly and allow to stand for about 10 minutes. Serve with vegetables.

HARISSA

⭐ **Preparation time:** 10 minutes
Total cooking time: none
Serves 6

3 1/2 oz dried red chili
pepper
6 cloves garlic, peeled
1/3 cup salt

1/2 cup ground coriander
1/3 cup ground cumin
2/3 cup olive oil

1 Wearing rubber or cotton gloves remove stems of chilies. Split in half, remove seeds and soften chilies in hot water.
2 Process garlic, salt, ground coriander and cumin seeds, and drained red chilies to a paste, slowly adding olive oil until well combined. Serve.

Note: Harissa is traditionally ground using a mortar and pestle. To give Harissa extra flavor, dry-fry the coriander and cumin seeds just before grinding.

brandy, rum or madeira. Mincemeat is traditionally a filling for Christmas tarts and pies.

Minestrone A hearty soup of Italian origin. Minestrone varies from region to region, but basically contains fresh vegetables and dried beans, simmered slowly in beef stock and thickened with pasta or rice.

Mint An herb with a strong fresh scent and flavor. There are many varieties. Most used in cooking is spearmint, which is made into jelly and sauce to accompany lamb, and goes well with peas and boiled potatoes. Finely chopped mint is used as an ingredient in Middle Eastern salads and dips, and flavors drinks. Apple mint, lemon mint and pineapple mint are often added to fruit salads. Peppermint oil is used to flavor candy.

Miso A thick, salty, nutty-flavored paste made from mashed and salted soy beans mixed with rice, barley or wheat grains, then fermented. Light or yellow miso, made with rice, is sweet and creamy and is used as a flavoring for soups and dressings. Red miso, made with barley, has a strong, salty taste and is used in soups, casseroles and general cooking. When using miso in hot dishes, add just before serving and do not allow the dish come to the boil.

Mixed Grill A dish consisting of several varieties of broiled meat and vegetables, such as lamb chops, steak, sausages, kidney, liver, bacon, tomato, onion and mushroom.

Mixed Spice Also known as pudding spice, a traditional English blend of sweet spices, generally nutmeg, cinnamon, cloves and ginger, but sometimes also including allspice and

coriander.
Mixed spice is used in rich fruit cakes, puddings and cookies.

Mocha A strongly flavored Arabian coffee bean originally grown near the Red Sea and named after the Yemenite seaport from which it was exported. In cooking, "mocha" refers to food, such as ice cream or cakes, which is flavored with coffee and chocolate.

B'STILLA (SHREDDED CHICKEN PIE)

⭐ ⭐ **Preparation time:** 45 minutes
Total cooking time: 2 hours 30 minutes
Serves 8 first course size

Filling
3¼ lb chicken
1 large onion, finely chopped
1 large bunch flat-leaf parsley, chopped
1 bunch fresh cilantro, chopped
¼ teaspoon ground turmeric
¼ teaspoon ground saffron
2 tablespoons vegetable oil
1 teaspoon ground cinnamon

1 teaspoon ground ginger
1½ cups water

Pie Pastry
5 eggs, lightly beaten
1 cup confectioners' sugar
ground cinnamon
ground pepper
1 lb frozen filo (phyllo) pastry, thawed
8 oz unsalted (sweet) butter, melted
1 cup ground almonds
ground cinnamon, extra
1 cup confectioners' sugar, extra

1 Preheat oven to 350°F. Place chicken, onion, parsley, cilantro, turmeric, saffron, oil, cinnamon, ginger and water in a roasting pan. Bake for 1½ hours. Remove chicken from pan and cool. Shred flesh, discard skin and bones.
2 Skim fat from the liquid in pan and transfer liquid to medium pan. Heat until simmering, add eggs, sugar, cinnamon and pepper to taste. Cook until thick.
3 Preheat oven to 375°F. Grease an 8 inch pie dish. Place a sheet of filo (phyllo) in pie dish. Brush with melted butter. Place a sheet on top, brush with butter. Repeat layering and buttering

with seven more sheets, sprinkling some of the combined ground almonds, cinnamon and confectioners' sugar on the last sheet of pastry.
4 Spread egg mixture and chicken filling on top, fold over pastry edges, brush again with butter. Butter and layer four more sheets, cut into a round, and cover pie. Butter more sheets of pastry and form into roses. Place on top of pie, brush with melted butter. Bake 30–45 minutes. Sprinkle with rest of combined almond mixture.

KHOBZ (WHOLE-WHEAT FLAT BREAD)

⭐ ⭐ **Preparation time:** 1 hour
Total cooking time: 12 minutes
Makes 16

1 cup whole-wheat flour
1½ cups all-purpose flour
1 teaspoon sugar
1 teaspoon salt
1 envelope active dry yeast
1¼ cups warm water

½ teaspoon sweet paprika
⅓ cup cornmeal
1 tablespoon oil
1 egg, lightly beaten
2 tablespoons sesame seeds

1 Preheat oven to 350°F. Combine ½ cup whole-wheat flour, sugar, salt, yeast and water in bowl. Stand covered in a warm place until foaming.
2 Sift remaining whole-wheat flour, flour, paprika and cornmeal into bowl, add oil. Stir in yeast mixture. Mix to firm dough. Knead until smooth. Stand covered in warm place 20 minutes.
3 Divide into sixteen, roll into balls, flatten into 4 inch rounds.
4 Place on a greased baking sheet. Brush with egg, sprinkle with sesame seeds. Stand, covered, until puffed. Bake 12 minutes.

SAFFRON CHICKEN

⭐ **Preparation time:** 30 minutes + overnight soaking
Total cooking time: 1¼ hours
Serves 6

12 chicken pieces	4 oz chickpeas (garbanzo
½ teaspoon sweet	beans), soaked
paprika	overnight
½ teaspoon ground	3 cups chicken stock
cumin	⅓ cup finely chopped
ground pepper	flat-leaf parsley
⅓ cup butter	1 tablespoon fresh lemon
1½ lb red or yellow	thyme
onions, sliced	8 oz rice, cooked
¼ teaspoon ground	lemon juice
saffron or turmeric	

1 Season chicken with paprika, cumin and pepper. Heat butter in a deep heavy-bottom pan, add onion and chicken, cook until chicken is golden.
2 Sprinkle chicken with saffron, add drained chickpeas and chicken stock. Simmer gently, uncovered, for 1 hour or until chicken is tender.
3 Add chopped parsley and thyme to chicken just before serving. Spoon rice into heated serving dish. Place chicken pieces on top and pour over the sauce. Sprinkle with lemon juice and serve.

OPPOSITE PAGE, ABOVE: B'STILLA (SHREDDED CHICKEN PIE); BELOW: KHOBZ (WHOLE-WHEAT BREAD). THIS PAGE, ABOVE: SAFFRON CHICKEN; RIGHT: PRESERVED LEMONS

PRESERVED LEMONS

⭐ **Preparation time:** 1 hour, spread over 3 days
Preserving time: 3 weeks
Makes 16

16 thin-skinned lemons	coarse salt
water	lemon juice

1 Wash lemons well. Place in a large glass, stainless steel or plastic container. Cover with cold water and allow to soak for 3–5 days, changing water daily.
2 Drain lemons. Insert the point of a sharp knife into peel, ¼ inch from the bud end of each lemon and make four incisions lengthwise to within ¼ inch of the other end. Then cut through incisions so that lemons are cut completely through both sides, but are still held together at both ends.
3 Insert ¼ teaspoon coarse salt into the center of each lemon, and arrange lemons in sterilized preserving jars and sprinkle with 1 tablespoon coarse salt. Add the strained juice of 1 lemon to each jar and pour in enough boiling water to cover the lemons. Store in a cool dry place for at least 3 weeks.
To use: Rinse well; serve with Middle Eastern fish or meat dishes. Use peel only.

Mock Cream A cream substitute used as a filling for cakes and buns. It is generally made with confectioners' sugar and butter beaten until stiff and fluffy.

Molasses A thick, dark brown syrup produced in the refining of cane sugar. Molasses is used to make baked goods and beans.

Mole A Mexican sauce made with onion, garlic, chili peppers, ground seeds and a small amount of unsweetened chocolate.

Monosodium Glutamate (MSG) A salt with little flavor of its own. It occurs naturally in many foods and is manufactured for use as a flavor enhancer.

Monterey Jack A Cheddar-style, cow's milk cheese, pale yellow in color. See also Jack Cheese.

Mornay Sauce A béchamel sauce flavored

with Gruyère or Parmesan cheese and used to coat seafood, egg and vegetable dishes that are to be browned under the broiler or in the oven.

MUFFINS

Muffins are classified as quickbreads—quickly made and quickly eaten. They can be sweet or savory, even high fiber and healthy. Serve them for breakfast or lunch, with morning coffee, and with soup for a light evening meal.

BELOW, FROM TOP: BRAN, PUMPKIN AND PRUNE, CHOCOLATE, BERRY.

These muffins are surprisingly easy to make: you simply add the combined liquid ingredients to the combined dry ingredients, stirring together with a fork in a few quick strokes. The mixture will look rather lumpy but light, fine-textured muffins will be the result. Overmixing will result in a tough texture. Use deep muffin pans, straight-sided, with a non-stick finish. Brush oil only over the base of tins: un-oiled sides allow the batter to climb while baking and also help to form rounded tops.

Muffins are best eaten as soon as possible after they are made, and served warm with butter. If storage is necessary, they may be kept for up to 2 days in an airtight container and reheated in a low oven before serving. Muffins freeze well for up to 3 months and can be wrapped in foil and reheated in a moderate oven for 10–12 minutes.

BASIC MUFFINS

Preheat oven to 400°F. Brush oil into base of 12 muffin tins. Place 2 cups all-purpose flour into a bowl. Add ¼ cup sugar, 2 teaspoons baking powder and ¼ teaspoon salt. Mix together well. Melt ⅓ cup butter, place it in another bowl with 1 egg and 1 cup milk. Beat the mixture well.

Add liquid all at once to dry ingredients and stir gently with a fork until mixture is just combined; the batter should look quite lumpy. Spoon the batter evenly into tins, filling each two-thirds full. Bake for 20–25 minutes, until golden brown. Loosen muffins with a spatula and remove at once to a wire rack to cool. Serve warm.

VARIATIONS

■ BERRY: Add 1 cup of fresh blueberries or chopped strawberries to dry ingredients.

■ WHOLE-WHEAT: Use 1 cup whole-wheat flour and 1 cup all-purpose flour instead of all all-purpose flour; add 1 teaspoon mixed spice and ½ cup sultanas to the dry ingredients.

■ SPICY APPLE: Add 1 teaspoon cinnamon, ¼ teaspoon nutmeg and 1 cup chopped, peeled and cored apples to the dry ingredients and increase the quantity of sugar to ⅓ cup.

■ CHEESE AND BACON: Cook 3 slices of finely chopped bacon until they are quite crisp; drain. Add the bacon with 1 cup grated Cheddar cheese to the dry ingredients. Reduce the quantity of sugar to 2 tablespoons.

■ ORANGE AND POPPY SEED: Add 1 tablespoon grated orange rind and 1-2 tablespoons poppy seeds to dry ingredients.

■ BANANA: Add 1 large mashed banana and ½ teaspoon mixed spice to the dry ingredients.

BRAN MUFFINS

Place 1 cup unprocessed wheat bran in a bowl, pour 1 cup boiling water over and leave to stand for 1 hour. Preheat oven to 400°F. Brush oil into base of 12 muffin cups.

Add to bran mixture 1 beaten egg, ½ cup soft brown sugar and ¼ cup vegetable oil. Mix well. Sift 1 cup all-purpose flour into another bowl. Add ⅓ cup nonfat dry milk powder, 2 teaspoons baking powder and 1 teaspoon baking soda. Mix together well. Add the bran mixture all at once; stir with a fork until just combined. Spoon mixture into muffin cups, filling each of them two-thirds full. Bake 20-25 minutes or until the muffins are golden.

VARIATIONS

■ CARROT AND PINEAPPLE: Add ½ cup shredded carrot, ½ cup well-drained, canned, unsweetened crushed pineapple and ½ teaspoon ground ginger at the same time as the egg is added.

■ PUMPKIN AND PRUNE: Add 1 cup cooked mashed pumpkin and ¾ cup chopped pitted prunes at the same time as the egg is added; increase brown sugar to ⅔ cup.

CHOCOLATE MUFFINS

Preheat the oven to 350°F. Brush oil into the base of 15 muffin cups.

In a mixing bowl, combine 2 cups all-purpose flour, ½ cup sugar, 4 oz grated milk chocolate, 2 eggs, 2 teaspoons baking powder, 1 teaspoon baking soda, ¼ teaspoon salt, 2 teaspoons vanilla, ⅓ cup unsalted butter, melted, and 1 cup sour cream. Using electric beaters, beat for 1 minute on low speed, increase speed and beat for 1 minute more.

Spoon half the mixture into cups, place 1 square of good quality dark chocolate in center of each muffin; add remaining mixture. Press chocolate chips all over the tops of the muffins. Bake for 15 minutes or until puffed and lightly browned.

When you serve chocolate muffins warm, the chocolate center will be runny and melted. If you prefer, let them cool on a wire rack and eat them after the chocolate has had sufficient time to harden. In any case, these muffins do not keep their fresh flavor for long and should be eaten on the day they are baked.

ABOVE, FRONT ROW, LEFT TO RIGHT: SPICY APPLE, BERRY, ORANGE AND POPPY SEED. SECOND ROW: BERRY, CHOCOLATE, BERRY. THIRD ROW: BERRY, BRAN.

Moroccan Food
Unlike its North African neighbors, Moroccan food is spiced with more subtlety. Lemon is a favorite flavor and preserved lemon peel is used in many of its most famous dishes. Cinnamon, coriander

and orange-flower water are also commonly used. The exception to this subtle flavoring is harissa, a fiery condiment used in Algeria and Tunisia as well. The main ingredients are chilies, garlic and coriander and it is served with couscous and soups.

Couscous is probably the most famous dish from north Africa. It is made from semolina and steamed over a rich stew of meat and vegetables, traditionally in a couscousier, a metal

pan topped with a steamer. The meat and vegetables cook in the bottom while the semolina cooks in the top. In Morocco, couscous is sometimes served as a sweet dish, flavored with cinnamon. Another example of the Moroccans' attraction to sweet dishes is tagine. It is a slow-cooked stew, often made with lamb or mutton and flavored with quinces and honey. In Morocco, food is eaten with the fingers.

MUFFINS

ENGLISH MUFFINS

★★ **Preparation time:** 20 minutes + 1 hour 10 minutes standing
Total cooking time: 16 minutes
Makes 18

1 envelope active dry yeast
1 teaspoon sugar
1 teaspoon all-purpose flour
1/4 cup warm water
4 cups all-purpose flour, extra
1 teaspoon salt
1 1/4 cups lukewarm milk
1 egg, lightly beaten
3 tablespoons butter, melted

1 Lightly dust two 13 x 11 inch baking sheets with flour. Combine the yeast, sugar, flour and water in a small bowl and blend until smooth. Stand, covered with plastic wrap, in a warm place for 10 minutes or until mixture is foamy.
2 Sift the extra flour and salt into a large bowl.

Make a well in the center, add the milk, egg, butter and yeast mixture. Using a knife, mix to a soft dough. Turn the dough onto a lightly floured surface, knead for 2 minutes or until smooth. Shape the dough into a ball, place in a large, lightly oiled bowl. Leave, covered with plastic wrap, in a warm place for 1 hour or until dough is well risen.
3 Preheat the oven to moderately hot 400°F. Knead dough again for 2 minutes or until smooth. Roll dough to 1/2 inch thickness. Cut into rounds with a 3 inch cutter. Place rounds on prepared baking sheets. Leave, covered with plastic wrap, in warm place for 10 minutes. Bake muffins for 8 minutes, turn muffins over and bake for another 8–10 minutes or until golden.

Note: Muffins are easy and quick to make. They can be served for breakfast or lunch or with morning coffee or tea. They are best eaten on the day they are made. Serve warm with butter. Muffins may be frozen for up to three months.

MUSHROOMS

SEASONED MUSHROOM CAPS

★ **Preparation time:** 15 minutes
Total cooking time: 20 minutes
Makes 16

16 medium mushroom
caps
2 tablespoons olive oil
2 slices bacon, finely
chopped
1/2 cup soft fresh bread
crumbs
1 clove garlic, crushed

2 scallions, finely
chopped
1/4 cup grated Parmesan
cheese
2 tablespoons finely
chopped flat-leaf parsley
1 egg, lightly beaten

1 Preheat oven to hot 475°F. Line a 13 x 11 inch baking sheet with foil; grease foil. Remove mushroom stems from caps; chop the stems finely. Arrange caps on baking sheet.
2 Heat oil in large frying pan; add bacon. Cook over medium heat for 3 minutes, stirring occasionally. Add chopped mushroom stems to pan with the bacon. Cook over high heat for 2 minutes. Remove pan from heat.
3 Transfer the mixture to a medium bowl. Add bread crumbs, garlic, scallions, cheese, parsley and egg; using wooden spoon, stir until combined.
4 Divide bacon and mushroom mixture evenly into 16 portions. Press mixture into each cap. Bake for 12 minutes or until lightly golden.

OPPOSITE PAGE: ENGLISH MUFFINS.
ABOVE: SEASONED MUSHROOM CAPS

MUSHROOMS PROVENCAL

★ **Preparation time:** 45 minutes
Total cooking time: 50 minutes
Serves 4–6

1 lb mushrooms
1 medium leek
1/4 cup butter
1 clove garlic, crushed
juice and grated rind of
1 lemon
pepper

1/2 cup chopped parsley
freshly grated nutmeg
11/2 cups soft whole-
wheat bread crumbs
2 tablespoons olive oil
1 garlic clove

1 Wipe over the mushrooms and cut them into slices. Trim the leek and wash well; cut into fine shreds. Preheat oven to 400°F, and grease an 8 inch ovenproof dish.
2 Melt butter in a heavy-bottom pan, add leek and cook, stirring, for 5 minutes over a low heat. Add sliced mushrooms and toss to coat in leek and butter mixture. Cover and cook 10 minutes. Remove lid, add crushed garlic and lemon rind and cook until most of the juices have evaporated, about 15–20 minutes.
3 Pour lemon juice over, reduce and season with pepper, parsley and nutmeg. Fold through 1/2 cup of the bread crumbs. Spoon into prepared casserole dish.
4 Heat oil in pan; add whole garlic and cook until garlic browns. Remove and discard garlic. Add remaining bread crumbs to oil, toss to coat crumbs.
5 Sprinkle crumbs over mushroom mixture. Bake for about 20 minutes or until mixture has heated through and crumb topping is crisp.

Mortadella A large, lightly smoked sausage made of pork or mixtures of either pork and beef or veal and ham. The meat is mixed with coarsely diced pork fat, seasoned, flavored with parsley and studded with green olives and pistachio nuts. It is served, thinly sliced, as an hors d'oeuvre, salad meat or sandwich filling.

Moussaka A baked dish of eggplant, ground lamb or beef and a topping of cheese sauce. It is popular in the Middle East, and most likely originated in Greece.

Mousse A rich, light sweet or savory dish that may include fruits or puréed fish, chicken or other ingredients. It has a smooth, foamy texture created from whisked egg white, whipped cream, or both. It may be served hot or cold.

Mousseline A mousse-like savory dish. Meat, seafood or poultry is folded into a cream and egg white mixture and cooked in small molds.

Mozzarella A rindless, unripened curd cheese, with a soft, plastic texture and a mild, slightly sweet, milky taste. Originally made from buffalo milk, it is now produced from cow's milk; it should be used within a few days of purchase. It is used in pizza and pasta dishes and melted as a topping.

Muenster Cheese A soft cow's milk cheese. The texture varies from smooth and waxy to dry and crumbly. It has a distinctive pungent taste and aroma.

Muesli A breakfast food of mixed raw cereals,

flakes, bran, wheat germ, nuts and dried fruit eaten with milk or yogurt.

Muffin Also known as a quick bread, a muffin is a light, sweet, soft bread baked in small, deep, round molds. Basic muffins are made from a

batter of egg, milk, flour and sugar. Sweet or savory flavorings can be added.

Mulberry A juicy berry, similar to a blackberry. Mulberries may be eaten fresh dusted with sugar and accompanied by

MUSHROOMS WITH GARLIC AND RED PEPPER SAUCES

★★ **Preparation time:** 30 minutes + 1 hour refrigeration
Total cooking time: 2 minutes each batch
Serves 8

1 lb 6 oz button
  mushrooms
⅓ cup all-purpose flour
3 eggs
1 cup dry bread crumbs
1 small red pepper
1 cup olive oil
2 egg yolks (or ¼ cup
  egg substitute)

1 teaspoon Dijon
  mustard
1 tablespoon lemon juice
1 small clove garlic, crushed
2 tablespoons plain
  yogurt
2 teaspoons finely
  chopped fresh parsley
olive oil for deep-frying,
  extra

1 Wipe the mushrooms with a damp cloth to remove any grit. Place flour in a large plastic bag, add mushrooms and shake until they are evenly coated in flour. Place eggs in a medium bowl and beat lightly. Dust excess flour from mushrooms. Divide mushrooms in half and coat first half well with egg. Repeat with second half.
2 Place dry bread crumbs in a large plastic bag. Add half the egg-coated mushrooms; shake to coat mushrooms thoroughly in bread crumbs.

Place crumbed mushrooms in a large bowl. Repeat with remaining mushrooms. Cover and refrigerate for 1 hour.
3 Brush red pepper with a little of the oil. Broil pepper until skin is black, then wrap in damp towel until cool. Rub off skin and place pepper in food processor or blender. Process to a smooth paste. Place egg yolks (or egg substitute), mustard and half the lemon juice in a medium mixing bowl. Using electric beaters, beat for 1 minute. Add oil, about a teaspoon at a time, beating constantly until mixture is thick and creamy. Increase addition of oil as mayonnaise thickens. Continue beating until all the oil is added; add remaining lemon juice. Divide mayonnaise between two bowls. Into one stir the garlic, yogurt and parsley; stir pepper purée into the other half.
4 Heat the extra olive oil in a medium heavy-based pan. Gently lower batches of mushrooms into moderately hot oil. Cook over medium-high heat for 1 minute or until golden brown. Remove with a slotted spoon and drain on paper towels. To serve, arrange the mushrooms on individual serving plates. Serve the sauces in separate bowls.

ABOVE: MUSHROOMS WITH GARLIC AND RED PEPPER SAUCES. OPPOSITE PAGE: CHINESE VEGETABLES WITH MUSHROOMS AND OYSTER SAUCE

CHINESE VEGETABLES WITH MUSHROOMS AND OYSTER SAUCE

Preparation time: 20 minutes
Total cooking time: 8 minutes
Serves 4

8 dried Chinese
    mushrooms
1 bunch Chinese green
    vegetables (bok choy,
    choy sum, gai lan)

2 tablespoons vegetable
    oil
2 tablespoons oyster sauce

1 Soak mushrooms in hot water. Thoroughly wash the green vegetables and drain well. Cut off thick stalks as these require longer cooking.
2 Trim stems from mushrooms, squeeze water from caps. Simmer in lightly salted water for 5 minutes; drain.
3 Bring a pan of water to the boil and plunge the vegetable stems in the water; cook for 1–2 minutes. Remove stems, drain. Briefly blanch the leafy parts and drain well.
4 Heat oil in a frying pan. Add well-drained vegetables and mushrooms and toss over moderate heat until well coated. Serve dressed with the oyster sauce.

MARINATED MUSHROOMS

Preparation time: 5 minutes
Total cooking time: 8 minutes
Serves 4

12 oz button mushrooms
¼ cup olive oil
1 clove garlic, crushed
1 tablespoon lemon juice
1 cup dry white wine or
    apple juice
1 bay leaf

1 tablespoon chopped
    fresh tarragon
freshly ground black
    pepper
1 tablespoon chopped
    fresh parsley

1 Wipe the mushrooms with a damp cloth and trim stalks level with caps. Heat oil in a medium pan, add garlic and mushrooms and toss over high heat until mushrooms have absorbed oil.
2 Add lemon juice, white wine, bay leaf, tarragon and pepper. Bring mixture to the boil and simmer for 5 minutes. Allow mushrooms to cool in liquid. Remove bay leaf. Sprinkle mushrooms with chopped parsley.
3 Drain mushrooms and serve on cocktail sticks as a first course or serve as a salad.

Note: Two peeled and chopped tomatoes can be added at the same time as the wine if desired.

MUSHROOM SOUP

Preparation time: 15 minutes
Total cooking time: 20 minutes
Serves 4

1 lb field mushrooms
    (open cap)
⅓ cup butter
1 large onion, chopped
1 clove garlic, crushed
2 tablespoons all-purpose
    flour

4 cups hot chicken stock
1 bay leaf
salt
freshly ground black
    pepper
½ cup heavy cream

1 Wipe mushrooms with a damp cloth and chop caps and stems. Melt butter in a large pan and add onion and garlic. Cook until onion is soft but not brown, add mushrooms and cook over high heat for 3 minutes while stirring.
2 Sprinkle flour over mushrooms, mix to combine, then stir in hot stock. Bring to the boil, add bay leaf and simmer for 10 minutes. Remove bay leaf and cool soup slightly.
3 Place soup in a food processor or blender and blend until smooth. (It may be necessary to do this in two batches.)
4 Return soup to rinsed pan, season with salt and pepper, heat until boiling. Stir in cream, serve.

whipped cream, puréed for sorbets and ice cream, stewed as a pie filling or made into jam. They are not usually commercially available since the berries are easily crushed, but

the tree is common in gardens and bears a copious crop each summer.

Mulligatawny
A spicy, soup-like dish of boiled rice topped with peppery, curry-flavored chicken or meat broth. The dish dates from the days of the British Raj in India.

Mung Bean A small bean with crisp, white, crunchy tendrils. Used in salads and stir-fries.

Mushroom Edible fungus found in a variety of shapes and sizes and ranging in taste from mild and nutty to strong and meaty. They may be eaten raw, in salads, or cooked. The most widely cultivated is the common mushroom with an umbrella-shaped cap that opens out as the mushroom grows. The youngest are sold as button mushrooms or champignons; next in size are cups (popular for stuffing); largest and with the most developed flavor are flats. The cèpe is a round-capped and stalked mushroom valued for its earthy flavor. The chanterelle or girolle, an apricot-colored, firm-fleshed, trumpet-shaped mushroom has a meaty flavor. The morel has a pointed, spongy, golden brown cap with a meaty flavor. Asian

mushroom varieties include the matsutake or pine mushroom, which has a dark brown cap and a thick meaty stem, lightly broiled it is considered a great delicacy in Japan. Also used in Japanese cooking is the enokitake or enoki, a tiny mushroom with a round cap atop a slender stem. Mild-flavored and crisp in texture, the enokitake is used in soups

and stews. The large floppy cap of the shiitake mushroom, usually sold dried, is used in Chinese and Japanese cooking.

Mussel A mollusk with a smooth almond-shaped shell. Like oysters, mussels are filter feeders, and so are subject to contamination. They should not be collected from areas where pollution is suspected.

MUSSELS

TOMATO GARLIC MUSSELS

⭐ **Preparation time:** 15 minutes
Total cooking time: 15 minutes
Serves 2–3

18 large live mussels
2 tablespoons butter
3 cloves garlic, crushed
3 large ripe tomatoes,
   chopped
1 tablespoon
   Worcestershire sauce
2 tablespoons tomato paste
¼ cup apple juice

1 Pick over mussels; discard those with damaged shells. Remove beards from mussels; wash away any grit. Pry open shells with small knife. Meat will be attached to one half-shell; discard other half.
2 Melt butter in large pan. Add garlic; cook 1 minute or until golden. Add tomato, Worcestershire sauce, tomato paste and apple juice; stir over medium heat 2 minutes. Bring to boil, reduce heat. Simmer, uncovered, 5 minutes.
3 Add mussels, cover and simmer 5 minutes or until mussels are tender.

BROILED MUSSELS

⭐ **Preparation time:** 10 minutes
Total cooking time: 5–10 minutes
Serves 2–4

1 lb mussels in shell
2 tablespoons lemon juice
1 clove garlic, crushed
1 small red chili pepper,
   finely chopped

1 Place mussels in pan of simmering water. Remove mussels as shells open; discard any that do not open.
2 Open out mussels and loosen from shells using scissors. Return mussels to half shells; discard other shells.
3 Combine lemon juice, garlic and chili; spoon over mussels. Place on broiler rack and broil 6–8 inches from heat until heated through. Sprinkle mussels with parsley to serve.

ABOUT MUSSELS

■ To remove all grit from mussels, immerse in salted water with a sprinkling of oatmeal or flour for at least 1 hour. The live mussels will digest the oatmeal, become plumper and expel grit.

1

2

3

MUSTARDS

CHICKEN DIJON

★ **Preparation time:** 10 minutes
Total cooking time: 20 minutes
Serves 6

6 boneless chicken breast   ¼ cup Dijon mustard
  halves   ¾ cup mayonnaise

1 Preheat oven to moderate 350°F. Lay a large piece of aluminum foil over a baking sheet. Lightly brush foil with melted butter or oil. Place chicken breasts, skin removed, side-by-side on prepared baking sheet.
2 Combine mustard and mayonnaise in small mixing bowl; stir until well combined.
3 Spoon the mayonnaise mixture over each chicken fillet.
4 Cover chicken with another large sheet of foil. Fold foil sheets together around edges until well sealed. Bake for 20 minutes or until chicken is tender.
5 To serve, spoon the juices over chicken. Serve with a green salad.

HERB MUSTARD

Place ¼ cup of white mustard seeds and 1 cup blanched almonds in a food processor and process until well ground. In a medium bowl, combine

OPPOSITE PAGE: TOMATO GARLIC MUSSELS.
ABOVE: CHICKEN DIJON

1 cup of oil, 1 cup of white vinegar and ¼ cup of sherry with 1 tablespoon each of chopped fresh chives, parsley and dill. Gradually pour through processor chute with the motor running. Process until mixture is thick and creamy. Spoon into sterilized jars. Seal and label the jars and store in a cool place for up to 4 weeks. This recipe makes about 2 cups of Herb Mustard.

HOT GRAIN MUSTARD

In a medium-sized heatproof bowl, combine ½ cup of black mustard seeds, ½ cup of yellow mustard seeds, 1 teaspoon of lightly crushed black peppercorns, 1 cup of oil, 1 cup of white vinegar, 1 cup of white wine and 2 teaspoons chopped fresh herbs of your choice. When you have mixed the ingredients well, place the bowl over a pan of simmering water. Gradually whisk in 2 beaten egg yolks and continue whisking until the mixture becomes thick and creamy. Remove the bowl from heat. When the mixture has cooled, spoon it into sterilized jars. Seal and label the jars and store in a cool place for up to two weeks. This recipe makes about 3 cups of Hot Grain Mustard.

DEVIL SAUCE

In a small bowl, mix together 1 teaspoon each of Dijon mustard, anchovy paste, Worcestershire sauce, white wine vinegar and sugar. Stir in 1 cup of whipped cream and serve with cold chicken.

Mussels are available live in the shell or canned, and are smoked, cooked or added to sauces.

Mustard A pungently flavored spice from the seeds of three members of the cabbage family and usually prepared as a condiment. White mustard, the mildest in flavor, is used in American mustard; brown and black mustard have more pungent seeds than white mustard. Black mustard seeds are used in Indian cooking and in pickles and chutneys. Brown and black mustard seeds, alone or combined, are ground into mustard powder and used to make English or French-style mustard.

Prepared mustard is made by softening seeds in liquid and pounding them to a paste. It is used to accompany meats, poultry and fish and as a flavoring in vinaigrettes, sauces and hot dishes.

Mustard Green The dark curly leaf of a young mustard plant. Small pieces add a peppery taste to salads.

Mutton The meat of a mature sheep, best suited to moist cooking.

N

Naan A puffy Indian bread made with wheat flour and ghee. It is traditionally baked plastered onto the inside walls of a clay oven.

Nacho A tortilla chip topped with melted cheese and chili peppers. Eaten as an appetizer.

Nam Pla See Nuoc Mam.

Napoleon A small pastry consisting of three layers of puff pastry filled with crème pâtissière or sweetened whipped cream, and topped with glazed icing decorated with lines of melted chocolate.

Nashi (Asian Pear, Apple Pear, Chinese Pear) A golden-green pear the shape and size of an apple. The pale translucent flesh is crisp, juicy and sweet. It may be eaten on its own or with cheese.

Nasi Goreng An Indonesian dish of fried rice garnished with chilies, thinly sliced meat, fried onions and slices of omelet.

NOODLES

BEEF SOUP WITH RICE NOODLES

★ ★ **Preparation time:** 30 minutes + 1 hour marinating
Total cooking time: 1 hour
Serves 4

12 oz beef tenderloin	6 cups beef stock
2 teaspoons soy sauce	2 tablespoons soft brown
1/4 cup coconut milk	sugar, extra
1 tablespoon crunchy	2 tablespoons fish sauce
peanut butter	(nuoc mam)
1 tablespoon soft brown	1 cup fresh bean sprouts
sugar	2 lettuce leaves, cut in
2 teaspoons sambal oelek	small pieces
or 1 small red chili	6 tablespoons finely
pepper, finely chopped	chopped fresh mint
1 teaspoon oil	leaves
4 oz rice vermicelli	1/2 cup roasted peanuts,
1 small, thin-skinned	finely chopped
cucumber	

1 Trim the meat of any fat and tendons. Slice meat across grain evenly into thin slices. Combine with the soy sauce, coconut milk, peanut butter, sugar and sambal oelek. Refrigerate, covered, for 1 hour.

2 Heat the oil in a pan. Brown the meat in small batches over high heat for 3 minutes. Remove from heat. Soak vermicelli in hot water 10 minutes; drain.
3 Cut cucumber in quarters lengthwise and then into thin slices. Heat the stock to boiling point. When boiling, add extra sugar and fish sauce.
4 Remove tails from bean sprouts. Place a tablespoon cucumber slices in each bowl. Divide sprouts, lettuce and mint leaves evenly between bowls. Place some vermicelli and a ladle of stock in each bowl, top with slices of cooked beef. Sprinkle with peanuts, serve immediately.

NOODLES WITH SHRIMP AND PORK

★ ★ **Preparation time:** 20 minutes
Total cooking time: 10 minutes
Serves 4

10 large cooked shrimp	1 tablespoon commercial
6 1/2 oz roast or Chinese	chili and ginger sauce,
barbecued pork	optional
1 lb fresh, thick noodles	1 tablespoon white
1/4 cup peanut oil	vinegar
2 teaspoons finely	1/4 cup chicken stock
chopped garlic	4 oz fresh bean sprouts,
1 tablespoon black bean	tails removed
sauce	3 scallions, finely sliced
1 tablespoon soy sauce	1/4 cup chopped fresh
	cilantro, for garnish

1 Peel and devein the shrimp. Cut the pork into thin slices. Cook the noodles in a pan of rapidly boiling water until just tender; drain and set aside.
2 Heat the oil in a wok or heavy-bottom frying pan, swirling gently to coat base and side. Add the garlic and cook, stirring, until it turns pale gold. Add the shrimp and pork, stir for 1 minute. Add the noodles to the wok with the black bean sauce, soy sauce, chili and ginger sauce, vinegar and chicken stock. Stir-fry over high heat until the mixture has heated through and all the sauce has been absorbed.
3 Add the bean sprouts and scallion and cook for a further minute. Serve immediately, garnished with cilantro.

Note: Chinese barbecued pork can be purchased from specialty Chinese stores.

ABOVE: BEEF SOUP WITH RICE NOODLES.
OPPOSITE PAGE: CRISP-FRIED THAI NOODLES

CRISP-FRIED THAI NOODLES

 Preparation time: 30 minutes
Total cooking time: 20 minutes
Serves 6 as a first course

oil for deep-frying	1 tablespoon fish sauce
4 oz rice vermicelli	(nuoc mam)
1 teaspoon chopped garlic	1 red chili pepper, seeded
8 oz ground pork	and finely chopped
8 medium uncooked	2 eggs, lightly beaten
shrimp, peeled and	4 oz fresh bean sprouts,
deveined	tails removed
2 tablespoons sugar	2 tablespoons fresh
2 tablespoons white	cilantro leaves
vinegar	

1 Heat the oil in a wok. Use tongs to lower small batches of vermicelli into the oil—the strands will instantly swell. Deep-fry each batch of noodles until they are golden, turning to color both sides. Drain on a paper towel. Cool the oil to room temperature.
2 Pour off all but 2 tablespoons oil from wok. Heat oil, add garlic and stir until golden. Add the pork. Cook over high heat for 3 minutes until meat is well browned and almost all of the liquid has evaporated. Add the shrimp, stirring for another 30 seconds. Add sugar, vinegar, fish sauce and chili. Bring to boil, stirring; add the eggs. Cook, stirring, until eggs are set.
3 Add the bean sprouts and noodles, tossing them thoroughly to combine. Scatter with cilantro leaves. Serve immediately.

Note: Do not try to speed things up by deep-frying too many noodles at a time— they will not become crisp. If still puffed and white, they will not stay crisp when returned to the sauce.

NOODLE SALAD

 Preparation time: 10 minutes +
10 minutes standing + refrigeration
Total cooking time: 20 minutes
Serves 4

8 oz fresh thick egg noodles	1 large carrot, cut into
2 red peppers, seeded, cut	fine strips, 2 1/2 inches
into quarters	long
2 green peppers, seeded,	1/3 cup olive oil
cut into quarters	2 tablespoons lemon juice
3 scallions, chopped	1 tablespoon finely
	chopped fresh mint

1 Cook noodles in a large pan of boiling water until just tender; drain and cool.
2 Place peppers on foil-lined baking sheet, skin-side-up. Broil 5 inches from the heat or until the skins blister and turn black. Remove from broiler, cover with clean damp towel and stand for 10 minutes.
3 Carefully remove skin from peppers. Cut flesh into 1/2 inch wide strips. Place in bowl with noodles, scallions and carrot; toss.
4 Whisk together the oil, lemon and mint in a small jug. Pour over the salad and mix well. Cover, refrigerate several hours or overnight. Toss again just before serving.

Navel Orange A seedless, sweet, flavorful orange with thick-rind. See also Orange.

Navy Bean (Yankee Bean) A small white legume used for canned pork and beans. See also Bean, Dried.

Nectarine A round, rosy pink thin-skinned

fruit with juicy flesh surrounding a large pit; it is a variety of peach. It can be eaten fresh, added to fruit salads, stewed or baked. Nectarines are in season in late summer.

Nesselrode Pie A chilled custard pie of chestnut purée, egg yolk, cream and sometimes candied fruit.

Neufchâtel Cheese A fresh unripened, soft, white cow's milk cheese made from whole or partly skimmed milk. It is similar to cream cheese, but is more moist and has a lower fat content and softer texture. It is eaten fresh or used for cheesecakes, mousses, icings and cake toppings.

Newburg Shellfish, usually lobster, sautéed. Served with cream, egg yolk and sherry sauce.

New York Steak
(New York Strip) A cut
of meat from the tender
beef short loin. It may
be grilled, broiled or
sautéed.

Niçoise, à la
A French term
for dishes
which have
tomato, garlic,
black olives,
anchovy and
olive oil in the
sauce. This style
of cooking originated
around Nice, in southern
France.

Noisette A French term
for dishes flavored with
or made of hazelnuts. It
is also used to describe a
thick slice from a boned
loin of lamb, rolled and
secured with a thin band
of fat, like a tournedos.

Noisette Butter A
sauce made by slowly
heating butter until
foaming and nut-brown,
adding lemon juice, then
immediately pouring
over fish, brains, eggs
or cooked vegetables.

Noodle A dough
of flour and water
(sometimes made with
egg yolk or whole egg)
cut into long, ribbon-
like strips and fried
or boiled. Noodles
originated in Asia
and are also used in
the Mediterranean,
particularly Italy, and
northern
Europe.
The name
comes from
the German
Nudel.

SEAFOOD NOODLE HOT POT

Preparation time: 15 minutes
Total cooking time: 14 minutes
Serves 4–6

2 tablespoons vegetable oil
1½ inch piece fresh ginger, peeled and grated
4 scallions, trimmed and sliced
½ small cabbage, shredded
8 cups water or fish stock
¼ cup soy sauce
2 tablespoons dry sherry
1 teaspoon sesame oil
6½ oz flat rice noodles
8 oz bottled oysters, drained
8 oz scallops
8 oz uncooked shrimp, peeled and deveined, tail intact
shredded green tops of scallion for garnish

1 Heat the oil in a large pan. Add the ginger, scallion and cabbage; cook gently until the cabbage is just soft.
2 Add the water, soy sauce, sherry and sesame oil to the ingredient in the pan. Bring to the boil, add the noodles and cook for 8 minutes. Reduce to a simmer, add the oysters, scallops and shrimp and cook for 3–4 minutes or until the shrimp are just cooked.
3 Place in a serving bowl, garnish with the shredded scallion and serve.

ABOVE: SEAFOOD NOODLE HOT POT; RIGHT: CRISP FRIED NOODLES AND CHILI VEGETABLES. OPPOSITE PAGE: SATAY LAMB WITH NOODLES

CRISP FRIED NOODLES AND CHILI VEGETABLES

Preparation time: 25 minutes
Total cooking time: 10 minutes
Serves 4–6

3⅓ oz packet rice vermicelli
oil, for deep-frying
1 teaspoon oil
2 teaspoons grated fresh ginger
1 tablespoon finely chopped cilantro
1 clove garlic, finely diced
1 onion, cut into thin wedges
1 green pepper, cut into strips
1 red pepper, cut into strips
1 large carrot, cut into thin strips
13 oz can baby corn, drained
13 oz can straw mushrooms, drained
½ cup soy sauce
¼ cup malt vinegar
2 teaspoons brown sugar
1 teaspoon preserved chopped chili
½ cup cilantro leaves, for garnish

1 Deep-fry rice vermicelli in hot oil. Drain on paper towel. Place on a large serving plate and keep warm.
2 Heat 1 teaspoon of oil in a large pan. Add the ginger, cilantro and garlic and cook for 2 minutes. Add onion, green and red pepper, and carrot. Stir-fry for 3 minutes. Add corn, mushrooms, combined soy sauce, vinegar, brown sugar and chili. Stir and cook over high heat for 3 minutes.
3 Spoon vegetables over the noodles and pour over any remaining sauce. Garnish with cilantro leaves and serve.

SATAY LAMB WITH NOODLES

⭐ **Preparation time:** 15 minutes
Total cooking time: 10 minutes
Serves 4

1½ lb lamb fillets
¼ cup peanut oil
3 large onions, cut in
   thin wedges
⅓ cup crunchy peanut
   butter
2 tablespoons hoisin sauce

½ cup coconut milk
¼ teaspoon garam masala
3½ oz dried egg noodles
3 teaspoons sesame oil
2 scallions, finely
   chopped

1 Trim lamb of any fat and sinew. Slice meat across grain evenly into thin slices. Heat 1 tablespoon of oil in a wok or heavy-bottom frying pan, swirling to coat base and side. Add the onions, stir-fry over high heat for 5 minutes. Remove from wok; keep warm.
2 Heat the remaining oil in the wok, swirling to coat base and side. Cook the meat quickly in small batches over high heat until browned but not cooked through. Remove and drain on a paper towel.
3 Combine peanut butter, hoisin sauce, coconut milk and garam masala in a small bowl. Add to the wok, stir over medium heat until the mixture boils. Return meat and onion to wok, stir until they are coated with sauce and just heated through.
4 Cook noodles in large pan of boiling water until just tender; drain. Toss with sesame oil and scallions. Serve topped with satay lamb.

MARINATED BEEF AND NOODLE SALAD

⭐ **Preparation time:** 20 minutes +
2 hours marinating
Total cooking time: 5 minutes
Serves 4–6

13 oz rare roast beef, cut
   into thin strips

Marinade
¼ cup lemon juice
¼ cup fish sauce (nuoc
   mam)
2 tablespoons soy sauce
1 tablespoon brown sugar
2 teaspoons sambal oelek
   (bottled red chilies)

Salad
10 oz fresh wheat
   noodles
1 cup mint leaves,
   coarsely chopped
1 cup cilantro, coarsely
   chopped
1 butterhead lettuce, torn
   into pieces
1 cucumber, peeled,
   seeded and sliced
1 red onion, sliced

1 Combine marinade ingredients; pour over beef, cover and marinate for 2 hours.
2 Cook noodles in boiling water until just tender; drain. While still hot add mint and cilantro, toss.
3 Place lettuce, cucumber and onion on serving plate, add noodles. Arrange meat slices on top and pour over remaining marinade.

EGG NOODLES WITH CHICKEN AND HAM

⭐ **Preparation time:** 20 minutes +
5 minutes soaking
Total cooking time: 5 minutes
Serves 4–6

10 oz egg noodles,
   soaked in water for
   5 minutes
oil, for deep-frying
1 tablespoon chopped
   ginger
2 scallions, chopped
10 oz can baby corn,
   drained

½ cooked chicken, meat
   removed and cut into
   thin strips
3½ oz ham from the
   bone, cut into thin
   strips
¾ cup chicken stock
2 tablespoons dry sherry
1 tablespoon soy sauce

1 Drain noodles well, then dry between sheets of paper towel. Deep-fry in oil until just crisp. Drain noodles and place onto large serving plate. Keep warm. Remove all but 2 teaspoons of oil from pan.
2 Add the ginger and scallions to pan, cook for 2 minutes. Add corn, chicken and ham. Stir in stock, sherry and soy sauce, cook 3–4 minutes.
3 Spoon chicken and ham mixture over noodles, top with sauce. Serve.

Nopales See Cactus Pads.

Nougat A chewy candy traditionally made of honey, sugar, egg white and nuts.

Nouvelle Cuisine
A style of cooking which emphasizes fresh, natural ingredients and flavors, simple cooking methods and imaginative presentation. Sauces are light and based on reduced stocks and purées rather than fats and flour.

Nuoc Mam (Nam Pla) Literally "fish water," a clear, amber-colored seasoning sauce with a pungent, salty taste. It is used in Vietnamese and Thai cooking to enhance the flavor in foods. Vietnamese nuoc mam is darker in color and has a stronger fishy taste than other types.

Nut A hard-shelled seed, particularly one with an edible kernel. They are among the earliest of human foods. Nuts are used in cakes, desserts and candy as well as in curries and stir-fries. Roasted nuts are a popular snack food.

Nutmeg A hard, brown oval seed which is ground into a pungent spice. It is most fragrant when freshly grated.

N NOODLES

Most Asian noodles are shaped in long narrow strings or flat strips, their length traditionally signifying long life. Different types of flour are used. Some noodles are made with eggs, and some need to be soaked before cooking.

Both dried and fresh noodles are sold: fresh ones can be kept for 3-4 days in the refrigerator; dried noodles will keep indefinitely in a cool, dry place. In Asian cuisines, noodles are served in soups and stir-fries, and can also be deep-fried.

WHEAT FLOUR NOODLES are made with or without eggs. Egg noodles range in color from light golden to deep yellow, while the eggless types are paler. Available fresh or dried, they are sold in compressed bundles and may be thick or thin, flat (for soups) or rounded (for frying). Cook fresh or dried varieties in a large pan of boiling water until just tender, testing frequently. When cooked, drain, run under cold running water, and drain the noodles again.

WHEAT NOODLES FROM JAPAN include: somen, very fine, thin and white, may be boiled, drained and eaten cold with a dipping sauce or simmered and served in clear, delicate soups; and udon, thick and buff-colored, used for heartier broths. They are sold in dried form, attractively bound in bundles and (less widely) fresh or in vacuum packs.

RICE FLOUR NOODLES, made from ground rice and water, come in various widths and thicknesses, but thin rice vermicelli (*mi fun*) and the flat, dried form known as *ho fun* or rice sticks are the most common. Rice vermicelli are soaked in hot water for 10 minutes before using in soups or stir-fries. For a crispy garnish, small bundles, direct from the pack, can be deep-fried in hot oil. Thicker noodles are soaked for 30-40 minutes, then cooked in boiling water for 6-10 minutes, testing frequently, until they are just tender.

FRESH RICE NOODLES, thick and pearly white, are sold in Asian stores. Some have a light coating of oil which is removed by pouring boiling water over them. Rice noodles can also be bought in the form of large rolled sheets, which are cut crosswise into ribbons. Soak noodles in boiling water for about 2 minutes until barely tender, drain well and add to stir-fries.

GROUND BUCKWHEAT plus a little wheat flour is the basis of Japanese soba noodles; usually beige colored, some are subtly flavored with green tea or beetroot. They can be purchased in dried form from Asian and health food stores: fresh soba noodles may be more difficult to find. Cook in boiling water until just tender, drain. Serve either hot in a broth or cold with a dipping sauce.

BEAN FLOUR NOODLES, made with soy or mung bean starch, are fine and semi-translucent. They are known as cellophane noodles or bean thread vermicelli. Soak noodles in hot water for 10 minutes or until softened, then drain well before adding to stir-fries. In small bundles (unsoaked), noodles can also be deep-fried.

RICE VERMICELLI

FRESH RICE NOODLES

HARUSAME (JAPANESE BEAN NOODLES)

CELLOPHANE/BEAN THREAD NOODLES

HARUSAME (JAPANESE BEAN NOODLES)

CHINESE NOODLES WITHOUT EGG

CHINESE NOODLES

FRESH CHINESE
EGG NOODLES

FRESH CHINESE
NOODLES

FRESH BUCKWHEAT
NOODLES

DRIED GREEN PEA BUCKWHEAT NOODLES

DRIED BUCKWHEAT NOODLES

UDON NOODLES

FRESH NOODLES
WITHOUT EGGS

SOMEN NOODLES

Oat Bran The coarse outer layers of the oat, removed in the milling process. Oat bran is used in cooking and is a good source of soluble fiber. It is sometimes added to breakfast cereals.

Oatcake A cake of unleavened bread made from oatmeal, water and a small amount of fat. Traditionally in northern England dollops of dough were cooked on a hot griddle until firm, then hung up until crisp and dry. In Scotland and Wales thin rounds of oatmeal paste were cooked slowly in a warm oven.

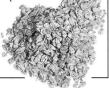

Oat Groats Oats that have been cleaned, toasted, hulled and cleaned again.

Oatmeal (Rolled Oats) Oat groats that have been steamed and flattened. Quick-cooking oatmeal is groats that have been cut up

OCTOPUS

MARINATED BABY OCTOPUS SALAD

⭐ **Preparation time:** 25 minutes + 1 hour marinating
Total cooking time: 10 minutes
Serves 4

1 lb 10 oz baby octopus
1/3 cup olive oil
2 cloves garlic, crushed
1 tablespoon Thai sweet chili sauce
1 medium red pepper, finely chopped
2 tablespoons chopped fresh cilantro
2 tablespoons lime juice

1 Clean the octopus with a small sharp knife: cut off head, or slit open, and remove gut.
2 Pick up the body, push beak up with index finger; remove and discard. Clean the octopus well under running water; pat dry with paper towel. Combine the octopus with oil and garlic. Cover with plastic wrap and marinate for 1–2 hours.
3 Heat the barbecue grill. When very hot, cook the octopus for about 3–5 minutes or until it is tender. Drain well on a paper towel. Combine the chili sauce, pepper, cilantro and juice in serving bowl. Add the octopus and stir. Serve warm or cold.

OCTOPUS IN RED WINE

⭐⭐ **Preparation time:** 20 minutes
Total cooking time: 35 minutes
Serves 4

2 lb baby octopus
1/3 cup olive oil
1 large onion, finely chopped
2 bay leaves
2 tablespoons dry red wine
2 tablespoons brown vinegar
1/2 teaspoon cracked black pepper
1/2 teaspoon dried oregano leaves

1 To clean the octopus, use a small, sharp knife to slit open head; remove gut. Pick up the body and use index finger to push beak up; remove and discard. Rinse the octopus under running water; pat dry with paper towel.
2 Place the octopus, oil, onion and bay leaves in large heavy-bottom frying pan. Cook, uncovered, over medium heat for 20 minutes or until almost all the liquid is absorbed, stirring occasionally.
3 Add remaining ingredients to pan. Bring to boil, reduce heat and simmer, covered, for 15 minutes or until octopus is just tender. Serve warm or cold with Greek salad.

ABOVE: MARINATED BABY OCTOPUS SALAD.
OPPOSITE PAGE, ABOVE: CRUMBED BRAINS;
BELOW: KIDNEYS AND BACON

OFFAL

KIDNEYS AND BACON

Preparation time: 10 minutes
Total cooking time: 10 minutes
Serves 4

4 slices bacon
8 lamb's kidneys
1/4 cup all-purpose flour
salt and freshly ground
 pepper
2 tablespoon butter
1 tablespoon olive oil

1/2 cup veal or chicken
 stock
2 teaspoons Dijon mustard
2 teaspoons lemon juice
1 tablespoon chopped
 parsley

1 Cook bacon in a hot dry pan. Transfer to a heated serving plate and keep hot. Wipe pan clean with paper towel.
2 Remove membrane and core from kidneys and slice kidneys across in half. Combine flour, salt and pepper and roll kidneys in flour, shaking off excess. Heat butter and oil in a heavy-bottom pan and cook kidneys over medium heat until browned; the inside should be faintly pink and moist. Remove from pan and keep warm.
3 Add stock, mustard, lemon juice and parsley to pan and simmer until sauce is reduced by half. Return the kidneys to the pan for a few seconds only to heat through.
4 Serve kidneys and sauce with bacon and accompany with hot buttered toast.

CRUMBED BRAINS

Preparation time: 20 minutes
Total cooking time: 12 minutes
Serves 4

4 sets lamb's brains
2 tablespoons all-purpose
 flour
salt and freshly ground
 pepper
1 egg

2 tablespoons milk
1/2 cup dried bread crumbs
light olive oil for shallow
 frying
cooked bacon for serving

1 Rinse brains under cold running water and carefully remove as much of the surrounding membrane and blood vessels as possible. Place brains in a pan of lightly salted water and bring to the boil. Reduce heat and simmer for 6–7 minutes; drain. Plunge brains into a bowl of iced water to prevent further cooking; drain again, then pat dry with paper towels. If desired, cut each set of brains through center horizontally to give two pieces.
2 Combine flour, salt and pepper on a sheet of waxed paper. Toss brains in seasoned flour; shake off excess. Beat egg in a small bowl, add milk and mix to combine. Dip brains into egg mixture. Coat with bread crumbs; shake off excess. Store, covered, in the refrigerator for 30 minutes before cooking.
3 Heat the oil in a heavy-bottom pan; fry brains until golden brown on all sides. Remove from pan; drain on paper towel. Serve brains hot with bacon.

before steaming and flattening. Oatmeal can be added to breads, muffins, cookie doughs and meatloaf. Cooked oatmeal is served warm as a breakfast cereal, usually with milk and sugar.

Octopus A tender-fleshed saltwater mollusk with eight tentacles, a large head with a strong beak, a small sac-like body and no internal

backbone; best for eating are the small varieties. Octopus should be either cooked slowly, simmered in wine or its own juices or stuffed and baked, or cooked rapidly over a high heat. It is popular in Asia, especially Japan, and Mediterranean countries. Pre-dressed fresh and frozen octopus is sold in many supermarkets and seafood shops. It is also sold smoked and canned.

Oeufs à la Neige (Eggs in the Snow) A dessert of French origin consisting of egg-sized spoonfuls of meringue poached in vanilla-flavored sweetened milk, drained and placed on top of a rich custard sauce made from the poaching milk.

Offal Also called variety meats. The general term used to describe the edible internal organs of an animal: heart, liver, tripe, kidneys, sweetbreads and brains as well as the tongue, tail, feet and head.

Oil, Vegetable The clear liquid extracted from various seeds, nuts and fruit, including almond, avocado, rape seed, coconut, cottonseed, grapeseed, hazelnut, corn, olive, peanut, pumpkin seed, safflower, sesame seed, soy bean, sunflower seed and walnut. Oils with fine flavor, such as olive, walnut, hazelnut, almond and pumpkin seed, are used to flavor cold foods, such as salads, and are added to hot foods such as pasta, fish or cooked vegetables just before serving to preserve the oil's aroma and taste. Oils used primarily for cooking include corn, safflower, peanut, coconut (high in saturated fats), cottonseed, sunflower and vegetable (a blend of oils sold as an all-purpose cooking oil).

Okra Also known as ladies' fingers, a long, rigid, five-sided, green seed pod, pointed at one end and containing numerous small white seeds. Okra has a gelatinous quality when cooked and is often used as a thickener. In Middle Eastern and Greek cooking the pod is usually left whole; in Cajun cooking it is cut into wheel-like discs and

VENETIAN LIVER

Preparation time: 15 minutes
Total cooking time: 30 minutes
Serves 4

1 lb calves' liver, trimmed
1/4 cup butter
4 medium white onions, sliced
3/4 cup dry white wine
salt and freshly ground pepper
1/4 cup butter, extra
parsley or chervil

1 Remove all the membrane from the liver and cut the liver into very thin slices, removing blood vessels. Cover and set aside.

2 Heat the butter in a heavy-based pan and cook onions until soft but not brown. Add wine and simmer gently, stirring occasionally, for 20 minutes or until pale golden in color. If necessary add a little water to pan to prevent the onions drying out. Add salt and pepper; remove onions to a serving dish and keep hot. Wipe pan clean with paper towel.

3 Heat the extra butter in the same pan until it turns a pale brown color. Cook the liver slices over a high heat for about 1 minute, turning once; the inside should be just cooked and still tender.

4 Arrange liver slices over onions and garnish with parsley or chervil.

TRIPE AND ONIONS

Preparation time: 25 minutes
Total cooking time: 2½ hours
Serves 4

2 lb tripe
1 small onion, chopped
3 tablespoons butter
2 medium onions, chopped, extra
1/4 cup all-purpose flour
1½ cups tripe stock (see method)
1 cup milk
salt, pepper and nutmeg to taste
2 tablespoons chopped parsley

1 To blanch tripe, wash well and place in a pan of cold water with a generous squeeze of lemon juice. Bring to the boil, pour off water and plunge tripe into cold water. Drain well.

2 Cut blanched tripe into small strips and place in a large pan with chopped onion. Add water to cover. Bring to boil, cover and simmer for about 2 hours or until tender. Drain tripe and reserve 1½ cups of liquid for stock.

3 Heat butter in a medium pan and cook extra onion until soft but not brown. Stir in flour and cook for 1 minute. Add stock and milk gradually to pan, stirring until mixture is smooth. Stir constantly over medium heat until sauce boils and thickens. Add tripe, salt, pepper, nutmeg and parsley and simmer for 5 minutes.

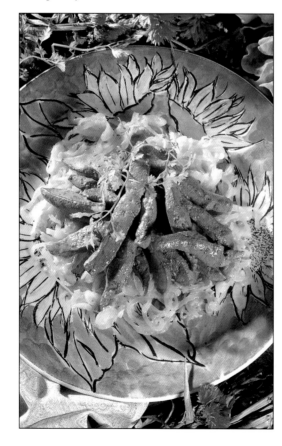

LEFT: VENETIAN LIVER; ABOVE: TRIPE AND ONIONS. OPPOSITE PAGE, ABOVE: CHICKEN WITH OKRA; BELOW: OKRA WITH ONIONS AND TOMATOES

OKRA

OKRA WITH ONIONS AND TOMATO

★★ **Preparation time:** 10 minutes +
4 hours soaking
Total cooking time: 1 hour 4 minutes
Serves 4

1 cup dried chickpeas (garbanzo beans)	1 tablespoon lemon juice
3 cups water	2 tablespoons red wine, optional
1 tablespoon olive oil	1 lb okra or 2 x 12 oz cans okra, drained
8 small pearl onions	
2 cloves garlic, crushed	
4 medium tomatoes, peeled and chopped	1 tablespoon chopped fresh oregano
1½ cups tomato juice	1 teaspoon ground pepper

1 Soak the chickpeas in water for 4 hours or overnight; drain. Heat the oil in a medium pan; add the onions and garlic. Cook on medium-high heat for 4 minutes or until golden. Add the chopped tomatoes, chickpeas, tomato juice, lemon juice and wine. Simmer, covered, for 40 minutes.

2 Add the okra and simmer for another 20 minutes. If using canned okra, add it to the tomato mixture in the last 5 minutes of cooking. Stir in the oregano and ground pepper. Serve with rice as a main meal or as an accompaniment to a meat dish.

CHICKEN WITH OKRA

★ **Preparation time:** 10 minutes
Total cooking time: 55 minutes
Serves 4

8 boneless chicken thighs (1½ lb)	14½ oz can diced tomatoes
2 tablespoons butter, melted	¼ teaspoon ground black pepper
2 cloves garlic, crushed	2 lb baby okra or 4 x 12 oz cans okra drained, not rinsed
¼ cup olive oil	
2 large onions, thinly sliced	

1 Trim the chicken thighs of excess fat and tendons. Place chicken on a cold, lightly oiled broiler rack. Cook 6–8 inches from the heat for 12 minutes or until tender, turning once. Brush with the combined butter and half the garlic several times during cooking. Remove from broiler; keep warm.

2 Heat oil in a heavy-bottom pan. Add onions and remaining garlic. Stir over high heat for 3 minutes. Reduce heat to low, cook for another 10 minutes, stirring occasionally. Add tomatoes and pepper. Simmer, covered, for 5 minutes.

3 Preheat oven to moderately hot 400° F. Top and tail okra and add to pan. Stir gently to combine. Simmer, covered, for 10 minutes. Pour okra mixture into a shallow ovenproof dish.

4 Arrange chicken over okra. Bake 15 minutes or until just heated through. Serve warm with bread, olives and cheese.

is often combined with tomato. It is used to flavor and thicken gumbo. Okra may be pickled, baked, deep-fried or served in sauces. It is used in many soups and stews in the south and the Caribbean. Native to tropical Africa, it was introduced during slave trade days. Okra is in season summer to autumn; look for crisp, bright-colored pods. It is also sold canned and frozen.

Olive The small, oval, oil-rich

fruit of an evergreen tree native to the Mediterranean region. Olives are picked unripe (green) and ripe (black). The flesh is treated to remove its bitterness and is then soaked in brine. Oil pressed from the ripe fruit has cosmetic and medicinal uses as well as an acclaimed culinary role. Green olives have a tart taste and come from fruit picked before fully mature. Olives are served as a finger food with drinks, a practice that goes back to Roman times, and in cooking with sauces, stuffings, pizzas, breads, salads and as a garnish.

The olive is the oldest tree in continuous cultivation and has been

ONIONS

Onions have been revered since ancient times. This pungent member of the lily family, with its slightly sweet flavor and savory aroma, will enhance most meat or vegetable dishes. Fried, baked or pickled, onions are also a versatile vegetable in their own right.

SPICY ONIONS AND TOMATOES

Peel and thinly slice 2 medium red onions. Heat 1 tablespoon butter, 1 tablespoon oil, ½ teaspoon each ground cumin, coriander, turmeric and garam masala. Add onions, cook 2–3 minutes. Stir in 2 chopped medium-ripe tomatoes. Cook for 3 minutes more until the onions are soft. Serve onions warm, sprinkled with chopped cilantro.

CURRIED ONION RINGS

SPICY ONIONS AND TOMATOES

GOLDEN BABY ONIONS

Peel 12 small onions, leaving base intact. Heat 2 tablespoons butter, 1 tablespoon oil and ¼ teaspoon sweet paprika in frying pan. Add onions, cook over medium heat for 5 minutes or until tender. Stir in ½ teaspoon soft brown sugar. Serve warm.

CURRIED ONION RINGS

Peel and slice 2 medium onions into thin rings. Heat 2 tablespoons olive oil in a frying pan. Add 2 teaspoons curry powder and onion rings. Cook for 5 minutes or until onion rings are tender. Stir in ½ teaspoon soft brown sugar. Serve warm.

GARLIC ONIONS

Peel and cut 2 medium onions into eight wedges. Heat 1 tablespoon butter and 2 tablespoons oil in a frying pan. Add 1–2 cloves crushed garlic and onions. Cook over medium heat for 5–6 minutes or until tender. Sprinkle with chopped chives. Serve warm.

GARLIC ONIONS

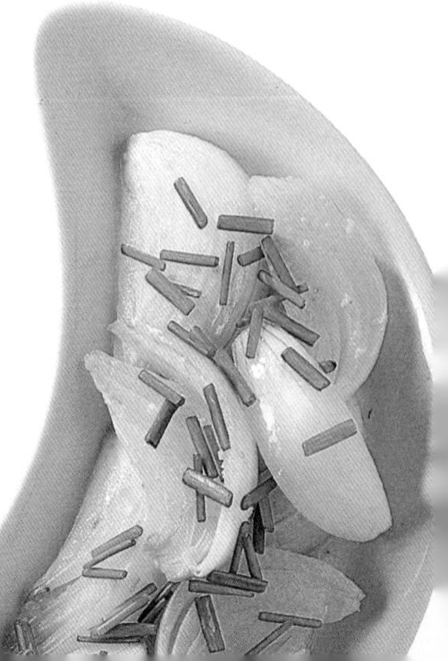

GOLDEN BABY ONIONS

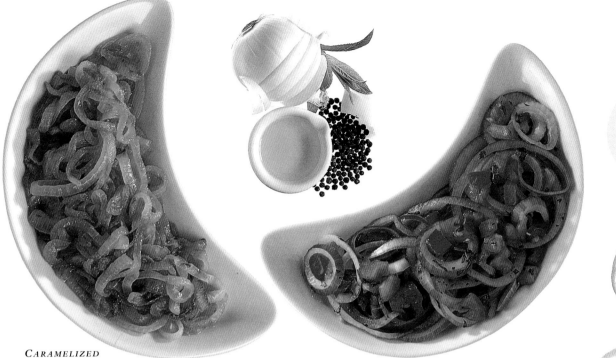

CARAMELIZED
ONIONS

QUICK ONION SALSA

THYME AND
ONIONS

BAKED ONIONS

CARAMELIZED ONIONS

Peel and cut 2 medium onions into thin rings. Heat 2 tablespoons butter and 1 tablespoon oil in heavy-bottom frying pan. Add onions, cook over low heat for 10–12 minutes or until onions are dark golden, stirring occasionally. Serve warm.

THYME AND ONIONS

Peel and cut 2 medium onions into eight wedges. Heat 2 teaspoons butter and 2 tablespoons oil in heavy-bottom frying pan. Add onions, cook over medium heat for 5 minutes or until tender and golden. Stir in 1 teaspoon each chopped fresh thyme and rosemary. Cook for 1 minute more. Drizzle with vinegar. Serve warm.

QUICK ONION SALSA

Peel and finely slice 1 large red onion. Combine with 2 tablespoons lime juice, 1 tablespoon olive oil, 1 teaspoon soft brown sugar, 1 tablespoon chopped fresh cilantro, 1 chopped tomato, and 1 finely chopped jalapeño chili pepper. Mix well and season. Cover and set aside at room temperature 10 minutes before serving.

BAKED ONIONS

Peel 8 small onions, leaving bases intact. Place in baking dish. Brush liberally with a mixture of 1 tablespoon melted butter and 1 tablespoon oil. Bake in a moderate 350°F oven for 30 minutes or until golden brown. Serve warm.

grown in the eastern Mediterranean for some 6,000 years. Egyptian paintings show olives being picked; ancient Crete, about 3,800 years ago, became the center of an export trade shipping olive oil to Egypt and Asia Minor. The olive was virtually indispensable in ancient times, valued for its fruit and the multipurpose oil it provided, as well as for its close-grained hardwood. Olives are sometimes available fresh but more usually are sold pickled whole (either loose or in jars and cans), pitted and stuffed with pimiento or almonds or salted and dried (either loose or in vacuum-sealed packs).

Olive Oil A pale yellow to deep green, monounsaturated vegetable oil pressed from the pulp of ripe olives. It has a fruity flavor and in cooking adds both flavor and nutrition to any dish in which it is an ingredient. Cold-pressed olive oil is produced by pressure only. Heat allows more oil to be extracted, but affects the taste. Olive oil is graded according to its level of acidity: the finest, extra virgin, with less than 1 per cent acid and deep green in

OLIVES

CHICKEN AND OLIVES

★★ **Preparation time:** 30 minutes + 1 hour standing
Total cooking time: 1 hour
Serves 6

12 chicken pieces	1 red pepper, chopped
1 teaspoon ground cinnamon	1/4 cup fresh cilantro,
1 teaspoon ground ginger	chopped
1/2 teaspoon ground	1 1/2 cups chicken stock
turmeric	4 strips preserved or
1 teaspoon sweet paprika	regular lemon rind,
1/2 teaspoon ground pepper	grated
1/4 cup olive oil	2 tablespoons lemon juice
2 onions, chopped	1 cup green olives

1 Combine chicken with spices in large bowl. Stand, covered, for 1 hour. Heat 2 tablespoons oil in a large pan. Cook chicken until well browned, but not cooked through. Transfer to larger pan.
2 Add remaining oil to first pan. Add onion and pepper. Cook over low heat for 5 minutes, stirring. Add to chicken pieces in larger pan.
3 Add the cilantro and stock, rind, juice and olives. Simmer, covered, for 40 minutes, until the chicken is tender and the liquid has reduced. Serve with rice.

MARINATED OLIVES

■ Whisk together virgin olive oil, crushed garlic, finely chopped orange rind, orange juice and freshly ground pepper. Add kalamata olives, sliced red onion and mix well. Cover and marinate for 2–3 hours before serving.

■ Crack green olives lightly with a meat mallet under a towel, or make small slits around the olive with a small sharp knife. Combine virgin olive oil, dry vermouth, bruised juniper berries, freshly ground black pepper. Add olives, whole blanched almonds and sliced lemons and mix well. Cover and marinate for 12 hours in refrigerator, stirring occasionally.

■ Combine olive oil, lemon juice, crushed garlic, chopped fresh oregano and a crumbled bay leaf. Add black olives, thinly shredded lemon rind, chopped celery, chopped red pepper and chopped flat-leaf parsley; mix well. Cover and marinate olives for 2–3 hours before serving.

■ Whisk together olive oil, crushed garlic, balsamic vinegar and freshly ground black pepper. Add some black olives, chopped sun-dried tomatoes, chopped fresh basil and pine nuts; mix well. Cover and marinate olives for 2–3 hours before serving.

ABOVE: CHICKEN AND OLIVES.
OPPOSITE PAGE: BLACK OLIVE AND ONION PIE

OLIVE AND ONION TART

★★ **Preparation time:** 1 hour +
30 minutes refrigeration
Total cooking time: 1 hour 25 minutes
Serves 8

1 cup all-purpose flour	*2 tablespoons butter, extra*
½ cup whole-wheat flour	*1 tablespoon brown*
½ cup butter, chopped	* mustard*
4–5 tablespoons iced	*1 cup sour cream*
* water*	*3 eggs, lightly beaten*
6 medium white onions	*½ cup pitted olives, sliced*

1 Combine flours in a bowl. Add ½ cup butter. Rub butter into flour until fine and crumbly. Add most of water, mix to a firm dough, add more water if needed. Turn onto a floured surface, knead until smooth. Roll out to fit a 9 inch fluted tart pan. Line pan with pastry; refrigerate 30 minutes.
2 Preheat oven to 350°F. Cut a sheet of parchment paper to fit tart pan. Place over pastry, cover with rice or dried beans. Bake 10 minutes, discard paper and rice, return pastry to oven for 10 minutes.
3 Peel and slice onions. Heat extra butter in saucepan, add onions. Cook, stirring occasionally, over medium-low heat 45 minutes. Set aside to cool.
4 Spread mustard over pastry. Spread onions over mustard. In a bowl, whisk together sour cream and eggs, pour over onions. Scatter olives on top. Bake 35 minutes or until filling has set. Stand 5 minutes before cutting.

OLIVE AND ROSEMARY FOCACCIA

★ **Preparation time:** 25 minutes +
1 hour proofing time
Total cooking time: 15–18 minutes
Makes 8

2½–3 cups all-purpose flour	*1 teaspoon sugar*
1 envelope active dry yeast	*½ teaspoon salt*
1 cup water	*3 tablespoons olive oil, extra*
1 tablespoon dried rosemary	*½ cup pitted olives, sliced*
3 tablespoons olive oil	

1 Combine 1 cup of the flour and yeast in a large bowl. Heat water, rosemary, 3 tablespoons olive oil, sugar and salt in a saucepan until warm (120–130°F). Add to flour mixture. Using an electric mixer, beat on a low speed for 30 seconds and on a high speed for 3 minutes. Stir in as much of the remaining flour as you can.
2 Turn dough onto a floured surface; knead for 10 minutes. Shape into a ball; place in a large, lightly oiled bowl. Stand, covered with plastic wrap, in a warm place 1 hour or until well risen.
3 Preheat oven to 425°F. Brush two large baking sheets with some of the extra olive oil. Knead dough until smooth. Divide into 8. Roll one portion at a time and shape into a flat 4 inch round. Repeat with remaining dough, press olives onto surface and brush with extra oil. Bake 15–18 minutes or until golden. Cool on a wire rack.

color, has the fullest flavor. Use it drizzled on pasta, salads and vegetables. Next is fine virgin olive oil with less then 1.5 per cent acidity. Virgin olive oil has less than 3 per cent. Pure olive oil, made from a blend of virgin oil and refined olive oil, has the same acid content as virgin olive oil. Refined olive oil is made by removing impurities from oils that do not meet the standards for extra virgin

or virgin olive oil: such blends have a milder flavor and are often labelled as "light".

Spain and Italy lead in the production of fine olive oil. It is available in bottles or large cans.

Omelet A dish of beaten eggs cooked in a frying pan and often folded over a filling. Omelets can be served at breakfast or as a light luncheon or supper dish; a sweet filling transforms it into a dessert. Omelets have been known in France since the Middle Ages.

Onion The bulb of a member of the lily family, related to garlic and leek, with pungently flavored flesh composed of thin, close layers. There are many onion varieties, varying in color, shape and intensity of taste, but in general the onion is sharp in flavor when raw and mellow when cooked. Many onions are juicy because of a high sugar content and can be used as an ingredient in salads or as a garnish; they can be boiled, fried or baked as a vegetable; or cooked in a wide variety of dishes. Simmered slowly in butter, they provide an almost sweet filling for the classic French onion tart and are also made into a famous French soup; onion rings dipped in batter and deep-fried are popular as a first course in Indian cooking and with steaks in western restaurants; and studded with cloves, the onion flavors sauces and stews. In stores, onions may be labeled white, yellow or red. Spanish onions are a large variety with a mild flavor. Pearl onions are small, white pear-shaped bulbs. Scallions are onions which are harvested when immature. Dried onion products include onion powder, onion salt, onion flakes and onion flavoring cubes. The birthplace of today's onion was probably central Asia.

OLIVE AND ROSEMARY PALMS

Preparation time: 20 minutes
Total cooking time: 15 minutes
Makes 30

½ cup chopped, pitted black olives	4 slices salami, chopped
⅓ cup grated Parmesan cheese	2 tablespoons oil
	2 teaspoons Dijon mustard
1 tablespoon chopped rosemary	2 sheets frozen puff pastry, thawed
	oil or melted butter

1 Preheat oven to moderately hot 400°F. Brush two baking sheets with melted butter or oil. Combine olives, cheese, rosemary, salami, oil and mustard in a blender or food processor. Process for 30 seconds or until mixture becomes a paste.
2 Roll out the pastry to ¼–½ inch thickness. Place a sheet of pastry on work surface and spread evenly with half the olive paste. Fold two opposite sides over to meet edge-to-edge in the center. Fold once again, then fold in half to give 8 layers of pastry.
3 Cut into ½ inch slices. Lay slices, cut side up, on prepared baking sheets, allowing room for spreading. Open slices out slightly at the folded end to give a "V" shape. Repeat with remaining pastry and olive paste. Bake for 15 minutes or until palmiers are golden brown.

CRUDITES WITH OLIVE PASTE

Preparation time: 15 minutes
Total cooking time: none
Serves 4–6

1 lb black olives	selection of fresh
⅓ cup olive oil	vegetables—snow peas,
2 cloves garlic, peeled	small radishes, pieces of
¼ cup basil leaves	cucumber, whole baby
1 tablespoon lemon juice	mushrooms
freshly ground pepper	

1 Remove pits from the olives. Place the olives, olive oil, garlic cloves, basil leaves and lemon juice into a blender or food processor.
2 Blend at a high speed until the mixture is a coarse paste—be careful not to overprocess or the mixture will become too smooth. Season to taste with freshly ground black pepper.
3 Serve the olive paste in a bowl, surrounded by a selection of fresh, seasonal vegetables of your choice.

Note: Olive Paste can be made 2–3 days before it is needed and stored in the refrigerator.

ABOVE: CRUDITES WITH OLIVE PASTE; LEFT: OLIVE AND ROSEMARY PALMS.

OPPOSITE, ABOVE: ORANGE GELATO; BELOW: ORANGE AND SPINACH SALAD

ORANGES

ORANGE AND SPINACH SALAD

★ **Preparation time :** 15 minutes
Total cooking time: none
Serves 4–6

4 medium oranges	½ cup pitted black olives
10–12 spinach leaves	⅓ cup olive oil
1 medium red onion, sliced	¼ cup red wine vinegar
	¼ cup toasted pine nuts

1 Place each orange on a board, cut a ¾ inch slice off each end to where the pulp starts. Peel, removing all white membrane. Separate the segments by carefully cutting between the membrane and the flesh with a small sharp knife. Do this over a bowl so that you don't lose any of the juice.

2 Tear spinach into bite-sized pieces, place into a large bowl. Add the sliced onion, orange and black olives.

3 Place the olive oil and vinegar in a small bowl. Whisk until well combined.

4 Pour the dressing over the salad and toss to mix well. Place in a serving bowl, sprinkle with toasted pine nuts and serve the salad immediately.

ABOUT ORANGES

■ Oranges keep well for many weeks, but once the skins develop soft spots, use them quickly.

■ Make orange juice by squeezing fruit and straining any seeds or pith. Juice can be frozen for several months: try freezing it in ice-cube trays.

ORANGE GELATO

★ **Preparation time:** 30 minutes + churning and freezing
Total cooking time: 20 minutes
Makes 6 cups

1¼ cups confectioners' sugar	2 tablespoons Cointreau or Grand Marnier liqueur
1½ cups freshly squeezed orange juice	2 egg whites
2 cups water	¼ cup confectioners' sugar, extra
1 tablespoon lemon juice	slices of orange to serve

1 Place confectioners' sugar, orange juice, water and lemon juice in a large pan. Stir over medium heat for 4–5 minutes or until sugar is dissolved. Bring to boil. Reduce heat. Simmer gently for 15 minutes; remove from heat.

2 Pour mixture into a large bowl; allow to cool. Stir in liqueur.

3 Using electric beaters, beat the egg whites until soft peaks form. Gradually beat in the extra sugar until the mixture is thick and glossy.

4 Gently fold the egg whites into the orange mixture. Pour into an ice cream machine and churn for about 30 minutes, or freeze until just the mixture is just solid.

5 To make by hand, prepare the mixture up to step 3. Before adding the egg whites, pour the mixture into a freezer tray and freeze until it is beginning to set around the edges.

6 Remove from freezer and beat well. Beat egg whites to soft peaks. Add extra sugar. Beat well. Fold into orange mixture. Return to tray and freeze until firm. Serve with slices of orange.

Orange A round citrus fruit with a bright orange skin and juicy, orange-colored, segmented flesh. Orange is eaten fresh as a fruit, chopped and added to fruit salads, cooked in both sweet and savory dishes and made into marmalade; its juice is a favorite at breakfast; and its rind is used fresh or dried to flavor desserts, cakes and savory sauces. There are three main types of orange: sweet oranges, including the large, thick-skinned navel, named for the navel-like growth at the blossom end; the smaller, thin-skinned Valencias, used for juicing and as a snack and dessert fruit; bitter oranges, including the Seville, which are used to make marmalade and tangy sauces; and blood oranges, with sweet, juicy, blood-red flesh, eaten as a dessert fruit and used for juicing.

The orange originated in southern Asia and has been cultivated in China for at least 4,000 years. The fruit was known to the Romans and grew in the ancient Middle East, where bitter oranges preserved in their skins in sugar may well be the forerunner of modern marmalade. The Moors planted orange orchards in Spain, from the eighth century on. The Spanish planted the first oranges in America in Florida in the sixteenth century. The fruit is now grown in tropical and sub-tropical regions world-wide. Oranges are available fresh all year

round and are also sold canned. Orange juice can be bought freshly squeezed or as a frozen concentrate; orange peel is sold dried and candied.

Orange Flower Water A fragrant liquid made from an essential oil extracted from the blossom of the bitter orange tree. Intensely flavored, it is added to cakes and candy.

Orange Pekoe A black tea with long leaves that makes a light brew.

Orange Roughy A fish in the perch family with firm, white flesh.

Oregano Also known as wild marjoram,

oregano is a hardy perennial herb similar in appearance and related to marjoram, but with a more robust

ORANGE BUN

⭐ **Preparation time:** 45 minutes + 1 hour 5 minutes standing
Total cooking time: 20–25 minutes
Makes one 9 inch round

2 cups all-purpose flour
1 envelope active dry yeast
1/3 cup mixed peel
1/2 teaspoon salt
1/4 cup sugar
2 teaspoons grated orange rind
1/3 cup warm milk
1/3 cup orange juice

2 tablespoons butter, melted
1 egg, lightly beaten

Glaze
1 tablespoon water
1 teaspoon sugar
1 teaspoon unsweetened gelatin

1 Brush deep 9 inch round cake pan with oil or melted butter. Sift half of the flour into a large mixing bowl. Add yeast, mixed peel, salt, sugar and orange rind; stir until combined. Make a well in the center.
2 Combine milk, orange juice and butter in a small saucepan. Heat until warm (120–130°F); add to flour mixture. Add egg. Beat with electric mixer on low speed 30 seconds. Beat on high speed 3 minutes. Stir in remaining flour. Turn onto lightly floured surface, knead 6 minutes or until dough is smooth and elastic.
3 Place dough into a large, lightly oiled mixing bowl. Leave, covered with plastic wrap, in warm place for 45 minutes or until well risen.

4 Knead dough again for 1 minute or until smooth. Press into prepared cake pan. Leave, covered with plastic wrap, in a warm place for 20 minutes or until well risen.
5 Preheat oven to moderate 350°F. Cut dough into eight wedges by carefully making deep cuts with a sharp, pointed, oiled knife. Be careful not to push out the air. If dough deflates, leave for another 5 minutes or until risen.
6 Bake for 20–25 minutes or until bun is golden brown and cooked through—bun should sound hollow when tapped. Turn onto wire rack.
7 To make Glaze: Combine water, sugar and gelatin in small mixing bowl. Place over a pan of simmering water, heat until sugar and gelatin are dissolved. Brush over bun while still hot.

ORANGE SESAME RICE SALAD

⭐ **Preparation time:** 40 minutes
Total cooking time: none
Serves 8

12 fresh asparagus spears
2 oranges
2 cups long-grain rice, cooked and cooled
1 medium cucumber, halved and thinly sliced
4 oz small pea pods
1 large red sweet pepper, cut into strips
2 large scallions, diagonally sliced
1 medium red onion, cut into thin wedges

Dressing
2 teaspoons finely grated orange rind
3/4 cup orange juice
3 teaspoons vegetable oil
1 tablespoon toasted sesame oil
1 tablespoon honey
2 teaspoons grated, pared fresh ginger
1 clove garlic, crushed

1 Cover asparagus spears with boiling water. Let stand 2 minutes. Drain, then plunge into a bowl of ice water. When cooled, drain; pat dry with paper towels. Cut asparagus diagonally into 1½ inch pieces.
2 Section oranges over a bowl to catch the juice.
3 Combine asparagus, orange sections, rice, cucumber, pea pods, pepper, scallions, and red onions in a large salad bowl. Add Dressing and toss until well combined.
4 To make Dressing: Place the orange rind, orange juice, vegetable oil, sesame oil, honey, ginger and garlic in a small jar. Cover tightly. Shake vigorously for 30 seconds or until ingredients are well combined.

ABOVE: ORANGE BUN.
OPPOSITE PAGE: OXTAIL SOUP

OXTAIL

OXTAIL SOUP

Preparation time: 10 minutes
Total cooking time: 3 hours
Makes 4 litres

1 oxtail (approximately 1½ lb)	2 stalks celery, finely chopped
2 tablespoons butter	1 large onion, finely chopped
1 large parsnip, peeled and finely chopped	2 tablespoons pearl barley
1 turnip, peeled and finely chopped	4 whole cloves
2 large carrots, peeled and finely chopped	¼ cup chopped parsley
	8 cups beef stock
	white pepper
	salt to taste

1 Trim oxtail and cut into 1 inch pieces.
2 Melt butter in a large heavy-bottom pan. Add oxtail in batches. Cook until browned; remove and drain. Add parsnip, turnip, carrots, celery and onion; stir until onion becomes transparent. Return meat to pan. Add barley, cloves, parsley, stock, pepper and salt.
3 Simmer for 2½ hours, skimming the froth off the surface as it rises in the pan. Serve Oxtail Soup in individual soup bowls, accompanied by bread or toast.

ABOUT OXTAIL

■ Oxtail requires long, moist cooking to tenderize the meat and reveal its distinctive texture. It is surrounded by a rich layer of fat which should be retained as it will contribute to the fine oxtail flavor. Froth from the fat will rise throughout cooking and should be regularly skimmed off with a spoon. Alternatively, cook oxtail the day before it is needed (this will also improve its flavor), and carefully lift away the cold fat when it has solidified on top.

■ As well as the classic soup, oxtail can be cooked as a casserole. The tail can also be boned, stuffed and braised slowly.

flavor. Used to flavor pizza toppings, tomato-based sauces, zucchini, eggplant and stuffings, oregano can be garden grown. It is also available fresh and dried.

Organic Food Food that is grown and processed without the use of chemical fertilizers, pesticides, artificial coloring or flavoring, and additives.

Osso Bucco A dish of braised veal shanks, with bone and marrow intact, which are sprinkled with a mixture of chopped parsley, garlic and grated lemon rind before serving with rice or pasta. The tasty bone marrow can be taken out with a toothpick. Osso bucco is a specialty of Milan, in northern Italy. The name means "bone with a hole."

Oven Fry To bake food in a hot oven so that it has the appearance and taste of fried food, but not the fat content. It is brushed lightly with oil, butter or margarine and coated with seasoned flour or bread crumbs before cooking.

Oxtail A flavorsome cut of meat consisting of the skinned tail of an ox or cow which requires long, slow cooking and is used to make soups and stews.

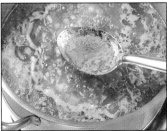

Oxtail soup is regarded as a traditional British dish, although some claim it crossed the Channel with French émigrés at the time of the French revolution.

Oyster A marine mollusk with a soft creamy-gray to creamy-tan body, encased in a rough, blue-gray, irregularly shaped, hinged shell. It is found adhering to rocks in shallow tidal waters around the world. Oysters are eaten raw, with a squeeze of lemon juice, bread and butter and a touch of freshly grated black pepper, or they can be fried, broiled or poached, or incorporated in soups, stuffings and sauces. Oysters have been gathered and eaten since the time of the earliest humans. There are ancient shell mounds on the coasts of North America and Australia. Native Americans seem to have always cooked them. Olympia oysters are still plentiful on the beaches of Oregon. The oysters often take their names from their harvesting area. Oysters are filter feeders, and are easily contaminated; they should not be collected where pollution is

OYSTERS

NEW ORLEANS OYSTERS

⭐ *Preparation time:* 10 minutes
Total cooking time: 4–6 minutes
Serves 4

24 large oysters, shell removed
1/4 teaspoon white pepper
1/4 teaspoon ground black pepper
1/4 teaspoon cayenne pepper
1/4 teaspoon thyme
1/4 teaspoon oregano
1/2 teaspoon dried paprika
1/4 teaspoon dried basil
1/2 cup all-purpose flour
1/2 cup vegetable oil
3 tablespoons unsalted (sweet) butter
lemon wedges and mayonnaise to serve

1 Dry the oysters on paper towel. In a shallow dish, mix the peppers, thyme, oregano, paprika and basil; set aside two teaspoons of the spice mix. Add the flour to the remaining spice mix and stir thoroughly.

2 Thread three oysters onto eight oiled skewers (choose thin bamboo or metal skewers) and coat with the spiced flour.

3 Heat the oil and butter in a wide pan. Cook the oysters until they are golden, turning several times, for about 6 minutes. Drain on paper towels. Sprinkle with the reserved two teaspoons of spice mix and serve with lemon wedges and dish of mayonnaise.

OYSTERS MORNAY

Heat 1 tablespoon butter in a small pan and add 2 tablespoons all-purpose flour. Stir over low heat for 2 minutes. Gradually add 1 cup milk to pan, stir until mixture is smooth. Stir over heat for 2 minutes until the mixture boils and thickens. Add 1/4 cup grated Cheddar cheese, 1/2 teaspoon Dijon mustard, 1 teaspoon lemon juice, salt and white pepper; stir until smooth. Spoon sauce over 24 oysters on the half shell, sprinkle with extra grated cheese and broil until lightly browned. Serves 2–4.

OYSTERS ROCKEFELLER

Heat 1 tablespoon butter in a medium pan and cook 1/4 cup finely chopped onion and 1 clove crushed garlic until onion is soft. Remove from heat and add 3/4 cup finely chopped cooked spinach (well drained), 3/4 cup thick sour cream, salt and freshly ground pepper. Spoon mixture over 24 oysters on the half shell. Mix 1/2 cup fine fresh bread crumbs with 1/2 cup grated Cheddar cheese and sprinkle mixture over the oysters. Broil oysters until the topping turns golden brown. Serves 2–4.

ABOVE: NEW ORLEANS OYSTERS.
OPPOSITE PAGE: SOUFFLE OYSTERS (LEFT) AND
OYSTERS WITH PINE NUTS AND BACON (RIGHT)

SOUFFLE OYSTERS

★★ **Preparation time:** 25 minutes
Total cooking time: 20 minutes
Serves 3

18 oysters on the half shell	1/4 teaspoon baking powder
1 tablespoon butter	1/2 cup milk
1 tablespoon all-purpose flour	2 teaspoons seed mustard
	1 egg, separated

1 Preheat oven to 350°F. Line a 13 x 11 inch baking sheet with foil. Place oysters on baking sheet and remove grit from surface of oyster flesh.
2 Heat butter in a small heavy-based pan; add the flour and baking soda. Stir over low heat for 2 minutes or until the mixture is lightly golden. Add milk gradually, stirring until the mixture is smooth. Stir constantly over medium heat for 5 minutes, or until the mixture boils and thickens. Boil for 1 minute, then remove from heat and cool. Stir in the mustard and egg yolk. Transfer to a medium mixing bowl.
3 Place egg white in a small, clean dry bowl. Using electric beaters, beat until firm peaks form. Using a metal spoon, fold beaten egg white gently into sauce mixture.
4 Spoon a heaped teaspoonful of the mixture onto each oyster and bake for 15 minutes or until slightly puffed and golden. Serve immediately.

OYSTERS WITH PINE NUTS AND BACON

★ **Preparation time:** 25 minutes
Total cooking time: 20 minutes
Serves 3

18 oysters on the half shell	1 teaspoon Worcestershire sauce
2 slices bacon, finely chopped	1 tablespoon finely chopped fresh chives
2 tablespoons pine nuts, coarsely chopped	

1 Preheat oven to 350°F. Line a 13 x 11 inch baking sheet with foil. Place oysters on baking sheet and remove grit from surface of oyster flesh.
2 Cook bacon in a small heavy-bottom pan over medium heat until browned. Add pine nuts and sauce, stir to combine well. Remove from heat.
3 Spoon onto each oyster. Sprinkle with chives. Bake 5–10 minutes. Serve immediately.

OYSTERS KILPATRICK

Combine 2 tablespoons Worcestershire sauce, 2 tablespoons tomato sauce, 2 teaspoons chopped parsley, 3/4 cup finely chopped bacon and ground black pepper in a small bowl. Spoon onto 24 oysters on the half shell and broil 4–5 inches from the heat or until cooked. Serves 2–4.

suspected. They are sold unshelled, on the half shell, or shucked and packed in clear oyster liquor. Oysters are also available canned, either plain or smoked. Refrigerate live oysters in a container covered with a damp cloth for up to 3 days.

Oyster Cracker A round bite-sized cracker.

Oyster Mushroom A fan-shaped mushroom with a pale to dark gray cap and grayish white stem. Their flavor is slightly peppery.

Oyster Sauce A thick, dark brown sauce originally made from oysters fermented in brine and then ground to a paste, but now usually thickened with cornstarch and darkened with caramel coloring. It has a strong, salty, slightly fishy flavor and is used as an all-purpose seasoning in Chinese cooking. Sold in bottles, jars and cans.

Oysters Bienville Baked oysters on the half shell with a béchamel sauce, pepper, cheese and bread crumbs.

Oysters Rockefeller Baked oysters on the half shell with spinach, butter, bread crumbs and seasonings.

P

Paella A dish of Spanish origin consisting of short-grained rice, olive oil, shellfish, chicken or game and vegetables, seasoned with garlic and colored with saffron. It takes its name from *paellera*, the shallow, two-handled pan in which it is traditionally cooked. Paella originated in the Valencia region of eastern Spain.

Palm Heart See Hearts of Palm.

Pan-broil To cook food in an ungreased pan. Fat released from the food is poured off. This method is used for fatty foods such as bacon and in low-fat diets.

Pancake A thin, flat cake made from a batter of flour, egg and milk cooked quickly on each side in a greased frying pan or on a griddle and then served hot, usually folded over or rolled

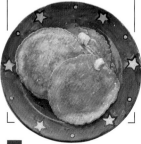

PANCAKES

SCOTTISH PANCAKES

★ **Preparation time:** 10 minutes
Total cooking time: 15 minutes
Makes 16 pancakes

1 cup all-purpose flour	³/₄–1 cup milk
2 tablespoons sugar	1 egg, lightly beaten
1 teaspoon baking powder	2 tablespoons butter,
¼ teaspoon baking soda	melted
½ teaspoon lemon juice or	extra melted butter
vinegar	

1 Sift flour, sugar, baking powder and soda into a medium-sized mixing bowl. Add juice or vinegar to the milk to sour it; allow to stand for 5 minutes.
2 Make a well in center of dry ingredients and add the egg, ³/₄ cup milk and the butter; mix to form a smooth batter. If batter is too thick to pour from the spoon, add remaining milk.

3 Brush base of frying pan lightly with melted butter. Drop 1–2 tablespoons of mixture onto base of pan, about ³/₄ inch apart. Cook over medium heat for 1 minute, or until underside is golden. Turn pancakes over and cook other side. Remove from pan; repeat with remaining mixture. Serve warm with curls or pats of butter.

ABOUT PANCAKES

■ Pancake batter improves with standing but does not keep well. Make only as much batter as you need, about an hour or two before cooking.
■ Add variety to batter by using different flours—try cornmeal, buckwheat or whole grain flours.
■ Pancakes can be eaten with either sweet or savory fillings. Fill with leftover casseroles, pasta sauces or mornays for a quick supper.
■ Use a soup ladle to transfer pancake batter from bowl to pan. Ideally, pancakes are cooked on a cast-iron griddle, but a heavy-bottom metal frying pan will do; the cooking surface should be very hot.

ROLLED PANCAKES

Preparation time: 15 minutes +
1 hour standing
Total cooking time: 5–10 minutes
Makes about 12

1 cup all-purpose flour   oil
pinch of salt   lemon juice and sugar to
1 egg   serve
1¼ cups milk

1 Sift the flour and salt into a medium bowl; make a well in the center. Add the egg and milk and whisk until smooth. Set mixture aside for 1 hour.
2 Heat a lightly oiled frying pan. Pour 3 tablespoons of mixture into the pan. Tilt pan to spread the mixture evenly. Gently lift edges with a knife. When underside of pancake is golden, turn over and cook the other side. Transfer to a plate and sprinkle with lemon juice and sugar. Roll up and serve hot.

Note: Instead of lemon juice and sugar, plain pancakes may be served hot with either whipped cream or ice cream. This basic recipe can be used to make a number of dishes based on sweet or savory rolled pancakes.

OPPOSITE PAGE: SCOTTISH PANCAKES
ABOVE: FLAPJACKS; RIGHT: ROLLED PANCAKES

FLAPJACKS (BASIC PANCAKES)

Preparation time: 20 minutes
Total cooking time: 20 minutes
Makes about 10

1 cup all-purpose flour   2 tablespoons butter,
2 teaspoons baking powder   melted
⅛ teaspoon salt   butter, extra
½–¾ cup milk   whipped butter and
2 tablespoons sugar   maple syrup to serve
1 egg, lightly beaten

1 Sift flour, baking powder and salt into a medium bowl; make a well in the center. Combine milk, sugar, egg and butter in a separate bowl; add to flour mixture.
2 Beat mixture until combined but the batter is still lumpy.
3 Heat a medium-sized frying pan, grease with a little butter. Pour ¼ cup batter into pan. Cook over medium heat 2 minutes, or until underside is golden. Turn over and cook other side. Transfer to a plate, cover with a towel. Keep warm.
4 Repeat with remaining batter, greasing the pan as necessary. Serve flapjacks topped with whipped butter and maple syrup.
5 To make whipped butter: Allow butter to soften to room temperature, then beat with electric beaters in a small bowl for 3–4 minutes or until light and creamy.

Notes: Flapjack batter will thicken as it stands. If you are making a large quantity of flapjacks you may need to stir in a little milk from time to time. True maple syrup is much more expensive than imitation maple syrup, but the flavor is so much better that it is worth the expense.

around a filling which can be either sweet or savory. Pancakes are similar to, but thicker than, crêpes. In North America pancakes stacked one upon the other and covered with maple syrup are a popular breakfast dish. Pancakes were traditionally cooked and eaten on Shrove Tuesday, also known as Pancake Day, a day of revelry before the fasting of Lent.

Pancetta Unsmoked bacon from the belly of a pig, cured with spices, salt and pepper. It is usually sold rolled into a sausage shape, and is served thinly sliced.

Panettone A cake made from sweet yeast dough enriched with egg yolk (which gives it its color), candied fruits and raisins. Usually made in the shape of a tall, round loaf, panettone is a specialty of Milan, in northern Italy, where it is now commercially produced for sale around the world. It is served with coffee for breakfast and is traditional Christmas fare.

Panforte A flat, very rich cake with a nougat-like texture containing nuts, honey, candied fruit and spices. It is a specialty of Siena, in Italy and, because of its energy-giving properties, is said to have been carried by the Crusaders on military expeditions.

Pan-fry To cook food in a pan smeared with a little fat.

Papaya Also known as pawpaw, a large, oval-shaped tropical fruit with smooth green to yellow skin, juicy golden flesh with a melon-like texture and a central cavity filled with small black seeds. Serve fresh and fully ripe with a sprinkle of lime juice for breakfast or as a dessert fruit, or add cubes to fruit salad (it combines especially well with passionfruit). Underripe papaya can be cooked as a vegetable. The fruit is native to the Americas and is thought to have been taken to Europe by Portuguese explorers; it now grows in tropical regions throughout the world. Papaya is in season in early summer. For eating choose fruit that is yellowish and feels soft when pressed.

Papillote, en A French term for a cooking method in which individual portions of food—meat, fish, poultry or vegetables—are wrapped in strong, greased paper or aluminum foil (often cut

SATAY VEGETABLE AND SPROUT PANCAKES

★ **Preparation time:** 35 minutes
Total cooking time: 15 minutes
Serves 4–6

Pancakes
1¼ cups all-purpose flour
1 teaspoon baking powder
1 egg
1½ cups milk
1 tablespoon oil

Filling
8 oz fresh snow pea sprouts
8 oz mung bean sprouts
6 scallions, finely sliced
8 oz button mushrooms, thinly sliced

1 large carrot, coarsely grated
1 cup roasted peanuts

Dressing
½ cup crunchy peanut butter
2 tablespoons cider vinegar
2 tablespoons lemon juice
2 teaspoons sambal oelek

1 To prepare Pancakes: Sift flour and baking powder into large bowl. Make a well in center. Combine egg, milk and oil, stir into flour; mix to a smooth batter. Pour mixture into a jug.
2 Brush a heated pancake pan with oil. Pour in batter to thinly cover pan base. Cook 2–3 minutes until the mixture sets. Turn over with a metal spatula, cook another 1–2 minutes. Remove to a plate, cover with waxed paper. Continue until all mixture has been used. Keep pancakes warm.
3 To make Filling: Combine vegetables and peanuts. Divide between the pancakes. Fold or roll the pancakes, place on serving plates.

4 To make Dressing: Combine all ingredients in a small bowl, whisking well. Pour over pancakes, or serve separately.

BLINI WITH SOUR CREAM AND SMOKED SALMON

★ **Preparation time:** 15 minutes
Total cooking time: 10–15 minutes
Makes about 50

Blini
1 cup all-purpose flour
¾ teaspoon baking powder
⅛ teaspoon salt
2 eggs, lightly beaten
½ cup milk
1 tablespoon sour cream

Topping
½ cup sour cream
2 tablespoons mayonnaise
2 teaspoons lemon juice
1 tablespoon finely chopped chives
1 tablespoon finely chopped mint
4 oz sliced smoked salmon

1 Sift flour, baking powder and salt into bowl, make a well in center. Add eggs, milk and sour cream; stir until mixture is smooth and free of lumps. Stand 10 minutes.
2 Heat large non-stick frying pan, brush with oil. Drop teaspoonfuls of mixture into pan. When bubbles appear on surface, turn blini and cook other side. Remove from pan, set aside. Repeat with remaining mixture.
3 To make Topping: Combine sour cream, mayonnaise, lemon juice, chives, and mint. Spoon some mixture on each blini. Top with smoked salmon. Decorate with lemon peel if desired.

THAI CORN PANCAKES WITH CILANTRO MAYONNAISE

★ ★ **Preparation time:** 15 minutes
Total cooking time: 3–5 minutes each
Serves 6

2 cloves garlic
1 small red chili pepper
3/4 inch piece fresh ginger
2 eggs
1/4 cup cornstarch
2 tablespoons fresh
  cilantro leaves
freshly ground black
  pepper
1 tablespoon sweet chili
  sauce
14 oz can sweet corn
  kernels, drained

1 tablespoon peanut oil

Cilantro Mayonnaise
2/3 cup mayonnaise
1/4 cup lime juice
1/3 cup cilantro leaves,
  chopped
8 scallions, finely chopped
freshly ground black
  pepper, to taste

1 Coarsely chop the garlic; chop the chili pepper and ginger. Place the eggs, cornstarch, cilantro leaves, garlic, chili, ginger, pepper, chili sauce and half the corn in a food processor. Process in short bursts for 30 seconds or until smooth. Transfer to a bowl and fold in remaining corn.
2 Heat the peanut oil in a large frying pan. Spoon two tablespoons of the corn mixture into the frying pan and cook over medium heat for

2–3 minutes or until golden. Turn over and cook the second side for 1–2 minutes or until the pancakes are cooked through. Repeat the process until all the mixture is used. Drain pancakes on paper towel.
3 To make Cilantro Mayonnaise: Combine the mayonnaise, lime juice, cilantro and scallions in a bowl. Mix well. Add pepper to taste. Serve the pancakes hot or cool with a dollop of Cilantro Mayonnaise.

CRAYFISH AND SHRIMP CREPE STACK

★ ★ **Preparation time:** 25–30 minutes
Total cooking time: 20 minutes
Serves 4–6

8 oz cooked crayfish meat
8 oz cooked shrimp
5 tablespoons butter
2 scallions, finely sliced
1/3 cup all-purpose flour
1 1/2 cups milk
3/4 cup yogurt
1 tablespoon lemon juice
pepper
3/4 cup grated Cheddar
  cheese

Crêpe Batter
1 cup all-purpose flour
2 teaspoons grated lemon
  rind
1 egg
2–2 1/2 cups milk
1 tablespoon butter,
  melted
butter for frying

1 Flake the crayfish meat and chop the shrimp into small pieces.
2 In a large saucepan melt the butter. Cook the scallions for 2-3 minutes. Add the flour. Cook for 1 minute. Slowly pour in the milk and stir until thick. Add the yogurt, lemon juice and pepper to taste. Mix well. Add the flaked crayfish and chopped shrimp.
3 To make Crêpe Batter: Sift flour into a bowl. Add lemon rind. In a separate bowl combine egg and milk; beat lightly. Add melted butter. Gradually pour egg mixture into flour. Stir until a smooth batter is formed.
4 Melt a little butter in a frying pan and cook the crêpes approximately 8 inches in diameter. When each crêpe is cooked, remove and stack them on a plate.
5 Preheat oven to slow 300°F. Prepare the crêpe stack by placing one crêpe on a serving platter and spreading evenly with some of the sauce mixture. Continue alternating pancakes with sauce until the crêpe stack is complete. Sprinkle the top with grated cheese and place in the oven for 10 minutes or until the cheese melts and the crêpe stack is heated through.

into a heart shape) and then baked, grilled or broiled. This technique preserves juices and flavor. Papillote is also the name of the paper frill used to decorate the bone end of a lamb or veal chop or a chicken drumstick.

Pappadam A thin, crisp wafer of Indian origin made from lentil, potato or rice flour. They are fried in hot vegetable oil, one at a time; held down with tongs for 3 seconds until the pappadams swell, bubble and turn

golden brown. Pappadams are best served hot, as an accompaniment to Indian meals. They are sold dried in packets, although varieties made especially to be microwaved are also available.

Paprika A seasoning made from the dried, ground flesh of a variety of sweet red pepper. Sweet paprika is piquant, rather than hot, and is used to flavor goulashes, ragoûts, stuffings and sauces. It is sprinkled on dips and egg, cheese and seafood dishes. The red pepper comes from a shrub native to

Opposite page: Blini with sour cream and smoked salmon. Above: Thai corn pancakes with cilantro mayonnaise

PASTA

Pasta is the Italian name for a dough made, in its most basic form, from flour and water. This most versatile of foods comes in a diverse range of shapes and sizes, bearing an even greater variety of names, some of which alter from one Italian region to another.

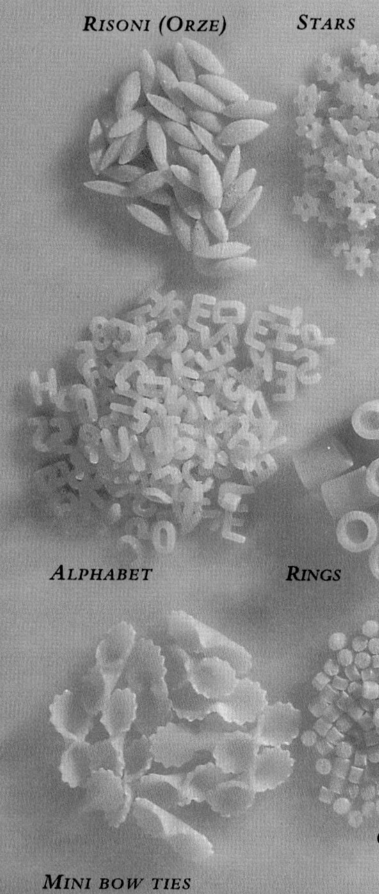

Some pastas, both dry and fresh, are flavored with herbs or spices, or colored with spinach or tomato purée.

Each pasta shape is ideally suited to a particular type of sauce. Spaghetti combines beautifully with rich tomato, butter and cream-based sauces which coat the strands well. Shorter pasta shapes like penne, rigatoni and fusilli are good with meaty, chunky sauces, since the pasta shapes trap the sauce and the meat is distributed throughout the dish. Vermicelli is ideal for creamy, cheese or egg sauces that cling to the thin strands. Flat, wide pasta, such as malfade are dressed with richly flavored tomato and game sauces. Smaller shapes like macaroni add substance to soups and ragouts. Bow ties and shells are best served with other attractive ingredients such as vegetable pieces, shrimp or mussels. Stuffed pasta such as ravioli and tortellini taste best when eaten with subtle sauces that do not overwhelm the main seasoning.

TO COOK PASTA

Essential equipment is a large, deep pot. Allow 4 cups water for each 4 oz pasta, add salt and a little oil, and bring water to a rapid boil. Add pasta gradually so that water does not stop boiling. When adding nests of dried pasta, unravel the pasta strands in the water with a fork. Cook uncovered for the time recommended by the manufacturer, but it should be *al dente* (firm but not hard in the middle). When pasta is cooked, drain quickly, place in a heated serving dish and toss with sauce, or return drained pasta to pan and add about 1 cup of sauce and a dash of olive oil. Mix well and serve topped with remaining sauce.

Cooking times: Start testing fresh pasta after 2 minutes for thin strips such as fettuccini, after 5 minutes for stuffed forms such as ravioli. Dry pasta takes longer—test after 5 minutes for tiny shapes, 7–8 minutes for larger shapes and 10–12 minutes for the very large shapes.

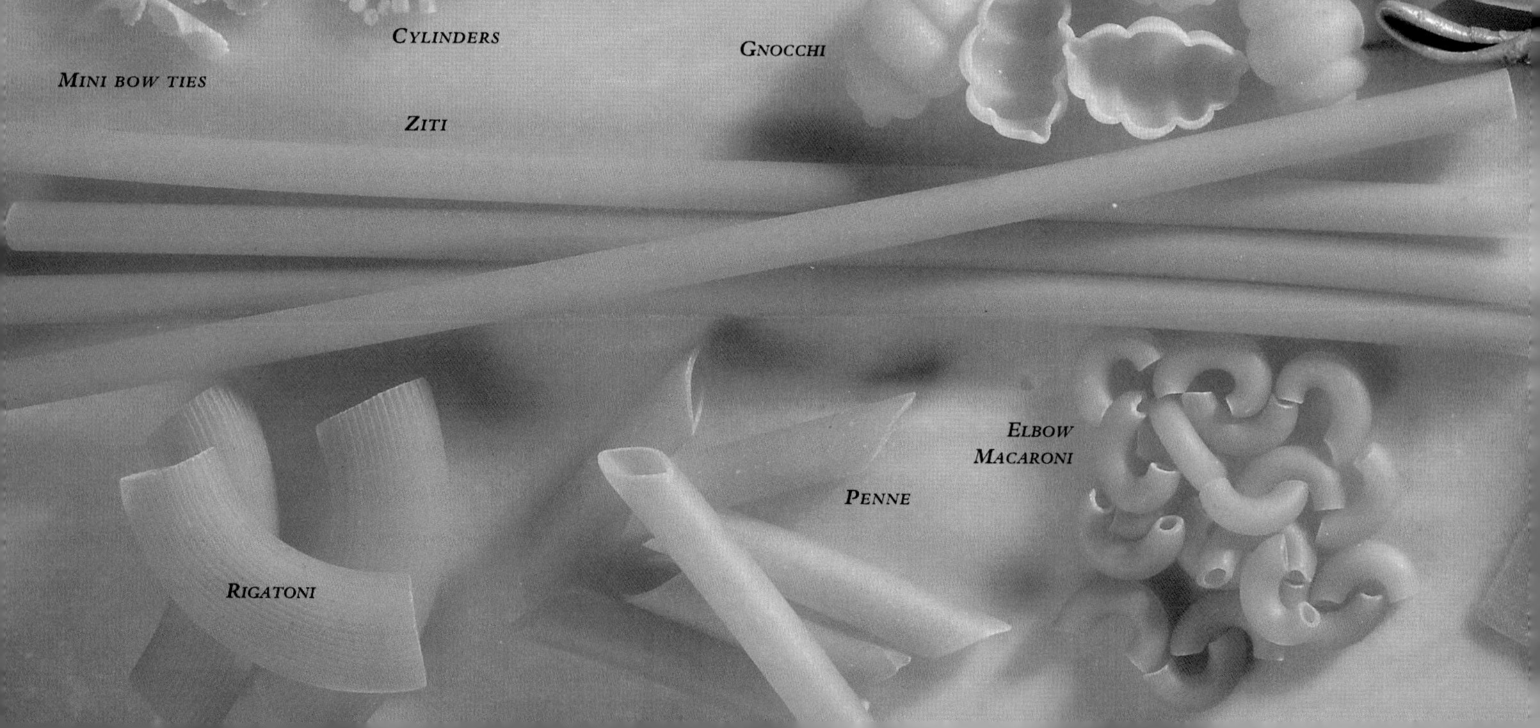

RISONI (ORZE)

STARS

ALPHABET

RINGS

MINI BOW TIES

CYLINDERS

ZITI

GNOCCHI

RIGATONI

PENNE

ELBOW MACARONI

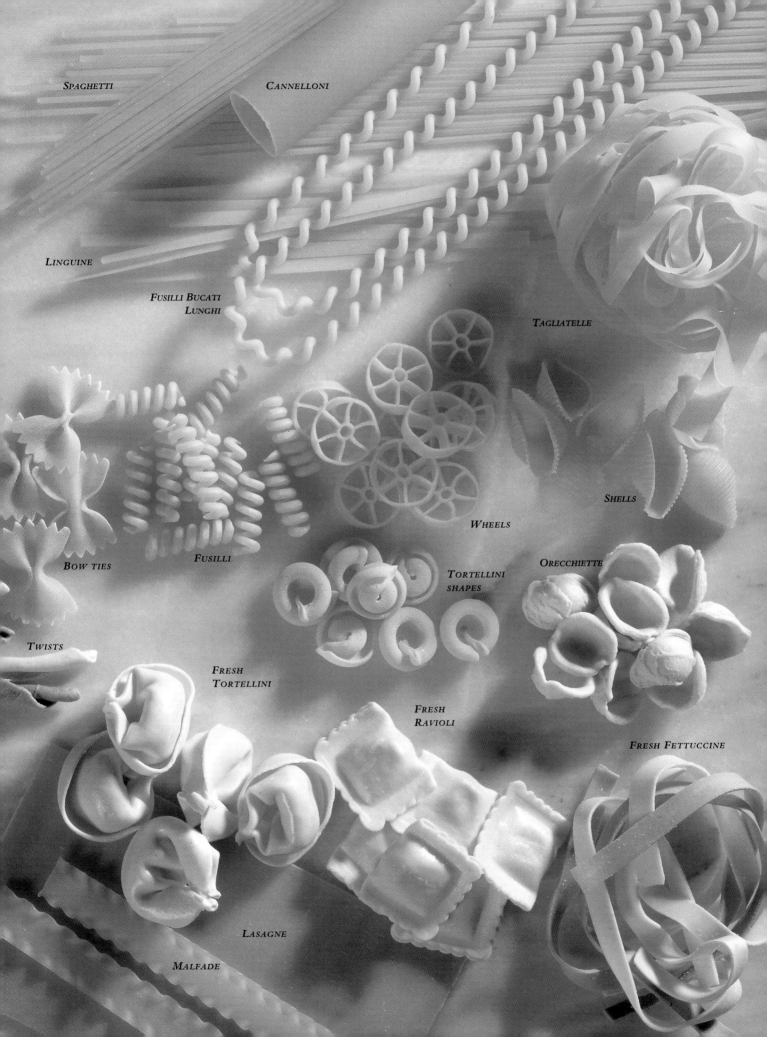

SPAGHETTI

CANNELLONI

LINGUINE

FUSILLI BUCATI
LUNGHI

TAGLIATELLE

WHEELS

SHELLS

BOW TIES

FUSILLI

ORECCHIETTE

TORTELLINI
shapes

TWISTS

FRESH
TORTELLINI

FRESH
RAVIOLI

FRESH FETTUCCINE

LASAGNE

MALFADE

Central America and has been known in Europe since the time of Columbus. The form used to make paprika developed in Hungary and is smaller and more pungently flavored than Spanish paprika, which is made from a milder red pepper. The name comes from the Hungarian word for "sweet pepper."

Paratha An unleavened, rich, flaky Indian bread made from a dough of whole-grain flour, ghee, salt and water, formed into a disk shape and fried on both sides; the dough can also be folded around a vegetable mixture to make a stuffed version. Parathas are usually reserved for special occasions; they are generally made at home but are sometimes available from Indian restaurants.

Parboil To partially cook food by boiling for a short time in water.

Parfait A chilled dessert served in a tall glass and eaten with a long-handled spoon. In America it consists of ice cream layered with flavored syrup and whipped cream. In France it is a frozen custard dessert.

PAPAYAS

SPICED PAPAYA

⭐ **Preparation time:** 15 minutes + overnight standing
Total cooking time: 40 minutes
Makes 4 cups

1 large ripe firm papaya	2 teaspoons whole allspice
sugar	2 inch piece cinnamon
white vinegar	stick
1 tablespoon whole cloves	

1 Peel papaya, cut into halves and scrape out the seeds. Cut each half into finger-length pieces. Weigh them and allow 1½ cups sugar for each 1½ oz fruit. Put fruit into a container, sprinkle the sugar over and leave overnight.
2 Put fruit and syrup into a large saucepan and heat gently, stirring until sugar has dissolved; simmer until papaya looks transparent (do not overcook). Drain syrup from fruit, reserving syrup. Measure and allow ¾ cup vinegar for every 2½ cups syrup. Add the vinegar to the syrup with cloves, allspice and the lightly crushed cinnamon stick.
3 Bring mixture to boil, cover and boil gently for 10 minutes. Set aside until cold; strain. Add syrup-vinegar mixture to the pan; add papaya and cook for 7 minutes.
4 Remove from heat, lift papaya slices out with a slotted spoon and put into sterilized jars. Bring syrup mixture back to boil and spoon over papaya. Cool before sealing. Label and date.

THAI PAPAYA SALAD

⭐ **Preparation time:** 15 minutes
Total cooking time: none
Serves 4–6

1 medium-sized papaya, about 1½ lb	6 tablespoons lime juice or lemon juice
¼ cup Chinese dried shrimp, soaked in boiling water for 10 minutes	6 tablespoons fish sauce 1–2 teaspoons sugar 1–4 teaspoons sweet chili sauce
1 teaspoon mashed garlic	scallions, for garnish

1 Peel papaya, remove seeds and cut into cubes. Using a mortar and pestle or food processor combine drained prawns (shrimp) and garlic. Process until finely chopped. Add half lime or lemon juice and half fish sauce. Process until smooth.
2 Toss shrimp mixture with papaya. Add remaining lime or lemon juice, fish sauce, sugar and chili sauce, tossing gently to coat.
4 Pile papaya mixture on a lettuce-lined plate. Garnish with thinly sliced scallions.

ABOUT PAPAYA

■ Ripe papaya is best cut just before serving; sprinkle with lime or lemon juice.
■ If refrigerating papaya, keep it closely covered to prevent its distinctive smell from tainting other foods, particularly dairy products.
■ Papaya contains an enzyme which is extracted and used to tenderize meat.

P A R S N I P S

P A R S N I P   C H I P S

Preparation time: 10 minutes
Total cooking time: 6 minutes
Serves 8

4 large parsnips
2 tablespoons lemon juice

oil for deep-frying

1 Peel parsnips. Cut parsnips diagonally into ⅛ inch slices. Place slices in a large bowl and cover with water. Add lemon juice to water. Set aside.
2 When ready to cook, drain parsnip slices and thoroughly dry with paper towel.
3 Heat oil in deep heavy-bottom pan. Gently lower a third of the parsnip slices into moderately hot oil. Cook over medium-high heat for 1–2 minutes or until golden; remove with tongs. Repeat with remaining parsnip slices. Drain chips on paper towels and serve immediately.

Note: For best results when deep-frying, use peanut, corn, safflower or soybean oil. These oils have a bland flavor and a high smoking point, which means that they can be heated to a very high temperature without burning or smoking.

OPPOSITE PAGE, ABOVE: SPICED PAPAYA; BELOW: THAI PAPAYA SALAD. THIS PAGE, ABOVE: PARSNIP CHIPS; RIGHT: PARSNIP SOUP

P A R S N I P   S O U P

Preparation time: 20 minutes
Total cooking time: 40 minutes
Serves 4–6

¼ cup butter
2 lb small parsnips, peeled and chopped
2 onions, chopped
1 teaspoon curry powder
½ teaspoon ground cardamom

½ teaspoon ground turmeric
4 cups vegetable stock
1 cup evaporated skim milk
croûtons or chopped herbs, to garnish

1 Melt butter in a large pan. Add parsnips and onions. Cover and cook over low heat for 3–4 minutes.
2 Add the curry powder, cardamom and turmeric. Stir to combine and cook for 1 minute. Pour in the vegetable stock. Bring to the boil, reduce heat and simmer, covered, until the vegetables are tender (about 30 minutes).
3 Remove the soup from the heat. Allow to cool for about 10 minutes. Blend in an electric blender or food processor until the soup is smooth. Return the liquid to the pan. Add evaporated milk. Stir over a low heat until the soup is heated through. Serve with croûtons or a sprig of fresh dill.

Note: Parsnips have a distinctively nutty flavor which has a sweetening effect in soups and other vegetable dishes, such as stews and casseroles. Choose parsnips which are small and firm. Larger parsnips may have a woody core—which will make them inedible.

Parker House Roll A light, puffy yeast roll that became well known in the late nineteenth century at a Boston hotel called The Parker House.

Parma Ham Fine quality salt-cured ham, also known as prosciutto, made from the hind legs of a variety of pig raised on a controlled food diet in the Parma region of northern Italy and cured in the traditional manner. Hams are rubbed with salt, left in a cool place for several weeks, then washed and allowed to dry out and mature in a cool, well-ventilated atmosphere for ten to twelve months. Rosy pink, marbled with lines of white fat, and only mildly salty, parma ham sliced wafer thin and served with melon or fresh figs is a popular antipasto not only in Italy but around the world.

Parmesan A very hard cow's milk cheese with a strong taste and grainy texture, famous as a grating cheese. Parmesan is made by the cooked curd method (the curd is "cooked" in heated whey) and is matured for up to three years. Because of its extremely low moisture content Parmesan can be stored at low temperatures almost indefinitely. It is used, grated, in cooking (it does not become stringy as most cheeses do) and as a garnish; young Parmesan can also be served as a table cheese with fruit. The cheese has been made in Parma, in northern Italy, for some eight hundred years and is now made around the world by the same method. Cheese carrying the stamp "parmigiano reggiano" comes from a select area of northern Italy. Parmesan is available in blocks and is best used freshly grated; it is also sold grated in vacuum-sealed packs.

Parsley An herb with bright green, fern-like leaves and a mild, celery-like flavor, widely used as a seasoning and a garnish. There are two

main varieties: curly-leaf and the larger flat-leaf or Italian parsley. Curly-leaf is best used as a garnish, either in sprigs or sprinkled, finely chopped, on food. The more flavorsome flat-leaf is preferable for cooking; it is the main ingredient in the Middle Eastern salad tabbouleh. Parsley

PASSIONFRUIT

PASSIONFRUIT VANILLA DESSERT

Preparation time: 35 minutes
Total cooking time: 20–25 minutes
Makes 9 squares

1 sheet frozen puff
pastry, thawed

½ teaspoon vanilla
extract

Custard
3 tablespoons cornstarch
⅓ cup sugar
1 cup heavy cream
1½ cups milk
3 egg yolks, beaten

Icing
¼ cup passionfruit pulp
or apple sauce
2 tablespoons unsalted
(sweet) butter
1½ cups confectioners'
sugar

1 Preheat oven to 400°F. Line two baking sheets with parchment paper. Roll pastry to 18 x 9½ inch rectangle. Cut in half crosswise. Place on baking sheets; prick with a fork. Bake 10–15 minutes or until golden and crisp. Cool on wire rack.
2 To make Filling: Blend cornstarch, sugar and cream in a heavy-bottom pan. Slowly add milk; stirring over medium heat until mixture boils and thickens. Stir a small amount of the hot mixture into beaten yolks. Return to saucepan. Cook and stir 2 minutes. Remove from heat, stir in vanilla. Cover surface of filling with plastic wrap to prevent skin forming. Cool completely.
3 Spread one sheet of pastry evenly with filling. Top with remaining pastry sheet, upside down.
4 To make Icing: Combine pulp and butter;

mix well. Add enough sugar to make spreading consistency. Spread evenly over pastry sheet. Refrigerate several hours or until pastry softens slightly. Cut into squares with a serrated knife.

PASSIONFRUIT AND PISTACHIO ICE CREAM

Preparation time: 15 minutes +
overnight freezing
Total cooking time: 15 minutes
Serves 8

½ cup milk
1½ cups heavy cream
6 egg yolks
1¼ cups sugar

pulp of 8 passionfruit
⅓ cup shelled pistachios,
chopped
passionfruit pulp for serving

1 Heat milk and cream until almost boiling.
2 Using electric beaters, beat yolks and sugar until pale and thick. Add milk and cream gradually. Return mixture to pan. Stir constantly over medium heat until lightly thickened (do not boil). Transfer to bowl, cool, stirring occasionally.
3 Reserve a quarter cup of passionfruit pulp, place remainder in pan. Warm over medium heat 1–2 minutes. Remove from heat; strain. Add passionfruit juice and reserved pulp to cream mixture. Pour into 6-cup capacity metal tray, freeze 3–4 hours or until just frozen around edges.
4 Transfer to large bowl. Beat until thick and creamy. Add nuts, mix well. Freeze overnight or until firm. Serve with passionfruit pulp.

LEFT: PASSIONFRUIT VANILLA DESSERT
ABOVE: PASSIONFRUIT AND PISTACHIO ICE CREAM.
OPPOSITE PAGE: RICOTTA-FILLED RAVIOLI WITH FRESH TOMATO SAUCE

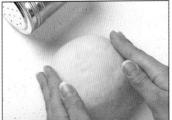

PASTA

RICOTTA-FILLED RAVIOLI WITH FRESH TOMATO SAUCE

⭐⭐ **Preparation time:** 45 minutes +
30 minutes standing
Total cooking time: 45 minutes
Serves 4–6

Ravioli Dough
1 cup all-purpose flour
1 egg
1 tablespoon oil
1 teaspoon water

Sauce
1 tablespoon oil
1 onion, chopped
2 cloves garlic, crushed
1 carrot, chopped
2 lb ripe tomatoes,
  skinned and chopped
1 tablespoon tomato
  paste

1 teaspoon soft brown
  sugar
1/2 cup chicken stock
1 tablespoon
  Worcestershire sauce
1/2 cup chopped fresh basil

Filling
1 lb ricotta cheese
4 oz prosciutto, finely
  chopped
1 tablespoon flat-leaf
  parsley
1 egg yolk

1 To make Ravioli Dough: Sift the flour into a bowl. Make a well in the center and add the egg, oil and water, gradually incorporating them into the flour to form a smooth dough. Turn dough onto a lightly floured board, knead until smooth and elastic. Cover dough and set aside for 30 minutes.

2 To make Sauce: Place oil in a large heavy-bottom pan. Add the onion, garlic and carrot. Cook over low heat for 5–7 minutes. Add the tomatoes, tomato paste, sugar, chicken stock, Worcestershire sauce and basil. Bring the mixture to the boil, reduce to simmer, cover and cook for 30 minutes. Purée the mixture in a blender and keep warm.

To make Filling: Combine ricotta, prosciutto, parsley and egg yolk. Mix well.

3 Halve dough and shape each half into a smooth ball. Roll out each portion thinly to a long rectangle. Place teaspoonfuls of filling in small mounds at 2 inch intervals, in regular lines, on one sheet of dough. Brush between the mounds of filling with water. Place the other sheet of dough carefully over the top. Press down between mounds of filling to seal. Use a pastry wheel or a sharp knife to cut into squares. Drop the ravioli into a pan of rapidly boiling water and cook for 8–10 minutes, or until tender. Remove ravioli from water using a slotted spoon and place into a heated serving dish. Cover with sauce and serve immediately with Parmesan shavings.

combines particularly well with salads, egg dishes, stews, vegetables, rice and pasta; deep-fried sprigs are used to garnish grilled meats and fish. Parsley is an ingredient in bouquet garni and the seasonings gremolata and persillade. The herb originated in southern Europe and has been cultivated since ancient times. Long valued for its medicinal as well as its culinary properties, it is rich in vitamin C and minerals and is sometimes called the "herb of health." The Romans wore wreaths of parsley to ward off the effects of alcohol.

Parsley Root A member of the parsley family often used in soups. It tastes like a combination of parsley and celery.

Parsnip A root vegetable with a carrot-like shape and creamy white flesh. When cooked it has a strong, slightly sweet flavor which goes well with roast meats. The parsnip originated in Eastern Europe and was introduced into North America in the seventeenth century.

Partridge A ground-dwelling game bird related to the pheasant and native to Europe. Partridge is hung unplucked and uncleaned for three to four days after killing to develop its flavor and to tenderize the flesh. In America a similar upland game bird is called bobwhite. Young birds can be grilled, broiled or roasted in the same way as chicken; older birds are best cooked slowly. Allow one bird per person. Partridge is available fresh and frozen from specialist game and poultry stores.

Pascal Celery A green celery with a crisp, leafy stalk.

Passionfruit Also called granadilla, the egg-shaped fruit of the passionflower vine with sharp-sweet, juicy, fragrant orange pulp studded with small black edible seeds. The leathery skin varies in color from pale yellow-green to pink, to

deep purple-brown; it is smooth and shiny when immature and deeply dimpled when ripe. Passionfruit can be eaten fresh (scooped from the shell with a spoon) or the pulp can be added to fruit salads, yogurt and ice cream, mousse and

FETTUCCINE BOLOGNESE

⭐ **Preparation time:** 10 minutes
Total cooking time: 1 hour 40 minutes
Serves 6

2 tablespoons oil	16 oz can tomatoes with
2 medium onions, chopped	their liquid, crushed
2 cloves garlic, crushed	1/2 cup tomato paste
1 lb ground beef	1 tablespoon chopped
8 oz small mushrooms,	fresh oregano
chopped	4 cups water
2 tablespoons chopped	1 lb dried fettuccine
fresh basil	

1 Heat the oil in a heavy-bottom pan, add the onion and stir over medium heat for 3 minutes or until the onion is soft. Add the garlic, stir for 1 minute. Add the ground beef and cook over high heat for 5 minutes until the meat is well browned and all the liquid has evaporated. Use a fork to break up any lumps of beef as it cooks.

2 Add the mushrooms, basil, crushed tomatoes with liquid, tomato paste, oregano and water. Bring to the boil, then reduce heat to a simmer. Cook, uncovered, for 1 1/2 hours, or until the sauce has reduced and thickened.

3 Bring a large pan of water to the boil. Add fettuccine and cook until just tender. Serve with meat sauce.

SPAGHETTI CARBONARA

⭐ ⭐ **Preparation time:** 20 minutes
Total cooking time: 10 minutes
Serves 6

4 cloves garlic	3/4 cup shredded
1 tablespoon oil	Parmesan cheese
6 slices bacon, chopped	freshly ground black
1/3 cup white wine	pepper to taste
4 eggs	1/4 cup chopped parsley
3/4 cup grated Cheddar	1 lb spaghetti, cooked
cheese	and kept warm

1 Peel and halve the garlic cloves. Heat the oil in pan, add garlic, stir until lightly golden, remove garlic and discard. Add the bacon to the pan and cook over medium heat until it is crisp and golden. Add the wine and cook for another minute.

2 Whisk eggs in a bowl; add cheeses, pepper and parsley.

3 To serve, place drained spaghetti in a large bowl, add the bacon with pan juices and toss together well. Add the beaten egg and cheese mixture, mix well. Serve pasta immediately, with extra Parmesan cheese, if desired.

ABOVE: FETTUCCINE BOLOGNESE.

OPPOSITE PAGE: PENNE WITH LAMB AND VEGETABLES

PENNE WITH LAMB AND VEGETABLES

★ **Preparation time:** 15 minutes
Total cooking time: 20 minutes
Serves 4

2 tablespoons oil
1 large onion, cut into
  eighths
2 garlic cloves, crushed
1 lb ground lamb
1 small red pepper,
  seeded and chopped
5 oz shelled fava beans
4 oz small mushroom
  caps, halved

16 oz can tomatoes,
  crushed
2 tablespoons tomato
  paste
1 lb dried penne
4 oz feta cheese
2 tablespoons shredded
  fresh basil

1 Heat the oil in a large heavy-bottom pan, add the onion and garlic and stir-fry over medium heat for 2 minutes or until lightly browned. Add the lamb; stir-fry over high heat for 4 minutes or until meat is well browned and all liquid has evaporated. Use a fork to break up any lumps as lamb cooks.
2 Add the chopped pepper, fava beans, mushrooms, undrained, crushed tomatoes and tomato paste; bring mixture to boil, reduce the heat to a simmer, cover and cook for 10 minutes or until the vegetables are tender; stir occasionally.

3 Cook the penne in a large pan of rapidly boiling water, with a little oil added, until it is just tender. Remove from heat and drain. Spoon the pasta into serving bowls and top with the lamb and vegetable sauce, crumble the feta cheese over the sauce and sprinkle with shredded fresh basil.

CHICKEN CANNELLONI WITH CHILI TOMATO SAUCE

★ ★ **Preparation time:** 20 minutes
Total cooking time: 45 minutes
Serves 4

1 tablespoon olive oil
1 small onion, finely
  chopped
2 teaspoons bottled
  crushed chili peppers
3 small carrots, finely
  diced
1/2 cup chopped
  parsley
28 oz can peeled
  tomatoes, chopped
1/4 cup white wine or
  chicken stock
1 egg, beaten

1 lb ground chicken
2 scallions chopped
1/2 cup heavy cream
2 tablespoons grated
  Parmesan cheese
8 cannelloni tubes,
  cooked and drained

Garnish

1 cup sour cream
2 medium avocados,
  sliced

1 Preheat oven to moderate 350°F. Lightly brush a 14 x 8 x 2½ inch shallow oblong baking dish with oil or melted butter.
2 Heat the olive oil in a pan. Add the onion, chili peppers and carrot, cook for 3–4 minutes or until the onion is tender. Add the parsley, tomatoes and wine or stock and bring to the boil, stirring all the time. Reduce heat and simmer, covered, for 10 minutes—the sauce should still be quite liquid.
3 Combine the egg, ground chicken, scallions, cream and Parmesan cheese; mix well. Place mixture into a piping bag which has been fitted with a large, plain nozzle. Carefully pipe the mixture into the cooked cannelloni tubes.
4 Spoon half the tomato mixture over the base of the prepared dish. Arrange the filled cannelloni tubes over the tomato mixture in a single layer. Top with the remaining tomato mixture. Bake for 30 minutes or until they are heated through. Serve garnished with sour cream and sliced avocado.

Note: Take care when piping filling into cooked cannelloni tubes as they are soft and very easy to rip or tear.

dessert sauces. The passionfruit vine is native to tropical America. Store at room temperature until ripe, then refrigerate. In season in late summer, it can usually be found

fresh through the year; pulp is available canned.

Pasta A dough or paste made of wheat flour, water, salt and sometimes egg, cooked in boiling water and served with many different sauces. Pasta is cut and shaped into a wide variety of shapes such as ribbons, bows, strings, rings, tubes, spirals and shells, each one known by a particular

name. It can be homemade or bought either fresh (*pasta fresca*) or dried (*pasta secca*). The size and shape of pasta dictates the way it is used. Long strands such as spaghetti, fettucine and linguine are boiled and drained. Wide flat pastas or large tubes such as lasagna and manicotti are often cooked and stuffed or layered with cheese sauces. Small intricately shaped pastas such as wheels, rings and alphabets are added to soups. Some pastas are made with only flour and water, other recipes include eggs. Flavored pasta can be made from egg pasta with the addition of

vegetables and herbs such as tomatoes which tint the pasta red, and spinach which tints it green. Egg pasta is associated with northern Italy; pasta made with durum wheat flour is from the south. Pasta is regarded as the national food of Italy. Simple to make and to cook, economical, nutritious and versatile, it has long been the food of rich and poor alike. The Roman writer Horace was fond of lasagna seasoned with leek and chickpeas; a similar dish is made in southern Italy today. Two hundred years ago pasta stalls sold hot pasta that was eaten with the fingers. The first pasta factories date from the nineteenth century.

Pastrami Lean beef, cured, spiced and rubbed with dried chili and black peppercorns. It is deep red in color and is served sliced as a cold meat or sandwich filling.

PASTA AND VEGETABLES

⭐ **Preparation time:** 20 minutes
Total cooking time: 50–55 minutes
Serves 4

1 tablespoon olive oil	2 cups bottled spaghetti
1 large onion, finely	sauce
chopped	salt and pepper to taste
1 clove garlic, crushed	1 tablespoon oil, extra
3 medium zucchini,	1½ cups dried pasta
sliced	(penne or spiral)
4 button mushrooms,	⅓ cup grated Parmesan
sliced	cheese
1 cup frozen peas	

1 Preheat oven to slow 300°F. Heat oil in frying pan. Add onion and garlic, cook over low heat for 4 minutes or until onion is soft. Add zucchini and mushrooms, cook for 3 minutes. Add peas and spaghetti sauce, cook for another 3 minutes. Season with salt and pepper. Remove from heat and set aside.
2 Bring a large pan of water to a rapid boil, add oil and pasta, cook 10–12 minutes or until pasta is just tender. Drain and add to vegetables in pan.
3 Spoon mixture into a casserole dish. Sprinkle with Parmesan cheese and bake, covered, for 20–30 minutes.

ABOVE: PASTA AND VEGETABLES;
RIGHT: FETTUCCINE WITH PESTO.
OPPOSITE PAGE: BEEF LASAGNE

FETTUCCINE WITH PESTO

⭐ **Preparation time:** 20 minutes
Total cooking time: 10 minutes
Serves 4

⅓ cup pine nuts	1 tablespoon butter,
2 cups fresh basil leaves,	softened
tightly packed	freshly ground black
½ cup olive oil	pepper to taste
2 cloves garlic	1 lb fettuccine, cooked
⅔ cup Parmesan cheese	

1 Place pine nuts in a dry pan, stir over moderate heat until nuts are lightly golden. Place in a food processor with basil leaves, olive oil and garlic. Blend until smooth. Transfer to a large bowl.
2 Add Parmesan cheese, butter and black pepper, mix well.
3 To serve, drain cooked pasta well, add the prepared pesto and toss. Serve immediately. Sprinkle extra Parmesan cheese on top before serving, if desired.

Note: Pesto sauce can be made up in larger quantities for later use. It will keep well in the refrigerator for at least a week if placed in a glass jar with a well-fitting lid. Pour a thin layer of olive oil over the surface of the sauce before replacing the lid. Pesto can also be stored in the freezer and will retain its flavor and color.

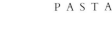

Pastry An unleavened dough made from fat (butter, margarine or lard), flour and sometimes sugar, and bound with water. Different types of pastry result from the kind of fat used and variations in the proportions of the ingredients.

Pastry, also called shortcrust pastry, forms the containers for sweet and savory pies, flans and tarts; crisp, filo (phyllo) pastry and flaky puff pastry are used for dishes ranging from sausage rolls to desserts such as strudel; hot-water crust pastry is used particularly for English game pies. Pastry is also a general term for sweet baked foods made with pastry dough.

Pastry Cream See Crème Pâtissière.

Pâté and Terrine Preparations of ground meat, poultry, game, fish or vegetables. In general, pâté is a fine-textured

paste or spread; the name "pâté" comes from the French *pâté en croûte*, a rich meat, poultry or game mixture cooked encased in pastry; the term is also applied to mixtures that have been baked or sautéed, then puréed to a

BEEF LASAGNE

★★ ***Preparation time:*** 45 minutes
Total cooking time: 1 hour 40 minutes
Serves 16

1¹/₂ lb lean ground beef	2 teaspoons dried basil
1¹/₂ lb ground pork sausage	1 teaspoon dried oregano
1 tablespoon oil	salt and pepper
2 onions, chopped	16 oz packages no-cook lasagna noodles
2 medium zucchini, chopped	
8 oz baby mushrooms, sliced	**Cream Sauce**
	¹/₂ cup butter
1¹/₂ lb bottle spaghetti sauce	²/₃ cup all-purpose flour
	6 cups milk
2 x 14¹/₂ oz cans crushed tomatoes	salt and pepper
	2 cups mozzarella cheese, grated
6 oz can tomato paste	¹/₂ cup grated Parmesan cheese
1 tablespoon sugar	
1 cup red wine	

1 Preheat oven to moderate 350°F. Grease two 13 x 9 x 2 inch baking dishes. In a large pan cook ground beef and sausage in batches until browned. Drain and transfer to bowl. Heat oil in the same pan, cook onion until soft. Add the zucchini and mushrooms, cook until just tender. Return the meat to the onion mixture, add the spaghetti sauce, undrained diced tomato, tomato paste, sugar, wine, basil, oregano and salt and pepper. Simmer, covered, for 30 minutes, stirring occasionally. Remove from heat and set aside.

2 To make Cream Sauce: Heat butter in a medium pan until melted. Add flour, cook, stirring over heat until mixture bubbles. Remove from heat, add milk gradually to pan, stirring, until smooth. Stir over heat until sauce boils and thickens. Add salt, pepper and cheese. Mix until smooth and cheese has melted.

3 To assemble lasagne, spread half a cup of tomato mixture over the base of each baking dish. Top with lasagna sheets to cover. Spread one-sixth of the cheese sauce over pasta. Spread a quarter of the tomato sauce over cheese sauce in each dish. Repeat layering with pasta, cream sauce, then tomato sauce, finishing with a pasta sheet topped with cream sauce. Sprinkle top with grated Parmesan. Bake lasagne for 45 minutes or until pasta is cooked through and the top is lightly browned.

creamy consistency. A terrine is usually coarser in texture and is served sliced. Pâté is usually served at room temperature, either spread on bread, toast or crackers as finger food, or cut into thick slices as a first course. A type of pâté was made in the days of ancient Rome, chiefly using pork, but sometimes with the addition of other ingredients such as spiced and marinated birds' tongues.

Pâte Brisée A pastry dough (pie crust) which is made from flour, butter, margarine or lard (or a combination of these), sugar, egg and water. It is mixed directly on the work surface by placing the wet ingredients into a well formed in the center of the dry ingredients. Using the fingertips, first the wet ingredients are mixed together, then the dry ingredients are gradually drawn in. It is called pâte brisée, which means literally "broken dough," because the ingredients are "broken" into one another. Pâte brisée is used in French cooking for both sweet and savory dishes.

SPAGHETTI MARINARA

⭐ **Preparation time:** 20 minutes
Total cooking time: 25–30 minutes
Serves 4

1 tablespoon olive oil
1 small onion, finely chopped
1 clove garlic, chopped
1 large carrot, diced
1 stalk celery, diced
28 oz can peeled tomatoes, puréed
¼ cup chopped parsley
½ cup white wine
12 oz marinara mix (see Note)
¼ cup heavy cream
1 lb spaghetti, cooked

1 Heat the oil in a pan. Add the onion, garlic, carrot and celery. Cook until the vegetables are tender. Add the puréed tomatoes, parsley and white wine. Simmer uncovered, stirring occasionally, for 15 minutes.
2 Add marinara mix to the sauce with the cream; stir to combine ingredients and cook for two minutes.
3 To serve, combine well-drained spaghetti with sauce. Serve immediately.

Note: Marinara mix is a mixture of seafood pieces (usually including octopus, shrimp, calamari and mussels) sold by fishmongers.

FETTUCCINE ALFREDO

⭐ **Preparation time:** 10 minutes
Total cooking time: 5–10 minutes
Serves 4

1 lb fresh fettuccine (plain, spinach or tomato)
1 cup heavy cream
¼ cup butter
⅔ cup grated Parmesan cheese
black pepper

1 Bring a large pan of water to the boil. Add a little salt. Drop in the fettuccine and cover the pot until the water returns to the boil—fresh fettuccine will take only a few minutes to cook. Drain in a colander.
2 Heat ⅔ cup of the cream along with the butter in a heavy casserole dish and simmer over medium heat for about 1 minute or until the cream has thickened slightly.
3 Transfer the drained fettuccine to the casserole dish, place over low heat, add the remaining cream, cheese and pepper. Toss until the fettuccine is thoroughly coated with the sauce. Serve immediately with extra Parmesan cheese if desired.

ABOVE: SPAGHETTI MARINARA.
OPPOSITE PAGE: VEGETABLE LASAGNE

VEGETABLE LASAGNE

★ ★ **Preparation time:** 20 minutes
Total cooking time: 1 hour 15 minutes
Serves 6

3 large red peppers	8 oz no-cook lasagna
2 large eggplants	noodles (8 noodles)
2 tablespoons oil	1 bunch spinach, chopped
1 large onion, finely	1 cup basil leaves
chopped	3¹/₂ oz sun-dried
3 cloves garlic, crushed	tomatoes, sliced
1 teaspoon dried mixed	¹/₄ cup grated Parmesan
herbs	cheese
1 teaspoon dried oregano	¹/₄ cup grated Cheddar
1 lb mushrooms, sliced	cheese
16 oz can whole	
tomatoes, crushed	**Cheese Sauce**
16 oz can red kidney	¹/₄ cup butter
beans, drained	¹/₄ cup all-purpose flour
1 tablespoon sweet chili	2 cups milk
sauce	1 lb ricotta cheese
salt and pepper, to taste	

1 Preheat oven to moderate 350°F. Brush a 14 x 11 inch ovenproof casserole dish with oil or melted butter. Cut peppers into quarters. Remove seeds and membrane. Place pepper pieces skin-side up on broiler rack and brush with oil. Broil 5 inches from heat for 5 minutes, or until skin is black and blistered. Cover with a damp towel until cool. Peel the skin off and cut pepper into long thin strips. Set aside. Slice eggplant into ¹/₂ inch rounds, place in a large pan of boiling water. Cook for 1 minute or until just tender; drain and pat dry with paper towel. Set aside.

2 Heat the oil in a large heavy-bottom frying pan. Add the onion, garlic and herbs. Cook over medium heat for 5 minutes or until the onion is soft. Add mushrooms and cook for 1 minute. Add tomatoes, beans, sauce, salt and pepper. Bring to boil, reduce heat. Simmer, uncovered, for 15 minutes or until sauce thickens. Remove from heat.

3 Dip lasagna sheets in hot water to soften slightly and arrange four sheets on base of prepared dish. Arrange half of each of the eggplant, spinach, basil, pepper, mushroom mixture and sun-dried tomatoes over pasta. Top with a layer of pasta and press gently. Repeat layers. Top with cheese sauce and sprinkle with combined Parmesan and Cheddar cheeses. Bake for 45 minutes or until pasta is soft.

4 To make Cheese Sauce: Heat butter in medium pan, add flour. Stir over medium heat for 2 minutes or until mixture is golden. Add milk gradually, stirring until mixture boils and thickens. Boil for 1 minute. Add ricotta and stir until smooth.

TORTELLINI WITH MUSHROOM CREAM SAUCE

★ **Preparation time:** 10 minutes
Total cooking time: 8 minutes
Serves 4

¹/₄ cup butter	pinch pepper
6 oz small mushrooms,	pinch nutmeg
sliced	3 tablespoons grated
1 clove garlic, crushed	Parmesan cheese
1 cup heavy cream	1 lb tortellini, cooked and
1 teaspoon grated lemon	kept warm
rind	

1 Melt the butter in a saucepan. Add the mushrooms and cook over medium heat for 30 seconds. Add the crushed garlic, cream, lemon rind, pepper and nutmeg to taste.

2 Stir over low heat for 1–2 minutes. Add the grated Parmesan and cook gently for a further 3 minutes.

3 To serve, combine well-drained pasta with sauce. Serve immediately.

Pâte Sucrée The dough for a sweet, crisp pastry (shortcrust) made from butter or margarine, sugar and egg yolk and used in French cooking for flan cases and tarts. It is mixed in the same way as pâte brisée.

Paupiette A thin fillet of meat, poultry or fish spread with a seasoned or herb stuffing mixture, rolled and secured with string or toothpicks then braised.

Pavlova A dessert consisting of a meringue case filled with whipped cream and topped with fresh fruit (usually including strawberries and passionfruit pulp). The dish is attributed to Herbert Sachse, chef at a leading hotel in Perth, Australia, who named it in memory of the 1929 visit to the city by the ballerina Anna Pavlova.

Pawpaw See Papaya.

Peach A round, yellow to rosy pink, downy-skinned fruit with a single pit and pale, fragrant, sweet, juicy flesh. There are two main types: freestone (the flesh separates easily from the pit), and clingstone (the flesh clings to the pit). In season from early summer to autumn, peaches are also available canned, in syrup.

PASTRY

The success of a tart, quiche or flan depends on the pastry base—it should be light, crisp and golden. Once you have mastered the techniques of pastry-making, you will have perfect results every time. For quiches and flans, use shortcrust (pie crust), filo (phyllo) or puff pastry. Ready-rolled pastry saves time and also gives an excellent result.

ABOUT SHORTCRUST (PIE CRUST) PASTRY

Plain (all-purpose) flour is the flour generally used to make shortcrust pastry; however, adding a little self-rising flour can give a much lighter result.

Although other shortenings can be used, butter produces the best flavor. Chop it into small (pea-size) pieces and make sure it is cold when you begin. Eggs make dough crumbly (short) and rich; milk gives a softer pastry that browns well.

Whether mixing by hand or with a food processor, work quickly and lightly to avoid melting the butter. Mixing dough for too long, handling it roughly or adding too much liquid will result in tough pastry.

Once you have rubbed the butter into the flour, add ice-cold water (or other liquid) a tablespoon at a time, until the mixture just comes together in a stiff dough.

Form the dough into a ball, cover with plastic wrap and chill for at least 30 minutes before rolling out. This will make the dough more manageable and prevent the pastry from shrinking as it cooks.

ABOUT CHOUX PASTRY

This is a very different pastry from shortcrust in that the flour is mixed with boiling liquid and then the eggs are added. The result is light puffs of pastry, hollow in the middle. Choux pastry is used for éclairs, cream puffs and profiteroles. Once cooked and filled they should be eaten immediately, otherwise they become soggy.

ABOUT PUFF PASTRY

Puff pastry is probably the most difficult to make but is considered the finest of all pastries. Good-quality commercial puff pastry is widely available, in blocks as well as packs of ready-rolled sheets. In this book, all recipes requiring puff pastry use the commercial type.

ROLLING OUT PASTRY

Use a marble or smooth wooden rolling pin. Divide the dough in half if necessary and form each half into a ball. Roll out dough on a smooth, lightly floured surface (marble is ideal), or between two sheets of plastic wrap or baking paper. Roll dough away from you, using short, quick strokes. Turn the dough a quarter turn after each roll, being careful not to stretch it. Roll out to an even thickness, about 1½ inches bigger than the size of the dish to be lined.

LINING THE DISH

Wrap rolled dough loosely around the rolling pin and lift it over the pie dish or flan pan; unroll dough gently, taking care not to stretch it.

Ease the dough into the pan and press it into the sides of the pan with the fingers. If using a metal dish, roll the pin over the top of the dish to cut off any excess dough. If using a ceramic dish, trim off the edges of the dough with a sharp knife.

DECORATIVE EDGES

For a decorative finish to the edges of open or closed pies, crimp or nip around the edge of the dough with fingers, mark with a fork, or cut at even intervals and fold each cut segment over.

To make a coin edge, trim dough to edge of dish and brush rim with water. From leftover dough, cut out ½ inch rounds and place, slightly overlapping, around rim, pressing gently.

Decorate open pies with lattice: make pastry for a two-crust pie, line dish, then roll the rest into a rectangle. Cut into 9 strips. Plait 3, join next 3 and plait, then repeat with last 3 strips. Moisten edge with water, place plait on rim and press gently.

BAKING BLIND

Baking an unfilled pastry shell is called "baking blind" and gives a crisp, firm base, even if the filling is a moist one. In some dishes, if the pastry shell is not baked blind, the filling will be cooked but the pastry base will be soggy.

Line pastry shell with a sheet of parchment paper and spread a layer of raw rice or beans evenly on top (the weight prevents the pastry rising). Preheat oven to 425°F and bake for 10–15 minutes. Remove paper and rice or beans and discard. Bake pastry for another 5–10 minutes or until it is light golden. The filling can now be placed in the pre-cooked pastry shell.

PASTRY TIPS

■ It is important to cook pastry at the correct temperature: if your oven tends to be cooler or hotter than normal, you may need to slightly adjust the baking time. Pastry should be crisp and golden-brown and the filling properly set.

■ Ceramic and glass pie plates or quiche dishes do not conduct heat as well as metal ones do. However, they are more attractive than metal dishes. To ensure your pastry becomes brown and crisp when baked in these dishes, put a baking sheet made of metal in the oven when preheating it. Place the ceramic or glass pie plate on the hot tray and the pastry on the bottom will cook faster.

■ An 8 inch pie will give 5–6 servings; if the pie is very rich, cut it into 7–8 pieces. A 9 inch pie will give 6–8 pieces (more if rich), and a 10 inch pie can be cut into 8–12 pieces or more.

PREPARING AHEAD

Ready-to-bake, pastry-lined dishes can be stored in the refrigerator or freezer. Line the dish with pastry, cover with heavy-duty aluminum foil or plastic wrap and freeze for up to 12 weeks. Alternatively, cover with plastic wrap and store in refrigerator for up to 24 hours. Before filling an unbaked frozen pastry-lined dish, bring it to room temperature, and bake blind at 425°F for 10–15 minutes. Or bake it straight from the freezer for 15–20 minutes.

PASTRY RECIPES

SHORTCRUST (PIE CRUST) PASTRY

This recipe uses mustard and is suitable for savory pies and tarts. For sweet dishes, omit the mustard and add 2 tablespoons sugar. Makes one 9 inch tart shell.

Put 2 cups all-purpose flour and ½ teaspoon dry mustard in a food processor with ½ cup cold butter, chopped into small pieces. Process until the mixture resembles coarse breadcrumbs. Slowly add 4–6 tablespoons cold water and process until the mixture comes together, adding a little more water if necessary. Cover the dough with plastic wrap, form into a rough ball and refrigerate for 30 minutes.

To make by hand: Sift the flour and mustard into a large bowl; add the butter. Using your fingertips, rub butter into flour for 3 minutes or until mixture is fine and crumbly. Add water and mix to a soft dough, adding more water if necessary. Form dough into a ball, cover with plastic wrap and refrigerate for 30 minutes.

RICH SHORTCRUST PASTRY

Use this for sweet pies and tarts. Makes one 9 inch tart shell. Place 2 cups all-purpose flour into a food processor with ½ cup cold butter, chopped into pieces, and 3 tablespoons of sugar. Process until the mixture resembles coarse bread crumbs. Add 1 egg yolk and 1 tablespoon iced water and process until mixture comes together, adding more water if necessary. Wrap in plastic wrap and chill for 30 minutes.

To make by hand: Sift the flour into large bowl; add butter. Rub the butter into the flour with the fingertips for 3 minutes or until the mixture is fine and crumbly; stir in the sugar. Add the egg yolk and water, mix to a soft dough; press into a ball. Cover with plastic wrap and refrigerate for 30 minutes.

MINI FRUIT DANISH

Using 2 ready-rolled puff pastry sheets, cut each sheet into 3 strips. Cut each strip into 3, giving 18 squares altogether.

In a small bowl, beat together 2 tablespoons softened butter with ⅓ cup confectioners' sugar until smooth. Add 1 egg yolk and ¼ cup ground almonds and beat until well combined.

Spread a little filling on each pastry square. Place two canned apricot halves side-by-side diagonally on each of the squares. Bring the remaining two corners of each square over the apricots; press corners together. Preheat oven to 415°F. Place pastries on baking sheets and bake for 15 minutes or until they turn golden brown; remove from oven.

In a small pan, heat together ½ cup apricot jam and 1 tablespoon water. Strain the mixture and brush as a glaze over the pastries. Allow to cool before serving.

CHOUX PASTRY

Sift 1 cup all-purpose flour, 1 teaspoon sugar and ¼ teaspoon salt onto a piece of wax paper. Place 1 cup water in a pan with ⅓ cup butter. Heat until the butter is melted, bring to the boil, remove from heat and add the flour mixture all at once. Stir vigorously with a wooden spoon until the mixture leaves the sides of the pan and forms a smooth ball.

Transfer the mixture to the small bowl of an

electric mixer and add 3 beaten eggs, a little at a time, beating well after each addition (the mixture should become smooth and glossy).

Place heaped teaspoonsful of mixture on a greased baking sheet, allowing room for spreading. Bake at 425°F for 10 minutes; reduce heat to 350°F and bake for another 15 minutes, until puffs are crisp and golden. Turn the oven off.

Make a small slit in the side of each puff. Place puffs in the oven with the door ajar for 10 minutes to dry out the centers. Cool puffs on a rack. Just before serving, split and fill as desired.

Food processor method: Place flour, sugar and salt in a food processor bowl fitted with a metal blade and process for a few seconds to aerate. Combine water and butter in a small pan, heat until butter melts, then bring to a fast boil.

With machine running, pour bubbling mixture through the feed tube onto the flour and process for a few seconds until the dough becomes thick and smooth. Allow to cool for 2 or 3 minutes. Pour beaten eggs in a slow, steady stream through the feed tube and process until the mixture is thick and glossy.

Place heaped teaspoonsful of mixture on a greased baking sheet, allowing room for spreading. Bake for 10 minutes, reduce heat to 350°F and bake for another 15 minutes until puffs are crisp and golden. Turn oven off.

Make a small slit in side of each puff. Place them in the oven with the door ajar for 10 minutes to dry out the centers. Cool puffs on a rack. Just before serving, split and fill as desired.

FILLINGS FOR CHOUX PUFFS

CREAM PUFFS: Fill puffs with whipped cream and dust with confectioners' sugar.

PROFITEROLES: Make smaller puffs. When cold, fill with Crème Pâtissière and serve with Chocolate Sauce (see Index for recipes).

SAVORY PUFFS: Omit sugar, fill with Salmon or Cheese Filling (recipes below).

Salmon Filling: Heat ¼ cup butter in a medium pan, and add ¼ cup all-purpose flour. Stir over low heat for 2 minutes or until the flour mixture is lightly golden. Add 1¼ cups milk gradually to pan, stirring until mixture is smooth. Stir continuously until mixture boils and thickens; boil for another minute, then remove from heat. Drain a 4 oz can red salmon, remove the skin and bones, and flake salmon. Add to mixture in pan along with 2 teaspoons lemon juice, 1 tablespoon mayonnaise and ⅓ cup finely chopped chives; stir gently until combined.

Cheese Filling: Heat 1 tablespoon butter in a medium pan, add 4 oz button mushrooms, thinly sliced, and cook over low heat for 3 minutes or until the mushrooms are just tender. Add ¼ cup all-purpose flour and 1 teaspoon freshly ground black pepper. Stir over low heat for about 2 minutes or until the flour mixture is lightly golden. Add 1 cup milk and ¼ cup heavy cream to the pan slowly, stirring until mixture is smooth. Stir continuously until the mixture boils and thickens; boil for another minute, then remove the pan from the heat. Stir in ½ cup grated Cheddar cheese and ¼ cup finely chopped parsley.

CLOCKWISE FROM TOP RIGHT: QUICHE LORRAINE (SEE RECIPE PAGE 362); MINCEMEAT TARTS (SEE PAGE 269); CHOUX PUFF; BLUEBERRY CHEESE TART (SEE PAGE 139); LEMON-LIME PIE (SEE PAGE 254); FRUIT FLAN (SEE PAGE 444) AND MINI APRICOT DANISH

Peach Melba A dessert consisting of peaches poached in vanilla syrup, chilled, then served with vanilla ice cream and fresh raspberry purée. The dish was created for the Australian opera star Nellie Melba by the esteemed French chef Auguste Escoffier.

Peanut Also called groundnut or goober, the edible seed of a legume encased in brittle, pale-brown pods that develop and ripen below ground. Peanuts can be eaten raw, roasted and salted as a savory snack, or coated in sweets or chocolate as a candy. Peanuts are important in the cooking of Southeast Asia where they are used in sauces for grilled meat or added whole to dishes. Peanuts are made into peanut butter and peanut oil is extracted from them.

Peanut Butter A spread made from ground, roasted peanuts and used in sandwiches (it combines well with celery, crisp bacon, raisins, honey and jam), on toast or as an ingredient in home-made satay sauce. It is available as either a smooth, creamy paste or

P A T E S

R E D   P E P P E R   P A T E

⭐ **Preparation time:** 8 minutes
Total cooking time: 35 minutes
Makes 1 cup

4 large red peppers
3 cloves garlic, unpeeled
2 tablespoons balsamic vinegar
1 tablespoon sweet chili sauce

2/3 cup butter, melted
pinch sugar
2 teaspoons finely chopped parsley

1 Preheat oven to 475°F. Line a baking sheet with foil. Cut the peppers in half lengthwise and remove seeds and membrane. Cut in half again. Arrange the pepper pieces on the baking sheet with the garlic cloves. Bake for 20 minutes. Remove from oven; cover peppers with damp towel until cool. Peel skins from pepper pieces and garlic cloves; discard skins.
2 Place the peppers, garlic, vinegar and chili sauce in a food processor and process until smooth. With the motor running, pour in the melted butter in a thin, steady stream; process until the mixture is thick and creamy.
3 Transfer the mixture to a small pan. Stir over low heat for 15 minutes. Remove from the heat and stir in the sugar and parsley. Serve with crackers or Melba toast. This pâté will keep in an airtight jar or container for up to three weeks.

Note: Red Pepper Pâté can be used on pizzas as a base sauce instead of tomato sauce. It is also delicious spread on blini and topped with ham, turkey or fresh herbs.

Q U I C K   S A L M O N   P A T E

⭐ **Preparation time:** 10 minutes
+ refrigeration
Total cooking time: none
Serves 4

1 x 7 oz can boneless, skinless salmon, drained
6½ oz soft cream cheese
1 onion, coarsely chopped
2 gherkins
2 tablespoons cream

1 tablespoon lemon juice
1 teaspoon whole grain mustard
few drops Tabasco sauce
freshly ground pepper, to taste

1 Place all ingredients in a together in a food processor and process until the mixture is a smooth consistency.
2 Spoon the mixture into a serving dish and refrigerate for several hours. Serve with crackers or Melba toast.

GRAND MARNIER PATE

⭐ **Preparation time:** 30 minutes
+ overnight refrigeration
Total cooking time: 10–15 minutes
Serves 8

1 lb chicken livers or duck livers	1/2 cup heavy cream
1/2 cup butter	2 teaspoons chopped fresh thyme
1 medium onion, chopped	2 teaspoons chopped fresh parsley or chives
2 scallions, chopped	
2 cloves garlic, crushed	salt and pepper
2–3 tablespoons Grand Marnier	Melba toast

1 Preheat oven to 350°F. Trim livers of sinew. Heat butter in a large heavy-based frying pan. Add livers, onion, garlic and Grand Marnier. Stir over medium heat until the liver is just cooked and the onion is soft. Bring to boil and simmer for 4–5 minutes. Remove from heat, allow to cool slightly.
2 Place mixture in a food processor. Process for 20–30 seconds or until smooth. Add cream; process for 10 seconds. Transfer mixture to a medium bowl. Stir in herbs. Season with salt and pepper, mix well. Spoon into small ramekins, or

OPPOSITE PAGE: RED PEPPER PATE.

ABOVE: GRAND MARNIER PATE

one large ramekin dish. Refrigerate overnight or until firm. Serve at room temperature accompanied by Melba toast.
3 To make Melba toast: Cut crusts from bread. Flatten slices with a rolling pin; cut each in half, or quarter diagonally. Bake 5–10 minutes or until crisp and lightly golden. Cool. Alternatively, toast sliced sandwich bread until golden, then remove the crusts. Split through the middle of the slice using a serrated knife. Cut each slice into quarters and brown the untoasted sides under a hot broiler.

Note: Grand Marnier may be replaced with the same quantity of cognac or port.

CHICKEN LIVER AND BRANDY PATE

⭐ **Preparation time:** 30 minutes
+ overnight refrigeration
Total cooking time: 10–15 minutes
Serves 4–6

1/2 cup butter	2 tablespoons heavy cream
1 large onion, chopped	
2 cloves garlic, crushed	1 tablespoon brandy
2 slices rindless bacon, chopped	2 tablespoons butter, extra, melted
8 oz chicken livers, trimmed	**Topping**
1/4 teaspoon dried thyme	1/4 cup butter, melted
freshly ground black pepper	2 tablespoons snipped chives

1 Melt butter in a pan, add onion, garlic and bacon. Cook until onion is tender and bacon is cooked.
2 Add chicken livers and cook, stirring occasionally, 5–10 minutes. Remove from heat. Stir in thyme, pepper, cream, brandy and melted butter.
3 Spoon the mixture into a food processor or blender, process until smooth. Pour into serving dishes.
4 To make Topping: Pour melted butter over pâté. Sprinkle top with chives. Refrigerate pâté overnight. Stand at room temperature 30 minutes before serving. Serve with toast, crackers or crusty French bread.

Note: Liver-based pâtés are quite strongly flavored and need the addition of well-balanced seasonings—onion, garlic, spices and alcohol. They improve if kept for two or three days before serving, and will keep for up to a week, covered, in the refrigerator.

a crunchy version containing pieces of crushed nut. Peanut butter was popularised in North America in the twentieth century.

Peanut Oil An oil made from peanut kernels, used for frying and to make salad dressings. Mildest in flavor is the European version; it is almost flavorless and used for dressing delicately flavored salads. American peanut oil has a more nutty taste. Asian oil is darker and more strongly flavored. It can be heated to a very high temperature, so is good for frying.

Pear A teardrop-shaped fruit with yellow, green or light brown skin and juicy white flesh. It can be eaten fresh, added to both fruit salads (it blends particularly well with raspberries and blackcurrants) and savory salads, poached in syrup or wine and used in many other desserts such as mousses, soufflés and tarts. The pear originated in Asia. It was

introduced into Europe by the ancient Greeks and was a popular fruit in ancient Rome.

Peas, Dried The seed of several varieties of the common garden pea grown specifically to be dried. They were an important vegetable before frozen peas became commonly available. Dried peas may be whole with wrinkled skins intact, or husked and split in two at the natural division (split peas). In India whole dried peas are roasted and spiced as a snack food; in England, where they are known as "mushy peas," they are soaked, simmered and served either with fish and chips or poured over hot meat pies. Split peas are prepared from the green and yellow field pea varieties of the common garden pea; they are sweeter and less starchy than whole dried peas. Split peas are used for pea soup, pease pudding and in Germany they are often baked with sauerkraut and sour cream.

Peas, Green Small, round, juicy green seeds encased in a green pod; a popular vegetable throughout the world. In most varieties the pod is discarded, although it can be used to make pea soup; some varieties such as the snow pea,

PEACHES

POACHED PEACHES WITH MARSALA CREAM AND VANILLA FINGERS

★ ★ **Preparation time:** 1 hour 10 minutes
Total cooking time: 30 minutes
Serves 8

5 cups water
1¼ cups sugar
8 medium peaches

Marsala Cream
4 egg yolks
⅓ cup sugar
⅓ cup marsala
1 cup heavy cream

Vanilla Fingers
¼ cup unsalted butter, softened
1 cup confectioners' sugar, sifted
2 egg whites
¼ teaspoon vanilla extract
⅔ cup all-purpose flour

1 Combine water and 1¼ cups sugar in a large, heavy saucepan. Stir over medium heat until sugar has completely dissolved. Bring to boiling; reduce heat slightly and add whole peaches. Simmer, covered, for 20 minutes, turning peaches occasionally to ensure even cooking. Using a slotted spoon, lift peaches carefully from syrup onto a plate and allow to cool. Remove skins gently with fingers. Chill, covered with plastic wrap, in the refrigerator. Let peaches stand at room temperature for 15 minutes before serving.

2 To make Marsala Cream: Using electric mixer, beat egg yolks and ⅓ cup sugar in a medium heatproof bowl for 1 minute. Place bowl over a saucepan of simmering water; beat constantly until just warmed through, about 2 minutes. Add marsala gradually to egg mixture, beating for about 3 minutes or until thick and foamy. Remove from heat, continue beating for 2 minutes or until mixture cools. Transfer to a clean bowl. Whip cream until stiff peaks form. Fold into egg yolk mixture. Cover and chill.

3 To make Vanilla Fingers: Preheat oven to moderate 350°F. Cut two pieces of parchment paper to fit two large baking sheets. Using a pencil and ruler, draw parallel lines 3 inches apart. Grease baking sheets and place paper pencil-side down. Using electric mixer, beat butter and confectioners' sugar until light and creamy. Add egg whites gradually, beating thoroughly after each addition. Add vanilla; beat until combined. Fold flour into egg white mixture.

4 Spoon mixture into a piping bag fitted with a ½ inch tip. Using drawn lines as a guide, pipe mixture into 3-inch lengths, leave 2 inches between each finger. Bake 10–12 minutes or until lightly golden. Leave on cookie sheet 1 minute, place on wire rack to cool. To serve, arrange a peach with a large dollop of Marsala Cream and three Vanilla Fingers on each plate.

ABOVE: POACHED PEACHES WITH MARSALA CREAM AND VANILLA FINGERS. OPPOSITE PAGE: PEACH MELBA

P E A C H   M E L B A

Preparation time: 15 minutes
Total cooking time: 8 minutes
Serves 4

2 cups water
1/2 cup sugar
1 small vanilla bean
4 ripe peaches (freestone)
8 oz raspberries
1/4 cup confectioners'
  sugar
2 teaspoons lemon juice
4 scoops vanilla ice cream

1 Place water, sugar and vanilla bean in a medium pan and heat while stirring to dissolve sugar. Simmer syrup for 2 minutes.
2 Cut peaches in halves, peel and remove pits. Poach peaches in syrup until barely tender; remove pan from heat and allow fruit to cool in syrup; chill well.
3 Purée raspberries in a food processor or electric blender with confectioners' sugar and lemon juice. Strain and chill.
4 Place a scoop of ice cream in each serving dish, top with two well-drained peach halves, spoon raspberry purée over the top. Serve immediately.

P E A C H   A N D   Z U C C H I N I   M U F F I N S

Preparation time: 8 minutes +
5 minutes standing
Total cooking time: 18 minutes
Makes 15 muffins

1 package 1-layer size
  cake mix (9 oz)
1 egg
2 teaspoons grated lemon
  rind
2/3 cup coarsely grated
  zucchini
1/2 cup finely chopped
  canned peaches in
  natural juice, well
  drained
1/4 cup unsalted (sweet)
  butter, melted

1 Preheat oven to moderately hot 400°F. Brush fifteen muffin cups with oil or melted butter.
2 Place the contents of the cake mix, egg, lemon rind, zucchini, peaches and butter in a large bowl. Using a wooden spoon, stir until ingredients are just combined—be careful not to overbeat the mixture.
3 Spoon the mixture into the prepared muffin cups, until they are two-thirds full. Bake for 18 minutes or until the muffins are puffed and lightly browned. Leave the muffins in cups for 5 minutes before turning then out onto a wire rack to cool. Decorate with Buttercream or Cream Cheese Icing (see Index for recipes), and extra fresh or canned peach slices, if desired.

P E A C H E S   A N D   C R E A M   P U D D I N G   P A R F A I T S

Preparation time: 10 minutes
Total cooking time: none
Serves 4

16 oz can sliced peaches,
  drained, chopped
6 teaspoons peach
  schnapps liqueur
1 pint vanilla ice cream
1 1/2 cups vanilla pudding
1/2 cup heavy cream,
  whipped
2 tablespoons sliced
  almonds, toasted

1 Place peaches and liqueur in a bowl and stand for 5 minutes.
2 Layer ice cream, peaches and custard into four parfait glasses. Top with whipped cream and sprinkle with almonds. Serve immediately.

Note: To vary, make up a 4-serving size package of orange jello. When set, chop into pieces and fold through pudding mixture.

A B O U T   P E A C H E S

■ Slightly underripe peaches are the best ones to use for cooking or baking and they are easier to peel.
■ To peel, immerse peaches in boiling water for 30 seconds. Remove peaches and plunge them immediately into iced water—the skins will loosen. Halve peaches and remove the pit before peeling them with a small knife. Rub the flesh with lemon juice to prevent discoloration.

have very tender pods that need only to be topped and tailed before cooking whole. Petits pois, a variety of tiny, sweet-tasting green peas popular in France, are shelled before use. Peas may be boiled, braised, steamed or microwaved and served hot as a vegetable or added to soups, casseroles and salads. The familiar green pea grown to be eaten fresh was developed in Italy in the seventeenth century; from there it was introduced into France.

Christopher Columbus is said to have planted the first peas in America. Fresh green peas are available for most of the year; green peas are also sold frozen and freeze-dried.

Pease Pudding Split peas, soaked, boiled, mashed and traditionally served with boiled salt pork. In bygone days butchers in the north of England sold slabs of pease pudding along with the pork for reheating at home.

Pecan An elliptical, smooth-shelled nut containing a ridged kernel (similar in appearance to a walnut kernel) with a sweet, buttery flavor. Whole pecan kernels can be eaten as a snack (either raw or roasted and salted) and are used whole in cookies, cakes, breads and the American favorite, pecan pie; chopped and ground nuts may be sprinkled on ice cream, used in pastry fillings or added to

candy. The pecan tree is native to south central North America, including Georgia, Oklahoma and Texas and as far north as Virginia. The nuts shelled or unshelled, stay fresh in airtight packs. When choosing unshelled pecans, look for clean, unblemished and uncracked shells. The kernel should not rattle when the shell is shaken. Unshelled pecans can be stored for up to 6 months in a cool dry place. Shelled pecans should be stored in an airtight container for up to 3 months or frozen for up to 6 months.

Pecorino A sheep's milk cheese which is made by the cooked curd method (the curd is "cooked" in heated whey). There are two varieties of pecorino: pecorino romano, the best known, is a hard, grating cheese (first made near Rome) which is similar in both taste and texture to Parmesan

PEANUTS

VIETNAMESE CHICKEN SALAD

★ **Preparation time:** 30 minutes
Total cooking time: 5 minutes
Serves 4

1–2 tablespoons vegetable oil
1½ cups shredded white radish
1 stalk celery, shredded
1 medium onion, thinly sliced
1 large carrot, grated
3 scallions, shredded
8 oz cooked chicken, shredded
lettuce leaves

2 tablespoons crushed roasted peanuts
fresh herbs (mint, parsley)

Dressing
2½ tablespoons nuoc mam or thin soy sauce
3 tablespoons lime or lemon juice
3 tablespoons vegetable oil
2 teaspoons sugar
1 clove garlic, crushed

1 Heat oil in a wok or heavy-bottom frying pan. Add radish and celery and stir-fry over medium heat for around two minutes until vegetables are softened; add onion, cook lightly for 1 minute longer. Remove from heat; cool.
2 Combine radish, celery, onion, carrot, green onion and chicken. Arrange on lettuce leaves and garnish with crushed peanuts and herbs.
3 To make Dressing: Combine all ingredients. Add to chicken several minutes before serving.

CHOCOLATE PEANUT BITES

★ **Preparation time:** 30 minutes
Total cooking time: none
Makes about 20

3 cups confectioners' sugar
1 cup soft brown sugar
½ cup butter, softened
2 cups peanut butter

1 cup unsalted peanuts (optional)
8 oz dark (semisweet) chocolate
1 tablespoon butter, extra

1 Beat together the powdered and soft brown sugar and butter until blended—the mixture will be crumbly. Mix in the peanut butter and peanuts, if using.
2 Press into an ungreased 13 x 9 x 2 inch pan, smoothing the surface.
3 Melt chocolate with the extra butter until smooth. Spread over peanut layer. Leave until set. Cut into 1 inch pieces.

ABOUT PEANUTS

■ Peanuts are easily shelled by hand and will keep for long periods. However, for convenience and immediate use in cooking, buy shelled raw peanuts.

■ To toast peanuts, spread out in a single layer on a baking sheet and place in a 350°F oven for about 10 minutes, or place under a hot broiler for around 5 minutes. Keep an eye on the nuts as they can burn quickly.

VEGETABLE LASAGNE

★★ **Preparation time:** 20 minutes
Total cooking time: 1 hour 15 minutes
Serves 6

3 large red peppers	8 oz no-cook lasagna
2 large eggplants	noodles (8 noodles)
2 tablespoons oil	1 bunch spinach, chopped
1 large onion, finely	1 cup basil leaves
chopped	3½ oz sun-dried
3 cloves garlic, crushed	tomatoes, sliced
1 teaspoon dried mixed	¼ cup grated Parmesan
herbs	cheese
1 teaspoon dried oregano	¼ cup grated Cheddar
1 lb mushrooms, sliced	cheese
16 oz can whole	
tomatoes, crushed	**Cheese Sauce**
16 oz can red kidney	¼ cup butter
beans, drained	¼ cup all-purpose flour
1 tablespoon sweet chili	2 cups milk
sauce	1 lb ricotta cheese
salt and pepper, to taste	

1 Preheat oven to moderate 350°F. Brush a 14 x 11 inch ovenproof casserole dish with oil or melted butter. Cut peppers into quarters. Remove seeds and membrane. Place pepper pieces skin-side up on broiler rack and brush with oil. Broil 5 inches from heat for 5 minutes, or until skin is black and blistered. Cover with a damp towel until cool. Peel the skin off and cut pepper into long thin strips. Set aside. Slice eggplant into ½ inch rounds, place in a large pan of boiling water. Cook for 1 minute or until just tender; drain and pat dry with paper towel. Set aside.

2 Heat the oil in a large heavy-bottom frying pan. Add the onion, garlic and herbs. Cook over medium heat for 5 minutes or until the onion is soft. Add mushrooms and cook for 1 minute. Add tomatoes, beans, sauce, salt and pepper. Bring to boil, reduce heat. Simmer, uncovered, for 15 minutes or until sauce thickens. Remove from heat.

3 Dip lasagna sheets in hot water to soften slightly and arrange four sheets on base of prepared dish. Arrange half of each of the eggplant, spinach, basil, pepper, mushroom mixture and sun-dried tomatoes over pasta. Top with a layer of pasta and press gently. Repeat layers. Top with cheese sauce and sprinkle with combined Parmesan and Cheddar cheeses. Bake for 45 minutes or until pasta is soft.

4 To make Cheese Sauce: Heat butter in medium pan, add flour. Stir over medium heat for 2 minutes or until mixture is golden. Add milk gradually, stirring until mixture boils and thickens. Boil for 1 minute. Add ricotta and stir until smooth.

TORTELLINI WITH MUSHROOM CREAM SAUCE

★ **Preparation time:** 10 minutes
Total cooking time: 8 minutes
Serves 4

¼ cup butter	pinch pepper
6 oz small mushrooms,	pinch nutmeg
sliced	3 tablespoons grated
1 clove garlic, crushed	Parmesan cheese
1 cup heavy cream	1 lb tortellini, cooked and
1 teaspoon grated lemon	kept warm
rind	

1 Melt the butter in a saucepan. Add the mushrooms and cook over medium heat for 30 seconds. Add the crushed garlic, cream, lemon rind, pepper and nutmeg to taste.

2 Stir over low heat for 1–2 minutes. Add the grated Parmesan and cook gently for a further 3 minutes.

3 To serve, combine well-drained pasta with sauce. Serve immediately.

Pâte Sucrée The dough for a sweet, crisp pastry (shortcrust) made from butter or margarine, sugar and egg yolk and used in French cooking for flan cases and tarts. It is mixed in the same way as pâte brisée.

Paupiette A thin fillet of meat, poultry or fish spread with a seasoned or herb stuffing mixture, rolled and secured with string or toothpicks then braised.

Pavlova A dessert consisting of a meringue case filled with whipped cream and topped with fresh fruit (usually including strawberries and passionfruit pulp). The dish is attributed to Herbert Sachse, chef at a leading hotel in Perth, Australia, who named it in memory of the 1929 visit to the city by the ballerina Anna Pavlova.

Pawpaw See Papaya.

Peach A round, yellow to rosy pink, downy-skinned fruit with a single pit and pale, fragrant, sweet, juicy flesh. There are two main types: freestone (the flesh separates easily from the pit), and clingstone (the flesh clings to the pit). In season from early summer to autumn, peaches are also available canned, in syrup.

PASTRY

The success of a tart, quiche or flan depends on the pastry base—it should be light, crisp and golden. Once you have mastered the techniques of pastry-making, you will have perfect results every time. For quiches and flans, use shortcrust (pie crust), filo (phyllo) or puff pastry. Ready-rolled pastry saves time and also gives an excellent result.

ABOUT SHORTCRUST (PIE CRUST) PASTRY

Plain (all-purpose) flour is the flour generally used to make shortcrust pastry; however, adding a little self-rising flour can give a much lighter result.

Although other shortenings can be used, butter produces the best flavor. Chop it into small (pea-size) pieces and make sure it is cold when you begin. Eggs make dough crumbly (short) and rich; milk gives a softer pastry that browns well.

Whether mixing by hand or with a food processor, work quickly and lightly to avoid melting the butter. Mixing dough for too long, handling it roughly or adding too much liquid will result in tough pastry.

Once you have rubbed the butter into the flour, add ice-cold water (or other liquid) a tablespoon at a time, until the mixture just comes together in a stiff dough.

Form the dough into a ball, cover with plastic wrap and chill for at least 30 minutes before rolling out. This will make the dough more manageable and prevent the pastry from shrinking as it cooks.

ABOUT CHOUX PASTRY

This is a very different pastry from shortcrust in that the flour is mixed with boiling liquid and then the eggs are added. The result is light puffs of pastry, hollow in the middle. Choux pastry is used for éclairs, cream puffs and profiteroles. Once cooked and filled they should be eaten immediately, otherwise they become soggy.

ABOUT PUFF PASTRY

Puff pastry is probably the most difficult to make but is considered the finest of all pastries. Good-quality commercial puff pastry is widely available, in blocks as well as packs of ready-rolled sheets. In this book, all recipes requiring puff pastry use the commercial type.

ROLLING OUT PASTRY

Use a marble or smooth wooden rolling pin. Divide the dough in half if necessary and form each half into a ball. Roll out dough on a smooth, lightly floured surface (marble is ideal), or between two sheets of plastic wrap or baking paper. Roll dough away from you, using short, quick strokes. Turn the dough a quarter turn after each roll, being careful not to stretch it. Roll out to an even thickness, about 1½ inches bigger than the size of the dish to be lined.

PEARS

FRESH PEARS POACHED IN WHITE WINE

 Preparation time: 15 minutes
Total cooking time: 20 minutes
Serves 4

4 ripe pears	1 cup sugar
2 cups water	1 cinnamon stick
1 cup good quality white wine	1 strip lemon rind

1 Peel the pears, leaving the stems attached. Remove the core section with an apple corer, leaving pear whole.
2 Place the water, white wine, sugar, cinnamon stick and lemon rind in a large pan. Bring to the boil. Add the whole pears and poach gently for 5–10 minutes, depending on the ripeness of the pears. The pears should be firm but tender when tested with a skewer. Carefully lift the pears out of the liquid with a slotted spoon. Set aside.
3 Boil syrup rapidly for about 5–10 minutes, or until it has thickened slightly. Spoon the syrup over pears. Serve warm or chilled.

OPPOSITE PAGE: VIETNAMESE CHICKEN SALAD.
ABOVE: FRESH PEARS POACHED IN WHITE WINE;
RIGHT: PEAR AND BRIE SALAD

PEAR AND BRIE SALAD

★ **Preparation time:** 15 minutes
Total cooking time: none
Serves 4

6½ oz Brie, at room temperature	3 tablespoons oil
3 medium pears	1 tablespoon tarragon vinegar
1 head butter lettuce	⅓ cup chopped pecans

1 Cut Brie into thin wedges. Cut pears into quarters and remove cores, then slice thinly—do not peel.
2 Wash and dry lettuce thoroughly. Tear into bite-size pieces and arrange on individual serving plates. Top with Brie and pears.
3 Place the oil and vinegar in a small screwtop jar and shake well. Drizzle the dressing over the salad and sprinkle with the chopped pecans. Serve immediately.

ABOUT PEARS

■ There are many varieties of pear throughout the world. Some are particularly suitable for cooking (among them the Conference Pear and American Bosc) and others (especially the *beurre*—meaning "buttered"—varieties) are best enjoyed in their natural state.

■ When buying pears, choose fruit with their stems intact (this helps to preserve them), and with flesh that yields slightly to pressure near the stem end.

and is used mostly in cooking. Pecorino fresco is a young, soft and mild-tasting version that can be used as a table cheese. Pecorino originated in southern Italy nearly 2,000 years ago and was traditionally made by shepherds; the name comes from the Italian word *pecora*, which means ewe.

Pectin A natural, water-soluble gelling agent that occurs in some fruits and vegetables. It is used for its thickening properties in the preparation of jams, jellies and preserves. When pectin-containing fruits are cooked with sugar they set firm. Black currants, red currants, citrus fruits, cooking apples, quinces, gooseberries and plums contain a high amount of pectin; strawberries and pears have very little. Underripe or just ripe fruit contains more pectin than over-ripe fruit.

Commercial pectin is available in powdered form.

Pekoe A variety of black Chinese tea made from immature leaves. Orange pekoe tea is a similar Indian tea.

PEAS & POTATOES

Frozen peas are used in these recipes. Fresh peas can be substituted but will take longer to cook. When cooking potatoes twice, for example boiling them before frying in oil, or boiling and mashing before baking, boil them on the day you are finishing the dish to avoid a stale taste.

MINTED PEAS

MINTED PEAS

Steam, microwave or lightly boil 2 cups frozen green peas. Toss with 1 tablespoon of finely chopped fresh mint and 1/4 teaspoon of soft brown sugar. Serve warm.

MASHED PEAS

MASHED PEAS

Steam, microwave or lightly boil 2 cups frozen green peas. Drain. Mash with a fork. Add 2 teaspoons butter and salt and freshly ground black pepper to taste. Stir to combine. Serve warm.

PEAS WITH BASIL AND TOMATO

Heat 2 teaspoons oil in heavy-bottom frying pan. Add 1 clove crushed garlic and 1/2 cup chopped canned tomatoes in juice. Cook for 1 minute. Add 2 cups frozen green peas and 1–2 tablespoons finely shredded basil. Cook for 2–3 minutes or until just tender. Serve warm.

PEAS WITH BASIL AND TOMATO

PEPPERED PEAS AND GARLIC

PEPPERED PEAS AND GARLIC

Heat 1 tablespoon oil in heavy-bottom frying pan. Add 2 cloves crushed garlic and 1 teaspoon cracked black pepper. Stir in 2 cups frozen green peas and 1/2 teaspoon sugar. Cook over medium heat 2–3 minutes or until tender. Drizzle with balsamic vinegar if desired. Serve warm.

*QUICK CHEESY
POTATO BAKE*

QUICK CHEESY POTATO BAKE

Peel and thinly slice 4 medium potatoes. Thinly slice 1 onion. Layer the potato and onion slices in an ovenproof baking dish. Sprinkle grated Cheddar cheese between each layer. Pour over combined ½ cup heavy cream, ¾ cup milk and 1 teaspoon dry mustard. Sprinkle top with extra grated cheese and chopped chives. Bake in moderate oven 350°F for 40 minutes or until potatoes are tender. Serve warm.

HASSELBACK POTATOES

Peel and halve 4 medium potatoes. Place the potatoes cut-side-down. Use a sharp knife to make thin slices in potatoes, taking care not to cut right through. Place potatoes cut-side-up in baking dish. Brush with 1 tablespoon olive oil combined with 1 tablespoon melted butter. Sprinkle with lemon pepper. Bake in 425°F oven for 45 minutes or until golden and slightly crisp. Serve immediately.

*HASSELBACK
POTATOES*

DUCHESS POTATOES

Peel and chop 4 medium potatoes. Cook in a large pan of boiling water until just tender; drain and mash. Add 3 egg yolks, 2 tablespoons cream and 2 tablespoons freshly grated Parmesan cheese. Mix thoroughly. Pipe the mixture in swirls onto greased baking sheets. Bake in 425°F oven for 20 minutes or until golden brown. Sprinkle with paprika. Serve warm.

FRENCH FRIES

Peel 4 medium potatoes. Cut lengthwise into ½ inch thick slices, then into ½ inch wide sticks, or peel long potato strips with a vegetable peeler. Cook in a pan of hot oil for 4–5 minutes for fries, 2–3 minutes for curls, or until crisp. Drain well on paper towels. Sprinkle lightly with salt. Serve hot.

DUCHESS POTATOES

FRENCH FRIES

Pemmican Dried buffalo meat and fruit carried as a food by native Americans.

Pepino Also known as the melon pear and tree melon, an apple-sized, melon-shaped vine fruit with smooth yellow-green skin streaked with purple and pale juicy flesh with a central cluster of edible seeds. Pepino can be eaten fresh in the same way as melon, diced and added to fruit salad, or lightly sautéed and served as an accompaniment to fish and meat. The fruit is native to Peru and Chile and was introduced into Florida in the late nineteenth century. It is in season from autumn to spring.

Pepper A pungent spice derived from the dried berry-like fruit (peppercorn) of a tropical climbing vine. Both white and black pepper come from the same plant, but are picked at different stages of maturity. Black pepper is picked while the berries are unripe; white pepper comes from berries that ripen before being harvested. They are soaked in water to remove their skins. Black and white pepper is used to flavor all types of savory food.

PEAS DRIED

PEASE PUDDING

⭐ **Preparation time:** 10 minutes + overnight soaking
Total cooking time: 2 hours
Serves 4

1 lb split peas, soaked overnight and drained	2 tablespoons butter, softened
1 onion, finely chopped	1/2 teaspoon white pepper
1 sprig fresh rosemary	salt to taste
2 eggs, lightly beaten	2 tablespoons malt vinegar

1 Preheat oven to moderate 350°F. Brush a 4-cup capacity ovenproof dish with melted butter or oil.
2 Place the peas, onion and rosemary sprig into a large pan. Cover with water. Place the lid on the saucepan and cook over low heat for 1 hour or until the peas are starting to soften.
3 Drain the peas in a strainer or colander. Discard the rosemary sprig. Mash the peas with a potato masher. Add the eggs, butter, pepper, salt and vinegar. Blend until the mixture is smooth.
4 Pour the pea mixture into the prepared dish and stand the dish in a large deep pan. Pour in hot water until it reaches halfway up the sides of the baking dish. Bake for 30–45 minutes or until pudding sets. Unmold to serve.

PEA AND HAM SOUP

⭐ **Preparation time:** 30 minutes + overnight soaking
Total cooking time: 1 1/2 –2 hours
Serves 6

8 oz split peas	freshly ground pepper
1 lb ham bones	1 teaspoon chopped fresh
2 medium onions, diced	thyme
2 medium carrots, diced	1 tablespoon lemon juice
1 cup sliced celery	3–4 frankfurters, sliced
2 bay leaves	(optional)
10 cups chicken stock or	chopped parsley for
water	serving

1 Rinse peas well and place in a medium bowl. Add sufficient water to cover and soak overnight. Drain peas and discard water.
2 Place peas in large, heavy pan with ham bones, onions, carrots, celery, bay leaves, stock or water, pepper and thyme. Bring to boil, cover; simmer gently for 1 1/2– 2 hours. Remove bay leaves.
3 Remove ham bones to a plate and scrape meat from them; chop meat and add to soup with lemon juice. Bring soup to the boil, add frankfurters and heat for 3 minutes.
4 Serve soup sprinkled with parsley.

ABOUT DRIED PEAS

■ Some cooking authorities maintain that split peas do not need to be soaked in water before they are cooked. However, if they are soaked in cold water for 8 hours or overnight, cooking time will be considerably reduced.

■ There are two ways to soak split peas and other pulses:

Slow soaking method: Place peas in a large bowl and cover with cold water. Pick off and discard any peas that rise to the surface. Leave to soak for 8 hours or overnight. If you plan to soak the peas for a longer time, place the bowl in the refrigerator or the peas may ferment.

Quick soaking method: Wash the peas and place in a large saucepan with plenty of cold water. Bring to the boil and boil for 2 minutes. Remove pan from heat, cover and set aside for 1–2 hours or until the peas have swelled.

■ Drain, place peas in a large pan and cover with fresh water. Bring to the boil very slowly— boiling too fast can produce hard peas.

■ Skim any scum that rises to the top of the pan with a slotted spoon. (Although some cooks do not bother with this, skimming does produce a finer-flavored dish.)

■ Dried peas form a complete protein when eaten with a grain such as rice.

For the best flavor, ground pepper should be added to hot dishes towards the end of cooking time; in long-cooking dishes, tie peppercorns in a cheesecloth bag and remove before

serving. Green peppercorns are the berries picked while still green; they are usually preserved in brine and used, sparingly, to flavor soups, stews, pâtés and sauces. Pink peppercorns are the soft, almost ripe, berries of an

unrelated South American tree; they are used more for their color than their flavor. Pepper is best used freshly ground, as it goes stale very quickly.

Peppermint An herb grown mainly for the oil distilled from its leaves and flowers. Peppermint essence is used to flavor candy, cake icings, and the liqueur crème de menthe. The leaves can be made into herb tea, or chopped and sprinkled over fruit salad.

Pepperoni A sausage of Italian origin, made from ground pork and beef and flavored with chili peppers and spices.

PEAS GREEN

SUGAR PEAS AND CARROTS IN LIME BUTTER

★ **Preparation time:** 10 minutes
Total cooking time: 10 minutes
Serves 4

4 oz carrots	1 tablespoon lime juice
4 oz sugar snap peas	1/2 teaspoon soft brown
3 tablespoons butter	sugar
2 cloves garlic, crushed	1 lime

1 Peel the carrots and cut into thin diagonal slices. Wash and string sugar snap peas. Heat the butter in a large heavy-bottom frying pan. Add the garlic and cook over low heat for 1 minute. Add the lime juice and sugar. Cook, stirring over low heat, until the sugar has completely dissolved.
2 Add the peas and carrots and cook over medium heat for 2–3 minutes, or until the vegetables are tender but still crisp. Serve hot, garnished with lime zest.

Note: To make lime zest, peel lime rind into

long strips with a vegetable peeler. Remove pith, cut rind into thin strips with a sharp knife.

PEPPERED PEAS AND GARLIC

Heat 1 tablespoon oil in heavy-bottom frying pan. Add 2 cloves crushed garlic and 1 teaspoon cracked black pepper. Stir in 2 cups frozen green peas and 1/2 teaspoon sugar. Cook over medium heat 2–3 minutes or until peas are tender. Drizzle with balsamic vinegar, if desired. Serve warm.

SAUTEED PEAS AND SCALLIONS

Heat 2 tablespoons butter in a heavy-bottom frying pan. Add 2 cups frozen green peas, 1 clove crushed garlic and 2 finely sliced scallions. Stir over medium heat 2–3 minutes, or until peas and onions are just tender. Serve warm.

SWEET CILANTRO PEAS

Heat 2 tablespoons butter in pan. Add 1 1/2 teaspoons lemon juice, 1/2 teaspoon sugar and 2 cups frozen green peas. Cook over medium heat 2–3 minutes until just tender. Add 2 tablespoons finely chopped fresh cilantro leaves and toss well.

OPPOSITE PAGE: PEASE PUDDING.
ABOVE: SUGAR PEAS AND CARROTS IN LIME BUTTER

Pepper, Hot See Chili Pepper.

Pepper, Sweet Also called Bell Pepper. A large, mostly hollow, shiny skinned fruit of a shrub native to tropical South America. Although a member of the same family as the fiery chili pepper, its crisp, moist flesh is mild in flavor and is used as both a salad and a cooked vegetable. Varieties include the red (the sweetest), green, yellow, orange and black. The stalk, white membrane and seeds should be removed before use. Sweet pepper is used raw and thinly sliced in salads and crudités, is cooked in casseroles, grilled or broiled or filled with various stuffings. It is an important ingredient in the cooking of Central America, the Mediterranean, the Middle East and Asia. Sweet peppers are available fresh throughout the year; sun-dried peppers in oil are sometimes available. Paprika is the ground and dried flesh of a variety of sweet pepper.

Persimmon A smooth-skinned, tomato-shaped fruit with yellow to orange-colored flesh that

PECAN NUTS

COFFEE PECAN SQUARES

Preparation time: 30 minutes
Total cooking time: 40 minutes
Makes 15

1½ cups all-purpose flour
½ cup confectioners' sugar
⅔ cup unsalted (sweet) butter

Topping
¼ cup heavy cream

¼ cup molasses or dark corn syrup
½ cup soft brown sugar
5 tablespoons unsalted (sweet) butter, melted
2 eggs, lightly beaten
1 teaspoon instant coffee powder
2 cups pecan halves

1 Preheat oven to moderate 350°F. Brush a 7 x 10¾ inch shallow rectangular pan with melted butter or oil. Line with parchment paper, extending over two sides. Place flour, powdered sugar and butter in food processor. Process for 1 minute or until mixture comes together. Turn out onto a floured surface and knead dough gently for 30 seconds or until smooth. Press into prepared pan and bake 15 minutes or until just golden. Cool completely in pan on a wire rack.
2 To make Topping: Combine cream, syrup, sugar, butter, eggs and coffee in a medium mixing bowl and beat with a wooden spoon until smooth. Add pecans and stir to combine.
3 Pour Topping over pastry base; bake for

25 minutes or until set. Cool completely in pan. Lift out and cut into squares, using a sharp knife.

PECAN CHICKEN

Preparation time: 30 minutes
Total cooking time: 10 minutes
Serves 4

4 boneless chicken breasts, skin removed
1 cup pecan halves
½ cup grated Gouda cheese
½ cup dry bread crumbs
½ cup fresh white bread crumbs

1 teaspoon ground sage
freshly ground black pepper
1 egg, lightly beaten
1 tablespoon water
¼ cup butter
2 tablespoons oil
watercress, for garnish

1 Pound chicken breasts flat between sheets of plastic wrap to ½ inch thickness.
2 Reserve 8 pecan halves; finely chop remainder. In a shallow bowl, mix chopped pecans, cheese, bread crumbs, sage and pepper to taste. In separate shallow bowl, beat egg and water together.
3 Coat chicken with half of the pecan mixture, dip them in the egg mixture, then coat with the remaining pecan mixture.
4 Heat butter and oil in large, shallow pan. Place fillets, two at a time, in pan; cook until golden brown and tender, turning once, 2–3 minutes per side. (Keep chicken warm while cooking the remainder.) Serve garnished with reserved pecans and watercress.

P E P P E R

B A R B E C U E D   P E P P E R E D   S T E A K S   W I T H   M A N G O   A N D   A V O C A D O   S A L S A

⭐ ⭐ **Preparation time:** 10 minutes +
30 minutes standing
Total cooking time: 6–16 minutes
Serves 6

6 beef tenderloin, about 4 oz each	**Mango and Avocado Salsa**
1–2 tablespoons whole black peppercorns	1 large ripe mango
1 tablespoon white mustard seeds	1 large ripe avocado
2 tablespoons oil	1 scallion, finely sliced
	1 tablespoon lime juice
	dash Tabasco sauce

1 Trim meat of excess fat and sinew. Flatten steaks to an even thickness. Nick edges to prevent curling. Crush peppercorns and mustard seeds briefly in a blender until coarsely cracked; or, place in a paper bag and crush with a rolling pin. Spread on a plate.
2 Rub oil over the steaks, then press on the peppercorn mixture to coat thoroughly. Store in refrigerator, covered with plastic wrap, for about 30 minutes.

OPPOSITE PAGE: COFFEE PECAN SQUARES.
ABOVE: BARBECUED PEPPERED STEAKS WITH MANGO AND AVOCADO SALSA

3 Place meat on a lightly oiled preheated grill. Cook over high heat for 2 minutes each side to seal, turning once. For rare, cook for another minute each side. For medium and well-done, move meat to a cooler part of the barbecue, cook for another 2–3 minutes each side for medium and 4–6 minutes each side for well-done. Serve with Mango and Avocado Salsa.
4 To make Mango and Avocado Salsa: Peel the mango and cut off cheeks from both sides; cut flesh into cubes. Peel avocado and cut into cubes. Combine mango, avocado, scallion, lime juice and Tabasco in a small bowl, toss well. Cover and refrigerate until required.

P E P P E R E D   B E E F   T E N D E R L O I N

⭐ **Preparation time:** 10 minutes
Total cooking time: 50 minutes–
1 hour 35 minutes
Serves 6

2 lb whole beef tenderloin or rib eye in one piece	**Green Peppercorn Sauce**
1 tablespoon soy sauce	½ cup chicken stock
2 tablespoons freshly cracked black peppercorns	½ cup heavy cream
3 tablespoons olive oil	2 teaspoons canned green peppercorns, rinsed and drained
	2 teaspoons brandy

1 Preheat oven to moderately hot 400°F. Tie the meat securely with string at regular intervals to retain its shape during cooking. Rub meat all over with soy sauce; roll meat in freshly cracked black peppercorns, pressing to coat the surface and ends.
2 Heat oil in deep baking dish on top of stove; add meat and brown all over on high heat. Transfer baking dish to oven.
3 Roast meat 45 minutes for rare, 1 hour for medium and 1 hour 30 minutes for well-done. Baste the meat occasionally with pan juices. Remove from oven. Leave in a warm place for 10 minutes, covered with foil. Remove the string before slicing. Serve with the Green Peppercorn Sauce.
4 To make Green Peppercorn Sauce: Add the chicken stock to the juices in the baking dish. Stir over a low heat on top of the stove until the mixture is boiling; add the cream and the drained green peppercorns. Boil the mixture for 2 minutes, stirring constantly; add the brandy. Boil for another minute; remove the dish from the heat.

is soft, sweet and jelly-like when fully ripe, but otherwise has a sharp, astringent taste. The ripe pulp of the persimmon can be eaten plain, added to fruit salad, mousses and custards, or used to top ice cream; it is also made into jam. The persimmon is native to Japan and China, where it has been cultivated for more than a thousand years. The sharon fruit is a variety which was developed in Israel; it can be eaten raw, even when firm and under-ripe. Persimmon is in season in late autumn and early winter; it is also available dried.

Pesto A thick, uncooked sauce made by blending together basil leaves, olive oil, garlic, pine nuts and Parmesan cheese. Traditionally pesto was made with a mortar and pestle, but it can also be made in a food processor. It is usually served over pasta, although in Genoa, where it originated (the sauce is also known as pesto alla Genovese), it is added to minestrone.

Petits Fours Fancy bite-sized cakes, cut into squares or circles and glazed or decorated with icing.

Pheasant A game bird with delicately-flavored white flesh, now raised commercially in many parts of the world. Young birds can be roasted (baste frequently to prevent the flesh from drying out); older birds should be casseroled or pot-roasted. Pheasant is available from specialty shops.

Phyllo See Filo.

Pickles and Relish Preserves made of vegetables such as onions, cucumber, cauliflower and sweet pepper. The vegetables are sliced if necessary, and soaked in brine, then rinsed, put into jars and covered with spiced vinegar. Eggs and walnuts can also be pickled.

Pie A sweet or savory mixture baked in, or served within, a top and bottom crust, or sometimes just a bottom crust. Pies can include main course chicken and meat pies; single crust pies can include custard filled and meringue-topped dessert pies—which sometimes are called tarts. Fruit pies can be made with a top crust of lattice or crumbs.

PEPPERS

HERB-MARINATED PEPPERS

★ **Preparation time:** 20 minutes + 2 hours marinating
Total cooking time: 5 minutes
Serves 4

4 red peppers
1/2 cup olive oil
2 tablespoons lemon juice
1 tablespoon chopped
  fresh basil
1 tablespoon chopped
  fresh parsley
2 teaspoons chopped fresh
  oregano
8 arugula leaves
8 romaine lettuce leaves
6 1/2 oz feta cheese

1 Cut each pepper into quarters; remove seeds and stems. Place skin-side up under a preheated broiler; cook until skin blisters and turns black. Cover peppers with a clean, damp towel and allow to stand for 5 minutes. Peel away skin.
2 Cut pepper pieces into 3/4 inch strips. Combine olive oil, lemon juice, fresh basil, parsley and oregano in a small jug.
3 Place pepper strips in a small bowl, pour oil mixture over; marinate for at least 2 hours, or preferably overnight. Serve with arugula and romaine lettuce leaves and some cubed feta cheese.

GARLIC PEPPERS

★ **Preparation time:** 15 minutes
Total cooking time: 15 minutes
Makes 4 cups

1 green pepper
1 red pepper
2 cloves garlic, peeled and
  cut into slices
1/2 cup sugar
2 cups white wine vinegar
2 teaspoons salt

1 Cut peppers lengthwise into quarters. Discard core, seeds and white pith. Blanch in boiling water until softened, about 1 minute. Drain and pack snugly into a jar with sliced garlic.
2 In a pan slowly heat sugar, vinegar and salt, stirring until the sugar has completely dissolved. Heat until boiling.
3 Pour hot liquid over peppers. Cover at once with an airtight lid. Label and date. Leave for 1 week before opening.

ABOUT PEPPERS

■ Peppers can be served either cooked or raw. The flavor is particularly complemented by tomatoes, eggplant, garlic, onion, herbs such as thyme and oregano, and olive oil.
■ Roasting or broiling peppers and peeling off the skin removes bitterness and intensifies the sweet flavor.

CHEESY RICE-STUFFED PEPPERS

⭐ **Preparation time:** 40 minutes
Total cooking time: 25 minutes
Serves 6

3 small red peppers	2 tablespoons tomato
3 small green peppers	paste
1 tablespoon olive oil	1 cup short-grain rice
1 small onion, chopped	2 cups water
1/4 teaspoon chili powder	10 oz can corn kernels,
1/2 teaspoon ground	drained
cumin	2 jalapeño chili peppers,
1 teaspoon instant	chopped
chicken bouillon	3/4 cup Cheddar cheese,
powder	grated

1 Preheat oven to moderate 350°F. Cut tops off the peppers and set tops aside. Carefully remove pith and seeds, taking care not to tear the pepper shells open.

2 Heat the olive oil in a medium pan. Stir in the onion, chili powder, cumin, bouillon powder, tomato paste and rice. Add water. Cover the pan with a tight-fitting lid. Bring slowly to boil; stir once. Reduce heat, simmer, covered until almost

OPPOSITE PAGE: HERB-MARINATED PEPPERS.

ABOVE: CHEESY RICE-STUFFED PEPPERS

all the water has been absorbed. Remove from heat. Stand, covered for 5 minutes or until all the water has been absorbed and the rice is just tender. Stir through the corn, chili peppers and 1/2 cup cheese.

3 Fill each pepper with the rice mixture. Sprinkle each with a little of the remaining cheese. Replace the tops. Place the peppers on a baking sheet and bake for about 15 minutes or until they have softened slightly. Serve the peppers warm. May be accompanied by tortillas and salad.

ROASTED PEPPERS AND OLIVE PIE

⭐⭐ **Preparation time:** 20 minutes
Total cooking time: 40 minutes
Serves 4–6

1 sheet refrigerated	1 yellow pepper
unbaked piecrust pastry	1 tablespoon oil, extra
1 cup pitted black olives	1 large red onion, cut
1 teaspoon olive oil	into thin wedges
2 cloves garlic, crushed	2/3 cup finely grated
1/2 teaspoon sugar	Gruyère cheese
1 medium red pepper	

1 Preheat oven to moderately hot 400°F. Lightly grease a 9 inch round fluted flan pan with melted butter or oil. Place the pastry on a lightly floured surface. Roll the pastry large enough to line the prepared pan. Ease the pastry into the pan, trim the edges with a sharp knife. Cut a sheet of parchment paper large enough to cover the pastry-lined pan. Spread a layer of dried beans or rice over the paper. Bake for 10 minutes, remove and discard the paper and the beans or rice, cook the pastry for another 10 minutes or until it is lightly browned.

2 Place the olives, oil, garlic and sugar in a food processor. Process until smooth. Spread the mixture over the base of the prepared pastry case. Cut the peppers into quarters. Place them skin-side up on broiler rack and broil until the skin blisters and turns black. Cover the peppers with a towel; cool slightly. Carefully peel away skin and cut the peppers into 1/2 inch strips.

3 Heat the extra oil in a small pan, add the onion wedges and cook over medium heat until soft. Add the sliced peppers and heat through. Sprinkle half the cheese over the olive mixture. Spoon the pepper and onion mixture over the cheese. Top with the remaining cheese, bake for 10 minutes or until cheese has melted and the pie is heated through.

Pigeon A small game bird with rich dark meat; a squab is a baby pigeon with milder-flavored meat. Commercially raised squab can be broiled or roasted and the breast meat served rare, thinly sliced, topped with a sauce. The flesh of older birds and wild pigeon or dove tends to be tougher. Allow one bird per person. Pigeon is available from specialty shops.

Pignoli See Pine Nuts.

Pigs in Blankets Sausage with a covering (blanket), such as cocktail sausages wrapped in pastry dough and baked, or breakfast sausages wrapped in pancakes.

Pikelet Also known as a Scottish pancake, a small, thick, sweet

pancake, served warm or cold with butter and jam or honey.

Pilaf (Pilau) Rice lightly browned in oil or butter then cooked in spiced stock; vegetables, meat, poultry or fish may be added halfway through the cooking process. The rice is served either fluffed with a fork and piled onto the plate or pressed into an oiled ring mold which is turned onto a serving plate. Pilaf

PICKLES & CHUTNEYS

Pickles and chutneys were originally made to preserve foods without the aid of refrigeration. Vegetables for chutneys are generally stewed in vinegar, sugar and spices until they are soft. Pickled vegetables are usually cooked for a shorter time and tend to retain their shape.

The quality of your pickles and chutneys depends upon the quality of the ingredients you use. Old limp vegetables, even when they are heavily seasoned with vinegar, spices and salt, will taste like old limp vegetables.

■ **VEGETABLES AND FRUIT:** Choose fresh, young, firm fruits and vegetables. Fruits may be pickled while they are still slightly underripe. Vegetables such as onions and cucumbers should be small and of even size. Wash them carefully to remove dirt and grit, which could cause bacterial action. The vegetables can be either raw or cooked, depending on the recipe. Raw fruit and vegetables are usually salted first to reduce their water content and to make the pickling process more effective.

■ **VINEGAR:** Use good quality vinegars that have an acid level of at least 5 per cent. Anything less may not preserve properly. Use malt vinegar for more strongly flavored raw ingredients, and cider and wine vinegars for more delicate pickles, especially fruit.

■ **PICKLING SPICES:** Unless ground spices are specifically stated in the recipe, use fresh, whole spices such as cloves, small hot red chili peppers, peppercorns, coriander seeds and mustard seeds for pickling, as they leave no sediment. Stale spices may give a musty flavor. For pickled fruits and vegetables and for spicing chutneys, tie the spices in a little piece of cheesecloth which can be extracted when cooking is complete.

■ **SALT:** Use coarse cooking salt or kosher salt when brining pickles: the iodine and other chemicals present in table salt may cause pickles to become cloudy and to darken in color.

PICKLES

PICKLED PEARS

Place 3 firm peeled, halved and cored pears in a pan with the juice and thin strips of rind from a lemon. Cover with cold water. Bring to the boil, reduce heat and simmer until the pears are just tender when tested with a skewer.

Meanwhile, in another pan, slowly heat ½ cup of sugar, 1½ cups white vinegar, 1 stick of cinnamon and 1 teaspoon whole cloves. Stir until sugar dissolves. Heat until boiling, then remove the pan from the heat.

Carefully pack the pears tightly into a warm, sterilized jar with cinnamon and cloves. Pour the hot sugar liquid over pears to cover them completely. Seal jar immediately. When cool, label and date jar. Keep for 2 weeks before opening. Pickled pears may be stored for up to 4 months. Serve with cold turkey or ham.

PICKLED VEGETABLES

Coarsely chop ½ small cauliflower, 1 red pepper, 2 unpeeled cucumbers, 1 carrot, 3 stalks celery and 2 onions. Place in a large bowl, cover with water and sprinkle with 10 oz coarse salt. Set the bowl aside, covered with a dry cloth, and leave to stand overnight. Drain, rinse and drain again. Combine in a large pan 5 cups of white vinegar, 5 whole dried chili peppers, ½ cup of sugar, 1 teaspoon of celery seeds and 1 tablespoon of mustard seeds.

Heat slowly, stirring, until the sugar is dissolved, then bring to the boil. Simmer 3 minutes, add vegetables and boil for another 12 minutes. Remove from heat; pack vegetables into warm sterilized jars using a slotted spoon. Return liquid to heat; bring to the boil. Pour boiling liquid over vegetables and seal. When cool, label and date jars.

Pickled vegetables can be used as part of an antipasto platter, or they can be finely chopped and mixed into tuna salad.

LIME CURRY PICKLE

Cut each of 12 limes into 8–10 wedges lengthwise, and then cut the wedges in half crosswise. In a glass bowl, layer the limes with 4 tablespoons of salt. Cover bowl with a clean cloth and let stand in a warm, dry place for 3 days, stirring occasionally. Drain and rinse the limes.

Combine, in a large pan, 1½ cups good quality olive oil, 1 tablespoon toasted and crushed yellow mustard seeds, 2 teaspoons ground cumin, 2 teaspoons ground ginger and ½ teaspoon coarsely ground pepper. Stir over low heat until hot. Add the limes with ⅓ cup white wine vinegar, 3 crushed garlic cloves and 2 long red chili peppers, seeded and chopped.

Stir over moderate heat for 5 minutes; stir in 3 tablespoons of sugar and heat until dissolved. Ladle pickle into warm, sterilized jars and seal. When cool, label and date. Serve with curries.

CHUTNEYS

TOMATO CHUTNEY

Peel and coarsely chop 2 lb ripe tomatoes, 3 onions and two green apples. Peel, halve and pit 3 peaches and chop coarsely. Place them all in a large pan or boiler. Add 2¾ cups dark brown sugar, 2 cups white vinegar, 1 tablespoon salt and

1 teaspoon each of mixed spice and Mexican chili powder. Bring slowly to the boil and simmer for about 2 hours, uncovered, until the mixture is thick. Stir occasionally. Remove chutney from heat and stand for 5 minutes. Spoon into warm sterilized jars; seal immediately. When cool, label and date.

VARIATIONS

■ Green tomatoes can be substituted for fully ripe ones, if preferred.
■ Add a large red or green pepper, peeled and chopped.
■ Use dark malt vinegar instead of white vinegar.

POINTS FOR SUCCESS

■ Seal pickles and chutneys as soon as possible after cooking, with non-corrosive lids. Plastic, plastic-coated metal, cork or wax coverings are all suitable, although transparent covers which let in the light are not suitable for chutney. It is important that metal lids are plastic-coated, as the acid in the vinegar will cause oxidation if the contents of the jar touch the lid.
■ Chutneys are best kept for at least a month after bottling in order to allow flavors to properly develop and mellow.
■ Pickles and chutneys can be stored for up to a year in a cool, dark place. It is not necessary to refrigerate until the jars have been opened.
■ Wash the jars well beforehand. Use warm, soapy water and rinse thoroughly. Dry off in a 275°F oven. Use while still hot, to prevent the jars from cracking when filled.

CLOCKWISE FROM ABOVE: LIME CURRY PICKLE, TOMATO CHUTNEY, TOMATO CHUTNEY WITH GREEN PEPPER, TOMATO CHUTNEY WITH DARK MALT VINEGAR, GREEN TOMATO CHUTNEY, PICKLED PEARS AND PICKLED VEGETABLES

can be a main dish or an accompaniment. The dish is of Middle Eastern origin; the name is derived from a Persian word for "boiled rice." Rice is prepared in a similar way in India and Pakistan.

Pimento Also known as allspice and Jamaica pepper, the dried and ground berries of a tree related to the myrtle and native to Jamaica. The term is sometimes also applied to the dried and ground flesh of the pimiento, a sweet pepper grown in Spain.

Pimiento A sweet pepper, long and thin in form and with mild-flavored flesh that is cut into strips and used to add color to a range of foods. Skinned pimiento strips are used in salads, as an accompaniment to cold meats, as a garnish and as a stuffing for pitted olives. Pimiento ranges in color from green to red, depending upon the ripeness of the fruit when picked; it is available bottled or canned in oil or brine. Its dried and ground flesh, *pimentón*, is a spice similar to paprika, much used in Spanish cooking.

Pineapple A large, cylindrical tropical fruit with thick skin, a crown of cactus-like

BACON, HERB AND VEGETABLE PIE

⭐ ⭐ **Preparation time:** 25 minutes
Total cooking time: 55 minutes
Serves 6

2 tablespoons butter	1 large carrot, chopped
1 clove garlic, crushed	1 parsnip, chopped
1 medium onion, chopped	2 leeks, thinly sliced
	1¼ cups heavy cream
1 tablespoon all-purpose flour	1 tablespoon chopped fresh rosemary
3½ oz button mushrooms, halved	2 sheets frozen puff pastry, thawed
5 oz bacon, chopped	1 egg, lightly beaten

1 Preheat oven to moderate 350°F. Heat butter in heavy-bottom pan, add garlic and onion. Cook over medium heat for 3 minutes or until golden. Add flour, stir 1 minute.
2 Add mushrooms and bacon, cook for 5 minutes. Add carrot, parsnip and leek. Gradually stir in cream and rosemary. Bring to boil, reduce heat, cover, simmer 15 minutes or until vegetables are tender.
3 Spoon the mixture into 9 inch pie plate. Cut each pastry sheet into twelve equal strips; weave the strips into tight lattice pattern, brushing with egg. Carefully lift the pastry and place over pie. Trim the edges with a sharp knife. Brush top of pastry with egg. Bake for 25 minutes or until golden.

CHICKEN PIE

⭐ ⭐ **Preparation time:** 40 minutes
Total cooking time: 1 hour
Serves 6–8

Pastry
2 cups all-purpose flour	2 tablespoons all-purpose flour
½ teaspoon salt	½ teaspoon ground nutmeg
½ cup butter	2 large leeks, chopped
1 teaspoon water	1 onion, thinly sliced

Filling
2 lb boneless chicken thighs, skin removed	¼ cup butter, melted
6½ oz ham	½ cup chicken stock
ground pepper	1 egg, for glazing
	½ cup heavy cream

1 To make Pastry: Sift flour into a bowl; add salt. Rub through the ½ cup butter until mixture resembles fine bread crumbs. Add water to form a stiff dough, knead lightly, refrigerate.
2 To make Filling: Trim fat from chicken, cut into 1 inch pieces; cut ham into ½ inch strips.
3 Preheat oven to 400°F. Grease a large shallow ovenproof dish with melted butter. Combine pepper, flour and nutmeg in a plastic bag, toss chicken pieces in flour mixture until well coated. Shake off excess flour.
4 Place half the leek and onion in layers over the base of the prepared casserole dish. Top with half of the ham and chicken pieces. Repeat

ABOVE: BACON, HERB AND VEGETABLE PIE.
OPPOSITE: CHICKEN PIE

layers using remaining onion, leek, ham and chicken. Drizzle the melted butter over the filling, add the stock.

5 Knead the pastry lightly, roll it out to fit the dish, allowing for a decorative edge. Glaze the edges of the casserole dish with a little of the beaten egg. Cover the pie with the prepared pastry. Decorate the edges of the pastry to form a seal on the pie, glaze with beaten egg. Cut three deep slits in the pastry to allow steam to escape— the cream will be added through these later. Bake for 1 hour, or until pastry is golden brown and the chicken is cooked. Remove from the oven and leave to stand for 5 minutes. Pour the cream into the slits and allow to stand for another 10 minutes before serving.

BLACKBERRY PIE

★ ★ **Preparation time:** 45 minutes
Total cooking time: 45 minutes
Serves 6–8

Filling
1/3 cup cornstarch
2 x 16 oz cans
  blackberries, drained,
  juice reserved
1/3 cup sugar
1 teaspoon finely grated
  orange rind

Pastry
2 cups all-purpose flour
2 tablespoons
  confectioners' sugar
1/2 cup chilled butter,
  chopped
1 egg, lightly beaten
2 tablespoons water
1 egg, extra, lightly
  beaten
1 tablespoon sugar

1 Preheat oven to moderate 350°F. Brush a 9 inch round ovenproof pie plate with melted butter or oil.

2 **To make Filling:** Blend the cornstarch with a small amount of the reserved blackberry juice in a small bowl until smooth. Combine the remaining juice, sugar, orange rind and cornstarch mixture in a medium pan. Stir over medium heat for 5 minutes, or until the mixture boils and thickens. Remove pan from heat and set aside. Allow mixture to cool.

3 **To make Pastry:** Place the flour, confectioners' sugar and butter in a food processor. Process for 15 seconds or until mixture is a fine, crumbly texture. Add egg and water, process for 15 seconds or until the mixture comes together, adding more liquid if necessary. Turn onto well-floured surface, knead for 2 minutes or until smooth. Store, covered with plastic wrap, in refrigerator for about 15 minutes.

4 Roll two-thirds of pastry out on a well-floured surface until large enough to cover base and sides of prepared pie plate. Spread cornstarch mixture evenly into pie shell, top with the blackberries. Roll the remaining pastry into a circle large enough to cover the top of the pie. Brush edges with extra egg to seal. Trim edges with a sharp knife. Brush the top of the pie with beaten egg. Using a fork, make a pattern around the edge. Sprinkle with the sugar. Bake in preheated oven for 35 minutes or until the pastry is crisp and golden. Let the pie stand for 5 minutes before cutting into wedges for serving. Serve pie hot with whipped cream or ice cream.

leaves and fragrant, sharply sweet, juicy, yellow flesh. Peeled, cored and sliced, pineapple can be eaten fresh, as a fruit; diced, it is added to fruit salad, savory salad and is an ingredient in sweet and sour dishes; chopped pineapple is used in cakes; grilled or broiled pineapple rings are a

traditional accompaniment for ham steaks (pineapple also combines well with chicken, pork and duck); puréed pineapple can be used in drinks and sorbets; and pineapple can also be made into jam. Raw pineapple contains an enzyme similar to that found in papaya (pawpaw) which stops it from setting in gelatin preparations; this enzyme is not present in the cooked or canned fruit. Pineapple is in season in spring, but can usually be bought fresh throughout the year; it is also available canned, juiced, glacéed and candied. The fruit was named for its resemblance to a large pine cone.

Pine Nut (Pignoli, Pignon, Pinon) The small, slender, soft, pale seed shed by the fully mature cone of certain types of pine tree. Pine nuts add richness to stuffings, sauces (such as pesto), salads, vegetable dishes, stews, cakes and cookies. They were a staple for native Americans, especially the Navajo and Zuni.

Pinto Bean A pink kidney bean common in Latin America. Used in stews, with rice and as the basis for refried beans.

Piroshki Tiny filled Russian savory pastries, served hot as a finger food, as a first course or with soup. They can be made with yeast dough, choux pastry, pie crust or puff pastry, and are filled with cheese, pork, fish, vegetables, game or poultry.

Pissaladière A savory similar to an Italian pizza, a crust of bread dough is filled with onions simmered in olive oil, garnished with

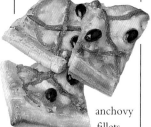

anchovy fillets and black olives, and baked. Pissaladière is a specialty of the Nice region of southern France.

Pistachio A small, oval nut with a brown shell and a green kernel with a mild, slightly sweet taste. The nuts may be

FAMILY MEAT PIE

⭐ **Preparation time:** 20 minutes
Total cooking time: 1 hour 10 minutes
Serves 4–6

1 tablespoon oil
1 medium onion, chopped
1½ lb ground beef
3½ oz button mushrooms, sliced
2 tablespoons tomato paste
1 cup beef stock

2 tablespoons all-purpose flour
1 sheet refrigerated piecrust pastry
1 sheet frozen puff pastry, thawed
1 egg, lightly beaten

1 Preheat oven to very hot 475°F. Heat oil in a heavy-bottom pan; add onion and beef. Stir over medium-high heat until meat is well browned and almost all liquid has evaporated. Use a fork to break up any lumps.
2 Add the mushrooms, tomato paste and stock. Reduce heat, simmer, uncovered, for 15 minutes. Mix the flour with a little cold water to make a smooth paste. Stir into meat, bring to the boil and cook until sauce has thickened. Cool.
3 Line a 9 inch pie plate with piecrust pastry. Fill with cold meat mixture. Roll out puff pastry until large enough to fit top of pie plate. Moisten edges of piecrust pastry with water, cover with puff pastry and press edges together. Trim excess pastry, decorate top if desired.
4 Brush top with beaten egg, cut a few steam holes. Place dish on a baking sheet; bake 10 minutes. Reduce oven temperature to 350°F and bake for 30 minutes or until pastry is golden.

VEGETABLE PIE

⭐ **Preparation time:** 40 minutes + 40 minutes refrigeration
Total cooking time: 55 minutes
Serves 4–6

Pastry
1½ cups all-purpose flour
½ cup butter, cubed
1 tablespoon iced water
1 egg yolk, lightly beaten
2 teaspoons lemon juice

6 spinach leaves, washed and chopped
½ teaspoon ground nutmeg
1 cup mashed potato (10 oz raw potato)
1 cup mashed pumpkin (6½ oz raw pumpkin)

Filling
2 tablespoons butter
1 small onion, finely chopped

2 large, firm tomatoes, sliced
1 cup grated Cheddar cheese

1 To make Pastry: Sift the flour into a large mixing bowl. Add the butter. Using fingertips, rub the butter into flour for 4 minutes or until the mixture is a fine, crumbly texture. Make a well in the center and mix in the combined water, egg yolk and lemon juice until the mixture clings together to form a ball. Place on a lightly floured surface and knead for 1 minute. Cover with plastic wrap and refrigerate for 30 minutes.
2 Preheat oven to moderately hot 400°F. Brush a deep, 8 inch pie plate lightly with melted butter or oil. Roll the pastry out between 2 sheets of waxed paper on a lightly floured surface. Line the prepared plate with pastry, being careful not to stretch pastry. Trim the excess from edge using a large, sharp knife. Chill for 10 minutes.
3 Line the pastry with wax paper, fill with rice, dried peas or beans. Bake for 12 minutes. Remove and discard the paper, rice, peas or beans. Return the pastry to the oven and continue to bake for 15 minutes or until the pastry is cooked and golden brown. Allow to cool for 5 minutes.
4 To make Filling: Melt the butter in a medium pan; add the chopped onion. Stir over medium- high heat for 2 minutes. Add the chopped spinach and nutmeg; cover and cook until the spinach is tender.
5 Spread the mashed potato over the base of the baked pie crust; top with spinach mixture, mashed pumpkin, tomato slices and cheese. Bake for about 20 minutes to heat thoroughly. Serve pie hot or cold.

ABOVE: FAMILY MEAT PIE.
OPPOSITE PAGE: GOURMET VEGETABLE PIZZA

eaten from the shell, salted or unsalted, as a snack; shelled pistachio nuts are added to pâtés, terrines, stuffings and spiced sausages and are used to garnish rice dishes; they are also used in candy, ice creams, cakes, sweet pastry fillings and cookies. The shells are sometimes dyed red, a practice that began in the United States in the 1930s to cover

blemishes. The pistachio nut is the fruit of a tree native to the Middle East which is now cultivated widely in the lands of the Mediterranean and in the south of the United States.

Pistou A vegetable and pasta soup, similar to minestrone. It is seasoned just before serving with a condiment of pounded basil leaves, mixed with oil and Parmesan cheese. A specialty of Provence, in southern France, pistou is closely related to the minestrone with pesto alla Genovese served across the Ligurian Sea in

northern Italy. The name pistou is derived from the Italian word for "pestle," and the soup is

PIZZAS

GOURMET VEGETABLE PIZZA

★★ **Preparation time:** 30 minutes + 30 minutes standing
Total cooking time: 1 hour
Serves 6

Pizza Dough
2 tablespoons cornmeal
1 envelope active dry yeast
1 teaspoon sugar
1½ cups all-purpose flour
½ cup warm water
1 teaspoon salt
⅓ cup basil leaves, finely chopped
1 tablespoon olive oil

Tomato Sauce
1 tablespoon oil
1 small red onion, finely chopped

1 clove garlic, crushed
1 large tomato, chopped
1 tablespoon tomato paste
½ teaspoon dried oregano

Topping
2 oz button mushrooms, finely sliced
3½ oz baby corn
1½ cups grated mozzarella cheese
2 oz spinach leaves, finely shredded
1 small red pepper, cut into short thin strips
2 tablespoons pine nuts

1 Brush a 12 inch pizza pan with oil and sprinkle with cornmeal.
2 To make Pizza Dough: Combine yeast, sugar and 2 tablespoons of the flour in a small

mixing bowl. Gradually add water; blend until smooth. Stand, covered with plastic wrap, in a warm place for about 10 minutes or until foamy.
3 Sift the remaining flour into a large mixing bowl. Add salt and basil, make a well in the center. Add yeast mixture and oil. Using a knife, mix to a soft dough.
4 Turn dough onto a lightly floured surface, knead for 5 minutes or until smooth. Shape dough into a ball, place in a large, lightly oiled mixing bowl. Leave, covered with plastic wrap, in a warm place for 20 minutes or until well risen. While dough is rising, prepare sauce.
5 To make Tomato Sauce: Heat oil in a small pan, add the onion and garlic and cook over a medium heat for 3 minutes or until soft. Add tomato, reduce heat and simmer for 10 minutes, stirring occasionally. Stir in tomato paste and oregano, cook for another 3 minutes. Allow sauce to cool before using.
6 Preheat oven to 425°F. Turn the dough out onto a lightly floured surface and knead for another 5 minutes or until smooth. Roll out to fit prepared pan.
7 Spread the sauce onto the pizza base; arrange the mushrooms and corn evenly on top. Sprinkle half the mozzarella over mushrooms and corn, followed by the spinach, pepper and remaining cheese. Sprinkle with pine nuts. Bake for 40 minutes or until crust is golden. Serve pizza, cut into wedges, immediately.

traditionally served with the basil sauce in a mortar in the center of the table to allow diners to season their soup to taste.

Pita Bread A slightly leavened, soft, flat, wheat flour bread baked until puffed and hollow.

Pita can be either cut in half across the middle or slit open at the edges; either way a pocket is formed which can then be filled with hot meat (such as lamb cubes), vegetable mixtures (such as falafel) or with salad. Cut or torn into smaller portions, pita bread is the traditional accompaniment to dips such as hummus bi tahini and baba ghannouj. It can also be used as a pizza base. Pita is of Middle Eastern origin.

Pizza A flat base of bread dough spread with various savory toppings (tomato sauce, cheese, salami, ham, seafood, chopped vegetables, anchovy and olives), seasoned with herbs and garlic, sprinkled with olive oil and baked,

TRADITIONAL PIZZA

⭐ ⭐   *Preparation time:* 1 hour
Total cooking time: 45 minutes
Serves 6

Pizza Dough
*2 teaspoons cornmeal or
  semolina*
*1 envelope active dry
  yeast*
1 teaspoon sugar
*1½ cups all-purpose
  flour*
½ cup warm water
1 teaspoon salt
1 tablespoon olive oil

Tomato Sauce
1 tablespoon olive oil
*1 small onion, finely
  chopped*
1 clove garlic, crushed
*1 large tomato, finely
  chopped*
1 tablespoon tomato paste
½ teaspoon dried oregano

1 Preheat oven to 425°F. Brush a 12-inch pizza pan with oil and sprinkle with cornmeal or semolina. Combine the yeast, sugar and 2 tablespoons of flour in a small mixing bowl. Gradually add water; blend until smooth. Stand, covered with plastic wrap, in a warm place for about 10 minutes or until foamy.
2 Sift remaining flour into a large mixing bowl. Add salt and make a well in the center. Add yeast mixture and oil. Using a knife, mix to a soft dough.
3 Turn dough onto a lightly floured surface, knead 5 minutes or until smooth. Shape dough into a ball, place in a large, lightly oiled mixing bowl. Leave, covered with plastic wrap, in a warm place 20 minutes or until well risen.
4 Turn dough out onto a lightly floured surface,

knead for another 5 minutes, until smooth and elastic. Roll out to fit prepared pan, cover with topping and cook in preheated oven for 30 minutes.
5 To make Tomato Sauce: Heat oil in a small pan, add onion and garlic and cook over a medium heat 3 minutes or until soft. Add tomato, reduce heat and simmer for 10 minutes, stirring occasionally. Stir in tomato paste and oregano, cook for another 2 minutes. Set aside to cool.

VARIATIONS

■ **Napolitana:** Spread 1 quantity Tomato Sauce on a pizza base. Sprinkle with 1 cup of grated mozzarella cheese and 1 tablespoon of chopped fresh oregano. Bake in preheated oven 30 minutes.
■ **Pepperoni:** Spread 1 quantity Tomato Sauce on a pizza base. Sprinkle with 1 cup of grated mozzarella cheese and 1 finely chopped red pepper. Top with 4 oz thinly sliced pepperoni. Bake in preheated oven 30 minutes.
■ **Four Seasons:** Spread ½ quantity of Tomato Sauce on a pizza base. Fry in oil, in separate batches, 2½ oz of sliced button mushrooms, 3 chopped bacon slices, 1 finely sliced onion. Place each of these on one quarter of pizza. Place 5 canned anchovy fillets over onion. On remaining quarter of pizza, arrange 3 sliced small balls of fresh mozzarella cheese and 1 tablespoon shredded fresh basil. Bake for 30 minutes.

ABOVE: TRADITIONAL PIZZA.
OPPOSITE PAGE: GARLIC BUTTER POLENTA

P O L E N T A

GARLIC BUTTER POLENTA WITH ROASTED PEPPER

 Preparation time: 30 minutes + 2 hours refrigeration
Total cooking time: 10–15 minutes
Serves 2–4

1¹/₃ cups chicken or vegetable stock
1 cup water
1 cup cornmeal
¹/₂ cup freshly grated Parmesan cheese
2 tablespoons butter
2 large red peppers

2 tablespoons butter, extra, melted
1 tablespoon olive oil
1 clove garlic, crushed
freshly grated Parmesan cheese, for serving
fresh ricotta cheese, for serving

1 Place the stock and water in a medium pan and bring to boil. Add cornmeal, reduce heat and stir constantly for 3–6 minutes or until very thick. Remove from heat, stir in Parmesan cheese and butter. Spread mixture into a foil-lined 8 x 8 x 2 inch baking pan; smooth surface. Refrigerate for 2 hours.
2 Cut peppers in half. Remove seeds and membrane. Place skin-side up on a broiler rack. Broil 4 inches from heat until skin blisters and blackens. Cover with a damp towel; cool. Carefully peel off the skin and discard. Cut flesh into thin strips.

3 Turn polenta out and cut into slices. Brush one side of slices with combined melted butter, oil and garlic.
4 Broil for 3–4 minutes or until slices are lightly browned. Repeat process on other sides. Serve hot with pepper strips, extra grated Parmesan cheese and fresh ricotta cheese.

A B O U T   P O L E N T A

■ Polenta is finely milled cornmeal which is simmered slowly with water and stirred constantly to produce a thick porridge-like mixture. It is a staple of Italian cooking with a variety of uses. Although rather bland in flavor, its versatile texture makes it adaptable to many sweet or savory dishes.

■ A popular alternative to potatoes, rice or pasta, polenta is easy to prepare and is often served with strong-tasting meats such as spicy sausages, sautéed liver or roast game, or with marinated, grilled vegetables.

■ Polenta can be enriched with milk or a soft cheese (such as chèvre), and stirred into soups or stews, or made into dumplings.

■ Alternatively, the polenta mixture can be spread over the base of a buttered baking dish. When it has cooled and set, it is cut into wedges or slices and fried or toasted. It can be eaten on its own with butter or cheese, or served as an accompaniment to savory dishes.

■ Polenta slices can be flavored after cooking: brush with olive oil, or spread with olive paste, mashed anchovies or feta cheese.

traditionally in a wood-fired oven. Pizza is eaten hot, as either a first or a main course; small portions or miniature pizzas can be served as finger food. Pizza originated in Naples, in southern Italy, where nineteenth-century street vendors vied with each other to attract customers to their tasty offerings. The classic Neapolitan pizza has a thin, crisp crust with a topping of tomato and mozzarella cheese. In Rome, pizza is made in large, rectangular pans, cut into pieces and sold by weight. Sicily is the home of the thick-crust or pan pizza, rolled thicker than the Neapolitan original and baked in a greased pan.

Plantain A tropical fruit closely related to the banana, but plumper and longer, with thick green skin and firmer, more fibrous flesh. Plantain is grilled, broiled, fried or barbecued and served as a vegetable, or it can be diced and added to curries, soups, casseroles and omelets; it can become bitter if overcooked. Raw plantain is never sweet, even when fully ripe. Young leaves can be used in soups and salads.

Plum A round fruit with smooth

shiny skin that ranges in color from deep purple to green, yellow or red, depending on the variety; it has sweet, juicy flesh and a flat pit. Raw plums can be eaten peeled or unpeeled as a snack; pitted, sliced and added to fruit salad; or puréed for use in sauces, ice creams and desserts. Plums may be stewed or poached, made into filling for pies and tarts, cooked in fruit puddings and cakes or made into jam; spicy plum sauce combines well with roast meats (especially pork) and poultry. There are several popular American varieties of plum. California horticulturalist Luther Burbank developed the Santa Rosa plum, which has deep crimson skin and accounts for about one-third of all American plums. Plums are in season in summer and early autumn; they are also available canned and dried as prunes.

Plum Pudding A rich steamed or boiled pudding made with dried fruit (prunes, raisins, sultanas and candied cherries), nuts and rum or whisky. It has a dense, moist, cake-like texture. Plum

POPPY SEEDS

POPPY SEED LOAF

★ **Preparation time:** 15 minutes
Total cooking time: 35 minutes
Makes 1 loaf

2½ cups all-purpose flour
1 teaspoon baking powder
¼ teaspoon salt
⅓ cup sugar
¼ cup poppy seeds
1 cup peeled, grated potato
⅔ cup butter, melted and cooled
2 eggs, lightly beaten
1 teaspoon poppy seeds, extra

1 Preheat oven to moderate 350°F. Brush an 8½ x 5½ x 2¾ inch loaf pan with melted butter or oil. Line the base and sides with parchment paper; grease paper.
2 Sift flour, baking powder and salt into large mixing bowl. Add sugar, poppy seeds and potato. Make a well in center. Add butter and eggs. Stir until just combined; do not overbeat.
3 Spoon mixture into pan; smooth surface, sprinkle with extra poppy seeds. Bake for 35 minutes or until skewer comes out clean when inserted in center of loaf. Leave loaf in pan for 3 minutes before turning it onto a wire rack to cool.

Note: Loaf will keep, refrigerated, for 4 days, or may be frozen successfully for up to 4 weeks. Can be served as accompaniment to a cheese/fruit platter.

ABOVE: POPPY SEED LOAF;
RIGHT: POPPY SEED TWISTS.
OPPOSITE PAGE: PORK WITH SOY ORANGE SAUCE

POPPY SEED TWISTS

★ ★ **Preparation time:** 20 minutes +
15 minutes refrigeration
Total cooking time: 15 minutes
Makes 24

½ cup all-purpose flour
3 tablespoons butter, chopped
2 tablespoons iced water
1 tablespoon poppy seeds
1 egg, beaten

1 Preheat oven to moderate 350°F. Brush a baking sheet with melted butter or oil. Place flour in a medium mixing bowl, make a well in the center and add butter. Using two knives, cut butter in a crossing motion until reduced to very small pieces. Stir in the water with a knife and mix to a firm dough. Turn out onto a lightly floured surface, knead for 1 minute or until smooth. Store, covered in plastic wrap, in refrigerator for 15 minutes.
2 On a lightly floured surface, roll pastry to a 10 x 6 inch rectangle. Sprinkle with poppy seeds and press them gently into the pastry with the back of a spoon. Fold pastry into three layers, and re-roll to a 12 x 5 inch rectangle. Cut crosswise into 24 strips.
3 Hold a strip at each end, and twist ends in opposite directions. Place on prepared baking sheet and brush lightly with beaten egg. Bake for 15 minutes or until golden. Cool on a wire rack. Serve as an appetizer or with soup.

PORK

PORK WITH SOY ORANGE SAUCE

★ **Preparation time:** 10 minutes + overnight marinating
Total cooking time: 30 minutes
Serves 8

8 boneless pork loin chops, about 6 oz each, butterflied	2 cloves garlic, crushed
	2 teaspoons dried rosemary
3/4 cup orange juice	1 tablespoon honey
1/4 cup soy sauce	1 tablespoon olive oil, extra, for frying
2 tablespoons olive oil	

1 Trim meat of excess fat and tendons. Place pork in a single layer in a large, shallow glass or ceramic dish. Combine orange juice, soy sauce, oil, garlic, rosemary and honey and pour over pork. Place in refrigerator to marinate for several hours or overnight.
2 Preheat oven to slow 300°F. Heat the olive oil in a large, heavy-based pan; remove pork from marinade, reserving marinade. Add pork to pan in batches, cook over medium heat 4–5 minutes each side. Remove from heat and drain on paper towels. Place cooked pork on a plate and cover loosely with foil. Keep cooked pork warm in oven.
3 Pour marinade in a pan. Stir over medium heat until mixture boils; reduce heat slightly and simmer for about 5 minutes or until reduced by half. To serve, place a pork medallion on each plate and spoon over a little of the sauce.

Accompany with a steamed green vegetable such as asparagus or snow peas.

Note: If preferred, white fish fillets can be used as a substitute for pork in this recipe. Reduce the marinating time to a couple of hours so that the high acid content of the marinade does not break up the flesh of the fish. Reduce the cooking time as well, cooking just until flesh flakes easily.

BARBECUED GINGER PORK SATAYS

★ **Preparation time:** 20 minutes + 1 hour marinating
Total cooking time: 10 minutes
Serves 6

1 lb boneless pork loin	1 teaspoon sesame oil
2 tablespoons grated fresh ginger	1 tablespoon lemon juice
	1 small onion, grated
1/2 teaspoon ground pepper	salt and pepper, to taste

1 Cut pork into even-sized cubes. Place grated ginger, pepper, sesame oil, lemon juice, onion and salt and pepper in a bowl and mix well. Mix pork cubes with marinade and leave for 1 hour.
2 Thread pork cubes onto skewers. Grill over medium-hot coals for 5 minutes each side or until pork is slightly pink on the inside. Serve with a salad and hot bread rolls.

Note: Pork loin is a delicate cut with little fat visible. If it is not available, choose another lean cut of pork.

pudding, decorated with holly, flamed with brandy and served with brandy butter, is traditional Christmas fare. Ice cream, whipped cream or custard can also accompany the pudding.

Poach To cook food by gently simmering it in liquid in a shallow pan.

Poblano Chili Pepper A dark green chili with a rich flavor (the darker the color, the richer the flavor). Dried poblanos are called ancho chili peppers.

Polenta Cornmeal cooked in water and butter until the consistency of thick porridge. It can be eaten hot, on its own, or mixed with Parmesan cheese, baked, broiled or fried and served in wedges as a side dish. The mixture can be varied with the addition of chopped meat or vegetables; slices of cold polenta are often fried in butter and served topped with a tomato sauce. Polenta has been a staple food in northern Italy since the arrival of corn from the Americas in the sixteenth century.

Pomegranate A round, reddish-golden skinned fruit about the size of an orange. It is divided by walls of bitter-tasting pith into several chambers, each containing numerous seeds embedded in sacs of sweet, deep pink, jelly-like pulp. The seeds and pulp can be scooped from the shell and eaten or may be added to fruit salad. Pomegranate juice is used to make grenadine syrup, a bright red, non-alcoholic drink used as a coloring and flavoring for cocktails, ice cream, fruit salad and other desserts. The pomegranate is of Asian origin and spread west to the African shores of the Mediterranean many thousands of years ago. It is in season in late autumn.

Pompano Any of several small saltwater fish with delicate flavor and texture. It is caught off the Florida and Gulf coasts. A small blue or green pompano is found off the California coast.

Popcorn A snack made by heating the kernels of a type of corn known as popping corn. The moisture in the kernel changes to steam, swelling the soft starchy interior until it bursts through the skin as a

PORK WITH CABBAGE AND PLUMS

★ **Preparation time:** 30 minutes
Total cooking time: 1 hour 30 minutes–1 hour 45 minutes
Serves 6-8

2 lb boneless pork loin (single loin)
2 tablespoons butter, softened
1 teaspoon ground allspice
1/2 cup water
2 tablespoons butter
1 large onion, thinly sliced
1 lb cabbage, shredded
1/3 cup lemon juice

Sauce
30 oz can whole, purple plums
2 tablespoons butter
4 scallions, finely chopped
1/3 cup red wine vinegar
1 teaspoon instant chicken bouillon powder
1/4 cup all-purpose flour
1 cup chicken broth

1 Preheat oven to 350°F. Trim pork of excess fat. Tie securely with string. Stir together softened butter and allspice; spread over pork. Place meat on rack in roasting pan. Insert meat thermometer. Pour water into pan. Roast 1 hour 30–45 minutes or until thermometer registers 160°F. Stand 10 minutes.

2 In a saucepan heat 2 tablespoons butter. Add onion; cook until tender and brown. Stir in cabbage. Add lemon juice. Cover; simmer 10–15 minutes until cabbage is tender. Set aside; keep warm.

3 To make sauce: drain plums, reserve syrup. Place plums in ovenproof dish; set aside. In a saucepan heat 2 tablespoons butter. Cook scallions in butter 1 minute; add vinegar; cook 1 minute more. Add plum syrup and bouillon granules to pan. Bring to boil; reduce heat. Simmer, uncovered, 5 minutes; set aside. Warm plums in 300°F oven for 15 minutes before serving.

4 Remove meat from pan, reserving drippings for gravy. Thinly slice meat; keep warm. Measure 1/3 cup of drippings. Transfer drippings to a skillet. Stir in flour. Cook and stir until flour browns. Add chicken broth and plum syrup mixture. Cook and stir for 1 minute more.

5 To serve, arrange cabbage on serving plate, overlap pork slices down center. Arrange warm plums around meat; pour a small amount of gravy over meat. Pass remaining gravy.

PORK WITH FENNEL

⭐ **Preparation time:** 35 minutes
Total cooking time: 1 hour 40 minutes
Serves 6

3 slices bacon, finely
  chopped
3 lb boneless pork loin
1 cup fresh white bread
  crumbs
1 cup finely chopped fresh
  fennel bulb
1 tablespoon chopped
  capers
2 tablespoons chopped
  fresh chives

1 egg, lightly beaten
2 tablespoons butter
1 tablespoon olive oil,
  extra
1/2 cup sweet sherry
1/2 cup orange juice
2 tablespoons red wine
  vinegar
1 teaspoon finely grated
  orange rind

1 Preheat oven to 350°F. Heat oil in a medium pan and cook the bacon over medium-high heat for 2 minutes or until crisp. Remove from pan and drain on paper towels.
2 Trim pork of excess fat. Cut through lengthwise to open out but do not cut right through. Open out, flatten with the palm of your hand.
3 Combine the bacon, bread crumbs, fennel, capers and chives in a medium bowl; add egg and stir to combine. Press the stuffing over the opened loin. Roll and tie securely with string.
4 Heat butter and oil in frying pan. Cook loin over medium heat 3–4 minutes until evenly browned. Remove from pan and place in a large baking dish.
5 Scrape sediment from pan. Add combined sherry,

orange juice, red wine vinegar and orange rind to pan. Simmer uncovered for 2 minutes. Pour over pork. Bake 1 1/2 hours or until slightly pink and a meat thermometer registers 160°F.
6 Remove string from pork, slice and place on serving platter, spoon pan juices over, serve.

CREAMY LEMON PORK

⭐ **Preparation time:** 10 minutes
Total cooking time: 45–50 minutes
Serves 4

1 1/2 lb diced pork
  tenderloin
2 tablespoons butter
6 oz button mushrooms,
  sliced
1 cup chicken stock
1 tablespoon all-purpose
  flour

1/2 cup heavy cream
1 tablespoon lemon juice
freshly ground black
  pepper to taste
1/2 small lemon, cut into
  small wedges
finely chopped fresh
  parsley

1 Trim meat of excess fat and sinew. Heat butter in heavy-bottom pan. Cook meat quickly, in small batches over medium-high heat until well browned; drain on paper towels.
2 Add mushrooms to pan and cook for 2 minutes. Return meat to pan with stock; bring to boil. Reduce heat to simmer, cook covered, 30 minutes or until meat is tender, stirring occasionally.
3 Mix together the flour and cream. Add to pan, increase heat, stir until the sauce thickens. Simmer for 2 minutes. Season with juice and pepper. Serve with noodles, decorate with lemon wedges and parsley.

OPPOSITE PAGE: PORK WITH CABBAGE AND PLUMS.
ABOVE: PORK WITH FENNEL

puffy white ball. Popcorn is eaten as a snack, either with melted butter and salt or with a sweet coating. Packs of popping corn for cooking on the stove-top (add to a little heated oil in a heavy lidded pan: it should start to pop in a minute or so and be ready in another minute) and a special pop-in-the-bag product for microwave ovens are available from supermarkets; cooked popcorn is sold in sealed bags or, freshly popped, in open cartons.

Popover An airy steam-raised quick bread made from a batter of flour, egg and milk that is very similar to the mixture used to make Yorkshire pudding. Popovers are baked in greased muffin tins or cups in a very hot oven so they rise quickly, forming a crisp, golden shell while the inside remains moist and mostly hollow. Popovers should be eaten hot, either with butter and jam or honey, or split open and filled with meat or vegetables; herbs, grated cheese or sugar may be added to the batter. Popovers can be frozen; reheat in a hot oven.

Poppy Seed The fine gray-blue seeds of the poppy plant. Poppy seeds have a strong, nutty flavor. They are often sprinkled on bread and savory crackers before baking. Poppy seeds can be added to pasta and potato dishes, and are

used to make the traditional Jewish poppy seed cake. The poppy is native to Asia.

Pork The meat of the domestic pig. Pale and succulent, it has long been prized for its richness and flavor. Suckling pig is an animal slaughtered at two months of age. Top quality pork should be pale pink, smooth and finely grained with white fat and smooth, thin skin. Pork is suitable for broiling, roasting, barbecuing, pan-frying and casseroling; pork joints can also be pickled. It is healthiest to choose lean cuts and trim off excess fat.

Pork is sold either fresh or processed. Chops and roasts are usually fresh; salt pork

SWEET AND SOUR PORK

⭐⭐ **Preparation time:** 20 minutes + 20 minutes marinating
Total cooking time: 12 minutes
Serves 4–6

1½ lb pork spareribs
1 tablespoon light soy sauce
1 tablespoon dry sherry
½ medium cucumber
2 tablespoons Chinese sweet mixed pickles
1 cup cornstarch
oil for deep-fat frying
¼ green pepper, shredded
¼ red pepper, shredded
1 medium onion, sliced top to base
1 cup water
½ cup white vinegar
⅓ cup sugar
¼ cup tomato sauce
1 tablespoon cornstarch
1 teaspoon instant chicken bouillon powder

1 Cut ribs crosswise into ½ inch strips so that each piece contains layers of pork and fat. Remove any small bones. Brush with soy sauce and sherry and set aside for 20 minutes.
2 Peel the cucumber; cut in half. Scoop out the seeds with a spoon and cut into thin slices. Finely chop pickles.
3 Coat pork pieces with the 1 cup cornstarch. Shake off any excess cornstarch.
4 Deep-fry pork in batches in hot oil (375°F) 2 minutes or until golden brown. Drain on a rack; cool. Place 3 tablespoons of the oil in a wok. Reserve remaining hot oil to fry pork again.
5 In a skillet with 3 tablespoons oil cook peppers and onion until tender. Add cucumber and chopped pickles and cook for 1 minute. Stir

together water, vinegar, sugar, tomato sauce, cornstarch and bouillon powder. Add to skillet. Cook and stir until thickened and bubbly. Cook and stir 2 minutes more.
6 Reheat oil for deep-frying. Deep-fry pork in hot oil about 2 minutes until golden brown and crisp.
7 Transfer to serving plate; spoon sauce over. Serve with rice.

PORK CHOPS WITH GRAINY MUSTARD CREAM

⭐ **Preparation time:** 15 minutes
Total cooking time: 12 minutes
Serves 6

6 boneless pork chops, about 6 oz each, butterflied
3 tablespoons all-purpose flour
½ teaspoon ground black pepper
¼ cup oil
1 medium onion, finely
chopped
¾ cup orange juice
1 chicken bouillon cube, crumbled
1 teaspoon soy sauce
2 teaspoons seeded mustard
1 teaspoon cornstarch
⅓ cup sour cream

1 Trim meat of excess fat and tendons. Combine flour and pepper on a sheet of wax paper. Toss chops in the seasoned flour until lightly coated; shake off excess.
2 Heat 2 tablespoons oil in a heavy-bottom pan; add meat. Cook over a medium heat 2–3 minutes each side or until tender, turning once. Remove from pan, drain on paper towels.

3 Heat the remaining oil in a pan. Add the onion and stir over medium heat 3 minutes or until soft. Add half of the orange juice, the bouillon cube, the soy sauce and mustard, stir until thoroughly combined. Blend the cornstarch with the remaining orange juice until smooth; add to pan. Stir over low heat until the sauce boils and thickens. Remove from heat; cool slightly. Add the sour cream, stir until smooth. Return meat; heat through and serve.

BARBECUED PORK MEDALLIONS WITH TAPENADE

Preparation time: 20 minutes
Total cooking time: 15 minutes
Serves 4

4 pork loin medallions, about 6 oz each, butterflied
2 tablespoons olive oil
1 tablespoon lemon juice
1 tablespoon fresh thyme leaves
1/4 teaspoon freshly ground black pepper

Tapenade
2 tablespoons olive oil
1/2 small onion, finely chopped
1 clove garlic, crushed

4 oz pitted black olives, finely chopped
2 anchovies, finely chopped
1 small, ripe tomato, peeled, seeded and chopped
2 teaspoons balsamic vinegar
1 medium red chili pepper, finely chopped
1 tablespoon chopped fresh basil leaves

1 Trim the meat of any excess fat and tendons.
2 Combine the olive oil, lemon juice, thyme and pepper; brush over meat.
3 Place the meat on a lightly oiled preheated grill. Cook over medium heat for 5 minutes on each side or until tender. Serve with Tapenade.
4 To make Tapenade: Heat the olive oil in a small pan, add the onion and garlic and stir over medium heat until the onion is tender. Add the olives, anchovies, tomato, vinegar, chili and basil, stir for 1 minute to make sure that all ingredients are thoroughly combined. Serve hot or cold.

Note: The pork for this recipe can be cooked under a preheated broiler. Unless it is cooked carefully at a moderate heat, pork can become dry and tough. Cuts such as those used in this recipe are done when the flesh feels fairly firm to touch; it should still be juicy and faintly pink.

To make butterfly medallions, trim the meat from the bone of the pork chops. Discard the bones. Using a sharp knife, carefully cut the meat horizontally through the center, starting at the fatty end. Ensure that you do not cut right through the meat. Open the meat out and press it firmly with your hands to flatten it slightly. The pork medallions are now ready to use in your recipe.

OPPOSITE PAGE, ABOVE: SWEET AND SOUR PORK; BELOW: PORK CHOPS WITH GRAINY MUSTARD CREAM. ABOVE: BARBECUED PORK MEDALLIONS WITH TAPENADE

and some hams are processed. Curing pork is done by pickling in a brine. Cured and smoked pork may require some cooking. Pork is complimented by the flavors of sage and juniper berries. Pork is the main meat in the cooking of China and Southeast Asia. In China and Vietnam the plump pig is a symbol of prosperity. For centuries pork was virtually the only meat eaten by the peasant communities of Europe, and nothing of the carcass was wasted, from the ears to the trotters. The nineteenth-century gastronomic writer Charles Monselet described the pig as "nothing but an immense dish that walks while waiting to be served." Moslems, Jews, Navajos, Laplanders  and the Yakuts of Turkey do not eat pork.

Pork and Beans A dish of navy beans or similar beans simmered with salt pork, onions, brown sugar and tomato sauce.

Porridge Oatmeal or rolled oats cooked in water or milk until thick and creamy. Porridge is usually served hot with milk or cream and sugar, for breakfast, but it can also be eaten cold with salt. Porridge is descended from gruel, which was a staple of peasant diets.

Port A rich, sweet, fortified wine used to flavor duck and game dishes, sauces such as Cumberland sauce, pâtés, and desserts such as jellies, creams and syrups for poached fruit. True port is made from a variety of grapes grown in northern Portugal and shipped through the town of Oporto.

Port Salut Cheese A semisoft, pasteurized cow's milk cheese with a smooth, savory taste, a creamy texture, a reddish-orange rind and a golden interior with a few tiny holes. Port Salut originated in north-western France, created by Trappist monks. In the years following World War II the monks, unable to keep pace with demand, sold the brand name Saint Paulin to commercial dairies to produce a similar cheese. Port Salut should be served at room temperature with fresh or dried fruit, as a snack cheese and in sandwiches; it is also used in cooking.

Potato A starchy, tuberous root vegetable with crisp white or yellow flesh and smooth brown, russet, yellow or purple skin. A remarkably versatile vegetable, it can be boiled, roasted, fried, baked or barbecued; it is

POTATOES

LAYERED POTATO AND APPLE BAKE

⭐ **Preparation time:** 20 minutes
Total cooking time: 45 minutes
Serves 6

2 large potatoes	1 cup heavy cream
3 medium green apples	1/4 teaspoon ground
1 medium onion	nutmeg
1/2 cup finely grated	freshly ground black
Cheddar cheese	pepper

1 Preheat oven to moderate 350°F. Brush a shallow 8-cup ovenproof dish with melted butter or oil. Peel potatoes and cut into 1/4 inch slices. Peel, core and quarter apples. Cut into 1/4 inch slices. Slice onion into very fine rings.
2 Layer potato, apple and onion in prepared dish, ending with a layer of potato. Sprinkle evenly with cheese. Pour cream over top, covering as evenly as possible.
3 Sprinkle with nutmeg and black pepper to taste. Bake for 45 minutes or until golden brown. Remove from oven and allow to stand for 5 minutes before serving.

Note: To prevent the sliced potato and apple from turning brown while assembling this dish, dip them in a bowl of cold water with a squeeze of lemon juice. Drain and pat dry with paper towels.

CRISP POTATO SKINS WITH CHILI CHEESE DIP

⭐ **Preparation time:** 30 minutes
Total cooking time: 1 hour 15 minutes
Serves 4–6

6 medium potatoes, about	1 clove garlic, crushed
2 1/2 lb	1 teaspoon mild chili
oil for shallow frying	powder
	3/4 cup sour cream
Chili Cheese Dip	2 cups grated Cheddar
1 tablespoon oil	cheese
1 small onion, finely	
chopped	

1 Preheat oven to moderately hot 400°F. Scrub potatoes and dry thoroughly; do not peel. Prick each potato twice with a fork. Bake for 1 hour, turning once, until skins are crisp and flesh is soft when pierced with a knife. Remove from oven and cool.
2 Cut potatoes in half and scoop out flesh, leaving about 1/4 inch of potato in the shell (save unused flesh for another use). Cut each potato half into three wedges.
3 Heat oil in a medium heavy-bottom pan. Gently lower batches of potato skins into moderately hot oil. Cook for 1–2 minutes or until golden and crisp. Drain on paper towels. Serve immediately with Chili Cheese Dip.
4 To make Chili Cheese Dip: Heat oil in a small pan. Add onion and cook over medium heat for 2 minutes or until soft. Add garlic and chili powder, cook for 1 minute, stirring. Add sour cream and stir until mixture is warm and thinned down slightly; add cheese and stir until melted and mixture is almost smooth. Serve hot.

ABOUT POTATOES

■ Potatoes are members of the nightshade family (as are tomatoes and eggplant). If exposed to light they can develop a greenish-tinged toxic compound under the skin which may cause illness in sensitive individuals. Unwashed potatoes will keep longer, because the soil helps keep out light. Discard potatoes which have turned green, or which have sprouting eyes.
■ Potatoes do not store well in the refrigerator— the low temperatures turn the flesh black as the starch converts to sugar. Store them in a cool, dark, dry place.
■ When deep-frying potatoes (for example when making French fries), a crisper result is obtained if the cut potatoes are soaked in water for about an hour beforehand to remove some of the starch. Dry well with paper towels before frying.

BAKED POTATOES AND FILLINGS

Pierce 2 large potatoes all over with a fork; place on a rack in moderately hot 400°F oven, bake 1 hour or until tender. Meanwhile, prepare topping. Make a deep slash or cross-cut in each cooked potato; squeeze to open and fill with topping. Serves 2.

Note: To microwave unpeeled potatoes, pierce them all over with a fork. Wrap each potato in a layer of paper towel and place directly on microwave turntable. Cook on high setting for 7–10 minutes. Leave for 2 minutes.

HOT CHILI

Cook 8 oz ground beef in skillet over medium-high heat for 5 minutes or until meat is brown and almost all the liquid has evaporated. Add 1 small sliced onion, 2 cloves of crushed garlic, 1 sliced red chili pepper, ½ medium red pepper, seeded and thinly sliced, 2 tablespoons of tomato purée and 1 cup of beef stock. Stir well to combine. Bring to boil, reduce heat and simmer, uncovered, for 20 minutes. Add freshly ground black pepper to taste. Make lengthwise slashes in 2 baked potatoes, squeeze slightly and top with meat mixture; garnish with extra chili slices. Serves 2.

OPPOSITE PAGE: CRISP POTATO SKINS.
ABOVE: BAKED POTATOES WITH FILLINGS

GARLIC MUSHROOMS

Cook 4 oz of quartered button mushrooms and 1 clove of crushed garlic in 2 tablespoons of butter in a medium pan until tender. Add 2 teaspoons finely chopped parsley and freshly ground black pepper to taste. Spoon mixture into 2 cross-cut baked potatoes. Serves 2.

NAPOLETANA

Peel and chop 2 medium, firm, ripe tomatoes. Place in a pan with 1 tablespoon olive oil and a pinch of dried oregano. Simmer for 10 minutes. Remove from heat, add freshly ground pepper to taste. Cut the tops off 2 baked potatoes. Fluff up centers with a fork. Top with tomato mixture, garnish with anchovy fillets and pitted black olives. Serves 2.

SPICY SHRIMP

Saute 8 oz of peeled, cooked medium shrimp, a pinch of turmeric and a pinch of ground coriander in 2 tablespoons of butter in a pan, over medium-high heat, for 1 minute. Add pepper to taste. Slash 2 baked potatoes lengthwise and fill with shrimp mixture. Serves 2.

BLACK RUSSIAN

Slash 2 baked potatoes lengthwise. Top each with 1 oz of sliced smoked salmon, half a slice of lemon and 1 tablespoon sour cream. Garnish with black caviar and serve. Serves 2.

the classic accompaniment to fish and meat courses or can itself form the basis of a main course. New potatoes are small, young potatoes; they have pearly, translucent skin (which need not be removed) and slightly waxy flesh and

are boiled whole and served with melted butter or used for making potato salad. Mature potatoes are floury and are best for boiling and mashing or for baking in their skins; they can also be used in soups and as pie topping. Slightly waxy potatoes roast well and are made into chips and French fries. Very waxy potatoes are ideal for potato salad. The potato is native to South America and was first cultivated high in the Andes as early as 5000 years ago. When introduced into England by Sir Francis Drake in the sixteenth century it soon

found favor in Ireland, where it flourished in the poor soils where other food crops failed; Sir Walter Raleigh is said to have planted the first potatoes in Ireland in 1586. Early in the eighteenth century the potato recrossed the Atlantic to America.

Potatoes are classified by age as well as variety. Freshly harvested potatoes are called "new" and are often small in size. Commercially grown potatoes include oval and round white and red potatoes. Store potatoes in a cool,

but not cold, dry place. Fresh potatoes are available year round; they are also available frozen, dehydrated and canned.

Potato Chip A popular snack food of very thin slices of potato deep-fried and salted.

Potpie A crusty meat or poultry pie baked with vegetables and gravy.

Pot Roast A less tender cut of beef that is browned and braised very slowly in a covered pot.

Poultry Domestic birds bred for their meat and eggs, such as chicken, duck, goose, guinea fowl and turkey. Chicken is the most widely eaten of all poultry, next is turkey. Poultry is available whole or in portions, either fresh, frozen or cooked.

Praline A candy made from almonds or pecans cooked in caramel, then cooled and crushed to a

SPICY POTATO PASTRIES

⭐ **Preparation time:** 40 minutes
Total cooking time: 25 minutes
Serves 4–6

4 large potatoes
　(2 lb 10 oz), peeled
　and cut into small cubes
2 tablespoons butter
1 clove garlic, crushed
2 teaspoons finely grated
　fresh ginger
1 medium onion, finely
　chopped
1 teaspoon turmeric
1 teaspoon garam masala

1 teaspoon ground
　cardamom
1 tablespoon lemon juice
¼ cup chopped fresh
　cilantro
¼ cup chopped fresh
　mint
4 sheets frozen puff
　pastry, thawed
1 egg, lightly beaten
2 teaspoons poppy seeds

1 Preheat oven to moderate 375°F. Line two baking sheets with paper towels or parchment paper. Cook potato in boiling water until just tender. Drain, set aside.
2 Heat butter in pan; add garlic, ginger, onion and spices. Cook over medium-high heat for 4 minutes or until onion is soft. Add potato, lemon juice, cilantro and mint; stir gently to combine. Remove from heat; cool.
3 Roll each pastry sheet to 14 x 14 inches. Cut each sheet into 9 even squares. Brush edges with beaten egg. Place 1 rounded tablespoon potato mixture in the center of each square, fold over to form a triangle and press edges to seal.
4 Brush top of each triangle with egg; sprinkle with poppy seeds. Place 1 inch apart on prepared baking sheets. Bake for 15–20 minutes.

POTATO AND CHEESE CAKES WITH APPLE

⭐ **Preparation time:** 25 minutes
Total cooking time: 20 minutes
Makes 18

2 cups mashed potato
4 oz Cheddar cheese,
　grated
2 tablespoons all-purpose
　flour
1 egg, lightly
　beaten
½ teaspoon ground
　nutmeg
2–3 tablespoons olive oil

Apple Sauce
2 large green apples,
　peeled and cored
2 tablespoons water
2 tablespoons chopped
　fresh mint
1 tablespoon white
　vinegar

1 Combine potato, cheese, sifted flour, egg and nutmeg in mixing bowl. Stir until the mixture is just combined; do not overbeat.
2 Heat olive oil in a medium, heavy-bottom pan. Spoon level tablespoonsful of prepared potato mixture into pan. Cook over medium high heat for 5 minutes. Turn over and cook for another 5 minutes or until Potato and Cheese Cakes are golden brown and cooked through. Top each Potato and Cheese Cake with a spoonful of Apple Sauce and serve immediately.
3 To make Apple Sauce: Cut apples into large cubes and place in a small pan. Add the water, cover and cook over low heat until apples are tender and all the water has evaporated. Mash well with a fork and add mint and vinegar. Stir until well combined.

POTATO AND SALAMI PANCAKES

⭐ **Preparation time:** 25 minutes
Total cooking time: 6 minutes per batch
Makes 18–20 pancakes

½ cup milk
1 teaspoon white vinegar
½ cup all-purpose flour
1 teaspoon baking soda
½ cup mashed potato
2 eggs, lightly beaten
2 tablespoons butter, melted

1½ oz salami, finely chopped
2 tablespoons butter, extra
1 oz sun-dried tomatoes, cut into fine strips, for garnish
fresh basil leaves, for garnish

1 Combine milk and vinegar in a small bowl and leave for 5 minutes. Sift the flour and soda into a medium mixing bowl. Make a well in the center; add mashed potato, beaten eggs and combined milk and vinegar. Stir with a wooden spoon until well combined.
2 Add melted butter and chopped salami, stir gently until combined.
3 Heat extra butter in medium pan; spoon level tablespoonsful of the mixture into pan, about ¾ inch apart.
4 Cook over medium heat 3 minutes each side or until golden. Serve warm garnished with sun-dried tomatoes and basil leaves.

OPPOSITE PAGE: SPICY POTATO PASTRIES.
ABOVE: POTATO AND SALAMI PANCAKES AND
POTATO AND TOMATO SOUP

POTATO AND TOMATO SOUP

⭐ **Preparation time:** 30 minutes
Total cooking time: 25 minutes
Serves 4–6

1 tablespoon butter
1 large onion, chopped
1 clove garlic, crushed
4 medium tomatoes (1 lb), sliced
2 medium potatoes (14½ oz), peeled and sliced
2 tablespoons chopped fresh chives or scallions
1 tablespoon tomato paste

1 teaspoon finely grated lemon rind
½ teaspoon ground thyme
1 bay leaf
4 cups chicken bouillon
freshly ground pepper
sour cream, to serve
fresh thyme sprigs, for garnish

1 Heat the butter in large pan; add onion and garlic. Cook over medium heat until onion is soft. Add tomato, potato, chives, tomato paste, rind, thyme, bay leaf and bouillon.
2 Bring to the boil, reduce heat and simmer, uncovered, for about 20 minutes or until potato is tender. Remove from heat; discard bay leaf. Allow to cool.
3 Place the mixture in batches in a food processor. Process 30 seconds or until the mixture is smooth. Return to pan, season with pepper to taste; heat through. Serve topped with a little sour cream and garnished with thyme sprigs.

POTATO SOUFFLE

⭐ **Preparation time:** 20 minutes
Total cooking time: 1 hour
Serves 2–4

2 large potatoes
⅓ cup sour cream
3 oz Cheddar cheese, grated
4 eggs, separated

pepper and salt to taste
4 scallions, finely chopped
pinch cream of tartar

1 Preheat oven to 350°F. Butter a 6-cup capacity soufflé dish.
2 Peel potatoes, cut each into 4 pieces, place in a pan, cover with water and boil until tender. Remove from heat, drain and mash (do not add butter or milk).
3 Add sour cream, grated cheese, egg yolks and pepper and salt to taste. Blend well and add the scallions.
4 Beat the egg white with cream of tartar until stiff. Fold into the potato mixture and spoon into the prepared dish. Bake for 45 minutes and serve hot.

powder and used as a decoration for desserts or baked into cakes and cookies. Praline also refers to a patty-shaped candy with pecans and brown sugar from Louisiana.

Prawn (Shrimp) A small clawless crustacean with long antennae, slender legs and a long plump body. Shrimp vary in

size and color (from yellow, green, bluish-brown to pale gray) according to species, but most become reddish-orange when cooked. Varieties are found from the tropics to the temperate and cold waters, in both fresh and salt water. The most widely eaten of all shellfish, their firm, moist, sweet flesh forms the basis of numerous dishes in the

cooking of many lands. Eaten hot or cold, they are cooked in many ways, as main dishes or finger food. Shrimp are available raw or cooked, with or without their shells, frozen or canned. In the USA shrimp that live in fresh water are called prawns, as are very large shrimp. Methods of preparation, however, are the same for both shrimp and prawns.

Pretzel A savory snack made with a yeast-leavened dough that is formed into the shape of a loose knot or a stick. It is boiled in water, drained and brushed with egg and sprinkled with coarse salt before baking. It may be either a crusty, soft-centered bread or a crunchy cracker. The pretzel originated in the Alsace region on the German border where it was traditionally served with beer.

Prickly Pear See Cactus Pad.

Profiterole A small, choux pastry puff with a sweet or savory

filling. Profiteroles are probably best known as a dessert, filled with crème pâtissière or chantilly cream and topped with chocolate, caramel or coffee sauce.

Prosciutto An Italian ham from the hind leg of the pig, rubbed with salt and other dry seasonings and matured for eight to ten months. It is deep pink, has a slight sheen and is usually served sliced wafer thin as a first course, although it may also be cooked as part of another dish. Best

PRAWNS (SHRIMPS)

SESAME PRAWNS WITH TANGY MINT CHUTNEY

★ **Preparation time:** 20 minutes
★★ **Total cooking time:** 2 minutes per batch
Serves 4

24 uncooked prawns, about 2 lb
1/4 cup all-purpose flour
1 egg, lightly beaten
2/3 cup dried bread crumbs
1/2 cup sesame seeds
oil for deep frying

Tangy Mint Chutney
1 cup fresh mint leaves, firmly packed
1/2 cup fruit chutney
2 tablespoons lemon juice

1 Peel prawns, leaving tails intact; cut down the back, devein and flatten slightly.
2 Toss prawns in flour; shake off excess, dip in beaten egg and coat with combined bread crumbs and sesame seeds.
3 Heat oil in a deep, heavy-bottom pan. Gently lower prawns into moderately hot oil. Cook over medium-high heat 2 minutes or until golden brown. Carefully remove from oil with tongs or a slotted spoon. Drain on paper towels.
4 To make Tangy Mint Chutney: Combine mint, chutney and lemon juice in a blender or food processor. Process for 15 seconds or until smooth. Serve as a dip for prawns.

SPANISH SHRIMP SALAD

★ **Preparation time:** 25 minutes
Total cooking time: none
Serves 6

1 lb medium shrimp, cooked
2 large oranges
1 small head romaine lettuce
1 small red onion, finely sliced
2 tablespoons red wine vinegar
1/4 cup olive oil
1/2 teaspoon finely grated orange rind
1 clove garlic, crushed

1 Peel shrimp, leaving the tails intact. Remove veins from back. Cut a slice off each end of orange to where flesh starts. Using a small knife, cut the skin away in a circular motion, cutting just deep enough to remove all the white membrane (reserve a little peel for grating). Separate the segments by cutting between the membrane and the flesh.
2 Wash and dry lettuce and arrange on individual plates or a serving platter, top with shrimp, orange segments and onion rings.
3 Place the vinegar, olive oil, orange rind and garlic in a small screw-top jar and shake well. Drizzle over salad and serve immediately with crusty bread.

ABOUT SHRIMP

■ Choose firm shrimp with crisp shells and a fresh, pleasant smell; stale shrimp will be limp and dry. Frozen shrimp are available but should not be substituted for fresh shrimp unless specified in recipes, because the the flesh is slightly mushy when thawed.

CRYSTAL SHRIMP

★ ★ **Preparation time:** 15 minutes +
30 minutes marinating
Total cooking time: 20 minutes
Serves 4

1½ lb medium uncooked
  shrimp
2 scallions, roughly
  chopped
2 teaspoons salt
1 tablespoon cornstarch
1 egg white, lightly
  beaten
1 small red pepper
4 oz sugar snap peas or
  snow peas

1 tablespoon oyster sauce
2 teaspoons dry sherry
1 teaspoon cornstarch,
  extra
1 teaspoon sesame oil
oil for deep-frying
½ teaspoon crushed garlic
½ teaspoon finely grated
  ginger

1 Peel the shrimp, and devein. Place the shells, heads and the scallions in a pan with water to cover; bring to the boil. Simmer, uncovered, for 15 minutes. Strain into a bowl. Reserve ½ cup of the liquid. Place the shrimp in a glass bowl. Add 1 teaspoon of salt and stir briskly for a minute. Rinse under cold, running water. Repeat this procedure twice more, using ½ teaspoon salt each time. Rinse thoroughly and pat the shrimp dry on paper towels.
2 Combine the cornstarch and egg white in a large bowl, and add the peeled, deveined shrimp. Leave the prawns to marinate for 30 minutes in the refrigerator.
3 Cut the pepper into thin strips; wash and remove the string from the sugar snap peas. Combine the reserved liquid, oyster sauce, sherry, extra cornstarch and sesame oil in a small bowl. Heat the oil in a wok or deep heavy-bottom frying pan. Gently lower the shrimp into the moderately hot oil. Cook over medium-high heat for 1–2 minutes or until lightly golden. Carefully remove the shrimp from the oil with tongs or a slotted spoon. Drain on paper towels and keep warm.
4 Pour off all but 2 tablespoons of the oil. Replace the pan over the heat and add the garlic and ginger. Stir-fry for 30 seconds, add the sugar snap peas and pepper, and stir-fry over high heat for 2 minutes. Add the combined sauce ingredients and cook, stirring constantly, until the sauce boils and thickens. Add the shrimp and stir gently to combine. Remove from the heat and serve immediately.

*OPPOSITE PAGE, ABOVE: SESAME PRAWNS WITH
MINT CHUTNEY; BELOW: SPANISH SHRIMP SALAD.
ABOVE: CRYSTAL SHRIMP*

SPAGHETTI CREOLE

★ **Preparation time:** 15 minutes
Total cooking time: 25–30 minutes
Serves 6

1 tablespoon oil
1 lb spaghetti
chopped fresh parsley to
  garnish

Sauce
¼ cup butter
1 lb uncooked shrimp,
  shelled and deveined

⅓ cup white wine
16 oz can peeled
  tomatoes, crushed
pinch black pepper
2 teaspoons curry powder
1 cup heavy cream
2 tablespoons freshly
  grated Parmesan cheese

1 Bring a pan of water, with the oil added, to boil. Add the spaghetti and cook for 10–12 minutes, or until firm and tender. Drain and rinse under warm water. Drain thoroughly and return the spaghetti to the pan. Add the shrimp sauce. Toss over low heat for 1–2 minutes. Serve garnished with chopped fresh parsley.
2 To make Sauce: Melt the butter in a frying pan. Cook the shrimp until they are just pink. Remove from the pan and set aside. Add the white wine, crushed tomato, pepper, curry powder, cream and grated Parmesan. Simmer for 10 minutes.

Note: Freshly grated Parmesan cheese is preferable to the packaged grated Parmesan.

known varieties are Parma ham (this particular curing process originated in Parma, in northern Italy) and San Daniele ham from the Friuli region in the north-east, reckoned by many to be the finest.

Provençale, à la, A French term for dishes, sauces and garnishes containing olive oil, garlic and tomatoes, typical of the Provence region of southern France.

Provolone A soft, yellow, cow's milk cheese with a mild to sharp taste (depending on age) and a smooth-textured interior free of holes. Provolone is made by the *pasta filata* or stretched curd method in which the curd is kneaded and manipulated under hot water or whey. The cheese originated in Campania, in southern Italy, and is descended from similar cheeses made in Roman times. Provolone can be served with fruit and is also a good cooking cheese.

Prune The dried fruit of certain varieties of plum tree. Prunes have a dark, wrinkled appearance and sweet, rich flavor. They are generally soaked and then gently stewed, and served as a dessert, with breakfast cereal or as a filling for tarts and pastries. Prunes can be wrapped with bacon and grilled to serve as finger food or can accompany main course dishes, such as pork. They can also be eaten as a snack, without the need to soak first. Sun-dried prunes have been known since the times of the ancient Romans; today dehydration is usually by artificial heat. Prunes are sold (either pitted or unpitted) in vacuum-sealed packs and cans.

Pudding A soft, creamy, sweet dessert made with eggs, milk and sugar. Puddings can be boiled, baked or frozen. Sweet puddings can be used in pies

and are often topped with cream. Thicker puddings can be steamed and range from rich fruit puddings eaten on festive occasions to rice pudding and bread pudding. The term originally referred to all boiled dishes.

Puff Pastry A rich, crisp, flaky pastry used for both sweet and savory dishes. Its airiness is achieved by a lengthy procedure of rolling and folding the dough to give it a multilayered form.

HOT AND SOUR THAI SHRIMP SOUP

⭐ **Preparation time:** 10 minutes
Total cooking time: 20 minutes
Serves 4

13 oz medium uncooked shrimp
1 tablespoon oil
6 cups water
1 teaspoon chopped garlic
3/4 teaspoon salt
4 red chili peppers
1 stalk lemon grass, thick base only, coarsely chopped

3 dried or fresh kaffir lime leaves
1 tablespoon roughly chopped fresh cilantro
2 scallions, finely sliced
1 red chili pepper, extra, finely sliced
6 teaspoons nuoc mam (fish sauce)
2 tablespoons lime juice

1 Peel and devein shrimp. Reserve heads and shells. Heat the oil in a pan and, when very hot, add the shells and heads. Cook over high heat until they turn pink. Add the water, garlic, salt, chilies, lemon grass and lime leaves. Bring to the boil, reduce to a simmer and cook, uncovered, for 15 minutes.
2 Strain the stock into a clean pan through a double thickness of paper towel placed in a sieve.
3 Add shrimp and heat until simmering. Continue simmering until they have turned pink. This will only take a few minutes. Remove from heat, add cilantro, scallions, chili, nuoc mam and lime juice. Serve at once.

SHRIMP CROUSTADE

⭐⭐ **Preparation time:** 45 minutes
Total cooking time: 35 minutes
Serves 6

1/2 loaf unsliced bread
1/2 cup olive oil
1 clove garlic, crushed

Filling
1 lb uncooked shrimp
1 1/2 cups water
2 slices lemon
1/4 cup butter
6 scallions, chopped

3 tablespoons all-purpose flour
ground pepper
1 tablespoon lemon juice
1 teaspoon dried dill
1/4 cup heavy cream
parsley and lemon, to garnish

1 Preheat the oven to moderately hot 400°F. Remove the crust from the bread, cut into 2 inch thick slices. Cut each slice diagonally to form 2 triangles. Cut a 1/2 inch border around the bread slices, scoop out the center, taking care to leave a base. This provides a cavity in which to place the filling. Heat the oil and garlic together in a small pan, and brush all over the bread cases. Bake for 10 minutes.
2 To make Filling: Shell and devein the shrimp and chop coarsely. Place in a small pan and cover with cold water. Add the lemon slices, and simmer for 15 minutes. Strain and reserve the cooking liquid.
3 Heat the butter in a small pan, cook the chopped scallions until soft, add flour and pepper. Stir over low heat for 2 minutes. Gradually add reserved liquid. Stir constantly over medium heat for 5 minutes or until sauce boils and thickens. Add the lemon juice, dill, cream and shrimp and heat gently for approximately 5 minutes.
4 To serve, spoon filling into bread cases, garnish with parsley and lemon.

PRUNES

BRAISED PORK MEDALLIONS WITH PRUNES

★ **Preparation time:** 15 minutes
Total cooking time: 30 minutes
Serves 4

4 pork loin medallions, about 6 oz each
2 cups chicken stock
2 tablespoons oil
1 large onion, cut into wedges
2 cloves garlic, crushed

1 tablespoon fresh thyme leaves
1 large tomato, peeled, seeded, finely chopped
½ cup heavy cream
16 pitted prunes

1 Trim meat of excess fat and tendons. Shape into rounds by securing a length of string around the medallions. Tie with a bow for easy removal. Place the stock in medium pan, bring to boil. Reduce heat to a simmer, cook, uncovered, for 5 minutes or until reduced to ¾ cup.
2 Heat oil in a heavy-bottom pan, add meat. Cook over high heat 2 minutes each side to seal, turning once; drain on paper towels.
3 Add onion and garlic to pan, stir for 2 minutes. Return meat to pan with thyme, tomato and stock, reduce heat to low. Cover the pan, bring to a simmer and simmer for 10 minutes or until meat is tender, turning once. Add cream and prunes. Simmer for 5 minutes longer and serve.

OPPOSITE PAGE, ABOVE: HOT AND SOUR THAI SHRIMP SOUP; BELOW: SHRIMP CROUSTADE. THIS PAGE: PRUNE AND NUT LOAF

PRUNE AND NUT LOAF

★ **Preparation time:** 40 minutes
Total cooking time: 1 hour
Makes 1 loaf

1 cup whole-wheat flour, sifted
1 cup all-purpose flour
1 cup rolled oats
¾ cup sugar
1 teaspoon baking soda
1 teaspoon pumpkin pie spice

½ cup butter, cubed
2 eggs
½ cup sour cream
¼ cup milk
1 cup chopped pitted prunes
⅓ cup walnut halves

1 Preheat the oven to moderately hot 375°F. Place the flours, oats, sugar, baking soda and pumpkin pie spice in a large bowl and mix well. Rub in the butter with fingertips until mixture resembles bread crumbs.
2 Whisk the eggs and sour cream together in a small bowl. Make a well in the center of the flour and oat mixture. Pour in the egg mixture and the milk and mix to a stiff but moist dough. Mix in the pitted prunes and walnut halves.
3 Spoon the mixture into a greased 5½ x 8½ inch loaf pan. Smooth top and decorate with the extra walnut halves if desired. Bake for about 1 hour or until cooked.
4 Cool loaf in pan for 5 minutes. Turn loaf out onto wire rack to cool completely. Store in an airtight container.

PRUNES IN PORT

★ **Preparation time:** 10 minutes
Total cooking time: 5 minutes
Makes about 4 cups

1½ lb prunes, pits carefully removed
3 cups port
¼ cup soft brown sugar

2 cinnamon sticks
rind of 1 lemon and 1 orange, cut into thin strips

1 Place the prunes in a bowl. Place the port, sugar, cinnamon sticks and rind in a pan. Heat until boiling point is reached.
2 Pour the mixture over prunes. Cool completely. Remove the cinnamon sticks.
3 Place the prunes in sterilized jars. Carefully pour the syrup over the prunes so that they are completely covered. Seal and label the jars. Store the jars in a cool place. Leave for about a week before opening for use. When properly stored, the prunes will keep for up to 12 months.

During baking the pastry rises up to four or five times its original thickness. Although the invention of puff pastry is widely attributed to the seventeenth-century French landscape painter Claude Lorrain, who in his youth trained as a pastry cook, it seems likely that puff pastry was made in the fourteenth century (the Bishop of Amiens listed puff pastry cakes in 1311) and may even have been known in ancient Greece. Puff pastry is similar to mille-feuille and pâte brisée Puff pastry is commercially available frozen in sheets.

Puftaloon Small cakes which are made by deep-frying rounds of a type of scone (biscuit) dough. They are served hot with butter, golden syrup or light corn syrup, or honey.

Pulses The edible seeds, usually dried, of pod-bearing plants; they include lentils, beans and peas. They are a rich source of protein, vitamins and minerals, making them important in a vegetarian diet. Pulses have been a staple food in many parts of the world for thousands of years.

Pumpernickel A solid, dark-colored, strongly flavored bread made from a mixture of rye flour, rye meal and cracked rye grains.

Pumpkin In America pumpkin is one of a variety of winter squash. It is the large, hard-skinned fruit of a trailing vine with golden, nutty-flavored flesh and a central cavity filled with flat, oval seeds. There are many varieties of winter

squash ranging from small, round golden nuggets, to bell-shaped butternuts, pear-shaped hubbards, cylindrical banana pumpkins and yellow spaghetti squash. Most pumpkins are sold in October for Halloween festivities. Pumpkins, like all winter squash, can be served as a vegetable, steamed, boiled (and mashed) or baked; it can be stuffed, made into soups, biscuits, pancakes, sweet pies, cheesecake, bread and chutney. The fragrant, trumpet-shaped blossoms can be chopped

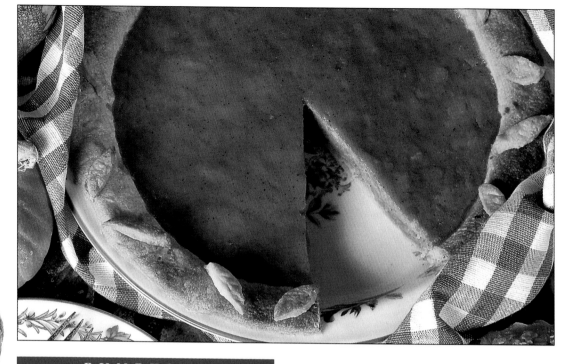

PUMPKINS

PUMPKIN PIE

★ ★ **Preparation time:** 20 minutes + 30 minutes standing
Total cooking time: 55 minutes
Serves 8

1¼ cups all-purpose flour	1 cup soft brown sugar
⅓ cup butter, chopped	1 lb can pumpkin
1 tablespoon sugar	½ cup heavy cream
4 tablespoons water, chilled	1 tablespoon sherry
1 egg yolk, lightly beaten	1 teaspoon ground cinnamon
1 tablespoon milk	½ teaspoon ground nutmeg
Filling	½ teaspoon ground ginger
2 eggs, lightly beaten	

1 Preheat oven to moderate 350°F. Sift the flour into a large mixing bowl; add the chopped butter. Using fingertips, rub the butter into the flour for 2 minutes or until the mixture is a fine, crumbly texture; stir in the sugar. Add almost all the water, mix to a firm dough, adding more liquid if necessary. Turn onto a lightly floured surface, knead for 1 minute or until the dough is smooth. Store, covered with plastic wrap, in refrigerator for at least 30 minutes.

2 Roll out the pastry between 2 sheets of plastic wrap, large enough to cover the base and sides of a 9 inch pie plate; reserve the pastry trimmings. Roll out the trimmings to ⅛ inch thickness and, using a sharp knife, cut into leaf shapes of

different sizes. Score vein markings onto leaves. Beat together the egg yolk with the milk, and brush onto the pastry edge. Arrange the leaves around the pastry edge, pressing gently to attach them. Brush the leaves lightly with the egg mixture.

3 Cut a sheet of wax paper large enough to cover the pastry-lined dish. Spread a layer of dried beans or rice evenly over the paper. Bake for 10 minutes, remove from oven and discard the paper and beans. Return the pastry to oven for 5 minutes or until it is lightly golden. Set aside to cool.

4 To make Filling: Whisk the eggs and sugar in a large mixing bowl. Add pumpkin, cream, sherry and spices and combine thoroughly. Pour into pastry shell and bake for 40 minutes or until set. If pastry edge begins to brown too much during cooking, cover with aluminum foil. Serve at room temperature.

ABOUT PUMPKINS

■ Whole pumpkins can be stored for longer than cut pumpkin. Cover cut pieces with plastic food wrap and store in the refrigerator.

■ Covering the surface of a cut pumpkin from which the seeds have been scooped with a layer of coarse milled black pepper will help prevent it going soft.

■ Raw pumpkin does not freeze well.

ABOVE: PUMPKIN PIE.

OPPOSITE PAGE, ABOVE: PUMPKIN BISCUITS;
BELOW: FRIED PUMPKIN RIBBONS

CURRIED PUMPKIN SOUP

Preparation time: 15 minutes
Total cooking time: 45 minutes
Serves 6

1 medium onion,
  chopped
1 clove garlic, crushed
¼ cup butter
1½–2 lb pumpkin,
  peeled, cubed, steamed
  and mashed
pinch each of sugar and
  nutmeg
1 tablespoon curry powder

1 bay leaf
4 cups chicken stock
2 cups milk (or skim
  milk if preferred)
¼ cup heavy cream
freshly ground black
  pepper and fresh chives
  to garnish

1 In a large saucepan, sauté onion and garlic in butter until very soft, about 5 minutes. Add mashed pumpkin, sugar, nutmeg, curry powder and bay leaf. Season to taste. Stir in stock and heat until boiling.
2 Reduce heat and simmer gently for 30 minutes. Remove from heat. Discard bay leaf.
3 Stir in milk and heat for 2–3 minutes. Serve with a swirl of cream, pepper and chopped chives.

FRIED PUMPKIN RIBBONS

Peel 1 lb pumpkin. Peel pumpkin into ribbons using a vegetable peeler. Heat a medium pan half-filled with oil. Deep-fry pumpkin ribbons in batches until crisp and golden. Drain on paper towels. Sprinkle with salt and pepper to taste. Serve warm.

PUMPKIN BISCUITS

Preparation time: 35 minutes
Total cooking time: 12 minutes
Makes 12

2 tablespoons butter
⅓ cup sugar
½ cup mashed pumpkin
1 egg, lightly beaten
¼ cup milk

2½ cups all-purpose
  flour, sifted
1 teaspoon baking powder
¼ teaspoon salt

1 Preheat oven to 425°F. Cream butter and sugar together until light and fluffy. Mix in pumpkin, egg and milk.
2 Lightly fold in flour, baking powder and salt and mix until a soft dough is formed.
3 Turn the dough out onto a floured board. Knead lightly. Press or roll out to form a round about ¾ inch thick.
4 Cut into rounds using a floured plain cutter. Place on greased baking sheet. Glaze with a little milk. Bake for 10–12 minutes. Serve warm with butter.

SWEET SPICED PUMPKIN

Peel 1 lb of pumpkin. Cut into thin slices. Place on a greased foil-lined baking sheet. Melt 3 tablespoons of butter. Brush over pumpkin. In a bowl, place ½ teaspoon each of ground cumin, ground coriander, ground ginger and 1 teaspoon soft brown sugar. Mix well and sprinkle over the pumpkin. Bake in moderate 350°F oven for 35 minutes or until cooked through. Serve warm.

into salads, fried in butter or stuffed; pumpkin seeds can be toasted, tossed in salt and eaten as a snack. Pumpkins are native to the Americas and were cultivated perhaps as early as 10,000 years ago. Pumpkins, like all winter squash, come in many sizes. Look for smooth, dry, dull rind that is free of dents, cracks or soft spots. Winter squash can be stored uncut for up to three months in a cool, dry place. Deep orange in color, pumpkins can weigh 200 pounds, but smaller, sweeter varieties are best used as pie fillings, or for other cooking.

Punch A hot or cold beverage consisting of a mixture of fruit juice, water, often carbonated liquid and sometimes alcohol. Apart from fruit juices, ingredients can include champagne, wine, spirits, lemonade, soda and mineral water.

Purée A thick, creamy liquid or paste made by processing a solid food in a blender or food processor or pushing it through a sieve.

Puri A flat, unleavened deep-fried whole-wheat Indian bread. The dough is rolled thin, cut into rounds and then deep-fried until puffed and golden brown.

Q

Quahog A round hard-shelled clam found on the Atlantic coast. Also known as cherrystone.

Quail A small game bird with mottled brown plumage found in flat open country in Europe, Asia, North America, Africa and Australia. Quail can be roasted (with a veal- or pork-based stuffing), split, flattened and broiled, barbecued, pan-fried (with grapes), or casseroled. It has delicate flesh and care should be taken not to dry it out. Baste frequently to keep the flesh moist. In northern Italy, quail is often marinated in wine, sage, rosemary and pepper, then simmered in the marinade and served on slices of broiled polenta. Quail is best in autumn, when the bird is plump and the flesh full-flavored. Serve two per person.

Quail eggs are plum-shaped and greenish-beige with dark brown markings, and about one-third the size of hen's eggs. They may be served hard-boiled in salads or in aspic, and are

QUICHES

QUICHE LORRAINE

★ **Preparation time:** 30 minutes + 20 minutes refrigeration
Total cooking time: 1 hour 10 minutes
Serves 10–12

Pastry
1½ cups all-purpose flour
6 tablespoons butter, chopped
1 egg
1 tablespoon water, approximately

Filling
10 slices bacon
6 eggs
⅔ cup milk
1¼ cups heavy cream
salt and pepper
½ cup grated Swiss cheese

1 To make Pastry: Place flour and butter in food processor. Process for 30 seconds or until mixture is fine and crumbly. Add egg and almost all the water, process for 20 seconds or until mixture just comes together when squeezed, adding more water if required. Turn onto a lightly floured board. Knead mixture gently to form a smooth dough. Refrigerate, covered with plastic wrap, for 20 minutes. Preheat oven to moderately hot 400°F.

2 Roll pastry on a floured board large enough to fit a 13 inch round loose-bottomed flan pan. Ease pastry into pan. Trim edge with a sharp knife. Cut a sheet of parchment paper large enough to cover pastry-lined pan. Place paper over pastry; spread a layer of dried beans or rice evenly over paper. Bake for 15 minutes, remove paper and beans; bake for another 10 minutes or until pastry is lightly browned; cool. Reduce oven temperature to moderate 350°F.

3 To make Filling: Reserve 4 slices of bacon. Chop the remaining bacon. Heat the pan, cook bacon until crisp; drain on paper towels. Combine the eggs, milk, cream, salt and pepper in a jug. Whisk well. Sprinkle the bacon into the pastry case, pour the cream mixture over. Cut the reserved bacon in half crosswise. Lay strips over the cream mixture and sprinkle with cheese. Bake for 40 minutes or until cooked through and golden. Serve hot or cold.

Note: Do not overwork the dough when making pastry in a food processor or the pastry will be tough.

ABOVE: QUICHE LORRAINE.
OPPOSITE PAGE: CHICKEN AND CORN QUICHE

CHICKEN AND CORN QUICHE

Preparation time: 35 minutes +
20 minutes refrigeration
Total cooking time: 1 hour
Serves 4

1 cup all-purpose flour
1/4 cup butter, chopped
1 egg yolk
1/2 cup grated Cheddar cheese
1–2 tablespoons iced water

Filling
2 tablespoons butter, chopped
1 medium onion, finely chopped

1 1/2 cups chopped cooked chicken
4 oz can corn kernels, drained
1/2 medium red pepper, chopped
2 eggs
1/2 cup heavy cream
1/2 cup milk
1/4 cup grated Cheddar cheese
1 tablespoon chopped

1 Place flour into a large mixing bowl; add chopped butter. Using fingertips, rub butter into flour until mixture is fine and crumbly. Add egg yolk, grated cheese and enough water to mix to a firm dough. Turn onto a lightly floured surface, knead gently for 30 seconds or until smooth. Refrigerate, covered with plastic wrap, for 20 minutes.
2 Preheat oven to moderately hot 400°F. Brush a

shallow 8 inch round cake pan with melted butter or oil. Roll out the pastry between two sheets of plastic wrap, large enough to cover base and sides of pan. Ease pastry into pan; trim edge with a sharp knife.
3 Cut a sheet of waxed paper large enough to cover pastry-lined pan. Line pastry with paper, spread a layer of dried beans or rice evenly over paper. Bake 10 minutes, remove from oven and discard the paper and beans. Return to oven for another 7 minutes or until lightly golden. Cool.
4 To make Filling: Reduce oven to moderate 350°F. Heat butter in small pan, cook onion until just soft; drain on paper towels. Spread onion, chicken, corn and pepper over pastry. Combine the remaining ingredients in a large bowl; mix well. Pour over chicken mixture. Bake 35 minutes, or until lightly browned and set. Stand in pan for 5 minutes before cutting for serving. Serve warm or cold with a green salad.

INDIVIDUAL SEAFOOD QUICHES

Preparation time: 30 minutes
Total cooking time: 30 minutes
Serves 8

8 sheets frozen filo (phyllo) dough, thawed
1/4 cup butter, melted
5 oz small, peeled, cooked shrimp
5 oz fresh scallops, cleaned and halved
3 eggs
3/4 cup heavy cream

1/2 cup milk
4 scallions, chopped
1/4 cup grated Cheddar cheese
2 tablespoons all-purpose flour
1 tablespoon chopped fresh lemon thyme

1 Preheat the oven to moderate 350°F. Brush eight 3 inch flan pans with melted butter or oil. Layer four sheets of filo (phyllo) together, brushing each layer with melted butter. Cut the stack of filo in half, cut each half into four squares. Repeat with the remaining pastry and butter. Line each flan pan with four squares of pastry placed at right angles to each other. Brush with any remaining melted butter.
2 Divide the shrimp and scallops between the prepared pans. In a large bowl combine the eggs, cream, milk, chopped scallions, cheese and flour; mix well. Pour the mixture over the prepared seafood, sprinkle with the chopped lemon thyme, and bake for 30 minutes or until golden brown and set. Leave to stand in the flan pans for 5 minutes. Serve warm with a green salad and hot crusty bread.

available pickled. Farm-raised quail (fresh and frozen) and quail eggs are available from specialist game and poultry stores.

Quark Lowfat curd cheese made in Austria and Germany. It can have a smooth consistency or be in the form of small curds, like cottage cheese.

Quatre Épices See Four Spices.

Queen of Puddings A baked dessert consisting of a layer of bread crumbs, milk and egg yolk, spread with strawberry jam, cooked and cooled, then topped with meringue and returned to the oven until meringue is crisp.

Quenelle A small, light, savory dumpling made from finely chopped or puréed fish, meat or poultry, bound with egg and flour, formed into an egg or sausage shape and poached. Quenelles are usually served with a rich sauce as a first course; small quenelles can also garnish soup. The name comes from the German *Knödel*, dumpling.

Quiche An open tart with a thin pastry shell (usually pie crust) filled with a rich savory egg custard flavored with ham, cheese, onion, leek, spinach, mushroom, asparagus or seafood. Quiche is usually served warm as a first or a light main course; miniature versions are often served as finger food; and cold quiche is a popular picnic food. The quiche originated in Nancy, in Lorraine, on the French-German border, where it was originally made with bread dough. Quiche Lorraine, with a filling of egg and ham or bacon, is a specialty of the region; true quiche Lorraine should never contain cheese, which is thought to be a Parisian addition. The name comes from the German *kuchen*, cake.

Quick Bread Bread that is quick to make because it is leavened with baking powder or baking soda.

Quince A large, fragrant, yellow-skinned fruit, round to pear-shaped and usually too hard and sour to eat raw. When cooked, quince has a

soft, pink, delicately sweet flesh with the slightly grainy texture of stewed pear. The quince is related to the apple and the pear. Quince is stewed slowly as a filling for pies and tarts, baked whole as a dessert, made into quince paste to serve with soft, ripe

VEGETABLE QUICHE

★★ **Preparation time:** 40 minutes + 20 minutes refrigeration
Total cooking time: 50 minutes
Serves 4–6

1 cup all-purpose flour
½ cup whole-wheat flour
⅓ cup butter, chopped
1–2 tablespoons lemon juice

1 small red pepper, cut into ¾ inch squares
1 medium onion, chopped
3 tablespoons butter
3 tablespoons all-purpose flour
1 cup milk
2 egg yolks
1 cup finely grated Cheddar cheese
freshly ground black pepper, to taste
4 oz canned corn kernels, drained

Filling
3½ oz broccoli, cut into small florets
2 small zucchini, cut into ¾ inch slices
5 oz pumpkin, cut into ¾ inch cubes
2 teaspoons oil

1 Place flours into a large mixing bowl. Using fingertips, rub butter into flour for 2 minutes or until mixture is fine and crumbly. Add almost all the lemon juice, mix to a firm dough, adding more liquid if necessary. Turn onto a lightly floured surface, press together until smooth. Brush an 8 inch fluted flan pan with oil. Roll out pastry large enough to cover base and side of pan. Ease pastry into pan; trim. Refrigerate, covered with plastic wrap 20 minutes.
2 Preheat oven to 350°F. Line pastry with a sheet of waxed paper large enough to cover; spread a

layer of dried beans or rice evenly over paper. Bake for 10 minutes, remove from oven and discard paper and beans. Return to the oven for 10 minutes more or until lightly golden. Set aside to cool.
3 To make Filling: Steam broccoli, zucchini and pumpkin until just tender. Drain. Heat oil in a heavy-bottom frying pan and cook peppers and onion over medium heat until soft. Set aside. Heat butter in a small pan; add flour. Stir over low heat 2 minutes or until mixture is just golden. Add milk gradually to pan, stirring until mixture is smooth. Stir constantly over medium heat until mixture boils and thickens; boil 1 minute and remove from heat. Beat in egg yolks until mixture is smooth; stir in cheese.
4 Place the cooked vegetables in a large bowl. Add corn and pepper. Pour hot sauce over; mix. Pour vegetable mixture into pastry shell. Bake for 20 minutes, until top is golden. Serve warm.

BLUE CHEESE QUICHE

★★ **Preparation time:** 50 minutes + 20 minutes refrigeration
Total cooking time: 50 minutes
Serves 4–6

1 cup all-purpose flour
½ cup ground walnuts
¼ cup butter, chopped
1–2 tablespoons water

Filling
5 oz blue cheese
½ cup heavy cream
2 eggs, lightly beaten
1 tablespoon chopped fresh parsley

1 Place flour into a bowl; add walnuts and butter. Rub butter into flour with your fingertips until the mixture is fine and crumbly. Add 1 tablespoon water; mix to a firm dough, adding more water if necessary. Turn the dough out onto a lightly floured surface and roll out large enough to cover base and side of an 8 inch flan pan. Ease pastry into pan; trim. Refrigerate for 20 minutes.
2 Preheat oven to moderate 350°F. Line pastry with a sheet of wax paper large enough to cover; spread a layer of dried beans or rice evenly over paper. Bake 10 minutes, discard paper and beans, return pastry to oven for another 10 minutes or until lightly golden. Cool.
3 To make Filling: Place the cheese in a mixing bowl and lightly mash. Add the cream, eggs and chopped parsley, whisking to combine. Pour into the prepared pastry shell and bake for 30 minutes, until the filling is puffed and golden. Serve warm.

4 Halfway through cooking time for the lamb, add the cooked onion, quinces and prunes. Serve the cooked lamb on a warmed serving dish.

Note: This is a Moroccan dish and one of the most successful combinations of meat and fruit. Substitute hot paprika if a spicier flavor is preferred. Dates can be used instead of prunes and pears instead of quinces.

QUINCE CONSERVE

✦ ✦   **Preparation time:** 30 minutes
Total cooking time: 1½ hours
Makes 6 cups

3 lb quinces	*¾ cup lemon juice*
3 quarts water	*5½ cups sugar, warmed*
2 teaspoons grated lemon rind	

1 Peel and core quinces and slice thinly. Place peel and cores in cheesecloth and tie.
2 Combine quinces, cheesecloth bag, water and rind in a large pan or boiler. Bring to the boil and simmer, covered, for about 50 minutes or until fruit is pulpy. Discard cheesecloth bag. Stir in the lemon juice.
3 Add the warm sugar and stir until dissolved. Boil rapidly, uncovered, for about 40 minutes or until setting point is reached.
4 Remove cooked conserve from heat, stand for 10 minutes. Pour into warm, sterilized jars and seal immediately. When cool, label and date jars.

QUINCE

TAGINE OF LAMB WITH QUINCES

✦   **Preparation time:** 50 minutes
Total cooking time: 1 hour
Serves 6

2 lb shoulder of lamb cut in ¾ inch cubes	*¼ teaspoon ground saffron*
2 large onions, chopped in ¾ inch cubes	*½ teaspoon ground ginger*
ground pepper	*1 lb quinces cored, halved and peeled*
½ teaspoon mildly hot paprika	*¼ cup butter*
1 bunch fresh cilantro, finely chopped	*1 cup pitted prunes, pre-soaked*

1 Place cubed lamb and one of the chopped onions in a large heavy-bottom pan. Season to taste with pepper and paprika and cover with water.
2 Add fresh cilantro, saffron and ginger. Bring to the boil, reduce heat, cover and simmer for about an hour, or until lamb is tender.
3 Cut the quinces into roughly the same sized pieces as the meat. Cook the quinces and the second onion together in butter in a pan until lightly golden.

OPPOSITE PAGE: VEGETABLE QUICHE. THIS PAGE, ABOVE: TAGINE OF LAMB WITH QUINCES; RIGHT: QUINCE CONSERVE

cheese, roasted whole as an accompaniment for game; and, pectin-rich, is often made into jellies, jams and conserves Quinces preserved in syrup are an old-time dessert favorite in northern Italy. In Middle Eastern cooking it is often stuffed with peas, beans or ground beef and spices.

The quince originated in Asia, and reached the eastern Mediterranean in ancient times. It was popular with the ancient Greeks, who ate it hollowed out and baked with honey. As the fruit travelled north and west, its name changed: in southern France *kydonia* became *cydonea*, in northern France, *coing*, and in England, quince. In Greek mythology the quince was the famous golden apple awarded by Paris to Aphrodite, goddess of love. Since the time of the ancients the fruit has been a symbol of love, marriage and fertility and in medieval Europe a gift of quinces was regarded as a declaration of serious ardor.

R

Rabbit A small, furred animal of the hare family. Young rabbit bred for the table has lean and tender white flesh similar to chicken; wild rabbit has darker, more stringy meat. Rabbit is often marinated in wine seasoned with shallots, garlic and thyme; it can be sautéed, stewed, roasted or casseroled. Rabbits can be bought ready to cook, fresh or frozen, from specialist butchers.

Rack of Lamb A portion of the rib section of lamb containing approximately eight ribs.

Radicchio A salad vegetable resembling a small head of red cabbage with peppery flavored leaves. The two main varieties are Verona (small and round) and Treviso (long leaves). Radicchio adds a bitter bite to mixed-green salads or it may be braised or grilled and served with meat or poultry. Originally from Italy, growers in the United States have only recently begun to

RASPBERRIES

RASPBERRY MOUSSE CAKE

★★ **Preparation time:** 35 minutes + refrigeration
Total cooking time: 15 minutes
Serves 8

⅓ cup all-purpose flour
3 tablespoons cornstarch
½ teaspoon baking powder
2 eggs
½ cup sugar

½ cup sugar
8 oz package cream cheese, softened
1 cup heavy cream
1 envelope unsweetened gelatin
2 tablespoons water

Raspberry Mousse
13 oz fresh or frozen raspberries
1 egg or ¼ cup egg substitute

confectioners' sugar for serving

1 Preheat the oven to moderate 350°F. Brush an 8-inch round springform pan with melted butter or oil.
2 Sift the flour and cornstarch 3 times onto wax paper. Using electric beaters, beat the eggs in a small mixing bowl for 3 minutes or until thick and pale. Add the sugar gradually, beating constantly until dissolved and mixture is pale yellow and glossy.
3 Transfer mixture to large mixing bowl. Using a metal spoon, fold in dry ingredients quickly and lightly. Spread mixture evenly into prepared pan.

Bake for 15 minutes or until sponge is lightly golden and shrinks from side of pan. Leave sponge in pan for 3 minutes before turning onto wire rack to cool.
4 To make Raspberry Mousse: Process 10 oz of the raspberries to a smooth texture in a blender or food processor, pass through a fine sieve. Reserve half of the purée for serving. Using electric beaters, beat the egg, or egg substitute, and sugar in a small bowl until creamy. Add the cream cheese, beat until smooth. In a separate bowl beat the cream until soft peaks form.
5 Combine gelatin with water in small bowl, stand bowl in hot water, stir until gelatin dissolves. Using a metal spoon, fold gelatin, half of the raspberry purée and remaining whole raspberries into cream cheese mixture, then fold in cream. Cover with plastic wrap and refrigerate for 10 minutes or until mixture has thickened, stirring occasionally.
6 To assemble, cut the cake in half horizontally. Return the first cake layer to the springform pan. Spread cake evenly with mousse. Top with the remaining cake layer, refrigerate until the mousse has set.
7 For serving, sift the confectioners' sugar over the top of the cake. Cut the cake into wedges. Place on individual serving plates and spoon the reserved raspberry purée around the cake.

ABOVE: RASPBERRY MOUSSE CAKE.
OPPOSITE PAGE: RASPBERRY CHICKEN SALAD

RASPBERRY AND STRAWBERRY RIPPLE

★ ★ Preparation time: 20 minutes + freezing
Total cooking time: none
Serves 8–10

1 lb strawberries
1½ cups sugar
2 tablespoons lemon juice
2¼ cups cream, lightly whipped

4 oz raspberries
½ cup sugar, extra
raspberries and strawberries, extra, for serving

1 Line the base and sides of a 7-cup capacity loaf pan with foil. Remove stems from strawberries. Place in a food processor with sugar and juice. Process for 30 seconds or until quite smooth.
2 Reserve ⅓ cup whipped cream, fold remaining cream into strawberry mixture. Pour into metal freezer tray. Freeze, stirring occasionally, until thick. Do not allow mixture to freeze solid.
3 Using a food processor, blend raspberries and extra sugar. Fold into the reserved cream and mix well.
4 Spoon a layer of strawberry ice cream over base of the prepared pan. Spoon the raspberry mixture and the remaining strawberry ice cream randomly over the base. Using a sharp knife or a skewer, swirl the mixtures together, being careful not to dig into foil. Freeze for 3–4 hours or overnight. Serve in scoops or remove from pan and cut into slices. Garnish with the extra raspberries and strawberries.

RASPBERRY CHICKEN SALAD

★ Preparation time: 15 minutes
Total cooking time: 10 minutes
Serves 4

4 medium boneless chicken breast halves, skinned, about 12 oz
1 cup white wine
1 cup water
1 bunch curly endive
1 bunch watercress
⅓ cup olive oil

3 tablespoons raspberry vinegar
½ teaspoon Dijon-style mustard
salt and freshly ground black pepper, to taste
1 pint fresh raspberries

1 Trim chicken of excess fat. Cover and bring to the boil. Reduce heat, add chicken to pan, cover and simmer gently 10 minutes or until cooked through. Remove from pan. Drain, cool and cut into slices.
2 Wash and dry endive, lettuce and watercress. Tear into bite-size pieces, discarding thicker stems of watercress. Place greens in a large mixing bowl.
3 Place olive oil, vinegar, mustard, salt and pepper in a small screw-top jar and shake well. Pour one-third of the dressing over leaves and toss lightly to combine. Place ⅓ cup of the raspberries and the remaining dressing in food processor. Blend or process, using the pulse action, until smooth. Arrange salad leaves on serving plates, top with chicken slices and remaining raspberries. Drizzle with raspberry dressing and serve immediately.

RASPBERRY JAM

★ Preparation time: 30 minutes
Total cooking time: 15 minutes
Makes 3 cups

2 lb raspberries
2 lb sugar, warmed

1 teaspoon cream of tartar

1 Check fruit and discard hulls and any leaves. Place raspberries in a large stainless steel pan and mash fruit lightly with a potato masher to release juice. Heat fruit gently until boiling, stirring occasionally.
2 Add warmed sugar, stir until it dissolves; return mixture to boil. Cook rapidly for 3 minutes, add the cream of tartar and boil for another 5 minutes or until setting point is reached.
3 Cool jam slightly and pour into hot sterilized jars. Seal jars, and when cool label and date. Store jam in a cool dark place.

cultivate it. A variety of chicory, radicchio is available fresh throughout the year.

Radish A root vegetable with peppery tasting crunchy white flesh. The roots range in size, shape and skin color from small, round and red to long, thin and white. Radish is eaten raw with dips, in salads and as a garnish; it can also be boiled or steamed as a vegetable. Daikon, a giant white radish, is an important ingredient in the cooking of Japan and China. The radish has been grown in China for more than 3000 years. Radish is available fresh throughout the year; daikon is sold fresh and pickled.

Ragoût A French term for a stew made from cubes of meat, poultry, fish, game or vegetables cooked in a thickened, well-seasoned broth.

Raisin A grape of a sweet variety dried either naturally in the sun or artificially. Raisins are sprinkled on

breakfast cereal, added to rice and salads and used in fruit cakes, candies and cookies. Varieties include: dark seedless grapes, golden seedless grapes, large sundried muscat raisins, soft sultanas and currants.

Rambutan A small oval fruit with a thick red skin covered with soft spines. Its pale-colored translucent flesh is similar in taste to a grape. Peeled and pitted, the rambutan is added to fruit salad, green salad or fish salad. Related to the lychee and longan, the rambutan is available canned.

Rape A member of the cabbage family with edible leaves. The source of rapeseed oil.

Rapeseed Oil See Canola Oil.

Rarebit Also known as Welsh rarebit, a hot snack consisting of cheese melted with beer, seasoned with mustard or Worcestershire sauce, spread on toast and browned under a broiler.

Raspberry The soft, fragrant, juicy fruit of a thorny plant related to the

rose. Raspberries can be served fresh, with cream

RASPBERRY COCONUT COOKIES

★★ **Preparation time:** 45 minutes
Total cooking time: 8–10 minutes (per batch)
Makes 28

Cookie Dough
1/4 cup unsalted butter
2/3 cup sugar
1 large egg
1 1/2 cups all-purpose flour
1 teaspoon baking powder
1/4 teaspoon salt

Icing
4 oz pink or white marshmallows
3 tablespoons butter
1/3 cup confectioners' sugar, sifted
2/3 cup finely grated coconut
1/2 cup raspberry jam

1 Preheat oven to moderate 350°F. Lightly grease two baking sheets; set aside.

2 To make Cookie Dough: Beat the butter and sugar in a large bowl until creamy. Beat in egg. Combine flour, baking powder, and salt; stir into butter mixture.

3 Turn dough onto lightly floured surface. Knead gently for 1 minute or until smooth. Roll out dough to 1/8 inch thickness (about 14 x 10 inches). Using a knife or fluted pastry wheel, cut into 2 x 2 1/2 inch rectangles. Place on prepared baking sheets about 1 inch apart. Bake for 10 minutes or until lightly golden around edges. Transfer to wire rack to cool.

4 To make Icing: In a medium saucepan combine the marshmallows and butter. Stir over low heat until the marshmallows and butter are melted and smooth. Stir in the confectioners' sugar; mix until smooth. Place the coconut on a sheet of wax paper. Working quickly, spread about 1/4 teaspoon of icing along each long side of the cookies, leaving a space in the center. Dip each iced cookie into coconut; shake off any excess coconut. In a small saucepan heat the jam until it is thinned and warm. Spread a little jam down the center of each cookie. Set aside until the jam has hardened.

RASPBERRY SAUCE

Heat 8 oz raspberries and 1 tablespoon sugar in a small pan, stirring until the sugar is melted. Purée in a blender or food processor or push through a sieve with a wooden spoon. Set aside until cool. This can be served over ice cream or as a sauce with rich chocolate cake or lemon tart. It is best made on the day you wish to serve it.

RIGHT: RASPBERRY COCONUT COOKIES

or ice cream, added to fruit salad, puréed for use in desserts and sauces or as a filling in tarts. Raspberries are available fresh summer to autumn, and can also be bought frozen.

Ratatouille A stew of vegetables from the Provence region of France, traditionally consisting of eggplant, zucchini, onion, summer squash, tomato and garlic. Sometimes red pepper is added and the mixture is simmered in olive oil.

Ravigote Sauce A seasoned, spicy sauce. Cold ravigote, a vinaigrette mixed with capers, herbs and onion, is served with cold meat and fish. Hot ravigote is made by cooking chopped shallots in wine vinegar, scallions, white sauce and chopped parsley, tarragon, chives and chervil. Ravigote butter is flavored with minced shallots, herbs and sometimes mustard.

Ravioli Small squares of pasta filled with meat, cheese or vegetable mixtures which are boiled in water. They are served with a sauce and sprinkled with grated Parmesan cheese as a first course or main dish. Ravioli can be made at home or bought fresh or frozen.

Red Beans and Rice
A Louisiana dish of kidney beans and ham hocks boiled and served over rice. Musician Louis Armstrong signed his letters, "Red beans and ricely yours".

Red Cabbage A red-leafed cabbage, similar in taste to green cabbage. It is often pickled or served raw in salads.

Red Currant See Currant.

Reduce To boil down a sauce or gravy to concentrate its flavor and thicken its consistency.

Refresh To plunge lightly boiled vegetables into cold water to halt the cooking process and maintain their color.

Rémoulade Sauce A spicy mayonnaise-based sauce flavored with tarragon, chervil, parsley, gherkins and anchovies. Served with cold poultry, fish, shellfish, meat and eggs.

Rendang A hot and spicy Indonesian curry made from cubed beef, mutton or chicken fried with spices and then cooked slowly in coconut milk until the meat is tender and the gravy thick and paste-like.

RATATOUILLE

RATATOUILLE

⭐ **Preparation time:** 30 minutes + 30 minutes standing
Total cooking time: 45 minutes
Serves 4–6

2 medium eggplant, (about 1 lb each)
salt
½ cup olive oil
1 large onion, chopped
2 cloves garlic, crushed
2 medium zucchini, cut into ¼ inch slices
2 tablespoons red wine vinegar

2 teaspoons sugar
freshly ground pepper
2 medium ripe tomatoes, peeled, seeded and chopped
¼ cup dry white wine
¼ cup grated Parmesan cheese

1 Cut eggplant into ½ inch slices. Sprinkle lightly with salt. Place in a colander and let stand for 30 minutes. Wash salt off eggplant and pat dry with paper towels.
2 In a large skillet heat the oil. Add the onion and cook until tender and brown. Add eggplant slices and garlic to onion mixture and cook until eggplant is brown, turning eggplant once. Remove from skillet. Add zucchini and cook until brown.
3 Transfer all vegetables to saucepan. Add vinegar, sugar and pepper. Stir in tomatoes and wine. Bring to boil; reduce heat. Cover; simmer 30 minutes. Sprinkle with Parmesan cheese before serving.

RATATOUILLE SQUARES

⭐ **Preparation time:** 15 minutes
Total cooking time: 45 minutes
Makes 4 tarts

2 sheets frozen puff pastry, thawed
1 egg, lightly beaten
1 tablespoon olive oil
1 medium onion, finely sliced
2 cloves garlic, crushed
2 medium long slender eggplant, cut into ½ inch slices

2 medium zucchini, cut into ½ inch slices
1 medium red pepper, cut into ¾ inch squares
1 medium green pepper, cut into ¾ inch squares
2 medium tomatoes, coarsely chopped

1 Preheat oven to moderate 350°F. Brush one pastry sheet with egg; top with the other sheet. Cut pastry into four squares. Place on large baking sheet and cook for 20 minutes until puffed and golden. Set aside to cool.
2 Heat the oil in a large heavy-based frying pan, cook the onion and garlic over medium heat for 5 minutes. Add the eggplant, zucchini and red peppers. Cook, covered, for 10 minutes, stirring occasionally.
3 Add the tomato and cook uncovered for 10 minutes, stirring occasionally, until most of the liquid has evaporated. To serve, cut a 3 inch round hole in the top of each of the pastry squares, and pull out the soft pastry in the center. Fill each of the cavities with ratatouille and serve immediately.

RHUBARB

SPICED RHUBARB AND PEAR COBBLER

⭐ **Preparation time:** 25 minutes
Total cooking time: 40 minutes
Serves 4

13 oz rhubarb
3 large pears, peeled
1 tablespoon finely grated orange rind
1 tablespoon finely grated lemon rind
1/2 teaspoon pumpkin pie spice
1/2 cup sugar
2 tablespoons marsala
2 tablespoons orange juice

Batter
1/4 cup flaked coconut
1/2 cup all-purpose flour

1/4 cup sugar
1/2 teaspoon baking powder
2 eggs, lightly beaten
2 tablespoons milk
2 tablespoons butter, melted

Topping
1 cup fresh white bread crumbs
1/2 cup sugar
4 tablespoons flaked or shredded coconut
1/4 cup butter, melted

1 Preheat the oven to moderate 350°F. Brush a deep, 6-cup capacity rectangular ovenproof dish with melted butter or oil. Wash the rhubarb, cut the stalks into 1¼ inch lengths. Cut the pears into ¾ inch cubes. Combine the rhubarb, pears, orange and lemon rinds, pumpkin pie spice, sugar,

OPPOSITE PAGE, ABOVE: RATATOUILLE; BELOW: RATATOUILLE SQUARES. ABOVE: SPICED RHUBARB AND PEAR COBBLER; RIGHT: RHUBARB FOOL

marsala and orange juice in a large pan. Cover and simmer for 10 minutes, stirring occasionally. Remove pan from heat. Keep warm.

2 To make Batter: Place the coconut, flour, sugar and baking powder into a medium mixing bowl; make a well in the center. Add combined egg, milk and butter all at once. Whisk until all liquid is incorporated and batter is smooth and free of lumps.

3 Pour hot fruit into prepared dish. Pour batter evenly over the top.

4 To make Topping: Combine the bread crumbs, sugar, coconut and butter in a small mixing bowl, and sprinkle over the batter. Bake the cobbler for 30 minutes or until a skewer comes out clean when inserted in the center. Serve immediately.

RHUBARB FOOL

Cut a bunch of rhubarb into ½ inch lengths, place in a colander and wash well. Place the rhubarb in a pan with just enough water to prevent it from sticking, 3 tablespoons sugar and a pinch of ground cinnamon. Cover and simmer for 15–20 minutes or until the rhubarb is very soft. Remove from the heat; beat with a wooden spoon until smooth. Leave to cool; add 5 fl oz lightly whipped cream and stir well. Serve as a dessert or with hot croissants for breakfast.

Rennet A substance made from the stomach lining of unweaned calves. It is used to coagulate milk in the making of junket and hard cheese. Rennet is available in tablet form (often in a variety of flavors) for making desserts and ice cream.

Rhubarb The pink, fleshy stalks of a leafy vegetable cooked, sweetened and eaten as a dessert or breakfast dish. The trimmed stalks are cut into short lengths and stewed, poached or baked in a sugar syrup until tender; serve warm or cold or use as a filling for pies, tarts and cobblers. The leaves contain poisonous oxalic acid and must not be eaten. Rhubarb is sold fresh all year but is best in autumn and winter.

Rice The small oval grain from a semi-aquatic grass cultivated in warm climates. An important food (it is the staple of more than half the world's people), it is always eaten cooked, either hot or cold. Brown rice is the whole kernel with just the inedible husk removed; it has a chewy texture and a slightly nutty flavor.

White (polished) rice is the inner kernel. Types of white rice include long-grain, with long narrow kernels. It is popular in Asia and when cooked the grains remain separate; it is used for plain boiled rice, rice salads and in stuffings. Most white rice now on the market is nutritionally enriched with a dusting of iron, niacin and thiamin. Do not wash this rice before cooking. Medium grain rice has plump oval kernels which when cooked are moist enough to hold together yet are still distinct. Short-grain rice, also called pearl or round rice has kernels that clump together when cooked; short

grained rice is used in Italy to make risotto and in Spain to make paella. An Asian short-grained variety is a glutinous or sticky rice and is the preferred rice for sweet dishes in Asia. Quick cooking rice has been cooked and then dehydrated. Parboiled rice is pressure steamed before packaging, and is fluffy after cooking. Converted rice is first parboiled, then dried; the starch content is reduced and the grain is especially fluffy. Wild rice is the seed of an aquatic grass, and is native to the lakes of Minnesota.

RICE

BALINESE-STYLE FRIED RICE

★ ★ **Preparation time:** 45 minutes
Total cooking time: 10–11 minutes
Serves 6

2 teaspoons vegetable oil
2 eggs, lightly beaten
2 medium onions, coarsely chopped
2 cloves garlic
3 tablespoons vegetable oil
1/4 teaspoon shrimp paste
8 medium shrimp, peeled and deveined
1/2 cup lean cooked beef cut into bite-size strips

1/2 cup cooked chicken cut into bite-size strips
1 tablespoon soy sauce
1 tablespoon fish sauce
1 tablespoon sambal oelek
1 tablespoon tomato paste
6 scallions, finely chopped
5 cups cold, cooked rice
scallions, 1 small cucumber, red chili peppers, for garnish

1 Heat 2 teaspoons of oil in a wok or a very large non-stick skillet over medium heat. Season eggs with a little salt and pepper. Add eggs to wok. Lift and tilt the wok to form a thin omelet.
2 Cook, without stirring, 2 minutes or just until set. Slide omelet onto cutting board to cool. Roll up jelly-roll style. Cut into 3/4 inch wide strips; place on plate and set aside.
3 Place onions and garlic in a food processor or blender. Cover and process until well combined or finely chop by hand using a sharp knife. Heat 3 tablespoons of oil in a wok over medium-high heat. Add onion mixture. Stir-fry for 4–5 minutes

or until onion is soft and lightly browned. Add the shrimp paste. Stir-fry for 1 minute.
3 Add shrimp, beef and chicken. Stir-fry 1 minute. Combine soy sauce, fish sauce, sambal oelek and tomato paste; add to wok. Add scallions and rice. Stir-fry 2 minutes or until heated through. Transfer to warm serving platter. Add omelet strips on top. Garnish with Green Onion Brushes, Cucumber Garnish and Chili Flowers.
4 To make Green Onion Brushes: Take a 3 inch piece of scallion; cut a thin crosswise ring of red chili. Thread scallion through chili ring. Make thin, parallel cuts from one end of the scallion using a sharp paring knife. Place scallion piece in iced water; the slashed end will open and curl back to resemble a brush. Repeat process to make more.
5 To make Cucumber Garnish: Run the tines of a fork down the length of a cucumber and cut cucumber crosswise into thin slices.
6 To make Chili Flowers: Start at the stem end and make thin cuts down the length of each chili to form petals using a sharp paring knife. Place chilies in a bowl of ice water for 30 minutes or until petals open. Repeat process to make more.

WILD AND BROWN RICE SALAD

★ **Preparation time:** 10 minutes
Total cooking time: 40 minutes
Serves 6

1/2 cup wild rice
1 cup brown rice
1/4 cup slivered almonds
1 tablespoon chopped fresh parsley
1 tablespoon chopped fresh chives

1 tablespoon chopped fresh basil
3 tablespoons light vegetable oil
2 teaspoons white wine vinegar

1 Cook wild rice and brown rice separately in large pans of boiling water until just tender. Drain, rinse under cold water and drain again thoroughly. Refrigerate. Rice should be quite cold and dry before assembling salad.
2 Preheat oven to 350°F. Spread almonds on a foil-covered baking sheet; cook 3 minutes until golden.
3 Combine cold wild and brown rice, parsley, chives, basil, oil and white wine vinegar in a serving bowl; top with cooled almonds just before serving.

ABOVE: BALINESE-STYLE FRIED RICE. OPPOSITE PAGE, BELOW: SAVORY RICE; ABOVE: VALENCIA-STYLE RICE

VALENCIA-STYLE RICE

Preparation time: 10 minutes
Total cooking time: 15 minutes
Serves 4–6

1¼ cups long-grain rice	2 teaspoons finely grated
1 tablespoon olive oil	orange rind
1 tablespoon butter	½ cup orange juice
1 medium onion, chopped	½ cup sweet sherry
	1½ cups chicken stock

1 Soak rice in cold water 10 minutes, drain, rinse with cold water; drain again.

2 Heat oil and butter in a medium pan over low heat. Add onion and cook until golden brown and soft; add rice, reduce heat to low. Stir rice for 2 minutes or until lightly golden.

3 Add the orange rind, juice, sherry and stock. Cover the pan with a tight-fitting lid. Bring to the boil; stir once. Reduce heat and simmer, covered for 8–10 minutes or until almost all of the liquid is absorbed. Remove the pan from heat and stand, covered for 5 minutes or until all of the liquid is absorbed. Separate rice grains with a fork and serve.

SAVORY RICE

Preparation time: 10 minutes
Total cooking time: 20 minutes
Serves 4

1 tablespoon ghee or oil	1 teaspoon salt
1 medium onion, finely	3 cups boiling water
sliced	
1½ cups long-grain rice	

1 Heat ghee in a medium pan with a well-fitting lid. Add onion, cook until golden brown; remove from pan and set aside on a plate. In the ghee remaining in the pan, lightly cook the rice, stirring, for 2 minutes.

2 Add salt and boiling water and cook, uncovered, until the water has evaporated sufficiently for the surface of the rice to show. Cover tightly, reduce heat to very low and cook for 15 minutes.

3 Remove lid from pan; fluff the rice with a fork and let the steam escape. Spoon onto a serving plate and garnish with reserved onions. Serve immediately.

ABOUT RICE

■ Rice comes in either brown or white versions and three main varieties: long-grain, medium-grain and short-grain. Brown rice (rice without the bran removed) takes at least twice as long to cook as white rice.

■ To make fluffy white rice in which grains remain separate, bring 8 cups of water to the boil, add 1 cup of rice and boil, uncovered, for 12–15 minutes. Strain in a colander. For pearly white rice, in which the grains stick together, place 1 cup rice in pan, add water to 1 inch above rice, bring to boil, reduce heat to very low, cover with tight-fitting lid, cook for 20 minutes or until water is absorbed.

■ Cooked rice can be stored in the refrigerator, covered, for a few days. It may be frozen and reheated, when required, in a microwave oven or in a colander over a pan of boiling water.

Rice Flour Also called rice powder, a flour ground from milled rice; used in Asia to make rice noodles and used commercially as a thickening agent in cakes and puddings.

Rice Paper A thin, almost transparent, edible paper made from the straw of rice. It is used to wrap sweet and savory foods; macaroons are often baked on rice paper because it doesn't need to be removed before serving.

Rice Vinegar A mild-flavored, pale yellow liquid made from fermented rice and used in oriental cooking.

Rice Wine Alcoholic beverage distilled from fermented rice. Sake, Japanese rice wine, is served warm.

Ricotta Cheese A soft, smooth, moist, white cheese with a bland, sweet flavor. Traditionally ricotta is made from whey, which when

heated coagulates in the same way as the white of an egg; sometimes skimmed or whole cow's milk is added, giving the cheese a creamier consistency and a fuller flavor. Ricotta can be served as a dessert with fruit or warm honey, used as filling for cheesecake, or mixed with a sharp-tasting soft cheese as a spread or filling for cannelloni. Ricotta is bought fresh and must be used quickly.

Rigani A variety of the herb oregano which is mostly used dried

rather than fresh. It is often used in Greek cooking.

Rillettes Also known as potted pork, a spread made from pork, rabbit, goose or poultry. Highly seasoned, it is cooked in lard, then pounded to a paste. It is served spread on bread or toast.

Risotto Short-grained Italian rice (arborio, found in specialty shops is best) sautéed in butter or oil and then simmered gently in stock until thick and creamy. A range of ingredients, especially shellfish, chicken liver, beef

TOMATO RICE CUPS

⭐⭐ **Preparation time:** 30 minutes
Total cooking time: 1 hour 30 minutes
Serves 4

8 large ripe tomatoes, about 3 lb
1/3 cup olive oil
3 large onions, finely chopped
2/3 cup short-grain rice
1/4 cup tomato paste

1 cup coarsely chopped flat-leaf parsley
salt and freshly ground black pepper; to taste
1/2 cup water
2 tablespoons olive oil, extra

1 Arrange tomatoes on a board, stem-side down. Cut bases from tomatoes with a sharp knife and set aside. Squeeze tomatoes gently to remove excess seeds; discard seeds. Use a small spoon to scoop out flesh and remaining seeds from tomato cups; chop flesh finely. Set cups aside.
2 Heat oil in heavy-bottom pan. Add onion, cook over low heat 20 minutes, stirring occasionally. Add rice, stir over low heat 3 minutes. Add chopped tomato and tomato paste. Bring to boil, reduce heat and simmer, covered, for 7 minutes. Remove from heat; cool slightly. Stir in parsley and season with salt and pepper.
3 Preheat oven to moderate 350°F. Spoon rice mixture evenly into tomato cups; use reserved bases to cover filling. Arrange tomatoes in a deep baking dish.
4 Pour water into dish. Drizzle oil over tomatoes. Cover dish with foil. Bake 30 minutes, remove foil and bake for another 30 minutes. Baste with pan juices just before serving. Serve warm.

DOLMADES

⭐⭐ **Preparation time:** 1 hour +
1 hour standing
Total cooking time: 55 minutes
Makes about 35

8 oz vine leaves in brine
3/4 cup (6 fl oz) olive oil
2 large onions, finely chopped
3/4 cup short-grain rice
6 scallions, chopped
1/3 cup coarsely chopped fresh dill

1 tablespoon finely chopped fresh mint
salt and freshly ground black pepper, to taste
1 1/2 cups water
1 tablespoon lemon juice

1 Rinse vine leaves in cold water; soak in warm water 1 hour; drain. Heat 1/2 cup oil in pan. Add onion. Cook over low heat 5 minutes; remove from heat, leave covered 5 minutes.
2 Add rice, scallions, herbs, salt and pepper to pan; mix well. Lay out a vine leaf, vein-side-up.
3 Place 3 teaspoons of mixture on center of leaf. Fold sides over mixture, roll towards leaf tip. Repeat process with remaining filling and leaves.
4 Place five vine leaves over base of medium heavy-bottom pan. Arrange rolled dolmades in the pan in two layers; drizzle with remaining oil. Place a plate on top of the dolmades; cover with water. Bring to boil, reduce heat and simmer, covered, for 45 minutes. Remove plate; drizzle with lemon juice. Serve warm or cold.

LEFT: TOMATO RICE CUPS; ABOVE: DOLMADES.
OPPOSITE PAGE: KEDGEREE

WARM RICE AND DATE SALAD

Preparation time: 25 minutes
Total cooking time: 1 hour
Serves 4–6

½ cup wild rice
¾ cup basmati or
  jasmine rice
1 cup chopped fresh dates
1 banana, sliced

Dressing
¼ cup olive oil

¼ cup lemon juice
2 teaspoons soft brown
  sugar
1 teaspoon French seeded
  mustard
⅓ cup toasted chopped
  macadamia nuts

1 Wash and drain wild rice. Add it to 14 fl oz boiling water. Cover and simmer for about 45 minutes or until tender.
2 Wash basmati rice well. Place in a pan with cold water to cover ½ inch above the level of the rice. Bring to the boil, then cover tightly and cook for 10–15 minutes, or until tender.
3 To make Dressing: Combine oil, lemon juice, brown sugar and mustard in a screw-top jar. Shake well to combine.
4 Combine rice, dates and banana. Pour dressing over rice mixture and stir gently to combine. Place on a serving plate and garnish with macadamia nuts. Serve immediately.

KEDGEREE

Preparation time: 15 minutes
Total cooking time: 30 minutes
Serves 4

1 lb smoked haddock or
  other smoked fish
1 teaspoon finely grated
  lemon rind
1 bay leaf
1½ cups cooked long-
  grain rice
3 hard-boiled eggs, finely
  chopped

¼ teaspoon ground
  nutmeg
pinch pepper
salt to taste
1 tablespoon lemon juice
3 tablespoons butter,
  chopped
¾ cup heavy cream

1 Preheat oven to moderate 350°F. Brush a shallow 6-cup capacity ovenproof dish with melted butter or oil. Cut fish into 1¼ inch cubes, place in large pan with lemon rind and bay leaf, cover with water and simmer until just cooked, about 6–8 minutes.
2 Using a slotted spoon, remove fish pieces from liquid. Flake fish with a fork.
3 In a large bowl, combine cooked rice, eggs, fish, nutmeg, pepper, salt and lemon juice.

4 Spoon mixture into prepared dish. Dot the top of the kedgeree with butter, pour the cream over. Bake for 20 minutes. Serve with buttered toast and lemon slices.

BAKED RICE CUSTARD

Preparation time: 20 minutes
Total cooking time: 1 hour
Serves 4

¼ cup short-grain rice
2 eggs
⅓ cup sugar
1½ cups milk
½ cup heavy cream
1 teaspoon vanilla

1–2 teaspoons grated
  lemon rind
¼ cup golden raisins or
  currants (optional)
¼ teaspoon ground
  nutmeg or cinnamon

1 Preheat oven to moderately slow 325°F. Brush a deep, 8 inch round ovenproof dish (6-cup capacity) with melted butter or oil. Cook rice in medium pan of boiling water until just tender; drain.
2 In a medium mixing bowl, whisk together the eggs, sugar, milk, cream, vanilla and rind for about 2 minutes. Fold in the cooked rice and raisins or currants. Pour the mixture into the prepared dish. Sprinkle with nutmeg or cinnamon.
3 Place filled dish into deep baking dish. Pour in warm water to come halfway up the sides. Bake for 50 minutes or until custard is set and a knife comes out clean when inserted in the center. Remove dish from baking dish immediately. Allow to stand for 5 minutes before serving. Serve with cream or stewed fruits.

marrow, savory sausages and vegetables, can be added. Risotto with Parmesan cheese and butter is served in Italy as an alternative to pasta. Risotto means "little rice."

Rissole A small ball of ground meat, poultry, fish or shellfish, coated in breadcrumbs and fried or baked.

Roast To cook food in the dry heat of an oven, a method most often used for larger cuts of meat, poultry or game. Roasting results in a browned, crunchy crust and a moist interior. Spit roasting involves rotating the food over a naked flame.

Rock Cake A small, firm-textured cake

containing dried fruit and with a rough, rock-like appearance.

Rock Cornish Hen See Cornish Hen.

Rockfish The largest of the Pacific coast fish families, this low-fat fish is divided into two categories—deep-bodied and elongated. The deep-bodied variety includes yellowtail, blue rockfish and goldeneye. This fish is firmer and has a fuller flavor than the elongated rockfish.

Rockfish average from 5 to 15 pounds and are sold as fillets or whole. Deep-bodied rockfish can be cooked by any method, but elongated rockfish must be gently baked or poached. Some rockfish are labelled "Pacific Snapper" but are not related to Atlantic red snapper. Striped bass is also called rockfish.

Rocky Road A candy flavor of chocolate, nuts and marshmallows. It is so named

because it resembles a "rocky road."

Rockmelon See Cantaloupe.

Roe Hard roe is the eggs of female fish and includes sturgeon roe (caviar), lumpfish roe and salmon roe. Milt or soft roe is the sperm of the male fish; the soft roe of cod and mullet is blended with cooked potato, olive oil and lemon juice to make the Greek dip taramasalata.

Rolled Roast A boneless or deboned cut of meat, usually rolled tightly and tied.

Rollmop A boned herring fillet rolled

CARROT PILAF

⭐ **Preparation time:** 15 minutes
Total cooking time: 30 minutes
Serves 4–6

2 cups long-grain rice
2 tablespoons butter
2 tablespoons olive oil
2 cups coarsely grated carrot
finely ground black pepper
1 tablespoon light corn syrup
2 1/2 cups chicken stock
1 cup white wine
1/2 cup chopped pistachios

1 Wash rice until water runs clear. Drain well.
2 Heat butter and oil in heavy-bottom pan. Add rice; fry 3–4 minutes. Add carrot and pepper; fry for 5 minutes, stirring constantly. Add corn syrup and mix thoroughly.
3 Add stock and wine. Bring to the boil, reduce heat to low, cover with tight-fitting lid and cook for 20–25 minutes or until rice is tender.
4 Place in serving bowl. Sprinkle pistachios over.

Note: Rice must be washed well under cold running water when preparing a pilaf, to ensure light fluffy rice grains.

PARSLEYED BROWN RICE

Stir 1 1/2 cups quick-cooking brown rice into plenty of rapidly boiling water and cook according to packet directions. Drain. Toss with 1 bunch chopped parsley, 1 1/2 tablespoons grated lemon rind and 1/2 teaspoon cracked black peppercorns.

RICE AND VEGETABLE PILAF

⭐ **Preparation time:** 20 minutes
Total cooking time: 35 minutes
Serves 4

3 tablespoons olive oil
1 medium onion, sliced
2 cloves garlic, crushed
2 teaspoons ground cumin
2 teaspoons paprika
1/2 teaspoon allspice
1 1/2 cups long-grain rice
1 1/2 cups vegetable stock
3/4 cup white wine
3 medium tomatoes, chopped
5 oz button mushrooms, sliced
2 medium zucchini, sliced
5 oz broccoli, cut into florets

1 Heat oil in a large heavy-bottom pan. Add onion, cook for 10 minutes, cover the pan with a tight-fitting lid. Simmer for 15 minutes. Remove the pan from heat.
Add the rice to the pan and stir until well combined. Add the vegetable stock, wine, tomato and mushrooms. Bring to the boil. Reduce the heat to low. Cover the pan with a tight-fitting lid. Simmer for 15 minutes. Remove the pan from heat.
3 Add the sliced zucchini and broccoli florets to the the pan. Cover and cook for 5–7 minutes or until just tender. Serve.

ABOVE: RICE AND VEGETABLE PILAF.
OPPOSITE PAGE, ABOVE: VEGETABLE RISOTTO;
BELOW: PORCINI MUSHROOM AND ONION RISOTTO

VEGETABLE RISOTTO

⭐ ⭐ **Preparation time:** 15 minutes
Total cooking time: 30 minutes
Serves 6

5 cups chicken stock	1 medium onion, finely
1 bunch asparagus, cut	chopped
into 1¼ inch lengths	1½ cups arborio rice
2 medium zucchini, cut	2 small tomatoes,
into ¾ inch slices	chopped
3½ oz snow peas, cut	½ cup grated Parmesan
into ¾ inch lengths	cheese
2 tablespoons olive oil	

1 Place the chicken stock in a medium pan. Cover and bring to the boil. Reduce the heat and simmer. Place the asparagus, zucchini and snow peas in a heatproof bowl and cover with boiling water. Allow to stand for 2 minutes, then drain. Refresh with cold water, drain well.

2 Heat the oil in a large heavy-bottom pan. Add the onion, stir over medium heat until golden; add the rice. Reduce heat to medium low, stir rice for 3 minutes or until lightly golden. Add a quarter of the simmering stock to the pan, stir constantly for 7 minutes or until all the stock is absorbed.

3 Repeat the process until all but ½ cup of the stock has been used, and the rice is almost tender. Add the vegetables with the remaining stock, stir for 5 minutes until all the liquid is absorbed and the vegetables are tender. Stir in the grated Parmesan. Serve.

PORCINI MUSHROOM AND ONION RISOTTO

⭐ ⭐ **Preparation time:** 10 minutes + 45 minutes soaking
Total cooking time: 45 minutes
Serves 4

½ oz sliced dried porcini	1½ cups arborio rice
mushrooms	4 oz fresh mushrooms,
4 cups chicken broth	chopped
¼ cup butter	⅓ cup grated Parmesan
2 onions, chopped	cheese
1 clove garlic, crushed	¼ cup chopped parsley

1 Soak porcini mushrooms in hot water to cover for 45 minutes; drain. In a saucepan bring chicken broth to a boil; reduce heat.

2 In a saucepan melt butter over low heat. Cook onion and garlic until tender and brown.

3 Add rice; stir until combined. Add 1 cup simmering chicken broth; bring to boil. Cook and stir until almost all the broth is absorbed.

4 Add another cup of chicken broth; cook and stir until almost all the broth is absorbed. Add porcini mushrooms and fresh mushrooms and continue adding stock, 1 cup at a time, as directed above. The total cooking time should be about 20 minutes.

5 Once all the broth has been added and absorbed, reduce heat to low. Stir in Parmesan cheese and parsley. Cover; cook for 2 minutes and serve immediately.

around a slice of onion or a gherkin, secured with a wooden toothpick, pickled in spiced vinegar.

Romaine Lettuce A lettuce with long, crisp leaves; the outer leaves are

dark and pungent, the inner leaves pale and mild in taste. Romaine lettuce used to make Caesar salad and is valued for its crispness.

Romano Cheese A hard grating cheese, usually made from cow's milk, similar in taste and texture to Parmesan. When made with sheep's milk the cheese is called pecorino romano.

Roquefort Cheese A creamy-textured, blue-veined, ewe's milk cheese with a strong aroma and a pungent, salty flavor. The cheese is matured for three months in the damp limestone caves of Roquefort-sur-Soulzon in south-eastern France. It is best served at room temperature.

Rose Water A liquid distilled from fragrant rose petals and used widely in the cooking of India and the Middle East. It flavors Indian desserts such as *gulab jamun* (rich, fried dumplings soaked in rose water syrup) as well as creams, jellies and ices. Rose water essence is much stronger than rose water and should be used sparingly.

Rosemary The long, thin, aromatic, gray-green leaves of a perennial shrub used fresh or dry. Rosemary combines well with lamb, veal, suckling pig, poultry and rabbit dishes. Fresh leaves can be chopped and added to stuffings or leafy twigs can be placed in the roasting pan or on the barbecue fire; a sprig in a bottle of vinegar flavors salad dressings; and the tiny, star-shaped, blue flowers can be added to salads or candied.

Rosette A small fried pastry made with a rosette iron dipped into a thin batter and cooked in hot fat. It is drained on paper towels and sprinkled with cinnamon sugar.

Rouille A fiery sauce made from dried red chili pepper, olive oil, bread crumbs and saffron pounded together. Rouille is served with bouillabaisse or grilled fish.

Roulade A food rolled around a filling. It can be meat, poultry or fish rolled around vegetables or other stuffing, a

RICOTTA

RICOTTA AND PESTO PIZZAS

⭐ ⭐ **Preparation time:** 1 hour
Total cooking time: 15 minutes
Makes 6 individual pizzas

Pizza Dough
1 envelope active dried yeast
1³/4 cups warm water
4–5 cups all-purpose flour
¹/2 teaspoon salt
2 tablespoons olive oil

Topping
2 cloves garlic
1 cup fresh basil leaves
¹/2 cup fresh parsley sprigs
¹/3 cup walnuts
³/4 cup grated Parmesan cheese
¹/3 cup olive oil
8 oz ricotta cheese
8 oz sun-dried tomatoes in oil, drained and sliced

1 Combine yeast and water. Stand in a warm place for 10 minutes. Sift 4 cups flour and the salt into a large bowl. Make a well in the center; add yeast mixture and oil. Mix well, until dough forms a soft ball. Add more flour, if necessary.
2 Knead dough on floured surface until smooth and springs back when touched. Transfer to large, lightly oiled bowl. Cover with plastic wrap; stand in a warm position until dough has doubled in bulk. Prepare Topping while dough is proofing.
3 Preheat oven to 400°F. Grease two baking sheets.
4 To make Topping: Combine garlic, basil, parsley, walnuts and Parmesan in blender or food processor. Blend mixture at medium speed, adding oil in a thin stream until a thick paste is formed.

5 Punch dough down; divide into six equal portions. Shape each piece into flat circles 5 inches in diameter. Lay circles on prepared baking sheets.
6 Spread ricotta cheese on each portion. Top with the basil mixture. Arrange slices of sun-dried tomatoes over basil mixture. Bake for 15 minutes or until dough is golden brown and cooked through. Remove pizzas from baking sheets immediately and serve with freshly made salad.

CHOCOLATE RICOTTA TORTE

⭐
⭐ ⭐ **Preparation time:** 30 minutes
Total cooking time: 40 minutes
Serves 8

Cake
¹/2 cup butter, softened
1 cup plus 2 tablespoons sugar
2 eggs
1¹/3 cups all-purpose flour
²/3 cup unsweetened cocoa powder
1 teaspoon baking powder
¹/4 teaspoon salt
1 cup water

Filling
8 oz ricotta cheese

1 oz candied mixed peel, finely chopped
1 oz candied cherries, finely chopped
¹/4 cup sugar

Topping
2 teaspoons instant coffee powder
2 tablespoons confectioners' sugar
1 teaspoon hot water
1¹/4 cups heavy cream
6 tablespoons brandy
1 cup slivered almonds, toasted

1 Preheat oven to 350°F. Beat butter with electric mixer until smooth. Add sugar; beat until fluffy. Beat in eggs, one at a time. Stir together flour, cocoa powder, baking powder and salt. Add flour mixture and water alternately to batter; beat until smooth. Beat 2–3 minutes more until light and fluffy.
2 Pour into a greased, floured 8 inch cake pan. Bake 40 minutes or until a toothpick inserted in center comes out clean. Cool in pan 10 minutes. Remove from pan; cool on wire rack. Cut into three layers.
3 To make Filling: Combine ricotta cheese, mixed peel, cherries and sugar.
4 To make Topping: Dissolve coffee and sugar in water. Combine cream and coffee mixture, beat with electric mixer until soft peaks form.
5 To assemble torte, place one cake layer on serving plate. Brush with 2 tablespoons brandy, spread with half ricotta. Top with cake layer; brush with 2 tablespoons brandy, spread with remaining ricotta. Top with last cake layer, brush with remaining brandy. Spread top and sides with cream mixture. Sprinkle almonds around top edge of cake.

ROCK CAKES

ORANGE AND CURRANT ROCK CAKES

⋆ **Preparation time:** 8 minutes
Total cooking time: 15–18 minutes
Makes 9 rock cakes

1½ cups all-purpose flour
1 teaspoon baking powder
¼ teaspoon salt
1 teaspoon grated orange rind

¼ cup unsalted butter, melted
½ cup currants
⅓ cup sugar
1 egg, lightly beaten
2 tablespoons orange juice
2 teaspoons sugar

1 Preheat oven to 400°F. Brush a baking sheet with melted butter or oil, line base with paper; grease paper.
2 Sift flour, baking powder and salt into small mixing bowl; add rind and butter. Using electric beaters, beat mixture on low speed for 2 minutes.
3 Add currants, sugar and combined egg and juice. Beat on high speed for 1 minute or until the ingredients are just combined.
4 Pile mixture in portions of approximately 2 level tablespoonfuls, on prepared baking sheet, about 2 inch apart. Sprinkle rock cakes with sugar. Bake for 15–18 minutes or until golden brown. Turn onto wire rack to cool. Serve warm or cool with butter and marmalade, if desired.

OPPOSITE PAGE: RICOTTA AND PESTO PIZZAS.
ABOVE: ORANGE AND CURRANT ROCK CAKES

ROCK CAKES

⋆ **Preparation time:** 30 minutes
Total cooking time: 10–15 minutes
Makes about 20

2 cups all-purpose flour, sifted
1 teaspoon baking powder
½ teaspoon ground ginger
¼ teaspoon salt
⅓ cup butter, cut into pieces

⅔ cup sugar
½ cup dried mixed fruit bits
1 tablespoon chopped mixed nuts (optional)
1 egg
⅓ cup milk

1 Preheat oven to hot 400°F. Brush two baking sheets with melted butter or oil, line bases with paper; grease paper. Place flour, baking powder, ginger and salt in a large bowl. Add pieces of butter and rub in with fingertips until mixture resembles bread crumbs.
2 Mix in sugar, fruit and nuts. Whisk the egg into milk and add to dry ingredients. Mix to a stiff dough.
3 Pile mixture, in portions of approximately 2 level tablespoonfuls, on prepared baking sheets. Bake for 10–15 minutes or until golden brown. Transfer to a wire rack to cool. Before serving, rock cakes can be split and buttered if desired.

VARIATIONS

■ Use 1 cup of whole-wheat flour instead of 1 cup of the white flour.
■ Sprinkle rock cakes with cinnamon, sugar or freeze-dried coffee before baking.

savory or sweet soufflé mixture baked, spread with a filling and rolled; or sponge cake wrapped around a sweet filling.

Roux A mixture of butter and flour cooked over a low heat and used to thicken sauces. Blended with milk it forms the basis of many white sauces.

Rum A spirit distilled from sugarcane and used to flavor sweet foods such as rich fruit cakes, pancakes and mousses.

Rum Baba See Baba au Rhum.

Russian Dressing A mayonnaise-based salad dressing with added chili and tangy ingredients such as pickles and horseradish.

Rutabaga A fleshy root vegetable, larger than a turnip with a strong cabbage-like flavor. It is boiled, baked, roasted with meat and puréed to use in savory pies.

Rye A cereal grain used to make bread, cakes and crispbreads. Cracked rye is cooked with milk or water as a breakfast food.

Rye Bread A dark, dense-textured bread with a slightly sour taste. It is commonly served with shellfish.

S

Sabayon Sauce A light, foamy sauce made with whipped egg yolks, sugar and a liquid (usually dry or sweet white wine or champagne), served warm and foaming with puddings, cakes or fruit; it is a French variation of the Italian dessert zabaglione.

Sacher Torte A dense chocolate cake with two layers separated by a thin filling of apricot jam and the whole covered with smooth chocolate. Created by Franz Sacher, chief pastry cook to the Austrian statesman Metternich during the Congress of Vienna (1814-15), the cake was later the cause of a protracted argument between Sacher's descendants and Vienna's famous Demel pâtisserie as to whether in its true form it had two layers or was simply a cake spread with jam and then iced.

Saffron A spice made from the dried, thread-like stamens of the saffron crocus. It is strongly fragrant and dark orange in color. Saffron is very expensive: the small crocus flower

SALADS

CAESAR SALAD

⭐ **Preparation time:** 20 minutes
Total cooking time: 15 minutes
Serves 4–6

1 clove garlic
1 tablespoon olive oil
3 slices thick bread
2 slices bacon
1 head romaine
3 tablespoons olive oil, extra

1 tablespoon lemon juice
1 tablespoon sour cream
1/2 teaspoon Worcestershire sauce
4 anchovies, chopped
3 oz Parmesan, thinly shaved

1 Preheat oven to moderate 350°F. Cut the garlic in quarters; place in a small bowl with 1 tablespoon oil. Let stand for 10 minutes, stirring occasionally. Discard garlic. To make croûtons, remove crusts from bread. Brush the bread with garlic-flavored oil; cut into small squares. Place on baking sheet and bake 10 minutes or until golden. Leave to cool.
2 Remove excess fat from bacon; cut into small strips. Cook over medium heat until crisp.
3 Wash and dry romaine leaves thoroughly. Use the larger leaves to line a serving bowl; tear remainder into bite-size pieces and place in bowl.
4 Place 3 tablespoons oil, juice, sour cream and sauce in a small screw-top jar; shake well. Drizzle

dressing over lettuce; add bacon, anchovies, croûtons and Parmesan to bowl (reserve a little Parmesan for garnish); toss to combine. Serve immediately.

COLESLAW

⭐ **Preparation time:** 15 minutes
Total cooking time: none
Serves 6

1/2 small cabbage, finely shredded
2 medium carrots, finely shredded
1 stalk celery, finely chopped
1 medium white onion, finely chopped
1 small red pepper, finely chopped

Dressing
1/2 cup mayonnaise
2 tablespoons white wine vinegar
1 teaspoon Dijon mustard

1 Place vegetables in a large mixing bowl and toss to combine.
2 To make Dressing: In a separate bowl, mix together dressing ingredients and toss with vegetables. Transfer to a serving bowl.

ABOVE: CAESAR SALAD. OPPOSITE PAGE, BELOW: WALDORF SALAD; ABOVE: SALAD NIÇOISE

SALAD NICOISE

Preparation time: 20 minutes
Total cooking time: none
Serves 4–6

5 oz fresh green beans
2 medium tomatoes, cut
into 8 wedges
1 small red onion, cut
into rings
3 hard-boiled eggs,
quartered
²⁄₃ cup black pitted
olives

2 x 9¹⁄₄ oz cans tuna,
drained
2 oz can anchovies,
drained
¹⁄₄ cup olive oil
2 tablespoon white wine
vinegar
1 clove garlic, crushed
¹⁄₂ teaspoon Dijon
mustard

1 Trim the green beans and cook in a large pan of boiling water for 1 minute. Drain and plunge into iced water. Drain well.

2 Arrange the beans, tomato, onion, egg, olives, tuna, olives and anchovies on a large serving platter or shallow bowl.

3 Place the olive oil, vinegar, garlic and Dijon mustard in a small screw-top jar and shake well. Drizzle the dressing over the salad. Serve immediately with crusty bread.

SEAFOOD SALAD

Preparation time: 20 minutes
Total cooking time: 2 minutes
Serves 4

8 oz calamari rings
1 lb cooked medium
shrimp
3¹⁄₂ oz can smoked
mussels
4 lettuce cups

¹⁄₂ cup Thousand Island
dressing
1 tablespoon heavy cream
1 teaspoon finely chopped
fresh parsley

1 Boil 1 inch water in a large skillet. Add the calamari rings; simmer 2 minutes, turning once. Do not overcook or calamari will become rubbery. Remove from the pan with a slotted spoon. Set aside to cool.

2 Peel and devein shrimp. Drain mussels.

3 Arrange seafood in lettuce cups. Combine Thousand Island dressing and cream and drizzle over seafood. Sprinkle parsley on top. Serve immediately.

WALDORF SALAD

Preparation time: 15 minutes
Total cooking time: none
Serves 6

3 medium red apples
2 medium green apples
2 celery stalks, sliced
¹⁄₃ cup walnut halves

¹⁄₃ cup mayonnaise
2 tablespoons vinaigrette
1 tablespoon sour cream

1 Quarter and core the apples and cut into ³⁄₄ inch chunks.

2 Place in a large mixing bowl with the celery and walnuts.

3 In a separate bowl combine mayonnaise, vinaigrette and sour cream; mix well. Add to apple mixture and fold through. Transfer to a lettuce-lined serving bowl. Serve immediately.

has only three stamens and each must be plucked by hand; it takes more than 150,000 fresh flowers to produce 2.2 pounds (1 kilogram) of dried saffron. Fortunately only scant amounts are needed to impart its unique flavor and color. Saffron is used in fish dishes, such as bouillabaisse; with rice (as in the Spanish dish paella; and saffron rice, popular in Indian and Asian cooking), in poultry and beef stews; in curries; tomato-based sauces; sweet breads and cookies. Saffron is best purchased as threads. To use, pound in a mortar and steep for about 5 minutes in warm liquid to bring out the flavor.

Sage An herb with gray-green aromatic leaves with a pungent, slightly bitter flavor, originally used medicinally but now used in cooking, especially in stuffings for poultry and pork and as a traditional flavoring for cottage cheese. In Italian cooking it flavors veal and other meat dishes; in Germany it is used in eel dishes; and in Greece sage tea is a popular beverage. Sage is native to the northern shores of the Mediterranean. It is available fresh or dried.

Sage Derby A close-textured cow's milk cheese flavored with fresh sage leaves, which give it a green hue with darker green streaks. It is a variant of the English cheese, Derby. Serve at room temperature on a cheese platter and as a snack cheese.

Sago Tiny balls of starch prepared from the starchy inner bark of the sago palm, a tree native to the swamps of Malaysia, the Philippines and India which, just before flowering at 15 years of age, builds up a large reserve of starch. Sago is used mainly as a dessert, cooked until transparent in sweetened milk, flavored water or coconut milk.

Saint Paulin Cheese A pasteurized cow's milk pressed curd cheese with a semisoft texture and a flavor ranging from buttery and slightly sweet to tangy. Now factory-made all over France, it is derived from Port Salut, a cheese first made in the early nineteenth century in the Port-du-Salut monastery in Brittany.

Sake A Japanese alcoholic drink made from fermented rice. A sweet sake, mirin, is an important flavoring in Japanese cooking; sweet sherry can be substituted.

ASIAN NOODLE VEGETABLE SALAD

⭐ **Preparation time:** 30 minutes
Total cooking time: 15 minutes
Serves 4–6

6 scallions
1 lb thick rice (or egg) noodles
4 ripe plum tomatoes
1 medium carrot
12 snow peas
4 oz canned baby corn, drained and halved (or fresh)
5 oz fresh bean sprouts
1½ oz roasted peanuts
soy sauce, optional

Dressing
2 teaspoons sesame oil
¼ cup olive oil
5 teaspoons white rice vinegar
1¼ teaspoons sugar
salt and cracked black pepper, to taste
1 teaspoon finely chopped fresh red chili pepper
1–2 tablespoons chopped fresh cilantro

1 Trim scallions, cut into thin diagonal slices. Cook noodles in large pan of boiling water for 3–4 minutes or until just tender. Remove from heat, drain. Rinse under cold water, drain again.
2 Mark a cross on the top of each tomato. Place in boiling water 1–2 minutes; plunge into cold water; drain. Peel down skin at cross. Cut tomatoes in half, remove seeds. Cut flesh into narrow strips. Peel carrot, cut into thin matchstick lengths. Trim snow peas, cut into diagonal slices.
3 If using fresh baby corn, boil in lightly salted water 3 minutes; drain. Plunge into cold water,

drain and set aside. Plunge bean sprouts into boiling water 1–2 minutes; drain. Combine all vegetables and peanuts in a salad bowl. Add Dressing and mix thoroughly. Chill briefly before serving. Drizzle with soy sauce, if desired.
4 To make Dressing: Combine oils, vinegar, sugar, salt, pepper, chili and cilantro in a screw-top jar; shake vigorously to combine.

ASPARAGUS AND PROSCIUTTO SALAD

⭐ **Preparation time:** 20 minutes
Total cooking time: 3 minutes
Serves 4

24 fresh asparagus spears (6 spears per person)
4 slices prosciutto
3 tablespoons olive oil

1 tablespoon tarragon vinegar
1 teaspoon poppy seeds
1 oz Parmesan cheese

1 Trim any woody ends from the asparagus and place in a large pan of boiling water. Cook for 1 minute, then drain and plunge into iced water. Drain well. Arrange asparagus on individual serving plates.
2 Place the prosciutto under a hot broiler for 2 minutes or until very crispy. Allow to cool.
3 Place the oil, tarragon vinegar and poppy seeds in a small screw-top jar and shake well. Drizzle dressing over asparagus and crumble the prosciutto on top. Using a vegetable peeler or sharp knife, shave strips of Parmesan over the prosciutto and serve immediately.

Note: Prosciutto is an Italian smoked meat, also known as Parma ham. It is available from delicatessens, usually sliced paper thin.

CURLY ENDIVE SALAD WITH CRISP PROSCIUTTO AND GARLIC CROUTONS

★ *Preparation time:* 20 minutes
Total cooking time: 5 minutes
Serves 4–6

1 large bunch curly endive
½ bunch red leaf lettuce
2 red onions
4 slices white or sliced brown bread
2 large cloves garlic, crushed
3 tablespoons butter, softened

1¼ oz Feta cheese, mashed
4–6 thin slices prosciutto
1 large avocado

Dressing
2 tablespoons olive oil
¼ cup sugar
¼ cup spicy tomato sauce
1 tablespoon soy sauce
⅓ cup red wine vinegar

1 Rinse endive and leaf lettuce in cold water. Shake lightly in a towel to absorb excess water. Tear endive and lettuce into pieces. Peel and slice onions; separate into rings. Combine endive, lettuce and onion rings in a salad bowl or wide shallow dish.
2 Toast bread one side only. Mash garlic, butter and Feta cheese into a paste, spread over the untoasted side of the bread. Remove crusts; toast

buttered side of bread until crisp and golden on the surface. Cut each slice into ½ inch cubes.
3 Place prosciutto under very hot broiler for a few seconds until crisp. Remove and cut into 2 inch pieces. Set aside. Peel avocado and cut into thin wedges.
4 To make Dressing: Whisk the oil, sugar, tomato sauce, soy sauce and vinegar together in a small bowl. Add the prosciutto and avocado to the salad and pour over half the dressing. Arrange croûtons on top and serve salad with remaining dressing.

CHEF'S SALAD

★ *Preparation time:* 15 minutes
Total cooking time: none
Serves 6

6 lettuce leaves
1 lb Swiss cheese, cut into thin strips
4 thin slices ham
1 cup cooked, chopped chicken

3 medium roma tomatoes
2 tablespoons chopped pimiento, optional
2 hard-boiled eggs, quartered
½ cup vinaigrette

1 Wash and dry lettuce thoroughly. Cut the cheese and ham slices into evenly-sized, fine strips. Cut each tomato into 6 wedges.
2 Combine the cheese, ham, chicken, tomatoes, pimiento and eggs in a mixing bowl. Toss to combine. Divide salad evenly between lettuce leaves. Drizzle the vinaigrette over salad and serve immediately.

OPPOSITE PAGE, ABOVE: ASIAN NOODLE VEGETABLE SALAD; BELOW: ASPARAGUS AND PROSCIUTTO SALAD. ABOVE: CURLY ENDIVE SALAD WITH CRISP PROSCIUTTO AND GARLIC CROUTONS

Salad A mixture of foods, either savory or sweet, such as vegetables (raw or cooked) and salad greens, fresh fruits, seafood, poultry, meats, egg, pasta and grains. Savory salads are usually served with a dressing. In North America a green salad is

often served after the first course and before the main course; in many parts of Europe it is served with the main course; in France it is served after the main course. Salads featuring green beans, corn, rice, tomato, potato or cabbage are often served as side dishes, while first and main course salads include Caesar salad, and salads of cheese, seafood, chicken, pasta and meats. Fruit such as grapefruit segments, grapes and cantaloupe can also be added to savory salads.

Salad Dressing A flavored liquid which is used to moisten and flavor a salad; it can be a sprinkling of lemon juice, a mixture of olive oil and vinegar or a cold sauce such as mayonnaise. The dressing can be served mixed through the salad, or it may be served separately as an accompaniment.

Salami A cured dry sausage made from ground pork and seasoned with garlic and other herbs and spices; it is sometimes smoked and can be flavored with red wine. Salami is served thinly sliced as finger food, in salads and sandwiches and as a pizza topping. The sausage is thought to have originated in the ancient city of Salamis, in Cyprus, but is now commonly associated with Italy; distinctive types of salami are also made in Denmark, Hungary, Austria, Spain and Germany.

Sally Lunn A sweet tea cake or layered with cream or butter.

Salmon A large fish that spends most of the year in cooler ocean waters, but swims up rivers to spawn in fresh water. It has delicately flavored, fatty pink flesh. Salmon may be broiled, grilled, baked or poached; the flesh may also be smoked or salted. It is used in many traditional dishes such as the Scandinavian gravlax (raw salmon salted and marinated with dill and pepper) and the Russian koulibiac (a fish and vegetable pie).

CHAR-GRILLED BEEF AND EGGPLANT SALAD

★ ★ **Preparation time:** 25 minutes + 30 minutes marinating
Total cooking time: 20 minutes
Serves 4

2 medium eggplant
2 tablespoons salt
3 medium zucchini
2 medium red peppers
4 oz button mushrooms
2 medium onions
1/3 cup olive oil

2 tablespoons lemon juice
1 lb sirloin or round steak
2 oz snow pea sprouts or watercress
1/4 cup shredded fresh basil

1 Cut eggplant in half lengthwise, lay cut side down and cut into long 1/2 inch slices. Spread out in a single layer on a plate and sprinkle with salt. Set aside for 15 minutes, place in a colander and rinse under cold water. Pat dry thoroughly with paper towels.
2 Cut the zucchini into 3/4 inch pieces. Slice the peppers into 3/4 inch strips. Cut the mushrooms in half. Slice the onions thickly. Combine all the vegetables with the olive oil and lemon juice in a large bowl. Cover with plastic wrap and leave to marinate for about 30 minutes at room temperature.
3 Remove excess fat and tendons from the meat. Place on a lightly greased grill rack. Cook over

high heat for 2 minutes each side, or until the meat is seared. Move the meat to a cooler part of the grill and continue to cook for another 2 minutes each side or until medium-rare. Transfer the meat to a platter, cover loosely with foil and allow to cool slightly. Slice meat thinly using a sharp knife.
4 Using a slotted spoon, remove the vegetables from the marinade. Grill in two batches for about 5 minutes each batch until the vegetables are just tender and lightly browned, turning once.
5 Arrange a pile of snow pea sprouts or watercress on individual serving plates. Top with sliced meat and vegetables. Garnish with shredded fresh basil. Serve immediately.

Note: The meat and vegetables can also be cooked under the broiler. Cook meat and vegetables 3–4 inches from the heat for about the same amount of time.

Eggplant, especially more mature ones, can contain bitter juices. When sprinkled with salt, as in this recipe, these juices are drawn out and the bitterness reduced. This salting process also reduces the amount of fat which is absorbed by the eggplant during cooking. Make sure you dry the eggplant well before cooking.

ABOVE: CHAR-GRILLED BEEF AND EGGPLANT SALAD. OPPOSITE PAGE: TUNA SALAD WITH GARLIC MAYONNAISE

TUNA SALAD WITH GARLIC MAYONNAISE

⭐ **Preparation time:** 25 minutes
Total cooking time: 10 minutes
Serves 6

6 small red potatoes, peeled
5 oz snow peas
1 bunch asparagus
8 oz cherry tomatoes
3 x 6½ oz cans tuna, drained

Garlic Mayonnaise
3 egg yolks or ¼ cup egg substitute
1 clove garlic, crushed
½ teaspoon Dijon mustard
2 tablespoons lemon juice
1¼ cups olive oil or vegetable oil

1 Cut the potatoes into ¾ inch cubes and cook in a large pan of boiling water until just tender. Drain and set aside. Place snow peas in a pan of boiling water. Cook 1 minute, drain and plunge into iced water. Drain and set aside. Trim ends from the asparagus, and repeat process as for snow peas.
2 To make Garlic Mayonnaise: Place the yolks or egg substitute, garlic, mustard and lemon juice in a food processor or blender container. Using the pulse action, process for 15 seconds or until blended. With motor running, add oil slowly in a thin stream until all oil is added and mixture is thick and creamy.
3 Arrange the potatoes, snow peas, asparagus, tomatoes and chunks of tuna on individual plates. Place spoonfuls of mayonnaise on each plate or pass around in a bowl. Serve immediately.

FRAGRANT RICE SALAD

⭐ **Preparation time:** 25 minutes
Total cooking time: 10 minutes
Serves 4

1 cup basmati or Thai fragrant rice
2 medium carrots, sliced diagonally
1 medium green pepper, cut into short, thin strips
7 oz can baby corn, cut into ¾ inch pieces

2 scallions, thinly sliced
6 oz Chinese barbecued pork, thinly sliced
¼ cup peanut oil
2 tablespoons sesame oil
2 tablespoons lime juice
2 tablespoons soy sauce

1 Bring a large pan of water to the boil. Add rice and cook until just tender. Drain and rinse under cold water, drain again thoroughly.
2 Combine the rice, carrot, pepper, baby corn, scallions and pork in a serving bowl. Toss to combine.
3 Place peanut and sesame oils, lime juice and soy sauce in a small screw-top jar and shake well. Drizzle over the salad and toss lightly to combine. Serve immediately.

Note: Barbecued pork is available from Chinese food stores.

TURKEY SALAD WITH CRANBERRY DRESSING

⭐ **Preparation time:** 15 minutes
Total cooking time: none
Serves 4

4 oz watercress
1 lb sliced cooked turkey
2 small oranges
¼ cup cranberry sauce

1 tablespoon oil
1 tablespoon white wine vinegar
¼ cup chopped pistachios

1 Wash and dry the watercress thoroughly. Break into large sprigs, discarding any thick stems. Arrange on a serving platter.
2 Arrange turkey slices in the center of the watercress. Using a sharp knife, peel the oranges, removing all the white pith, cut into slices and arrange around the turkey.
3 Place the cranberry sauce, oil and vinegar in a small bowl. Whisk until combined. Spoon the dressing over the turkey. Sprinkle with chopped pistachios and serve immediately.

Note: This recipe is an excellent way to use up leftover cooked turkey. For the leanest salad, choose breast meat.

Smoked salmon is served cold, thinly sliced, with lemon and capers, or with cream cheese or horseradish sauce, and often accompanied by bread, bagels, toast or blinis; it can also be included in various hot and cold dishes, including mousses, dips, crêpes, omelets and scrambled eggs, and tossed through pasta.

Salmon was once abundant in north Atlantic and north Pacific oceans, in rivers and lakes. There are several species of Pacific salmon: chinook or king; chum or dog; pink or humpback; coho or silver; and sockeye. Atlantic salmon is red to bright orange in color and slightly more oily. European salmon is found in the Baltic or Scottish streams. Salmon is now farmed in many parts of the world. Fresh salmon can be bought whole, or as steaks or fillets; it is also available smoked and in cans.

Salsa A highly seasoned, chunky sauce based on tomato, chili peppers, garlic and onion, served as an accompaniment to Mexican and Tex-Mex dishes. Salsas can be fresh or cooked and range in flavor from mild to spicy

to fiery. Commercially made varieties are available from supermarkets and specialist food stores.

Salsify A long, thin root vegetable with a delicate, oyster-like flavor. The most common variety has pale, almost white, flesh and light brown skin. A black-skinned variety, scorzonera, has cream-colored flesh. Salsify is usually boiled or sautéed and served tossed in butter and parsley, or with a béchamel sauce. It can also be added to stews.

Salt A white, odorless and sharp-tasting crystalline powder, sodium chloride, used as a seasoning and preserving agent. Table salt is finely ground rock salt with additives to make it free-flowing. Kosher salt is an evaporated salt with large, irregularly shaped crystals free from additives and iodine. Flavored salt has garlic or other seasonings added. Bay and sea salt, in the form of small, brittle chunks and flakes, has an intensely salty taste; it should be crushed before use. In America "rock salt" refers to non-edible salt used for ice cream machines.

Saltimbocca Thin slices of veal sautéed in butter, topped with ham or prosciutto and sage

MEDITERRANEAN SALAD

Preparation time: 40 minutes
Total cooking time: 2 minutes
Serves 8

1 medium eggplant
salt
2 tablespoons oil
8 oz cherry tomatoes, halved
2 small cucumbers, sliced
1 red onion, very thinly sliced
8 oz Feta cheese in 3/4 inch cubes
2/3 cup pitted black olives

1–2 tablespoons shredded fresh basil leaves

Dressing
1/3 cup olive oil
1 tablespoon balsamic vinegar
1 clove garlic, crushed
1 tablespoon chopped fresh oregano leaves

1 Cut eggplant into 1 inch cubes and spread out on a plate. Sprinkle with a little salt and let stand for 30 minutes. Rinse under cold water, pat dry with paper towels.
2 Heat the oil in a shallow pan, add eggplant. Stir over medium heat for 2 minutes or until eggplant is lightly browned and tender; drain on paper towels, allow to cool. Toss eggplant in a bowl with tomato, cucumber, onion, cheese, olives and basil.
3 To make Dressing: Place all ingredients in a small screw-top jar. Shake vigorously for 10 seconds or until combined. Add to salad, toss until mixed well.

SMOKED SALMON SALAD

Preparation time: 20 minutes
Total cooking time: none
Serves 4

2 oz watercress
6 1/2 oz smoked salmon slices
1 medium avocado, sliced lengthwise
1 small onion, finely sliced into rings

1 stalk celery
1/3 cup olive oil
1 tablespoon lemon juice
1/3 cup soft cream cheese
2 tablespoons heavy cream
1 tablespoon finely chopped fresh dill

1 Wash and dry the watercress thoroughly. Break into large sprigs. Arrange the sprigs on individual plates or a serving platter. Arrange salmon, avocado and onion over sprigs. Cut the celery into 2 inch lengths, then into long strips. Scatter over salad.
2 Combine olive oil, lemon juice and cream cheese in a food processor or blender and process until smooth. Stir in cream and chopped dill. Drizzle dressing over salad and serve immediately with crusty breadsticks.

CITRUS WALNUT SALAD

Preparation time: 20 minutes
Total cooking time: none
Serves 8

2 oranges
2 grapefruit
4 oz sugar snap peas
1/2 bunch arugula, leaves torn
1/2 bunch leaf lettuce, shredded
1 large cucumber, sliced
1/3 cup walnut pieces

Walnut Dressing
2 tablespoons walnut oil
2 tablespoons oil
2 teaspoons tarragon vinegar
2 teaspoons seeded mustard
1 teaspoon sweet chili sauce

1 Using a sharp knife, peel the oranges and grapefruit, removing all of the white pith. Carefully separate the fruit into segments, remove any seeds. Cover the sugar snap peas with boiling water and allow to stand for 2 minutes. Plunge immediately into iced water. Drain and pat dry with paper towels. Combine the fruit segments, sugar snap peas, arugula, shredded lettuce, cucumber and walnut pieces in a large bowl.
2 To make Walnut Dressing: Combine oils, vinegar, mustard and chili sauce in a screw-top jar and shake well.
3 Pour the dressing over salad ingredients and toss lightly until combined.

TRICOLOR PASTA SALAD

★ **Preparation time:** 20 minutes +
1 hour standing
Total cooking time: 10 minutes
Serves 6

2 tablespoons olive oil
2 tablespoons white wine
  vinegar
1 small garlic clove,
  halved
12 oz tricolor pasta
  spirals
1 tablespoon olive oil,
  extra

3/4 cup sun-dried
  tomatoes in oil, drained
1/2 cup pitted black olives
3 1/2 oz Parmesan cheese
1 cup quartered artichoke
  hearts
1/2 cup shredded fresh
  basil leaves

1 Combine olive oil, vinegar and garlic in a small
screw-top jar. Shake well to mix and allow to
stand for 1 hour.
2 Bring a large pan of water to the boil. Slowly
add the pasta spirals and cook until just tender.
Drain in a colander and toss with extra olive oil
while still hot. Allow to cool completely.
3 Cut sun-dried tomatoes into fine strips and cut
olives in half. Cut Parmesan cheese into paper-
thin slices.
4 Place pasta, tomato, olives, cheese, artichokes
and basil in a large serving bowl. Remove garlic,
pour dressing over. Toss gently to combine.

OPPOSITE PAGE: MEDITERRANEAN SALAD.
ABOVE: TRICOLOR PASTA SALAD

GARDEN SALAD

★ **Preparation time:** 15 minutes
Total cooking time: none
Serves 8

8 oz mixed green lettuce
  leaves
4 oz red cabbage
1 medium carrot

1 large stalk celery
1 small green pepper
1/4 cup vinaigrette

1 Wash and dry lettuce leaves thoroughly; tear
into bite-size pieces.
2 Finely shred cabbage; grate carrot and finely
slice celery and pepper. Combine in a large
serving bowl, add the vinaigrette and toss lightly
to combine. Serve immediately.

RED LEAF SALAD

★ **Preparation time:** 15 minutes
Total cooking time: none
Serves 6

5 oz mixed red lettuce
  leaves
3 oz fennel bulb
1 small red onion

2 tablespoons olive oil
1 tablespoon balsamic
  vinegar

1 Wash and dry lettuce leaves thoroughly, and
tear into bite-size pieces.
2 Thinly slice fennel and onion. Combine lettuce,
fennel and onion in serving bowl. Drizzle oil, then
vinegar over salad. Toss lightly. Serve immediately.

and braised in white
wine, it is rolled up or
left flat, and secured
with a toothpick.

Salt Pork The fatty top
part of a leg of bacon,
smoked and salted, cut
into small cubes and used
to flavor cooked dishes.

Sambal An
accompaniment
to an
Indonesian
curry or
rice meal.
Sambals
are made
with chili
peppers, minced
onion, oil and
lime juice.
They are often
varied by the
addition of
other
ingredients
such as shrimp
paste or
tomato.

Sambal Oelek
A hot chili relish which
is used in Indonesian
and Malaysian cooking.
Sambal oelek is available
in specialty shops, or it
can be made in a food
processor by blending
about 20 fresh red chilies,
roughly chopped, with
1 to 2 tablespoons of
vinegar. Place the
mixture in a sterilized jar;
it can be stored in the
refrigerator for up to one
month. Sambal oelek can
be used to
replace
fresh
chilies
in
almost
any dish.

Samosa A small savory snack of Indian origin consisting of a spiced and seasoned mixture of ground meat and chopped vegetables encased in a semi-circle of pastry and fried in ghee or

oil. Samosas should be served hot, accompanied by mint or cilantro chutney.

Samp Coarsely ground cornmeal; hominy grits.

Sandwich In its simplest form a sandwich is a savory or sweet filling or spread contained between two slices of bread to make an eat-in-the-hand meal. There are many variations, including Danish or open sandwiches, with substantial toppings piled high; rolled sandwiches, with the bread rolled around a filling; ribbon sandwiches made from three layers of bread, alternate slices of white and brown; the club sandwich, also made with three

slices of bread; and sandwiches with hot fillings of bacon, roast beef or broiled steak. In France the name has been adopted for a

THAI POTATO SALAD

⭐ **Preparation time:** 15 minutes
Total cooking time: 5 minutes
Serves 8

2 lb new potatoes

Dressing
1 clove garlic
¼ cup lime juice
2 tablespoons oil
2 tablespoons chopped fresh mint

2 tablespoons chopped fresh cilantro
1 tablespoon nam pla (see Note)
2 teaspoons sweet Thai chili sauce
1 teaspoon sugar

1 Scrub potatoes under cold water. Cut potatoes in half and cook in boiling water for 5 minutes or until just tender. Drain, rinse under cold water and allow to cool.
2 To make Dressing: Crush clove of garlic into a bowl. Add lime juice, oil, chopped fresh mint and cilanro, nam pla, chili sauce and sugar; stir until well combined.
3 Pour mixture into a small screw-top jar; shake for 30 seconds until mixed. Place potatoes in a bowl, pour dressing over; toss until well combined.

Note: Nam pla is the Thai version of fish sauce. It is available in specialty food stores and most supermarkets.

BEAN SALAD

⭐ **Preparation time:** 10 minutes
Total cooking time: none
Serves 6

5 oz green beans
17 oz can lima beans
16 oz can red kidney beans
15 oz can butter beans

1 small red onion, finely sliced
2 tablespoons chopped fresh parsley
¼ cup vinaigrette

1 Trim the green beans and cut into 1½ inch lengths. Place green beans in a small pan of boiling water. Cook for 1 minute; drain and plunge into iced water. Drain well.
2 Drain the lima, kidney and butter beans in a colander; rinse well under running water. Leave to drain. Combine the beans, onion and chopped fresh parsley in a serving bowl. Pour over the dressing and stir gently until all ingredients are thoroughly combined.

Note: Any combination of beans can be used for this salad; look for a good contrast in color and size.

ABOVE: THAI POTATO SALAD. OPPOSITE PAGE, BELOW: QUICK CHICKEN SALAD; ABOVE: CILANTRO SALAD

QUICK CHICKEN SALAD

Preparation time: 20 minutes
Total cooking time: none
Serves 4

1 head red leaf lettuce	1/3 cup mayonnaise
1 cooked whole chicken	1/3 cup buttermilk
1 avocado, peeled, pitted and sliced	1 tablespoon tarragon vinegar
2 stalks celery, cut into 1/4 inch slices	1/3 cup chopped pecans or walnuts

1 Wash and dry the lettuce thoroughly. Tear into bite-size pieces and arrange on a serving platter. Cut the chicken off the bone, and divide into pieces, leaving the skin on (if desired). Cut the larger sections of chicken so that the pieces are of a roughly uniform size

2 Arrange half of the chicken pieces on the lettuce, top with half the avocado. Repeat layering with the remaining chicken and avocado; scatter celery slices over the top.

3 Place the mayonnaise, buttermilk and tarragon vinegar in a small screw-top jar and shake until well combined. Drizzle the dressing over the chicken mixture. Garnish with chopped pecans or walnuts. Serve the salad immediately with warm whole grain bread rolls or crunchy French bread.

CILANTRO SALAD

Preparation time: 15 minutes + 20 minutes soaking
Total cooking time: 1 minute
Serves 6

1/3 cup bulgur (cracked wheat)	1/2 teaspoon honey
1/2 cup orange juice	2 tablespoons balsamic vinegar
1 cup fresh cilantro leaves	1/4 cup olive oil
6 1/2 oz red cabbage, finely sliced	1 small clove garlic, crushed
1 small red onion, finely sliced	1/4 teaspoon Dijon mustard

1 Place the bulgur in a small mixing bowl. Heat the orange juice in small pan until it is hot; pour over the bulgur. Allow to stand for 20 minutes or until all of the juice is absorbed.

2 Place the bulgur, cilantro, cabbage and onion in a large bowl and mix well.

3 Place the honey, vinegar, oil, garlic and mustard in a small jar. Screw the lid on tightly and shake vigorously until all of the ingredients are well combined.

4 Pour the dressing over the salad, and toss well to coat. Transfer to a serving bowl. This salad may be served with grilled or barbecued meat, chicken or fish.

length of crusty baguette, split open and filled with pâté, ham or cheese. The sandwich takes its name from the Earl of Sandwich (1718-92) who, during a long gambling session,

asked his man-servant to keep him supplied with sliced beef between two pieces of bread.

Sapodilla A round fruit with thin, leathery green to brown skin and pale, sweet flesh with a custard-like texture tasting somewhat like soft brown sugar. It can be eaten scooped from the shell, chopped into fruit salad or puréed and added to ice cream. The sapodilla tree is native to Central America and the Caribbean. Chicle, a milky latex obtained from its bark, is used for making chewing gum.

Sapote A tropical fruit from Central America. The black sapote, also known as the chocolate pudding fruit, is similar in size and shape to a persimmon. It has green skin and soft, sweet, dark brown flesh. It can be eaten scooped from the skin, puréed as a sauce or added to ice cream. The white sapote, also green-skinned, has pale yellow, buttery-textured sweet flesh.

SALAD DRESSINGS

A salad dressing is the making of a salad—even a bowl of torn lettuce leaves can taste delicious when tossed with the right dressing. The addition of extra ingredients to a basic vinaigrette or mayonnaise gives the dressings their distinctive flavor and aroma.

The dressing should enhance the flavor of a salad without overpowering its other components. The success of a dressing depends very much on the quality of the ingredients and the subtle balance between them.

- A good olive oil, not too fruity, is the basis.
- Vegetable or nut oils can be used in conjunction with olive oil; the distinctive taste of sesame or chili oil enhances a salad with Asian ingredients.
- Wine vinegars are made from both red and white wine; herb-flavored vinegars are delicious when used in moderation, as are fruit vinegars such as raspberry vinegar.
- Lemon juice can be used in place of some or all of the vinegar.
- Rice vinegars from China and Japan are sweet and mild and go well with cabbage and carrots.
- Add dressing to salad just before serving so that leaves don't wilt. Don't drown salads—use just enough dressing to moisten leaves.

VARIATIONS

- The sharp taste of vinaigrette can be reduced by the addition of $1/2$ teaspoon sugar, if desired.
- Use freshly squeezed citrus juice instead of vinegar. This is particularly good in poultry or game salads.
- Add 1 tablespoon of finely chopped fresh herbs such as chives, parsley, marjoram, thyme.
- As a dressing for shredded raw, green vegetables such as cabbage or spinach, add 1 tablespoon of freshly grated Parmesan cheese.
- The addition of the finely chopped white and sieved yolk of a hard-boiled egg will give the vinaigrette a smoother and thicker texture.

MAYONNAISE

BASIC MAYONNAISE

Place 2 egg yolks, 2–3 teaspoons white vinegar and white pepper to taste in food processor or blender. Process for 15 seconds or until blended. With motor running, add 1 cup olive oil slowly in a thin steady stream and blend until mixture is thick and creamy. Adjust the flavor with more vinegar if you wish. If mixture is too thick, lighten its texture by adding a little hot water. This recipe makes approximately $1 1/4$ cups.

VINAIGRETTE

BASIC VINAIGRETTE

In a small screw-top jar, place $1/4$ cup oil, 2 tablespoons of white wine vinegar, 1 teaspoon seeded mustard and some freshly ground black pepper to taste. Shake well until all the ingredients are evenly mixed. Alternatively, mix in a bowl with a fork or small whisk. Use immediately. This will make $1/2$ cup dressing.

VARIATIONS

▪ A lighter sauce can be made using equal quantities of olive oil and a good vegetable oil.

▪ Add the mashed pulp of 1 avocado and fold it gently through the mayonnaise.

▪ To make a less rich mayonnaise, add 2–3 tablespoons of plain yogurt.

▪ Add 2 tablespoons tomato paste and 1 tablespoon chopped fresh basil.

▪ Mix ⅔ cup heavy cream with 2 tablespoons mayonnaise. Serve with salads containing fruit.

THOUSAND ISLAND DRESSING

Thousand Island Dressing is usually served on lettuce leaves. Place mayonnaise in a bowl and stir in 2 teaspoons tomato purée, 1 teaspoon Dijon mustard, a pinch cayenne pepper, 1–2 teaspoons Worcestershire sauce, 1 tablespoon finely chopped celery, 1 tablespoon chopped sweet pickle, 1 teaspoon chopped capers, 1 chopped hard-boiled egg, salt and freshly ground black pepper to taste.

MAYONNAISE SAUCES

Variations to mayonnaise are often used as sauces, particularly with fish dishes, rather than as salad dressings.

AIOLI

Aïoli is a Mediterranean sauce which is served with fish soups or vegetables. Combine egg yolks with 3 cloves crushed garlic and ½ teaspoon salt in a blender, then proceed as with basic recipe; after oil has been added, adjust flavor with 3–4 teaspoons lemon juice rather than vinegar.

TARTAR SAUCE

Place 1 cup basic mayonnaise in a bowl; stir in 4 tablespoons finely chopped capers, 6 tablespoons chopped gherkins, 2 tablespoons chopped fresh parsley and 2 tablespoons heavy cream or sour cream. Adjust flavor with salt and pepper to taste. Serve with fried or grilled fish.

GREEN SAUCE

Green Sauce goes particularly well with fish such as salmon and trout, and with cold egg dishes. Blanch 10 sprigs of watercress in boiling water. With 1 cup basic mayonnaise, blend ¼ cup cooked spinach leaves, strained and finely chopped, watercress and 4 sprigs each of fresh tarragon and parsley.

GREEN GODDESS DRESSING

Green Goddess Dressing often accompanies shellfish. Make the basic mayonnaise recipe and place in a small bowl. Stir in 3–4 chopped anchovy fillets, 1 clove finely chopped garlic, ¼ cup sour cream and ¼ cup chopped fresh mixed herbs.

FROM LEFT: TARTAR SAUCE, RASPBERRY VINEGAR, VIRGIN OLIVE OIL, FRESH HERB VINAIGRETTE, CITRUS VINAIGRETTE, TARRAGON OIL

Sardine A small, silvery, saltwater fish with tender, strong-flavored, dark, oily flesh. Fresh sardines are best broiled or dusted with flour, quickly pan-fried and served hot with boiled potatoes and a wedge of lemon. The sardine is a member of the herring family. From ancient times in southern Europe it was salted for use in inland areas. In medieval France, sardines preserved in oil or

vinegar were packed into earthenware jars for distribution in areas far from the sea. The fish is named after the Mediterranean island of Sardinia, which was once the center of a fishing industry based on this small fish. Sardines are available fresh, frozen and canned.

Sashimi A dish of Japanese origin consisting of slices of raw, very fresh fish cut into small cubes (tuna or salmon) or sliced paper thin (flounder and sea bream), garnished with grated daikon (giant white radish), shredded lettuce, cucumber, thin

SALMON

POACHED SALMON STEAKS

⭐ **Preparation time:** 5 minutes
Total cooking time: 15 minutes
Serves 4

1½ cups fish stock or bottled clam juice
½ teaspoon salt
½ teaspoon cracked black pepper
pinch ground nutmeg
½ cup dry white wine
2 scallions, finely chopped
4 salmon steaks
2 tablespoons finely chopped fresh parsley

1 Combine fish stock, salt, cracked pepper, ground nutmeg, white wine and chopped scallions in a shallow medium pan. Bring the ingredients in the pan slowly to the boil; boil for 1 minute.
2 Place the salmon steaks in the fish stock in a single layer and simmer, covered, for 10 minutes. Carefully remove the salmon steaks to individual serving plates with a slotted spoon; keep warm.
3 Boil the fish stock for a further minute and then add the chopped fresh parsley. Spoon the fish stock liquid over the salmon and serve immediately.

SALMON WITH DILL MAYONNAISE

⭐ **Preparation time:** 30 minutes
Total cooking time: 15–20 minutes
Serves 4

3 lb whole salmon
2 cups fish stock or bottled clam juice
1 cup homemade mayonnaise
2 tablespoons finely chopped fresh dill
freshly ground black pepper

1 Scale, wash and trim salmon. Place in a fish kettle or large pan. Pour the fish stock over the salmon. Poach till flesh flakes, approximately 15 minutes. Do not turn.
2 Remove salmon and chill well.
3 Place mayonnaise, fresh dill and pepper in a mixing bowl and stir until combined. Transfer mixture to a serving bowl and garnish with a sprig of fresh dill.
4 Skin salmon on one side and serve from each side of the backbone with a spoon and fork.

Note: Use a pair of heavy-duty kitchen scissors to trim away the fins and tail of fish.

ABOVE: POACHED SALMON STEAKS. OPPOSITE PAGE: SALMON AND CAMEMBERT CROQUETTES

SALMON AND CAMEMBERT CROQUETTES

★★ **Preparation time:** 40 minutes +
3 hours standing
Total cooking time: 30–35 minutes
Makes 16

3 large potatoes, about 2 lb, peeled and chopped	1 tablespoon vinegar
1 small onion, finely chopped	1 egg, lightly beaten
	freshly ground pepper
2 x 7 oz cans boneless pink salmon, drained and flaked	2 oz Camembert cheese, cubed
	¼ cup all-purpose flour
1 tablespoon chopped fresh parsley	ground pepper, extra
	2 eggs, lightly beaten, extra
2 teaspoons finely grated lemon rind	1½ cups fresh white bread crumbs
¼ cup lemon juice	oil, for deep-frying

1 Cook the potato in a large pan of boiling water until just tender; drain and mash. Transfer to a large mixing bowl. Add the onion, salmon, parsley, lemon rind and juice, vinegar, egg and pepper to taste. Stir to combine. Divide mixture into 16 evenly sized portions. Form each portion into a sausage shape about 2¾ inches long, working a piece of Camembert in the center of each, making sure that the Camembert is completely enclosed.

2 Combine flour and pepper on a sheet of waxed paper. Toss the croquettes in the seasoned flour; shake off the excess. Dip in beaten egg, then press into the crumbs to coat them evenly; shake off excess. Store, covered, in the refrigerator for 3 hours.

3 Heat oil in deep, heavy-bottom pan. Gently lower a few croquettes at a time into moderately hot oil. Cook over medium-high heat for 5 minutes or until golden brown. Carefully remove from oil with tongs. Drain on paper towels and keep warm. Repeat with remaining croquettes. Serve as a first course, an accompaniment or as a main meal with vegetables or salad.

ABOUT SALMON

▧ Fresh salmon is available whole, cut into steaks or fillets. It has a deep pink flesh and is prized for its delectable flavor.

▧ Whole salmon is wonderful if poached or baked and can be served hot or cold.

▧ Fresh salmon is ideal for marinating and serving raw. Use fresh ginger and herbs to flavor.

▧ Pâtés made from salmon look attractive because of the pretty color. The taste is superb.

▧ Canned salmon is very popular for use in cooking and as a sandwich filling.

strips of carrot or finely chopped ginger and accompanied by a dipping sauce of wasabi (a pungent horseradish sauce), dark soy sauce and sweet cooking wine. Sashimi is generally served as a first course.

Satay (Saté) A dish consisting of small morsels of marinated beef, lamb, pork, poultry or seafood, threaded on bamboo or wooden skewers and grilled. Satays are served hot, accompanied by peanut sauce and cubes of cucumber as a first course. Satays are found in the cooking of Southeast Asia, especially Indonesia, Malaysia and Singapore,

where they are often cooked on small charcoal braziers by street vendors.

Sauce A hot or cold seasoned liquid which is served with a dish to add flavor. A sauce may be thick or thin, strained or chunky. Classic French sauces may be based on a roux of butter and flour (béchamel, brown sauce), on a butter emulsion (Béarnaise, Hollandaise), or on a cold emulsion of oil and egg yolks (mayonnaise); all can be varied with the addition of a great variety of other ingredients. Other sauces are based on puréed vegetables or fruit (coulis), ground nuts (satay sauce), cooked tomato (ketchup), cream, yogurt, cream cheeses and oils. Sweet sauces include custards, rich cream sauces and fruit purées. Many sauces are commercially available, either bottled, canned or dry in packets to be mixed with water, milk or stock.

Sauerbraten A dish of German origin consisting of beef or pork marinated (for one to three days) in a spiced vinegar or red wine mixture, then cooked slowly in the mixture. It is served hot and thinly sliced, traditionally accompanied by the thickened marinade, dumplings and red cabbage.

Sauerkraut White cabbage, sliced wafer-thin, salted to draw out moisture then fermented in brine for four to six weeks. Braised or stewed (sometimes with additional ingredients such as sliced apple, onion or juniper berries) sauerkraut is the classic accompaniment to roast goose, boiled pork, frankfurter and smoked sausage. Fermented cabbage was eaten by workers on the Great Wall of China more than 2,000 years ago. In

GRAVLAX

⭐ **Preparation time:** 20 minutes + 2 days standing
Total cooking time: none
Serves 8

2 salmon fillets, each about 10–16 oz
3 tablespoons sea salt
1½ tablespoons sugar
1 teaspoon white pepper
1 cup coarsely chopped fresh dill, with stems

1 Wash fillets thoroughly. Do not skin.
2 In a bowl combine salt, sugar and pepper. Mix well. Thoroughly rub salt mixture into each flesh side of the fillets.
3 In a shallow dish place one of the salmon fillets skin-side down. Sprinkle the dill over it. Place the other fillet on top of the first fillet with the skin-side up. Place a heavy dish on top of the salmon to weigh it down, and cover the dishes with plastic wrap.
4 Place salmon in refrigerator for 48 hours. Turn the fish over every 12 hours. Baste it periodically with liquid from the fish.
5 To serve, scrape off the dill and salt mixture. Pat the fish dry and slice thinly at an angle (as you would smoked salmon). If desired, press extra very finely chopped dill leaves over the fish before separating the slices, so each slice is edged with dill. May be served with a mustard sauce, freshly made toast and a green salad.

SALMON STEAKS WITH ORIENTAL MAYONNAISE

⭐ **Preparation time:** 10 minutes
Total cooking time: 5 minutes
Serves 4

Oriental Mayonnaise
1 cup homemade or good commercial mayonnaise
2 tablespoons chopped fresh cilantro leaves
2 teaspoons finely grated fresh ginger
2 teaspoons honey, warmed
1 teaspoon soy sauce
½ teaspoon sesame oil
3 tablespoons vegetable oil
2 teaspoons balsamic vinegar
freshly ground pepper
4 x small salmon steaks

1 To make Oriental Mayonnaise: Prepare 30 minutes in advance. Place mayonnaise in a small bowl, add remaining ingredients; mix well.
2 Whisk vegetable oil, vinegar and pepper in a shallow dish, add salmon and turn to coat fish.
3 Heat a heavy-bottom pan until very hot and cook salmon over high heat 2–3 minutes each side. Salmon should be slightly pink and moist in the center. Serve with Oriental Mayonnaise.

SALMON AND NOODLE BAKE

⭐ **Preparation time:** 10 minutes
Total cooking time: 45–50 minutes
Serves 4–5

8 oz dried wheat flour noodles
6½ oz can red salmon, undrained
1 tomato, peeled and finely chopped
2 teaspoons finely chopped fresh dill
1 tablespoon lemon juice
1 cup finely chopped broccoli
2 eggs, lightly beaten
6½ oz ricotta cheese, sieved
3 scallions, finely chopped
⅔ cup grated Cheddar cheese

1 Cook noodles in large pan of boiling water until just tender; drain, cool. Preheat oven to moderate 350°F. Remove bones from salmon, mash salmon in bowl using a fork. Add tomato, dill, juice and broccoli; mix well.
2 Combine noodles with eggs, ricotta and scallions until well coated. Press half noodle mixture over base of paper-lined and greased 8 inch springform pan. Press salmon mixture over noodles, smooth over with back of spoon. Top with remaining noodle mixture. Sprinkle with cheese, bake for 35 minutes or until golden.

SANDWICHES

OPEN-FACED SANDWICH TOPPINGS

Open-faced sandwiches must be eaten with a knife and fork (they're much too messy to be eaten with the hands). Because of this they are usually piled high with ingredients and garnished with herbs or nuts.

▓ Spread slices of rye or pumpernickel bread with butter. Combine equal quantities of mayonnaise and thick sour cream and add chopped hard-boiled eggs. Pile mixture on bread, top with slices of smoked salmon and a spoonful of salmon roe or black caviar. Garnish with a sprig or two of dill.

▓ Spread whole-grain bread with butter and top with lettuce and slices of rare roast beef. Add sliced mango or ripe papaya, a generous spoonful of grain mustard and garnish with watercress or alfalfa sprouts.

▓ Spread sliced bagels or croissants with butter and top with arugula leaves. Mix chopped cooked chicken with a little mayonnaise, chopped apple, celery and scallions and pile on top of the arugula. Top with pecans just before serving.

▓ Spread rye or pumpernickel bread with butter, add a lettuce leaf and pile smoked trout on top.

Add a spoonful of horseradish cream and garnish with a tiny slice of lemon and a parsley sprig.

▓ Spread rye bread with butter and top with lettuce leaves, sliced tomato and thinly sliced cucumber. Add whole peeled shrimp, finely sliced red onion rings and a spoonful of tartar sauce.

▓ Slice a French baguette diagonally and spread with butter. Top with watercress, lightly cooked green asparagus spears, thinly sliced prosciutto and a sliced hard-boiled egg. Add a spoonful of mayonnaise and sprinkle with paprika.

▓ Spread whole-wheat bread thickly with cottage cheese and top with grated carrot, slices of pastrami or corned beef, sliced pickled dill cucumbers and sliced red pepper.

▓ Spread split horseshoe rolls with butter and top with lettuce leaves. Top with sliced avocado, sliced tomato and crisply cooked bacon.

▓ Spread walnut or cracked wheat bread generously with cream cheese or ricotta cheese and add some sliced fresh pear, sliced fresh figs and finely chopped candied ginger. Top with a walnut half or two.

▓ Spread rye or pumpernickel bread with creamy blue cheese and top with sliced apple and chopped celery. Scatter with finely chopped scallions.

▓ Spread rye crispbread with butter and top with shredded lettuce leaves. Add slices of ham, sliced Swiss cheese and sliced tomato. Scatter chopped scallions on top.

OPPOSITE PAGE: GRAVLAX.

ABOVE: OPEN-FACED SANDWICH TOPPINGS

Gaul, food, including cabbage, was salted for the winter. By medieval times salted, fermented cabbage was a staple throughout central and Eastern Europe.

Sausage Ground meat or poultry, seasoned and mixed with a little ground cereal or bread crumbs, usually stuffed into a tube-like casing. Sausages are an ancient way of ensuring that every edible part of the carcass was used (including the intestine, traditionally used as casing). The mixture was often preserved by salting; "sausage" comes from the Latin word *salsus*, salted.

Sausage Roll A sausage encased in puff or flaky pastry and baked. Sausage rolls are eaten hot as a snack or finger food. They

originated as a way of using up leftovers.

Sauté To cook food in a frying pan in a small amount of hot butter or oil until brown.

Savarin A large ring-shaped cake made of baba dough without raisins. After baking, it is soaked with rum-flavored syrup and the center filled with crème patissière, custard or Chantilly cream and fruit. Serve hot and cold.

Saveloy A small, plump sausage made with pork, seasoned with pepper and garlic and sometimes smoked.

Savory, Summer and Winter Two similar aromatic herbs with a delicate, peppery flavor similar to sage and mint. They are used in stuffings and marinades and are often added to cooked fava beans. Summer savory, an annual, has silvery green leaves and a sweeter taste. Winter savory is a perennial with stiffer leaves.

Scald To heat a liquid, especially milk, to the temperature when tiny bubbles appear at the edge of the pan. The term also means to plunge fruit or vegetables into boiling water to remove impurities or make peeling easier.

Scallop A mollusk with a distinctive, ribbed, fan-shaped, hinged shell. There are many species,

including bay and sea scallops. It propels itself

S A R D I N E S

SARDINES WITH TOMATO SAUCE

⭐ **Preparation time:** 30 minutes
Total cooking time: 15 minutes
Serves 4–6

Tomato Sauce
1 tablespoon olive oil
2 cloves garlic, crushed
16 oz can tomatoes, crushed
1/4 cup white wine
2 tablespoons tomato paste
1/4 cup chopped fresh basil

1 lb small fresh sardines or 12 oz canned sardines
1/2 cup all-purpose flour
1/2 teaspoon ground pepper
1/3 cup olive oil
lemon and lime wedges

1 To make Tomato Sauce: Heat the oil in a medium pan; add garlic. Cook over low heat for 2 minutes. Add the tomato, white wine, tomato paste and basil. Simmer, uncovered, for 10 minutes.
2 Cut heads from sardines and discard. Clean and rinse body under cold running water, pat dry.
3 Combine flour and pepper in bowl. Toss sardines lightly in seasoned flour. Shake off excess. Heat oil in a medium pan; add sardines. Cook over medium heat for 2 minutes each side. Drain on paper towels.
4 Place sardines on large serving plate, top with Tomato Sauce and serve immediately with lemon and lime wedges if desired.

HERBED SARDINES

⭐ **Preparation time:** 10 minutes
Total cooking time: 5 minutes
Serves 2–4

2 x 3½ oz cans sardines
1/4 cup butter
2 tablespoons chopped mixed fresh herbs (parsley, chervil, lemon thyme, chives)

1 clove garlic, crushed
2 teaspoons lemon juice
freshly ground pepper
4 large slices brioche, French or Italian bread

1 Drain sardines well and pat gently with paper towels to remove excess oil.
2 Beat butter in a small bowl until very soft and add chopped mixed herbs, garlic, lemon juice and pepper.
3 Toast brioche or bread slices on one side until golden. Arrange sardines on untoasted side. Carefully spread butter mixture over sardines and broil until butter is melted and sardines are hot. Serve immediately.

FRIED SARDINES WITH SAMBUCA

⭐ **Preparation time:** 15 minutes
Total cooking time: 3 minutes
Serves 4

8 large sardines
all-purpose flour for dusting
2 eggs, lightly beaten
2 tablespoons sambuca
2 tablespoons chopped fresh parsley

2 tablespoons grated Parmesan cheese
freshly ground black pepper
1/4 cup butter
lemon wedges

1 Cut the heads from sardines. Cut along underside of fish, open out and press flat. With skin-side-up, press along backbone, pull backbone away. Wash; drain.
2 Dust sardines with flour. Combine eggs, sambuca, parsley, cheese and pepper. Add fish; toss to coat.
3 Melt butter in frying pan and add sardines in a single layer. Fry on both sides for 1 minute or until lightly browned. Drain on paper towels. Serve with lemon wedges.

Note: Sambuca is an Italian liqueur with the taste of aniseed. It is usually drunk with two coffee beans floating in the glass.

ABOVE: SARDINES WITH TOMATO SAUCE.
OPPOSITE PAGE, BELOW: COCONUT LAMB SATAYS;
ABOVE: PORK SATAYS

SATAYS

PORK SATAYS

★ **Preparation time:** 30 minutes + overnight marinating
Total cooking time: 8 minutes
Makes 8 satays

1½ lb lean boneless pork	1 teaspoon ground cumin
1 large onion, coarsely chopped	½ teaspoon ground fennel
2 cloves garlic	1 tablespoon ground coriander
1 stick lemon grass, thick base only, chopped, or 2 strips lemon rind	1 teaspoon ground turmeric
2 thick slices galangal, optional	½ teaspoon salt
	1 tablespoon soft dark brown sugar
1 teaspoon finely chopped, pared fresh ginger	1 tablespoon lemon juice, malt vinegar or tamarind liquid

1 Trim fat from pork. Place pork in freezer for 30 minutes to make slicing easier. Slice across grain into very thin, even strips. Place onion in food processor, process until almost smooth.
2 Add garlic and lemon grass. Cover and process until combined. Add a little water to make blending easier, if necessary. Transfer to a large bowl.
3 Stir in the galangal, ginger, cumin, fennel, coriander, turmeric, salt and lemon juice.
4 Add meat; stir to coat with onion mixtue. Cover meat; refrigerate 6–24 hours. Drain, reserving marinade. Bring marinade to boil in small saucepan. Reduce heat; stir and simmer 2 minutes.

5 Thread meat strips onto bamboo skewers. Cover ends with foil to prevent burning. Preheat broiler. Place skewers on unheated rack of broiler pan. Place under the broiler 3–4 inches from heat 6–8 minutes or until cooked through.
6 Turn skewers occasionally, basting with the reserved marinade several times.

COCONUT LAMB SATAYS

★ **Preparation time:** 10 minutes + 2 hours standing
Total cooking time: 3 minutes
Serves 4

4 lamb shoulder chops, about 1 lb 10 oz	1 tablespoon light soy sauce
1 small onion	1 teaspoon sambal oelek
1 clove garlic, crushed	¼ cup flaked coconut
1 tablespoon tamarind sauce	2 tablespoons oil
1 tablespoon vinegar	1 teaspoon sesame oil

1 Remove fat and bones from lamb chops and cut meat into ¾ inch cubes.
2 Chop onion. Place in bowl, combine with lamb, garlic, tamarind sauce, vinegar, soy sauce, sambal oelek and coconut. Cover and leave to marinate in refrigerator 2 hours or overnight.
3 Thread lamb onto skewers, brush with combined oils; cook under preheated broiler 3 minutes, turning occasionally.

by using a large muscle to successively open and shut its shell; it is this muscle, creamy-white to creamy-pink in color, that is eaten; the pinky-orange roe, also edible, is sometimes discarded.

Scallops are generally cooked and served on the shell. The term also refers to a wavy border made as a garnish for pastry, melon or other foods.

Scaloppine A small thin slice of boneless veal cut across the grain and flattened (in France known as *escalope*, in Germany as *Schnitzel*, used in the famous dish *Wienerschnitzel*). The term "scaloppine" is often extended to include a dish of northern Italian origin in which the slices are coated in flour, fried in butter or oil and served with a tomato or wine sauce.

Scampi The Italian name for a large shrimp with long, thin claws. When cooked they have delicately flavored white flesh and are often served cooked in butter, garlic, white wine and herbs or fried in batter (scampi fritti). The French name is *langoustine*.

CLASSIC SAUCES

Sauces are used to flavor, coat or accompany a dish; some are used to bind the ingredients together. A fine, smooth, well-flavored sauce will improve both the taste and appearance of the dish with which it is served.

Here are six basic sauces. Once the techniques of preparation are mastered, the range of variations is almost endless.

BASIC WHITE SAUCE

Melt 2 tablespoons of unsalted (sweet) butter in a small heavy-bottom pan, blend in 2 tablespoons all-purpose flour and cook the mixture gently for 1 minute, whisking all the time. Remove pan from the heat; gradually whisk in 1 1/4 cups lukewarm milk and bring the mixture slowly to the boil. Continue to cook gently, whisking all the time, until the sauce comes to the boil and thickens. Simmer the sauce very gently for another 2–3 minutes. Season sauce with salt and white ground pepper. Makes 1 1/4 cups. Serve over vegetables, such as cauliflower and broccoli, or with fish, shellfish, or corned beef.

VARIATIONS

■ **MORNAY (CHEESE) SAUCE:** Follow the basic recipe but before seasoning, stir in 1/2 cup finely grated Gruyère or Cheddar cheese, 1 teaspoon Dijon mustard and a pinch of cayenne pepper.

■ **CAPER SAUCE:** Follow basic recipe, using half milk and half meat stock. Before seasoning, add 1 tablespoon capers and 1–2 teaspoons lemon juice. Reheat gently.

■ **BECHAMEL SAUCE:** For this classic French sauce, place the milk in a pan with a slice of onion, 1/2 stalk celery and 1/2 carrot, both chopped, a bay leaf and 3 black peppercorns. Bring slowly to the boil, remove from heat, cover and set aside to infuse for 30 minutes. Strain, reserving the milk, and proceed as for basic recipe.

BEARNAISE SAUCE

Put into a pan 4 tablespoons white wine vinegar, 2 finely chopped shallots and a few chopped tarragon sprigs. Boil gently until liquid has reduced by one-third. Set aside to cool, then strain into a heatproof bowl or the top of a double boiler. Add 2 egg yolks to vinegar and heat over gently simmering water. Whisk until thick and smooth. Gradually add 1/2 cup softened butter, a small piece at a time, whisking until each piece has been absorbed and sauce has thickened. Season. Serve warm. Makes 2/3 cup. Serve with steak, chicken or fried fish.

HOLLANDAISE SAUCE

Melt ¾ cup unsalted (sweet) butter in a small pan. Skim froth from top and discard. Allow melted butter to cool, but not re-set. Combine 2 tablespoons water and 4 egg yolks in a small, heavy-bottom pan; whisk 30 seconds or until pale and creamy. Place pan over low heat and continue whisking for 3 minutes, until mixture is thick. Remove from heat and add cooled butter a little at a time, whisking after each addition. (Discard whey in bottom of the pan.) Stir in 2 tablespoons lemon juice, season to taste. Serve warm. Makes 1 cup. Serve with asparagus, broccoli, poached eggs (Eggs Benedict), poached or grilled fish.

VARIATIONS

■ **MOUSSELINE:** Stir 3 tablespoons heavy cream into sauce just before serving.

■ **LIGHTER HOLLANDAISE:** Just before serving, fold in 2 stiffly beaten egg whites.

■ **SAUCE MALTAISE:** Stir in grated rind of 1 orange and 4 tablespoons of orange juice in place of lemon juice.

BEURRE BLANC

Place 1 cup white wine and 1 tablespoon finely chopped shallots in small heavy-based pan. Boil to reduce to 2 tablespoons. Remove from heat. Cut 1 cup chilled butter into small cubes. Add 2 cubes to wine mixture, whisk in vigorously. Return pan to low heat and continue whisking in butter, a piece at a time. The sauce will thicken to the consistency of light cream. Remove from heat. Makes 1 cup. Serve with grilled fish or asparagus.

RICH TOMATO SAUCE

Heat 2 tablespoons olive oil in a heavy-bottom pan, add 1 finely chopped onion and cook over medium heat for 5 minutes, until onion is lightly golden, stirring occasionally. Add 2 cloves crushed garlic and cook for 1 minute. Add 1 tablespoon red wine vinegar and 2 lb large ripe tomatoes which have been peeled and chopped; bring to boil. Reduce heat to low and simmer, uncovered, for 25 minutes, stirring occasionally. Add ¼ cup tomato paste, 1 teaspoon sugar, 1 teaspoon dried basil leaves and 1 teaspoon dried oregano leaves. Simmer 15 minutes, stirring often. Use as a topping for pizza or a sauce with pasta, or serve warm with sausages or steak. Makes 1½ cups.

SAUCE ESPAGNOLE

Melt ½ cup butter in a large pan. Add 1 tablespoon each of finely chopped celery, carrot, onion and bacon. Stir over medium heat 10 minutes or until well browned. Add 2 tablespoons all-purpose flour. Stir over low heat 8–10 minutes or until browned. Remove from heat; blend in 8 cups beef stock and 2–3 tablespoons tomato paste. Add a bouquet garni. Simmer, partially covered, over low heat for 1½ hours, skimming off surface regularly, or until liquid has reduced by about half. Remove from heat. Add salt and pepper to taste. Strain and reheat. Makes 2 cups. Serve with grilled steak, cutlets, roasted game or vegetables. To make a richer sauce, stir in 1 tablespoon of sherry or Madeira.

CLOCKWISE FROM TOP LEFT: BEARNAISE SAUCE, RICH TOMATO SAUCE, BECHAMEL SAUCE, SAUCE MALTAISE, HOLLANDAISE SAUCE. CENTER: SAUCE ESPAGNOLE

Schnitzel See
Scaloppine.

Scone A small plain
cake made from a simple
flour and milk dough
raised with baking
powder or baking soda;
in North America a
similar cake is known by
the term "biscuit" and
the term "scone" refers
to a plain or sweet quick
bread made from a richer
dough that usually
contains egg.

Scones are served
freshly baked, split in
half, with butter or
cream and jam or honey
as a snack; scones with
clotted cream (a thick
cream formed by heating
and cooling milk) and
strawberry jam are the
basis of Devonshire tea.
Dried fruit can
be added
to the
dough
or, for a
savory
scone,
flavorings can
include onion, cheese or
herbs. In North America
scones or biscuits are
often served with a meal
or they may be split
open to sandwich fillings
such as smoked turkey
and ham.

Scones originate from
Scotland where they
were cooked on a thick
flat iron with a handle,
called a griddle.

Score To make small
incisions on the outer
surface of a food in order
to decorate it or to allow

SAUCES SWEET

CARAMEL SAUCE

Bring 1 cup water to boil in medium pan. Add 1 cup sugar and stir until dissolved. Return pan to heat and bring to the boil. Cook rapidly (without stirring) until golden brown, occasionally brushing sugar crystals from inside of pan with a pastry brush dipped in cold water. Place pan in a sink and, with hand covered with a towel, add $1/2$ cup water to pan—the mixture will splatter. Return pan to heat and stir until caramel is dissolved. Chill sauce before serving.

VANILLA CREAM SAUCE

Heat 1 cup heavy cream and $1/2$ cup milk in a pan until almost boiling. Using electric beaters beat 3 egg yolks, 1 teaspoon cornstarch and 2 tablespoons sugar in a small bowl and pour hot cream mixture over yolks while beating. Return mixture to pan and heat gently while stirring to a smooth sauce—do not boil. Strain the sauce into a cold bowl; add $1/2$ teaspoon vanilla extract, chill.

RUM OR BRANDY SAUCE

Using electric beaters beat 1 egg yolk and 2 tablespoons sugar in a small bowl until light in color. Stir in 2 tablespoons rum or brandy and $1/2$ cup lightly whipped cream. Fold in 1 stiffly beaten egg white. Serve within 30 minutes of preparing.

HOT FUDGE SAUCE

Break $3 1/2$ oz dark (semisweet) chocolate into pieces and place in a small pan with 2 tablespoon butter, 2 tablespoons corn syrup, $1/2$ cup soft brown sugar and $1/2$ cup cream. Stir over low heat until ingredients have melted. Bring to boil and remove from heat. Serve warm or hot.

STRAWBERRY SAUCE

Place 8 oz hulled strawberries in a blender with 2 tablespoons sugar and 1 tablespoon lemon or orange juice. Blend until smooth; strain if desired. Chill before serving.

HARD SAUCE

Beat $1/2$ cup unsalted (sweet) butter in a bowl until it is soft. Gradually add 2 cups sifted confectioners' sugar and beat until mixture is light and creamy. Beat in 1 tablespoon brandy, whisky or rum. Cover, refrigerate until firm.

BUTTERSCOTCH SAUCE

Place $1/4$ cup butter in a medium pan with 1 cup soft brown sugar, 1 cup heavy cream and 2 tablespoons light corn syrup. Heat gently while stirring until smooth. Bring to the boil and simmer sauce for 1 minute. Cool.

ABOVE: ICE CREAM SUNDAE WITH STRAWBERRY SAUCE. OPPOSITE: BLACK PUDDING WITH CABBAGE AND APPLE

BLACK PUDDING (BLOOD SAUSAGE) WITH CABBAGE AND APPLE

★ **Preparation time:** 15 minutes
Total cooking time: 20–25 minutes
Serves 4

2 slices bacon
1 lb black pudding
2 tablespoons butter
1 small onion, diced
3 cups shredded cabbage

2 tart green apples,
  peeled and sliced
2 tablespoons stock
ground pepper
buttered toast, to serve

1 Cut bacon slices into strips. Skin black pudding and cut diagonally into ½ inch thick slices.
2 Heat the butter in a pan. Add the bacon and cook for 2–3 minutes and remove from the pan. Add the black pudding to the pan, cook for 5 minutes, remove and keep warm.
3 Cook the diced onion for 1 minute, add the bacon, cabbage, apple, stock and ground pepper. Cover the pan and cook gently for about 10–15 minutes.
4 Arrange cabbage mixture over base of a serving plate. Top with warm black pudding and serve with toast.

SPICY SAUSAGE AND BACON PAELLA

★ **Preparation time:** 20 minutes
Total cooking time: 45 minutes
Serves 6

4 chorizo or other spicy
  sausages, sliced
  diagonally
4 slices bacon, chopped
1 medium onion, sliced
1 medium green pepper,
  sliced

1 clove garlic, crushed
1½ cups long-grain rice
16 oz can tomatoes
¾ cup chicken stock
1 teaspoon turmeric
salt and pepper

1 Cook the sausages and bacon in a large pan until they are well browned (about 5 minutes). Remove from the pan; drain on paper towels.
2 Add the onion, pepper, garlic and rice to the pan. Cook over medium heat, stirring for 3 minutes.
3 Add the canned tomatoes with their juice and stir well. Add stock and turmeric, stir to combine. Cover pan with a tight-fitting lid.
4 Bring to boil; stir once. Reduce the heat and simmer, covered, for 25 minutes or until the

liquid is almost absorbed and the rice is tender. Add the sausage and bacon mixture; heat through. Season with salt and pepper.

BARBECUED BEEF AND MINT SAUSAGES

★ **Preparation time:** 15 minutes
Total cooking time: 10 minutes
Makes 12 sausages

1½ lb ground beef
8 oz ground sausage
2 tablespoons cornstarch
1 egg, lightly beaten
1 medium onion, finely
  chopped
2 cloves garlic, crushed
2 tablespoons chopped
  fresh mint

1 teaspoon sambal oelek
  (bottled red chilies)
1 teaspoon ground cumin
1 teaspoon garam masala
½ teaspoon ground
  cardamom
½ cup mango chutney

1 Combine ground beef and sausage in a bowl. Add cornstarch, egg, onion, garlic, mint, sambal oelek, cumin, garam masala and cardamom; mix well.
2 Divide the mixture into 12 even-sized portions. Using wet hands, mold each portion into sausage shapes.
3 Place sausages on lightly oiled preheated grill. Cook over medium heat for 10 minutes or until cooked through, turning sausages occasionally during cooking. Serve with mango chutney, peas and mashed potato if desired.

the penetration of a marinade. The skins of some fruits, such as apples, are scored to prevent them from splitting during baking.

Scotch Egg A hard-boiled egg which is shelled and encased in ground sausage. It is then coated with bread crumbs and deep-fried. Scotch

eggs may be eaten hot or cold.

Scottish Food Scotland is popularly identified with the uncomplicated and sustaining foods needed to face its brisk weather. Steaming porridge, warming broths, oatmeal cakes and haggis are traditional fare of the Highland farming communities and are a response to the climate which, although inhospitable in so many ways, is ideal for growing the staple, oats. The region is also the home of some fine food, based on high-quality local ingredients and which shows in its preparation the influence of the old alliance between Scotland and France. For centuries the kitchens of Highland landed gentry have produced dishes such as cream soups, game braised in wine, rich sauces and pastries; estate streams teem with salmon and trout; the heaths supply grouse and the forests and fields venison and hare. In the Lowlands and the cities of Glasgow and Edinburgh,

where wheat flour has always been more widely used, there are delicious breads, buns, scones and cakes.

In Scotland the day often begins with a nourishing cooked breakfast of oatmeal porridge (traditionally eaten without sugar), fried ham and eggs, or fresh fish, kippers or perhaps finnan haddie (smoked haddock, a specialty of the northeastern coast, which is delicious poached in milk), followed by toast, oatcakes or warm baps (buns) with marmalade and tea or coffee. The main meal of the day is taken at midday and usually includes soup (which, if it is a thick broth or a meat soup, may be served over a boiled potato as the main course)

and fish (such as trout, salmon, haddock, halibut or cod), meat (beef or lamb),

PORK SAUSAGE ROLLS WITH MUSTARD CREAM

⭐ **Preparation time:** 20 minutes
Total cooking time: 10 minutes
Serves 6

2 lb ground pork
1 small onion, finely chopped
1 cup fresh bread crumbs
2 cloves garlic, crushed
1 egg, lightly beaten
1 teaspoon dried sage
6 long crusty bread rolls

Mustard Cream
1/2 cup sour cream
1 tablespoon whole-grain mustard
2 teaspoons lemon juice

1 Prepare and heat grill. Place pork in large mixing bowl. Add onion, bread crumbs, garlic, egg and sage. Using hands, mix to combine thoroughly. Divide the mixture into 6 equal portions; shape into sausage shapes about 6½ inches long.
2 Place meat mixture on hot, lightly oiled grill. Barbecue for 5–10 minutes, or until no longer pınk, turning occasionally.
3 Place pork on a long crusty roll with Mustard Cream. Garnish with chives and serve with a salad, if desired.
4 To make Mustard Cream: Place sour cream, whole grain mustard and juice in a small bowl and stir to combine.

CHICKEN AND CORN SAUSAGES WITH SALSA CRUDA

⭐ **Preparation time:** 20 minutes + refrigeration
Total cooking time: 35 minutes
Makes 12

1 lb 10 oz ground chicken
1 cup fresh bread crumbs
4 oz canned creamed corn
1 tablespoon fresh chives, finely chopped
1/4 cup cornmeal

Salsa Cruda
2 large tomatoes, finely chopped
1 medium onion, finely chopped
1 clove garlic, crushed
2 tablespoons fresh cilantro, finely chopped
1 tablespoon orange juice

1 Preheat oven to 350°F. Line a baking sheet with foil; brush lightly with oil. Place chicken, bread crumbs, corn, chives and cornmeal in a large mixing bowl; combine thoroughly. Divide into 12 equal portions and shape into sausages 5 inches long. Mixture will be quite moist.
2 To make Salsa Cruda: Combine all ingredients in a bowl; refrigerate for at least 1 hour. Serve at room temperature.
3 Place sausages on prepared baking sheet; bake 35 minutes, turning occasionally. Serve with Salsa Cruda.

SCALLOPS

HERBED SCALLOP KABOBS

⭐ ⭐ **Preparation time:** 1 hour
Total cooking time: 5–10 minutes
Serves 8

24 scallops	2 teaspoons lemon juice
6 large scallions, green part only	1 tablespoon white wine
2 zucchini	2 teaspoons mixed dried herbs
2 medium carrots	¼ teaspoon onion powder
1 tablespoon butter, melted	

1 Wash scallops and remove vein; pat dry with paper towels. Cut scallion greens in half lengthwise, then into 3 inch lengths. Line a baking sheet with aluminum foil. Using a vegetable peeler, slice zucchini and carrots lengthwise into thin ribbons. Plunge vegetable strips into a bowl of boiling water, leave 2 minutes; drain, then plunge in bowl of ice water. When cold, drain. Pat dry with paper towels.
2 Roll a scallop in a strip of onion, carrot and zucchini; secure with small skewer. Repeat this process with the remaining scallops and vegetables. Cover the ends of the skewers with

foil to prevent burning.
3 Combine the butter, juice and wine in a mixing bowl. Brush over the scallops. Sprinkle with the combined herbs and onion powder. Place under hot broiler 4–5 inches from heat 5–10 minutes or until the scallops are tender and cooked through.

SCALLOP SALAD WITH LIME AND GINGER

⭐ **Preparation time:** 20 minutes
Total cooking time: 2 minutes
Serves 4

13 oz scallops	½ teaspoon honey
1 tablespoon peanut oil	3 medium zucchini, cut into matchsticks
¼ cup peanut oil, extra	2 medium carrots, cut into matchsticks
1 tablespoon lime juice	
1 teaspoon grated fresh ginger	2 scallions, cut into ½ inch diagonal slices
1 tablespoon chopped fresh cilantro	

1 Wash scallops and remove brown vein. Pat dry with paper towels. Heat oil in heavy-bottom pan, add scallops. Cook on high heat 2 minutes or until golden, turning once. Remove from pan and keep warm.
2 Place extra peanut oil, lime juice, ginger, cilantro and honey in a screw-top jar. Shake well.
3 Arrange a bed of vegetables on a serving platter or individual plates. Pile the scallops on top, pour dressing over and serve immediately.

OPPOSITE PAGE, ABOVE: PORK SAUSAGE ROLLS WITH MUSTARD CREAM; BELOW: CHICKEN AND CORN SAUSAGES WITH SALSA CRUDA.
ABOVE: HERBED SCALLOP KABOBS

game or meats prepared in sausages (such as haggis), pies or black puddings. Steamed and baked puddings or fruit (especially berry) tarts complete the meal. A light supper, which is called "high tea" and may consist of foods such as cold meats, shepherd's pie, fish and chips or bacon and eggs is eaten in the evening. Cakes, scones, buns and cookies are always on hand; specialties include butter-rich shortbread and the almond

encrusted Dundee cake. The national drink, of course, is whiskey.

Scrapple A breakfast dish made of a mixture of cornmeal, pork and spices, cut into slices and fried.

Scrod A small white fish of the cod family.

Seafood A collective term for edible fish and shellfish. A mixture of seafood, usually including squid, shrimp, crab and lobster meat. Used with tomato sauce for spaghetti marinara, or sprinkled on dough to make seafood pizza. A mixture of two or three types of seafood is often served accompanied by a mayonnaise-based sauce.

SCONES

CHIVE SCONES WITH BACON BUTTER

⭐ **Preparation time:** 12 minutes + 30 minutes standing
Total cooking time: 15–18 minutes
Makes 16

Bacon Butter
1/3 cup butter, softened
2 teaspoons bacon bits

Chive and Onion Scones
3 cups all-purpose flour
1 envelope French onion soup mix

2 teaspoons baking powder
1/2 teaspoon salt
1/4 cup butter
1 cup milk
1 egg yolk
2 tablespoons freshly chopped chives
2 tablespoons milk, extra

1 To make Bacon Butter: Combine the butter and bacon bits in a bowl; mix well. Store, covered with plastic wrap in the refrigerator, for 30 minutes.
2 Preheat oven to 425°F. Line a baking sheet with parchment paper. Place the flour, soup mix, baking powder, salt and butter in a food processor. Process in short bursts for 15 seconds. Add the milk, yolk and chives to bowl, process 5 seconds or until mixture almost forms a dough.
3 Turn dough onto a lightly floured surface; knead for 30 seconds. Roll mixture evenly into a 8 x 8 inch rectangle. Place on a floured board. Using a sharp knife, cut dough into 16 pieces. Brush tops with extra milk.
4 Arrange pieces spaced evenly apart on prepared baking sheet. Bake for 15–18 minutes, or until

scones are well risen and browned. Serve warm with chilled bacon butter.

DEVONSHIRE SCONES

⭐ **Preparation time:** 15 minutes
Total cooking time: 15–18 minutes
Makes 12

3 cups all-purpose flour
2 teaspoons baking powder
1/2 teaspoon salt
2 tablespoons sugar

1/4 cup butter, chopped
1 cup milk
beaten egg, for glaze
strawberry jam and whipped cream, to serve

1 Preheat oven to moderately hot 400°F. Brush a baking sheet with melted butter or oil. Sift the flour, baking powder and salt into a mixing bowl, add sugar. Using your fingertips, rub in butter until mixture resembles bread crumbs. Make a well in the center and pour in milk, mix to form a soft, slightly sticky dough.
2 Turn the dough out onto a floured surface, knead lightly. Pat or roll to a thickness of 3/4 inch. Cut into 2½ inch rounds with a cutter and place close together on prepared baking sheet.
3 Brush scones with beaten egg. Bake for 15–18 minutes. Serve the scones hot, with jam and whipped cream.

LEFT: DEVONSHIRE SCONES;
ABOVE: CITRUS ROUND.
OPPOSITE PAGE: POTATO KNOTS

Sear To quickly brown the surface of a food, usually meat, using a very high heat. It is done to seal in the juices.

Seasoning An ingredient added to a food to heighten its natural flavor.

Sea Urchin A marine animal with a soft body encased in a hard, spherical shell. The edible part is the bright red-orange roe, which has a salty taste and the consistency of raw egg.

Seaweed A variety of edible sea plant used in Japanese cooking.

Semolina A food made by coarsely grinding hard durum wheat. Semolina is used to make milk puddings, cakes, custards and cookies. Semolina flour, milled from the heart of durum wheat, is used to make pasta.

Sesame Oil A strongly flavored amber-colored oil pressed from roasted sesame seeds. It is used in Chinese cooking, mainly as a flavoring; in Japan sesame oil is blended with other oils to fry tempura. When heated, sesame oil loses much of its flavor. Cleopatra is said to have

CITRUS ROUND

⭐ **Preparation time:** 20 minutes
Total cooking time: 20 minutes
Makes 8 wedges

2 cups all-purpose flour
1½ teaspoons baking
  powder
¼ teaspoon salt
¼ teaspoon baking soda
¼ cup butter
2 tablespoons chopped
  candied peel

2 tablespoons sugar
2 teaspoons grated lemon
  rind
⅓ cup wheatgerm
1 egg, beaten lightly
1 tablespoon lemon juice
¼ cup milk

1 Preheat oven to 425°F. Sift flour, baking powder, salt and baking soda in a large bowl, add the butter; rub in lightly with fingertips. Mix in candied peel, sugar, lemon rind and wheatgerm.
2 Combine egg, lemon juice and milk. Make a well in the center of the flour and pour in liquid all at once. Mix quickly to form a soft dough. Turn onto floured surface and knead lightly.
3 Shape dough into a round about 8 inches in diameter, place on greased baking sheet. With a floured knife, cut through to the bottom to form eight wedges. Glaze top with a little milk.
4 Bake round for 20 minutes. Cool on a wire rack 5 minutes, serve with butter and marmalade.

POTATO KNOTS

⭐ **Preparation time:** 20 minutes
Total cooking time: 20–25 minutes
Makes 8 large scones

1½ cups all-purpose flour
1½ teaspoons baking
  powder
¼ teaspoon salt
¾ cup cold, mashed
  potato

2 tablespoons butter,
  softened
⅔ cup milk
milk, extra
½ cup coarsely grated
  Cheddar cheese

1 Preheat oven to 400°F. Grease a baking sheet with melted butter or margarine; dust with flour. Sift the flour, baking powder and salt into a bowl. Add the mashed potato and stir to combine. Add the butter and milk and mix to form a soft dough. Turn onto a lightly floured surface.
2 Knead lightly. Divide into eight portions. Roll each portion into a thin roll about 10 inches long. Shape into knots. Place on prepared baking sheet.
3 Brush the knots with the extra milk, sprinkle with the Cheddar cheese. Bake for 20–25 minutes until golden and cooked through. Serve warm, spread with butter.

Note: Potato knots are delicious served with a hearty casserole.

used it as a skin oil; thirteenth-century Venetian traveller Marco Polo praised it as the best oil he tasted during his journeys. Sesame oil is available from most supermarkets and Asian food stores.

Sesame Seeds Also known as benne seeds, the small oval seeds of a semi-tropical plant. Lightly toasted seeds can be tossed through salads, vegetable dishes, stuffings and stews; raw seeds are often sprinkled on bread, buns and cookies before baking. In the Middle East ground sesame seeds are used to make the candy halva and the dressing tahini. In Africa the seeds are roasted and eaten like peanuts and are also ground into a flour. In Japan and Korea freshly roasted then lightly crushed seeds are added to dips and dressings; in China whole roasted seeds are used as a garnish and are ground into a brown, nutty-flavored paste.

Shallot A small onion, similar in shape to a large clove of garlic, with a reddish-brown skin and purple-tinged white flesh with a mild flavor. Shallot bulbs and leaves are used

raw, finely chopped in salads, and are cooked; they are widely used in the cooking of northern

France, where they are used to flavor sauces and casseroles.

Shark Any of several species of firm, meaty fish, often broiled or grilled.

Shashlik The Russian name for cubed mutton or lamb marinated in vinegar and oil flavored with thyme, nutmeg, onion and bay leaf, then broiled or grilled. Shashlik is similar to the Middle Eastern kabob.

Shellfish An edible marine animal with a shell or carapace. There are three main classes: crustaceans,

including lobsters, crabs, prawns, shrimp and crayfish; mollusks, including oysters, scallops, mussels, clams and whelks; and cephalopods (with a reduced internal shell and technically classed as mollusks), namely, squid, cuttlefish and octopus.

Shepherd's Pie A dish consisting of finely chopped or ground cooked lamb, fried onion and stock, seasoned with Worcestershire sauce, thickened with flour and simmered; the mixture is transferred to a pie dish, topped with mashed

SCOTTISH CLASSICS

SCOTCH BROTH

⭐ *Preparation time:* 25 minutes + overnight soaking
Total cooking time: 2 hours
Serves 4–6

¼ cup dried peas
2 tablespoons pearl barley
6 lamb neck chops, (1½ lb)
6 cups water
1 leek, cut into ¾ inch pieces
1 turnip, cut into ½ inch cubes

1 large carrot, cut into ½ inch cubes
1 stalk celery, sliced
2 cups shredded cabbage
salt, pepper
¼ cup chopped fresh parsley

1 Place whole dried peas in a large bowl. Cover with warm water; stand, uncovered, overnight. Rinse peas twice and drain thoroughly.
2 Place the peas, barley, chops and water in a large heavy-bottom pan. Bring to boil, skim the froth from the top. Add the leek and turnip. Reduce the heat to low and simmer, covered, for 1½ hours.
3 Add the carrot and celery to pan. Simmer, uncovered, for another 30 minutes.
4 Add the shredded cabbage. Stir until the cabbage is just heated through and tender. Season to taste. Stir in the chopped fresh parsley just before serving.

OAT CRACKERS

⭐ *Preparation time:* 5 minutes
Total cooking time: 25 minutes
Makes 25

2½ cups oatmeal
½ teaspoon baking powder
½ teaspoon salt

1 teaspoon sugar
¼ cup lard or butter, melted
½ cup warm water

1 Preheat oven to moderate 350°F. Line two baking sheets with parchment paper. In food processor grind 1½ cups oatmeal until fine. Combine fine and regular oatmeal, baking powder, salt and sugar in a large mixing bowl. Make a well in the center; add lard or butter and water.
2 Using a flat-bladed knife, work mixture into a firm dough. Turn dough out onto a surface lightly sprinkled with fine oatmeal or flour; press into a flattish square.
3 Roll out to a 12 x 12 inch square, ⅛ inch thick, sprinkling with extra oatmeal if necessary. Cut into 2½ inch diamonds. Repeat with leftover dough.
4 Place oatcakes on baking sheets about ¼ inch apart; bake 25 minutes. Allow to cool on baking sheets. Serve warm with butter.

LEFT: SCOTCH BROTH; ABOVE: OAT CRACKERS.
OPPOSITE PAGE, ABOVE: HOTCH POTCH;
BELOW: CRUMBED TROUT WITH PARSLEY BUTTER

CRUMBED TROUT WITH PARSLEY BUTTER

Preparation time: 15 minutes +
20 minutes refrigeration
Total cooking time: 4 minutes
Serves 6–8

2 large trout fillets (about
   1 lb), skin removed
2 teaspoons milk
½ cup oatmeal, ground
¼ cup oil

Parsley Butter
¼ cup butter, softened
1 tablespoon lemon juice
¼ teaspoon cracked black
   peppercorns
1 scallion, finely chopped
1 tablespoon finely
   chopped fresh parsley

1 Cut each trout fillet evenly into four pieces. Brush each with milk, then coat with the ground oatmeal. Repeat process with the remaining trout fillets, milk and oatmeal. Arrange the coated trout on a tray. Cover with plastic wrap and refrigerate for 20 minutes.

2 To make Parsley Butter: Place the softened butter in a small bowl; mash with a fork. Gradually mix in the lemon juice and cracked peppercorns. Add the scallion and parsley; mix well. Serve in dollops or form into a log shape and cut into rounds.

3 Heat oil in medium nonstick frying pan; add trout pieces. Cook over medium heat for 2 minutes on each side or until lightly golden. Serve with parsley butter.

HOTCH POTCH (LAMB STEW)

Preparation time: 25 minutes
Total cooking time: 1 hour 45 minutes
Serves 4–6

1 tablespoon oil
3 lamb shanks, about
   2 lb
1 large onion, chopped
1 large turnip, chopped
1 stalk celery, chopped
4 cups water
2 teaspoons salt
1 teaspoon cracked black
   pepper

10 oz cauliflower,
   chopped
2 carrots, chopped
1 cup frozen peas,
   thawed
2 cups shredded lettuce
2 tablespoons finely
   chopped fresh parsley

1 Heat oil in a large heavy-bottom pan; add lamb. Cook over medium heat for 10 minutes or until well browned. Add onion, turnip, celery, water, salt and pepper. Bring to boil, reduce heat to low; simmer, covered, for 1 hour, stirring occasionally.

2 Add cauliflower, carrots and peas to pan. Simmer, uncovered, for 30 minutes.

3 Carefully transfer lamb from pan to chopping board with slotted spoon or tongs; cool slightly. Remove all flesh from bones and chop coarsely. Discard the bones.

4 Return lamb to pan with lettuce and parsley. Stir over low heat for 3 minutes, or until just heated through.

potato and then browned under a broiler. Cottage pie is a similar dish using beef. Both were created to use up leftover roast meat.

Sherbet A smooth, iced dessert made of milk, sugar, sometimes gelatin or egg white and a sharp-tasting fruit flavoring, usually citrus or berries. Sherbet is softer and less rich than ice cream and although similar, it lacks the biting fruity flavor of sorbet, which does not include milk. Sherbert can be served topped with a few spoonfuls of champagne or liqueur and accompanied by sliced fresh fruit. Both sherbet and sorbet have their origins in ancient Persia. The word "sherbet" comes from *sharbia*, the Arabic word for "drink." Sherbet is commercially available or can be made at home.

Sherry A fortified wine usually served before dinner. Both dry sherry and sweet sherry are used in sauces, stews and in chicken dishes, when it is usually added just before serving; also used in sweet dishes and desserts. Sherry was imported into England after the sixteenth century from the Spanish port of Jerez de la Frontera.

Shish Kabob See Kabob.

Shoofly Pie A very sweet Pennsylvania Dutch molasses and brown sugar pie. It is so sweet that one must "shoo away" the flies.

Shortbread A rich, buttery, slightly sweet, thick cookie made from flour, sugar and butter only. Shortbread

originated in Scotland; it is usually baked in a round pan, scored into segments before baking, but can also be cut in rectangular fingers. In Britain it is traditional Christmas fare.

Shortcake A cake made from a dough similar to that used for scones or biscuits but enriched with butter, sugar and milk or cream. Sponge cake or pound cake can also be used. Shortcake is usually served as a dessert,

QUEEN MARY'S TART

★ *Preparation time:* 8 minutes + 20 minutes refrigeration
Total cooking time: 50 minutes
Makes 9 inch round

1 sheet frozen puff pastry, thawed	½ cup chopped candied mixed peel
2 tablespoons apricot jam	¼ cup golden raisins
⅓ cup butter	1 tablespoon all-purpose
½ cup sugar	flour, sifted
4 eggs, lightly beaten	

1 Preheat oven to 400°F. Brush a deep 9 inch flan pan with melted butter. Roll out pastry to line base and side of prepared pan; trim edges. Refrigerate for 20 minutes. Prick pastry evenly with a fork; bake for 10 minutes. Remove from oven; spread base with jam.
2 Using electric beaters, beat the butter and sugar in a small mixing bowl until light and creamy. Add the eggs gradually, beating thoroughly after each addition—the mixture will appear curdled. Add the mixed peel, raisins and flour; beat on low speed for 20 seconds until the ingredients are just combined.
3 Pour the mixture into the cooled pastry case. Reduce the temperature to 375°F, bake tart for 30–40 minutes, or until a skewer comes out clean when inserted into the filling. Serve the tart warm or cold.

ATHOLL BROSE

★ *Preparation time:* 5 minutes + 30 minutes standing
Total cooking time: none
Makes 4 cups

1½ cups oatmeal, ground	½ cup Drambuie
1 cup warm water	½ cup heavy cream
2 teaspoons honey	

1 Place the oatmeal in a medium mixing bowl. Make a well in the center. Gradually add the water, stirring with a wooden spoon. Set aside, covered with a towel, for 30 minutes.
2 Place the oatmeal mixture in a coarse strainer and push the liquid through into a clean jug, pressing until the oatmeal is dry; discard the oatmeal. Reserve the liquid and strain it for a second time through a fine strainer into a clean jug.
3 Add honey, Drambuie and cream. Whisk thoroughly. Pour into sterilized jars or bottles, and shake well. Store, sealed, in a cool dark place until ready to use. Always shake well before using.

Note: Atholl Brose is traditionally drunk at Christmas, Hogmanay and Burns Night in Scotland.

ABOVE: QUEEN MARY'S TART.
OPPOSITE PAGE: SEAFOOD MORNAY CASSEROLE

SEAFOOD MORNAY CASEROLE

Preparation time: 25 minutes
Total cooking time: 40 minutes
Serves 4–6

3 medium white fish
   fillets
8 oz medium green
   shrimp
6¹/₂ oz scallops
13 oz mussels
1 small onion, cut in half
2 bay leaves
¹/₂ lemon, sliced
¹/₂ cup good-quality white
   wine

Sauce
3 tablespoons butter
1 stalk celery, chopped
1 large carrot, finely
   chopped

2 tablespoons all-purpose
   flour
1¹/₂ cups milk
4 oz Gruyère cheese,
   grated
1 cup frozen peas

Topping
1 cup fresh white bread
   crumbs
¹/₂ cup flaked almonds
2 teaspoons finely grated
   lemon rind
¹/₂ teaspoon freshly
   ground black pepper
¹/₄ cup butter, chopped

1 Preheat oven to moderate 350°F. Remove skin and bones from fish fillets; cut fish into 1¹/₄ inch cubes. Peel and devein shrimp. Wash scallops, remove brown vein. Remove beards from mussels and wash away any grit. Pry open shells,
remove mussels; discard shells. Place fish, shrimp, scallops and mussels in pan. Cover with cold water; add onion, bay leaves, lemon and wine. Bring slowly to the boil. Cover; reduce heat to low and simmer for 3–4 minutes. Remove seafood from cooking liquid. Place in lightly greased casserole dish.

2 To make Sauce: Heat butter in medium pan; add celery and carrot. Cook for 1 minute; add flour. Stir over low heat for 2 minutes or until flour mixture is lightly golden. Add milk gradually, stirring until mixture is smooth. Stir constantly over medium heat for 3 minutes, or until mixture boils and thickens. Boil for another minute, remove from heat. Cool.

3 Add cheese and peas to sauce and stir. Pour sauce over mixed seafood; toss gently to combine.

4 To make Topping: Combine bread crumbs, almonds, lemon rind and pepper in bowl, mix well. Spread evenly over top of seafood mixture. Dot with butter. Bake for 20 minutes or until casserole is heated through and topping golden brown. Serve garnished with a sprig of dill.

VARIATIONS

■ Use fresh white fish only and omit shellfish for an economical version of this dish. For special occasions, add shelled lobster and fresh oysters.

■ Use a mixture of cornflake crumbs and Parmesan cheese to make topping.

split horizontally and filled with sweetened whipped cream and sliced fruit such as strawberries, blueberries or peaches; the top is also spread with cream and fruit. Shortcake is American in origin and gets its name from the "short" (rich and crumbly) dough used in its preparation.

Shortcrust Pastry (Pie Crust) A rich pastry made by rubbing fat (butter, margarine or lard) into flour, then stirring in just enough liquid (usually water) to hold the mixture together; the dough should be chilled before use. Used for pie crusts and tart bases, shortcrust can be sweetened with sugar, enriched with egg or made savory by the addition of herbs or grated cheese. Ready-made frozen shortcrust pastry (pie crust) is available in supermarkets.

Shortening A fat used for frying and baking, usually made from vegetable oils although animal fat is sometimes added. Shortening makes pastries rich and flaky; it prevents proteins and carbohydrates from becoming too hard. Shortening is used in doughs, pastries, breads and cakes. It is used to make crisp pie crusts.

Short Soup (Wonton Soup) A Chinese soup consisting of chicken stock, noodle dumplings filled with ground meat and sometimes garnished with chopped scallion.

Shrimp A shellfish with a large tail and 10 tiny legs. Pink shrimps are found on the Atlantic coasts of northern Europe and the west coast of North America; they are used in bisques and salads. In North America extremely large shrimp, as well as freshwater shrimp, are sometimes called prawns.

Shrimp Paste An very pungent seasoning paste made from sun-dried, salted shrimp or prawns. In the cooking of Southeast Asia it flavors curries and dipping sauces; use sparingly.

Siena Cake See Panforte.

Sift To pass ingredients through the small holes of a sieve to remove any large pieces.

Silver Beet See Swiss Chard.

Simmer To cook food in a liquid that is just below boiling point. When a liquid is simmering bubbles form but they usually burst before they reach the surface.

SEAFOOD WITH NOODLES

⭐ **Preparation time:** 35 minutes
Total cooking time: 30 minutes
Serves 4–6

1 lb large uncooked shrimp
2 boneless fish fillets, about 8 oz
4 small squid hoods
2 tablespoons olive oil
3 cloves garlic, crushed
1 teaspoon sweet paprika
1 teaspoon chopped red chili pepper

3 small ripe tomatoes, peeled and chopped
2 tablespoons tomato paste
1 cup fish stock
1 cup red wine
1 teaspoon soft brown sugar
1 lb pasta

1 Shell and devein the shrimp, leaving the tails intact. Cut fish into 1¼ inch pieces. Using a sharp knife, cut squid into thin rings. Set aside.
2 Heat the oil in wok or pan; add the garlic, paprika and chili. Cook on medium-high heat for 2 minutes. Add the shrimp, fish and squid and toss over high heat for 3-4 minutes. Remove and set aside.
3 Add tomato, tomato paste, fish stock, red wine and brown sugar to pan. Bring slowly to the boil, reduce heat and simmer, uncovered, for 10 minutes. Return seafood to pan and mix well.
4 Cook pasta in a large quantity of boiling water until just tender. Drain well. Combine seafood mixture with pasta and serve immediately.

SEAFOOD SALAD

⭐ **Preparation time:** 50 minutes
Total cooking time: 10 minutes
Serves 4

1 lb uncooked large shrimp, peeled and deveined
1 small cooked crayfish
8 oz scallops
2 tablespoons lemon juice
2 medium firm-fleshed white fish fillets

salt
¼ teaspoon dried red chili flakes
freshly ground pepper

1 head romaine lettuce
1 avocado, peeled, pitted and sliced
2 hard-boiled eggs, 1 chopped, 1 left whole
2 tablespoons finely chopped parsley

Dressing
5 tablespoons olive oil
1 tablespoon lemon juice

1 Bring a large pan of salted water to the boil, add the shrimp and cook for about 3 minutes, or until they turn pink. Remove immediately and plunge into a bowl of iced water.
2 Cut the crayfish in half, remove flesh from shells and cut flesh into small pieces.
3 Poach scallops in water with lemon juice added for a minute or two until tender; drain. Poach fish in the same water for 5 minutes or until tender. Drain and flake into large pieces.
4 To make Dressing: Mix together in a large bowl the oil, lemon juice, salt, chili flakes and pepper. Add the drained seafood and toss gently until well coated.
5 Tear lettuce into pieces and line the bottom of a large china or glass salad bowl. Remove seafood from bowl with a slotted spoon to drain away dressing and place a layer of seafood on top of lettuce, followed by avocado slices and some of the chopped egg. Continue layering in this way, ending with a layer of seafood.
6 Sieve the yolk of the remaining hard-boiled egg and mix it with the parsley. Discard the white, or chop and add it to the salad if desired.
7 Sprinkle the salad with egg and parsley mixture and serve with Green Goddess Dressing (see Index for recipe).

Note: The layered arrangement of this dish makes it look spectacular when served in a glass bowl. However, it can also be served simply with all ingredients mixed together and spread on a large platter, over a bed of lettuce or with bowls of lettuce served separately. Alternatively, pile salad into halved and hollowed-out avocados.

ABOVE: SEAFOOD WITH NOODLES.
OPPOSITE PAGE: SEAFOOD BAKE

SEAFOOD

SEAFOOD BAKE

★ **Preparation time:** 25 minutes
Total cooking time: 25 minutes
Serves 10–12

2 tablespoons butter	½ teaspoon cracked black
2 tablespoons all-purpose	peppercorns
flour	2 lb uncooked shrimp
2 tablespoons dry white	1 lb scallops
wine	2 lb boneless white fish
1 tablespoon lemon juice	fillets
1 tablespoon tomato paste	2 cups croûtons
1 cup heavy cream	1 cup grated Swiss cheese
2 teaspoons seeded mustard	2 tablespoons sliced
	almonds

1 Preheat the oven to moderately hot 400°F. Heat the butter in a pan; add the flour. Stir over low heat for 1 minute or until the flour mixture is golden. Add the combined white wine, lemon juice and tomato paste to the pan, stir until smooth. Add the cream, stirring over medium heat for 3 minutes or until the mixture boils and thickens. Remove from heat, stir in the mustard and peppercorns; cool.

2 Peel and devein the shrimp; rinse and drain well. Rinse the scallops and remove the vein, leaving coral intact; drain well. Cut the fish fillets into 1¼ inch cubes. Combine the seafood, sauce, 1½ cups of the croûtons and ¼ cup of the cheese in a large mixing bowl; mix well.

3 Spoon the mixture into a shallow ovenproof dish; sprinkle with the remaining croûtons, remaining cheese and the almonds. Bake for 20 minutes or until the top is golden and seafood is just cooked through.

Note: Croûtons are crisp toasted cubes of bread, available packaged in supermarkets or delicatessens. To make your own, you will need six slices of thick toasting bread. Cut off crusts and discard. Cut remaining bread into ½ inch cubes. Scatter on a foil-lined baking sheet, bake in moderate oven for 15 minutes or until golden, turning occasionally. Cool on baking sheet.

ABOUT SEAFOOD

■ Fresh scallops should be white and firm to the touch with a bright orange coral and fresh smell. Do not freeze—when thawed they often shrink, become waterlogged and develop a stale odor.
■ The cooked flesh of the lobster has a slightly sweet yet salty flavor. They are best cooked quickly (by frying, baking, boiling, steaming, poaching or barbecuing) to retain moisture. Place live lobsters in the freezer for at least six hours before cooking to stun them.
■ Mussels should have tightly closed shells when bought fresh. They can be stored, wrapped in a damp cloth, in the refrigerator for one day. Remove from cooking liquid as soon as the shells open; discard any unopened shells.

Simnel Cake A rich fruit cake sandwiched and coated with almond paste. In England it is traditionally associated with Easter.

Sirloin A cut of beef from between the rump and the ribs.

Skewer A long, thin, pointed rod made of metal or wood that is most often used to hold small pieces of meat or vegetables in place during cooking.

Skim Milk Milk after the cream content has been removed.

Slump An old-fashioned New England dessert made with fruit, usually berries, and a biscuit dough topping. It is also known as "grunt."

Smørrebrød See Danish Open Sandwich.

Snail A small, soft-bodied, land-dwelling mollusk. Some snails are prized as food, especially in Europe where they are usually cooked with garlic butter and served in the shell. Snails are commercially raised, often on a diet of cabbage, wheat or oats.

411

Most highly regarded in France is the Burgundy, or Roman, snail which is fed on vine leaves from the Burgundy vineyards. The Romans were probably the first to farm snails. Snails are available canned; the shells are sold separately. Snails are called *escargots* in France.

Snap Beans (String Beans) The name for any of a variety of green beans or yellow wax beans.

Snow Peas and Sugar Snap Peas Bright green varieties of pea with sweet, delicately flavored pods that are eaten whole. Snow peas are harvested when the peas are still immature; sugar peas are fully mature but the pod is so tender that they can be cooked and eaten unshelled. Both snow peas and sugar snap peas can be added raw to salads. To prepare either pea, break off the stalk end and remove any string; lightly boil or steam and serve while still crisp. Snow peas are popular in Asian cooking.

Soda Bread A bread in which the leavening agent is a combination of baking soda and buttermilk, or some other acid ingredient,

SEAFOOD STEW

⭐ **Preparation time:** 20 minutes
Total cooking time: 50 minutes
Serves 4–6

10 oz uncooked shrimp
1/4 cup olive oil
2 medium onions, finely chopped
2 medium carrots, chopped
2 stalks celery, finely chopped
2 cloves garlic, crushed
6 medium tomatoes, about 2 lb, peeled and chopped
1/4 cup good-quality white wine

2 tablespoons tomato paste
2 lb boneless fish fillets, cut into 1 1/4 inch pieces
salt and pepper
12 mussels, beards removed
1/4 cup good-quality white wine, extra
2 tablespoons chopped parsley
1 tablespoon fresh thyme leaves

1 Peel and devein shrimp, leaving tails intact. Heat oil in a pan. Cook onion for 10 minutes. Add carrots, celery and garlic. Cook, stirring, for 10 minutes.
2 Add the tomatoes and wine. Bring to the boil, reduce heat and simmer, covered, for 20 minutes. Stir in the tomato paste. Add the shrimp. Cover and simmer for another 3 minutes. Add the chopped fish, salt and pepper; simmer for 2 minutes more.
3 Place mussels in a large pan, add extra wine and herbs. Cover, cook over medium heat for 2–3 minutes until mussels open. Strain liquid from mussels into tomato mixture and combine. Arrange mussels on top.

SEAFOOD WITH MANGO SALSA

⭐ ⭐ **Preparation time:** 30 minutes + 1 hour refrigeration
Total cooking time: 3 minutes
Serves 6

1 dozen oysters on the shell
2 medium tubes calamari, about 10 oz
1 tablespoon butter
1 tablespoon lemon juice
1 tablespoon finely chopped fresh parsley
12 cooked shrimp, unpeeled

Mango Salsa
1 large ripe mango
1 small fresh red chili pepper
1 stalk lemon grass

1 teaspoon finely chopped cilantro
1 teaspoon finely grated fresh ginger

Dill Vinaigrette
2 tablespoons white wine vinegar
1/2 cup oil
1 teaspoon Dijon mustard
2 teaspoons finely chopped fresh dill
2 teaspoons honey
salt and white pepper, to taste

1 Remove any grit from the surface of oyster flesh. Slice the calamari tubes into rings about 1/2 inch wide. Melt butter in a medium frying pan, add calamari and lemon juice and stir over medium heat for about 3 minutes, or until calamari is opaque. Add parsley and stir. Remove mixture from the pan and set aside to cool. Refrigerate, along with the shrimp and oysters, until required.
2 To make Mango Salsa: Peel the mango, remove the seed and cut the flesh into small cubes. Cut the chili in half lengthwise, remove the seeds and slice finely. Cut a 3/4 inch piece of the white part from the lemon grass stalk and chop finely. Mix together the mango, chili, lemon grass, cilantro and ginger in a small bowl and refrigerate for 1 hour. Allow the salsa to stand at room temperature for 10 minutes before serving.
3 To make Dill Vinaigrette: Place the vinegar, oil, mustard, dill and honey in a small jar. Shake vigorously for 1 minute or until all ingredients are well combined. Add salt and pepper to taste.
4 To serve, divide the oysters, calamari and shrimp evenly between individual serving plates. Add a tablespoon of Mango Salsa to each plate. Pour Dill Vinaigrette into bowls to accompany each plate, or pass a small jug of dressing around separately for guests to help themselves.

ABOVE: SEAFOOD STEW.
OPPOSITE PAGE: TRADITIONAL SHORTBREAD

SHORTBREAD

TRADITIONAL SHORTBREAD

★ ***Preparation time:*** 20 minutes
Total cooking time: 25–30 minutes
Makes 8 or 12 wedges

1 cup butter, softened
½ cup confectioners'
sugar, sifted
1¾ cups all-purpose
flour
⅓ cup rice flour

1 In a bowl beat the butter with an electric mixer until it is soft. Add the sifted confectioners' sugar and beat until fluffy. With a wooden spoon stir in the all-purpose flour and rice flour. Shape the dough into a ball and knead gently until smooth.
2 Press the dough into a 9 inch round baking pan or place it on a baking sheet and gently pat into a 9 inch circle. Flute the edge, if desired. Using a sharp knife, score the dough into 8 or 12 wedges. Pierce the top of the dough with a fork.
3 Bake the shortbread in a warm 325°F oven for 25–30 minutes, or until it is set and light brown. Cool the shortbread slightly on a wire rack. Cut or break into wedges while still warm (use a bread knife to avoid crumbling). Allow it to cool completely. Store the shortbread in an airtight container.

ABOUT SHORTBREAD

■ There are many variations on the shortbread theme. Traditional Scottish tea favorites include petticoat tails (round shortbreads inspired by the petticoat hoops worn by nineteenth century women), Ayrshire shortbread (made with cream) and oatmeal shortbread. All use very fresh, high-quality ingredients for the best results.
■ Handle shortbread dough lightly—overworking it will give a tough, chewy texture.
■ Candied peel and almonds are popular traditional decorations for shortbread.

which react together to generate bubbles of carbon dioxide. Traditional Irish soda bread contains only local wholemeal flour, buttermilk, baking soda

and salt;
it is scored on top with a deep cross to ensure even baking.

Sole Any of several species of flatfish with fine, white, mild flesh. Dover sole, the finest of these fish, is imported into the United States.

Sorbet A smooth, sharp-tasting iced dessert which consists of sugar syrup and fruit juice or sometimes a liqueur.
Sorbets can be served in a tall glass or a shallow dish, and topped with a few spoonfuls of liqueur or champagne, garnished with frosted fruits or accompanied by a puréed fruit sauce. Sometimes a small scoop is served between

courses to refresh the palate; a savory sorbet (such as thyme, rosemary, avocado or olive) can be served as an accompaniment to a meat course.

Both sorbet and its relative, sherbet, reached Europe through ancient Persia; their names come from *Sharbia*, the Arabic word for "drink".

Sorghum A cereal which is a staple food in parts of Africa and Asia where it is cooked like rice, or ground into flour and used in porridge and flat cakes. A fermented drink is made from its seeds. Ground sorghum is used in stews or as a porridge. Sorghum syrup, made from the juice of the stem of the sugar sorghum, is similar to molasses.

Sorrel A green, leafy plant with a bitter, slightly

lemony flavor. Sorrel is usually cooked, like spinach; it can be puréed as an omelet filling or made into a soup; very young and tender leaves can be added (sparingly) to a green salad; and it is often used as a stuffing for fish.

Sorrel is native to Europe; in ancient times it was eaten to offset the richness of some foods. It is especially popular in the cooking of

GREEK SHORTBREAD

⭐ **Preparation time:** 20 minutes
Total cooking time: 15 minutes
Makes about 48

2/3 cup oz butter
1 cup confectioners' sugar, sifted
1 teaspoon finely grated orange rind
1 egg
1 egg yolk
2 1/2 cups all-purpose flour

1 1/2 teaspoons baking powder
1 teaspoon ground cinnamon
8 oz blanched almonds, toasted, finely chopped
confectioners' sugar, extra

1 Preheat oven to 325°F. Line a baking sheet with parchment paper. Using electric beaters, beat butter, sugar and rind in a small mixing bowl until light and creamy. Add egg and egg yolk, beating in thoroughly.
2 Transfer mixture to large mixing bowl. Using a metal spoon, fold in sifted flour, baking powder, cinnamon and almonds; mix until well combined.
3 Shape level tablespoons of mixture into crescent shapes. Place on prepared baking sheet. Bake 12–15 minutes or until lightly golden. Stand 5 minutes before transferring cookies to wire rack to cool. While still warm, dust with confectioners' sugar. Just before serving, dust heavily again with confectioners' sugar.

ABOVE: GREEK SHORTBREAD;
RIGHT: GINGER SHORTBREAD CREAMS.
OPPOSITE PAGE: CHOCOLATE PECAN BARS

GINGER SHORTBREAD CREAMS

⭐ **Preparation time:** 25 minutes
Total cooking time: 10–12 minutes
Makes 22

1 cup all-purpose flour
2 tablespoons cornstarch
6 tablespoons unsalted butter, chopped
2 tablespoons soft brown sugar
1 teaspoon baking powder
1/4 teaspoon salt

Filling
1/4 cup unsalted (sweet) butter
1/3 cup confectioners' sugar
1 tablespoon finely chopped candied ginger

1 Preheat oven to moderate 350°F. Line two baking sheets with parchment paper. Place flours, butter and sugar, baking powder and salt in food processor. Process for 30 seconds or until mixture comes together. Turn onto a lightly floured surface, knead for 20 seconds.
2 Roll level teaspoons of the mixture into 3/4 inch balls. Place on baking sheets, press with a fork in a crisscross pattern. Bake 10–12 minutes, until golden. Transfer to wire rack to cool before filling.
3 To make Filling: Beat the butter and sugar until light and creamy; add the ginger, beat well. Spread half the cookies with filling, sandwich with the others.

SLICES (BARS)

CHOCOLATE PECAN BARS

⭐ **Preparation time:** 30 minutes +
30 minutes refrigeration
Total cooking time: 5–10 minutes
Makes 50

8 oz chocolate cream
cookies (about 20),
crushed
1/2 cup flaked coconut
1 cup pecans, coarsely
chopped
1 tablespoon unsweetened
cocoa powder, sifted
3 oz dark (semisweet)
chocolate, chopped
1/3 cup unsalted (sweet)
butter

1/4 cup light corn syrup
extra pecans, for
decoration
2 oz dark (semisweet)
chocolate, extra

Icing
3 oz dark (semisweet)
chocolate, chopped
3 tablespoons unsalted
(sweet) butter

1 Line base and sides of shallow 8 x 8 inch square
baking pan with foil. Combine cookie crumbs,
coconut, pecans and cocoa in medium mixing
bowl. Make a well in the center.
2 Combine chocolate, butter and syrup in small
heavy-bottom pan. Stir over low heat until
chocolate and butter have melted and mixture is
smooth. Remove from heat. Pour onto dry
ingredients. Combine well with wooden spoon.
Press into pan. Refrigerate for 30 minutes.
3 To make Icing: Stir the chocolate and butter
in small bowl over a pan of simmering water
until melted and smooth; cool. Spread over the
bars. Refrigerate. When completely set, cut
into squares. Top with pecans dipped in extra
melted chocolate.

COCONUT JAM BARS

⭐ **Preparation time:** 20 minutes
Total cooking time: 35 minutes
Makes 25 squares

1³/4 cups all-purpose
flour
1/2 cup unsalted (sweet)
butter
2/3 cup confectioners'
sugar

Topping
1/2 cup sugar
1 egg
2 cups flaked coconut
1/2 cup blackberry jam

1 Preheat oven to moderate 350°F. Lightly grease
and flour a 9 x 9 x 2 inch or an 8 x 8 x 2 inch
square baking pan.
2 Place the flour, butter and confectioners' sugar
in a food processor bowl. Using the pulse action,
process until the mixture forms fine crumbs.
Spread the crumbs evenly over the base of
the prepared pan, pressing firmly to form
a crust. Bake for 15 minutes or until lightly
golden; cool.
3 To make Topping: In a medium mixing
bowl, beat sugar and egg until just combined. Stir
in coconut. Spread jam over cooled base. Spread
topping over jam, pressing down with the back of
a spoon. Bake for 20 minutes, until golden. Cool
on a wire rack; cut into 25 squares.

Provence, in southern
France. The name is
derived from the Greek
word for sour.

Soufflé A light and
fluffy egg dish, either
savory or sweet. There
are two types: hot and
cold. The airy texture of
a hot soufflé is achieved
by folding stiffly whisked
egg whites through a
warm sauce or purée; air
trapped in the white
causes the soufflé to rise
when baked. Hot soufflé
must be served
immediately. A cold
soufflé is a mousse-like
mixture lightened with
whipped egg whites; it is
set in a mold with sides
extended by foil.

Soup A liquid food
made from meat, poultry
or fish, usually with
vegetables, or from one
or more vegetables and
usually served hot. A
soup
course is
often
served
at the
start of a
meal, or, if
thick and

hearty, may be a meal in itself. The wide range of soups includes clear consommés; puréed vegetables with cream; meat and vegetable mixtures thickened with a roux and cold soups.

Sour Cream Cream to which a special culture has been added to give it a sharp, slightly sour taste. It is

thicker than pure fresh cream. Sour cream is used in soups, savory dips and salad dressings; as a topping for baked potatoes and in cheesecake. It is used particularly in Eastern European cooking.

Sourdough Fermented dough, saved when making a batch of bread and used instead of yeast as a starter when making the next batch.

Soursop Also called prickly custard apple.

Soybean An oval bean, about the size of the common pea, borne in hairy pods on a bush native to China. Most common is the creamy-yellow

CHOCOLATE CARAMEL TRIANGLES

✦ ✦ ***Preparation time:*** 15 minutes
Total cooking time: 20 minutes
Makes 24 triangles

1 cup (about 22) crushed vanilla wafers	½ cup butter
⅓ cup unsalted butter, melted	½ cup sugar
	½ cup light corn syrup
3 tablespoons flaked coconut	1⅓ cups milk chocolate chips
14 oz can sweetened condensed milk	1 tablespoon vegetable shortening

1 Line a 12 x 8 inch or 13 x 9 inch baking pan with foil, extending foil beyond sides. Lightly grease foil; set aside.
2 In a bowl combine vanilla wafer crumbs, melted butter and coconut. Press mixture evenly into prepared pan; smooth surface.
3 In a medium saucepan combine condensed milk, butter, sugar and corn syrup. Stir over low heat 15 minutes or until sugar has dissolved and mixture is smooth and thick. Remove from heat; cool slightly. Pour over cookie layer; smooth surface.
4 In a small saucepan heat milk chocolate pieces and shortening; stir constantly until smooth. Spread chocolate mixture over caramel. Allow to partially set before marking into 24 triangles. Refrigerate until firm.

WALNUT BROWNIES

✦ ***Preparation time:*** 10 minutes + 20 minutes standing
Total cooking time: 35 minutes
Makes 20 diamonds

6 tablespoons unsalted (sweet) butter	¼ teaspoon baking soda
¾ cup soft brown sugar	½ cup chopped walnuts
¾ cup water	⅓ cup chocolate chips
¼ cup golden raisins, chopped	chopped walnuts
2 cups all-purpose flour	
1 teaspoon baking powder	***Icing***
1 teaspoon ground cinnamon	¼ cup unsalted (sweet) butter
2 tablespoons unsweetened cocoa powder	1 cup confectioners' sugar
	1 tablespoon unsweetened cocoa powder
	1 tablespoon milk

1 Preheat oven to moderate 350°F. Brush shallow 11 x 7 inch rectangular pan with oil. Cover base with parchment paper, extending over two longer sides; grease paper. Combine butter, sugar, water and raisins in pan. Stir over low heat 5 minutes until butter melts and sugar dissolves; remove from heat.
2 Sift flours, cinnamon and cocoa into a bowl;

ABOVE: CHOCOLATE CARAMEL TRIANGLES.
OPPOSITE PAGE: MOIST CHOCOLATE BROWNIES

add nuts and chocolate chips. Make a well in center. Add butter mixture. Stir until just combined. Spoon into pan. Bake 30 minutes or until skewer comes out clean when inserted in center. Stand 20 minutes before turning onto a wire rack to cool.

3 To make Icing: Beat butter until light and creamy; add sugar, cocoa and milk. Beat until smooth. Spread over brownie. Cut into diamonds, top each with chopped walnuts.

MOIST CHOCOLATE BROWNIES

★★ **Preparation time:** 20 minutes
Total cooking time: 45 minutes
Makes 36 squares

1½ cups all-purpose
  flour
¼ cup unsweetened cocoa
  powder
1 teaspoon baking
  powder
½ teaspoon baking soda
½ cup chopped
  macadamia nuts
½ cup unsalted (sweet)
  butter
6½ oz dark (semisweet)
  cooking chocolate,
  chopped

1 cup sugar
2 eggs, lightly beaten
⅓ cup sour cream
⅓ cup chopped
  macadamia nuts, extra

***Chocolate Cream
Topping***
5 oz dark (semisweet)
  cooking chocolate,
  chopped
½ cup sour cream

1 Preheat oven to moderate 350°F. Brush a shallow, 9 inch square cake pan with oil or melted butter. Line the base and sides with paper; grease paper. Sift flour with cocoa, baking powder and baking soda into a large mixing bowl; add the nuts. Make a well in the center.
2 Place the butter and chocolate in a medium heatproof bowl. Stand the bowl over a pan of simmering water and stir until the chocolate and butter have melted and the mixture is smooth. Remove from heat; add the sugar, eggs and cream. Beat with a wire whisk until all ingredients are well combined and the mixture is thick and smooth. Add chocolate mixture to the dry ingredients. Using a wooden spoon, stir until well combined—do not overbeat. Spread mixture into the prepared pan. Bake for 40 minutes or until a skewer comes out clean when inserted in the center of the slice. Leave to cool in the pan.
3 To make Chocolate Cream Topping: Place the chopped cooking chocolate in a medium heatproof bowl. Stand the bowl over a pan of simmering water and stir until all the chocolate has melted. Remove from heat and leave for 2 minutes. Add cream to the chocolate and beat with a wire whisk until the mixture is thick and glossy. While mixture is still warm, spread Chocolate Cream Topping over the cooled slice and sprinkle with nuts. Allow the Topping to set before cutting the slice evenly into 1½ inch squares.

variety, but they can also be red, purple, brown or black. Soybeans are valued for their high vegetable protein content and can be eaten in a number of ways: fresh, dried, sprouting, ground and as bean curd and soybean milk. Miso, widely used in the cooking of Japan, is a paste of fermented, salted soybean. Dried soybeans are used in soups, stews and casseroles.

Soybean Curd See Tofu.

Soy Sauce A dark, salty sauce of Chinese origin made from fermented roasted soy beans, another grain (usually wheat) and brine; the mixture is aged for up to two years, then filtered and bottled. Dark soy sauce is aged longer and towards the end of processing is tinted and flavored with molasses. Soy sauce is indispensable in Asian cooking; it is used as a seasoning and marinade and adds flavor and color to many dishes. Chinese cooking uses both dark and light soy sauce: light is used with seafood, chicken, vegetables, soups and in dipping sauces; dark soy sauce is used in red meat dishes. Japanese soy sauce, *shoyu*, is usually sweeter and less salty than the Chinese variety; in Indonesia, *kecap manis*, a thick, dark, sweetened soy sauce, is often used.

A seasoning made from fermented soybeans, known as *shih*, was in use in China more than 2,000 years ago. A strained sauce similar to the version in use today has been made since the sixth century. Soy sauce is available from supermarkets and Asian food stores.

Spaghetti Pasta in the form of long strands, made from a flour and water

dough.
It is best with oil-based sauces that allow the strings to remain slippery and separate. Spaghetti has been made in southern Italy for many hundreds of years; commercially made spaghetti is available in dried fresh and refrigerated or frozen form.

Spanish Food
Spain shares with its Mediterranean neighbors access to myriad fish and shellfish, the use of aromatic hillside herbs and the Roman legacy of olives. From the Phoenicians came the chickpea (garbanzo bean) and the salting of fish. However, what makes

BRANDY ALEXANDER BARS

★ **Preparation time:** 20 minutes + 3 hours refrigeration
Total cooking time: 5 minutes
Makes 12 bars

1/3 cup unsalted (sweet) butter, chopped
2 oz dark (semisweet) cooking chocolate, chopped
8 oz chocolate wafer cookies, crushed (about 2 cups)
10 oz ricotta cheese
1/4 cup heavy cream
1/3 cup confectioners' sugar, sifted
1/2 cup grated milk chocolate
1 tablespoon brandy
1 tablespoon crème de cacao liqueur
1/2 teaspoon ground nutmeg
2 oz dark (semisweet) chocolate

1 Brush a shallow 12 x 8 inch pan with oil. Line base and sides with parchment paper. Place butter and chocolate in a small heatproof bowl. Stand bowl over a pan of simmering water. Stir until chocolate has melted and mixture is smooth. Remove from heat. Place cookie crumbs in a small bowl, add chocolate mixture and stir, using a flat-bladed knife. Press cookie mixture evenly over base of prepared pan; set aside.
2 Using electric beaters, beat cheese, cream and sugar in small mixing bowl on medium speed for 3 minutes or until mixture is light and creamy. Add chocolate, brandy and liqueur. Beat on low speed for another minute.

3 Spread cheese mixture over prepared base; sprinkle with nutmeg. Refrigerate several hours or overnight. Cut into 12 bars. Place chocolate in small heatproof bowl and stand over simmering water until chocolate has melted. Use to pipe a design on top of each bar.

PRUNE AND CREAM CHEESE SCROLLS

★ ★ **Preparation time:** 30 minutes + 30 minutes refrigeration
Total cooking time: 15 minutes
Makes 20

1 1/2 cups all-purpose flour
1 tablespoon cornstarch
1/3 cup unsalted (sweet) butter
1/4 cup sugar
1 egg yolk
2–3 tablespoons milk

Prune Filling
4 oz cream cheese
1/3 cup sugar
2 teaspoons grated lemon rind
1 cup chopped, pitted prunes

1 Brush two 13 x 11 inch cookie sheets with oil or melted butter. Place the flour, cornstarch, butter and sugar in a food processor. Using pulse action, press button for 15 seconds or until the mixture is fine and crumbly. Add the egg yolk and milk; process for 15 seconds or until mixture comes together. Turn onto a lightly floured

ABOVE: BRANDY ALEXANDER BARS.
OPPOSITE PAGE: CHOCOLATE CARROT TRIANGLES

surface; knead for 1 minute or until smooth. Roll out the dough on a sheet of baking paper to form a 12 x 11 inch rectangle.

2 To make Prune Filling: Beat cream cheese, sugar and rind in small bowl until light and creamy. Spread over dough. Top with prunes.

3 Roll dough from one long side into the center. Roll dough from opposite side to meet in center. Refrigerate 30 minutes or until firm. Heat oven to moderate 350°F. Cut roll into ⁵⁄8 inch slices. Place onto cookie sheets, allowing room for spreading. Bake 15 minutes or until lightly golden. Transfer to wire racks to cool.

CHOCOLATE CARROT TRIANGLES

⭐ **Preparation time:** 15 minutes
Total cooking time: 30 minutes
Makes 32

1 cup all-purpose flour	¹⁄3 cup unsalted (sweet)
1 teaspoon ground	butter, melted
cinnamon	¹⁄3 cup chopped walnuts
³⁄4 teaspoon baking	
powder	***Cream Cheese Frosting***
1 cup sugar	4 oz cream cheese
¹⁄2 cup finely grated carrot	2 tablespoons unsalted
1 cup mixed dried fruit	(sweet) butter
¹⁄2 cup chocolate chips	1¹⁄2 cups confectioners'
¹⁄3 cup flaked coconut	sugar, sifted
2 eggs, lightly beaten	1 teaspoon hot water

1 Preheat oven to moderate 350°F. Brush a shallow 9 inch square cake pan with oil or melted butter; line the base and sides with parchment paper. Sift the flour, cinnamon and baking powder into a large mixing bowl. Add the sugar, carrot, mixed fruit, chocolate chips and coconut; stir until the ingredients are just combined. Add the beaten eggs and butter, stir until just combined.

2 Spread mixture evenly into prepared pan; smooth the surface. Bake for 30 minutes or until golden. Cool in the pan, then turn out onto a flat surface.

3 To make Cream Cheese Frosting: Using electric beaters, beat together the cream cheese and butter in a small bowl until smooth. Add the confectioners' sugar and beat for a further 2 minutes or until the mixture is light and fluffy. Add the hot water and beat until combined. Spread the slice with the Cream Cheese Frosting, using a flat-bladed knife. Sprinkle with the chopped walnuts. Cut into 16 squares, then cut each square into triangles.

CHOC RUM BARS

⭐ **Preparation time:** 25 minutes + 2–3 hours refrigeration
Total cooking time: none
Makes 16 bars

8 oz chocolate wafer	²⁄3 cup sweetened
cookies, crushed (about	condensed milk
2 cups)	1 teaspoon ground
1 cup mixed fruit or	cinnamon
golden raisins	2 tablespoons rum
¹⁄2 cup walnuts, chopped	4 oz semisweet chocolate,
¹⁄2 cup butter	chopped

1 Brush a 9 inch square baking pan with melted butter or oil.

2 Combine cookie crumbs, fruit and walnuts in a large mixing bowl. Make a well in the center.

3 Combine butter and condensed milk in a small pan. Stir over low heat until butter has melted; remove from heat and whisk in cinnamon and rum.

4 Add butter mixture to cookie crumb mixture; stir with a wooden spoon until well combined.

5 Press mixture evenly into prepared pan.

6 Place chocolate in a glass bowl. Stir over barely simmering water until melted; remove from heat.

7 Spread chocolate evenly over bars. Score into squares. Refrigerate, covered, until firm (see Note). Cut into squares to serve. Store, covered, in the refrigerator.

Note: The bars will cut better if refrigerated.

Spanish cuisine distinct is the Muslim/Arab influence of the Moors, who ruled the country from the eighth to the fifteenth century. From this period comes the emphasis on spices and seasonings, with an array introduced including nutmeg, cloves, saffron, cumin, cinnamon, turmeric and vanilla. The Moors were keen agriculturalists; they built irrigation systems to open up farming lands and planted citrus groves, especially the orange, throughout Spain; they also introduced eggplants and asparagus,

apricots and pomegranates, almonds and pistachios, rice and sugar; Arab culinary influence is also seen in Spain's syrup-soaked pastries.

The next major strand in the development of Spanish cuisine was the introduction of new foods from the Americas: sweet pepper, chili pepper and tomato— all now firmly identified with national dishes, and potato and chocolate (chocolate drinks were long-favored in Spain as a daily energizer before coffee became widely available). Regardless of all these influences, Spanish cooking is still

SOUFFLES

Baked soufflés are made by combining a rich sauce or purée with stiffly beaten egg whites, and baking them in special deep, straight-sided ovenproof dishes. They emerge dramatically from the oven, puffed and golden, and must be served at once, before they begin to sink.

THIS PAGE, CENTER ROW, FROM LEFT: COFFEE; BLUEBERRY; SPINACH; BOTTOM: HERB. OPPOSITE PAGE, TOP: CHOCOLATE; CENTER ROW, FROM LEFT: RASPBERRY, MOCHA, CHEESE; BOTTOM: SALMON

Savory or sweet, soufflés can be baked in one large dish or in small ones for individual servings. When buying dishes for soufflés, choose attractive ones because hot soufflés are usually served in the same dish they are cooked in. For successful soufflés it is important to beat the egg whites just before cooking. If you let them stand before folding them into the sauce or if you let the soufflé stand before baking, the egg whites will sink and become watery. Hot soufflés are best served with a simple salad. Sweet soufflés are delicious when served with vanilla ice cream or freshly whipped cream.

until well combined. Add 1 cup grated Cheddar cheese, salt, pepper and 1/2 teaspoon Dijon mustard. Allow sauce to cool slightly. Beat the 4 egg whites until stiff peaks form. Fold one-third of the egg white into the cooled sauce, using a metal spoon, then add the rest, folding very gently. Pour the mixture gently but without delay, into the prepared dish, filling it to within 1/2 inch of the rim. Sprinkle with a tablespoon freshly grated Parmesan cheese. Bake soufflé for 40–45 minutes for a large soufflé, 25–30 minutes for individual dishes. Serve immediately.

CHEESE SOUFFLE

Preheat the oven to 350°F. Grease one 7 inch soufflé dish or four small (1-cup) dishes generously with butter, then dust with fine, dry bread crumbs. Melt 1/2 cup butter in a pan and add 1 cup all-purpose flour. Stir well to combine and cook over low heat; stirring, for 1 minute. Remove the pan from the heat, add 1 cup warm milk, stir or whisk until smooth, then return to the heat and stir until the mixture boils and thickens. Remove the pan from heat. Beat 4 egg yolks until very well mixed, add to sauce, stirring constantly,

VARIATIONS

■ **HERB SOUFFLÉ:** Add 1 tablespoon finely chopped shallot and 1 tablespoon finely chopped fresh herbs (chervil, parsley, marjoram or chives) at the same time as the cheese.

■ **SPINACH SOUFFLÉ:** Replace Cheddar cheese with 1/2 cup cooked spinach, finely chopped (after chopping, squeeze with your hands to remove as much moisture as possible), a pinch of grated nutmeg, 1 tablespoon grated Parmesan cheese and 2 tablespoons grated Swiss cheese. Add these to the cooked sauce before adding the egg whites.

■ **SALMON SOUFFLÉ:** Replace Cheddar cheese with an 8 ounce can of red salmon, drained and flaked, and 2 tablespoons finely chopped fresh chives. Stir these into the cooked sauce before adding the egg whites.

BASIC SWEET SOUFFLE

Preheat the oven to 375°F. Grease an 8 inch soufflé dish and dust with sugar. Melt 3 tablespoons butter in a small pan, ¼ cup all-purpose flour and stir over low heat for 1 minute or until smooth. Remove pan from heat and gradually add 1 cup warm milk, stirring constantly. Add ¼ teaspoon salt, ½ cup sugar and 1 teaspoon vanilla, return pan to heat and stir continuously until mixture becomes thick and smooth. Set the sauce aside to cool. Beat 4 egg yolks and add them gradually to the cooled sauce, stirring well between each addition. Beat 5 egg whites until stiff and then fold them gently into the sauce using a large metal spoon. Pour the mixture carefully into the prepared soufflé dish filling to within ½ inch of the rim. Stand the soufflé in a deep baking dish that is half filled with hot water. Bake in the preheated oven for 15 minutes, then reduce the temperature to 350°F and bake for another 25 minutes. Serve immediately.

POINTS FOR SUCCESS

■ Fold flavorings into the basic sauce before adding beaten egg whites.

■ Eggs should be at room temperature.

■ To beat egg whites successfully, they must be free of any trace of yolk. The bowl and beaters must be dry and free of any trace of grease. If any of the egg yolk slips into the white during separation, carefully remove it with half an egg shell or a teaspoon.

■ For best results, beat the egg whites with a wire whisk rather than using electric beaters.

■ Egg whites should be beaten only until the moment that stiff peaks form. When ready, the mixture should stay in a peak when you hold the whisk upright. Do not overbeat egg whites because they will break up when you fold through the sauce and the soufflé will not rise properly.

VARIATIONS

■ **COFFEE SOUFFLÉ:** Substitute ½ cup strong black coffee for half the milk.

■ **CHOCOLATE SOUFFLÉ:** Melt 2 oz dark (semisweet) chocolate over hot water and stir into the sauce before you add the egg yolks.

■ **BLUEBERRY SOUFFLÉ:** Purée 6½ oz fresh blueberries in a food processor until smooth. Fold into the sauce with the egg yolks.

■ **RASPBERRY SOUFFLÉ:** Purée 8 oz raspberries in a food processor. Strain to remove seeds. Fold into sauce with the egg yolks.

■ **MOCHA SOUFFLÉ:** Dissolve 1–2 tablespoons instant coffee in 1 tablespoon of hot water. Melt 2 oz dark (semisweet) chocolate over hot water, mix with coffee. Allow to cool and fold into sauce before adding egg yolks.

■ Fold the beaten whites lightly and quickly into the warm sauce.

■ To ensure even cooking of your soufflé place a baking sheet in the oven until it is hot and stand the soufflé dish on it.

■ Remove a shelf from the oven to allow room for the soufflé to rise.

■ If you open the oven door while soufflé is baking, do so carefully to avoid drafts.

■ A good soufflé is slightly creamy in the center, never dry throughout. The creamy center becomes a sauce. Serve everyone some of the thoroughly cooked soufflé and a little of the creamy, soft center.

fairly basic, relying on quality fresh produce and the flavors of garlic, onion, pepper, olive oil, saffron and cumin, rather than complicated techniques. Pork is the common meat of the region.

The traditional start to the day is a breakfast of churros (sugared twists of fried pastry) with coffee or thick, chocolate-flavored milk. At midday Spaniards meet friends in cafés, pick at tapas (platters of finger food that can include olives, pickled vegetables, fried and marinated seafoods and savory pastries) before taking the main meal of the day (comida), a leisurely affair that can stretch over several hours.

It is traditional for the Spanish to begin their meals with a green salad, a habit which seems to date from the time of Moorish rule. In the early evening the cafés fill once more and the tapas ritual is repeated.

Spareribs Pork spareribs are cut from the belly area and consist of long narrow strips with small bones and layers of fat and tasty lean meat. The term is also used for

SNOW PEAS

SNOW PEA SALAD

⭐ **Preparation time:** 20 minutes
Total cooking time: 5 minutes
Serves 8

6¹/2 oz snow peas, sliced diagonally
1 large red pepper, sliced
10 leaf lettuce leaves
8 oz cherry tomatoes
2 oz watercress sprigs
Parmesan cheese, to serve

Garlic Croûtons
3 slices white bread

1/4 cup olive oil
1 clove garlic, crushed

Dressing
2 tablespoons olive oil
1 tablespoon mayonnaise
1 tablespoon sour cream
2 tablespoons lemon juice
1 teaspoon brown sugar
cracked pepper, to taste

1 Wash the lettuce and tomatoes. Tear lettuce into pieces. Combine the snow peas, red pepper, lettuce, tomatoes and watercress in a large mixing bowl.
2 To make Garlic Croûtons: Remove the crusts from the bread slices. Cut the bread into 1/2 inch squares. Heat the olive oil in a small, heavy-bottom pan, add the garlic. Stir in bread. Cook until the bread squares are golden and crisp. Remove from heat; drain on paper towel.
3 To make Dressing: Whisk all ingredients together in a small mixing bowl for 2 minutes. Just before serving, pour the Dressing over the salad, toss. Top with garlic croûtons and shavings of Parmesan cheese.

STIR-FRIED BEEF AND SNOW PEAS

⭐ **Preparation time:** 10 minutes
Total cooking time: 5 minutes
Serves 4

13 oz round or sirloin steak, finely sliced
2 tablespoons soy sauce
1/2 teaspoon grated ginger
2 tablespoons peanut oil
6¹/2 oz snow peas, topped and tailed

1¹/2 teaspoons cornstarch
1/2 cup beef stock
1 teaspoon soy sauce, extra
1/4 teaspoon sesame oil

1 Place meat in a dish. Combine soy sauce and ginger, sprinkle over meat and stir to coat well. Heat oil in a wok or heavy-bottom frying pan, swirling gently to coat base and side.
2 Add the beef and snow peas and stir-fry over high heat for 2 minutes, or until the meat browns.
3 Dissolve cornstarch in a little stock. Add to wok with remaining stock, extra sauce and sesame oil. Stir until sauce boils and thickens. Serve with steamed rice.

SNOW PEA AND ASPARAGUS SALAD

⭐ **Preparation time:** 15 minutes
Total cooking time: 5 minutes
Serves 4–6

6¹/2 oz snow peas
1 bunch asparagus spears

Dressing
2 tablespoons peanut oil

3 teaspoons sesame oil
3 teaspoons rice vinegar or red wine vinegar
1/2 teaspoon sugar
1 tablespoon sesame seeds

1 Top and tail the snow peas. Trim any woody ends from the asparagus. Cut spears diagonally in half. Place in a pan of boiling water. Leave for 1 minute, then drain asparagus and plunge into iced water. Drain well.
2 To make Dressing: Place peanut oil, sesame oil, vinegar and sugar in a small screw-top jar and shake well. Place the asparagus and snow peas in a serving bowl. Pour dressing over the vegetables ; toss to combine.
3 Place the sesame seeds in a dry frying pan. Cook over medium heat for 1–2 minutes until they are lightly golden. Sprinkle over salad and serve immediately.

ABOVE: SNOW PEA AND ASPARAGUS SALAD.
OPPOSITE PAGE: COCK-A-LEEKIE

SOUPS

MULLIGATAWNY

⭐ **Preparation time:** 30 minutes
Total cooking time: 1 hour 10 minutes
Serves 6

2 lb chicken pieces, such
as thighs, drumsticks,
breasts
2 tablespoons all-purpose
flour
2 teaspoons curry powder
1 teaspoon turmeric
1/2 teaspoon ground ginger
1/4 cup butter

6 cloves
12 peppercorns
1 large apple, peeled and
diced
6 cups chicken stock
2 tablespoons lemon juice
1/2 cup heavy cream
boiled rice and chutney to
serve

1 Wipe the chicken pieces with paper towels. Combine the flour, curry powder, turmeric and ground ginger; rub the mixture all over the chicken pieces.
2 Heat butter in a heavy-bottom pan and lightly brown chicken on all sides. Add cloves, peppercorns, apple and stock; bring to the boil, and simmer, covered, for 1 hour.
3 Remove chicken pieces from pan and discard peppercorns and cloves. Skin chicken and cut flesh into small pieces. Return to soup with the lemon juice and cream; gently reheat.
4 Serve in heated bowls, accompanied by hot boiled rice and chutney offered separately for stirring into soup, if desired. Other accompaniments, such as coconut, raisins or chopped peanuts can also be offered.

COCK-A-LEEKIE

⭐ **Preparation time:** 20 minutes
Total cooking time: 1 hour 45 minutes
Serves 6–8

2 1/2 lb whole chicken
2 large leeks, chopped
6 cups water
1 bay leaf
1 teaspoon fresh thyme
leaves

1 small bunch parsley
2 teaspoons salt
1 teaspoon cracked black
pepper
12 pitted prunes

1 Rinse the chicken thoroughly, both inside and out, under cold running water; drain well and pat dry with paper towels. Trim off excess fat and cut chicken in half.
2 Place chicken, leeks, water, herbs and salt in a large heavy-bottom pan. Bring slowly to the boil; reduce heat to low. Simmer, uncovered, for 1 1/2 hours, skimming froth from the top occasionally. Discard bay leaf and parsley.
3 Carefully remove chicken halves from the pan; cool slightly. Shred flesh coarsely, discarding the skin and bones.
4 Return chicken flesh to pan with pepper and prunes; stir until just heated through.

breast ribs after the outer cuts have been removed. Sold individually or in sets called racks. Ribs are often broiled or barbecued, and are valued for the sweet, nutty flavor of the meat that clings to them.

Spatchcock A small chicken or game bird that has been split down the back and flattened, then often threaded onto skewers before being broiled or roasted.

Spearmint The most commonly used member of the mint family. It is used in mint sauce to accompany lamb, adds flavor to boiled peas and potatoes and is also an important ingredient in Thai cooking. Mint leaves dry well, keeping their color and smell.

Speculaas Thin, crisp cookies which are spiced with ginger, cinnamon and allspice and topped with slivered almonds. The dough is pressed into wooden molds before baking. The cookies are often made in the shape of legendary and traditional characters. Speculaas are popular in the Netherlands and in southern Germany, from where they originated.

Spice The aromatic seeds, fruit, bark, roots or flowers of trees and shrubs, almost always dried, used to flavor both sweet and savory dishes. Most spices grow in tropical and semi-tropical climates, especially in India and Southeast Asia (the Moluccas, a group of islands off Indonesia and original home of the clove and nutmeg trees, were long known as the Spice Islands). For thousands of years spices reached Europe along trading routes through south-western Asia. Among the first to reach the Mediter-ranean were pepper and cinnamon. Spices were rare and expensive; they were used in innumerable dishes and sauces, both sweet and savory. For centuries the lucrative trade was monopolized by Venetian merchants. It was the desire to find the source of the spices that launched the fleets of Dutch and Portuguese ships. These voyages of discovery not only found their goal, the fabled Spice Islands of Southeast Asia, but also reached the shores of the Americas.

Spices are available

BEEF CONSOMME

★ ★ **Preparation time:** 45 minutes
Total cooking time: 4–5 hours
Serves 6

1 large carrot, chopped	2 teaspoons salt
1 large onion, chopped	bouquet garni
3 stalks celery, chopped	10 peppercorns
4 lb sawn beef and veal bones	2 egg whites crushed shells of the eggs
1 lb beef shanks, chopped	1/4 cup dry sherry
12 cups cold water	

1 Place carrot, onion and celery in a large baking pan; scatter bones and meat on top. Roast in a moderate oven 350°F, turning occasionally, for 1 hour or until meat and vegetables are well browned but not dark.
2 Transfer meat and vegetables to a large stock pot and cover with cold water. Add salt, bouquet garni and peppercorns and bring slowly to boil, skimming surface well. Simmer stock gently, half-covered, for 3–4 hours, skimming surface occasionally. Strain stock through a colander lined with cheesecloth or a fine sieve. Cool stock, then refrigerate until jellied. Remove all fat from surface.
3 To clarify, place de-fatted stock in a large clean pan with egg whites and crushed egg shells. Bring to boil slowly, whisking occasionally with a wire whisk when liquid gradually rises in pan. Simmer gently for 20 minutes. Strain stock through a cheesecloth-lined colander or sieve.
4 Place in a clean pan and reheat gently; add sherry. Serve consommé in heated soup bowls.

WATERCRESS SOUP

★ **Preparation time:** 40 minutes
Total cooking time: 15 minutes
Serves 8

1 large onion	2 1/2 cup water
4 scallions	sour cream and watercress
1 lb watercress	sprigs, for garnish
1/3 cup butter	
1/2 cup all-purpose flour	
3 cups chicken stock	

1 Coarsely chop onion, scallions and watercress. Melt butter in a large heavy saucepan; add onions and watercress. Cook and stir over low heat for 3 minute or until watercress is wilted. Add flour; stir until well combined.
2 Stir together chicken stock and water. Add mixture gradually to saucepan, stirring until

mixture is smooth. Stir constantly over medium heat for 10 minutes or until mixture bubbles and thickens. Cook and stir for 1 minute more; remove from heat. Set aside to cool.
3 Place one-third of the soup mixture in food processor bowl. Using the pulse action, process for 15 seconds or until mixture is smooth. Return soup to saucepan. Repeat twice more. Gently heat soup through. Garnish each serving with a dollop of sour cream and a watercress sprig.

VICHYSSOISE

★ **Preparation time:** 25 minutes +
1 hour refrigeration
Total cooking time: 30 minutes
Serves 6

2 large leeks, chopped	fresh chives
2 medium potatoes, about 14 1/2 oz, peeled and chopped	3 cups chicken stock 1 cup milk 1/2 cup heavy cream
2 tablespoons chopped	grated nutmeg

1 Place leek, potato, chives and stock in a large pan. Bring to the boil, reduce heat. Simmer, covered, until vegetables are tender, about 30 minutes. Add milk. Allow to cool.
2 Place soup in food processor. Process 30 seconds or until smooth. Transfer to large bowl; stir in cream. Cover and refrigerate for 1 hour or overnight. Serve sprinkled with nutmeg.

Note: Traditionally served chilled, this soup can also be gently reheated and served warm.

CHICKEN NOODLE MUSHROOM SOUP

Preparation time: 15 minutes +
15 minutes soaking
Total cooking time: 20 minutes
Serves 4–6

2 teaspoons sesame oil	1/2 cup sliced dried
2 teaspoons vegetable oil	mushrooms, soaked 15
3 boneless chicken breast	minutes in hot water
halves, cut into cubes	3 1/2 oz cellophane
5 cups chicken stock	noodles, soaked in
2 tablespoons soy sauce	water for 15 minutes
1 slice fresh ginger	1/3 cup snipped chives, for
	garnish

1 Heat oils in large pan, add chicken and cook until golden brown. Remove from pan; pour out any remaining oil from pan.
2 Return chicken to pan, add stock, soy sauce, ginger and mushrooms. Bring to the boil and simmer, uncovered, for 10 minutes. Add well-drained noodles and simmer for 5 minutes longer. Remove the slice of ginger.
3 Pour into a large serving bowl. Garnish with chives. Serve immediately.

Note: Cellophane noodles are made from soy or mung bean flour and are also known as bean thread vermicelli. They can be found in Asian food stores and most large supermarkets.

RISONI (ORZO) SEAFOOD SOUP

Preparation time: 20 minutes
Total cooking time: 20 minutes
Serves 4–6

1/4 cup olive oil	10 oz assorted fresh
1 onion, chopped	seafood
2 cloves garlic, crushed	ground black pepper
2 tablespoons chopped	
parsley	**Bread Slices**
1 cup red wine	1 small Vienna loaf,
1 cup tomato purée	sliced thinly
2 cups water	1/3 cup olive oil
2 tablespoons tomato	extra 2 cloves garlic,
paste	crushed
3/4 cup risoni (orzo)	

1 Heat oil in a large pan, add onion and garlic, and cook until golden. Add parsley and wine, cook 5 minutes. Add the tomato purée, water and tomato paste. Bring to boil, sprinkle in the risoni and gently boil until risoni is just tender.
2 Stir in the seafood and cook for 3 minutes. Serve with crisp Bread Slices.
3 To make Bread Slices: Place slices of bread on baking sheet. Combine oil and garlic and brush over each bread slice. Bake at 400°F until crisp and golden brown.

OPPOSITE PAGE: WATERCRESS SOUP.
LEFT: CHICKEN NOODLE MUSHROOM SOUP
ABOVE: RISONI SEAFOOD SOUP

whole or ground, but because ground spices lose flavor quickly it is best to grind it in small quantities as needed or regularly replace commercially ground spices.

Spinach Also called English spinach, a vegetable with dark green leaves. It is often served with butter and a sprinkle of nutmeg as an accompaniment to poultry and veal; used in stuffings, soufflés and quiches; and raw leaves may be added to salads. It probably originated in southwestern Asia and was taken by the Moors

to Spain in the eleventh or twelfth century. Spinach grows best in cool climates. It is available fresh most of the year and can also be bought frozen, preserved in glass jars or canned.

Split Pea The dried pea, yellow or green in color and with husks removed, split in two at the natural division. Split peas are used to make pea and ham soup and pease pudding. In India yellow split peas are made into dhal.

Sponge Cake A cake with a light and fluffy texture. This airiness is achieved from the addition of well-beaten eggs and lightly folded in flour. There are several types of sponge cake. They can be flavored with vanilla, citrus peel, cocoa or orange flower water; after baking, the cake may be moistened with a liqueur or thin syrup. Sponge cakes are often used

for layer cakes, filled with jam and cream and dusted with confectioners' sugar.

Sponge Fingers Airy finger-shaped cookies made using sponge cake mixture; firm on the outside and soft in the center, the tops are dusted with confectioners' sugar before baking. Sponge fingers are served with chilled cream desserts, ice cream and fruit purées and can be used as a border for cold charlottes.

Spoon Bread A soft fluffy quick cornmeal bread; the batter-like dough is baked in, and served from, a deep pan.

Spotted Dick A steamed or boiled suet pudding studded with currants, sultanas or other dried fruit. Usually served hot, spotted dick is a traditional English dessert.

CREAM OF CHICKEN AND VEGETABLE SOUP

⭐⭐   **Preparation time:** 20 minutes
Total cooking time: 1 hour 45 minutes
Serves 6

Stock
2 lb chicken
6 cups water
$^{1}/_{2}$ stalk celery, chopped
6 peppercorns
1 bay leaf
1 clove garlic, sliced
1 small onion, chopped

Soup
1 medium carrot
1 tablespoon oil
1 medium onion, sliced

$6^{1}/_{2}$ oz button
   mushrooms, sliced
$^{1}/_{4}$ cup all-purpose flour
$^{2}/_{3}$ cup milk
1 cup cream
$3^{1}/_{2}$ oz snow peas, thinly
   sliced
3 medium tomatoes,
   peeled, seeded, chopped
1 tablespoon soy sauce
salt and freshly ground
   black pepper, to taste

1 To make Stock: Wipe the chicken and dry with paper towel. Cut chicken into breasts, thighs, legs and wings. Place in a large heavy-bottom pan with water, celery, peppercorns, bay leaf, garlic and onion. Bring to boil; reduce heat and simmer, covered, for 1¼ hours. Remove from the heat and cool slightly. Strain, reserving the chicken and 5 cups of stock; discard the onion mixture.

2 To make Soup: Cut the carrot into matchstick strips. Heat the oil in large heavy-bottom pan, add the onion, carrot and mushrooms. Cook, stirring, over low heat until the onion is tender. Stir in the stock, blended flour and milk. Bring to boil. Reduce heat and simmer, stirring, until slightly thickened.

3 Cut the reserved chicken into thin strips. Add chicken, cream, snow peas, tomato and soy sauce to soup. Stir until heated through. Season to taste. Serve hot.

CORN AND CHEESE CHOWDER

⭐   **Preparation time:** 15 minutes
Total cooking time: 30 minutes
Serves 8

$^{1}/_{3}$ cup butter
2 large onions, finely
   chopped
1 clove garlic, crushed
2 teaspoons cumin seeds
4 cups chicken stock
2 medium potatoes,
   peeled and chopped
1 cup canned creamed
   corn
2 cups fresh corn kernels

$^{1}/_{4}$ cup chopped fresh
   parsley
1 cup grated Cheddar
   cheese
salt and freshly ground
   black pepper to taste
$^{1}/_{4}$ cup heavy cream,
   optional
2 tablespoons chopped
   fresh chives

1 Heat the butter in a large heavy-bottom pan. Add the onion and cook over medium-high heat for 5 minutes or until golden. Add the garlic and cumin seeds and cook for 1 minute, stirring constantly. Add the chicken stock. Bring to boil. Add potato; reduce heat and simmer, uncovered, for 10 minutes.

2 Add the creamed corn, corn kernels and parsley. Bring to boil, reduce heat and simmer for 10 minutes more.

3 Stir in the grated cheese, salt and pepper to taste, and cream. Heat gently until the cheese melts. Serve immediately, sprinkled with chopped chives.

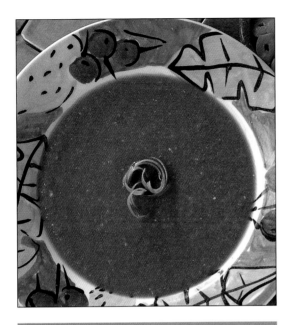

SPANISH CLASSICS

GAZPACHO

★ **Preparation time:** 15 minutes +
1–2 hours refrigeration
Total cooking time: none
Serves 4–6

3 slices white bread,
crusts removed
8 large ripe tomatoes,
peeled, seeded and
chopped
1 cucumber, peeled,
seeded and chopped
1 small onion, chopped
1 small green pepper,
chopped
1/3 cup chopped fresh mint
2 cloves garlic, crushed
2 tablespoons olive oil
2 tablespoons red wine
vinegar

2 tablespoons tomato
paste
1–2 cups iced water

Garnish
1 medium red pepper, cut
into thin strips
1 medium onion, thinly
sliced
1 small cucumber, peeled,
seeded and chopped
2 hard-boiled eggs,
chopped
1/2 cup sliced green olives

1 Combine all ingredients, except iced water and
garnishes, in a large bowl.
2 Place one-third of vegetable mixture into food
processor bowl. Using the pulse action, process
for 30 seconds or until smooth. Pour into large
bowl; repeat with remaining two batches. Thin
mixture to desired consistency using iced water.
Cover with plastic wrap and refrigerate 1–2 hours.

*OPPOSITE PAGE, ABOVE: CHICKEN AND VEGETABLE
SOUP; BELOW: CORN AND CHEESE CHOWDER.
THIS PAGE, ABOVE: GAZPACHO; BELOW: POTATO
AND ONION OMELETTE*

3 Serve soup in large bowls with ice cubes.
Garnishes are placed in small bowls and passed
around for guests to add to soup, as desired.

POTATO AND ONION OMELET

★ **Preparation time:** 15 minutes
Total cooking time: 20 minutes
Serves 4–6

2 tablespoons olive oil
2 large potatoes, cut into
1/2 inch cubes
1 medium onion,
chopped

4 eggs
1/4 teaspoon sweet paprika
1 tablespoon olive oil,
extra

1 Heat oil in a medium heavy-bottom skillet; add
potato and onion. Cook over medium-high heat
until golden brown and well coated with oil.
Reduce heat, cover pan and cook for 5–6
minutes, stirring occasionally, until the potato
is cooked.
2 Remove potato and onion from pan. Drain on
paper towels. Beat eggs and paprika in a medium
bowl until frothy; stir in potato and onion mixture.
3 Heat extra oil in a clean skillet. Add egg
mixture and cook, covered, over medium heat
for 15–20 minutes or until mixture is firm. Broils
3–4 inches from heat until golden brown.
4 Cut into wedges and serve hot or cold with a
green salad.

Note: The success of this omelet relies on slow,
even heat, which is why a heavy-bottom skillet is
required. A nonstick skillet may also be used, but
reduce the amount of oil by half.

Spring Onion (Green
Onion) Also known as
scallion, a variety of
onion with small, white,
mild-flavored bulbs and
long, green, grass-like
leaves. They are eaten
raw and finely sliced in
salads.

Spring Roll (Egg Roll)
A layer of thin dough
wrapped around a filling
of cooked vegetables and
meats, rolled up
and deep-
fried
until
crisp and
golden.
Spring rolls are usually
served with a dipping
sauce, as finger food or a
first course. Variations
are eaten throughout
Southeast Asia. They are
traditionally served
during Lunar New Year
celebrations.

Spring Roll Wrapper
Pliable, paper-thin sheet
of white rice flour dough
usually sold frozen in
packs. When using, keep
wrappers covered with a
cloth.

Sprout A grain, seed or
pulse, germinated to
grow as a plant and used
as a food.
Sprouts most
commonly used
include mung
beans, soy beans and
alfalfa. Small and
crunchy,
sprouts
can be
added to
salads and are
often an ingredient in

Chinese stir-fries. When sprouting seeds at home, use dried seeds sold as food (seeds sold for gardening may have been treated with fungicides). Sprouts are also available fresh or canned.

Spumoni An Italian frozen dessert consisting of ice cream layers assembled in a mold and then frozen. Spumoni usually has a layer of chocolate ice cream, a strawberry or raspberry ice cream layer and a green layer of pistachio ice cream; the inner layers can also consist of whipped cream or liqueur-soaked fruits, candied fruits or nuts. The dessert is served sliced.

Spun Sugar Also known as angel's hair, gossamer-fine threads of syrup made from sugar boiled to a light caramel. Spun sugar is used as a decoration or garnish for ice creams, special desserts and festive cakes. *Croquembouche*, the traditional French wedding cake, is a high pile of choux pastry puffs glazed with spun sugar.

Squab A young pigeon, about four weeks old. Its dark, sweet, succulent flesh, which is served rare, can be broiled or roasted. Care should be taken not to overcook it.

PAELLA

⭐ ⭐   *Preparation time:* 25 minutes
Total cooking time: 20 minutes
Serves 4–6

1 tablespoon olive oil
4 boneless, skinless chicken thighs, each cut into 4 pieces
1 large red pepper, chopped
1 tablespoon chopped parsley
1 tablespoon olive oil, extra
2 cloves garlic, crushed
1 medium onion, sliced, top to bottom
1 cup long grain rice
2 cups chicken stock
¼ teaspoon saffron threads
1 cup frozen peas
12 oz assorted seafood
4 oz salami, thinly sliced
1 lemon, cut into 6 wedges

1 Heat oil in large heavy-bottom skillet, add chicken pieces. Cook over medium-high heat for 2–3 minutes or until golden brown, turning once. Remove from pan, drain on paper towel. Add pepper and parsley to skillet and stir for 1 minute over medium-high heat. Remove mixture and set aside.
2 Heat extra oil in skillet; add garlic and onion, cook over medium heat 1 minute or until golden. Add rice, stir well, making sure rice grains are well coated with oil. Stir in saffron and stock and cover pan with tight-fitting lid.
3 Bring to a boil; stir once. Add chicken. Reduce heat. Cover and simmer for 15 minutes. Add frozen peas, assorted seafood, salami and pepper mixture. Cover and cook 10 minutes more or

until chicken and rice are tender and seafood is cooked.
4 Remove from heat. Let stand, covered, 5 minutes before serving. Separate rice grains with a fork just before serving on a large platter garnished with lemon wedges.
Note: Paella is the best-known rice dish from Spain. It takes its name from the shallow round pan or *paellera* that it is cooked in. Any shallow pan will make a suitable substitute. There are many variations to the basic paella recipe. You can choose any combination of seafood that you like such as shrimp, scallops, mussels, clams, squid and lobster.

MIXED VEGETABLES WITH GARLIC MAYONNAISE

⭐   *Preparation time:* 30 minutes
Total cooking time: 15 minutes
Serves 4–6

Garlic Mayonnaise
2 egg yolks or ¼ cup egg substitute
4 cloves garlic, crushed
1 cup olive oil
pinch pepper
2 tablespoons lemon juice

Vegetables
4 small eggplants
4 medium red peppers
4 medium firm tomatoes
4 small onions
⅓ cup olive oil
⅓ cup chopped fresh parsley
1 clove garlic, crushed
¼ teaspoon ground pepper

1 To make Garlic Mayonnaise: Place egg yolks or egg substitute and garlic in a medium mixing bowl. Whisk together for 1 minute. Add oil, about 1 teaspoon at a time, whisking constantly until mixture is thick and creamy. Increase the speed at which oil added as mayonnaise thickens. Stir in pepper and lemon juice. Stir in pepper and lemon juice. Set aside.
2 Place whole unpeeled vegetables on a lightly oiled broiler rack. Broil 3–4 inches from heat 6–8 minutes, turning once, until they are black all over. Remove, cover with a damp towel, allow to cool. Peel blackened skin from vegetables and cut into ¾ inch cubes. Arrange in a serving dish.
3 Combine oil, parsley, garlic and pepper in a small bowl and pour over vegetables. Serve, warm, or at room temperature with Garlic Mayonnaise and bread.

ABOVE: MIXED VEGETABLES WITH GARLIC MAYONNAISE.

OPPOSITE PAGE, ABOVE: ORANGE AND CARAMEL CUSTARD; BELOW: CHICKEN SPANISH STYLE

CHICKEN SPANISH STYLE

Preparation time: 30 minutes
Total cooking time: 25 minutes
Serves 6

1½ lb boneless, skinless
  chicken breasts
6 thin slices ham
¼ cup butter
1 small onion, chopped
1 small carrot, finely
  chopped
1 tablespoon all-purpose
  flour

1½ cups chicken stock
1 cup apple cider
¼ teaspoon ground
  pepper
¼ teaspoon ground
  nutmeg
¼ cup toasted pine nuts,
  optional

1 Preheat oven to moderate 350°F. Using a sharp knife, make a deep incision into the thickest section of each breast. Insert a slice of ham, secure with toothpicks. Cover with plastic wrap and refrigerate until required.
2 Heat butter in saucepan; add onion and carrot. Cook 4 minutes over low heat until soft. Add flour, stir over low heat until lightly golden. Add combined stock and apple cider gradually to pan, stirring until mixture is smooth. Add pepper and nutmeg. Stir constantly over medium heat 3 minutes or until sauce boils and thickens; boil 1 minute more. Remove from heat.
3 Place chicken in a single layer in a shallow ovenproof dish. Pour sauce over, cover and bake 20–25 minutes or until chicken is no longer pink.
4 Remove toothpicks from chicken, serve with a spoonful of sauce. Top with toasted pine nuts.

ORANGE AND CARAMEL CUSTARD

Preparation time: 30 minutes +
8 hours refrigeration
Total cooking time: 45 minutes
Serves 4–6

Caramel
½ cup water
1 cup sugar

Custard
1 cup milk

1 cup light cream
1 teaspoon finely grated
  orange rind
3 eggs
3 egg yolks
⅓ cup sugar

1 Preheat oven to 325°F. Brush a deep 8 inch round pan or ovenproof dish with melted butter.
2 To make Caramel: Combine water and sugar in small saucepan. Stir over low heat until mixture boils and sugar has dissolved. Simmer, uncovered, without stirring, 5 minutes or until mixture is dark golden brown. Pour evenly over base of prepared pan.
3 To make Custard: Heat milk, cream and rind in small saucepan until almost boiling. Cool and strain. Beat eggs, yolks and sugar in a bowl with electric beaters until thick and pale. Add milk mixture gradually to egg mixture, beating constantly.
4 Pour through fine strainer over caramel in pan. Stand pan in deep baking dish. Pour in hot water to come halfway up sides. Bake 45 minutes or until set. Remove pan from hot water bath. Cool; refrigerate for at least 8 hours. Serve.

Squash A general term for edible members of the gourd family, native to the Americas. They are usually divided into summer squash and winter squash. Summer squash, soft-skinned and quick-growing, are picked young and include zucchini, patty-pan, scalloped, baby sunburst and yellow straightneck squash; small summer squash may be steamed or boiled. Winter squash are the larger, slow-growing, hard-skinned varieties, such as acorn, spaghetti squash and pumpkin.

Squid Known as calamari in Italy, squid is a saltwater mollusk with a long cylindrical body and ten tentacles surrounding a parrot-like beak. It is prized for its delicately flavored, firm, white flesh. Squid is found in temperate waters throughout the world. It has long been an important ingredient in the cooking of Asia and the Mediterranean.

Star Anise The dried, star-shaped fruit of a tree native to southern China, used as a spice. It has a strong aniseed flavor. Star anise has long been used in Asian cooking to flavor meat and poultry dishes and is one of the components of five-spice powder; it has been known in Europe since the early seventeenth century. It is available whole or ground.

Star Fruit See Carambola.

Steak A slice of meat, usually beef, taken from between the rump and the rib. Steak cuts include T-bone, porterhouse and sirloin; fillet or tenderloin comes from beneath the lower backbone. Steak can be

broiled or pan-fried, and is sometimes served with a sauce.

Steak Tartare Raw ground beef seasoned with salt and pepper and raw egg yolk, onions and parsley.

Steam To cook food by using the concentrated moist heat of steam given off by steadily boiling water. Steaming can be done in a double

SPARERIBS

MEXICAN-STYLE BEEF SPARERIBS

★ *Preparation time:* 15 minutes
Total cooking time: 1 hour
Serves 4

3 lb beef spareribs	*1 tablespoon white sugar*
2 bay leaves	*2 tablespoons cider vinegar*
1½ cups water	*14 oz can tomato puree*
¼ cup soft brown sugar	*1 tablespoon Mexican*
1 clove garlic, crushed	*style chili powder, or to taste*
Sauce	*1 teaspoon dried oregano*
1 tablespoon vegetable oil	*1 teaspoon ground cumin*
½ cup chopped onion	*bottled hot pepper sauce*
1 clove garlic, crushed	*to taste*

1 Place spareribs and bay leaves in a large pan. Combine water, brown sugar and garlic, pour over ribs. Heat until boiling, reduce heat and cover. Gently simmer, turning ribs occasionally, until tender, about 30–45 minutes.

2 To make Sauce: Heat the oil in a small pan, add the onion and garlic; cook until soft. Stir in the sugar, vinegar, puree, chili powder, oregano, cumin and sauce. Heat until boiling, reduce heat. Simmer, stirring occasionally, for 5 minutes. Cover and keep warm.

3 Drain ribs, pat dry on paper towels. Grill directly over medium-hot coals. turning and basting frequently with sauce, about 10–15 minutes. Serve with remaining sauce.

BARBECUED PORK SPARERIBS

★ *Preparation time:* 5 minutes +
2 hours marinating
Total cooking time: 20 minutes
Serves 4

6 lb pork spareribs	*½ cup lemon juice*
¼ cup tomato paste	*½ cup honey*
¼ cup hoisin sauce	*2 tablespoons sesame*
¼ cup chili sauce	*seeds, toasted*

1 Trim any excess fat from ribs. In a bowl or jug, combine the tomato paste, hoisin sauce, chili sauce, lemon juice and honey. Place the spareribs in a large, shallow dish and pour the marinade over. Store in the refrigerator, covered with plastic wrap, for 2 hours or overnight, turning occasionally.

2 Drain the meat, reserving the marinade. Place the spareribs on a lightly oiled preheated grill. Cook directly over medium coals for 20 minutes or until the meat is tender, turning occasionally.

3 Heat the remaining marinade in a small saucepan over a low heat; do not allow to boil. Pour the marinade over the ribs just before serving.

4 Sprinkle the ribs with the toasted sesame seeds. Spareribs may be served with boiled or fried rice and steamed green vegetables.

ABOVE: BARBECUED PORK SPARERIBS. OPPOSITE PAGE, BELOW: SPINACH FRITTERS WITH WALNUT SAUCE; ABOVE: SPINACH AND AVOCADO SALAD

S P I N A C H

SPINACH FRITTERS WITH WALNUT SAUCE

⭐ **Preparation time:** 20 minutes
Total cooking time: 6–8 minutes
Serves 6

12 spinach leaves, stems removed	⅓ cup oil
2 eggs	**Sauce**
2 cups whole-wheat bread crumbs	½ cup toasted ground walnuts
1 cup walnuts, ground	1 cup plain yogurt
4 drops Tabasco sauce	pinch of ground saffron

1 Wash spinach under cold running water. Chop coarsely and place in a pan. Cover, cook until spinach is tender. Drain; cool. Using hands, squeeze spinach to remove excess moisture. Chop finely.
2 Place spinach in a bowl, add lightly beaten eggs, breadcrumbs, ground walnuts and Tabasco sauce. Mix well to combine. Divide mixture into twelve equal portions. Shape each into a round. Heat oil in shallow pan. Add fritters and cook over a medium heat, turning once, until fritters are golden brown on both sides.
3 While fritters are cooking, prepare sauce by combining walnuts, yogurt and saffron. Stir well to mix. Serve fritters with walnut sauce.

Note: If fresh spinach is not available substitute a 9 oz package of frozen chopped spinach. Thaw, remove excess moisture using paper towels.

SPINACH AND AVOCADO SALAD

⭐ **Preparation time:** 15 minutes
Total cooking time: none
Serves 6

12 large spinach leaves	2 tablespoons walnut oil
2½ oz walnuts, chopped	3 teaspoons white wine vinegar
1 medium avocado, sliced	

1 Wash and dry spinach thoroughly. Place in a serving bowl with the walnuts and avocado.
2 Place oil and vinegar in a small screw-top jar and shake well. Pour over salad ingredients; toss lightly. Serve immediately.

CREAMED SPINACH

Tear 1 bunch of spinach into pieces. Heat 1 tablespoon butter in heavy-bottom frying pan. Add 1 finely sliced small onion. Cook 2–3 minutes or until onion is soft. Add spinach, cook 1 minute. Stir in ¼ cup heavy cream, heat through. Sprinkle with nutmeg and grated Cheddar cheese. Serve warm.

SHREDDED SPINACH AND BACON

Finely shred 1 bunch of spinach. Cut 2 slices of bacon in thin strips. Heat 2 teaspoons olive oil in a frying pan. Add the bacon strips, fry on medium-high heat until almost crisp. Add the shredded spinach, toss through until just wilted. Serve warm.

saucepan; in a covered basin set in a pot of boiling water; or, as in China and South-East Asia, in multilayered metal or bamboo steamers.

Steamboat A Chinese meal consisting of small portions of meat and seafood cooked at the table in simmering stock. Each diner uses chopsticks or a long-handled small wire basket to add or retrieve food; when cooked, each portion is dipped in sauce and eaten. Meat is cooked first, then seafood, then vegetables. As a final course, noodles are cooked in the remaining broth and served with it as soup. The dish is traditionally cooked in a Mongolian fire pot, a tabletop cooking device which has a moat (for the stock) around a chimney-like funnel and is set over glowing coals. A fondue set or saucepan and gas ring may be substituted. This style of cooking is believed to have originated with the nomadic Mongolians of northern China.

Steamed Pudding A British specialty, the steamed pudding is cooked in a deep covered basin over boiling water. The basic pudding mixture usually consists of flour, fat, sugar and eggs; dried or fresh fruits, spices and flavorings such as coffee, vanilla and chocolate, may be added. Steamed puddings range from the dense and fruity plum (Christmas) pudding to light, cake-like puddings. Steamed ginger pudding probably evolved as a less expensive version of the traditional plum pudding, is made with a layer of honey or sweet syrup (golden syrup or

light corn syrup) at the bottom of the basin; this soaks into the batter and forms a syrupy topping sauce when the pudding is unmolded.

Stew A dish made from a selection of meat, poultry or fish and vegetables, with herbs and seasonings added, which is cooked slowly with liquid in a covered container (either on the stove-top or in the oven) until the meat and vegetables are tender. Many less expensive, tougher cuts of meat are suitable for stewing.

SPINACH AND SALMON TERRINE

★★ **Preparation time:** 35 minutes
Total cooking time: 10 minutes
Serves 8

2 x 9 oz packages frozen chopped spinach
2 tablespoons butter
1/2 cup chopped scallions
1 tablespoon chopped fresh dill
nutmeg and pepper to taste
6 eggs
1 tablespoon cornstarch
1 tablespoon lime juice
1/4 cup grated Parmesan

Filling
1/4 cup chopped scallions
1 teaspoon chopped fresh dill
1 tablespoon lime juice
1 tablespoon horseradish
8 oz Neufchâtel cheese
6 1/2 oz sliced smoked salmon

1 Preheat oven to moderate 350°F. Brush a shallow 12 x 10 inch jelly roll pan with melted butter or oil. Line the base and sides with baking paper, extending 2 inch extra at the ends. Thaw spinach and squeeze out the excess moisture using paper towels. Heat the butter in a medium pan. Add the scallions and dill, stir over medium heat for 1 minute. Add the spinach, heat through. Season with nutmeg and pepper. Remove from the heat.
2 Beat the eggs in medium bowl. Blend the cornstarch and lime juice in small bowl until smooth. Combine with eggs and spinach mixture. Pour into prepared pan. Bake for 7 minutes or

until firm to touch. Turn onto a damp towel covered with a sheet of baking paper and sprinkled with cheese. Cover with a cloth and leave to cool.
3 To make Filling: Place scallions, dill, juice, horseradish and cheese in food processor. Process 30 seconds or until smooth.
4 Cut the spinach base into three strips. Place one strip on board. Spread with a layer of Filling, top with one-third of the smoked salmon slices. Spread the second strip with a thin layer of Filling. Place cheese-side down on salmon. Repeat this procedure with next layer. Decorate with rolled smoked salmon slices. Cut the terrine into 3/4 inch slices to serve. Serve cool as a first course, with a light salad as an accompaniment.

BASIL SPINACH SALAD

Tear 1 bunch of spinach into pieces. Combine in a large bowl with 1/4 cup of shredded basil leaves and 2 tablespoons of toasted pine nuts. Finely slice 1 slice of bacon. Cook bacon in a small pan until crisp. Remove from pan and drain on paper towels. In a small bowl, combine 2 tablespoons oil, 1 tablespoon white wine vinegar, 1 tablespoon sour cream, 1/2 teaspoon sugar and 1 clove crushed garlic. Mix well and drizzle over salad. Top with bacon and Parmesan cheese.

ABOVE: SPINACH AND SALMON TERRINE.
OPPOSITE PAGE: VEGETARIAN MINI SPRING ROLLS

SPRING ROLLS

VEGETARIAN MINI SPRING ROLLS

★ **Preparation time:** 35 minutes + 30 minutes standing
Total cooking time: 20 minutes
Makes 20

4 dried Chinese mushrooms
5 oz fried tofu
1 tablespoon oil
6 scallions, finely chopped
1 teaspoon crushed garlic
3/4 teaspoon finely grated ginger

3 cups shredded Chinese cabbage
1 large carrot, grated
1 tablespoon soy sauce
5 large spring roll wrappers
oil, extra, for deep-frying

1 Place mushrooms in a bowl and cover with hot water. Leave for 30 minutes. Drain, squeeze to remove excess liquid. Remove stems; chop caps finely. Cut tofu into small cubes and set aside. Heat oil in wok or heavy-based frying pan, swirling gently to coat base and side. Add scallions, garlic, ginger, cabbage, carrot, mushrooms and tofu. Stir-fry for 5 minutes over a moderate to high heat until vegetables are softened. Add the soy; stir to combine. Allow to cool.

2 Cut each spring roll wrapper into four squares. Work with one square at a time, keeping the remainder covered with a clean, damp towel. Place 2 teaspoonfuls of the filling on the wrapper and fold one point over. Fold in the two side points, then roll up towards the last point, forming a log shape. Seal point with a little flour and water paste. Repeat process with remaining wrappers and filling.

3 Heat the extra oil in a wok; deep-fry the rolls, four at a time, until golden, for about 3 minutes. Remove rolls from oil with a slotted spoon; drain on paper towels. Serve warm.

Stilton A creamy-textured, blue-veined, semi-firm cow's milk cheese. It is creamy-white to amber in color and has a strong aroma. Stilton dates from the seventeenth century, when it was sold to coach passengers who stopped at the Bell Inn in the village of Stilton, in eastern England. The cheese should be served at room temperature at the end of a meal.

Stir-fry To rapidly and uniformly cook chopped food (vegetables, meat, poultry or seafood) in a small amount of hot oil, in either a wok or a frying pan over a high heat, while continuously turning the mixture with a spatula. Stir-frying seals in the flavors of the food and ensures it retains its crispness.

Stock A thin, clear, flavored liquid obtained by simmering vegetables, herbs and spices with meat, poultry or seafood. The liquid is then strained and chilled so that any fat which rises to the top can be removed. Stock is used to enrich soups, stews, casseroles and sauces. Excellent stock can be home-made but it is also available in cans, as a powder and as a cube.

Stollen A German yeast cake made with dried fruits, candied peel and almonds, and sprinkled with sugar before baking. It is traditionally eaten at Christmas.

Strawberry The red, heart-shaped, juicy berry of a ground-hugging plant related to the rose, cultivated throughout the world. Strawberries can be added to fruit and savory salads, eaten with a little cream or a dusting of sugar and a squeeze of lemon juice, and used whole or sliced to garnish cakes and desserts. They are pureed for use in ice cream and sorbets, and cooked as jams, jellies, preserves and fillings for tarts and pies.

Strawberries have been cultivated in Europe since the thirteenth century. Most varieties available today are descended from the scarlet Virginia strawberry which came to France from North America in the early eighteenth century. Wild strawberries have a more intense flavor.

Streusel A crumbly topping of flour, sugar, butter and spices that is sprinkled on cakes, breads and muffins.

Stroganoff A traditional Russian dish consisting of strips of beef fillet, lightly sautéed and

SQUID (CALAMARI)

FRIED SQUID (CALAMARI) WITH TARTAR SAUCE

★
★★
Preparation time: 20 minutes
Total cooking time: 1 minute per batch
Serves 4

1 lb small, cleaned
    calamari tubes
2 tablespoons cornstarch
2 eggs, lightly beaten
2 cloves garlic, crushed
2 teaspoons grated lemon
    rind
1 cup dried bread crumbs
oil for deep frying

Tartar Sauce
1 cup mayonnaise
2 tablespoons chopped
    fresh chives
2 tablespoons chopped
    dill pickle
1 tablespoon seeded
    mustard

1 Slice calamari thinly. Place cornstarch on a plate. Combine eggs, garlic and rind in a bowl. Place bread crumbs on another plate. Toss calamari in cornstarch; shake off excess. Dip in egg mixture. Coat with bread crumbs; shake off the excess.
2 Heat oil in a deep heavy-bottom pan. Gently lower small batches of calamari into moderately hot oil. Cook over medium-high heat for 1 minute or until just heated through and lightly browned. Carefully remove from oil with a slotted spoon. Drain on paper towels, keep warm. Repeat with remaining calamari.
3 To make Tartar Sauce: Combine mayonnaise, chives, pickle and mustard. Mix well. Serve as a dip.

GREEK STYLE SQUID (CALAMARI)

★
Preparation time: 30 minutes
Total cooking time: 35 minutes
Serves 6–8

2 lb medium tubes
    calamari

1 egg, lightly beaten

Stuffing
1 tablespoon olive oil
2 scallions, chopped
1/3 cup pine nuts
1/2 cup currants
2 tablespoons chopped
    fresh parsley
2 teaspoons finely grated
    lemon rind
1 1/2 cups cooked rice

Sauce
1 tablespoon olive oil
1 onion, finely chopped
1 clove garlic, crushed
4 large ripe tomatoes,
    peeled and chopped
1/4 cup good quality red
    wine
1 tablespoon fresh
    chopped oregano

1 Preheat oven to moderately slow 325°F. Wash and dry calamari tubes. Combine oil, scallions, pine nuts, currants, parsley, lemon rind and rice in a bowl. Mix well. Add enough egg to moisten all ingredients.
2 Three-quarters fill each tube. Secure end with a toothpick or skewer. Place in single layer in a casserole dish.
3 To make Sauce: Heat oil in pan; add onion and garlic and cook over low heat 2 minutes or until onion is soft. Add tomato, wine and oregano. Cover; cook over low heat 10 minutes.
4 Pour sauce over calamari; cover and bake 20 minutes or until tender. Remove toothpicks; slice thickly. Spoon sauce over just before serving.

STEAK

STEAK DIANE

⭐ **Preparation time:** 5 minutes
Total cooking time: 15–20 minutes
Serves 6

6 beef tenderloin steaks,
about 4 oz each
½ teaspoon ground black
pepper
3 tablespoons butter
1 tablespoon butter,
extra
2 scallions, finely chopped

4 cloves garlic, crushed
2 tablespoons
Worcestershire sauce
1 tablespoon brandy
½ cup heavy cream
2 tablespoons finely
chopped fresh parsley

1 Trim the meat of excess fat and sinew. Flatten the steaks to an even thickness and nick the edges to prevent curling. Sprinkle each steak with pepper. Heat the butter in a pan; add steaks. Cook over high heat for 2 minutes each side to seal, turning once. For rare, cook for another minute each side. For medium and well-done, reduce heat to medium, cook for another 2–3 minutes each side for medium and 4–6 minutes each side for well done. Remove from the pan and drain on paper towels.
2 Heat the extra butter in pan. Add the chopped scallions and garlic; cook for 3 minutes. Add the Worcestershire sauce and brandy and stir

Opposite page, above: Fried squid; below: Greek style squid. This page, above: Steak diane; right: Steak with cilantro butter

---

to dislodge any crusty pieces from the bottom of pan. Stir in the cream and simmer for 5 minutes. Return steaks to the pan with parsley and heat through.

STEAK WITH CILANTRO BUTTER

⭐ **Preparation time:** 20 minutes
Total cooking time: 5–15 minutes
Serves 8

6 oz beef rib eye steaks

Cilantro Butter
⅔ cup butter, softened
2 tablespoons finely
chopped fresh cilantro

1 tablespoon finely
chopped fresh mint
1 teaspoon grated orange
rind
2 teaspoons finely grated
ginger

1 Trim meat of excess fat and tendons.
2 To make Cilantro Butter: Beat the butter in a small bowl until creamy. Add the cilantro, mint, rind and ginger. Beat until combined. Place in a log shape on a piece of foil. Roll up and refrigerate until firm.
3 Place the steaks on an oiled, preheated grill. Cook over high heat for 2 minutes each side to seal, turning once. For rare, cook for another minute each side. For medium and well-done, move meat to cooler part of grill, cook another 2–3 minutes each side for medium and 4–6 minutes each side for well done. Slice Cilantro Butter into ½ inch thick rounds. Place on top of hot steaks to serve.

---

coated with a sauce of sour cream; it sometimes contains mushrooms and onions. Stroganoff is often served over noodles. It has been known since the eighteenth century and is said to have been created

for a member of the Stroganov family, wealthy merchants originally from Novgorod.

Strudel A dessert or savory dish consisting of a wafer-thin pastry dough that is spread with a filling and rolled as a jelly roll, then baked (traditionally bent into a crescent or horseshoe shape). It is usually served warm. Sweet fillings can include apple, sour cherry, and cream cheese.

Savory strudels with fillings such as chopped, boiled beef with bacon and onions are popular in Austria.

Stuffing (Dressing) A savory mixture of bread crumbs, corn bread, rice, ground meat, poultry or fish, with chopped fruit or vegetables, herbs and spices, which is bound with milk or egg and used to add bulk, shape and flavor to meat, fish, poultry and vegetables by filling a cavity created by the removal of innards or seeds.

Sturgeon A freshwater and saltwater fish with white to pink flesh. It can be roasted, broiled or stewed. Caviar is sturgeon roe.

Succotash A dish of North American origin consisting of a mixture of corn kernels and lima beans. It is served as an

accompaniment to meat or poultry. Succotash descends from the *misickquatash* of the Narraganset Indians, made with corn and kidney beans cooked in bear fat.

Suckling Pig Also known as sucking pig, a young pig slaughtered when no more than eight weeks old, prized for its sweet, rich, succulent meat. Suckling pig may be spit-roasted whole over a barbecue or oven-roasted.

Suet The white fat which surrounds lamb and beef kidneys. It is firm, dry and non-greasy

STEAK AND KIDNEY PUDDING

⭐
⭐ ⭐ **Preparation time:** 30 minutes
Total cooking time: 4 hours 10 minutes
Serves 4

1 lb round or rump steak	fresh parsley
6½ oz lamb kidneys	1 bay leaf
2 tablespoons all-purpose flour	
2 tablespoons butter	**Suet Pastry**
1 tablespoon oil	1½ cups all-purpose flour
1 medium onion, sliced	½ teaspoon baking powder
1 clove garlic, crushed	⅛ teaspon salt
4 oz button mushrooms, quartered	⅓ cup suet, skinned, finely grated
½ cup red wine	½ cup water, approximately
1 cup beef stock	
2 tablespoons chopped	

1 Trim meat of excess fat and tendons. Cut meat evenly into 1 inch cubes. Peel skin from kidneys, cut kidneys into quarters, trim off any excess fat and membranes. Place flour in a plastic bag, add meat and kidneys and toss to coat. Shake off any excess flour.
2 Heat butter and oil in heavy-bottom pan. Add onion and garlic, stirring until soft, remove. Add meat and kidneys in small batches, cook quickly over a medium-high heat until well browned on

all sides; drain on paper towels.
3 Return onion, garlic, meat and kidneys to pan. Add mushrooms, wine, stock, parsley and bay leaf; bring to boil. Reduce heat to a simmer, cook, covered, 1 hour or until the meat is tender, stirring occasionally. Allow mixture to cool.
4 To make Suet Pastry: Sift flour, baking powder and salt into a bowl, stir in the grated suet. Add sufficient water to mix to a firm dough. Knead on a lightly floured surface until smooth. Roll two-thirds of suet pastry to fit the base and side of an 8-cup ovenproof bowl; brush the top edge with water.
5 Spoon cooled meat filling into pastry. Roll remaining pastry to cover bowl, press edges of pastry firmly together to seal. Grease a sheet of wax paper large enough to cover the top of the bowl plus about 2 inches all round. Place the paper over top of pudding.
6 Place a sheet of foil over the top of the paper, secure tightly with string. Place bowl on a trivet in a large pan. Add enough water to come halfway up side of bowl. Bring to boil, reduce heat to a simmer and cook, covered, 3 hours. Turn out onto a plate, cut into wedges to serve.

STEAK TARTARE

⭐ **Preparation time:** 15 minutes
Total cooking time: none
Serves 4

1 lb beef top sirloin	2 tablespoons chopped capers
salt and pepper	
4 egg yolks	2 tablespoons chopped fresh parsley
1 medium white onion, finely chopped	pumpernickel bread or toast triangles for serving

1 Trim meat so that no tendons or fat are evident. Chop or grind beef finely in a meat grinder or food processor; it should not become pulp. Season meat well with salt and pepper.
2 Divide into four portions, shape into round cakes and place on serving plates. Using the back of a soup spoon, make a shallow impression in the top of each cake, slide in a whole egg yolk.
3 Serve each steak with a small mound of onion, capers and parsley on the side and accompany with pumpernickel bread or toast triangles.

Note: Some people like to serve Steak Tartare with Tabasco or chili sauce.

ABOVE: STEAK AND KIDNEY PUDDING.
OPPOSITE PAGE: STRAWBERRY SHORTCAKE

STRAWBERRIES

STRAWBERRY SHORTCAKE

✶ **Preparation time:** 20 minutes
Total cooking time: 18–20 minutes
Makes one 8 inch round cake

2 cups all-purpose flour
2 teaspoons baking
  powder
1/8 teaspoon salt
1/4 cup sugar
1/2 cup butter

1 egg lightly beaten
2/3 cup milk
1 1/2 cups cream, whipped
  strawberries, halved, or
  other sliced fresh fruit

1 Preheat oven to 425°F. Brush an 8 inch round cake pan with butter or oil. Coat base and side evenly with flour; shake off excess. Place flour, baking powder, salt and sugar in a large bowl. Cut in butter until coarse crumbs.
2 Combine egg and milk. Add to dry ingredients and stir until just moistened. Spread in prepared cake pan. Bake for about 20 minutes. Turn cake out onto wire rack to cool.
3 Split cake horizontally using two forks. Spread cut side of bottom half with half of the whipped cream. Place most of the halved strawberries or other sliced fresh fruit over the cream. Top with other half of cake. Spread remaining cream on top and decorate with remaining strawberries or fruit.

STRAWBERRY CONSERVE

✶ **Preparation time:** 15 minutes + overnight soaking
Total cooking time: 30–40 minutes
Makes 1 1/2 cups

1 lb strawberries   1 1/2 cups sugar

1 Wash and drain fruit; remove stems. Cover fruit with 1/2 cup sugar and leave to stand overnight.
2 Strain liquid from strawberries. Place liquid in pan, add remaining sugar and stir over low heat for 10 minutes. Do not allow to boil.
3 Add fruit, cooking until setting point is reached, about 20–30 minutes. Ladle into warm, sterilized jars. When cool, seal and label jars.

STRAWBERRY SUNSET

Soften 1 quart of rich vanilla ice cream by placing in refrigerator for about 30 minutes. Place ice cream in a medium bowl and stir very gently until smooth. Fold in 1/2 cup partially frozen orange juice concentrate and 2 tablespoons of orange liqueur (for example, Grand Marnier). Arrange the hulled strawberries in four stemmed glasses and the spoon orange cream over the fruit. Sprinkle with ground cinnamon and serve immediately.

to handle and is used as fat in the cooking of pastries and rich boiled puddings.

Sugar A sweet-tasting food used mainly as a flavoring. It is extracted from many plants, principally sugar cane (in tropical regions) and sugar beet (in cooler climates); lesser quantities are obtained from certain maple and palm trees and the sorghum plant. To process sugar from cane the juice is extracted and boiled until it crystallizes (candies); centrifugal machines are used to separate the raw sugar crystals from the liquid molasses. For beet sugar the juice is extracted from the root. There are various types of sugar. Brown sugar is soft and moist with a characteristic flavor that comes from a film of

molasses surrounding each crystal; it is used especially in baking chewy cookies and dark cakes. Raw sugar, made directly from the clarified juice of sugar cane, has coarse, straw-colored crystals. White or granulated sugar, with medium-sized crystals, is refined from sugar cane and is used as a general sweetener. Superfine

(caster) sugar has finer crystals and dissolves more quickly than white sugar and so is best for meringues, and some cakes and puddings. Powdered or confectioners' sugar is granulated sugar milled to a fine powder. Palm sugar (jaggery) is extracted from a species of low-branched palm tree and has a strong flavor; it gives deep color and rich flavor to a number of sweet and savory Indian, Malaysian and Indonesian dishes.

Sugar cane, a perennial grass, probably originated in southern India. The plant spread from there south to Malaysia and Indonesia, and north and west to ancient Persia. The "sweet reed" and crystals that could be obtained from its juice, were also known to the Greeks and Romans. Sugar reached Europe with the Crusaders returning from southwestern Asia in the thirteenth century but it did not displace honey as a general sweetener until the eighteenth century, when it inspired the development of elaborate French candies and pâtisseries.

Sukiyaki A stew-like dish of Japanese origin consisting of finely sliced meat (usually beef, but pork, chicken and

STRAWBERRY CHARLOTTE RUSSE

⭐ **Preparation time:** 1 hour + 4 hours refrigeration
Total cooking time: 45 minutes
Serves 12

1 cup all-purpose flour
1 teaspon baking powder
1/4 teaspoon salt
3 large eggs
1 cup sugar
1/3 cup warm milk
1/3 cup flaked coconut
3 tablespoons unsalted butter, melted and cooled
2 teaspoons vanilla
1 cup strawberry jelly

2 cups halved strawberries
24 ladyfingers

Strawberry Mousse
1 envelope unflavored gelatin
1/2 cup orange juice
2 cups sliced strawberries
1/2 cup sugar
1 1/2 cups heavy cream, whipped

1 Preheat oven to moderate 350°F. Grease one 9 inch round springform pan. Line bottom with wax paper circle. Dust side lightly with flour, tapping out excess. Sift the flour, baking powder, and salt onto wax paper.
2 Add sugar gradually, 1 tablespoon at a time, beating constantly about 10 minutes or until the sugar has dissolved and the mixture is pale yellow and glossy. Transfer mixture to a large mixing bowl. Add milk, coconut, melted butter, vanilla and sifted dry ingredients; using a metal spoon, fold in quickly and lightly. Spread the mixture evenly into prepared pan. Bake for 45 minutes or until cake springs back when touched lightly in center.

Leave the cake in pan for 10 minutes before turning onto wire rack to cool. Remove paper.
3 To make Strawberry Mousse: Combine gelatin with orange juice in a small saucepan. Heat and stir over medium heat until gelatin dissolves. Remove from heat; cool. Place gelatin mixture, 2 cups sliced strawberries and sugar into food processor bowl. Using the pulse action, press button for 20 seconds or until mixture is smooth. Transfer mixture to a large mixing bowl. Fold in whipped cream. Line the side of springform pan with parchment paper. Cut dome off cake horizontally to give a level surface. Place cake in lined pan. Pour Mousse evenly into prepared pan to cover cake. Cover, refrigerate several hours or until set.
4 Place the jelly in a small saucepan. Stir over medium heat until melted; remove pan from the heat. Decorate the top of the mousse with the halved strawberries. Brush with half of the jelly. Remove cake from the pan. Remove paper. Place on a serving plate.
5 Cut ladyfingers to the height of the cake. Press carefully around the edges of the cake.

STRAWBERRY MALLOW

Place 1/2 cup of chopped marshmallows in a medium bowl and stir in 1 cup of plain yogurt. (Use wet scissors to chop marshmallows easily.) Add 8 oz sliced fresh strawberries and mix well. Cover and refrigerate for 1 hour. Spoon mixture into 4 dessert dishes and sprinkle with toasted flaked almonds before serving.

STROGANOFF

BEEF STROGANOFF

⭐ **Preparation time:** 25 minutes
Total cooking time: 15 minutes
Serves 6

2 lb piece beef tenderloin
⅓ cup all-purpose flour
¼ teaspoon ground black pepper
¼ cup olive oil
1 large onion, chopped
1 lb small mushrooms
1 tablespoon sweet paprika

1 tablespoon tomato paste
2 teaspoons Dijon mustard
½ cup good quality dry white wine
¼ cup chicken stock
¾ cup sour cream
1 tablespoon finely chopped fresh parsley

1 Trim meat of excess fat and tendons. Slice meat across the grain evenly into short, thin pieces. Combine flour and pepper on a sheet of wax paper. Toss meat in seasoned flour; shake off the excess.
2 Heat 2 tablespoons oil in a heavy-bottom pan. Cook meat quickly, in small batches, stirring over medium-high heat until well browned; drain on paper towels.
3 Add remaining oil to pan. Add the onion, cook over a medium heat for 3 minutes or until soft. Add mushrooms, stir over medium heat for 5 minutes. Add the paprika, tomato paste, mustard, wine and stock to pan, bring to the boil. Reduce heat and simmer for 5 minutes, uncovered, stirring occasionally.
4 Return meat to pan. Add sour cream, stir until combined and just heated through. Sprinkle with parsley just before serving.

CHICKEN STROGANOFF

⭐ **Preparation time:** 20 minutes
Total cooking time: 15 minutes
Serves 6

2 tablespoons butter
2 tablespoons oil
2 onions, thinly sliced
2 cloves garlic, crushed
8 boneless chicken thighs, sliced
8 oz mushrooms, sliced

2 teaspoons sweet paprika
1 cup sour cream
¼ cup tomato paste
freshly ground black pepper
2 tablespoons chopped fresh parsley

1 Heat the butter and oil together in a large frying pan. Add the onion and garlic and cook over a medium heat for 3 minutes or until the onion is soft.
2 Add chicken slices. Cook, stirring, until chicken is tender. Stir in mushrooms and paprika. Cook until mushrooms are tender.
3 In a bowl, combine the sour cream, tomato paste and pepper. Stir into pan. Simmer gently until heated through. Sprinkle with chopped parsley. Serve with boiled rice or noodles.

OPPOSITE PAGE: STRAWBERRY CHARLOTTE RUSSE.
ABOVE: BEEF STROGANOFF

seafood can also be used) and vegetables, soy sauce and sake cooked at the table (this can be done in an electric frying pan). Traditionally each diner breaks a raw egg into an individual bowl, beats it with chopsticks and then dips the hot food into it before eating.

Sultana The dried fruit of a white grape which is softer and sweeter than both the raisin and currant. Sultanas are baked in cakes, cookies, biscuits, breads and puddings, they can be added to stuffings, casseroles and curries, or sprinkled on breakfast cereals and tossed with salads. They originated in Crete, where in ancient times sweet, seedless

grapes were sun-dried and exported throughout the Aegean.

Summer Pudding A cold dessert made by lining a basin with slices of bread, filling it with a lightly poached soft fruit (such as raspberries, red currants, black currants, loganberries and blackberries) then chilling it overnight, until the

juice soaks into the bread, flavoring and coloring it. The whole is turned out and served with whipped cream. Summer pudding is a traditional English dessert.

Summer Sausage Any of several types of dry sausage that do not require refrigeration.

Sundae A dessert or sweet snack consisting of ice cream topped with a flavored syrup and sometimes fruit, often sprinkled with crushed nuts and whipped cream and served in a long, shallow glass dish. It originated in the United

States in the nineteenth century where it was a special Sunday treat.

Sunflower Seed Small, flat, oval seed from the center of the huge yellow flowerhead of the sunflower plant. The seeds can be used raw in soups, stir-fries, pasta and rice dishes. Roasted, they add crunch to salads and cooked vegetables; boiled, they can be added to cakes or cookies. Sunflower seeds are often used as bird

S T R U D E L S

CREAMY CHICKEN STRUDEL

⭐⭐ **Preparation time:** 30 minutes
Total cooking time: 40 minutes
Serves 4

1 tablespoon oil
1 large onion, chopped
2 garlic cloves, crushed
8 oz ground chicken
1 tablespoon curry powder
1/3 cup ricotta cheese
1/4 cup sour cream
10 sheets frozen filo dough, thawed

1/3 cup butter, melted
1 stalk of celery, finely chopped
1 small red pepper, finely chopped
1 small avocado, sliced
1 tablespoon sesame seeds

1 Preheat oven to moderate 350°F. Brush a baking sheet with melted butter or oil. Heat oil in heavy-bottom pan, add onion and garlic, cook over medium heat for 2 minutes or until lightly browned. Add ground chicken, cook over high heat 4 minutes or until chicken is well-browned and all liquid has evaporated. Use a fork to break up any lumps of chicken as it cooks. Add curry powder, cook 1 minute, remove pan from heat; cool mixture. Combine chicken mixture with ricotta cheese and sour cream.
2 Cover filo dough with a damp towel. Remove one sheet of pastry, place on work surface, brush all over with melted butter. Place another sheet on top, brush with butter. Repeat with remaining pastry and most of the butter.

3 Spoon chicken mixture along the long side of the pastry. Top with celery, pepper and avocado.
4 Roll up, tucking in ends. Place, seam-side down, on prepared baking sheet, brush with butter, sprinkle with sesame seeds. Bake 30 minutes or until pastry is golden brown. Serve sliced.

CREAM CHEESE STRUDEL

⭐⭐ **Preparation time:** 15 minutes
Total cooking time: 25 minutes
Serves 6

8 oz cream cheese, softened
1 tablespoon lemon juice
1/4 cup sugar
1/4 cup all-purpose flour

1/3 cup golden raisins
2 sheets frozen puff pastry, thawed
2 tablespoons milk
1 tablespoon sugar, extra

1 Preheat oven to moderate 350°F. Beat the cream cheese, lemon juice and sugar together until smooth. Lightly stir in the flour and the golden raisins.
2 Place the pastry sheets on a work surface. Roll out until 1/4 inch thick. Place half the cheese mixture along one side of each pastry sheet, about 2 inches in from the edge. Roll up as for a jelly roll. Press ends together to seal.
3 Place on a greased baking sheet. Brush with milk and sprinkle with extra sugar. Bake the strudels for abouy 25 minutes, or until it is golden brown.

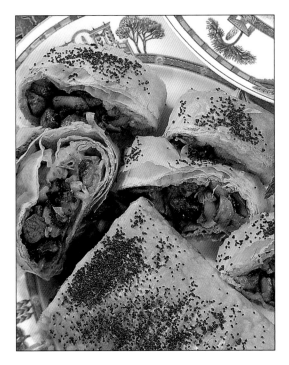

MUSHROOM STRUDEL

⭐ **Preparation time:** 20 minutes
Total cooking time: 25 minutes
Serves 4–6

1 tablespoon butter	8 sheets frozen filo
1 clove garlic, crushed	dough, thawed
2 teaspoons lemon juice	1/3 cup butter, extra,
1 lb medium mushroom	melted
caps, sliced	1/2 cup grated pecorino
2 teaspoons finely grated	cheese
lemon rind	6 scallions, sliced
freshly ground pepper	2 teaspoons poppy seeds

1 Melt butter in a medium-sized pan. Add garlic and lemon juice and cook over a low heat for 2 minutes. Add mushrooms, rind and pepper. Cook until mushrooms are just tender; cool.
2 Cover filo pastry with a damp towel. Remove one sheet of pastry, place on work surface, brush all over with melted butter. Place another sheet on top, brush with butter. Repeat with remaining pastry and most of the butter.
3 Place the cooled filling along the center, parallel with long sides of pastry. Sprinkle with cheese and scallions. Roll up pastry, tucking in the ends. Place on a well-oiled baking sheet, with the seam underneath. Brush top and sides with butter, sprinkle with poppy seeds.
4 Bake at 400°F for 8 minutes. Reduce heat to 350°F and cook for another 15 minutes.

OPPOSITE PAGE: CREAM CHEESE STRUDEL.
ABOVE: MUSHROOM STRUDEL

APPLE STRUDEL

⭐ ⭐ **Preparation time:** 20 minutes
Total cooking time: 30 minutes
Serves 8

1/2 cup ground walnuts	6 sheets frozen filo
1 tablespoon soft brown	dough, thawed
sugar	1/4 cup butter, melted
1 teaspoon ground	15 oz can apple pie
cinnamon	filling
	1/2 cup golden raisins

1 Preheat oven to moderately hot 400°F. Combine the walnuts, sugar and cinnamon.
2 Work with one sheet of filo at a time, keeping remainder covered with a damp towel to prevent drying out. Brush first pastry sheet with a little melted butter; sprinkle 2 teaspoonfuls of walnut mixture over the pastry. Repeat procedure with remaining pastry sheets, layering the buttered sheets one on top of the other and sprinkling all but the last layer with walnut mixture.
3 Combine the apple and raisins. Spread mixture down the center of pastry. Fold in the narrow ends to meet; fold over the long ends to make an envelope. Place seam-side down on a lightly greased baking sheet. Brush the top and sides with butter. Make diagonal slits across the top at 1 1/4 inch intervals.
4 Bake strudel for 15 minutes. Reduce the heat to moderate 350°F and cook for another 15 minutes or until crisp and golden. Serve warm.

CHERRY STRUDEL

Drain a 15 oz can of cherries. Pit and halve cherries; set aside in a colander to drain. Combine 3/4 cup of very finely chopped walnuts, 1/2 cup of sugar, 1 tablespoon of grated lemon rind and 1 teaspoon each of ground cinnamon and ground allspice in a large bowl. In another bowl, combine 3/4 cup of soft, white breadcrumbs with 1/4 cup of melted butter. Add bread-crumb mixture to nut mixture; stir well.

Lay a sheet of puff pastry on a work surface and roll until 1/4 inch thick; brush with a little melted butter. Spread with the nut mixture, followed by the cherries, leaving a 2 inch margin on each side. Fold over lengthwise and press the edges together firmly. Tuck in the short ends. Brush all over with melted butter, sprinkle with poppy seeds, if desired, and place on a greased baking sheet. Bake for 10 minutes in a hot 400°F oven, reduce heat to 350°F and bake for another 25–30 minutes or until the strudel is golden. Serve warm with whipped cream.

feed. A flour ground from the roasted seeds is available from health food stores. Oil pressed from the seeds is used in cooking, and in salad dressings, margerines and shortenings. The sunflower plant is believed to have originated in Central America. It was taken to Spain in the sixteenth century and spread throughout Europe.

Supreme of Chicken
The breast and wing of a chicken, removed and cooked in one piece, It is often served with a rich cream sauce.

Sushi A dish of Japanese origin which consists of small rolls of seaweed containing cooked rice and savory fillings such as a thin slice of raw fish (usually tuna) or omelette, or a vegetable. Other shapes are also made. Sushi featuring seaweed is called *maki*, that made with fish or seafood is called *nigri*, and that made with omelette is called *fukusu*. In Japan sushi is sold in small specialty restaurants or at a separate counter in larger restaurants. Sushi is served cold, with wafer-thin slices of pickled ginger, and is usually eaten with the fingers. The dish originated as a fishermen's snack.

Swede See Rutabaga

Sweet and Sour Sauce
A sauce of Chinese origin which combines sweet and tart ingredients, such as sugar and vinegar, usually thickened with cornstarch and often also containing fruit juice, pineapple pieces or sweet pepper.

Sweetbread Classed as offal or variety meat; sweetbreads can be either the thymus gland (in the throat) or the pancreas (near the stomach) of calves and lambs. Valued for their delicate flavor, sweetbreads must be soaked in several changes of water and blanched before use. They may be poached, sautéed, braised, or broiled and served with a sauce.

Sweet Corn See Corn.

Sweet Pepper See Peppers, Sweet.

Sweet Potato A starchy tuber, no relation to the potato, and often confused with the yam. There are three main varieties which differ in color: white, orange (also known as kumara) and red. All are cooked in the same way as the potato, although sugar is sometimes added to emphasize their natural sweetness.

SWEET POTATOES

TWO-POTATO HASH BROWNS

⭐ **Preparation time:** 20 minutes
Total cooking time: 25 minutes
Serves 4–6

3 slices bacon, finely chopped (optional)	2 tablespoons olive oil
1 lb potatoes, peeled	salt and freshly ground black pepper, to taste
8 oz orange sweet potato, peeled	sour cream
1 large onion, finely chopped	2 tablespoons chopped fresh chives

1 Preheat oven to moderate 350°F. Brush a baking sheet with melted butter or oil. Grease an egg ring to use as a mold. Place bacon in small pan. Cook over medium-high heat for 3 minutes. Drain on paper towels. Cut potato and sweet potato in half. Cook in boiling water for 10 minutes, or until just starting to soften. Drain well and grate them both.
2 Place potatoes, onion, bacon, oil, salt and pepper in a bowl. Toss well to ensure even mixing. Press spoonfuls of mixture in egg ring on oven tray. Level the top surface. Remove ring and repeat with remaining mixture. Or, shape by hand into patties.
3 Bake for 20 minutes or until crisp and golden. Serve immediately, topped with sour cream and chopped fresh chives.

CHILI SWEET POTATO AND EGGPLANT CRISPS

⭐ **Preparation time:** 5 minutes
Total cooking time: 20 minutes
Serves 4–6

1 orange sweet potato, about 10 oz	¼ teaspoon ground chili powder
1 slender eggplant, about 12 oz	¼ teaspoon ground coriander
oil for deep frying	1 teaspoon salt

1 Peel sweet potato. Cut sweet potato and eggplant into long thin strips of similar size. Place in a large bowl, mix.
2 Heat oil in a deep heavy-bottom pan. Gently lower half the combined sweet potato and eggplant into the moderately hot oil. Cook over medium-high heat for 10 minutes or until golden and crisp. Carefully remove the crisps from the oil with tongs or slotted spoon. Drain on paper towels. Repeat cooking process with remaining sweet potato and eggplant.
3 Combine the chili powder, coriander and salt in a small bowl. Sprinkle all the mixture over the hot crisps. Toss until the crisps are well coated. Serve immediately.

ABOUT SWEET POTATOES

■ Sweet potatoes have either orange, white or yellow flesh and have a sweet flavor.
■ If cut into chips and deep-fried, sweet potatoes make an interesting alternative to potatoes.

SWISS ROLLS
(JELLYROLLS)

CHOCOLATE RASPBERRY SWISS ROLL (JELLY ROLL)

★★ **Preparation time:** 25 minutes
Total cooking time: 12–15 minutes
Makes one jelly roll

½ cup all-purpose flour
¼ cup unsweetened cocoa powder
1 teaspoon baking powder
⅛ teaspoon salt
4 eggs
⅔ cup sugar

¼ cup grated dark (semi-sweet) chocolate
1 tablespoon hot water
1 tablespoon sugar, extra
1¼ cups heavy cream
1 tablespoon sugar
2 cups fresh or frozen raspberries

1 Preheat oven to 375°F. Brush a 15 x 10 x 1 inch jelly roll pan with oil. Line base and sides with parchment paper; grease paper. Sift flour, cocoa, baking powder and salt three times onto waxed paper. Using electric beaters, beat eggs 4–5

OPPOSITE PAGE, ABOVE: TWO-POTATO HASH BROWNS; BELOW: CHILI SWEET POTATO AND EGGPLANT CRISPS. THIS PAGE: CHOCOLATE RASPBERRY SWISS ROLL

minutes until thick and pale. Add sugar gradually, beating constantly until pale yellow and glossy.
2 Transfer mixture to large bowl. Using a metal spoon, fold in sifted flour mixture, chocolate and water quickly and lightly. Spread mixture into pan; smooth surface. Bake 12–15 minutes, until lightly golden and springy.
3 Place sheet of wax paper on a dry towel. Sprinkle with extra sugar. Turn cake onto paper; stand 2 minutes. Carefully roll warm cake up with paper; let stand 5 minutes. Unroll, discard paper. Whip cream with 1 tablespoon sugar; fold in raspberries. Spread cake with whipped cream mixture; re-roll. Trim ends of roll.

ABOUT SWISS ROLLS
When the cake is cooked it will have shrunk a little from the sides of the pan. A cake is cooked when a skewer inserted into the center comes out clean. This should only be tried at the very end of the cooking time. Making a hole in a partially cooked sponge cake can cause it to collapse.

A Swiss roll is rolled up with its paper while still warm because if it cools before being rolled it will crack. The paper prevents the cake from sticking together making it easy to unroll for filling. It can be filled with jam while still hot, but if you attempt to fill a hot cake with cream, the cream will become oily.

Swiss Chard A leaf vegetable that has large, bubbly, spinach-flavored leaves and fleshy white stems. The green leaves are cooked and eaten like spinach, or may be added to salads.

Swiss Roll (Jelly Roll) A thin sheet of sponge cake that is spread with jam or another sweet filling before being rolled up. The finished cake is then sprinkled with

confectioners' sugar and sliced.

Syrup A sweet liquid, usually a solution of sugar and a liquid. Corn syrup is the liquid form of sugar refined from corn. Light corn syrup is less sweet than sugar; dark corn syrup has caramel coloring and

flavoring added and tastes similar to molasses. See also Golden Syrup and Maple Syrup.

Szechwan Pepper Also known as Chinese pepper, a fragrant, intensely flavored (but not fiery hot) spice made from the dried berries of the Chinese prickly ash.

T

Tabasco A thin, red, fiery-tasting sauce made by fermenting chili peppers with salt in oak barrels for four years, then straining it and adding vinegar. Tabasco sauce is used sparingly to add a hot flavor to sauces, salad dressings, tomato juice, meat, crab and lobster dishes, and is an essential ingredient in Cajun cooking. It was first made in Louisiana in 1868 and is named for the Tabasco region in Mexico, original home of the chili peppers used. The sauce is sold around the world in distinctive, small bottles.

Tabbouleh (Tabouli, Tabooley) A salad of Middle Eastern origin made with cracked wheat (bulgur), finely chopped fresh flat-leaf parsley, diced tomato, olive oil, mint and lemon juice.

Traditionally wrapped in

TARTS

FRUIT FLAN

★ **Preparation time:** 40 minutes + refrigeration
Total cooking time: 30 minutes
Makes 2 x 9 inch flans

2¹/2 cups all-purpose flour
¹/4 cup sugar
²/3 cup butter, chopped
1 egg
1 egg yolk
1 tablespoon water

Custard
2¹/2 cups milk
3 eggs
2 tablespoons all-purpose flour
2 tablespoons cornstarch
¹/2 cup sugar

2 teaspoons vanilla extract

Topping
2 kiwifruit, sliced
16 oz can peach halves, sliced
14 black or red seedless grapes
8 oz strawberries, halved
¹/2 cup strawberry jam
1 tablespoon brandy

1 Place the flour, sugar and butter in food processor. Using the pulse action, process for 30 seconds or until mixture is fine and crumbly. Add the egg, egg yolk and water and process for a further 20 seconds or until the mixture just comes together when squeezed. Turn onto a lightly floured board and knead gently to form a smooth dough. Refrigerate, covered with plastic wrap, for 20 minutes.

2 Preheat oven to moderately hot 400°F. Halve the pastry, wrap one portion in plastic wrap and set aside. On a floured board, roll the other half of the pastry to fit a 9 inch round loose-bottomed flan pan. Ease the pastry into pan, trim edge with a sharp knife. Repeat with the remaining half of pastry and a second flan pan. Cut a sheet of parchment paper to cover each pastry-lined pan. Place the paper in each pan and spread a layer of dried beans or rice evenly on top. Bake for 10 minutes. Remove the paper and rice or beans, bake for another 10 minutes or until lightly browned; cool.

3 To make Custard: Whisk ¹/2 cup milk with eggs, sifted flour, cornstarch and sugar in medium bowl. Heat remaining milk in a pan until warm, remove from heat. Gradually whisk into egg mixture. Return mixture to pan, whisk over heat until custard boils and thickens. Simmer for 3 minutes. Stir in vanilla. Remove from heat and cool. Spread into pastry shell.

4 To make Topping: Arrange fruit decoratively over custard. Heat jam and brandy together in pan, then strain through a sieve; brush over fruit. Refrigerate flan before serving.

ABOVE: FRUIT FLAN.

OPPOSITE PAGE: PASSIONFRUIT RICOTTA TART

PASSIONFRUIT RICOTTA TART

 Preparation time: 30 minutes +
1 hour 20 minutes refrigeration
Total cooking time: 20 minutes
Serves 6

1¼ cups all-purpose flour
⅓ cup butter, chopped
¼ cup sugar
2 tablespoons iced water

Filling
1½ cups ricotta cheese
½ cup sugar
3 eggs
½ cup heavy cream
3 passionfruit
2 teaspoons confectioners'
    sugar

1 Sift flour into large mixing bowl, add butter. Using fingertips, rub butter into flour for 2 minutes or until mixture is fine and crumbly; stir in sugar. Add almost all the water, mix to a firm dough, adding more water if necessary. Turn onto a lightly floured surface, press together until smooth. Roll out and line an 8-inch deep round flan pan. Cover with plastic wrap and refrigerate for 20 minutes.

2 Preheat oven to moderate 350°F. Cut a sheet of wax paper large enough to cover pastry-lined pan. Place over the pastry and spread a layer of dried beans or rice evenly over the paper. Bake for 10 minutes then remove from oven and discard the paper and beans. Return to the oven for 10 minutes, or until pastry is lightly golden. Allow to cool.

3 To make Filling: Place the ricotta, sugar, eggs and cream in food processor. Using pulse action, press button for 20 seconds or until mixture is smooth. Add passionfruit pulp and process for 5 seconds. Pour into pastry shell and bake for 1 hour or until set and lightly golden. Cool and refrigerate for 1 hour. Dust with powdered sugar before serving.

APPLE AND SOUR CREAM FLAN

 Preparation time: 35 minutes +
30 minutes refrigeration
Total cooking time: 45 minutes
Serves 4–6

1 cup all-purpose flour
¼ cup finely grated
    Cheddar cheese
2 tablespoons butter,
    chopped
1–2 tablespoons iced
water

Filling
2 small green apples

1 egg, lightly beaten
⅓ cup sugar
2 tablespoons cornstarch
1 teaspoon vanilla
    extract
¾ cup sour cream
2 tablespoons butter,
    melted
2 tablespoons apricot jam,
    warmed and sieved

1 Place flour, cheese and butter in a food processor. Using the pulse action, press button for 20 seconds or until mixture is fine and crumbly. Add almost all of the water and process for another 15 seconds or until the mixture comes together. Turn onto a lightly floured board and knead gently. Brush an 8-inch round flan pan with oil or melted butter. Roll out pastry large enough to cover base and side of pan. Ease pastry into pan; trim. Cover with plastic wrap; refrigerate for 30 minutes.

2 Preheat oven to moderate 350°F. Cut a sheet of waxed paper large enough to cover pastry-lined pan. Place over pastry and spread a layer of dried beans or rice evenly over the paper. Bake for 10 minutes, remove from the oven and discard the paper and beans. Return to the oven for another 10 minutes or until the pastry is lightly golden. Set aside to cool before filling.

3 To make Filling: Peel the apples, remove cores and slice thinly. In a medium mixing bowl, combine the egg, sugar, cornstarch, vanilla and sour cream until smooth. Pour the mixture into the pastry base and arrange the apple slices on top; brush with melted butter. Bake for 25 minutes or until the apples are lightly golden. Brush tart with apricot jam while warm. Serve warm or cold.

romaine lettuce leaves and eaten with the hands, tabbouleh is often served as an accompaniment to broiled meat and poultry.

Taco A tortilla made of corn which has been folded and fried until crisp. It is traditionally served with a spicy meat filling; refried beans, grated cheese, chopped tomato, shredded lettuce and chili-based sauce may be added. Ready-made taco shells are available from supermarkets.

Taffy A candy made from boiled syrup which is pulled and worked into long strands; the pulling incorporates air and gives taffy its light and creamy texture. The taffy is then twisted and cut into bite-sized pieces and wrapped so that it doesn't get sticky during storage.

Tagine A highly spiced Moroccan stew of meat, vegetables or fruit, often served at banquets.

Tagliatelle (Fettuccine) Long, flat ribbon pasta, often colored and flavored with spinach or tomato, boiled in water and served with a sauce. It is a specialty of northern and central Italy and is said to have been inspired by the flaxen hair of Lucrezia Borgia.

Tahini (Tahine) A thick, smooth, paste of roasted, ground sesame seeds. In the Middle East it is mixed with lemon juice, garlic and chickpeas (garbanzo beans) to make a dip served with flat bread. Tahini is also used in cakes, cookies and the candy halva; it can be bought in jars from supermarkets.

Tamale A sweet or savory cornmeal cake steamed inside a corn husk. A Mexican specialty, it is often served hot as a first course. The tamale is made by spreading a dough of ground dried corn and water (called *masa*) on a corn husk, adding a sweet or savory filling, then wrapping it up and steaming until cooked. Banana leaf or aluminum foil may be substituted for the corn husk.

Tamales are a traditional festival food and were once considered to be a gift from the gods. Tamale pie is a baked dish made with layers of cornmeal and spicy ground meat.

Tamarillo An egg-shaped fruit with glossy, deep red skin and soft, tart-tasting flesh with tiny seeds. The bitter skin is removed by blanching; the flesh can be added to sweet and

CARAMEL NUT TARTLETS

★★ ☆ **Preparation time:** 30 minutes
Total cooking time: 40 minutes
Makes about 18

½ cup all-purpose flour
1 tablespoon sugar
3 tablespoons butter
1 tablespoon milk

Filling
8 oz unsalted mixed nuts
½ cup sugar
¼ cup water
¼ cup cream

1 Preheat oven to moderate 350°F. Sift flour into a medium bowl; add sugar. Add butter and rub into flour with fingertips for 2 minutes or until mixture is fine and crumbly. Add milk, mix to a soft dough. Knead on lightly floured surface 1 minute or until smooth.
2 Roll pastry out thinly; cut into circles using a 2½ inch fluted cutter. Press into greased muffin cups, prick evenly with fork. Bake 10 minutes or until lightly golden.
3 To make Filling: Spread nuts on a baking sheet. Bake 10 minutes or until they are lightly golden. Combine sugar and water in a medium pan. Stir constantly over low heat until sugar has dissolved. Bring to boil. Reduce heat; simmer, uncovered, without stirring, for 10 minutes or until mixture turns golden brown. Remove from heat, add cream and stir. (If syrup sets in lumps when the cream is added, return pan to heat for 1 minute or until the mixture is smooth.) Add the nuts and stir. Spoon into pastry shells; cool before serving.

INDIVIDUAL HERB TARTS

★ ☆ **Preparation time:** 15 minutes
Total cooking time: 35 minutes
Makes 18

18 slices white bread, crusts removed
2–3 tablespoons butter, softened

Filling
2 eggs
2 tablespoons milk
2 teaspoons chopped fresh chives
1 teaspoon chopped fresh dill
1 teaspoon chopped fresh thyme
1 tablespoon chopped fresh parsley
½ cup heavy cream
2 tablespoons grated Parmesan cheese

1 Preheat oven to moderately hot 400°F. Brush two muffin pans with melted butter or oil. Cut bread into rounds using a 3 inch plain round cookie cutter. Flatten out each round with a rolling pin. Spread both sides of each round with butter and gently press them into the muffin pans. Bake for about 10 minutes, or until the bread rounds are lightly browned and crisp. Take care not to overcook the rounds or they will become brittle.
2 To make Filling: Reduce heat to moderate 350°F. Combine the eggs, milk, herbs and cream in a bowl; mix well. Pour the egg mixture into prepared bread cases and sprinkle with Parmesan cheese. Bake for 25 minutes or until the tart filling is lightly browned and set. Serve immediately.

TERRINES

RED PEPPER TERRINE

★ ★ **Preparation time:** 30 minutes +
45 minutes standing
Total cooking time: 30 minutes
Serves 8

3 large red peppers	1/3 cup oil
1 1/2 lb eggplant	1 lb spinach
salt	1/3 cup pesto

1 Preheat oven to moderate 350°F. Cut peppers in half and remove seeds. Place peppers cut side down on a baking sheet. Broil for 5 minutes or until skin blisters and browns. Cover with damp towel, cool; peel off skins.
2 Cut the eggplant into 1/4 inch slices. Sprinkle with salt and set aside for 45 minutes. Rinse the eggplant under cold water, drain and dry with paper towel.
3 Heat 1 tablespoon of the oil in a pan, add a layer of eggplant slices. Cook over medium heat for 2 minutes each side until the eggplant is lightly browned. Drain. Repeat with remaining oil and eggplant.
4 Remove the stems from the spinach leaves, place leaves in a medium bowl, cover with hot water. Stand for 1 minute, then drain and rinse under cold water. Line a 12 x 5 inch loaf pan with a double layer of spinach leaves, allowing the leaves to drape over sides of pan.
5 Place a quarter of the eggplant in overlapping slices along base of pan. Top with a third of the peppers, spread with a quarter of the pesto. Repeat layering with remaining eggplant, pepper and pesto.
6 Enclose filling completely with spinach leaves. Bake for 30 minutes or until the terrine is tender; set aside to cool. Store the terrine, covered with plastic wrap, in the refrigerator. Turn out of pan to serve.

PORK AND VEAL TERRINE

★ ★ **Preparation time:** 30 minutes
Total cooking time: 2 hours
Serves 6

1 lb ground pork	1 cup dry white wine
1 lb ground veal	salt and freshly ground
2 eggs, beaten	pepper
1 onion, finely chopped	1/2 teaspoon chopped fresh
1 clove garlic, finely	thyme
chopped	1/2 teaspoon ground mace
2 tablespoons melted lard	6 slices bacon

1 Preheat oven to slow 300°F. In a large bowl, mix together minced pork and veal. Add beaten eggs, onion, garlic, lard, wine, salt, pepper, thyme and mace.
2 Line base and sides of a terrine or 9 x 5 inch loaf pan with bacon. Spoon prepared mixture into the pan and fold the ends of the bacon over to cover the top.
3 Cover the pan with a lid or foil and place in a roasting pan half-filled with water. Bake terrine for 2 hours. Remove from the oven, cool and refrigerate.
4 When the terrine is cold, turn it out of the pan and cut into slices. Serve at room temperature with crusty bread or a crisp salad.

ABOUT TERRINES

■ Traditionally terrines are baked in a special earthenware mold (called a terrine) with a tight-fitting lid. Some versions are baked uncovered, cooled, then pressed with a weight to compact the mixture for slicing.
■ Pork has long been the favored ingredient for both terrines and pâtés. Nowadays there are many recipes, including vegetable and fish terrines, which use less fatty mixtures.
■ Terrines with interesting layers or textures, or colorful ingredients, look very attractive when sliced. Serve with crackers, toast or fresh bread.

OPPOSITE PAGE: CARAMEL NUT TARTLETS.
ABOVE: RED PEPPER TERRINE

savory salads or sweetened and cooked for use in tarts and hot puddings. The tamarillo is native to Peru; there are also yellow varieties.

Tamarind Sour-sweet pulp from the seed pods of a tropical tree, used to give a bite to curries, stews and chutneys and as an ingredient in

Worcestershire sauce. It is available from Asian food stores in the form of dried pulp or a paste. Also called the Indian date.

Tandoori A traditional Indian method of cooking in which chicken or lamb is marinated in a spicy red paste, threaded onto long skewers and cooked in a tandoor or clay oven. Tandoori paste is available from specialist food stores.

Tangelo A citrus fruit which has pale, yellow to orange, sharp-tasting, juicy flesh. The fruit has orange-colored peel that is easily removed. It is produced by crossing the grapefruit with the tangerine (or mandarin).

Tangerine A type of mandarin, a small, loose-skinned variety of orange with sweet, juicy, easily separated segments. The fruit is named after the seaport of Tangier in Morocco, where it has long been grown.

Tapas Platters of hot or cold bite-sized savory snacks, olives, nuts, pickles, stuffed or broiled vegetables, sliced meats and dry sausages eaten with drinks, especially sherry. Tapas originated in Spain.

Tapenade A savory spread made by puréeing pitted black olives with anchovies, capers, garlic, lemon juice and olive oil. It is served with crusty bread, or can be diluted with olive oil and used as a

dressing for broiled sweet pepper or eggplant. Tapenade originated in Provence in southern France and the name derives from the local word *tapeno*, meaning capers.

Tapioca Tiny balls of starch prepared from the tuberous root of the cassava plant which is grown in tropical America, the Pacific Islands, Indonesia, the Philippines and Africa. Tapioca is cooked in sweetened milk or water as a dessert, in pies or to thicken soups and stews.

T O F U

ASIAN-STYLE TOFU SALAD

★ **Preparation time:** 20 minutes + 1 hour marinating
Total cooking time: none
Serves 4

2 teaspoons Thai sweet chili sauce
½ teaspoon grated ginger
1 clove garlic, crushed
2 teaspoons soy sauce
2 tablespoons oil
8 oz firm tofu

3½ oz snow peas, cut into 1¼ inch lengths
2 small carrots, cut into matchsticks
3½ oz red cabbage, finely shredded
2 tablespoons chopped peanuts

1 Place the chili sauce, ginger, garlic, soy and oil in a small screw-top jar and shake well. Cut the tofu into ¾ inch cubes. Place the tofu in a medium bowl, pour marinade over and stir. Cover with plastic wrap and refrigerate for 1 hour.
2 Place the snow peas in a small pan, pour boiling water over and leave to stand for 1 minute, then drain and plunge into iced water. Drain well.
3 Add the snow peas, carrots and cabbage to tofu and toss lightly to combine. Transfer to a serving bowl or individual plates, sprinkle with nuts and serve immediately.

DEEP-FRIED SPICED TOFU

★ **Preparation time:** 10 minutes
Total cooking time: 10 minutes
Serves 4

12 oz block firm tofu
½ cup rice flour
2 teaspoons ground coriander

1 teaspoon ground cardamom
1 clove garlic, crushed
½ cup water
oil, for deep frying

1 Drain tofu, cut into ½ inch thick slices.
2 Combine the flour, coriander, cardamom and garlic in a bowl. Add water and stir until smooth.
3 Heat oil in a pan. Dip tofu slices into the spice mixture, coating thickly.
4 Lower tofu slices into heated oil, three at a time, and cook over medium heat for 1 minute on each side, or until slices are crisp and golden brown; drain on paper towel. Repeat with remaining slices. Serve hot with a tomato-chili dipping sauce.

ABOUT TOFU

■ Tofu is sometimes also called bean curd or soy cheese. Like tempeh (made from cooked and fermented soy bean paste), it is a protein food used in many recipes instead of meat.
■ Tofu should be kept in the refrigerator, covered with water, and will keep fresh for up to a week if the water is changed regularly.
■ Tofu is available in different textures; firmer varieties hold their shape better for stir-fried dishes or salads.

TOMATOES

WARM TOMATO AND HERB SALAD

⭐ **Preparation time:** 20 minutes
Total cooking time: 15 minutes
Serves 6

1 clove garlic, crushed
1 tablespoon olive oil
12 slices French bread, cut ³/4 inch thick
1 tablespoon olive oil, extra
8 oz cherry tomatoes
8 oz yellow pear tomatoes

¹/4 cup shredded basil leaves
1 tablespoon chopped fresh tarragon
¹/4 cup chopped fresh parsley
salt and freshly ground black pepper, to taste

1 Preheat oven to moderate 350°F. Combine garlic and oil in a small bowl. Brush mixture lightly on one side of bread slices; place on a baking sheet, bake for 7 minutes. Turn bread over, brush other side and bake for another 5 minutes. Set aside to cool.
2 Heat extra oil in frying pan. Add tomatoes and

OPPOSITE PAGE, ABOVE: ASIAN-STYLE TOFU SALAD; BELOW: DEEP-FRIED SPICED TOFU.
ABOVE: WARM TOMATO AND HERB SALAD

stir over medium heat 2 minutes, until just soft.
3 Add basil, tarragon, parsley and salt and pepper, stir-fry for 1 minute more until combined. Serve warm with croûtons.

PESTO-TOPPED CHERRY TOMATOES

⭐ **Preparation time:** 35 minutes
Total cooking time: none
Makes about 50

1 cup chopped fresh parsley, firmly packed
2 cloves garlic
2 tablespoons pine nuts
¹/4 cup olive oil
²/3 cup grated Parmesan cheese

¹/4 cup fresh basil leaves
1 tablespoon butter at room temperature
freshly ground pepper, to taste
1 lb cherry tomatoes

1 Place parsley, garlic, pine nuts and oil in a food processor or blender and process until mixture forms a purée.
2 Add remaining ingredients, except tomatoes. Process until well combined.
3 Slice tops from tomatoes. Spoon a small mound of pesto mixture on top of each tomato. (A small amount of flesh may be scooped out to allow for more pesto filling.) Refrigerate until required.

Taramasalata A creamy dip made by puréeing *tarama*, the dried, salted and pressed roe of mullet, with bread, garlic, onion, olive oil and lemon juice. A Greek and Turkish specialty, taramasalata is served chilled  on thin toast or pita bread. Tarama is available in specialty stores.

Taro The starchy tuber of a tropical plant with rough, brown, hairy skin and firm, nutty-flavored white to violet flesh. It is widely used in the cooking of the Pacific and Southeast Asia, either boiled or baked and served as a vegetable, or steamed and sweetened and made into a pudding.

Tarragon A herb with a subtle liquorice-like flavor that combines well with chicken and is mixed with chervil, chives and parsley to make the classic *fines herbes* blend. Tarragon vinegar is an important ingredient in Béarnaise sauce and mayonnaise. French tarragon has an intense flavor and aroma; Russian tarragon is inferior in flavor. The dried form of the herb loses its flavor quickly.

Tart A sweet or savory single-crust pie, either full-sized or made in an individual serving size.

Tartar Sauce A cold, mayonnaise-based sauce containing finely chopped chives,

scallions, parsley, gherkin and capers. It is served with seafood.

Tarte Tatin An upside-down apple tart. Caramelized apples are topped with a layer of pastry; when baked the tart is inverted and served hot, fruit-side-up. Named for the Tatin sisters, who ran a restaurant in the French town Lamotte-Beuvron, they are said to have created the dish to repair a baking error. Similar fruit tarts are an ancient specialty of the region.

Tasso Cured pork or beef seasoned with red pepper, garlic, filé powder and seasonings. A Cajun specialty.

Tea A drink made by steeping tea leaves (the dried leaves of a shrub in the

T O M A T O A N D P E P P E R S T E W

⭐ **Preparation time:** 15 minutes
Total cooking time: 15 minutes
Serves 4–6

2 tablespoons olive oil
1 large red onion, chopped
2 large red peppers, chopped

1 large green pepper, chopped
4 large ripe tomatoes, peeled and chopped
2 teaspoons soft brown sugar

1 Heat oil in medium pan; add onion. Cook over low heat until onion is soft.
2 Add chopped red and green peppers, cook over medium heat for 5 minutes, stirring constantly.
3 Stir in tomato and brown sugar. Reduce heat, cover and cook for 6–8 minutes until vegetables are tender.

T O M A T O A N D O L I V E C R I S P B R E A D

⭐ **Preparation time:** 20 minutes
Total cooking time: 20–25 minutes
Serves 8

1/2 oz butter
2 teaspoons olive oil
2 large onions, sliced in rings

1/3 cup pimiento-stuffed olives
1/3 cup oil-packed sun-dried tomatoes, drained
2 sheets lavash bread

1 Preheat oven to 350°F. Line two baking sheets with aluminum foil. Heat butter and oil in a heavy-bottom frying pan. Add onion, cook over medium-high heat until dark golden brown. Remove from heat. Drain on paper towel.

2 Place olives and tomato in food processor. Using pulse action, press button for 20 seconds or until mixture is fairly smooth. Spread mixture evenly over bread. Top with onion rings, place on prepared baking sheets. Bake for 20 minutes or until dark and crisp.
3 Leave to stand for 5 minutes before removing from baking sheets. Cut into squares or triangles to serve.

R O A S T T O M A T O S A L A D

⭐ **Preparation time:** 15 minutes
Total cooking time: 20 minutes
Serves 6

6 medium ripe tomatoes
1 tablespoon olive oil
2 tablespoons white wine vinegar
1/4 cup olive oil, extra

1/2 teaspoon Dijon mustard
12 basil leaves, finely shredded

1 Preheat oven to moderate 350°F. Brush shallow baking pan with oil. With a very sharp knife, cut cores from tomatoes. Place cut-side down on prepared pan. Score a large cross in skin of each, taking care not to cut into flesh. Brush with a little oil, bake for 20 minutes; cool.
2 Place the vinegar, extra oil and mustard in a small screw-top jar; shake well. Peel the tomatoes. Gently place on serving platter or individual plates. Pour a little dressing over each and top with basil.

FRESH TOMATO RELISH

⭐ **Preparation time:** 20 minutes
Total cooking time: 20 minutes
Serves 6

1 tablespoon olive oil
1 small red onion, finely
   chopped
3 ripe tomatoes, peeled
   and chopped
1/2 cup red wine vinegar
2 teaspoons soft brown
   sugar
2 zucchini, chopped

1 green pepper, chopped
1/2 cup black olives,
   pitted, chopped
1 tablespoon capers
2 tablespoons pine nuts
2 tablespoons finely
   chopped flat-leafed
   parsley

1 Heat the oil in a large pan, add the onion, cover and cook over low heat for 1 minute. Add the chopped tomato, cover and cook over low heat until the tomato is soft. Add the vinegar and brown sugar and simmer, uncovered, for about 10 minutes or until the sauce has reduced and thickened.
2 Add the zucchini and green pepper; cover and cook until the vegetables are just tender. Allow to cool for 10 minutes. Add the black olives, capers, pine nuts and finely chopped parsley and mix well to combine.

OPPOSITE PAGE, ABOVE: TOMATO AND PEPPER STEW; BELOW: TOMATO AND OLIVE CRISPBREAD. ABOVE: GRILLED TOMATOES WITH BRUSCHETTA

GRILLED TOMATOES WITH BRUSCHETTA

⭐ **Preparation time:** 15 minutes
Total cooking time: 35 minutes
Serves 4

1 loaf Italian bread
4 large ripe tomatoes
1/2 teaspoon dried
   marjoram leaves
salt and freshly ground
   black pepper, to taste
2 tablespoons olive oil
2 tablespoons red wine
   vinegar

1 teaspoon soft brown
   sugar
2 tablespoons olive oil,
   extra
1 clove garlic, cut in half
1/2 cup chopped marinated
   artichokes, drained
1 tablespoon finely
   chopped flat-leaf
   parsley

1 Cut bread into thick slices. Preheat broiler. Cut tomatoes in half and gently squeeze out seeds. Place tomatoes cut-side-up in a shallow ovenproof dish. Place marjoram, salt and pepper, oil, vinegar and sugar in a small screw-top jar and shake well. Pour dressing over tomatoes.
2 Broil tomatoes 6–8 inches from heat for 30 minutes; turn halfway through cooking. Remove from heat; keep warm.
3 Brush bread slices liberally with oil on both sides; toast until golden. Rub cut surface of garlic over bread. Place the cooked tomatoes onto the bread slices, top with artichokes and sprinkle with parsley. Serve immediately.

camellia family) in just-boiled water. It is served hot, with or without milk, or iced. Tea cultivation is thought to have originated in China some 5,000 years ago. The main types of tea are green, black or oolong. Many commercial teas are blends of these teas. Herb teas or tisanes are infusions made with fresh or dried leaves or blossoms and include mint, rose hip, hyssop, sage and camomile, and are used as beverages or for medicinal purposes.

Tea Cake A light cake eaten warm, sliced and buttered. The traditional English tea cake is a round, yeast dough bun.

Tempura A Japanese dish consisting of pieces of seafood and vegetables dipped in batter and deep-fried. Tempura is served hot with soy sauce for dipping.

Tenderloin See Fillet.

Teriyaki A Japanese dish of meat, poultry or fish marinated in mirin and soy sauce then broiled or barbecued. Teriyaki sauce is sold in bottles.

Terrine A preparation of ground meat, poultry, game, fish or vegetables cooked in a deep, straight-sided earthenware container

lined with thinly sliced pork fat to keep the mixture moist, and sealed with a tight-fitting lid.

Tex-Mex A food term describing the combination of Texan and Mexican cultures. Examples include: nachos, burritos and tacos.

Thai Food The cooking of Thailand is characterized by subtle blending of hot, sweet, salty, bitter and sour flavors. It shows influences from China, India, Java, Cambodia and Sri Lanka. The chili pepper did not reach Thailand until the sixteenth

century; now, with mint, basil, scallion, cilantro and coconut milk, it is a central flavor of Thai cuisine. A traditional Thai meal consists of a variety of dishes: a soup, a curry, a steamed dish, a fried dish and a salad, selected for a balance of flavors, textures and colors. All dishes are served at the same time and eaten warm or at room temperature, using a spoon and fork; rice is always served. The main meal is followed by fresh fruits and cakes and desserts

STUFFED TOMATOES

⭐ **Preparation time:** 20 minutes + 15 minutes standing
Total cooking time: 40 minutes
Serves 6

1/4 cup bulgur (cracked wheat)	2 tablespoons tomato paste
1/3 cup hot water	1 tablespoon barbecue sauce
1 tablespoon oil	1 teaspoon dried oregano
1 small onion, finely chopped	1 tablespoon finely chopped parsley
1 lb ground beef	6 large firm tomatoes
2 oz oil-packed sun-dried tomatoes, finely sliced	2 teaspoons olive oil

1 Preheat oven to 350°F. Brush a deep baking dish with oil. Place bulgur in a small bowl and add hot water. Set aside for 15 minutes. Squeeze excess moisture from bulgur. Heat the oil in a heavy-bottom frying pan; add chopped onion and beef, cook for 5 minutes. Use a fork to break up any lumps as beef cooks. Remove from the heat and drain off the excess liquid. Transfer to a mixing bowl.
2 Add bulgur, sun-dried tomato, tomato paste, barbecue sauce and herbs to beef mixture.
3 Cut a 3/4 inch slice from the base of each tomato and scoop out seeds and membrane. Fill cavity with beef mixture and replace tops.
4 Brush each tomato all over with olive oil and place about 1 inch apart in prepared dish. Bake for 35 minutes.

TOMATO AND BROWN LENTIL SOUP

⭐ **Preparation time:** 10 minutes
Total cooking time: 40 minutes
Serves 4

1 large onion	2 small dried chili peppers
1 cup brown lentils	1 bay leaf
1/4 cup olive oil	4 cups water
1 clove garlic, crushed	salt and freshly ground black pepper, to taste
1/4 cup tomato paste	

1 Finely chop onion. Rinse lentils in cold water; drain well.
2 Heat oil in a large heavy-bottom pan. Add the onion and garlic and stir over low heat for 10 minutes.
3 Add tomato paste, chilies, bay leaf, lentils and water; bring to boil. Reduce heat and simmer, covered, 30 minutes or until the lentils are soft.
4 Remove chilies and bay leaf and discard. Add salt and pepper to taste. Serve soup with fresh, crusty bread.

*ABOVE: TOMATO AND BROWN LENTIL SOUP
LEFT: STUFFED TOMATOES.
OPPOSITE PAGE, ABOVE: CHEESY SUN-DRIED
TOMATO HOT BREAD; BELOW: TOMATO PASTA SALAD*

TOMATO PASTA SALAD

★ **Preparation time:** 20 minutes
Total cooking time: 12 minutes
Serves 10

1/2 cup oil-packed sun-dried tomatoes, drained
1–2 cloves garlic, crushed
1 tablespoon balsamic vinegar
2 tablespoons oil, from sun-dried tomatoes
1/2 cup olive oil
1 lb bow-tie pasta

1 bunch fresh asparagus
8 oz cherry tomatoes
8 oz yellow pear tomatoes
1/3 cup chopped flat-leaf parsley
salt and pepper
fresh basil leaves, to garnish

1 Combine sun-dried tomatoes, garlic, vinegar and oils in food processor. Process for 20 seconds or until all ingredients are combined.
2 Cook the pasta in a large pan of boiling, salted water for 12 minutes or until it is just tender; drain.
3 Plunge the asparagus spears into a bowl of boiling water. Leave them for 2 minutes until they turn a vibrant green color and are slightly tender. Drain asparagus, then plunge into a bowl of ice water. When cold, drain and pat dry with paper towels. Cut into 1 inch lengths. Cut the cherry tomatoes and pear tomatoes in half, lengthwise.
4 Assemble the salad while the pasta is still warm: combine the pasta, tomatoes, asparagus and parsley in a large serving bowl; mix in the tomato dressing. Add salt and pepper, to taste. Garnish with basil leaves and serve.

CHEESY SUN-DRIED TOMATO HOT BREAD

★ **Preparation time:** 15 minutes
Total cooking time: 15 minutes
Serves 10

1/4 cup butter, softened
1/3 cup grated Parmesan cheese
2 tablespoons sun-dried tomato paste

1 tablespoon chopped basil
2 French baguettes

1 Preheat oven to moderately hot 400°F. Combine the butter, grated Parmesan cheese, sun-dried tomato paste and chopped basil in a small mixing bowl.
2 Slice the bread almost through at 1/2 inch intervals, leaving the base intact. Spread butter mixture between the slices, then press back into a loaf shape.
3 Wrap the bread in foil. Bake for 10 minutes, open foil and bake for another 5 minutes or until bread is crisp.

Note: Cheesy Sun-Dried Tomato Hot Bread can be assembled several hours ahead and baked just before serving. Sun-dried tomato paste is available from some delicatessens or from specialty food stores.

made from mung bean flour, rice, coconut, palm sugar and eggs. Water and tea accompany the meal.

Thyme A fragrant herb with small, oval, grayish-green leaves that have a strong aroma and a pungent, clove-like taste. Used in marinades for lamb, beef and poultry; with bay leaf and parsley, thyme is part of a bouquet garni. It is added to stuffings and tomato-based sauces, and combines well with rabbit. Thyme leaves can be bought fresh, dried or ground.

Tilsit Cheese A smooth, semihard, cow's milk cheese, pale yellow in color, with a fruity, mild to medium-sharp flavor. It is a good snack cheese, teaming well with fruit and salad vegetables, or used in sandwiches. It melts well for use in sauces.

Timbale A custardy mixture of meat, poultry, seafood or vegetables cooked in individual molds and usually served with a sauce as a first course. Timbales are named after the deep, round molds in which they are cooked.

Tipsy Cake A dessert, similar to trifle, consisting of sponge cake liberally sprinkled with sherry, brandy or sweet white wine, decorated with slivered blanched almonds and topped with whipped cream.

Tiramisù A rich Italian dessert consisting of lady fingers dipped in marsala or brandy and topped with layers of zabaglione, coffee-flavored mascarpone cheese and whipped cream; it is served chilled. Tiramisù was created in Siena, where it was called *zuppa del Duca*, the Duke's soup; because of its popularity with the expatriate English in nineteenth-century Florence it became *zuppa inglese*, English soup; tiramisù means "pick me up," a relatively recent name.

Tisane An herbal tea, usually drunk for its medicinal properties. Tisanes include angelica to help digestion; camomile for an upset stomach and to aid sleep; lemon balm to calm the nerves and aid digestion; peppermint tea to ward off colds; and rose petals and violets with honey for soothing a cough.

Toast To brown or crisp food by exposing it to dry heat. Toasting will develop a fuller flavor in nuts and seeds. The term also refers to a slice of bread exposed to heat so

T R O U T

TROUT WITH ALMONDS

★ **Preparation time:** 15 minutes
Total cooking time: 15 minutes
Serves 4

4 cleaned lake trout, about 6 oz each)	1/3 cup lemon juice
1/3 cup all-purpose flour	1/3 cup butter
1/2 teaspoon dried dill	1/2 cup blanched almonds, halved crosswise
1/4 teaspoon dry mustard freshly ground black pepper	1/2 cup dry white wine fresh dill (optional)

1 Using scissors, remove the fins from the trout and trim the tail. Rinse the fish and pat dry with paper towels. Stir together the flour, dill, and mustard; season with freshly ground black pepper.
2 Brush the surface of the fish with the lemon juice and reserve any excess. Coat the whole trout in the seasoned flour mixture to form a crust. Shake off the excess flour.
3 In a large skillet cook the butter and almonds until golden. Remove the almonds with a slotted spoon and drain on paper towels. Add the fish to the skillet and cook over medium-high heat until the fish flakes easily when tested with a fork, carefully turning the fish once. Drain on paper towels.
4 Add the remaining lemon juice to the skillet with the pan drippings. Stir in the wine. Bring to

the boil and cook over high heat until the mixture is reduced by half. Stir in the reserved almonds and pour over the fish at once. Garnish with fresh dill, if desired.

SMOKED TROUT WITH KIWIFRUIT SALAD

★ **Preparation time:** 20 minutes
Total cooking time: none
Serves 4

3 whole smoked trout	2 tablespoons hazelnut oil
2 kiwifruit	
1 large ripe avocado	assorted greens (butter lettuce, romaine, curly endive)
juice and rind of 1 lime	
1 tablespoon white wine vinegar	1/4 cup hazelnuts, finely chopped

1 Skin the trout and gently remove the fillets from each side. Cut each fillet into two pieces. Peel and slice the kiwifruit and avocado.
2 Combine the lime juice and rind, vinegar and hazelnut oil.
3 Wash the greens and arrange on either one large serving platter or individual serving plates.
4 Arrange the smoked trout fillets, sliced kiwifruit and avocado on top of the greens and lightly drizzle with the lime and hazelnut dressing. Sprinkle with the finely chopped hazelnuts and serve immediately.

MOROCCAN-STYLE TROUT WITH DATES

★ **Preparation time:** 30 minutes
Total cooking time: 20 minutes
Serves 2

2 medium trout
1 cup chopped dates
¼ cup cooked rice
1 onion, finely chopped
¼ cup chopped almonds
2 tablespoons chopped
  fresh cilantro
½ teaspoon ground
  cinnamon

2 tablespoons butter,
  melted
¼ teaspoon ground
  pepper
¼ teaspoon ground ginger
1 teaspoon sugar
¼ teaspoon ground
  cinnamon

1 Preheat oven to 315°F. Clean trout, rinse under cold water. Dry with paper towel.
2 Combine dates, rice, onion, almonds, cilantro and cinnamon in a bowl.
3 Spoon seasoning mixture into fish cavities; close opening with metal skewers. Place on shallow baking pan.
4 Brush fish with melted butter, sprinkle with combined pepper, ginger and sugar. Bake for 20 minutes, or until golden. Sprinkle fish with cinnamon before serving.

OPPOSITE PAGE: TROUT WITH ALMONDS.
ABOVE: MOROCCAN-STYLE TROUT WITH DATES

ABOUT TROUT

■ Trout has a very delicate taste which can be easily overwhelmed by stronger flavors. It is usually cooked whole. The flesh is slightly dry and should not be overcooked.
■ The color of trout (and salmon) flesh is influenced by what the fish eats; it can be varied in farmed trout by a controlled diet.
■ It is usual to remove the skin from trout before eating. The flesh comes away very easily from the backbone, which can be removed, once half the fish has been eaten.
■ One of the simplest and most delicious ways to serve trout is to fry it in olive oil. Make sure the fish is absolutely fresh. Rinse cleaned trout inside and out under cold running water and dry well with paper towel. Cut off all the fins with scissors or a sharp knife. Dip trout in all-purpose flour seasoned with salt and pepper; shake off any excess. Cover the base of a pan large enough to comfortably hold the trout with a shallow layer of olive oil. Heat the oil and add trout. Cook over high heat to sear the outside, then lower the heat slightly. After about 3 minutes, turn the trout over. Increase the heat again to sear the skin, then reduce it and cook the trout for another 3 minutes, or until the fish is cooked through. Remove and drain on a dish lined with paper towels. Serve with lemon wedges and a mayonnaise and sour cream mixture.

that its surfaces become brown and dry. Toasted bread, spread with butter or other spreads, is served at breakfast, or used to make toasted sandwiches.

Toffee A rich, sticky, usually brown candy which is made by adding butter to a boiled mixture of sugar and water. It can be soft and chewy or hard and crunchy, depending on cooking time and temperature.

Tofu Soybean curd, a white to cream-colored, smooth-textured and bland-flavored food made by adding a setting agent to a thin liquid of ground boiled soya beans and water. It is valued for its high vegetable protein content and is widely used in the cooking of China, Japan and Southeast Asia. Tofu absorbs the flavors of foods cooked with it. Tofu, either soft or firm, is available fresh and in sealed packs.
See also Soybean Curd.

Tomato A round, smooth-skinned, juicy, seed-filled fruit with a rich, slightly sweet flavor, used as a vegetable. It is eaten raw as a salad vegetable, cooked in a variety of sauces and dishes, or made into juice. Types include the common tomato, used in salads; plum tomatoes, with dense, flavorsome flesh, good for soups and sauces; the tiny cherry tomato, used whole in salads and as a garnish; and pear-shaped yellow tomatoes, noted for low-acidity and used in salads and preserves.

Tongue Classed as a variety meat, usually beef, but lamb's tongue is also eaten. Tongue is boiled, pickled, smoked, baked, or pressure-cooked, served hot or cold with a sauce, sliced, and with pickles.

Torte A rich, dense-textured cake, made with little or no flour. Ground nuts or bread crumbs, eggs, sugar and flavorings are used.

Tortellini Small rings of pasta, usually stuffed with finely chopped seasoned meat, often served with a cream or tomato sauce.

Tortilla A paper-thin Mexican flat-bread made from corn or wheat flour quickly cooked, but not

T U N A

TUNA STEAKS WITH OLIVE PASTE

★ **Preparation time:** 15 minutes + 1 hour marinating
Total cooking time: 4 minutes each steak
Serves 6

Marinade
1/3 cup olive oil
2 tablespoons dry white wine
2 tablespoons lemon juice

6 tuna steaks, about 6 oz each

Olive Paste
1 cup pitted black olives
2 teaspoons capers
1 clove garlic, crushed
1 tablespoon olive oil
1 tablespoon finely chopped parsley
6 teaspoons sour cream

1 Combine olive oil, white wine and lemon juice in a small screw-top jar and shake vigorously for 30 seconds. Place tuna steaks in a single layer in a shallow ceramic or glass dish. Pour marinade over and refrigerate for 1 hour, turning tuna over halfway through marinating time.
2 To make Olive Paste: Combine olives, capers, garlic and oil in food processor and, using pulse action, process for 30 seconds or until well combined. Refrigerate until required.
3 Remove tuna steaks from dish, reserve marinade. To barbecue, place tuna on a preheated lightly greased grill. Grill over high heat for 2–3 minutes on each side, basting occasionally with marinade. Alternatively, broil steaks on a foil-

lined broiler rack under high heat for 2–3 minutes each side, basting occasionally with marinade. Stir chopped parsley into Olive Paste and set aside for 10 minutes at room temperature.
4 To serve, place one tuna steak on each plate, top with a level tablespoon of Olive Paste and a teaspoon of sour cream. Serve immediately.

TUNA TERIYAKI

★ **Preparation time:** 10 minutes + 30 minutes marinating
Total cooking time: 10 minutes
Serves 4

1 lb tuna steak

Teriyaki Marinade
3/4 inch piece ginger, finely grated

2 tablespoons soy sauce
1 tablespoon lemon juice
2 tablespoons dry sherry
1/2 cup fish stock

1 Remove any skin from the tuna. Cut into four even pieces.
2 To make Marinade: In a shallow dish, combine the grated ginger, soy sauce, lemon juice, dry sherry and fish stock.
3 Place the tuna into the dish with the marinade and allow to stand for at least 30 minutes. Turn the tuna during marinating time.
4 Place the tuna on a foil-lined broiler rack and broil until the flesh flakes, this will take approximately 2–3 minutes each side. Baste the fish during cooking, using all the marinade. Serve immediately.

FRESH TUNA WITH HERBS AND BALSAMIC VINEGAR

⭐ **Preparation time:** 5 minutes
Total cooking time: 10 minutes
Serves 4

2 tablespoons olive oil	1 tablespoon chopped
4 tuna steaks	basil
1 tablespoon chopped	2 tablespoons balsamic
parsley	vinegar

1 Heat the oil in a large frying pan. Add tuna steaks to the pan in a single layer and cook on both sides over medium heat for about 10 minutes, or until the fish is cooked through. (Cooking time will depend on the thickness of tuna steaks.)
2 Transfer tuna steaks to a serving plate. Sprinkle with chopped parsley and basil and drizzle with balsamic vinegar.

Note: Tuna is an oily fish and should be eaten as fresh as possible. Tuna steaks are usually cooked with the skin on.

OPPOSITE PAGE: TUNA STEAKS WITH OLIVE PASTE.
ABOVE: FRESH TUNA WITH HERBS AND
BALSAMIC VINEGAR

FRESH TUNA CROQUETTES

⭐ **Preparation time:** 20 minutes
Total cooking time: 10–15 minutes
Serves 4

1 lb tuna steak	2 tablespoons finely
1 medium onion, finely	chopped parsley
chopped	seasoned all-purpose flour
1½ cups mashed potato	1 egg, beaten
1 tablespoon finely	dry bread crumbs
chopped pimiento	oil for shallow frying
pepper	

1 Skin the tuna. Cut into small pieces. Grind in a food processor or chop very finely.
2 Put the tuna into a bowl. Add the onion, potato, pimiento, pepper and parsley. Mix well. Mold spoonfuls of the mixture into croquettes.
3 Coat the croquettes with flour. Dip in beaten egg and roll in bread crumbs.
4 Lower a few croquettes at a time into hot oil. Shallow-fry until golden, turning once. Drain on paper towels and serve.

FRESH TUNA FETTUCCINE

⭐⭐ **Preparation time:** 15 minutes
Total cooking time: 15–20 minutes
Serves 6

1½ lb fettuccine	3 cloves garlic, crushed
2 large, ripe tomatoes	2 onions, sliced
4 oz fresh asparagus, cut	¼ cup finely sliced basil
into 1 inch lengths	leaves
½ cup olive oil	¼ cup chopped capers
1 lb tuna steaks	

1 Cook fettuccine in a large pan of rapidly boiling salted water until just tender; drain and toss with a little oil to keep strands separate.
2 Peel tomatoes and chop. Cook asparagus in a small pan of rapidly boiling water for 2 minutes or until just tender; drain, rinse under cold water and drain again.
3 Heat 1 tablespoon of the oil in large frying pan. Add tuna steaks and cook for 2 minutes on each side or until golden brown on the outside but still moist on the inside; remove from pan. Using a fork, shred tuna and remove any bones; set aside.
4 Heat remaining oil in pan. Add the garlic and onion, stir over medium heat for 3 minutes or until onion is tender. Add cooked fettuccine, asparagus, tuna, chopped tomato, basil and chopped capers; stir over medium heat until all ingredients are combined and heated through.

browned, on a griddle or in a pan. Tortillas may serve as a wrapper for fillings, or as an edible scoop or plate.

Tostada A crisp, fried tortilla topped typically with refried beans, avacado, lettuce, cheese, and sauce.

Tournedos Also known as filet mignon, a small, round, thick steak cut from a fillet of beef, usually pan-fried and served on a round of fried bread accompanied by a rich sauce.

Treacle A thick, dark, strong-tasting syrup, also called golden syrup, it comes in light and dark varieties.

Trifle A traditional English dessert consisting of layers of sponge cake sprinkled with sweet sherry, interspersed with fruit or fruit jam, cream, rich egg custard and crushed nuts.

Tripe The stomach lining of cattle. Tripe is blanched, then boiled. It can be served with onions or in the style of Caen, northern France, in a casserole.

Trout A freshwater fish of the salmon family with delicately flavored flesh, available fresh, frozen and smoked.

Truffle, Chocolate A small, very rich candy made from chocolate, butter, cream and liqueur, formed into small balls and rolled in cocoa powder or chopped nuts. Truffles are usually served with coffee. They are named for their similarity in appearance to the fungi, black truffle.

Truffle, Fungi An edible fungus that grows underground in forests in France and Italy. Truffles are prized for their musky fragrance and delicate flavor similar to garlic. They are used in pâtés, added to pasta and as a filling for omelets. There are two types of truffle: the black truffle, available fresh in France, bottled or canned in specialty shops elsewhere, and the white truffle, found in Italy.

Truss To secure the legs, wings and front opening of poultry, before roasting, to maintain the bird's shape and prevent the loss of stuffing during cooking.

Tuile A thin, curved, crisp cookie made of sugar, slivered

T U R K E Y

ROAST TURKEY WITH SOUR CHERRY SAUCE

★ *Preparation time:* 20 minutes
Total cooking time: 2–3 hours
55 minutes
Serves 8–10

8 lb self-basting turkey
3 tablespoons butter
1 large onion, finely chopped
8 oz can water chestnuts, drained, chopped
2 tablespoons chopped blanched almonds
1 medium apple, peeled, chopped
2 scallions, chopped
salt and pepper
2 tablespoons finely chopped flat-leaf parsley
1 egg

1 cup cooked long-grain rice
2 cups water

Sour Cherry Sauce
16 oz can pitted tart red cherries
1/4 cup red currant jelly
2 teaspoons balsamic vinegar
2 cups pan juices, strained
salt and pepper
1/4 cup cornstarch
1/3 cup water

1 Preheat oven to moderate 350°F. Remove excess fat from turkey, rinse well. Pat inside and out with paper towel. Tuck wing tips to underside. Place turkey, breast-side-up, on rack in a deep baking dish. Melt butter in pan; add onion. Stir over low heat for 5 minutes or until onion is soft. Add water chestnuts and almonds, cook for 5 minutes, stirring occasionally. Add apple and scallions; stir until heated through. Remove from heat, add salt and pepper, parsley, egg and rice; mix well. Spoon into turkey cavity; secure with string or skewer. Pack remaining mixture in neck cavity; secure. Add water to pan.
2 Bake turkey for 2–3 hours, basting occasionally with pan juices. Prick all over with a fork, bake another 30 minutes or until a meat thermometer registers 180°F. Remove from oven, reserve pan juices. Rest turkey for 15 minutes. Carve and serve with seasoning and Sour Cherry Sauce.
3 To make Sour Cherry Sauce: Drain cherry juice into a heavy-bottom pan; reserve cherries. Add jelly, vinegar and juices to pan. Stir over medium heat 10 minutes or until mixture boils and reduces slightly. Add cherries, boil 2 minutes; season. Blend cornstarch with water in a bowl to form a smooth paste and add to pan. Stir over medium heat until sauce boils and thickens.

RIGHT: ROAST TURKEY
WITH SOUR CHERRY SAUCE

almonds, butter and eggs, shaped by draping the hot, pliable cookie over a rolling pin.

Tuna A large saltwater fish with dark, compact meat which turns pink when cooked and has a rich, gamey flavor. Fresh tuna may be poached, baked, broiled or grilled; it is also served raw: diced or sliced wafer-thin as in the Japanese dish sashimi. In ancient times the fish was a favorite of the Phoenicians. In ancient Greece and Rome it was roasted and then sprinkled with salt and oil. Tuna is available fresh and frozen, usually as boneless steaks, and also canned, in oil or water

Turkey A large, heavy-bodied domestic fowl native to the Americas and now bred throughout the world. It is valued for its plump breast, which provides a higher proportion of white to dark meat than other poultry. Whole turkey can be stuffed and roasted; it is also available in pieces and boneless roasts that are rolled, tied and ready to cook. Breast slices and cutlets can be sautéed like a veal escalope. Thighs, drumsticks and wings can be roasted. The meat can be prepared as turkey pastrami, turkey salami, turkey ham and smoked turkey sausage. In the United States roast turkey with stuffing is traditionally eaten on Thanksgiving Day. The American wild turkey still exists; it weighs about 15 pounds and is hunted as a game bird.

Turkish Delight A gummy, sugary candy with a firm, smooth

texture which can be colored pink, white or green. It is made by thickening a sugar and lemon juice syrup with cornstarch and flavoring it with peppermint or rose water; when cool it is cubed and coated with confectioners' sugar. It is also known as "lokum."

Turmeric A bright yellow powdered spice ground from the dried roots of a tropical plant related to ginger. It has a mild, bitter-sweet flavor. Turmeric is an essential

ingredient in curry powders and pastes and is used in pickles, chutneys and prepared mustard.

Turnip A globe-shaped, white-fleshed root vegetable used in soups,

CURRANT-GLAZED ROAST TURKEY

⭐ ⭐   *Preparation time:* 1 hour
Total cooking time: 1 hour 30 minutes
Serves 8

⅓ cup currant jelly
¼ cup dark corn syrup
⅓ cup brown sugar
1 x 4 lb whole turkey breast
3 tablespoons butter, melted

Gravy
¼ cup all-purpose flour
1 cup chicken stock

Apple Stuffing
¼ cup butter
1 large onion, finely chopped
2 medium green apples, peeled and finely chopped
4 scallions, finely chopped
⅔ cup chicken stock
8 slices dry bread, cubed
2 tablespoons chopped chives
1 tablespoon lemon juice

1 Preheat oven to 325°F. Combine jelly, corn syrup and brown sugar in a bowl. Stir until smooth. Brush turkey with melted butter; place on roasting rack in shallow baking pan. Insert meat thermometer. Cover with foil, bake 1 hour 10 minutes. Remove foil; brush turkey liberally with jelly mixture. Bake, uncovered, 20 minutes more or until thermometer registers 180–185°F. Brush again with jelly mixture. Remove from oven; transfer turkey to a carving board. Cover with foil and stand for 10 minutes before carving.
2 To make Gravy: Preheat broiler. Sprinkle flour over large baking sheet. Broil 4 inches from heat until golden. Add flour to pan juices; stir over low heat 2 minutes. Add stock gradually, stirring until mixture is smooth. Stir over medium heat 5 minutes until the mixture bubbles

and thickens. Cook and stir for 1 minute more. Serve warm with turkey.
3 To make Apple Stuffing: Melt the butter in a heavy-bottom pan. Add the onion, apples and scallions; stir over medium heat until the apple is tender. Add the stock; bring to the boil. Add the remaining ingredients; stir until the bread is moistened. Cover, heat through for 2–3 minutes. Serve warm with turkey.

DEVILED TURKEY STIR-FRY

⭐   *Preparation time:* 10 minutes
Total cooking time: 7 minutes
Serves 4–6

1 red pepper
1 green pepper
1 celery stalk
1 carrot
2 tablespoons peanut oil
4 cups coarsely chopped cooked turkey

2 tablespoons bottled mango chutney
1 tablespoon Worcestershire sauce
1 tablespoon Dijon mustard

1 Cut peppers in half, remove seeds and membrane. Cut into thin strips. Slice celery diagonally, cut carrot into thin slices. Heat oil in a frying pan. Add peppers, celery and carrot. Stir-fry over medium-high heat 5 minutes.
2 Add turkey to pan and toss for 1 minute.
3 Combine chutney, Worcestershire sauce and mustard in a bowl; add to pan. Cook, stirring, for 1 minute until ingredients are well coated and heated through. Serve with rice or noodles.

stews and casseroles. In Italy caramelized turnip is served as a dessert. The tops have a sharp spinach like flavor and are boiled as greens.

Turnover A square or circle of pastry turned over a filling, sealed and baked or deep-fried. Turnovers can be large or individual-sized, sweet or savory and may be eaten hot or cold as a finger food, snack or main meal.

Tzatziki A tangy yogurt and cucumber dip of Greek origin. It is served as finger food or a first course with toasted

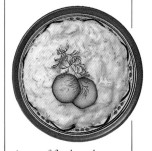

TURNIPS

TURNIP AND BACON SOUP

⭐ **Preparation time:** 20 minutes
Total cooking time: 1 hour 25 minutes
Serves 4–6

1 tablespoon dripping	1½ lb turnips, peeled
3 large onions, peeled,	and thinly sliced
cut into ½ inch cubes	6 cups chicken stock
8 oz bacon cut into	ground pepper
½ inch squares	ground nutmeg
2 medium potatoes,	chopped parsley, for
cut into ½ inch cubes	garnish

1 Heat the dripping in a large pan, cook the onion until transparent. Add the bacon and continue cooking for about 10 minutes, or until the bacon is crisp.
2 Add the potatoes and turnips, stir. Cover the pan, reduce the heat and cook slowly for 10 minutes.
3 Add the chicken stock. Bring to boil,

uncovered, reduce the heat and simmer for 1 hour.
4 Season to taste with pepper and nutmeg. Serve in a heated soup tureen, garnished with parsley.

HONEYED BABY TURNIPS WITH LEMON THYME

⭐ **Preparation time:** 10 minutes
Total cooking time: 7 minutes
Serves 4

1 lb baby turnips	½ teaspoon grated lemon
3 tablespoons butter	rind
¼ cup honey	3 teaspoons chopped fresh
3 teaspoons lemon juice	lemon thyme leaves

1 Rinse and lightly scrub turnips under water. Trim tips and stalks. Cook in boiling water for 1 minute. Drain; rinse under cold water, drain.
2 Heat butter in pan; add honey. Bring to boil, add juice and rind. Boil over high heat for 3 minutes. Add turnips to mixture. Cook over high heat for 3 minutes or until turnips are almost tender and well glazed (test with a skewer).
3 Add the lemon thyme. Remove pan from heat and toss until the turnips are well coated with honey mixture. Serve warm.

pieces of flat bread or fresh vegetables; as a salad dressing; or as an accompaniment to fried or grilled fish or barbecued meat.

Upside-down Cake A fruit-topped cake popular as a dessert. A layer of softened fruit (traditionally pineapple rings, but also peaches, apricots, apples, pears or cherries) and sometimes nuts is arranged in the bottom of a cake pan, covered with a butter and sugar syrup, topped with cake batter and baked. The cooked cake is inverted and served warm with cream.

OPPOSITE PAGE, ABOVE: RED CURRANT-GLAZED ROAST TURKEY; BELOW: DEVILED TURKEY STIR-FRY. ABOVE: HONEYED BABY TURNIPS

V

Vacherin A cold dessert consisting of a ring or basket of meringue or almond paste filled with layers of softened ice cream and fresh fruit, such as strawberries or peaches.

Candied (crystallized) fruits and chestnut purée may also be used, and topped with sweetened whipped cream. Sometimes ice creams of various flavors are used as the filling instead of fruit.

Vanilla The fragrant, slender seed pod, called a "bean," of a climbing orchid. Vanilla is used to flavor creams and ice creams, sweet sauces, custards, syrups, cakes and drinks (especially milk-based chocolate drinks). Vanilla beans can be used more than once; they are infused in hot liquid until the desired strength of flavor is reached, then removed, rinsed and dried for further use. Vanilla sugar is made by burying a vanilla bean in a

V E A L

WIENER SCHNITZEL

⋆ **Preparation time:** 20 minutes + 30 minutes refrigeration
Total cooking time: 8 minutes
Serves 4

4 veal cutlets	light olive oil for frying
¼ cup all-purpose flour	4 slices lemon
freshly ground pepper	2 teaspoons capers
1 egg, beaten	chopped fresh parsley
1 cup fresh bread crumbs	

1 To flatten veal, place cutlets between two sheets of plastic wrap and gently flatten with a rolling pin, taking care not to break meat. Make small nicks about every 2 inches around edge of each cutlet with scissors to prevent veal from curling during cooking.
2 Combine flour and pepper on wax paper. Coat veal with flour; shake off excess. Dip in beaten egg. Coat with bread crumbs, pressing crumbs firmly onto meat. Place veal on a flat tray and refrigerate for 30 minutes before cooking.
3 Heat the oil in a heavy-bottom pan. Add two scallops and cook for about 2 minutes each side, until they are golden brown. Remove from pan, drain on paper towels and keep hot. Cook remaining veal.
4 Serve veal cutlets hot, topped with a slice of lemon, a few capers and a sprinkling of chopped fresh parsley.

VEAL WITH WINE AND MUSTARD SAUCE

⋆ **Preparation time:** 10 minutes
Total cooking time: 20 minutes
Serves 6

6 veal steaks, about 4½ oz each	2 teaspoons oil
½ cup all-purpose flour	1 cup good quality white wine
1 teaspoon ground mustard seeds	⅔ cup chicken stock
3 tablespoons butter	3 teaspoons seed mustard

1 Trim meat of fat and tendons. Combine flour and ground mustard seeds on a sheet of wax paper. Toss meat in seasoned flour; shake off excess. Reserve 3 teaspoons of seasoned flour.
2 Heat the butter and oil in a large heavy-bottom frying pan. Add steaks to pan. (Unless you have a very large pan you will have to cook them in batches.) Cook meat over medium-high heat 3 or 4 minutes each side. Remove from pan; drain on paper towels and keep warm. Repeat with remaining steaks.
3 Add the combined wine, stock, mustard and reserved seasoned flour to the pan, stirring to incorporate any browned bits from the bottom of the pan. Stir until the mixture boils and thickens. Place the veal on serving plates and pour the sauce over.

ABOVE: VEAL WITH WINE AND MUSTARD SAUCE.
OPPOSITE PAGE: VEAL MARSALA

VEAL MARSALA

Preparation time: 10 minutes
Total cooking time: 10 minutes
Serves 4

4 veal steaks, about 6 oz each	1/3 cup chicken stock
2 tablespoons all-purpose flour	1 tablespoon soy sauce
2 tablespoons oil	2 teaspoons plum conserve
1/3 cup marsala	1 scallion, finely chopped

1 Trim the meat of all excess fat and tendons. Place the veal steaks between two sheets of plastic wrap and gently flatten them to an even thickness using a rolling pin, taking care not to break the meat. Spread the flour on a sheet of wax paper. Toss the veal lightly in flour; shake off any excess.
2 Heat the oil in a heavy-bottom pan; add the meat. Cook over a medium heat for 2–3 minutes each side, turning once. Remove the veal steaks from the pan and drain on paper towels. Leave, covered with aluminum foil, in a warm place.
3 Add the marsala and chicken stock to the pan and bring to the boil. Boil the mixture for 1 minute, uncovered, stirring constantly. Add the soy sauce and plum conserve, stir until combined and heated through. Return the veal steaks to the pan, heat through in the sauce for about 1 minute. Serve immediately, sprinkled with the finely chopped scallion. May be served with boiled new potatoes.

VEAL AND MUSHROOM CASSEROLE

Preparation time: 20 minutes
Total cooking time: 2 hours
Serves 4

1 1/2 lb veal steaks	1/2 cup good-quality white wine
1/4 cup all-purpose flour	1 tablespoon chopped fresh thyme
2 tablespoons butter	1 cup chicken stock
1 clove garlic, crushed	12 oz button mushrooms, halved
1 tablespoon Dijon mustard	
1 cup heavy cream	

1 Trim meat of excess fat and tendons. Cut into 1/2 inch strips. Toss meat with flour in plastic bag, shake off excess flour. Heat butter and garlic in heavy-bottom pan. Add meat and cook quickly in small batches over medium heat until well browned. Drain on paper towels.
2 Return meat to pan. Add mustard, cream, white wine, thyme and stock. Bring mixture to boil, reduce heat. Simmer, covered, 1 1/2 hours, stirring occasionally.
3 Add mushrooms; cook for another 15 minutes or until meat is tender. May be served with pasta and steamed julienned vegetables.

Note: Seeded mustard or hot English mustard may be used instead of Dijon mustard. This recipe may be made one day ahead and kept in an airtight container in refrigerator. Reheat gently.

jar of sugar; the longer it is left, the stronger the flavor becomes.

The vanilla orchid is native to Central America. The pods are gathered, drenched in hot water, and left in the sun to dry out. They shrivel, darken and produce a coating of vanillin, the strongly scented crystalline substance which gives vanilla its distinctive aroma and flavor. The finest beans are deep-brown, pliable and covered with a frosting of vanillin. Vanilla extract, a liquid made from the bean which is very powerful and should be used sparingly, and vanilla sugar are also available. Imitation vanilla extract is a chemical attempt to synthesize the flavor of true vanilla.

Variety Meats The non-fleshy part of an animal. Included are: brain, heart, liver, intestines, kidney, sweetbread and tongue. See also Offal.

Veal The meat of a young calf, unweaned or just weaned, reared for slaughter. The meat of milk-fed veal is very pale pink and delicately grained, with a little satiny white fat; meat from animals that have started to eat grass is darker and coarser, but lacks the rich flavor of beef. Veal is a lean, tender meat; it has little natural fat and is best cooked slowly. Braising and moist heat cooking methods are ideal; roasting and broiling should be at a lower heat than for other meats. Like chicken, veal has no strong flavor of its own but absorbs those of the vegetables and herbs cooked with it. It is also good with tangy sauces. Thin slices of veal cut across the grain (in France known as *escalope*, in Italy, *scaloppine* and in Germany, *Schnitzel*) can be fried in butter and served with various sauces or garnishes or rolled around a flavorsome filling and braised. Veal parmigiana is an Italian-style American dish of baked or fried veal coated with bread crumbs and topped with Parmesan cheese.

Vegetable Any edible part of a plant: leaf, stem, bud, flower, seed, root, bulb or tuber that is cultivated as a food. Some fruits are used as vegetables, including the tomato, pumpkin and squash, zucchini, eggplant and sweet pepper. Seed and pod vegetables include peas, beans and lentils;

ITALIAN VEAL POT ROAST

★★ **Preparation time:** 30 minutes
Total cooking time: 1 hour 50 minutes
Serves 4–6

3 lb breast or shoulder of veal, pocketed
1 tablespoon olive oil
1 onion, grated
1 clove garlic, crushed
½ small red chili pepper, chopped finely
1 large carrot, grated
½ cup ground almonds
¼ cup pine nuts
⅓ cup chopped raisins
1 egg yolk
1 tablespoon chutney
1 tablespoon olive oil, extra
2 cups good quality red wine
1 cup beef stock

1 Remove any excess fat or tendons from meat. Heat olive oil in pan, add onion, garlic and chili and fry for 2–3 minutes. Add grated carrot and cook for 2 minutes longer, stirring to combine. Remove pan from heat; add ground almonds, pine nuts and chopped raisins. Allow the mixture to cool slightly and add combined egg yolk and chutney. Mix well to combine.
2 Place stuffing mixture in pocket of meat, pushing in firmly with back of spoon. Secure with string.
3 Heat extra oil in large pan. Add meat and cook until well browned all over. Add wine and stock, bring to the boil and then reduce heat. Simmer covered until meat is tender, about 1½ hours.
4 Remove meat from the pot. Bring liquid to the boil and simmer gently until sauce has reduced and thickened. Serve meat in slices with sauce spooned over. This recipe is delicious when served with whole new potatoes and onions, cooked, and steamed seasonal vegetables.

OSSO BUCCO

★ **Preparation time:** 30 minutes
Total cooking time: 2 hours
Serves 6

8 veak shanks, chopped
½ cup all-purpose flour
⅓ cup olive oil
1 large onion, chopped
1 large carrot, sliced
1 clove garlic, crushed
1 cup chicken stock
½ cup good quality white wine
16 oz can tomatoes, crushed
2 tablespoons finely chopped fresh parsley
1 tablespoon finely grated lemon rind
1 clove garlic, finely chopped, extra

1 Preheat oven to 350°F. Place flour in a plastic bag or freezer bag; add shanks pieces, a few at a time and shake bag gently until shanks are covered with flour. Shake off excess flour.
2 Heat oil in a heavy-bottom pan. Cook the veal quickly over medium-high heat until well browned; drain on paper towels.
3 Place the veal in 6-cup capacity casserole dish. Add the onion, carrot, garlic, stock, wine and tomato with juice. Cover and bake 1½ hours or until the veal is tender.
4 Serve sprinkled with the chopped parsley, grated lemon rind and extra chopped garlic. (This mixture is called gremolata.)

ABOVE: OSSO BUCCO; LEFT: ITALIAN VEAL POT ROAST. OPPOSITE: VEAL BIRDS IN TOMATO SAUCE

VEAL BIRDS IN TOMATO SAUCE

★ ★ **Preparation time:** 12 minutes
Total cooking time: 40 minutes
Serves 6

6 veal cutlets, about
  3½ oz each
12 thin slices prosciutto
1 cup grated mozzarella
  cheese
1½ oz cans anchovies in
  oil, drained
2 tablespoons all-purpose
  flour

¼ teaspoon ground black
  pepper
2 tablespoons oil
⅓ cup dry white wine
⅓ cup chicken stock
½ cup bottled chunky
  tomato sauce
1 teaspoon capers
1 tablespoon chopped
  fresh parsley

1 Preheat oven to moderate 350°F. Place the veal cutlets between two sheets of plastic wrap and gently flatten to an even thickness of about ⅛ inch with a rolling pin, taking care not to break the meat. Place 2 slices of prosciutto over each cutlet. Sprinkle 2 tablespoons cheese over the prosciutto and top with 3 anchovies.

2 Roll up the cutlets and tie securely with string at regular intervals to retain their shape during cooking. Combine the flour and pepper on wax paper. Toss the meat lightly in seasoned flour; shake off excess.

3 Heat the oil in a heavy-bottom pan. Cook the rolled up cutlets quickly over medium heat until they are well browned all over. Arrange the meat in a single layer over the base of a shallow casserole dish. Add the white wine, stock, tomato sauce and capers to pan; bring to the boil. Pour the sauce over the meat. Cover the dish and transfer to oven, cook for 35 minutes. Remove string just before serving. Serve sprinkled with chopped parsley.

ABOUT VEAL

■ Veal does not have a strong flavor of its own so it is often teamed with foods such as anchovies or capers. Sauces featuring lemon, wine or tomato and a variety of herbs help keep the veal moist and enhance its flavor.

spinach, lettuce and cabbage are leaf vegetables; celery is a stem; carrots, turnips and parsnips are fleshy roots; yams and potatoes are tubers; bulbs include onions, shallots and fennel; and broccoli and cauliflower are heads of tightly massed flower buds. Mushrooms and other fungi are generally included with vegetables. Vegetables are eaten raw as salads, and cooked either as a soup, an accompaniment to a main course, or a dish in their own right. They are also often pickled as a condiment.

Vegetable Marrow A sausage-shaped vegetable belonging to the same family as the zucchini. Young marrows have the best flavor and most delicate flesh and can be cooked in the same way as zucchini.

Velouté Sauce A basic white sauce made with lightly browned roux and a well-flavored, reduced veal, chicken or fish stock. The name comes from the French word for velvety.

Venison Meat from any kind of deer or animal from the deer family, with hooves and antlers, such as elk, reindeer, moose and antelope. Venison is a dark red,

ASIAN VEGETABLES

The wide and exotic range of vegetables found in Asian food stores and supermarkets sometimes can be daunting. Many already have a place in Western cuisines, while others have yet to be discovered. Here is a brief introduction to these vegetables and ways to enjoy them.

BEAN SPROUTS (NGA CHOY)

Crisp, white, short sprouts are the most tender but are highly perishable: use within 3 days of purchase. Rinse and remove any sprouts that are limp or brown; traditionally the root and growing tip are trimmed, but the tip contains most nutrients. Serve raw in salads, lightly steamed and seasoned with sesame oil or soy sauce, or add to stir-fries.

BITTER MELON OR CUCUMBER (FOO GWA)

Yellow-green melon which looks like a small, warty cucumber. To prepare: rinse well, cut in half lengthwise, remove and discard seeds, slice melon crosswise. Blanch melon pieces for 3 minutes, drain and use in stir-fries with a Chinese sauce, black beans or garlic. As the name suggests, it does have a bitter flavor, and is definitely an acquired taste. However, cooked with beans or meat, the bitterness can be somewhat mitigated.

CHILI PEPPERS, RED AND GREEN

Highly flavored and very spicy; the smaller and redder the chili, the hotter it is. Used as a spice, rather than as a vegetable, they are rarely eaten whole. For a milder chili flavor, add a washed whole chili pepper to the dish and remove it just before serving, or slit the chili open and remove the seeds and membrane (which are the hottest parts). When chopping chilies, wear plastic gloves to avoid skin irritation. If you cook with chilies often, it is best to keep a board aside especially for chopping them.

CHINESE BROCCOLI (GAI LAN)

Fleshy stems, dull green leaves and small white flower heads are all eaten. Regarded as a gourmet vegetable, it is similar in flavor to Western broccoli but has a slightly earthier taste. In Chinese restaurants it is most often lightly steamed and served with oyster sauce. It can also be blanched and used in stir-fries, especially with pork or in mixed vegetable dishes.

CHINESE CABBAGE (CHINESE CHARD, BOK CHOY)

Use the crisp olive green leaves and the thick white celery-like stems (sliced) in meat or seafood stir-fries or soups. Or steam rinsed bundles briefly to retain texture, and serve with oyster sauce. The stalks have a mild, slightly sweet, flavor and the leaves are tangy.

CHINESE FLOWERING CABBAGE (CHOY SUM)

Tender fleshy white stems, bright green leaves (similar to bok choy) but harvested when the bright yellow flowers appear. All these parts are eaten, but cook stems for longer; steam or blanch and serve with oyster or mushroom sauce, or as an accompaniment to meat dishes.

CHINESE LETTUCE (WONG BOK, CELERY CABBAGE)

The elongated pale green leaves have a slight mustard flavor and are used in Chinese and Japanese cooking. Tear into bite-size pieces and steam until barely tender, add to stir-fries or braise with other Asian vegetables in oyster sauce. Also used to make kimchi, the fiery Korean pickle.

CHRYSANTHEMUM LEAVES (SHUNGIKU, TONG HO)

A close relative of the common flowering plant, but the aromatic dark green leaves are entirely edible. In Japanese and Chinese cooking they are usually parboiled and tossed in sesame oil or used as a pot herb when cooking meat. In Chinese cooking, they are stir-fried and are popular in steamboats. The leaves must be rinsed very well to rid them of excess sand.

DAIKON (JAPANESE RADISH, LOH BOK, CHINESE WHITE TURNIP)

This large white cylindrical radish with a sweet fresh flavor is mostly eaten raw in salads. Peel and slice finely, cut into matchsticks or grate. In Japan, daikon is often served with fried foods such as tempura. In Chinese dishes it is served sliced or cubed and braised with meat, which helps to tenderize the flesh. Daikon can be pickled in white vinegar or brine and is sometimes dried.

FUZZY MELON (CHIT KOU, FUZZY SQUASH)

Of Chinese origin, this small 6–10 inch long cylindrical melon has a dark green skin that is covered with a fine downy fur. Before using, peel and remove the stem end. Shred the creamy-colored medium-firm flesh and steam, boil or stir-fry. The mild taste of the fuzzy melon complements sweet and sour dishes and readily absorbs the flavors of whatever other foods it is cooked with.

SCALLION (JSUNG, GREEN ONION)

Mostly sold in bunches with roots intact. To prepare, remove root and base of stem and any damaged parts of leaves; wash well; slice diagonally into even-sized pieces. Most flavor is in the white stem. They add color and subtle onion flavor to salads, stir-fries or soups. They need little cooking.

SNAKE BEAN (DOH GOK, ASPARAGUS BEAN)

These stringless beans which grow up to 12 inches are cut into 2 inch lengths and used in stir-fries, curries and soups. They can also be cooked in the same ways as other types of green beans, but have less flavor.

SNOW PEA (HO LAN DOW, SUGAR PEA, MANGE TOUT)

Bright green, crisp pods are blanched and used whole in salads, stir-fries and soups. To prepare, soak in cold water, pull off stem end and any string from edge of pod. Add to dishes only at the last moment.

TARO ROOT (WOO TOW, DASHEEN)

Large tan-colored bulb with tough outer skin marked by rings, and white flesh. Store in a cool dark place (not in refrigerator). Peel, slice and steam or boil until tender before adding to rich or fatty meat stews. Like potatoes, it can be boiled, mashed, baked or sautéed with garlic. When cooked, the flesh is grayish.

WATERCRESS (SAI YEUNG CHOY)

At its prime when leaves are a dark green-purple color, stems crisp with no unpleasant smell. To prepare, rinse well, then chop entire plant or just snip off leaves and discard stems. In Asian cuisines it is usually blanched in boiling water, then refreshed in cold water and served with a dressing such as soy sauce or sesame oil. Can be puréed with vegetable stock to make a cool, refreshing, peppery soup or steamed with other vegetables. A useful garnish.

very lean meat with a fine grain. Farm-raised venison is milder in flavor and more tender than the game version. Game venison should be larded before roasting; it can be braised and casseroled. Farm venison can be roasted, pan-fried or broiled and allowed to rest before serving. Venison should not be overcooked since it will dry out. Forequarter cuts are best slowly simmered to make curries and stews.

Vermicelli These long, thin strands of pasta dough are sometimes coiled into nests, boiled and served with a sauce or broken into short lengths and added to soup. In Chinese cooking, vermicelli made with soybean flour is boiled or fried for use in soups and vegetable dishes and fine strands white rice flour vermicelli are added to soups or fried in oil for use as a garnish. The name comes from the Italian for "little worms."

Vermouth A wine used as an aperitif or as a cocktail ingredient, made by infusing a base wine (red or white) with herbs, spices, barks or peels, then fortifying the result with distilled spirits. It can be used to flavor stuffings, sauces and poaching stock, and in place of wine in some chicken dishes.

VEGETABLES

SWEET VEGETABLE CURRY

⭐ **Preparation time:** 20 minutes
Total cooking time: 40 minutes
Serves 4

2 medium carrots
1 medium parsnip
1 medium potato
2 tablespoons oil
2 medium onions, chopped
1 teaspoon ground cardamom
1/4 teaspoon ground cloves
1 1/2 teaspoons cumin seeds
1 teaspoon ground coriander
1 teaspoon turmeric
1 teaspoon brown mustard seeds

1/2 teaspoon chili powder
2 teaspoons grated fresh ginger
1 1/3 cups vegetable stock
3/4 cup apricot nectar
2 tablespoons fruit chutney
1 medium green pepper, cut into 3/4 inch squares
6 1/2 oz small button mushrooms
10 oz cauliflower, cut into small florets
1/4 cup ground almonds

1 Cut carrots, parsnip and potato into 3/4 inch pieces. Heat oil in large heavy-bottom pan. Add onion, cook over medium heat for 4 minutes or until just soft. Add cardamom, cloves, cumin seeds, coriander, turmeric, mustard seeds, chili powder and grated ginger; cook, stirring, 1 minute until aromatic.

2 Add carrot, parsnip, potato, stock, nectar and chutney. Cook, covered, over medium heat, stirring occasionally, for 25 minutes.

3 Stir in pepper, mushrooms and cauliflower. Simmer for another 10 minutes or until vegetables are tender. Stir in ground almonds. Serve.

Note: Any vegetables may be used in this curry. For example, broccoli, zucchini, red pepper or orange sweet potato would be suitable. May be served with steamed rice. Add one can of chickpeas (garbanzo beans) to make this a complete meal.

WHITE WINTER VEGETABLE CASSEROLE

⭐ **Preparation time:** 5 minutes
Total cooking time: 1 hour 20 minutes
Serves 4

8 new potatoes, halved
2 medium rutabagas, peeled and sliced
4 baby onions, halved
6 1/2 oz cauliflower, cut into florets
1/4 cup butter

1/3 cup all-purpose flour
13 1/2 oz can chicken consommé
1 1/2 cups milk
1/2 cup freshly grated Parmesan cheese

1 Preheat oven to moderate 350°F. Place the potato, rutabaga, onion and cauliflower in a greased 6-cup capacity casserole dish.

2 Heat butter in a medium pan; add flour. Stir over low heat 2 minutes or until flour mixture is lightly golden in color.

3 Add chicken consommé and milk gradually to pan, stirring until mixture is smooth. Stir constantly over medium heat for 2 minutes or until sauce boils and thickens.

4 Pour sauce over vegetables. Cover and bake for 1 hour. Sprinkle with Parmesan cheese and bake, uncovered, for 10 minutes, or until cheese is golden and vegetables are soft.

MEDITERRANEAN-STYLE VEGETABLES

★ **Preparation time:** 30 minutes + 1 hour 15 minutes standing
Total cooking time: 15 minutes
Serves 6

1 large eggplant	1 small green pepper, chopped
1 tablespoon salt	
8 oz cherry tomatoes	3 oz button mushrooms, halved
1 tablespoon olive oil	
1 medium red pepper, halved	2 tablespoons chopped fresh oregano leaves
1/3 cup fresh basil leaves	2 tablespoons balsamic vinegar
2 medium zucchini, sliced	1 tablespoon olive oil, extra

1 Preheat oven to moderate 350°F. Brush a shallow baking pan with oil. Cut eggplant lengthwise into thin slices, spread out in a single layer on a board; sprinkle with salt. Set aside for 15 minutes; rinse and dry thoroughly. Place eggplant slices in a single layer on pan.

2 Score a small cross on each tomato, place on pan with eggplant. Brush eggplant and tomatoes with oil; bake for 10 minutes. Remove from oven and allow to cool. Cut eggplant into strips.

3 Remove seeds from red pepper; brush skin with oil. Broil until skin is black, then wrap in a damp towel until cool. Rub off skin, and slice. Shred fresh basil leaves. Place zucchini in a small heatproof bowl. Cover with boiling water, stand for 1 minute, drain and plunge into cold water, drain well.

4 Combine all vegetables and herbs in a large mixing bowl. Sprinkle balsamic vinegar and oil over vegetables and toss well to combine. Allow to stand for 1 hour for flavors to combine, then serve at room temperature.

Note: Salting eggplant reduces the bitterness and the amount of fat absorbed during cooking. Scoring tomatoes prevents them from bursting when baked. This dish teams well with baked lamb and beef. You can change the flavor by varying the herbs or adding a clove of crushed garlic when adding oil.

OPPOSITE PAGE: SWEET VEGETABLE CURRY.
ABOVE: MEDITERRANEAN-STYLE VEGETABLES

Verte, Sauce Literally "green sauce," mayonnaise containing finely chopped herbs and leaf vegetables such as spinach, watercress, tarragon, parsley and chervil. It is served with cold fish, eggs and vegetable dishes.

Vichyssoise A soup made by cooking potatoes and the white part of leeks in chicken stock. The mixture is then puréed and cream is added. It is usually served chilled, topped with chives. The soup was created in the early 1900s at New York's Ritz-Carlton Hotel.

Victoria Sponge A sponge cake used as the base for a jam sandwich cake. It was named after Queen Victoria, who was served the cake at tea parties.

Vidalia Onion A round, yellow onion with a mild, sweet flavor. It was developed in Georgia.

Vinaigrette A thin oil and vinegar dressing, often containing herbs, spices, mustard or finely chopped onion. It is served with green salads, and can also be used to dress some vegetable, meat, poultry and fish dishes.

Vine Leaf The leaf of the grape vine, much used in Greek and Middle Eastern cooking; it has a slightly bitter flavor which is lessened by blanching. Leaves for cooking should be medium-light green and not too young; used to wrap fish and small game birds before braising, they add a slightly lemony taste. They are probably best known for their use in dolmades (small cylindrical packages of rice, ground lamb, finely chopped onion, nuts and seasonings). Vine leaves are available fresh or preserved in brine.

Vinegar A sharp-tasting liquid obtained when the alcohol in wine, or alcoholic solutions from grains, apples and other sources, is changed by fermentation into acetic acid. Wine vinegar is fermented from fresh wine, cider vinegar from apple cider, malt vinegar from malt liquor and sweet-sour vinegars from rice wine; the quality of the vinegar depends upon the quality of the wine or other alcohol from which it has been made.

Vinegar is used in salad dressings, mayonnaise, mustards, mint and horseradish sauces, and in marinades; to add bite to soups, sauces and stews, and for

GRILLED VEGETABLES WITH GARLIC MAYONNAISE

★★ **Preparation time:** 30 minutes
Total cooking time: 15 minutes
Serves 8

2 medium eggplants, cut into thin slices lengthwise
salt
4 small leeks, halved lengthwise
2 medium red peppers, cut into eighths
4 small zucchini, halved lengthwise
8 large flat mushrooms

Dressing
2 tablespoons balsamic vinegar
3 tablespoons Dijon mustard

2 teaspoons dried oregano leaves
1 cup olive oil

Garlic Mayonnaise
2 egg yolks or ¼ cup egg substitute
1 tablespoon lemon juice
2 cloves garlic, crushed
1 cup olive oil
1 tablespoon chopped fresh chives
1 tablespoon chopped fresh parsley
1 tablespoon water

1 Sprinkle eggplant slices with salt, allow to stand 30 minutes. Rinse under cold water, pat dry with paper towel. Place eggplant, leek, peppers and zucchini in a single layer on a flat broiler rack, brush with dressing.
2 Broil 4–5 inches from the heat for 5 minutes, turning once; brush occasionally with dressing. Add mushrooms, cap-side-up, to broiler rack,

brush with dressing. Continue to cook vegetables for 10 minutes or until tender, turning mushrooms only once. Brush vegetables with dressing during cooking. Serve with Garlic Mayonnaise.
3 To make Dressing: Combine vinegar, mustard and oregano in a small bowl; gradually whisk in oil.
4 To make Garlic Mayonnaise: Place egg yolks (or egg substitute), lemon juice and garlic in a food processor or blender, blend for 5 seconds until combined. With motor constantly operating, add oil slowly in a thin, steady stream until all oil is added and mayonnaise is thick and creamy. Add chives, parsley and water, blend for 3 seconds until combined.

FILO (PHYLLO) VEGETABLE POUCHES

★ **Preparation time:** 45 minutes
Total cooking time: 35–40 minutes
Makes 12

Filling
3 cups grated carrot
2 large onions, finely chopped
1 tablespoon grated ginger
1 tablespoon finely chopped fresh cilantro
1 cup water

7½ oz can water chestnuts, sliced
1 tablespoon miso
¼ cup tahini paste
pepper, to taste

8 sheets frozen filo (phyllo) dough, thawed
½ cup butter, melted

1 To make Filling: Combine carrot, onion, ginger, cilantro and water in large pan. Cover, cook over low heat 20 minutes. Uncover, cook for another 5 minutes or until all liquid has evaporated. Remove from heat, cool slightly. Stir in water chestnuts, miso and tahini paste. Season with pepper.

2 Preheat oven to moderate 350°F. Brush two shallow baking pans with melted butter or oil. Cover filo (phyllo) pastry with a damp towel to prevent drying out. Remove one sheet of pastry and place on work surface. Brush lightly with butter. Top with another three pastry sheets, brushing each layer with butter. Cut into 6 even squares. Repeat process with remaining pastry, giving 12 squares in total.

3 Divide filling evenly between the squares, placing filling in the center. Bring edges together and pinch to form a pouch. Brush the lower portion of each pouch with butter. Place on prepared pans. Bake for 10–12 minutes or until golden brown and crisp. Serve warm with sweet chili sauce, if desired.

Note: Tahini paste is an oily paste made from sesame seeds. It may separate on standing. If this should occur, stir well before using.

OPPOSITE PAGE: GRILLED VEGETABLES WITH GARLIC MAYONNAISE. THIS PAGE, ABOVE: FILO VEGETABLE POUCHES; RIGHT: SPICY CHICKPEA AND VEGETABLE CASSEROLE

SPICY CHICKPEA (GARBANZO BEAN) AND VEGETABLE CASSEROLE

Preparation time: 25 minutes + overnight soaking
Total cooking time: 1 hour 30 minutes
Serves 4

1 1/2 cups dried chickpeas (garbanzo beans)
2 tablespoons oil
1 large onion, chopped
1 clove garlic, crushed
3 teaspoons ground cumin
1/2 teaspoon chili powder
1/2 teaspoon allspice
16 oz can peeled tomatoes, crushed
1 1/2 cups vegetable stock
10 oz pumpkin, cut into 3/4 inch cubes
5 oz green beans, topped and tailed
6 1/2 oz pattypan squash, quartered
2 tablespoons tomato paste
1 teaspoon dried oregano

1 Place the chickpeas in a large bowl, cover with cold water and soak overnight; drain thoroughly in a colander. Heat the oil in a large pan, add the onion and garlic; stir-fry for 2 minutes or until tender. Add the cumin, chili and allspice and stir-fry for 1 minute.

2 Add the chickpeas, crushed tomatoes and stock to the pan. Bring to boil, reduce the heat and simmer, with the pan covered, for 1 hour, stirring occasionally.

3 Add the cubed pumpkin, green beans, pattypan squash, tomato paste and oregano. Stir to combine. Simmer, covered, for another 15 minutes. Remove the lid from the pan and simmer uncovered for another 10 minutes to reduce and thicken sauce slightly.

pickling and preserving.

Flavored vinegars, which have herbs or fruits added, are also available, or can be made at home.

Red wine vinegars are used to make demi-glace sauces for game, beef and lamb dishes, and in vinaigrette; white wine vinegars can be made into dressings for fish dishes and used in vinaigrette, mayonnaise and hollandaise sauce, and as a base for herbed vinegars. Raspberry vinegar can be used in vinaigrette, teamed with cream to dress fruit, or used in place of lemon when cooking veal or chicken. Lemon balm vinegar can be used in salad dressings. Tarragon vinegar is an essential ingredient of Béarnaise sauce. It is also used in mayonnaise and in marinades for chicken, fish and seafoods.

Rosemary vinegar is good in lamb stew and in sauces for fish and shellfish. Dill vinegar is used in sauces for fish, in sour cream and yogurt sauces and dressings, and for pickling cucumbers. Sherry vinegar, smooth, rich and slightly tart, makes flavorsome gravies and combines well with nut oils in vinaigrette.

Balsamic vinegar, made from the juice of the sweet Trebbiano grape and aged in aromatic hardwood casks, is deep-colored and mellow-flavored; it is used to dress berries, to deglaze roasting pans for gravy, and as a salad dressing. Cider vinegar, slightly sweet and with a faint apple flavor, is used to make sauces for roast pork and roast duck, in vinaigrettes, and can be substituted for rice vinegar in Chinese cooking. Malt vinegar, dark-colored and too strongly flavored for use in salad dressings, is used as a condiment on fish and chips, is an ingredient in Worcestershire sauce, and is used for pickling onions and walnuts. White or distilled vinegar (usually distilled malt vinegar) is colorless and sharp-flavored; it is used in the pickling of gherkins and cocktail onions and in the manufacture of sauces and chutneys. Spirit vinegar, the strongest of all vinegars, differs from distilled vinegar in that it contains a small amount of alcohol; it is used for pickling. White rice vinegar, mild-flavored, pale and clear, is distilled from fermented rice; it is used to flavor the rice in the Japanese dish sushi and can be used as a dressing for raw vegetables such as cabbage and carrots, in vinaigrettes and as a marinade for fish and chicken. Chinese black vinegar, usually made from wheat, millet or sorghum, has a mild

VEGETABLE FRITTERS WITH TOMATO SAUCE

⭐ **Preparation time:** 30 minutes
Total cooking time: 40 minutes
Makes 12

2 medium potatoes, peeled
1 medium carrot, peeled
2 zucchini
4 oz sweet potato, peeled
1 small leek
1/4 cup all-purpose flour
3 eggs, lightly beaten
oil for frying

Tomato Sauce
1 tablespoon oil
1 small onion, finely chopped
1 clove garlic, crushed
1/2 teaspoon ground paprika
3 ripe medium tomatoes, finely chopped
1/4 cup finely shredded fresh basil

1 Grate potatoes, carrot, zucchini and sweet potato. Using hands squeeze out as much moisture as possible from the vegetables. Slice leek finely, add to grated vegetables and combine.
2 Sprinkle flour over vegetables; stir. Add eggs; mix well. Heat 1/4 inch of oil in a pan; drop in 1/4 cup of mixture. Form mixture into a 4 inch round. Fry 2–3 at a time, 3 minutes each side, over medium heat until crispy. Drain; keep warm. Repeat with remaining mixture.
3 To make Tomato Sauce: Heat oil in pan. Add onion, garlic and paprika; cook over medium heat 3 minutes or until soft. Add tomato, reduce heat; cook 10 minutes, stirring occasionally. Stir in basil.

MUSHROOMS EN CROUTE

⭐⭐ **Preparation time:** 40 minutes
Total cooking time: 20–25 minutes
Makes 48

8 slices white bread
5 tablespoons butter, melted
1 tablespoon olive oil
1 clove garlic, crushed
1/2 small onion, finely chopped
12 oz small button mushrooms, finely sliced

salt and pepper, to taste
1 tablespoon dry sherry
2 teaspoons cornstarch
1/3 cup sour cream
1 tablespoon finely chopped fresh parsley
1 teaspoon finely chopped fresh thyme
1/4 cup shredded Parmesan cheese

1 Preheat oven to moderate 350°F. Cut the crusts from the bread. Brush both sides of bread with the melted butter. Cut each slice into 6 small rectangles or squares. Place bread squares on a foil-lined baking pan. Bake 5–10 minutes or until golden and crisp.
2 Heat the oil in a large frying pan; add the garlic and onion. Cook, stirring over low heat, until onion is soft. Add the mushrooms and cook over medium heat for 5 minutes or until tender. Season with salt and pepper.
3 Pour in the sherry. Blend the cornstarch and

ABOVE: VEGETABLE FRITTERS WITH TOMATO SAUCE. OPPOSITE PAGE: RICE AND RATATOUILLE WITH CHEESE CRUST

flavor and is widely used in the cooking of northern China, especially in long-braising dishes. Chinese red vinegar, a wine vinegar with a delicate, tart flavor, is used mainly as a dipping sauce.

In Roman times vinegar

diluted with water was the common drink of soldiers. The name comes from the French *vin aigre*, sour wine.

Virginia Ham A ham that is produced from pigs fed on nuts; salted and smoked over hickory or apple wood fires.

Vol-au-Vent A round shell of puff pastry filled after baking with chicken, seafood, veal or mushrooms bound in a creamy sauce. It is served hot as a first course or in bite-sized portions as finger food. The cases should be filled just before serving, or the pastry will lose its crispness. The vol-au-vent was created by nineteenth-century Parisian chef and pastrycook Carême, who wanted a puff pastry first course so delicate that "it flew away in the wind." Ready-cooked vol-au-vent shells are available from supermarkets.

sour cream, add to mushroom mixture and stir until mixture boils and thickens. Remove pan from heat and stir in the parsley and thyme. Set aside to cool.

4 Spread the mushroom mixture on each square. Top with the Parmesan. Place on a baking pan, bake 5 minutes until they are heated through.

RICE AND RATATOUILLE WITH CHEESE CRUST

★ **Preparation time:** 45 minutes
Total cooking time: 55–60 minutes
Serves 4–6

2 large eggplants	1 teaspoon sugar
1 teaspoon salt	1 cup water
1½ lb tomatoes	1 cup tomato juice
⅓ cup olive oil	½ cup long-grain rice
6 cloves garlic, chopped	
2 large onions, cut in	**Topping**
¾ inch cubes	3 eggs
salt and pepper to taste	½ cup heavy cream
2 large red peppers, cut	2 teaspoons Dijon mustard
in ¾ inch squares	1 cup grated Cheddar
1 large green pepper, cut	cheese
in ¾ inch squares	salt and pepper
2 zucchini, about 1 lb,	
cut in ¾ inch slices	

1 Preheat oven to moderate 350°F. Peel the eggplant and cut into 1 inch cubes. Place the eggplant in a colander. Sprinkle well with salt and leave to stand for 15 minutes. Rinse under cold water and drain well. Pat dry with paper towels. Score a small cross on each tomato. Place the tomatoes in boiling water for 1–2 minutes and then plunge them immediately into cold water. Remove them from the water and remove the skins by peeling down from the cross. Cut the peeled tomatoes in quarters.

2 Heat the oil in a large heavy-bottom pan. Add the eggplant, garlic and onion, cook over medium heat for 5 minutes. Season with salt and pepper. Add the red and green peppers, sliced zucchini, tomato quarters and sugar, cook for another 5 minutes. Remove from heat.

3 Add water, tomato juice and rice, mix well. Transfer mixture to an 8-cup capacity ovenproof dish. Cover and bake for 20–30 minutes or until rice has absorbed the liquid and is tender.

4 To make Topping: Whisk together the eggs, cream and Dijon mustard in a large jug. Stir in the Cheddar cheese and season with salt and pepper. Pour the Topping over the cooked vegetables and rice. Return to the oven and bake for a further 15 minutes or until the Topping is set. Leave the casserole to stand for 5 minutes before serving.

Note: The cheese topping in this recipe is a bit like a thin custard which sets on top of the dish. For added flavor, you can add 1 tablespoon of chopped fresh oregano or marjoram and a little freshly grated Parmesan cheese.

W

Wafer A small, thin, crisp cookie or cracker, often served with ice cream; while hot, they are sometimes shaped into rolls or cones.

Waffle A flat, crisp cake made by baking an egg batter in a special hinged iron with a honeycomb-patterned grid. Waffles are served hot, topped with jam, honey or maple syrup, and cream or ice cream.

Waldorf Salad A salad made with chopped apples, celery and walnuts, with a mayonnaise dressing. Usually served on lettuce, as a side dish, it was created at the Waldorf-Astoria Hotel.

Walleye A freshwater fish, with white flaky flesh. It is the largest of the perch family.

Walnut (English Walnut) A nut encased in a hard, round shell and consisting of two deeply ridged lobes of creamy-white, mild-flavored flesh. Eaten as a snack, chopped and added to stuffings and salads, cakes, cookies and

WALNUTS

WALNUT COOKIES

★ ★ **Preparation time:** 10 minutes
Total cooking time: 25 minutes
Makes 20

2/3 cup butter, softened
2/3 cup sugar
2 tablespoons orange
  flower water
2 cups all-purpose flour,
  sifted

Walnut Filling
1/2 cup walnuts, chopped
1/3 cup sugar
1 teaspoon ground
  cinnamon

1 Preheat oven to 325°F. Brush a baking sheet with melted butter or oil, line base with parchment paper; grease paper. Beat butter and sugar together in a small mixing bowl until light and creamy.
2 Transfer the mixture to a large bowl. Using a metal spoon, fold in the orange flower water and the sifted flour until they are well combined. Press with your hands until the mixture comes together to make a stiff dough.
3 To make Walnut Filling: Mix the walnuts, sugar and cinnamon together in a medium bowl.
4 Roll heaping tablespoonfuls of the dough into balls. Press a hollow in the center of each ball of dough with your thumb. Place 1 teaspoon of Walnut Filling into each hollow. Place on baking sheets, flatten the balls slightly without folding the

dough over filling. Bake for 25 minutes or until the cookies are golden. Cool on a wire rack.

WALNUT AND HERB SALAD

★ **Preparation time:** 15 minutes
Total cooking time: none
Serves 4–6

1 head Boston lettuce
1 head leaf lettuce
1/2 bunch watercress
1 bunch fresh oregano
1 bunch fresh basil
1/2 bunch fresh mint
1/2 bunch fresh cilantro
1 cup walnut halves

Dressing
1/4 cup tarragon vinegar
2 tablespoons walnut oil
1/2 teaspoon freshly
  ground pepper

1 Wash the lettuces and watercress; dry thoroughly. Prepare herbs by breaking into sprigs or removing leaves from tough stalks. Wash and dry thoroughly.
2 Arrange lettuce, watercress and herbs in a large salad bowl. Add walnuts and toss to combine.
3 To make Dressing: Combine vinegar, oil and pepper in a small bowl and whisk to combine.
4 Pour dressing over salad just prior to serving.

ABOVE: WALNUT COOKIES.
OPPOSITE PAGE, ABOVE: SWEET AND SPICY
WALNUTS; BELOW: WALNUT AND HERB SALAD

CHOCOLATE WALNUT RING

⭐ **Preparation time:** 35 minutes
Total cooking time: 35 minutes
Makes one 10 inch ring cake

2 cups all-purpose flour
1 teaspoon baking soda
1 teaspoon baking powder
1/8 teaspoon salt
1/2 cup unsweetened cocoa
  powder
1 cup sugar
1/3 cup soft brown sugar
1 teaspoon vanilla
  extract
2 eggs

1 1/4 cups buttermilk
2/3 cup milk
1/4 cup unsalted butter,
  melted
1/2 cup chopped walnuts

Chocolate Sauce
3 oz dark chocolate,
  chopped
1/3 cup heavy cream

1 Preheat oven to moderate 350°F. Brush a deep 10 inch fluted tube pan with melted butter. Mix flour, soda, baking powder, salt and cocoa in a large bowl; add sugars. Make a well in the center.
2 Add combined vanilla, eggs, milks and butter to dry ingredients. Using electric beaters, beat mixture on low 3 minutes, or until just moist.
3 Beat on high for 5 minutes until smooth and increased in volume. Fold in walnuts. Pour into prepared pan. Bake 35 minutes or until skewer comes out clean. Leave cake in pan 10 minutes before turning onto a wire rack to cool.
4 To make Chocolate Sauce: Combine choco-

late and cream in a pan. Stir over low heat until chocolate melts and mixture is smooth. Cool to room temperature. Pour sauce over cake. Decorate with two-toned chocolate curls and powdered sugar, if desired.

SWEET AND SPICY WALNUTS

⭐ **Preparation time:** 5 minutes
Total cooking time: 10 minutes
Serves 8

1/4 cup butter
1 teaspoon ground
  cinnamon

1 teaspoon ground
  cardamom
2 cups walnut halves
1/4 cup sugar

1 Preheat oven to 400°F. Melt butter in a pan; remove from heat. Add cinnamon and cardamom to pan; stir until combined.
2 Add walnuts, stir until coated in spice mixture. Spread, in a single layer, on baking pan. Bake 8 minutes until lightly browned; remove from oven.
3 Place sugar in a bowl. Add hot walnuts, stir until well coated. Serve warm or cold as a snack.

ABOUT WALNUTS

■ Store walnuts in an airtight container. Shelled walnuts will keep for about 6 months in the refrigerator and can be frozen for about 12 months.
■ If you buy 1 lb unshelled walnuts the yield will be about 1/2 lb.

quick breads, walnuts are available in the shell, shelled in cans or packs, or pickled.

Walnut Oil A fragrant, clear, pale golden oil pressed from walnut kernels and used mainly in dressings for salads and cooked vegetables.

Wasabi A pungent, powerfully flavored root, not unlike the horseradish root, used in Japanese cooking as an ingredient in sushi and mixed with soy sauce as an accompaniment to sashimi. Wasabi is available from Asian markets in powdered form or as a pale green paste in tubes.

Water Chestnut A crisp, white-fleshed, delicately flavored root vegetable valued as an ingredient in Chinese cooking because it remains crunchy after cooking. Water chestnuts have a brown husk that should be removed before eating, they are available fresh or canned.

Watercress A plant with small, deep green, peppery-tasting leaves and stems which are used in salads and soups, and as a garnish. Watercress is available fresh throughout the year.

Watermelon A large melon with a hard, smooth, mottled-green skin and sweet, juicy, red flesh studded with dark seeds; it is eaten fresh as a fruit and added to fruit salads. The rind can be pickled, and the seeds roasted as a snack. Watermelons grow on a trailing vine.

Waterzooi A stew made with chicken or fish.

Welsh Rarebit See Rarebit.

Western Omelette An omelette with minced ham, onions and green pepper.

Wheat A cereal grain, staple for half the world's population. It is ground into flour and used to make bread, pasta, cakes, cookies, and as a breakfast cereal.

Whitebait Tiny, silvery fish, the young of several species, such as herring and sprat, they are dusted with flour and deep-fried.

White Sauce A sauce based on a roux of butter and flour with milk (béchamel sauce) or chicken, veal or fish stock (velouté sauce).

Whole-Wheat Flour A coarse-textured flour ground from the entire wheat kernel and used to make bread, cakes, cookies and pasta.

WONTONS

WONTONS WITH CHILI DIP

⭐ ⭐ **Preparation time:** 40 minutes
Total cooking time: 10–15 minutes
Makes 48

8 oz lean pork
3 1/2 oz uncooked shrimp, peeled
2 oz bamboo shoots, drained
3 scallions, chopped
1/2 inch piece fresh ginger, peeled
salt and white pepper
1/4 cup chopped unsalted peanuts
1/2 teaspoon sugar

1 tablespoon chopped fresh cilantro
48 round egg pastry wonton wrappers
oil for deep frying

Chili Dip
1/4 cup honey
1/4 cup sweet chili sauce
1 teaspoon chopped fresh ginger
1 teaspoon rice vinegar

1 Trim pork of fat and tendons. Cut into cubes. Process pork, shrimp, bamboo shoots, scallions and ginger in food processor for 20–30 seconds. Add salt, pepper, peanuts, sugar and cilantro.
2 Place 1 teaspoon of the mixture in the center of each wonton wrapper. Brush edges with water. Bring wrapper edges together to form pouches; squeeze to secure.
3 Heat the oil in a deep, heavy-bottom pan. Lower wonton pouches into moderately hot oil. Cook in batches over medium heat for 1 minute or until golden, crisp and cooked through. Remove from oil with slotted spoon, drain on paper towels.
4 To make Chili Dip: Combine honey, sauce, ginger and vinegar in a bowl. Mix well.

STEAMED SHRIMP WONTONS

⭐ ⭐ **Preparation time:** 40 minutes
Total cooking time: 20–30 minutes
Makes 12

8 large shrimp
8 oz ground pork
1 1/2 oz can water chestnuts, drained, finely chopped
1 1/2 oz can bamboo shoots, drained, finely chopped
1 tablespoon oyster sauce
1 tablespoon hoisin sauce

1 tablespoon Chinese soy sauce
1 tablespoon Chinese rice wine or dry sherry
1 tablespoon sesame oil
1 egg white, lightly whisked
1 tablespoon rice flour or cornstarch
12 wonton wrappers

1 Peel the shrimp and chop very finely. Combine with ground pork, water chestnuts, bamboo shoots, oyster sauce, hoisin sauce, soy sauce, rice wine or sherry, sesame oil, egg white and rice flour or cornstarch.
2 Place 1 teaspoon of the shrimp mixture in the center of each wrapper. Brush the edges of the wrapper with a little water. Bring the edges together to form pouches and squeeze gently to secure.
3 Lay a piece of aluminum foil on the base of a steamer; brush with oil, and place wontons on top. Steam for 20–30 minutes until cooked. Serve wontons from the steamer accompanied by a piquant sauce.

ABOVE: WONTONS WITH CHILI DIP.
OPPOSITE PAGE: VEGETABLE WONTONS WITH CHILI SAUCE

VEGETABLE WONTONS WITH CHILI SAUCE

★ ★ **Preparation time:** 40 minutes +
30 minutes soaking
Total cooking time: 20 minutes
Makes 25

8 dried Chinese mushrooms	1 tablespoon soy sauce
1 tablespoon peanut oil	2 tablespoons water
1 teaspoon sesame oil	6½ oz wonton wrappers
1 teaspoon grated ginger	oil for deep frying
2 scallions, finely chopped	
1 medium carrot, finely chopped	**Chili Sauce**
	1 tablespoon peanut oil
1 medium parsnip, finely chopped	1 clove garlic, crushed
	¼ cup sweet chili sauce
3 oz broccoli, cut into small florets	2 tablespoons soy sauce
	2 tablespoons sherry
2 tablespoons bread crumbs	1 tablespoon lemon juice

1 Soak mushrooms in hot water 30 minutes. Drain, squeeze out liquid. Discard stems. Slice caps finely.

2 Heat oils in wok or heavy-based frying pan. Add ginger and scallions. Cook 1 minute over medium heat. Add mushrooms, carrot, parsnip and broccoli; stir-fry 3 minutes or until vegetables are just softened. Stir in bread crumbs, soy sauce and water. Remove from heat; cool.

3 Place a heaped teaspoonful of the vegetable mixture in the center of each wrapper. Brush edges of pastry with water and pinch edges together to seal. Heat oil in a wok or deep-fryer. Cook wontons in batches (no more than four at a time), for 2 minutes or until golden. Remove with a slotted spoon. Drain on paper towels. Serve with Chili Sauce.

4 To make Chili Sauce: Heat oil in a pan, add garlic. Cook until golden. Add chili and soy sauces, sherry and juice, stir until heated.

Note: If wrappers are not used immediately, cover unused ones with a damp towel.

1   2   3

Wild Rice The long, dark-brown, nutty-flavored, chewy grain of an aquatic grass which grows in the Minnesota lakes of North America. Wild rice is boiled or steamed and served with poultry or fish; sautéed onions, mushrooms or nuts are sometimes added for flavoring. It is hand harvested, sometimes by Native Americans.

Wine The fermented juice of grapes, it is used in cooking to add flavor to both savory and sweet dishes.

Witloof See Belgian Endive.

Wonton A Chinese snack made of a savory filling inside a small square or round of paper-thin dough. Wontons can be steamed or deep-fried. Wrappers can be made like pasta and rolled out until almost transparent; they are also sold fresh at Asian food stores. See Short Soup.

Worcestershire Sauce A thin, brown-black, piquant sauce made from a secret recipe but thought to contain soy sauce, anchovy sauce, vinegar, molasses, chili, ginger, tamarind, shallots and garlic.

Y

Yabby Freshwater crayfish found in creeks, rivers, waterholes and dams across Australia and related to similar species native to France (*écrevisse*) and North America (crawfish). Its cooked meat, mostly in the tail and claws, is white, sweet, moist and delicately flavored; it is best served with a mild-flavored sauce or a splash of extra virgin olive oil, freshly grated black pepper and a squeeze of lemon juice. Yabbies commercially farmed in Australia are exported live around the world. Best cooked live, stun them first for 20 minutes in the freezer. Crawfish, an American freshwater crustacean, resembles the yabby, but does not have claws; only the tail is used.

Yakitori A Japanese dish consisting of small pieces of chicken threaded on bamboo skewers and grilled over glowing coals while being basted with a soy sauce-based marinade.

YEAST COOKERY

SAVORY PIZZA SNAILS

★
★ ★

Preparation time: 1½ hours,
Total cooking time: 40 minutes
Makes about 32

1 tablespoon olive oil
1 onion, finely chopped
½ cup finely chopped green pepper
¼ cup finely chopped black olives
1 envelope active dry yeast
1 teaspoon sugar
½ cup whole-wheat flour
1¼ cups warm water
2¼ cups all-purpose flour
½ cup rye flour
1 teaspoon salt
¼ cup tomato paste
2 teaspoons dried sweet basil leaves
1 cup grated Cheddar cheese

1 Heat oil in a pan. Add onion and peppers and cook over low heat for about 8 minutes or until soft. Add olives to pan and cook for 2 minutes. Remove from heat and leave to cool.

2 Combine yeast with sugar and whole-wheat flour in a bowl. Gradually add water, blend until smooth. Cover bowl with plastic wrap, leave in warm place 10 minutes or until mixture is foamy.

3 Stir remaining flours into a large mixing bowl and add salt. Make a well in the center and add yeast mixture. Mix to a soft dough.

4 Turn onto a lightly floured surface. Knead for 5 minutes or until the dough is smooth. Shape into a ball, place in a large, clean, lightly oiled bowl. Leave, covered with plastic wrap, in a warm place for about 30 minutes or until dough is well-risen.

5 Knead the dough again for about 3 minutes or until smooth. Roll out onto a lightly floured surface to a 12 x 18 inch rectangle. Spread the dough evenly with tomato paste. Top with the cooled vegetable mixture. Sprinkle with basil and grated cheese.

6 Roll up lengthwise tightly across the rectangle to make a long roll. Using a sharp knife, cut through roll to base at ½ inch intervals. Arrange "snails" on lightly oiled baking pan about 2 inches apart. Cover with plastic wrap and leave in a warm place for 20 minutes or until snails are well-risen.

7 Bake at 375°F for 15 minutes or until golden and crisp. Leave snails on pans for 5 minutes before transferring to a wire rack to cool.

DOUGHNUTS

★ ★

Preparation time: 1½ hours,
Total cooking time: 15 minutes
Makes 22–24

4 cups all-purpose unbleached or bread flour
2 envelopes active dry yeast
¼ cup sugar
1 teaspoon salt
1 egg, beaten
1¼ cups warm milk
⅓ cup butter, melted
light olive oil for frying
¾ cup sugar, extra
1½ teaspoons cinnamon

1 Combine the flour, yeast, sugar and salt in a medium mixing bowl. Combine the egg, milk and butter and gradually add to flour mixture; mix to a soft dough. Turn dough onto a lightly floured surface and knead for 10 minutes, until dough is smooth and elastic. Shape dough into a ball and place in a large, lightly oiled mixing bowl. Leave, covered with plastic wrap, in a warm place for 45 minutes or until ball has doubled in volume.

2 Knead the dough for 1 minute until smooth; rest the dough for 5 minutes. Roll out to ¼–½ inch thickness and cut into circles with a doughnut cutter, or use a 3 inch and a 1½ inch round cutter to make doughnut rings. Place the doughnuts on lightly floured baking sheets, cover and leave in a warm place for about 20 minutes to rise.

3 Heat oil to a depth of 2½ inches and fry doughnuts for 1–2 minutes on each side until golden brown and cooked through. Drain on paper towels.

4 Combine the sugar and cinnamon and toss the doughnuts in the mixture until they are well coated.

BABA AU RHUM

★★ **Preparation time:** 1½ hours
Total cooking time: 25 minutes
Serves 8

2 cups all-purpose
  flour
½ teaspoon salt
¼ cup sugar
1 envelope active dry
  yeast
½ cup lukewarm milk
3 eggs, beaten

¼ cup butter, melted
½ cup chopped raisins

Syrup
1½ cups water
1 cup sugar
½ cup rum

1 Brush a deep 9 inch, 5-cup capacity baba or savarin pan or ring mold with melted butter, dust with flour. Combine flour, salt, sugar and yeast in a medium mixing bowl; make a well in the center. Add milk, eggs and butter and mix to a thick batter.
2 Using your hand, beat and slap the mixture against the side of the bowl for 6 minutes or until it is still quite tacky but smooth and glossy. Scrape down from side of bowl during this process. Leave, covered with plastic wrap, in a warm place for about 1 hour or until the mixture has doubled in volume.
3 Preheat the oven to moderately hot 400°F.

Add the raisins and stir dough to incorporate fruit. Spoon into the prepared pan. Leave, covered with plastic wrap, in a warm place for about 30 minutes, until the dough has doubled in size. Bake for 20 minutes, until well browned and cooked through.
4 Turn baba immediately onto a wire rack placed over a shallow baking pan. Prick well with a fork or skewer; spoon hot syrup liberally over baba until it is well soaked.
5 To make Syrup: Place water and sugar in a pan and stir over moderate heat until the sugar has dissolved. Bring to the boil and simmer for 5 minutes. Remove from heat and add rum.

Note: For best results, use unbleached or bread flour for this recipe.

ABOUT YEAST

■ Fresh (compressed) yeast loses its effectiveness with age. It should be stored in the refrigerator for no longer than two weeks, or can be frozen for up to two months. Dry yeast can be stored for longer, in a cool, dry place.
■ Test compressed yeast for freshness by dissolving it in warm water with a teaspoon of sugar—within 10 minutes it should be frothing.
■ Yeast depends for its action on the temperature of the dough. If it is too cold, yeast activity will be slowed, while high temperatures will kill the yeast organisms.

OPPOSITE PAGE: SAVORY PIZZA SNAILS.
ABOVE: BABA AU RHUM

Yam The starchy brown-skinned, pale-fleshed tuber of a tropical vine which originated in China and is now found throughout the Pacific, Africa and the Caribbean. Yams are not widely available in the United States; sweet potatoes are often confused with, and mislabeled as, yams.

Yarrow A member of the daisy family with deep green lacy leaves and a pungent odor and taste. The slightly bitter leaves can be steamed or braised and eaten as a vegetable, made into soup or chopped and added to salads. It may also be used to make tea.

Yeast A tiny, single-celled organism that multiplies rapidly in warm and moist environments. Bakers yeast is used as the leavener in various kinds of dough, where it ferments the sugar in the dough to produce the bubbles of carbon dioxide gas which make the mixture rise. Yeast has been used in bread-making since its accidental discovery more than 4,000 years ago. It is available in two forms: compressed (fresh) yeast which is partially dried and formed into a cake, and dried or granular yeast. Yeast is also used in brewing and wine-making.

Yogurt A thick, creamy, slightly acidic milk product made by coagulating milk with a bacterial product. Yogurt can feature in all parts of a meal. It is the base of a number of Middle Eastern dips and is used to thicken and enrich soups, stews and curries. Yogurt has a cooling effect on the palate and is often served with chopped cucumber as an accompaniment to a spicy meal; it is also used in salad dressings and in sauces for hot cooked vegetables. Tenderizing yogurt marinades are used in many Indian dishes, particularly in tandoori dishes and korma curries. As a dessert, yogurt can be sweetened with honey or mixed with fresh or stewed fruit, or it can be baked in cakes, cheesecakes, cookies and biscuits.

Natural yogurt containing cultures such as *Lactobacillus acidophilus* and *Bifidobacteria bacterium* is considered to have beneficial effects on the digestive system. These cultures are believed to help restore a healthy balance in the intestines by re-establishing bacteria which are normally

H O T   C R O S S   B U N S

⋆⋆ **Preparation time:** 2 hours
Total cooking time: 30–35 minutes
Makes 12

4 cups all-purpose flour	1/4 cup butter, melted
1 teaspoon pumpkin pie spice	1 egg, beaten
1/4 teaspoon salt	1 1/4 cups warm milk
2 envelopes active dry yeast	1 cup dried mixed fruit, chopped
1/2 cup sugar	

1 Place flour, spice, salt and sugar in food processor and process for 1–2 minutes. Dissolve yeast in warm milk; add egg and butter. With motor running, add liquid to dry ingredients, process until combined. Turn mixture onto floured board, knead in dried fruit, then knead 5–10 minutes, until dough is smooth and elastic.
2 Place the dough in greased bowl, cover with cloth. Leave in a warm place for 1 hour or until doubled in bulk.
3 Brush a 13 x 9 x 2 inch pan with oil or melted butter. Divide dough into 12 round buns. Arrange in pan, 1 inch apart. Cover with cloth and allow to rise 45 minutes.
4 Preheat oven to 375°F. Pipe a cross on each bun. Bake 30–35 minutes, or until golden brown. If necessary, cover with foil to prevent over-browning. Brush glaze over buns while still hot.

Note: For crosses, fill a piping bag with a mixture made from 1/4 cup all-purpose flour, 1/4 teaspoon baking powder, and 3 tablespoons water. Glaze: Stir 1/4 teaspoon unflavored gelatin, 2 teaspoons honey and 1 tablespoon water in a small pan over low heat until dissolved.

P A N E T T O N E

⋆ **Preparation time:** 1 hour 40 minutes
⋆⋆ **Total cooking time:** 1 hour 15 minutes
Makes one 8 inch loaf

3/4 cup mixed fruit, coarsely chopped	2 tablespoons lukewarm water
2 tablespoons candied mixed peel	3 cups all-purpose flour
2 tablespoons orange juice	1/4 cup butter, chopped
1 envelope active dry yeast	3 eggs, lightly beaten
1 teaspoon sugar	1/4 cup sugar
	1/2 cup lukewarm milk
	extra milk for glazing

1 Brush an 8 inch charlotte pan or 9 x 5 inch loaf pan with oil or melted butter. Combine fruit, peel and orange juice in a small bowl and set aside while preparing the rest of the cake.
2 Combine the yeast, sugar and water in a bowl; blend until smooth. Leave, covered with plastic wrap, in a warm place for 10 minutes or until foamy.
3 Sift flour into large mixing bowl, add butter. Rub butter into flour with fingertips for 2 minutes or until mixture is fine and crumbly. Add fruit mixture, stir until well mixed.
4 Combine eggs, sugar and milk; stir in yeast mixture. Make a well in center of flour, add liquid. Mix to a soft dough.
5 Turn the dough out onto a lightly floured surface. Knead for 5–10 minutes or until the dough is no longer sticky. Place in a bowl and leave, covered with plastic wrap, in a warm place for 30 minutes or until well risen. Shape the risen dough into a loaf. Place in pan, and let rise in a warm place for 30 minutes.
6 Preheat oven to moderately hot 400°F. Brush the dough with extra milk, bake for 15 minutes; reduce the heat to moderate 350°F, bake for 1 hour more or until the Panettone is well browned and cooked through. If necessary, cover it loosely with foil to prevent over browning. When cooked it will sound hollow when tapped.

ABOVE: HOT CROSS BUNS. OPPOSITE PAGE, ABOVE: CURRIED YOGURT CHICKEN; BELOW: YOGURT CAKE WITH LEMON SYRUP

Y O G U R T

CURRIED YOGURT CHICKEN

 Preparation time: 20 minutes + marinating
Total cooking time: 40–45 minutes
Serves 6

1 cup plain yogurt	1 teaspoon finely grated
1/2 cup coconut milk	lime rind
1/4 cup fresh cilantro,	1 tablespoon curry powder
chopped	freshly ground black
1 onion, finely chopped	pepper
1 clove garlic, crushed	2 lb chicken pieces
1 tablespoon lime juice	1 cup plain yogurt, extra

1 Combine yogurt, coconut milk, chopped cilantro, onion, garlic, lime juice and rind, curry powder and pepper in a large, shallow glass or ceramic dish. Add the chicken pieces. Mix to coat completely.
2 Cover dish with plastic wrap. Marinate the chicken for several hours, or overnight, in the refrigerator.
3 Remove chicken from marinade. Place chicken in a shallow baking pan. Bake in a moderate oven 350°F for 40–45 minutes.
4 Garnish with fresh cilantro leaves and serve with extra yogurt and rice or salad.

YOGURT CAKE WITH LEMON SYRUP

★★ **Preparation time:** 20 minutes
Total cooking time: 1 hour 10 minutes
Serves 8–10

2 1/2 cups all-purpose	**Lemon Syrup**
flour, sifted	1 1/4 cups sugar
1 teaspoon baking powder	3/4 cup water
1/4 teaspoon salt	rind of 1 lemon cut into
1 cup sugar	thin strips
1 cup vanilla yogurt	1/4 cup lemon juice
1 cup milk	lemon rind, extra, cut
2 eggs, lightly beaten	into thin strips, to serve
	whipped cream, to serve

1 Preheat oven to 350°F. Brush a deep 9 inch round cake pan with oil or melted butter. Line the base with paper; grease paper. Place the flour, baking powder, salt and sugar into bowl. Pour over combined yogurt, milk and eggs. Beat with electric beaters on low speed for 2 minutes, then on high speed 5 minutes.
2 Spoon into pan. Bake for 1 hour or until a skewer comes out clean when inserted into the center. Immediately pour half of the prepared Lemon Syrup over the top of the cake; leave for 10 minutes. Serve with extra lemon strips, extra syrup and cream.
3 To make Lemon Syrup: Stir all the ingredients together in a pan over low heat until the sugar dissolves; do not boil. Simmer for 10–15 minutes or until thick. Keep warm. Remove the lemon strips before serving.

present but may have been destroyed by infections or drugs such as penicillin.

Yogurt has been used in the Middle East for many thousands of years, and its therapeutic properties are often cited as the reason for the famed longevity of the people of the Caucasus. Commercially available yogurt may be made from fat-free, reduced-fat or full-cream milk, and may be either natural, flavored with vanilla or other sweeteners, or mixed with fruit. Flavored frozen yogurt and drinking yogurt are also available.

Yorkshire Pudding A light, crisp, baked batter served with roast beef. In Yorkshire, in the north of England, where it originated, the pudding is traditionally served before the meat.

Youngberry A sweet, purple fruit

which is a cross between several types of blackberry.

Yule Log Also called *Bûche de Noël*, a traditional French Christmas cake with a number of popular variations in other countries. A rolled sponge cake is filled and coated with chocolate butter cream frosting and the surface decorated to resemble bark.

YOGURT & FRESH CHEESES

Yogurt and soft, fresh, cottage-style cheeses are easy to make and nutritious. The fat content depends on the kind of milk used. Powdered milk (whole or skim) can be added to homemade yogurt to increase the protein and calcium content and improve texture.

FROM LEFT TO RIGHT, BELOW: BLUEBERRY SWIRL, CREME FRAICHE, LASSI, HERB CHEESE ROLL, SOFT CHEESE

YOGURT

Yogurt is eaten with many combinations of fresh or stewed fruits or chopped nuts. It can be used as a tenderizing marinade for meats and poultry, to thicken and enrich casseroles, stews and some soups, and as a sauce with hot vegetable dishes.

Natural yogurt containing the "friendly" bacteria *Lactobacillus acidophilus* and *Bifidobacteria bacterium* is thought to assist the functioning of the digestive system by supplementing the body's natural bacteria.

THICK CREAMY YOGURT

Combine 2¾ cups milk with ⅓ cup powdered whole milk in a saucepan and heat gently to boiling point until the froth rises. Reduce the heat and allow the milk to simmer very gently for 20 minutes. Remove from heat and set aside to cool until lukewarm. For best results, test the milk with a thermometer—it should read 90°F. Remove the skin from the top of the milk and discard, then gently stir in ⅓ cup natural yogurt combined with ¼ cup milk. Pour the mixture into sterilized jars and seal. Stand the jars in a saucepan and fill the saucepan with hot tap water. Wrap a blanket around the saucepan to keep in the warmth and set aside for at least 6 hours. Chill the yogurt well for 3–4 hours before using it. Makes 2 cups.

Yogurt can be stored in the refrigerator for up to a week.

Note: An electric yogurt maker can be used if you have one—follow the manufacturer's instructions.

BLUEBERRY SWIRL

Purée 6 oz fresh blueberries in a food processor until smooth. Taste, and if necessary add 1–2 teaspoons of sugar. Place a dollop of plain yogurt in a tall glass and, tilting the glass, fill with alternating spoonfuls of blueberry purée and yogurt, ending with blueberries. Makes 4 glasses.

CREME FRAICHE

Crème Fraîche is the rich, slightly tart cream used with fresh seasonal fruits, fish, and some soups, sauces and savory dishes. It is available commercially, but can be made at home easily. Combine equal quantities of heavy cream and sour cream in a bowl. Cover the bowl and set it aside to stand at room temperature until the cream mixture has thickened—this will take 1–2 days. Cover and refrigerate before using. Crème Fraîche will keep in the refrigerator for up to a week.

MINT LASSI

In a large bowl or jug, whisk together ⅓ cup plain yogurt, 3–4 teaspoons of sugar and 1 tablespoon chopped fresh mint. Gradually add 2⅓ cups ice water or soda water and whisk again until well combined. Pour over ice cubes into a tall glass. To vary, add ⅓ cup mango purée and omit the mint, if desired. Serves 4 as a refreshing drink.

FRESH CHEESES

HERB CHEESE ROLL

Using electric beaters, beat 1 lb cream cheese until smooth and creamy. Add 6 oz fresh ricotta cheese; beat well. Spread evenly over a sheet of parchment paper into a 10 inch square. Combine 2 tablespoons finely chopped chives, 1 tablespoon each finely chopped lemon thyme and oregano, 1–2 teaspoons grated lemon rind and 2–3 tablespoons finely grated fresh Parmesan cheese. Sprinkle mixture on top of cheese square, then slide square and parchment paper onto a flat tray. Cover and refrigerate 2–3 hours. Using parchment paper as a guide, carefully roll cheese mixture, jelly roll style. Lift roll onto plastic wrap. Wrap up tightly and refrigerate overnight. Roll in ground toasted almonds or walnuts. Serve sliced or in a log with crackers or breads.

SOFT CHEESE

Press 8 oz cottage cheese and ½ cup sour cream through a fine sieve. Gradually beat in 2 teaspoons chopped chives, 2 teaspoons chopped parsley and 2 cloves crushed garlic. Add salt and freshly ground black pepper. Pack into a cheesecloth-lined sieve or draining mold over a bowl. Fold cheesecloth over cheese, place small weight on top and refrigerate 24 hours. Unmold and serve with capers, green salad and Melba toast.

TO MAKE SOFT CHEESE: PRESS CHEESE AND SOUR CREAM THROUGH SIEVE UNTIL SMOOTH

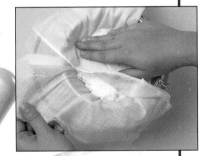

PACK MIXTURE INTO A CHEESECLOTH-LINED SIEVE OR DRAINING MOLD; FOLD CHEESECLOTH OVER

Z

Zabaglione A foamy Italian dessert sauce made with whole eggs, egg yolk, sugar and marsala. These are whisked together over gentle heat in the top of a double boiler. Zabaglione can be served warm with sweet, crisp cookies or wafers or spooned over strawberries, or chilled. Zabaglione can also be made with other dessert wines or liqueurs; in Spain it is made with sherry, and in France a similar sauce made with sweet white wine or champagne is known as *sabayon*. The name zabaglione is derived from a Neapolitan dialect word which means "to foam."

Zest The thin, colored, outside rind of a citrus fruit. It contains volatile oils that add fragrance and concentrated flavor to both sweet and savory foods.

Ziti A long tubular pasta (macaroni) that is often served with meat or mushroom sauce.

Zucchini A small, slender vegetable, a type of summer squash. It has

ZUCCHINI

ZUCCHINI, APPLE AND APRICOT BARS

★★ **Preparation time:** 20 minutes +
10 minutes standing
Total cooking time: 1 hour
Serves 8

½ cup butter	¼ cup boiling water
½ cup soft brown sugar	20 oz can apple pie
2 egg yolks	filling
1½ cups all-purpose	1 small zucchini, grated
flour	½ cup rolled oats
¼ cup wheatgerm	½ cup flaked coconut
½ teaspoon baking	2 tablespoons honey
powder	2 egg whites, stiffly
⅛ teaspoon salt	beaten
¼ cup finely chopped	
dried apricots	

1 Preheat oven to 350°F. Brush a 13 x 9 x 2 inch pan with oil or melted butter. Line base and sides with waxed paper; grease paper.
2 Beat butter and sugar in a small bowl with an electric mixer until light and fluffy. Add egg yolks, beat until combined. Using a metal spoon, fold in flour, wheatgerm, baking powder and salt. Press evenly over base of pan.
3 Soak apricots in boiling water 10 minutes or until plump and almost all liquid is absorbed.
4 Spread apple pie filling over prepared base. In a bowl, combine undrained apricots with zucchini, oats, coconut and honey. Fold in egg whites with a metal spoon.

5 Spoon mixture over apple and smooth the surface. Bake for 1 hour or until golden and cooked through. Leave to cool in pan. Cut into bars. Serve with flavored yogurt, if desired.

ZUCCHINI WITH CUMIN CREAM

★ **Preparation time:** 5 minutes
Total cooking time: 12 minutes
Serves 4–6

1 lemon	½ teaspoon cumin seeds
4 large zucchini	½ cup heavy cream
2 tablespoons butter	salt and freshly ground
1 tablespoon oil	black pepper, to taste

1 Grate rind from lemon to make ½ teaspoonful and squeeze 2 teaspoons lemon juice. Set aside. Cut zucchini into ¼ inch thick diagonal slices. Heat butter and oil in a large frying pan and add half the zucchini slices. Cook over medium-high heat for 2 minutes on each side or until golden. Remove from pan; drain on paper towel; keep warm. Repeat with remaining zucchini slices.
2 Add the cumin seeds to the pan, stir over low heat for 1 minute. Add the lemon rind and juice; bring to boil. Add the cream to the pan and boil for 2 minutes or until sauce thickens slightly; season to taste. Do not boil sauce for too long as it may curdle.
3 Return zucchini slices to pan. Stir over low heat for 1 minute or until just heated through. Serve warm or cold.

ZUCCHINI SWIRLS

Preparation time: 12 minutes +
1 hour refrigeration
Total cooking time: 15 minutes
Makes 25

2 medium zucchini,
  coarsely grated
1 small onion, grated
2 oz salami, finely
  chopped
1 clove garlic, crushed

½ cup grated fresh
  Parmesan cheese
4 sheets frozen filo
  (phyllo) dough, thawed
2 tablespoons butter,
  melted
⅓ cup dried packaged
  bread crumbs

1 Brush two shallow baking pans with oil or melted butter. Combine the zucchini, onion, salami, garlic and Parmesan cheese in a medium mixing bowl.
2 Lightly brush each pastry sheet with butter and layer them on top of each other. Spread zucchini mixture over pastry sheets leaving a 2 inch border along one long side; sprinkle bread crumbs evenly over zucchini mixture.
3 Roll pastry up tightly over filling towards side with border. Brush roll all over with remaining butter; cover with plastic wrap, refrigerate 1 hour. Preheat oven to moderately hot 400°F. Using a sharp knife, cut roll into 25 slices; arrange on prepared pans. Bake 15 minutes or until slices are crisp and brown. Cool on pans.

ZUCCHINI AND CHEESE PIE

Preparation time: 30 minutes
Total cooking time: 30 minutes
Serves 4–6

4 large zucchini, coarsely
  grated
8 oz feta cheese
8 oz ricotta cheese
2 tablespoons chopped
  mint

8 sheets frozen filo
  (phyllo) dough, thawed
2 tablespoons olive oil
2 tablespoons poppy seeds

1 Preheat oven to 400°F. Combine the zucchini with the cheeses and mint. Mix together using a wooden spoon.
2 Brush each sheet of filo (phyllo) pastry with oil and fold in half to form a smaller rectangle. Place one folded sheet in a well-oiled 9 inch pie plate, brush with oil, then top with a second sheet. Spread one-third of the filling on top. Repeat until all of the pastry and filling have been used, finishing with a sheet of folded pastry. Brush top with oil and sprinkle with poppy seeds.
3 Bake for 10 minutes, then reduce oven temperature to 350°F and cook for another 20 minutes, or until the pastry is crisp and golden. Cut into wedges and serve.

OPPOSITE PAGE: ZUCCHINI WITH CUMIN CREAM
ABOVE: ZUCCHINI AND CHEESE PIE
LEFT: ZUCCHINI SWIRLS

thin green or yellow skin and pale flesh with a central cluster of small, soft edible seeds. Very young zucchini are the sweetest and most tender. Zucchini can be eaten raw in salads or cut into lengths and served with dips; they are steamed, braised or boiled and served as a vegetable, and can be stuffed and baked. Zucchini combine particularly well with tomato. The male flower can be picked while still firmly closed and used in cooking, usually stuffed then dipped in batter and fried, or stuffed and baked (the female flower, with its thicker stem, is left to mature into the vegetable). The zucchini was developed in Italy from seed brought back from the Americas by Christopher Columbus. It is available fresh all year round.

Zwieback A bread made from slightly sweetened yeast dough (sometimes flavored with lemon or cinnamon) baked then cut into thin slices and returned to a slow oven until crisp and golden.

INDEX

Page numbers in **bold** indicate main entries, including recipes and illustrations; *italics* indicate other illustrations; ***bold italics*** refer to dictionary (marginal) entries.